FROM
HIGHER
AIMS
TO HIRED
HANDS

FROM HIGHER AIMS TO HIRED HANDS

The Social Transformation

of American Business Schools

and the Unfulfilled Promise

of Management as a Profession

RAKESH KHURANA

PRINCETON UNIVERSITY PRESS

PRINCETON AND OXFORD

Published by Princeton University Press, 41 William Street,
Princeton, New Jersey 08540
In the United Kingdom: Princeton University Press, 6 Oxford Street,
Woodstock, Oxfordshire OX20 1TW
press.princeton.edu

Third printing, and first paperback printing, 2010
Paperback ISBN: 978-0-691-14587-7

The Library of Congress has cataloged the cloth edition of this book as follows

Khurana, Rakesh, 1967–
    From higher aims to hired hands : the social transformation of American business schools
and the unfulfilled promise of management as a profession / Rakesh Khurana.
        p. cm.
    Includes bibliographical references and index.
    ISBN 978-0-691-12020-1 (hardcover : alk. paper)   1. Business education—United States.
2. Business schools—United States.   3. Management—Vocational guidance—United States.
I. Title.
    HF1131.K45 2007
    650.071′173—dc22   2007014497

British Library Cataloging-in-Publication Data is available

This book has been composed in Minion with GillSans display
Printed on acid-free paper. ∞

Printed in the United States of America

10   9   8   7   6   5   4   3

To Stephanie—

For her insight, companionship, and unconditional love

Contents

FROM
HIGHER
AIMS
TO HIRED
HANDS

Business Education and the Social Transformation

of American Management

Modern management has long been one of the most powerful but invisible of American institutions—invisible not in the sense of being out of the public eye but in the sense that its control of many of society's most powerful organizations has become so taken for granted, and its influence so pervasive, that it has evaded searching scrutiny.

This idea might seem counterintuitive today, when in less than a decade we have gone from the era of the charismatic, superstar CEO of the likes of Lee Iacocca and Jack Welch to a historical moment that has seen not just the deflation of erstwhile icons such as Carly Fiorina and "Chainsaw" Al Dunlap but the conviction and imprisonment of others, such as Jeffrey Skilling and Bernie Ebbers, who turned out to have used their celebrated business acumen to enrich themselves while defrauding investors. Yet the dramatic contrast between the CEO as superhero and the CEO as antihero has obscured the underlying links between these two types, which have appeared on the scene only in the last twenty-five years or so. Moreover, not even the profusion of corporate scandals since the beginning of the current decade has prompted the question why it is that managers run corporations.

As the late Alfred Chandler has detailed in a series of famous studies, modern industrial capitalism in the United States was rooted not so much in the rough-and-tumble world of the robber barons (the original incarnation of the charismatic business leader) as in a more complex, depersonalized environment in which technological advances made possible both previously unimaginable economies of scale and the creation of a national market. Realizing the economic advantages of these new technologies, Chandler argued, rested on the efforts of a new type of individual working in the upper and middle ranks of large organizations, a figure who did not fit into conventional economic distinctions between capital and labor. Neither owner nor worker, this new economic actor, the manager, performed work that, while not as visible and tangible as the factories built by financial capital or the tasks performed by those who labored in them, was nonetheless critical to the development of the large-scale business enterprise. Managers' work involved administrative tasks such as directing personnel, defining procedures for selling their firm's goods, and organizing processes for distributing those goods across the nation. In the process of carrying out these duties, managers gradually, but decisively, appropriated the authority of the entrepreneurs who had started businesses, and then that of the shareholders who owned their stock. In contrast to much microeconomic theorizing, Chandler noted, management was not subordinate to the authority of Adam Smith's *invisible hand.* Rather, this group constituted a *visible hand* operating in a new system of managerial capitalism, one in which the discipline of the market was attenuated and the scope for managerial choice considerable. Nevertheless, as the post–World War II American economy delivered twenty-five years of prosperity, widespread economic advancement, labor peace, and overall contentment with the American economic system, the managers who led and administered American corporations attracted little public notice outside of their local communities, making up what C. Wright Mills recognized as a critical order-bestowing group, an essential but invisible structure of postwar American society.[1]

It was the economic crisis of the 1970s that began to bring management out from backstage and into the limelight. Lower rates of profit and concerns about U.S. economic competitiveness catalyzed a wave of deregulation intended to improve productivity and profitability. Rarely, if ever, in American history had there been such a wholesale reinterpretation of economic history as that which occurred during the subsequent decades of the 1980s and 1990s.[2] As the narrative was revised, managerial capitalism was portrayed no longer as the key to America's economic success but, rather, as a liability.[3] A popular theme was that American executives were unwilling or unable to make the difficult choices necessary to revitalize their corporations. The prevalent systems of economic and psychological motivation within the corporation were seen as no longer providing sufficient incentives for managers to act in the corporation's best interests. Rather, mechanisms that lay at the heart of bureaucratic administration were seen as distorting corporate goals and diverting managerial attention and effort from the most productive uses of capital. In such a context, it was argued, only the restoration of Adam Smith's invisible hand, through the creation of a market for corporate control, could ensure profit maximization and economic efficiency.[4] Corporate takeovers came to be seen as a means of restoring power to the group now believed to be the only one with a legitimate claim to the value created by corporations—shareholders. Conventional corporate executives, especially in the largest public companies, were portrayed by many economists and policy advocates as unwilling to set aside their own personal interests and align their efforts with the goal of maximizing shareholder value. The result was a wholesale transformation in the relations between executives of large, publicly traded companies and shareholders and the appearance of a new type of chief executive, along with the development of a new kind of corporate model in which the interests of corporate executives and shareholders were to be closely linked. The full economic and societal implications of this new model, sometimes described as investor capitalism, are only just beginning to be understood. Yet even as the image of the ideal executive was transformed from one of a steady, reliable caretaker of the corporation and its many constituencies to that of the swashbuckling, iconoclastic champion of "shareholder value" (and is now probably in the process of being transformed once again, in ways it does not yet seem possible to predict), a larger story has remained untold and largely uncomprehended.

This larger story stretches back beyond the transition from the era of the bland, more or less anonymous corporate statesman of the postwar world to that of the star CEO of the more recent past. Long before they became the nameless, inoffensive, taken-for-granted corporate functionaries of postwar managerial capitalism, managers were controversial or, at the very least, members of a new and unfamiliar economic and social group whose role required explanation. Lacking legitimate authority, managers needed to prove their social worth and legitimate their authority, not only to others, but to themselves. When salaried managers first appeared in the large corporations of the late nineteenth century, then began to proliferate, it was not obvious who they were, what they did, or why they should be entrusted with the task of running corporations. It was only after a sustained quest for social and moral legitimacy—finally achieved through the linkage of management and managerial authority to existing institutions viewed as dedicated to the common good—that management successfully defined its image as a trustworthy steward of the economic resources represented by the large, publicly held corporation. Once management had successfully pursued its claims to legitimacy and control over corporations, the awareness that this was neither inevitable nor inherent in the nature of things began to vanish—although it has flickered at the edges of America's collective consciousness at moments of crisis such as the Depression (when business leaders were implicated by many in the stock market crash), the economic crisis of the 1970s (when shareholders began to rise up against managers held responsible for inadequate corporate performance), and, most recently, the spate of business scandals of the early years of the twenty-first century.

One of the key factors in management's successful effort to establish its claims to the legitimacy and authority it enjoys to this day was another institution—once new and obscure, now familiar and powerful—whose sources of legitimacy and authority have become largely invisible: the university-based business school. When they first emerged, business schools were highly controversial institutions. The profit-maximizing imperatives of business were seen to be at odds with the more disinterested mission of universities. Business education came to be an accepted and uncontroversial part of the university only through the efforts of a vanguard of institutional entrepreneurs, both academics and managers, who saw the need for creating a managerial class that would run America's large corporations in a way that served the broader interests of society rather than the narrowly defined ones of capital or labor.

Like contemporary executives, business schools today are not exactly out of the public eye. The MBA has become the second-most popular graduate degree in America and a virtual requirement for entry into the upper echelons of management in large, established corporations, as well as into such lucrative occupations as consulting, investment banking, and private equity.[5] As a result, publications including *BusinessWeek* and the *Wall Street Journal* regularly trumpet their rankings of the top business schools in the country. Business magazines and the business pages of major newspapers advertise the panoply of full-time MBAs, part-time MBAs, and executive education programs offered by leading business schools. Nor has it gone unnoticed during the recent corporate scandals that corporate felons such as Skilling and Andrew Fastow have degrees from some of America's most prestigious business schools at some of the country's leading universities.[6]

Yet just as the rationale for managerial authority in corporations has sunk from sight, so that it is now barely possible to examine and reevaluate it even amid mounting discontent with managerial behavior among shareholders, employees, regulators, and citizens, so too the rationale for enlisting the resources and reputations of American universities in the education of corporate managers, financiers, and the like has become obscure with the passage of time and the consolidation of the power and influence of business schools. In 1926, C. P. Biddle, an assistant dean at Harvard Business School, provided one framing of what was, at the time, the highly contested question of whether and why business schools belonged in universities:

> The basic consideration of what constitutes graduate work in business administration seems to me to lie in the purpose of the graduate training. If its purpose is to train "hands," or technicians, or merely successful money-makers, in my judgment the course has no place in a graduate department of a university. On the other hand if its purpose is to train "heads" or future leaders in business, it has no difficulty in justifying its existence or place.[7]

Although, as I hope to show in the course of this book, the choice for business schools that Biddle presented nearly a century ago has yet to be decisively made, a number of factors suggest that all is not well within the institution of the university-based business school: recent events and trends in the corporate world; a mounting chorus of criticism directed at business schools from within their own ranks; and the implicit challenge represented by the rise of for-profit, online, and other alternatives to the traditional MBA. Biddle's implicit question is as relevant today as it ever was. For business schools and for management itself, the times seem ripe for reopening the question of what exactly this institution is for, what functions we as a society want it to perform, and how well it is performing them.

The rationale for placing the institutions of management and business schools side by side is not just that business schools shape the identity, outlook, assumptions, and aspirations of individuals who go on to become influential actors within powerful economic institutions. At a more fundamental level, the relationship between management and business schools is about how they have shaped each other *as* institutions and influenced other ones, in the sense in which sociology uses the term *institutions*.[8] That is, institutions are the complex and interacting systems of norms, structures, and cultural understandings that shape individual and organizational behavior. The two institutions of management and business education, for example, have reciprocally defined the ultimate ends of the corporation and shaped the means through which management seeks to achieve them. They have given rise to the contemporary understanding that the purpose of management is to maximize shareholder value, thereby legitimating practices such as the liberal granting of stock options and a focus on share price as the measure of managerial and organizational achievement. Grasping the nature of business education is therefore essential for our understanding of the function of management in the

American economy and American society today, and of how the institution of management can be not only critically evaluated but also, if deemed necessary, reshaped to make for a better fit with overall social aspirations.

To understand the nature of business education, and how it has shaped and been shaped by the larger business context, we need to go back to its beginnings. For the institutional entrepreneurs who invented the university business school—both those who came to the project from the business side and those who came to it from the academy—the primary purpose of this new institution was to legitimate and institutionalize the new occupation of management. To achieve this purpose, these institutional entrepreneurs framed management as an emerging profession, much like medicine and law. Using this frame, they successfully mobilized societal support, financial resources, and personnel for the development of this innovative educational enterprise, the university-based business school. To be sure, the incorporation of management education into the American university was part of a larger historical and social process in which the American research university—itself a relatively young institution at the end of the nineteenth century and the beginning of the twentieth—gained support and legitimacy by extending its mission beyond that of the religious liberal arts colleges of the seventeenth, eighteenth, and early nineteenth centuries to include preparation for the many practical occupations demanding increasingly sophisticated training amid the scientific and technological advances transforming the country in the late nineteenth century. Today, just over 125 years after the invention of the university-based business school, the relationship between the university and the business school has been largely reversed. Having undertaken, in a previous incarnation, to confer on management the academic charisma it sought in order to become respectable, the thoroughly rationalized, bureaucratized, disenchanted (in the Weberian sense) university of today, as some have said, looks to management for guidance on how to be respected.[9]

Yet if the university has been significantly transformed by its relationship with the institution of management, management has arguably been transformed just as decisively by its relationship with the university via the university-based business school.[10] It is now hardly a secret that, for example, the related scandals of outsized executive pay and options backdating have grown out of a belief that the way to motivate managers to act in the best interests of shareholders is to design a compensation structure that provides them with an incentive to increase the share price. Less well understood, perhaps, is the role that economic theories developed and disseminated within business schools have played in advancing this belief, or the extent to which such theories upended what had hitherto been the dominant paradigm within business schools of the nature and purpose of management. Still less fully grasped is how both what had been the reigning paradigm in university business education, and the challenge to this logic represented by doctrines such as shareholder primacy and the need to "incent" managers to maximize benefits for shareholders, were grounded in the fundamental relationship of management as a subject of study to the intellectual, pedagogical, and social traditions and practices of the university, and in the changing relationship of the university to the larger society.

To telescope the argument I make in the pages that follow: university business schools were originally created to be "professional schools" not in the loose sense in which we now use the term to refer to graduate schools in any area outside the arts and sciences, but in another, more complex sense reflecting a very specific, historically grounded understanding of what constitutes a "profession." This notion comprised, among other things, a social compact between occupations deemed "professions" and society at large, as well as a certain set of relations among professional schools, the occupational groups for which they serve as authoritative communities, and society. Business schools were thus intended not just to prepare students for careers in management but also to serve as the major vehicles of an effort to transform management from an incipient occupation in search of legitimacy to a bona fide profession in the sense in which the creators of the university business school understood that term. The history of the university-based business school is thus framed in these pages as a professionalization project undertaken, transformed, and finally abandoned over a period stretching from the founding of the Wharton School at the University of Pennsylvania in 1881 up to the present.

In the course of this history, the logic of professionalism that underlay the university-based business school in its formative phase was replaced first by a managerialist logic that emphasized professional knowledge rather than professional ideals, and ultimately by a market logic that, taken to its conclusion, subverts the logic of professionalism altogether. From this historical perspective, business schools have evolved over the century and a quarter of their existence into their own intellectual and institutional antithesis, in a process of development that is, as yet, little understood and generating consequences that we are only now beginning to comprehend and reckon with.

To illuminate this process of development, its consequences, and the significance of both for how we think about the role and purpose of business education today, I must first describe my approach to two subjects of fundamental relevance: (1) the concept of professionalism in sociology; and (2) the significance of how institutions arise and develop for our understanding of their nature and function in the present.

Professionalism

Professionalism and professions are powerful ideas and institutions. Sociologists and economists have recognized professions as an important subset of the labor market and professionals as a vital subset of the workforce. Professions are laden not only with economic implications but also with cultural meaning.[11] They often occupy the highest-status positions in an occupational hierarchy. In cultural terms, they are carriers of important societal norms and values concerning such matters as the relationship between knowledge and power and the maintenance of trust.

In sociology, the study of professions has a venerable lineage. Its earliest roots can be traced to European social thinkers including Tocqueville, Marx, Weber, and Durkheim. In American sociology, the early study of professions was closely linked to the functionalist perspective of Talcott Parsons and Robert Merton that defined the emergence of professions by how they fulfilled societal needs.[12] The functionalist approach was often taxonomic, identifying characteristics that distinguish a profession from an occupation and a professional from other members of the labor force.[13] Researchers in this tradition often asked, "What are the differences between doctors and carpenters, lawyers and autoworkers, that make us speak of one as professional and deny the label to the other?"[14] Functionalists like Harold L. Wilensky and William J. Goode focused their attention on structural attributes of professions, such as how professional work is organized and governed, and the types of training prerequisite to the practice of a particular occupation.[15] Wilensky, for example, studied the stages of development undergone by eighteen different professions and devised a model for the evolution of an occupation into a profession. Some of the critical points he analyzed were the following: the development of a training school, which indicates that an aspiring profession's work requires unique abilities and specialized preparation; the establishment of a professional association as a community of practitioners who share convictions and distinct practices; and a "self-conscious" definition of the core tasks that constitute the work of the profession.[16]

During the 1970s, a significant number of sociologists and economists expressed skepticism about the functionalist account of professions. These researchers argued that the functionalist perspective, particularly the focus on a profession's structures and distinguishing traits, uncritically assumed a tight coupling between a profession's formal structures and claims, on the one hand, and its actual activities, on the other. They moved away from an occupation-based view of professions to a class-based one. In particular, these critics maintained that the functionalist account obscured what they took to be the one true goal of professions, the creation of monopolies. If professions and professionals had anything in common, these scholars argued, it was the way in which they insulated themselves from market forces. Instead of offering a different research approach to understanding professions, the class-based critics simply reinterpreted many of the attributes of professions identified by the functionalists. Phenomena such as university training, professional associations, and licensing, for example, came to be seen as means of gaining and maintaining monopoly power.[17] Sociologists, represented by Magali Larson, Randall Collins, and others influenced by critical theory, emphasized the social closure and credentialism dimensions of professional status and its contribution to economic stratification.[18] The neoclassical economists who came to be known as the Chicago school portrayed professionals as monopolists fundamentally interested in restraining trade and maximizing profit by limiting the freedom of consumers to hire whomever they wanted to do a certain type of work or perform a particular service.

While both the economic and sociological critiques of professions emphasized their monopolistic aspects, sociologists focused their attacks not just on the structural features of the professions that tended toward monopoly but also on their cognitive and normative claims. The focus on the cognitive claims of professions is elaborated in Andrew Abbott's cultural and process account, *The System of Professions*. The key to understanding a profession, Abbott argues in his landmark book, lies not in its structural attributes or the explanations it gives to the public as to why those structures are important, but, rather, in the dynamics of its claims to knowledge and professional prerogatives in the arenas within which a profession claims expertise and seeks to exercise control. Of particular interest, Abbott argues, are boundary disputes between professions over which problems fall into their domains, what knowledge is relevant to their solution, and which occupational tasks fall to which groups: for example, the struggle between conventional medicine and osteopathy, or engineers and technicians, or, in my field, management researchers and management consultants. As Abbott notes, any occupation wishing to achieve professional autonomy and exercise professional authority must find a defensible knowledge basis for its jurisdictional claims. It is in the process of achieving exclusive jurisdiction over a particular class of problems or tasks and then continually defending (or expanding) this territory that a profession emerges. That a profession can claim control over a particular set of problems at one point in history is no guarantee that another profession will not dispute such control later on, and if the latter can establish its own knowledge claims, jurisdictional boundaries between professions can shift.[19]

Even before Abbott's work undermined the notion that a profession's cognitive claims can be grounded on any absolute claim of expert knowledge, Magali Larson took aim at the normative claims of professions in her book *The Rise of Professionalism.* In Larson's view—quite characteristic of the debunking spirit of much American social science in the 1970s—professional claims over a particular knowledge base are used for achieving professional status, then deftly manipulated to allow a profession to define the standards by which its competence is judged.[20] Meanwhile, professional norms prescribing orientation toward service (e.g., the Hippocratic oath) are seen as ideological facades masking the fundamentally self-interested motives of professions.[21]

The focus on knowledge and normative claims and their uses in claiming professional prerogatives—a focus that characterizes Abbott's and Larson's important work—is the starting point for my own inquiry into business education. The goal of the professionalization project in American management, carried out by the university-based business school, was to achieve control in a specific area—the large, publicly traded corporation—and protect that control from competing groups, namely, shareholders, labor, and the state.

Managers' challenge to the claims of shareholders, workers, or the state for various decision rights with respect to the corporation was made in the face of powerful ideological headwinds: for example, the idea that property rights should determine prerogative in the control of the business firm. This challenge was also set forth at a time when the large business corporation itself was seen (correctly) as a historically unprecedented institution, uniquely powerful and troubling in its capacity for overturning existing economic, social, and political institutions, and therefore in need of the most enlightened administration possible. Thus it was useful, and perhaps essential, for managers to attach to their claims of cognitive exclusiveness a strongly normative component. This they did by allying themselves with existing institutions—not just the professions but also the closely related institutions of science and the university—whose own cognitive claims were closely interwoven with normative values that were portrayed as aligned with broader social aspirations and the public's interest.

My research approach takes very seriously Larson's ideas about how professional structures and ideologies can obscure underlying interests, but it also reconceptualizes certain elements of the functional perspective on professions, viewing the structural and normative traits exhibited by professions as important markers in a professionalization project. While I agree with critics like Larson and Freidson when they argue that such traits do not help explain the development of professions, and can serve to enhance their monopoly status, these traits do point us toward a set of well-established cultural markers—for example, university training for professionals, codes of ethics—that are often used by external agents to evaluate the state of an occupation and its professional claims. These external agents, moreover, have bargaining power in negotiations with groups seeking recognition as professions, and it is fallacious to assume that they are simply duped by bids for monopoly status dressed up as expert knowledge or professional norms and values, as class-based critics suggest.

To clarify my own assumptions here, I take it that ideational interests can be important factors in a professionalization project, and that statements of them must sometimes be taken at face value to illuminate the dimension of shared meaning that, along with social roles and private (material or power) interests, constitutes the raw material from which professions are created. When we are ill, for example, we often defer to physicians' judgments about diagnosis and treatment mostly out of a presumption that they are acting in accord with the standards of practice articulated by the professional medical community. Moreover, I share the viewpoint of Everett C. Hughes, a scholar of the modern occupational structure, who described the status of professions in American society as the result of a type of social contract: professions are given extraordinary privilege in exchange for their contributions to the enhancement of social order.[22] (Similar ideas about professions holding a socially negotiated occupational status that mediates between the imperatives of the market and the needs of society can be found in the writings of Talcott Parsons, Robert K. Merton, and most recently Eliot Freidson, who has reconsidered his earlier class-based critique of professions.)[23] Again, the external agents involved in evaluating and passing judgment on claims to professional autonomy and authority have bargaining power that they are capable of using to reinforce social values as well as to ensure the competent performance of particular kinds of work. Finally, I take it that institutions like professions—or business schools—are not just efficient solutions to problems or vehicles for the advancement of interests but also order-creating institutions. This last assumption requires particular elaboration, for it informs the approach I take in this book to the study of the university-based business school as an institution.

▐ Institutionalization and the Creation of Social Order

The study of institutions has occupied social scientists from the inception of the social sciences themselves, although its theoretical underpinnings have undergone significant development in recent decades. From the 1920s until about the 1960s, the dominant approach was functionalism, which sought to understand institutions by describing the interrelated roles they played in enabling the smooth functioning of society.[24] The functionalist approach, which was often comparative, focused on the structural features of institutions as well as the norms and socialization processes that enabled individuals to carry out prescribed institutional roles. In functionalist theory, institutions are seen as efficient solutions to particular social problems, solutions that emerge through a competitive process and enable particular tasks. Although the focus on efficiency in functionalist theory exhibits a certain economistic bias, the assumption that an institution's survival is evidence of its efficiency, or that the causes of certain social arrangements can be explained by the consequences of those arrangements, is also characteristic of the functionalist approach to institutions in sociology.

As the heyday of functionalist theory passed in the 1960s, scholars engaged in the study of institutions in fields such as organizational theory began to focus on the increasingly evident limitations of functionalism and the competitive selection model of institutional behavior that underlay it. They pointed to such frequently observed phenomena as the unintended consequences of organizational designs, the decoupling of organizational practices from stated goals, and the tendency of organizations to resemble one another despite the diversity of their origins and stated goals, raising questions about whether institutions really pursue rational objectives or are more driven by normative conventions.[25]

Scholars constituting the theoretical school known as the "new institutionalism" have built upon earlier work in the study of institutions that originated principally in the fields of economics and political science (and that, in sociology, is partly rooted in the study of the professions). In sociology, the principal ideas behind the new institutionalism have been developed by Paul DiMaggio, John Meyer, Walter Powell, Richard Scott, and Philip Selznick.[26] Scott, in his review of the field, provides the most complete and succinct definition of an institution as these scholars use the term. "Institutions," Scott writes, "consist of cognitive, normative, and regulative structures and activities that provide stability and meaning to social behavior."[27] Most institutional analysis focuses on four facets of institutions: institutional actors, institutional fields, institutional logics, and legitimacy.

Institutional actors consist of both individual entrepreneurs and groups of social actors. Those institutional actors that regularly interact to "constitute a recognized area of institutional life, such as key suppliers, resource and product consumers, regulatory agencies and other organizations that produce similar services or products," make up an *institutional field*. In the automotive industry, for example, a field consists of not only the automobile manufacturers, but their customers, suppliers, regulators, and unions that define the rules and standards within which they operate. Institutional actors exert influence primarily in two ways. First, they are active agents capable of exercising power, mobilizing resources, and altering rules so as to affect the behavior of other agents. Second, they are reproducers of institutions: the ways in which existing institutions look and behave, and the values they espouse, shape new entrants' understandings as to how they themselves ought to look and act.

The third aspect of institutions that researchers emphasize is *institutional logic*. Roger Friedland and Robert R. Alford define an institutional logic as the set of "organizing principles" that provide "not only the ends" to which behavior is oriented but the "means by which those ends are achieved."[28] They constitute the "underlying assumptions, deeply held, often unexamined, which form a framework within which reasoning takes place."[29] Institutional logics construct and inform a perceptual frame in which those who inhabit an institution locate themselves and gain their understanding of the world.[30] A society's traditions affect institutional logics. Changing historical conditions may mean that principles and policies developed under one societal consensus can no longer be seen as valid under another.[31] Focusing on an era's prevailing institutional logics helps researchers understand the belief system and taken-for-granted assumptions in a particular era and how they have evolved.

The fourth element emphasized by the new institutionalism is *legitimacy*. Parsons described legitimacy as the "appraisal of action in terms of shared or common values in the context of the involvement of the action in the social system."[32] Jeffrey Pfeffer and John Dowling define legitimacy as a situation of "congruence between the social values associated with or implied by [an organization's] activities and the norms of acceptable behavior in the larger social system."[33] Powell and DiMaggio similarly describe legitimacy as the social standing granted to an institution by virtue of its conformity to widespread social norms, values, and expectations.[34] A legitimate corporate board, for example, is one that is perceived as having members attend legally required meetings, but also as behaving so as to represent the company's long-term interests. Given this normative dimension, efficiency and performance are not sufficient to establish societal legitimacy.

Legitimacy is the currency of institutions. For an aspiring institution, acquiring the halo of legitimacy is a difficult achievement often requiring effort and commitment and the steady observance of exacting standards over an extended period of time. But, like trust, legitimacy can vanish very quickly and, once lost, is difficult to regain. When an institution loses legitimacy, external observers call even everyday activities into question, and perfectly sincere actions may be interpreted as disingenuous or masking a hidden agenda. For organizations in general, legitimacy is an important aspect of the social fitness that enables them to secure advantages in economic and political markets and improve their chances of survival. Because legitimacy justifies an institution's role and helps attract resources and the continued support of constituents, it is both a goal and a resource, and institutions like professions may compete with one another to establish their claims to legitimacy.[35] The process in which new institutions strive to conform to generally accepted beliefs and rules in order to gain legitimacy gives rise, in turn, to the phenomenon of *isomorphism*, the tendency toward increased homogeneity within organizational fields.[36]

Institutional theory and its concepts have contributed significantly to sociological understanding of the relationship between existing organizations and their environment. Much less is known about the origins and development of new institutions, institutional logics, forms, and behaviors. Researchers have paid relatively little attention to the question: where do new institutions come from? In recent years, one of the field's most eminent scholars, Paul DiMaggio, has suggested that to answer this question, it is essential to examine an institution's birth—its emergence out of an interaction with the larger society and culture, the evolution of its internal dynamics, and the interface between the two. We must learn from what strata of society the institution's entrepreneurs and subsequent leadership have been drawn, with what existing institutions it has had to legitimate itself, the competing institutions and groups it had to contend with, and how it had to justify its existence and actions ideologically in the social and political environment in which it arose.[37] The key here is to show organizations responding to particular problems posed by history.

The reasons why institutions emerge are complex, but one explanation lies in the basic human desire to reduce uncertainty and increase order. Anthropologists and sociologists have observed that a fundamental characteristic of humanity is the propensity to impose order and meaning on its surroundings and interactions. While some institutions achieve this end in merely an instrumental or utilitarian sense, others serve to create and impose more complex forms of order and meaning. As the philosopher Eric Voeglin has observed, "The order of history emerges from the history of order. Every society is burdened with the task, under its concrete conditions, of creating an order that will endow the fact of its existence with meaning in terms of ends divine and human."[38] Alfred Schutz starkly frames the role of institutions such as the family, community, and religion as barriers against the alienation and anomie of life without meaning or purpose. The view that even economic institutions need to be understood with reference to religious or other noneconomic phenomena can be traced to *The Protestant Ethic and the Spirit of Capitalism*, where Weber showed that one could not adequately understand the development of economic relations apart from the most fundamental norms and beliefs that govern the lives of individuals in society. That we are still not used to thinking of a seemingly instrumental institution like the university-based business school in this way is a testament to the power of the institutionalization process to erase our awareness of origins and relegate questions of meaning and purpose to the margins of our attention.

The Business School as an Institution

As I hope to show in these pages, the development of the university-based business school over the approximately 125 years from its invention in the late nineteenth century, to its institutionalization in the post–World War II era, to its taken-for-granted yet not unchallenged status today exhibits many features better explained by institutional theory than by assertions of purposiveness and efficiency. For example, as I have already suggested, the history of American business schools from their beginnings to the present reveals a decoupling, over many decades, of business school practices from a mission that originally centered on the professionalization of business management, and that is still generally said to entail social purpose. I argue that the final, most decisive phase of this decoupling of practice from stated purpose can be traced to the unintended consequences of the large-scale reform of American business education undertaken in the post–World War II period and described in part 2.

Moreover, as I show in parts 2 and 3 of the book, the divergence of the American business school after World War II from the course set for it by its founders and early proponents came about through its susceptibility to influence from external actors (e.g., foundations, the press, the corporate sector) in the institutional field. As revealed in the founding period that I examine in part 1, the adoption of professionalism as an institutional logic calls attention to the importance of norms and values (as opposed to purely instrumental goals such as training individuals to perform particular functions in corporations) in the formation of the institution of the university-based business school. For as I argue in this first part of the book, the professionalization project undertaken by the founders of university business education depended to a critical degree on the ability of business schools (to borrow Philip Selznick's definition of the institutionalization process) to infuse the new occupation of management with values beyond the technical requirements of the job.[39]

Beyond these particular considerations, the founding and development of the university-based business school presents an especially fascinating study in the process of institutionalization because the institutional entrepreneurs who invented and launched it were highly conscious of the nature of their efforts. These individuals—many, but not all, of whom came from socially elite backgrounds—were self-consciously aware that the creation of institutions was a critically important task for the maintenance of social order. Through the establishment of this new institution, they sought a solution to what presented itself as one of the major social questions of their times: by what means, and for whose benefit, should large corporations be run? In choosing the professionalization of management as the path to the institutionalization of the university business school, these institutional entrepreneurs, as we shall see, sought to yoke their enterprise to those of other institution builders in late nineteenth- and early twentieth-century America whose efforts were part of what the historian Robert H. Wiebe called the "search for order" in this period.

The importance of the institutional context of the rise of the university-based business school is further emphasized by one of the unique features of this enterprise as a professionalization project. Professions, as we have seen, are in one of their dimensions occupational groups that claim jurisdiction over particular arenas of work. In order to successfully claim such jurisdiction, a profession must, as Andrew Abbott puts it, ask "society to recognize its cognitive structure through exclusive rights."[40] Other scholars who have studied the professions argue that societal recognition of such claims is usually achieved through the legal system and/or in the realm of public opinion.[41] Law and medicine are professions that rely on both the legal system (i.e., state licensing boards) and their standing with the public for their ability to monopolize particular types of work. Journalism and social work are examples of professions that are more dependent on public opinion alone. In this context, "professional management" is unique in that it has relied on neither legal authority for, nor public endorsement of, its claims of jurisdiction over managerial tasks in large publicly held corporations, investment banks, and so forth. Instead, its jurisdictional authority has been achieved through an interdependent relationship between university-based business schools—which derived their own legitimacy from institutions including the established, "high" professions and the university itself—and the corporate workplace. Viewed from this perspective, business schools cannot be regarded as stand-alone objects. Rather, they must be seen as part of a pattern of collective behavior, linked to other institutional sectors in society through the interaction of individuals within them with other actors and systems in society—hence the importance of an institutional field perspective.

Although institutional theory recognizes the importance of such links and interactions, it has not always paid enough attention to the emergence and development of institutions in their historical contexts as well as in their organizational and institutional fields.[42] Yet origins are crucial for our understanding of institutions. New institutions are often proposed and created in periods of instability and conflict, while these institutions themselves represent efforts on the part of individuals and groups to stabilize a situation in a way that aligns with their interests and values. Thus new institutions are both a source of social contention and a mechanism for resolving social conflicts.[43] They are means through which a society adjusts to new conditions.

To understand this crucial aspect of an institution, then, requires a deep familiarity with the social context of the period of its founding and development, and with the debates in which a set of institutional entrepreneurs were engaged, as well as an understanding of why it is that particular stances gained acceptance from resource providers.

Hence the method of this book, which, though chronological in structure, is not a history of business schools but, rather, uses historical data to develop an argument about the development of an institution. As the book's subtitle suggests, my use of sociological concepts and historical data to understand the origin of business education is directly inspired by Paul Starr's definitive account of the origins and development of American medicine, *The Social Transformation of American Medicine*. While this study does not approach the scope and breadth of Starr's analysis, my orientation and goal are the same: to use the historical record—as found in primary and secondary sources—as the raw material from which a more complete institutional understanding can be fashioned. As in Starr's work, this sociological approach toward history is particular and interpretative. It deals in depth with specific, concrete events and then tries to understand the meanings that different social actors attached to these events. As I observe in the "Bibliographic and Methods Note," it is from a detailed examination of particular historical circumstances and meanings, in turn, that sociology develops and refines its perspectives and general concepts. Such concepts then allow us to formulate explanations as to the cause of recurrent human phenomena, such as war or revolution, or the typical developmental process of important institutions, like government or business. The origins and development of university business education, which form my subject here, are inextricably intermixed with the messy stuff of history, including competing groups with their material and ideational interests, as well as time-bound cultural conceptions. I have attempted to understand these phenomena not for their purely historical interest but in order to shed light on a set of contemporary institutions that have powerful claims on our attention today.

Plan of the Book

I have divided this study into three parts to emphasize three distinct movements in the development of American business education: the professionalization project that led to the emergence and diffusion of business schools; the

institutionalization of business schools that took place during an era of reform and standardization; and the shift of business schools away from an
orientation toward professionalization. These three movements fall roughly
into three time periods. The professionalization project stood at the center of
business schools' agenda during the period from 1881 until America's entry
into World War II in 1941, an age in which business schools emerged and diffused throughout America's colleges and universities. The period of reform
and subsequent institutionalization took place from about 1941 to the economic recession of the early 1970s. Part 3 of the book takes us from the 1970s
to the present day, a time in which the imperatives of professionalism in business education were replaced by market imperatives.

Chapters 1 and 2 provide some historical and contextual perspective for
the emergence of business schools and the idea of management as a profession. It is no accident that the rise of university-based business education coincided with the astonishing economic and social transformations effected
by the rise of large-scale industrialism and corporate capitalism in the last
three decades of the nineteenth century, and with Progressives' "search for
order" in the wake of these upheavals.[44] The attempt to establish business as
a subject of professional education was, in fact, a quintessential Progressive
era phenomenon, for the Progressive response to the disorder unleashed by
industrial capitalism manifested itself not just in politics and law, but in attempts to bring a wide range of social phenomena, including management,
under the broader power of science, rationality, and expertise.

Chapter 3 shows that business education arose not from centralized
organizations, like the government or large corporations, but from an entrepreneurial vanguard of academics and forward-thinking managers.
These individuals sought to associate management with elite education
partly for status reasons, but also out of an idealistic belief that a certain
kind of education—professional education that emphasized the importance
of service and calling—could ensure that large corporations were run in the
best interests of society.

Chapter 4 describes the challenges of constructing management as a
profession. I examine, among other phenomena, the formation and early development of the American Association of Colleges and Schools of Business
(AACSB) and its struggles to professionalize managerial education through
efforts led by educators rather than practitioners.

Chapters 5 and 6 take us from World War II to the early 1970s, when
various important actors outside universities attempted to improve on the

prewar work of the AACSB. I look, in particular, at the Ford and Carnegie foundations, which issued critical reports on the academic limitations of business schools and provided generous funding to make them more intellectually competitive with standard academic departments. They succeeded, but at the price of distancing business schools from frontline practices in the world of business.

Chapter 7 begins with the economic crisis of the 1970s. It highlights the shift in business school logic away from the managerialist orientation inspired by the foundations, with its focus on abstract expertise, and toward an outlook dominated by the discipline of economics and the logic of the market. I attempt to show how this move undermined the ideals of professionalism that had long guided business schools.

Chapter 8 considers the business school in the contemporary marketplace. In so doing, the chapter returns to the enduring problem of defining the purpose of business education, now made especially difficult by the diverse and sometimes conflicting views, interests, goals, and educational challenges presently characteristic not only of business schools, but of universities.

In my epilogue, I do not offer any simple solutions for the challenges that business schools face—there are no silver bullets. I do suggest, however, that as business schools attempt to rebalance their relationships with students, faculty, business, and society at large, the ideals of professionalism and professional leadership should serve as a guide, as they so often have in the past.

The Professionalization Project in American Business Education, 1881–1941

An Occupation in Search of Legitimacy   **I**

The enormous cadre of salaried managers who administer the affairs of large corporations has become such a dominant and taken-for-granted presence that it requires considerable historical imagination to recognize that there was nothing inevitable about its appearance and development. It was not until the late 1870s that the equivalent of today's modern, salaried manager emerged as a significant, if still vaguely defined, entity. By 1900, the number of managers in organizations had grown dramatically. National statistics are difficult to find, but in the transportation and communications industries, for example, the number of proprietors, officials, managers, and inspectors increased from 12,501 in 1870 to 67,706 in 1900—more than 500 percent.[1] On the eve of World War I, a University of Michigan professor, who would later have an instrumental role in the founding of that institution's business school, reflected on a phenomenon that was attracting the attention of many Americans: "There has begun to emerge a special class of administrators, who are not capitalists, but stand midway between the multitude of stock and bond owners on the one side, and the wage-earning classes and public as consumers on the other."[2] By the early 1920s, managers constituted a sizable and universally recognized occupational group—the 1920 United States occupational census estimated that there were 2,612,525 executive and manager positions in business[3]—whose control of corporations and their resources was firmly established.[4] How did this group invent itself virtually ex nihilo and then rise to such heights of power, all in less than fifty years?

▚ The Rise of Management in American Society

Like any institution that achieves dominance in a society, management has risen to power partly by vesting itself in a series of changing ideological

23

mantles that, over time, have obscured this institution's historically contingent origins. One purpose of this book is to describe why and how this was accomplished.

Previous accounts of the rise and eventual triumph of management as an occupation have affirmed, albeit unintentionally, that there was something both inevitable and inherently right about this historical trajectory. One of the most influential such accounts was put forth by the Harvard business historian Alfred D. Chandler, Jr., in his classic *The Visible Hand*.[5] For Chandler, as for other scholars working in the tradition he represents, modern management grew naturally out of the large corporations that arose to take advantage of the national markets created by late nineteenth-century advances in manufacturing, transportation, and communications. Before the Civil War, Chandler notes, there was no such thing as "big business" by any modern definition. The typical business organization was a small enterprise, usually run by an individual owner or a few partners. Such firms often focused on one or two economic activities and operated within a restricted geographic realm. Chandler suggests that the small-firm structure was inherently unreliable and inefficient. Slight and unanticipated changes in the business cycle often doomed a business; indeed, most businesses, then as now, died in infancy. Moreover, Chandler argues, the quality and quantity of goods produced by such enterprises were unpredictable because workers largely controlled the manner and pace of work. Chandler and others working from this perspective claim that the replacement of the market's invisible hand by the "visible hand" of management in the modern business firm represented a kind of Darwinian triumph. A superior form of organization, better suited to evolving economic conditions, had replaced its unreliable and inefficient predecessor. Chandler wrote:

> [M]odern business enterprise took the place of market mechanisms in coordinating the activities of the economy and allocating its resources. In many sectors of the economy the visible hand of management replaced what Adam Smith referred to as the invisible hand of market forces. The market remained the generator of demand for goods and services, but modern business enterprise took over the functions of coordinating flows of goods through existing processes of production and distribution, and of allocating funds and personnel for future production and distribution. As modern business enterprise acquired functions hitherto carried out by the market, it

became the most powerful institution in the American economy and its managers the most influential group of economic decision makers. The rise of modern business enterprise in the United States, therefore, brought with it managerial capitalism.[6]

Chandler argued, specifically, that the visible hand of managers rationalized the structure and operations of business firms in ways that reduced costs and raised productivity:

> By routinizing the transactions between units, the costs of these transactions were lowered. By linking the administration of producing units with buying and distributing units, costs for information on markets and sources of supply were reduced. Of much greater significance, the internalization of many units permitted the flow of goods from one unit to another to be administratively coordinated. More effective scheduling of flows achieved a more intensive use of facilities and personnel employed in the processes of production and distribution and so increased productivity and reduced costs.[7]

Amid the increased scale and complexity of business in the late nineteenth century, the Chandler argument concludes, it was management's ability to perform crucial economic functions that the market carried out inefficiently—and that owner-entrepreneurs and their partners could no longer perform for themselves—that gave rise to the novel phenomenon of managers running enterprises they did not own.[8]

Writing in an era in which, as we shall see in part 3, the managerial capitalism whose origins he documented was coming under fierce attack, Chandler adhered to the then-current assumption among institutional economists that (as Frank Dobbin has recently summarized it) "history is efficient when it comes to institutions."[9] That is to say, Chandler offers a teleological view of organizational history in which, if particular organizational forms survive, it is because they perform some function more efficiently than other forms do. The history of organizational change thus recounts a march of progress to ever more efficient modes of organizing.

More recent research, however, suggests that the transition from entrepreneurial to managerial capitalism was hardly as simple, smooth, or inevitable as Chandler's characterization implies. Examining the emergence of the large corporation from a historical and sociological perspective, legal theorists, sociologists, and organizational behavior researchers take as their point of departure Chandler's economic interpretation of the rise of large corporations. Focusing on the social and political context of the late nineteenth and early twentieth centuries, these scholars note that the period saw a wholesale reconstruction of American society and its institutions. Thus, they argue, explaining the rise of large corporations only in economic terms offers a limited view.

Analyzing the period's economic, political, and legal discourses, these researchers find that concerns about the role of the corporation were among the preeminent issues in national politics during the late nineteenth and early twentieth centuries.[10] Leading politicians, economists, jurists, and public intellectuals saw the emergence of large corporations as much more than a natural economic event or an objective consequence of technical development. They considered its implications for the law, the role of government, the position of labor, and the relationship between the economy and society. Questions about who should control the large corporation were intertwined with competing economic, social, and political interests that went beyond the issue of the large corporation's efficiency (although shareholders, foreshadowing contemporary debates about corporate control, questioned whether a managerially controlled corporation would act in more economically efficient ways than shareholder-controlled companies). Debate centered on the nature of claims over corporate property, the economic and political consequences of separating ownership from control, class relations, democratic values, and the public interest, as well as on the legitimacy of a new system of social authorities in the form of management and large-scale bureaucracy. Thus researchers seeking to go beyond Chandler's efficiency hypothesis focus on the numerous points beyond the market at which large corporations intersected with society, including legal and political institutions. For example, institutional scholars have emphasized how organizations conform to the normative expectations of other actors in the environment, irrespective of considerations of efficiency.[11] Network theorists have demonstrated how economic relations are embedded in social relations.[12] Scholars examining the role of power underscore how the dynamics of power between state regulators and corporate executives affect organizational structure and strategy.[13]

The development of economic institutions, in other words, is not simply a function of their efficiency; rather it often results from the outcome of contests in the legal, political, social, and cultural realms.[14] Understanding why institutions such as large corporations and professional management evolved as they have therefore requires us to consider two phenomena that Chandler largely neglects.

The first of these is social context. Examination of the social context in which the large corporation arose, and of how this new entity was regarded by society, shows that the birth of the corporate structure represented more than a simple adaptation by firms to new technological and market conditions. It was also linked to emerging social, intellectual, and cultural conditions and, indeed, to the disruption of an entire social order. Some of the social conditions coincident with the rise of the large corporation are already so well known as to require no further elaboration here—for example, the rapid population growth in American cities (the result of both immigration and internal migration from rural areas between 1880 and 1900), which was not only a response to industrialization but also a spur to its advance. Other social conditions played critical (though perhaps less obvious) roles in creating the conditions necessary for the emergence of managers and managerial activities. For example, the rapid spread of literacy in the decades following the Civil War[15] created a cadre of individuals capable of performing the new kinds of managerial tasks that Chandler describes, such as establishing detailed work steps, devising organizational structures and timetables for achieving necessary results, monitoring those results, and providing policies and procedures to monitor work activity.[16]

The second important phenomenon associated with the creation of any new institution, but marginalized by Chandler, is agency. Chandler's account of the rise of the large corporation and of management ignores the role of specific individuals, groups, or classes so completely that a reader might think organizations were unaffected by the interested actions of human beings who populate organizational structures.[17] The efficiency explanation of the origins of the modern corporation and of contemporary management ignores, in particular, the agency of what Paul DiMaggio refers to as institutional entrepreneurs, and how such actors create institutions in an effort to make the environment more amenable to their interests.[18] As DiMaggio writes, "[it is] necessary to bring interest and agency more centrally onto the institutional stage, to recognize that institutions have never 'developed and operated without the intervention of interested groups, groups . . . which have different degrees of power.'" Here he is quoting the organizational sociologist Alvin W. Gouldner, who further observed that the persistence of an institution often represents the "outcome of a contest between those who want it and those who do not."[19] Social scientists studying the emergence of new institutions must, therefore, examine the role of agents' claims and how these are conditioned by individual biography, institutional affiliations, vested interests, and the social location of the agents themselves. Applied to the institutions with which we are here concerned—large corporations and management—this approach requires consideration of how managers actively created the necessary conditions for expansion of both their organizations and their own managerial power in contests that were not just economic but also political, cultural, and social in nature.[20]

Recent study of the early history of the large corporation in America and the history of management has focused attention, for example, on legal and political contests over the concentration of economic power in corporations and the question of who should be permitted to wield this power. The outcomes of such contests, scholars have shown, were crucial to both corporate expansion and the legitimation of managerial authority.[21] While managerial control over large corporations has been recognized since the 1932 publication of Berle and Means's classic volume, *The Modern Corporation and Private Property*, it was the legal scholar Mark J. Roe who first argued, some sixty years later, that this control was a hard-won prize, not an uncontested benefice. Establishing managerial authority required managers to wrest control of their organizations from entrepreneurial owners and controlling shareholders, many of whom remained suspicious of these newcomers even as they became increasingly reliant on them for running their enterprises.[22] Roe's emphasis on the legal context of the large, multidivisional firm's emergence grounds his argument in historical contingency that Chandler largely neglects. Roe demonstrates, for instance, that, as nonowner executives exerted greater control over American corporations, a counterforce of well-organized and resourceful financial interests sought, through recourse to politics and the legal system, to retain their own control over these organizations. Shareholders, in other words, did not passively accept managerial control over the corporation. Many believed that managerial control was neither desirable in itself nor more efficient than the available alternatives. Large financial intermediaries such as investment banks, insurance firms, and trusts pooled resources in a concerted effort to exert their property rights. They did this through a combination of mechanisms: wielding political influence to modify state incorporation laws in favor of owners; pyramiding ownership through trusts, cross-shareholding, and interlocking directorates; and controlling corporate proxies.[23] While ultimately unsuccessful, their efforts demonstrate how interested actors, not just abstract considerations of efficiency and productivity, operated during the rise of managerial capitalism.

Three recent sociological studies—although dealing only indirectly with the issue of managerial authority and control—lend substantial support to Roe's focus on the legal context in his account of the rise of the modern corporation and contemporary management. These studies demonstrate that the institutionalization of the large corporation and of managerial control over it was, at its root, a political process reflecting the relative power of the organized interests and social actors who mobilized around, and were mobilized *by*, those interests. Neil Fligstein, for example, has suggested that legislation such as the Sherman Antitrust Act, although framed by its supporters as a constraint on the growth of large corporations, actually facilitated a merger and consolidation wave in the United States by making coordination among firms in similar industries unlawful.[24] Using a large, multi-industry sample of early twentieth-century corporations, William G. Roy has found no statistical support for Chandler's primary hypothesis that firms in technologically advanced industries with the fastest-growing markets were able to significantly reduce costs through economies of scale. His research suggests, in fact, that the major link between scale and firm profitability was via market power, which reduced overall competition in particular industries. Roy has also demonstrated that the merger wave that swept across several American industries in the early twentieth century was not a function of scale economies but, rather, a consequence of changes in state incorporation laws that enabled corporations to own other corporations.[25]

In a third study, Charles Perrow has traced the political activities of New England's textile industry magnates over the course of the nineteenth century and demonstrated how powerful industrial interests won legal judgments that profoundly reshaped property and trading rights.[26] These legal victories favored large organizations over small ones and weakened the control that local communities and state legislatures had over corporations. As Perrow writes, "In a few decades, the basic laws governing large organizations were remade. The national political leaders and then the lawyers in the legislatures and judgeships paved the way for untrammeled organizational growth and the accompanying centralization of wealth and power. Political values were remade, traditions were founded rapidly, and the setting was ready for . . . really big organizations."[27] "Really big" organizations required large numbers of managers, which in turn created more leverage for management vis-à-vis owners. The political and legal decisions that removed constraints on corporate growth thus aided managers in their struggle with owners for control of the corporation.

The contest between managers and owners for corporate control was not the only obstacle to the triumph of managerialism that is ignored or glossed over by proponents of the efficiency hypothesis. While the mechanization of production might not have directly translated into profitability for large firms via improvements in productivity, it exerted a profound impact on workers, who then mounted their own challenge to the establishment of managerial authority.[28] The increasing mechanization of the factory, of course, dramatically undermined the power of workers in relation to employers by rendering the workers less instrumental to the production process. It particularly disadvantaged skilled workers. Steelworkers, for example, saw the processes of heating, roughing, catching, and rolling—time-honored skills of their trade—being automated. Meanwhile, the production process itself began to be viewed as a machine to be designed and maintained by engineers (considered by most scholars to be the prototypes of modern managers, although some have recently reached back to antebellum America to posit slave overseers as candidates for this role).[29] This new concept presented a direct challenge to the authority of factory foremen.[30] As scholars now note, management's eventual victory in this battle for control of the shop floor—a contest with factory foremen and craft workers who resisted new technologies and de-skilling techniques—owed much to the ideology of Frederick W. Taylor's "scientific management." Taylor's methods essentially served to cast managers as the brains of organizations and workers as the brawn, inviting all of the hierarchical implications suggested by that model. Yet Taylor himself professed an intent, not to subdue workers, but rather to effect a "mental revolution" in workers and managers alike so that they might cooperate in pursuit of their common interest in the rationalization of production. Inasmuch as Taylor was concerned with efficiency—which is what scientific management appeared, on its face, to be about—that concern served as an incentive for cooperation. More efficiency meant a larger financial pie to be shared among owners, managers, and workers.[31] Moreover, even if Taylorism was often used, in practice, to subordinate workers to managers under the banner of efficiency, it was championed during the Progressive era by Taylor and others (including future Supreme Court justice Louis Brandeis and the reformer Morris L. Cooke) as a solution to the conflict between capital and labor. Labor strife was widely viewed—along with the vicissitudes of the business cycle that helped usher in such conflict—as the principal social problem engendered by the new industrial order.[32] In sum, a struggle for economic, social, and political power, not simply a development in the direction of greater efficiency, provided the background for the rise of managerial authority vis-à-vis workers as well as in relation to owners.

The impact on American workers of the large corporation's rise posed particular challenges to the legitimation of management. Yehouda Shenhav, summarizing the work of scholars of American labor history, has noted the paradox that the United States has had one of the least radical labor movements in the world and yet also one of the highest strike rates and levels of labor-related violence. He also argues that "in the decades surrounding the turn of the century, rational rhetorics of the systems paradigm—including accountancy, production control, and organizational structure, as well as scientific management—initially emerged and intensified during periods of labor unrest," and that the rise of what Shenhav refers to as the "systems paradigm," which encompassed the concept of managerial authority, "cannot be understood except in this context."[33] By 1900, American factory employers had come to rely on harsh and sometimes arbitrary supervision to establish control over workers; factory managers would threaten layoffs and even resort to violence at times.[34] According to sociologist Mauro Guillén, "blacklisting, parallel unionization, strikebreaking, arbitrary firings, spying, coercion, and physical violence became common employer practices" in the United States.[35] To the extent that managers were identified with owners in the public's mind, they inherited a system of authority widely held to be of questionable legitimacy, a suspicion deriving from the actions of the previous era's so-called robber barons and their seeming disregard for the larger society.[36] While violence, as Max Weber noted, offers the ultimate means of social control, it is not normally a stable basis of social order, particularly when the state claims, as the foundation of political order, a monopoly on legitimate violence. With no credibility to borrow from owners, in whose interests they were theoretically acting, managers faced the challenge of justifying their forceful domination of workers to a wider group of stakeholders. The challenge was more daunting in that this audience, which included both lawmakers and the general public, viewed labor strife as a social ill caused by the modern corporation itself.[37] To understand the strategy that managers eventually chose to explain and legitimate their actions, we must consider how the large corporation as an institution was perceived in its formative decades.

⬛ The Large Corporation and the Disruption of the Social Order

To large segments of society, including groups that would make up the heart of Progressivism, the corporation threatened an evil that went far beyond the oppression and degradation of American workers—it threatened the very foundations of the social order.[38] The gigantic corporations that emerged in America toward the end of the nineteenth century not only altered the economic landscape but, along with other phenomena of the second industrial revolution, helped to transform a taken-for-granted way of life.[39] This way of life was profoundly affected by the era's tremendous technological innovations, by the new industrial and commercial systems powered by those innovations, and by socioeconomic transformations, such as urbanization, immigration, and increased upward and downward economic mobility, that accompanied these developments. Together, these changes shook the foundations of individual and community life, but the corporate form of economic organization was itself the cause of further change as it became more prevalent in America. The advance is evident both in the numbers of corporations formed, which rose from dozens to hundreds annually in key states from the 1860s through the 1890s (fig. 1.1), and in the social attention paid to corporations in the public sphere, suggested by a tenfold increase in mentions in *New York Times* stories from the 1880s through the early 1900s (fig. 1.2).

Large corporations acted on society and the body politic in a number of ways. First, as corporations grew in scope and scale to be national rather than merely local enterprises, they disrupted the social structure of communities. Local business ownership and community leadership had, prior to the advent of corporations, overlapped to a large degree.[40] Moreover, as local businesses were supplanted and the center of authority in the corporations that replaced them became both physically and emotionally removed from local communities, the relationship between employee and employer became more impersonal. The harmoniousness of employer-employee relations had never, even in the best of times, been guaranteed by more face-to-face arrangements. Now, with the swelling of the unskilled workforce, power also tilted increasingly toward these distant employers. C. Wright Mills observed that institutions such as the family, the church, small business, and the local community appeared puny and trivial in the face of the corporation.[41] This imbalance was amplified by a series of gradual changes in the legal status of corporations whereby, instead of being held to the terms of charters that

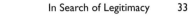

Number of Incorporations

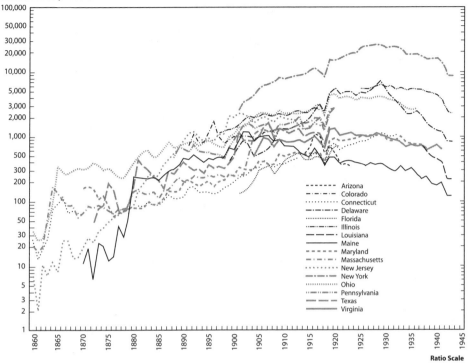

Figure 1.1
Business incorporations, sixteen states annually, 1860–1943. Adapted from George Heberton Evans, Jr., *Business Incorporations, in the United States*, 1800–1943 (New York: National Bureau of Economic Research, 1948).

obliged them to serve a public purpose, they began to be regarded before the law as "natural persons" with all the legal rights of individuals.[42] Let us examine each of these developments in turn.

For a country that still cherished the Jeffersonian ideals embodied in the small farmer, the independent merchant, and the self-sufficient, rural community—a world in which neither peasants nor aristocrats in the European sense had ever existed, and local communities largely governed themselves in their social and economic affairs—the change precipitated by industrialization itself in the course of the nineteenth century was epochal. Small farmers and small-town merchants diminished as a proportion of total workers. While the character and ideology of this group continued (and continues) to be celebrated in political rhetoric, by the late nineteenth century

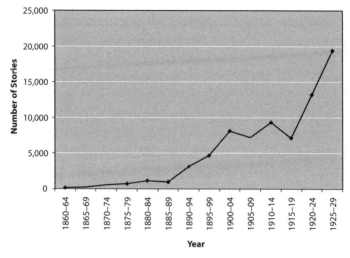

Figure 1.2
Social attention to corporations and business in the *New York Times*, 1860–1929.

these local players no longer stood at the center of the American economic story. Mills documented the breakdown of nineteenth-century American social structure by examining the changing social and economic position of farmers and small-town entrepreneurs. He argued that the rapid decrease in the number of farmers in the United States and the economic marginalization of small entrepreneurs could be traced directly to the rise of the large corporation. With the emergence of the corporation, these two groups no longer served their classic role as integrators in the community social structure. Local, small-scale entrepreneurs, for example, once employed most of a community's workforce. By the late 1920s, however, most workers in the United States were employed in large industrial factories, often located within or just outside major cities. Even the local retail merchant, who had once served as the hub of a community's social, political, and civic life, was transformed, Mills argued, into an outlet for branded products, merely one node in a vast, impersonal network of distributors.[43] The loss of commercial identity for merchants translated to a corresponding loss of social stature and a marginalized social role. Meanwhile, a new national ruling class, consisting of industrial tycoons such as Andrew Carnegie and John D. Rockefeller and financiers like J. P. Morgan, was emerging along with the corporate structure. The power wielded by these new monarchs would make them a central target of the Populist and Progressive movements.[44]

In addition to reducing the prominence of local business owners in community structure, the rise of the corporation also introduced a new relationship between employee and employer, engendered by the creation of a permanent wage labor class in the late nineteenth century. Wage labor itself was not, of course, a new phenomenon by the last quarter of the nineteenth century. What *was* new was the degree of dependency of workers on the corporation— a dependency exacerbated as economic activity once conducted by relatively small, locally owned enterprises was increasingly undertaken by large corporations. In the eighteenth and early nineteenth centuries, wage work had been not a permanent condition but a transitional state, part-time and seasonal. Writing about the early New England mills, the first large employers of wage labor, Charles Perrow notes that the original employees were often women and children from rural communities who would work in the nongrowing season. In contrast, by the early 1870s, a new, primarily undifferentiated and unskilled, wage-dependent class was being created. Whereas one's work had previously been one's own, now it was merely a commodity, an input for a distant, impersonal owner or manager.[45] The existence of a permanent class of wage laborers was also viewed—"far more widely than we have realized," according to Christopher Lasch—as posing a profound challenge to American democracy itself, which since before the Civil War had been widely believed (again in Lasch's words) to have "no future in a nation of hirelings."[46] The labor violence that began to afflict the nation in the late 1870s thus aggravated what was already a deep sense of social and political unease about the plight of workers in American industry. There was genuine concern that the nation as a whole might collapse under the weight of the struggle.

While the public at large, or at least large segments of it, worried about the position of labor in relation to the large corporation and what this meant for the future of democracy, many elites were also troubled by the threat that large corporations posed to the nation's other institutions.[47] The transformations in community life and worker relations wrought by the rise of corporations convinced many contemporary observers that the new entities had simply become too large and too powerful. Existing institutions such as government, religion, and the many organs of civil society seemed incapable of restraining the negative influences of these new behemoths. Henry Adams, a contemporary observer of the large corporation's rise in the late nineteenth century (and, by his own account, one of its "earliest victims"), declared that "the Trusts and Corporations . . . were revolutionary, troubling all the old conventions and values, as the screws of ocean steamers must trouble a school of herring. They tore society to pieces and trampled it under foot."[48] Harvard University's president, Charles W. Eliot, summed up the influence of the corporation on society when he said that "the activity of corporations, great and small, penetrates every part of the industrial and social body, and their daily maintenance brings into play more mental and moral force than the maintenance of all the governments on the [American] Continent combined."[49]

Beyond its impact on particular economic and social institutions, the large corporation was striking for its totality and apparent self-sufficiency. As a result, there prevailed a general suspicion of "Big Business" that often bordered on hysteria. " 'Big Business,' and its ruthless tentacles, have become the material for the feverish fantasy of illiterate thousands thrown out of kilter by the rack and strain of modern life," Walter Lippmann wrote in 1914. "[A]ll the frictions of life are readily ascribed to a deliberate evil intelligence, and men like Morgan and Rockefeller take on attributes of omnipotence."[50] The sheer size of the largest industrial corporations persuaded many Americans, as Roland Marchand has noted, that "the nexus of social institutions within which they lived had been radically transformed." Words such as *virtue, duty,* and *benevolence* seemed irrelevant to descriptions and evaluations of the corporation.[51] For many, the corporation symbolized a body of strange customs and new traditions where familiarity and trust were replaced by impersonality and guile. The failure of many corporate leaders to acknowledge any responsibility for the broader society was epitomized by J. P. Morgan's quip, "I owe the public nothing."[52] Moreover, as the corporation became one of society's central actors, it appeared to impose its ethical and social indifference on the whole nation, not just on corporate employees. Richard Hofstadter described a widely felt "fear founded in political realities—the fear that the great business combinations, being the only centers of wealth and power, would be able to lord it over all other interests and thus to put an end to traditional American democracy."[53] The momentous new imbalance in social forces, along with a prolonged period of economic stagnation and depression from the early 1880s to the mid-1890s and many instances of corporate malfeasance and abuse of power, created a crisis of legitimacy for large corporations in the late nineteenth and early twentieth centuries. In 1905, popular magazines published exposés on the insurance, drug, and beef industries. In 1906, Upton Sinclair published his widely read fictionalized account of the U.S. meatpacking industry, *The Jungle.* Congress subsequently initiated regular hearings not only on the food industry but also on utilities, railroads, and financial institutions. Yet another series of hearings focused on

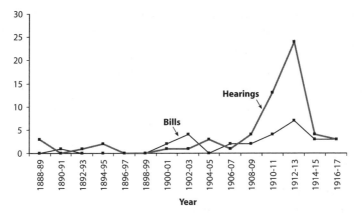

Figure 1.3
Federal hearings and bills on antitrust issues, 1880–1917. Source: Neil Fligstein, *The Transformation of Corporate Control* (Cambridge: Harvard University Press, 1990), 91.

the subject of how best to regulate large corporations, through antitrust laws, among other means (fig. 1.3).

The core problem for corporations was not one of legal legitimacy.[54] Although antitrust legislation sought to contain corporate power within prescribed limits, the corporate form of organization itself *had* come to be accepted.[55] By the mid-nineteenth century, incorporating a business no longer required a special act by a state legislature.[56] The growing legal recognition of corporations as "natural persons" with the legal rights of individuals (a doctrine based not on any court decision but merely on a brief remark made by Chief Justice Morrison Waite prior to the commencement of oral arguments in the 1886 U.S. Supreme Court case *Santa Clara County v. Southern Pacific Railroad*) interacted with the ensuing competition among states to lower the requirements for incorporation; the result was a reduced likelihood that corporate charters would be used to require corporations to act in the public interest.[57] This series of legal and political decisions enhancing the power of corporations in the last decades of the nineteenth century thus greatly contributed to the establishment in America of what James Coleman has labeled the "asymmetric society"—a condition that was keenly felt in what Richard Hofstadter has titled "The Age of Reform," the political era of Populism and Progressivism.

Populism and Progressivism, however, took very different stances toward the corporation. While Populist sentiment in the United States sought to cripple and, indeed, dismantle large corporations, Progressive reformers tended to view corporations as a means of addressing some of society's most vexing problems. Progressives recognized organizations as a new force shaping society in ways that could be beneficial: Herbert Croly, for example, called attention to their potential for advancing social welfare by enhancing productivity, and Louis Brandeis noted their capacity to create social order in modern societies.[58] As historian Robert H. Wiebe observed in his influential account of the "search for order" in American society during this period, the emerging middle class that formed the backbone of the Progressive movement embraced the new world of organizations that the Populists before them had rejected:

> Most of [the Progressive reformers] lived and worked in the midst
> of modern society and, accepting its major thrust, drew both their
> inspiration and their programs from its peculiar traits. Where
> their predecessors would have destroyed many of urban-industrial
> America's outstanding characteristics, the new reformers wanted to
> adapt an existing order to their own ends. They prized their organi-
> zations not merely as reflections of an ideal but as sources of every-
> day strength, and generally they also accepted the organizations that
> were multiplying about them. . . . The heart of progressivism was the
> ambition of the new middle class to fulfill its destiny through bu-
> reaucratic means.[59]

Also central to Progressivism was the concept of social order—a recognition that human beings have a preference for certainty and predictability. Indeed, many historians and social scientists have compellingly argued that the expansion of government and regulatory institutions in the twentieth century came about in response to the "crisis of order" that accompanied the dramatic changes of the late nineteenth century.[60] Instead of trying to eliminate the new business enterprise model, Progressive reformers sought to rationalize it to serve society's interests. In contrast to Populists, who saw large organizations, especially corporations, as the betrayers of America's core values, Progressives endeavored to infuse these leviathans with those very values. ("Progressivism, at its heart, was an effort to realize familiar and traditional ideals under novel circumstances," Richard Hofstadter wrote.)[61] For Progressives, the problem was not whether large corporations should exist or how large they should be, but rather where moral agency should be located in such a world. To whom was authority to be granted and *by* whom was it to be exercised? This line of questioning created an opening for the management class—if the group could overcome the obstacles in its way—to present itself as the best candidate for the job of running corporations in the best interests of society. If managers could successfully present themselves as agents of the rationalizing process that was required for corporations to achieve societal legitimacy, managers would, in turn, greatly advance their own quest for legitimacy.

Legitimizing Management: Obstacles and Strategies

One of the most articulate explicators of the age that witnessed the transition from the robber barons to a wholly new kind of business leader was Walter Lippmann, who believed that the salaried managers running large American corporations represented a new breed of enlightened businessman. In his 1914 book, *Drift and Mastery*, Lippmann devoted a chapter to the contemporary revolution in American business. There he observed that "in big business, . . . the real government is passing into a hierarchy of managers and deputies, who, by what would look like a miracle to Adam Smith, are able to cooperate pretty well toward a common end."

> They are doing that, remember, in the first generation of administrative science. They come to it unprepared, from a nation that is suspicious and grudging. They have no tradition to work with, and the old commercial morality of the exploiter and profiteer still surrounds these new rulers of industry. Perhaps they are unaware that they are revolutionizing the discipline, the incentives, and the vision of the business world. They do brutal and stupid things, and their essential work is obscured. But they are conducting business on a scale unprecedented in history.
>
> The real news about business, it seems to me, is that it is being administered by men who are not profiteers. The managers are on salary, divorced from ownership and from bargaining. They represent the revolution in business incentives at its very heart. For they conduct gigantic enterprises and they stand outside the higgling [*sic*] of the market, outside the shrewdness and strategy of competition. The motive of profit is not their personal motive. That is an astounding change. The administration of the great industries is passing into the hands of men who cannot halt before each transaction and ask themselves: what is my duty as the Economic Man

looking for immediate gain? They have to live on their salaries, and
hope for promotion, but their day's work is not measured in profit.
There are thousands of these men, each with responsibilities vaster
than the patriarchs of industry they have supplanted. It is for the
commercial theorists to prove that the "ability" is inferior, and talent
less available.[62]

"Perhaps they are unaware that they are revolutionizing the discipline,
the incentives, and the vision of the business world"—Lippmann's insight
here encapsulates some of the most subtle as well as crucial challenges that
managers faced in explaining, to themselves as well as to society, what role
they might play in the construction of a new social order for the age of the
large industrial corporation. Salaried managers might not always have been
as unconcerned about profit as Lippmann portrays them,[63] but his presenting them in this way created its own kind of social reality. Thus it appeared
that management's quest for legitimacy might indeed converge with American society's search for order, if only managers could use the resources they
now commanded to change the social and political order in ways that secured their own interests.

The resistance that managers encountered in this quest derived from a
variety of factors. First and perhaps most obvious was the doubtful legitimacy of large American corporations themselves—with which managers
were closely identified in the public's mind—at the beginning of their historical ascendancy.[64] Yet managers also faced certain challenges pertaining to
the nascent state of their occupation itself: in particular, the difficulty of explaining to the public what exactly managers did; a fragmented market for
managerial services; and the lack of a shared identity as a fulcrum for collective action. At the same time, they encountered the social disturbance that
inevitably follows when an emerging social group vies for power and resources.[65] As we have already seen, this took the form of resistance to managerial claims to authority by those, such as workers and shareholders, who
stood to lose from their successful prosecution.

The challenges posed to managers by the difficulty of explaining their
occupation and by the fragmented market for managerial services were
closely interrelated. When managers first appeared in business firms, the general public had little understanding of managerial work and activities, and no
precedents existed to show just what managers were capable of doing or how
effective they could be.[66] Most early managers, not having been formally

trained,[67] possessed no educational credentials or other formal warrant of expertise. Managers claimed an authority based on ability rather than on tradition, inherited position, or achieved wealth, but they had no ready means of demonstrating this ability. While members of the new managerial elite sometimes also invoked social Darwinist ideas to defend their qualifications and justify managerial authority, these arguments held little sway with a skeptical public, muckraking journalists, and a growing and increasingly restless working class.[68]

The difficulty managers had in defining their work in ways both understandable and acceptable to the public affected their status both inside firms and in the labor market. Because management was not a widely recognized skill with a broadly acknowledged value, markets for managerial services had to be created. The limited markets that already existed were fragmented and firm-specific; there was a need to standardize managerial work, and establish the criteria by which it could be evaluated, in order to define the occupational jurisdiction that is central to what Andrew Abbott has called the "system of professions."[69] But creating a managerial market was not an easy task, precisely because what a manager produces is not easily understood or measured, let alone standardized. Managerial work, like any other kind of professional labor, is what sociologist Magali Larson characterizes as "a fictitious commodity."[70] It cannot be easily detached from the rest of life to be cataloged, inventoried, and shipped. It is intangible and bound to the person of the producer.

For managers, the task of defining and standardizing their work so as to present themselves as candidates for leadership in a new social order was rendered all the more formidable by their having, even in their own eyes, no common identity. Although the opposition managers faced from both owners and workers may well have helped to give them an incipient sense of group consciousness and identity, it was not necessarily a positive one and therefore hardly a basis for collective action.[71] At the same time, managers were keenly motivated by a sense of status inferiority enforced on them by the economic and social elites whom their emergent power threatened to displace.

Managerial control of corporations signified a new distribution of economic power, with managers presenting themselves as fresh claimants for the control of economic resources at a time when a highly disproportionate segment of the nation's wealth was still controlled by a small elite.[72] While an 1893 government report, for instance, found that 9 percent of the nation's families still controlled more than 70 percent of the wealth,[73] managers were now capturing an increasingly large amount of the firm's profits in the form of greater salaries. The most reliable estimates of wage data indicate that, by the first decade of the twentieth century, management's remuneration exceeded even that of skilled workers by a considerable amount. Senior managers—the group that had the greatest stake in the legitimation of management as an occupation, and that would play an active role in trying to advance this goal—made on average about $10,000 a year.[74] Yet the status of even senior managers—what we would call *executives*—was lower than their class position, which created a distinct strain. Members of the new managerial elite were satisfied with their wealth, but not with their socially ambiguous position. They were ill at ease with the old social elite of merchants, financiers, and high professionals, such as jurists, doctors, and clergymen—a class whose members saw themselves as the guardians and transmitters of culture, art, and ideas, while viewing the businessmen (whether entrepreneurial or managerial) who had replaced the traditional mercantile elite as self-interested and craven parvenus.[75] Businessmen themselves often internalized this projection of their own social and even ethical inferiority in comparison with learned professionals, as Walter Lippmann explained:

> We say in conversation: "Oh, no, he's not a business man—he has a profession." That sounds like an invidious distinction, and no doubt there is a good deal of caste and snobbery in the sentiment. But that isn't all there is. We imagine that men enter the professions by undergoing a special discipline to develop a personal talent. So their lives seem more interesting, and their incentives more genuine. The business man may feel that the scientist content with a modest salary is an improvident ass. But he also feels some sense of inferiority in the scientist's presence. For at the bottom there is a difference of quality in their lives—in the scientist's a dignity which the scramble for profit can never assume. The professions may be shot through with rigidity, intrigue, and hypocrisy: they have, nevertheless, a community of interest, a sense of craftsmanship, and a more permanent place in the larger reaches of the imagination. It is a very pervasive and subtle difference, but sensitive business men are aware of it. They are not entirely proud of their profit-motive: bankers cover it with a sense of importance, others mitigate it with charity and public work, a few dream of railroad empires and wildernesses tamed, and some reveal their sense of unworthiness

by shouting with extra emphasis that they are not in business for their health.[76]

Yet even if business suffered a lack of prestige in comparison with the traditional professions, contemporary society was beginning to draw on occupation as a substitute for more traditional markers of identity and social position. This development created the option of establishing the occupation of management on a basis that would enable it to compete more effectively for social status. Meanwhile, even as the new managerial elite bore the taint of being engaged in nothing more than a venal "scramble for profit," the group benefited from a Progressive belief that enlightened administration of large organizations, public and private, held the key to establishing a new social order on a scientific and rational footing.

Given these openings, management had a clear opportunity to legitimize itself if it could shift the ground of the argument from the legitimacy of the corporation to the value of managers as the natural leaders of the emerging corporate order. For management to take advantage of this moment, it would be necessary to offer the public an explanation of what managers did and to standardize managerial work, and the market for it, by standardizing its producers. In other words, managers would have to be adequately trained and socialized to present themselves as providing distinct services for exchange in the labor market. At the same time, managers would need to construct a collective identity for themselves and infuse it with content that served to portray management as an ordering institution producing clear benefits for society. As soon as these requirements for the explanation and identity of management came to be understood, circumstances were ripe for the emergence of a vanguard of what DiMaggio calls "institutional entrepreneurs"— interested actors who would dedicate themselves to framing this new reality for others.[77]

Just such a vanguard did, in fact, start to coalesce early in the history of American management. A dominant group of academics and a small but influential group of business leaders who regarded themselves as forming a differentiated new group in society—one that would take its place alongside society's most fundamental institutions, such as the professions and the state—began working together to establish management as an ordering institution worthy of respect and advancement as such. How did these institutional entrepreneurs arise and come together from such distinct social realms? As it happens, the waning traditional elite and the emerging business elite found that this joint pursuit served to shore up the power of the first group while fostering the rise of the second.

A large section of this group of institutional entrepreneurs consisted of members of pedigreed New England families in the intellectual and professional classes. This group constituted the nation's true upper class. Many of its members were descended from families that had been wealthy before the Civil War and, as sociologist E. Digby Baltzell has documented, exerted enormous influence in the large metropolitan centers of Boston, New York, and Philadelphia, where they were regarded as the pillars of their communities.[78] In Massachusetts, for example, being a member of the Eliot, Adams, Lowell, Lawrence, or Lodge clan signified that one stood at the pinnacle of New England's political, social, and cultural pecking order. It also meant that one was quite likely to occupy a position of leadership in one or more important cultural and social institutions. This was no less true in higher education, where being descended from this group was a virtual prerequisite for becoming head of any major university. Harvard's Charles W. Eliot and Abbott Lawrence Lowell, the University of Pennsylvania's Robert Ellis Thompson, and Dartmouth's William Jewett Tucker, for example, were examples of eastern establishment elites leading universities. What motivated such individuals to lend support to the cause of institutionalizing and legitimating management was a complex mix of status anxiety with respect to the new business elite; long-standing investment in, and ongoing commitment to, established social institutions, particularly higher education; and the spirit of Progressive reform, which highlighted the social and status issues raised by the ascendance of the large corporation and the emerging corporate elite.

The first of these factors, status anxiety, arose as the economic transformations of the late nineteenth and early twentieth centuries created a misalignment between the new distribution of economic power and the old distribution of social prestige and political power. Those traditional elites whose tenuous places in the new economic order were incommensurate with their positions in the old social and political order became increasingly anxious about their place in American society.[79] In his book *The Age of Reform*, historian Richard Hofstadter wrote about the "alienation" of traditional elites who felt themselves being displaced during the Progressive era by the new class of business tycoons that had arisen in the late nineteenth century.[80] In eastern seaboard cities like Boston, many members of this elite claimed descent from an eighteenth-century mercantile class that had created what Hofstadter elsewhere described as an "ideal of the man of business as a civilized man and a civilizing agent."[81] Samuel Eliot Morison, in recollections of his boyhood in Boston at the end of the nineteenth century, stressed that many members of the city's "Brahmin" elite, once their family fortunes were secure, carried on the civilizing traditions of their class so as to distance themselves from the occupation of business, investing their talents as well as their fortunes in other institutions:

> Someone explaining the decay of American cities since 1940 observed that we had no solid core of nobility and bourgeois, as in Amsterdam, Strasbourg, Bordeaux, Bristol, and Milan, who insisted on living in town, interested themselves in local politics and supported cultural activities. But Boston had just that sort of group in my childhood. Not nobility, of course, but families that endowed Harvard and other universities, founded the Museum of Fine Arts, the Symphony Orchestra and the Opera House, and took pride in supporting great charitable foundations. . . . And Boston had something more than that. Despite all the sneers and jeers at "Proper Bostonians," "Boston Brahmins," and the like, there was a remarkable pattern of living here that existed nowhere else in the United States. When a family had accumulated a certain fortune, instead of trying to build it up still further, to become a Rockefeller or Carnegie or Huntington and then perhaps discharge its debt to society by some great foundation, it would step out of business or finance and try to accomplish something in literature, education, medical research, the arts, or public service. Generally one or two members of the family continued in business, to look after the family securities and enable the creative brothers or cousins to carry on without the handicap of poverty.[82]

For almost thirty years after assuming the presidency of Harvard in 1869, Charles W. Eliot, a prototypical Boston Brahmin, ignored repeated calls to establish a school of business (even as he was making the improvement of professional education a major focus of his reform efforts at the university), arguing that such a project would be anathema to the university's educational purpose of teaching students how to live worthy lives.[83] By the turn of the century, however, a new trend among Harvard students was becoming apparent, one that Eliot found impossible to ignore: more than half of all Harvard College graduates were going into business. In 1897, Eliot described the growing overlap between the old order to which he belonged and the new business elite: "In my own class [1853], which numbered only 89, fifteen men succeeded eminently in business, being a larger proportion of decided success than my classmates obtained in any other calling. . . . Most of the desirable business corporation appointments in Boston are filled by our graduates. . . . It stands to reason that thorough mental training must give a man an advantage in any business which requires strong mental work."[84] Yet neither a growing recognition by educators like Eliot of the desirability of "mental training" for business nor an influx of college-educated youth from "good" families into managerial work was enough, by itself, to imbue the new occupation with social status. A generation after the growing popularity of business among Harvard graduates had convinced the university fathers to establish a graduate school of "business administration" at Harvard in 1908, Harvard Business School dean Wallace B. Donham was lamenting the relatively low repute in which business was still held among the upper classes, especially when compared with other occupations, such as medicine and law. "This country has suffered less, perhaps, than England from an attitude which looks down on business as a calling," Donham observed, "but even here young men enter business too frequently because they do not feel competent or inclined to enter any of the so-called learned professions, rather than from a positive desire to enter upon a business career. Business has thus become in part a catch-all and a dumping ground into which in the case of many families inferior sons are advised to go."[85]

Raising the esteem enjoyed by business as an occupation thus promised to shore up the status of marginal members of the traditional elite even while providing access to increased occupational status for upwardly mobile managers. Specifically, it created a bridge for the natural aristocracy of intellectual talent to take its rightful place at the helm of the large corporation. As we shall see, the establishment of business schools at institutions such as the University of Pennsylvania, Dartmouth, and Harvard would provide a setting for the education of a new kind of manager who, instilled with the sense of social obligation derived from an elite background, would run corporations in a way consistent with the broader interests of the country. At the same time, as we shall also see, defining this mission for management allowed the study of business to be incorporated into the university as more than merely a concession to student and alumni demand. Indeed, business education could now be characterized as an instrument of Progressive-style reform, both of the corporation and of American society more broadly.

While traditional elites contemplated the potential advantages of elevating the status of business and management, members of a vanguard of enlightened business owners and managers were coming to view education as an emblem of high status *and* an increasingly necessary condition for both stabilizing managers' position and administering business. The emerging era of Progressivism saw an amplified call for "college-educated" men to help rationally administer society; in business, this was manifest in a growing view that managers were distinct from common workers and owners, and that managerial work did indeed require what Harvard's Eliot called "mental training." While academics like Eliot were contemplating how to bring business into the university's sphere of influence, an emerging group of business leaders was beginning to reach inside the university to exert widening influence. In 1899, Edward Tuck, the world-renowned international financier and railroad magnate, a member of Dartmouth's class of 1862, wrote to his college classmate William Jewett Tucker, who was now president of Dartmouth College. Tuck inquired about establishing some kind of graduate school at Dartmouth and asked his old friend how the school was preparing its graduates for the new industrial world. Tucker replied to Tuck that he had been entertaining the idea of a new kind of graduate school at Dartmouth, given a recent shift in the career trajectories of its students: "I have noticed the growth in numbers of our graduates who go into business. Can we give them a better training, commensurate with the larger meaning of business as it is now understood? Can we enlarge our constituency in this direction?"[86] Tuck himself was quite receptive to the idea—he wrote back to Tucker that he had familiarized himself with the Wharton School and had been closely following the growth in Harvard undergraduate courses focused on transportation and railway issues. In short, Tuck was eager to pursue the possibility of offering business training at Dartmouth.

Similar feelers were being sent out by businessmen across the United States as they began to establish closer relations with higher education. Daniel A. Wren, in his analysis of higher-education philanthropy, shows that American business leaders took a particular interest in higher education.[87] Of the gifts to universities and colleges in excess of fifty thousand dollars between 1869 and 1900, 80 percent were given by individuals who had earned their wealth as either founders or top executives in large business concerns. Several of these gifts were specifically directed toward scientific, technical, or "practical" education; the donors shared Tuck's, Tucker's, and Eliot's view that many colleges and universities were not doing enough to prepare people for the new industrial economy.[88]

These efforts by business leaders, including managers, to achieve influence within universities suggest that the significant cleft between the economic and status positions of managers motivated members of this group to pry open society's foundational institutions to secure a place for management in the social structure. Through supporting higher education, managers could establish for themselves a legitimacy that could not have been attained through profit-making activities. What linked this group of managers with the traditional elites with whom they became allied, however, was not just the overlap in interests of the two groups in securing their respective places in the emerging social order. They also shared a rational commitment to a common system of values that each group believed the emerging industrial order should embody. Both groups' interests, that is, were not solely material but also embraced what Weber called *ideational* interests, those "involving a conscious belief in the absolute value of some ethical, aesthetic, religious [idea] . . . entirely for its own sake and independently of any prospects of external success."[89] This lent a strong moral overtone to their efforts to impose a new social order, one to be based on such principles of Progressivism as political liberalism, rational administration, education for character and competence, and meritocracy. In many ways, this combined institutional vanguard embodied Weber's concept of a "charismatic" group[90] as it engaged in what its members believed to be a pioneering venture to offer solutions to a new range of problems. What is more, the cultural, economic, and political capital of these visionaries rendered them ideally suited for their roles as institutional entrepreneurs. Their social positions gave them the credibility to advocate norms that promised to improve the social order. Such credibility forms a critical part of institution-building activity, especially as it increases the likelihood that institution builders' solutions will be accepted by the various groups, interests, and individuals who constitute society as a whole. The ability of this particular group of institutional entrepreneurs to identify and articulate a direction for the nation's new economic order filled an important void amid the age's economic and social upheavals.

The values embraced by those attempting to legitimate management were reflected in the existing institutions with which they allied themselves. Institutional theory suggests that legitimating explanations, justifications, and strategies for new institutions are not created ab ovo. Rather, they are usually extracted from the external environment, grafted on to the new institution, and then voiced from within it. In examining the origin of rational bureaucracies, Weber argued that new authority structures emerge from collective efforts to present that authority as conforming to existing categories and practices that give meaning to the social world.[91] Edward Shils postulated that systems of authority capable of demonstrating that their objectives are directed toward collectively valued purposes are more likely to be seen by a society as legitimate.[92] And as Richard H. Brown has observed, all new social forms, to some degree, are unique and shape their own identities, "but . . . never . . . from raw cloth; indeed, for the most part they get their worlds ready to wear."[93] In order to secure public acceptance of its moral right to occupy a place within the foundational structures of society, the leaders of the managerial project absorbed and incorporated significant elements of existing social institutions, so that management would be viewed as reflecting parts of the traditional social order even while laying claim to a constitutive role in the new one.

More particularly, in the years between 1880 and 1941, this institutional vanguard—leveraging its existing social and economic resources—succeeded in articulating a new public account of the role of management in society by locating it within three institutions that had recently come to be seen as pillars of this new social order: science, the professions, and the university. These three institutions, which would become the building blocks of the modern institution of management, were taken to constitute rational, necessary, and adequate sources of legitimacy for the new occupation. By incorporating the logics of these existing, already-legitimated institutions into its own cognitive framework, symbolic constructions, and practices, this set of institutional entrepreneurs sought to persuade society of the functional utility of the managerial role in the absence of actual proof. In effect, the collective legitimacy of these other institutions was appropriated to support the creation of the new institution of management. The centerpiece of the project was to be a wholly new invention: the university-based business school.

In the creation of business schools as an effort to appropriate the legitimacy of science, the professions, and the university, we find the following process at work. First, the champions of business schools attempted to present management as a "science," both to furnish solutions to problems of efficiency and control, and to provide management with an aura of objectivity that removed the discussion of managerial claims from the turbulent and subjective realms of politics and markets. Second, they created intellectual parallels between the emerging occupation of management and more established, high-status occupations—specifically the age-old professions of the clergy, medicine, and the law—not only to advance the practice of management but also to cast themselves as a disinterested, socially oriented group and, not incidentally, to carve out a place for managers in an emerging stratification system wherein status was increasingly tied to occupation.[94] Finally, they associated themselves with the new institution of the American research university as a way not only of enabling the creation of appendages paralleling those of the existing professions, such as a professoriat, academic journals, and academic associations, but also of appropriating for management something of the status and even quasi-sacred character of an institution that combined utilitarianism with a sense of social and moral purpose. Indeed, science and the professions continued to advance their own positions partly by an increasingly close association with the university. The American university—which oversaw the invention, more or less from scratch, of the modern business school—to a large degree subsumed the institutions of science and the professions, and would ultimately act as the fulcrum for the legitimation of modern management.

Yet before we consider *how* the inventors of university-based business schools appropriated the institutions of science, the professions, and the university for their own institutional project (the subject of chapter 3), we must establish why they focused on these three institutions in particular. Why, in the late nineteenth- and early twentieth-century context, did these institutional entrepreneurs believe that management would benefit if it were seen as a science, a profession, and a candidate for study within the university? More directly, what were the roles and logics of these three institutions in the creation of social order in this period?

Ideas of Order: Science, the Professions, and the University in Late Nineteenth- and Early Twentieth-Century America

2

In their effort to establish management as not only a legitimate occupation but also a pillar of social order amid the turbulent economic and social conditions of the late nineteenth century in the United States, the institutional entrepreneurs described in the preceding chapter resorted to three institutions that, like the large corporation and its control by "professional" managers, are now entirely taken for granted as foundational structures of contemporary society. Science, the professions, and the American research university, however, also resemble the modern corporation and contemporary management in having assumed their present forms at a point in history—the very same that gave birth to the large corporation and the occupation of management—when such institutions presented themselves as filling a gaping void in the social order. Characterizing the era's reaction to the phenomena of "nationalization, industrialization, mechanization, [and] urbanization," Robert H. Wiebe observed that "to almost all of the people who created them, these themes meant only dislocation and bewilderment. America in the late nineteenth century was a society without a core. It lacked those national centers of authority and information which might have given order to such swift changes."[1] It was to establish such sources of "authority and information" that a host of institutional entrepreneurs in the last quarter of the nineteenth century transformed science, the professions, and higher education from the loosely organized, more or less marginal entities they had been since the nation's founding into powerful and pervasive institutions that came to enjoy a virtually sacred status.

Science and the Search for Order

Beginning in the late nineteenth century, the United States took the lead among Western nations in providing institutionalized support for scientific activity.[2] By the first decade of the twentieth century, America was resolutely making science a definitive force not only in education and research but also in political reform, social policy, and economic activity. This represented a significant transformation of attitudes toward science prevalent only a decade or two earlier.

Americans had, of course, engaged in scientific activity almost since the establishment of the first English settlements in New England. The Puritan divine John Cotton wrote that "to study the nature and course, and use of all God's works, is a duty imposed by God on all sorts of men," and many of the earliest New England colonists were active in scientific pursuits.[3] Connecticut governor John Winthrop, Jr., for example, was elected a fellow of the Royal Society of London in 1663 (the year of the society's first regular election) and had brought with him to New England a telescope that Isaac Newton had once used, an instrument Winthrop later donated to Harvard College. In 1745, Benjamin Franklin, the best known of America's eighteenth-century natural philosophers, cofounded the American Philosophical Society, which would later define its purpose as the pursuit of "all philosophical Experiments that let Light into the Nature of Things, tend to increase the Power of Man over Matter, and multiply the Conveniencies or Pleasures of Life"; while the avowed purpose of the establishment of the American Academy of Arts and Sciences in 1780 (by a group that included John Adams, John Hancock, and other leaders of the American Revolution) was "to cultivate every art and science which may tend to advance the interest, honour, dignity, and happiness of a free, independent, and virtuous people." Science thus had a history of support in America, from colonial times, as a source of public benefit, although (as elsewhere in the Western world during this period) scientific study and experimentation remained essentially private, loosely organized activities conducted by cultivated, gentlemanly amateurs.[4]

The advent of Jacksonian democracy in the early nineteenth century was fueled partly by a disdain for the gentlemanly culture of the Early Republic in all its manifestations, political and otherwise. The man who defeated Jackson for the presidency in 1824 and whom Jackson, in turn, defeated four years later—John Quincy Adams—was, in Richard Hofstadter's words, both "the last President to stand in the old line of government by gentlemen" and, eventually, "the chief victim of the reaction against the learned man." Besides possessing his own scientific interests, Adams (who served as president of the American Academy of Arts and Sciences both before and during his term in the White House) made federal support for science and technology the object of several proposals outlined early in his administration.[5] Half a century after the rise of Jackson, Simon Newcomb—a mathematician, physicist, astronomer, and economist who was one of the most passionately outspoken advocates for science and the scientific method in the second half of the nineteenth century in America—described the persistence, and lasting consequences, of the Jacksonian belief that science was valuable only to the extent that it was accessible to the average man:

> If, now, one enters upon a critical examination of the judging faculty of the American people, as shown by their reasoning on subjects of every class, one can hardly avoid being struck by a certain one-sidedness in its development, having an important bearing on its fitness for scientific investigation. Within a certain domain, usually characterized as that of practical sagacity and good sense, they have nothing to be ashamed of. Where the conclusion is reached by a process so instinctive that it is not reduced to a logical form, and where there is no need of an analysis of first principles, we may not unfairly claim to be a nation of good reasoners. But, if we pursue any subject of investigation into a region where a higher or more exact form of reasoning is necessary—where first principles have to be analyzed, and a concatenation of results have to be kept in the mind—it must be admitted that we do not make a creditable showing. It might almost seem as if the dialectic faculty among us had decayed from want of use. The plain "common-sense" of the fairly intelligent citizen has in most cases so completely sufficed for all the purposes where judging capacity was required, that the need of more exact methods of thought has never been felt by the nation at large.[6]

As Newcomb acknowledged, however, while arguing in 1876 for more organized support for science in the United States (Germany having by now been the world's leader in this regard for half a century), the nation had made a start in this direction under the impetus, initially, of the mechanization of weaponry in the Civil War. (The National Academy of Sciences had been chartered by Congress in 1863, Newcomb explained, as an extension of an advisory board formed early in the war when "the government was overwhelmed with inventions of improved machinery of war, the practicability of which could not be judged without the aid of scientific experts.")[7] The swift progress of science and technology in the years following the Civil War, and the rapidly spreading impact of this progress on economic, social, and political life, gave new and increasing impetus to this effort, so that, in the last quarter of the nineteenth century and the years just before World War I, the United States created the paradigm for the organization, support, and usage of scientific activity that would be followed by the rest of the world.[8]

In the process, the old Jacksonian suspicion of expertise gave way to what became one of the principal hallmarks of the Progressive era: a profound, widely shared faith in scientific expertise and the scientific method as instruments of social progress. Between the late nineteenth century and the end of World War I, social reformers had embraced science, the new cultural authority of which was soon brought to bear on a variety of institutions that had previously been immune to its influence. For example, in a famous 1908 Supreme Court case, *Muller v. Oregon*, the Massachusetts lawyer Louis Brandeis introduced a then-novel form of legal argumentation that incorporated extensive sociological and economic data to defend an Oregon law prohibiting women from working more than ten hours a day. Combining keen legal analysis and data demonstrating the relationship between long work days and women's maladies into an argument for the role of government in promoting social welfare, Brandeis won the case. He later used the same technique to defend laws limiting child labor and industrial monopolies. Meanwhile, Americans generally had increasingly come to accept that—as Simon Newcomb had asserted in calling for "a wider diffusion of the ideas and modes of thought of the exact sciences" in the America of the 1870s—"[a] large fraction of our public occupations consist in examinations and discussions of social phenomena, in which no certain result can be obtained without a logical exactness of investigation to which everyday life is an entire stranger."[9]

It is important to note that no distinction was made during this period between "pure" and "applied" science.[10] The strongest advocates for science saw a close relationship between the discipline's value as a window into natural phenomena and its utility for solving problems. John Dewey, one of the most vocal champions of a science-based social policy, argued that science paralleled other modes of problem solving in everyday life. Society needed to abandon "once for all the belief that science is set apart from all other social interests," Dewey wrote, maintaining that "economic power" was the only interest from which science needed to be separated to safeguard its promise of societal usefulness.[11] As Dewey's statement implies, the institutionalization of scientific authority, in late nineteenth- and early twentieth-century America, derived partly from the many tangible, practical benefits that science and technology were delivering to society, including some that contributed directly to the effort to solve particular social problems. Yet it is not possible to fully grasp the nature of this authority without understanding that, beyond these pragmatic considerations, science in this era was widely viewed as not only a means of solving concrete problems but also an intrinsically moral and even quasi-religious activity. The scientist's dedicated search for truth was seen to resemble the religious believer's zealous pursuit of spiritual truth, and for many Americans whose traditional religious faith was weakening under the onslaught of Darwinian evolutionary theory and German higher criticism of Scripture, science became an attractive surrogate for such faith. At the same time, the drive for social progress through science offered an outlet for a distinctly Protestant moral fervor. American society's embrace of scientific authority, then, represented as much a cognitive and ideational revolution as it did a revolution in problem-solving methods.[12]

Science and the values perceived as underlying it became, during this period, highly serviceable vehicles for the creation of a new social order. The institutionalization of science at a time of intense social upheaval and transformation in America recalls the process by which new views of, and foundations for, knowledge were constructed in seventeenth- and eighteenth-century Europe in what is still often called the Scientific Revolution. As Steven Shapin has observed of the seventeenth century's reaction to centuries of religious wars in Europe (culminating in the devastating Thirty Years War of 1618–1648), "It is just when the authority of long-established institutions erodes that the solutions to [fundamental] questions about knowledge come to have special point and urgency."[13] Much as the pioneering scientists of early modern Europe conceptualized a basis for knowledge that promised deliverance from murderous conflicts inspired by religious dogmatism, Americans in the late nineteenth century and the Progressive era sought a cognitive and normative framework within which to resolve the often intense social conflicts caused by the disruption of traditional communities, stratification systems, and mores by such forces as industrialization, urbanization, and the rise of the large corporation.

Observing the astonishing technological revolution that the Western world had undergone by the middle of the nineteenth century, even radicals such as Karl Marx and Friedrich Engels had had to marvel at the scientific and technological achievements of the age: "Subjection of Nature's forces to man, machinery, application of chemistry to industry and agriculture, steam navigation, railways, electric telegraphs, clearing of whole continents for cultivation, canalization of rivers, whole populations conjured out of the ground."[14] Because science itself was concerned primarily with discovering the true constitution of the natural and social worlds, its most passionate advocates believed that it represented a prescription for society's ills.[15] Some of the more tangible social ills of the period were, indeed, ameliorated by concrete, empirically demonstrable benefits flowing from the progress of science. Thus we find that the widespread embrace of science by social reformers, institutional entrepreneurs, and ordinary citizens at the end of the nineteenth century in America was inspired by the utilitarian possibilities suggested by advances both in basic scientific disciplines and in what Joseph Ben-David calls "quasi-disciplines"—fields of study that adopted the methods and social structures of basic science to pursue questions that were extrinsic to the core disciplines.[16] To take one example, progress in biology-based disciplines (which included problem-focused research agendas in topics such as sanitation or infectious disease) was already leading to significant discoveries in the areas of medicine and public health. Medicine was being revolutionized as a result of discoveries in disease pathology,[17] and new findings in bacteriology were being adopted and applied by departments of public health with considerable success.[18] Agriculture and engineering, meanwhile, increasingly benefited from the guidance of state-supported agricultural stations and the Army Corps of Engineers (which engaged in civil engineering research, dam construction and power generation, and the promotion of flood control), facilitating the development of applied science in these fields. Even industrial production was being transformed by "science" through Frederick W. Taylor's system of scientific management.

As the instance of scientific management suggests, the application of scientific ideas and method to the physical world and to efforts to subdue and change it extended to the study of human organizations as well. Yehouda Shenhav has shown how organizational theory (including Taylorism) grew out of the attempts of mechanical engineers to standardize engineering tools, processes, and systems as part of the overall effort to legitimate their discipline.[19] Nor was the rationalization of organizations an undertaking unique to business and industry in this era. On the administrative side of government, civil service reform—one of the key Progressive government initiatives—capitalized on the rhetoric of scientific principles and scientific management to enlist public support for expanding federal and state authority. Magazines and newspapers heralded the application of scientific management to political administration; an editorial in the *New Republic* noted, for example, that "the business of politics has become too complex to be left to the pretentious misunderstandings of the benevolent amateur."[20] Within the university—where, increasingly, scientific activity itself was concentrated—the organization of faculty into schools and departments reflected the growing specialization of science. The subject of natural history, for example—once taught by gentlemen who collected butterflies and visited exotic locales—was being broken down into the distinct fields of biology, botany, zoology, and anthropology. (Analogous cleavages even appeared in the humanities, where curricula began reflecting specialized courses and narrowed fields of interest.)

It was in the professionalization of science itself, however, that the application of scientific concepts and methods to the organization of human activity came full circle. As science came under the wing of the universities and even, to a certain extent, of the federal and state governments, it ceased to operate as a private activity, based on personalized ways of creating collective knowledge and supported by individual patrons. Instead, science evolved into a public institution dependent on complex institutional structures for creating knowledge,[21] supported by organized funding (public as well as private), and explicitly dedicated to the greater good. The new, more public kind of scientific activity and sponsorship assumed many forms, including government-sponsored research institutions; the planning and systematic diffusion of experiments through scholarly journals; the establishment of university-based departments, schools, and institutes of scientific research; foundation support for research that promised specific public benefits; and a proliferation of professional academic associations (see fig. 2.1).[22]

America's embrace of science in the late nineteenth century and the Progressive era was illustrated, in all of its dimensions, by the rise of the social sciences during this period.[23] Because science had been recast as public service rather than an idle indulgence for the elite, both social scientists and natural scientists—even as the social scientists were still defining their disciplines—enjoyed a new kind of social stature and prestige. As expert advisers, social scientists started to influence public policy.[24] They provided research to help inform policy makers concerning trends in immigration, poverty, education, international trade, the national economy, and public health. They developed their own systems of prizes and medals that then became intimately linked to emerging career patterns in universities. All of this was enabled by the successful development of analogies between social science and the natural sciences. One typical analogy was introduced by Jesse Macy, the president of the American

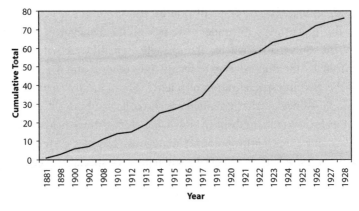

Figure 2.1
Founding of academic associations, 1880–1928. Source: *The Encyclopedia of Associations* (Thompson Publications).

Political Science Association, in an annual address to the society in 1917; Macy found explicit parallels between the natural sciences, which deal "with oxygen, hydrogen, and gravitation," and political science, which attends to "cities, states, and numerous other political and social institutions."[25] Both the natural sciences and political science, Macy argued, "furnish occasion for the exercise of the same spirit and method. Each county, each city is but an experiment station for the guidance of all others. Politics, like chemistry, might in this way be made an experimental science."[26]

While political scientists and economists divided between their two disciplines the subject matter that had once constituted political economy, the emerging sciences of sociology and psychology delved into the consequences, for individuals and society, of the vast social and psychological dislocations caused by the new industrialized, urbanized, rationalized society struggling to be born. Urbanization and the high rate of geographic mobility created by, and fueling, the second wave of industrialization in America combined to shape a society that registered a deep sense of loneliness and confusion. The resulting strains on individuals and society gave rise, in fact, to the new social sciences. Psychology occupied itself with studying the personal demoralization that surfaced as a symptom of these social changes, and sociologists focused on the implications for social order. Both agreed, based on widespread evidence, that modern man was in need of achieving integration in this new context, and that social science held the key to an understanding of how individuals and society could be made sound and whole again. Consider these remarks made in 1904 by G. Stanley Hall, first president of the American Psychological Association, founder of the *American Journal of Psychology*, and first president of Clark University, on the promise of psychology:

> We have great reason to congratulate ourselves on the progress of psychology . . . during the last quarter of a century. Not only have students, teachers, text-books, journals, societies, laboratories and monographs increased, and new fields have opened and old ones widened, but our department has been enriched by original contributions that have profoundly modified our views of mind and even of life itself. For the first time in this field American investigators have borne an important and recognized part in advancing man's knowledge of the soul.[27]

As such a statement makes clear, the extension of "science" from the physical world into realms embracing mind and society involved more than just the application of a particular cognitive framework and research methodology to new areas of inquiry. When a social scientist like Hall proffered what he called the "modest claim" that science "really does properly include logic, ethics, religion, aesthetics, epistemology, and metaphysics,"[28] he was proclaiming an essential role for science within the social and moral order. In her history of the progressive "marginalization" of moral education in the late nineteenth- and early twentieth-century American university, historian Julie A. Reuben summarizes why university leaders, trying to salvage their traditional mission in the face of declining religious belief and the rise of science, entertained the idea that science could replace religion as a basis for moral instruction and character formation:

> In the late nineteenth and early twentieth centuries, science itself seemed to be a powerful source of moral guidance. University reformers thought that scientific inquiry encouraged good personal habits, identical to those advanced by liberal Christianity. They conceived of the progress of scientific knowledge in utopian terms. Scientists confidently expected to produce broad unifying theories that would explain everything from the most basic physical events to the intricacies of advanced human societies. They thought that scientific research fueled social progress and proved that traditional moral values, such as temperance and monogamy, served the survival of the human race. They also believed that science would help solve difficult new ethical

problems created by modern industry. Advocates of scientific inquiry believed in the union of the good and the true, and expected that by producing better knowledge, they would become better people.[29]

In devising a curriculum to further this end, Reuben explains, advocates mapped out a moral "continuum" with the physical sciences at one end (being the least applicable to moral aims) and the social sciences on the other; in the middle of this continuum were the biological sciences. "University leaders," she writes, "looked primarily to the biological and social sciences to give substance to the ideal of the unity of truth"—that is, to what was viewed as "the unity of moral and intellectual purpose."[30]

How exactly did science come to be perceived not merely as a source of practical benefits and solutions to social problems but as an ordering institution that might actually take the place of religion?[31] Many scholars have noted the close linkages—evident in the biographies of nineteenth-century social scientists as well as in their professional discourse—between the aims and ambitions of the new social sciences and a distinctly Protestant moral fervor inherited from a pre-Darwinian age. Thomas L. Haskell observes that, for many of its proponents, science had an appeal much like that of religion. Scientism, Haskell points out, particularly captivated "the better-educated members" of American society, who were suffering "rampant doubt and uncertainty" during this period, their "Christian cosmology weakened by the rude shock of Darwin's evolutionary theory."[32] As Haskell comments:

> The point of departure for the professionalization of social science was a pervasive mood of doubt and uncertainty, triggered certainly by Darwin and historical criticism of the Bible, but rooted also in the intellectual quicksand of an increasingly interdependent social universe. By depriving sensitive thinkers of the opportunity for easy, unambiguous causal attribution that had enabled earlier generations to be serenely confident in their judgments of men and social affairs, the growing interdependence of society contributed to an erosion of confidence that made men receptive to claims of social science expertise. The collapse of confident belief gave rise to a movement of . . . reform which intended to construct safe institutional havens for sound opinion.[33]

Edward Shils, writing about late nineteenth-century American academics inspired by their experience of the German research university, described them in terms that also apply to social scientists in this era: "Their own falling away from the basic theological and historical tenets of Christianity in their literal form did not dissolve the more general bearing and active force of character that such belief engendered."[34] Or, as the historian Dorothy Ross has observed of the generation of "militant" social scientists who began coming to the fore of their disciplines in the 1880s (a group that included the economist Richard Ely, psychologist G. Stanley Hall, and sociologists Albion W. Small and Edward A. Ross), these individuals were motivated both by an acute sense of social crisis and by "family backgrounds in which the Protestant evangelical tradition had wielded a powerful influence. In part, the failure any longer to believe literally in Christianity, or the inability to achieve the religious experience some evangelical sects demanded, led them to pour their energy into the fervor for moral betterment."[35] Before his falling away from traditional Christian belief, G. Stanley Hall, for example, had undergone a religious conversion while an undergraduate at Williams College, and had gone on to take a degree from Union Theological Seminary and perform missionary work in the slums of New York. The economist Robert Ellis Thompson, who successively held professorships in mathematics, social science, and history and English literature at the University of Pennsylvania (and was an influential teacher of social science at Penn's Wharton School, founded in 1881), was a licensed Presbyterian preacher and historian of the Presbyterian Church in America. Albion W. Small, founder of the first sociology department in the United States (at the University of Chicago), was the son of a minister and had a seminary degree. James McKeen Cattell, the first professor of psychology in the United States (at the University of Pennsylvania), was also the son of a minister.

The pervasive influence of evangelical Protestant moralism within nineteenth-century American social science manifested itself in the character and activities of many of the newly established social science associations. Economists founded their professional association in 1885; psychologists in 1892; political scientists in 1903; and sociologists in 1905. In the writings, speeches, and histories of these associations, the words *science, method, reform, moral,* and *guidance* all recur frequently. Even historians of the era conceived the pursuit of their discipline as an effort "to conquer every social evil from crime to pauperism" through the use of history's investigative method. The American Economic Association and its first president, Richard Ely, as Haskell has written, "unquestionably regarded the organization as an instrument of reform. . . . [T]here was a striving for righteousness and perhaps here and there might have been [members] who felt a certain kinship with the old Hebrew prophets."[36] Sociologists viewed their discipline as "a means of promoting the development of a just and adequate social philosophy, and an element of strength and support in every wise endeavor to insure the good of men."[37] Together, these associations offered an overarching vision that combined social welfare and science to successfully convey a "conviction that in all its physical and social manifestations the world was responsive to human purpose—specifically, that the process of [scientific] inquiry could alter the world."[38]

Despite the more or less explicit strain of religious moralism in the reform programs of nineteenth-century social scientists, however, the legitimacy of social science as an instrument for ensuring social order depended on strict adherence to the canons of objectivity, reliance on evidence, and skepticism that came to define science as a mode of thinking. Even the most reformist social scientists insisted on a solid line of demarcation between a zeal for reform and advocacy for religious or moral rather than scientific principles, as when Albion Small—in the thick of the fight to establish sociology as a new social science—had to contend with a group of reformists marching under the banner of "Christian sociology."[39] The languages of religion and of scientific rationalism could be tightly interwoven, as they were when the astronomer Henry Smith Pritchett, who served as president of MIT from 1900 to 1906, and subsequently as the first president of the Carnegie Foundation, proclaimed in 1910, "The great function of science to humanity is to search out the laws of the universe and to point men to the consequences of their disobedience; to deliver men from fear and to bring mankind into a larger and clearer faith—a faith in the truth as the outcome of brave and honest thinking."[40] Yet it was clear which of the two voices—that of religion or that of science—had the final say when principles of personal conduct and social action were invoked. As the historian David A. Hollinger has observed, for example, "Not only were social scientists encouraged to extend to the social realm the search for facts pioneered by practitioners of the physical sciences; persons of any station confronting issues in politics and morals were encouraged to face them 'scientifically.' "[41]

The question of how, exactly, science came to assume this kind of specifically moral authority remains unsettled. Part of science's moral appeal—separate, that is, from its utilitarian benefits and the rhetoric of science as a moral activity—derived from its organizational structure, for science was conducted in a community setting where individuals were bound together through intense socialization, shared values, and common norms.[42] In a discussion of rationality in modern society, John Meyer points out that in an increasingly bureaucratic age, the scientist was not perceived as an organizational agent in any easily defined, modern sense of the term. Since science portrays itself as governed by a professional community of interest, it is presumably not easy for a practicing scientist to identify a principal client to whom he or she is accountable. This being the case, the goals of science were viewed as collective and rooted in the disinterested pursuit of truths about nature—"a matter of general virtue in terms of highly collective goods and the use of knowledge discovered to advance highly collective goods having to do with human social progress and equality."[43] Science, with its emphasis on an ideology of truth, service, and community, thus stood in stark contrast to an increasingly bureaucratic and materialistic culture that arguably dominated the motives of others in society. Moreover, Meyer and Scott note, scientific rhetoric framing phenomena as natural "laws" governing the physical and social worlds provided positive reassurance in an ambiguous, uncertain, and complex world. Indeed, scientists tend to produce not tangible products but, rather, ideas taking the form of principles and norms. Thus the perceived "virtue" of scientific activity had as much to do with questions of method and "objectivity" as it did with the motivation of practitioners and the material products of their efforts.[44]

By adducing its own methods, motives, and social structures, science in the late nineteenth and early twentieth centuries successfully presented itself as a cognitive framework offering a disinterested and apolitical means for solving the kinds of social problems and conflict with which the period was rife.[45] Indeed, the idea of science as a unique social institution in which empirical and rational arguments, not interests or violence, inform choices and policies prevailed as a core theme among science's strongest advocates. Scientists like Simon Newcomb portrayed themselves, and were characterized by others, as disinterested actors advancing the public good. By championing the new ideology of scientism with its guarantees of disinterestedness and objectivity, advocates for science provided what Joseph Ben-David and Gad Freudenthal have called a "symbol of and guide to truth and the improvement of human fate."[46] Science became their faith, the laboratory was their temple, and the scientific method was the path to salvation, envisioned as a new era of social order and social harmony. The adoption of this normative orientation created the conditions that enabled scientists to extend their cultural authority beyond the boundaries of the natural world studied by chemistry, physics, and biology, and into the social world, thereby gaining both legitimacy and resources.[47] In the process, as Julie Reuben has noted, "[e]ven the most utilitarian science, such as agricultural research, took on moral value."[48] Such connections, in turn, between the pure scientific disciplines and such "applied" or "quasi" disciplines[49] as agriculture, engineering, education, and management helped link science to the second major nineteenth-century institution with which management would align itself in search of legitimacy: the professions.

⮑ The Revival of the Professions

The last three decades of the nineteenth century and the early years of the twentieth witnessed the rise—or, to be more historically precise, the rebirth—of the professions. Partly because of their practical efficacy, but equally because they were depicted as order-creating mechanisms, professions came to occupy dominant and privileged positions in American society in the late nineteenth century and on through much of the twentieth; the Progressive era has been called "the golden age of professionalism in America." It is noteworthy that widespread acceptance of professionalism as a cognitive and normative framework preceded both the attempt of two of the traditional professions (medicine and law) to reassert weakened claims to authority and the emergence during this period of many new professions that offered strong claims to utilitarian efficacy.[50] Claims to practical efficacy, indeed, played only a relatively minor role in the revival of professions in the period we are examining here.

The "high" or "learned" professions of divinity, medicine, and law are obviously of ancient origin and had existed in America from the time of the Puritans. In the era of the Framers, professionals, along with merchants and landowners, were acknowledged as constituting the governing classes of the new nation. Yet the professional class in America faced major challenges to its legitimacy in the course of the nineteenth century—and particularly during the Jacksonian period—that closely parallel attitudes toward American science in that era. Paul Starr states that Jacksonian democracy valued science as a form of knowledge but saw it as one that could and *should* be accessible to all.[51] Thus it is not surprising that, to the extent professionals were believed to hoard expert knowledge for the sake of maintaining their own power and privilege, they were the object of widespread social contempt. As Hofstadter observed, "[The Jacksonian movement's] distrust of expertise, its dislike for centralization, its desire to uproot the entrenched classes, and its doctrine that important functions were simple enough to be performed by anyone, amounted to a repudiation not only of the system of government by gentlemen which the nation had inherited from the eighteenth century, but also of the special value of the educated classes in civic life."[52] The decline of professionalism as an institution in the course of the nineteenth century is reflected in trends in the education or training of professionals, as well as in their licensing. In neither medicine nor law did professional education exist in anything like its present form at the beginning of the century. A handful of university medical schools had been founded in the 1700s, but throughout the early nineteenth century they played no significant role in the training of doctors, who continued to prepare for their profession through apprenticeships to practicing physicians.[53] A similar situation existed in the law, where the profession itself clung to the apprenticeship model and disdained the idea that the practice of law required academic preparation, even as university law schools, in the course of the 1800s, increasingly aimed to combine academic with practical education. Moreover, university-based medical and law schools in the nineteenth century each competed with proprietary schools whose emphasis was wholly practical, and where standards were often nonexistent. The high rates of medical school foundings and dissolutions in the period highlight their unstable position. Between 1810 and 1876, seventy-three proprietary medical schools were established. Between 1876 and 1890, that number almost doubled. In total, almost four hundred medical schools were founded and dissolved in the United States between 1800 and 1900.[54] Abraham Flexner described the state of American medical education during this period:

> The schools were essentially private ventures, money-making in spirit and object. A school that began in October would graduate a class next spring; it mattered not that the course of study was two or three years; immigration recruited a senior class at the start. Income was simply divided among the lecturers, who reaped a rich harvest, besides, through the consultations which the loyalty of their former students threw into their hands. . . . No applicant for instruction who could pay his fees or sign his note was turned down. . . . The school diploma was itself a license to practice. The examinations, brief, oral, and secret, plucked almost none at all. . . . The man who had settled his tuition bill was thus practically assured of his degree,

whether he had regularly attended lectures or not. Accordingly, the business throve.[55]

If proprietary schools were turning out satisfied customers rather than professional graduates, this formula was not threatened by the relatively low—in some cases nonexistent—educational and licensing requirements for lawyers and doctors. For example, in 1800, three-quarters of the states maintained educational requirements for the practice of law; by 1860, only a quarter of them had any such requirements.[56] The egalitarianism of Jacksonian America had precipitated a spirited attack on professional licensing as a conspiracy against the public interest and as an obstruction of the individual's right to enter any occupation he pleased. Licensing laws, while rarely granting monopoly power to the professions, had played a pivotal role in publicly endorsing the distinction between rightful and wrongful practice. Moreover, licensing laws reflected a degree of public recognition when it came to the legitimacy of the professions' claims to authority and honor. Yet political populists now found that they could gain favor by denouncing such laws as aristocratic, monopolistic, and even anti-American. Thus, for example, in 1800 almost every state had medical licensing laws, while by 1860 none of them did.[57] This situation gave rise to an early nineteenth-century linguistic usage, noted by H. L. Mencken, whereby anyone who claimed to make a living using a supposedly specialized skill—a group that might include barbers, dancing masters, tailors, phrenologists, acrobats, or music hall piano players—could and did make use of the title "Professor." As Wiebe observed, "The so-called professions meant little as long as anyone with a bag of pills and a bottle of syrup could pass for a doctor, a few books and a corrupt judge made a man a lawyer, and an unemployed literate qualified as a teacher."[58]

The effort to reestablish the authority of the professions in America began in earnest during and just after the Civil War. Morris Janowitz has documented the professionalization of the U.S. armed forces that started during the Civil War, as the mechanization of weaponry and the wholesale slaughter that it wrought in that conflict were putting an end to chivalric conceptions of the soldier's calling, and the nation's military academies shifted their focus away from producing heroic leaders and to the education of military "managers," often trained as engineers.[59] A bellwether of change in medicine and law was the effort of the great educational reformer Charles W. Eliot, on assuming the presidency of Harvard in 1869, to significantly raise admissions and academic standards at Harvard Medical School and Harvard Law

School. The civil service reform movement that began immediately following the Civil War (eventually resulting in passage of the Pendleton Civil Service Reform Act of 1883) aimed to professionalize government administration, turning the patronage system that had characterized civil service hiring under Jacksonian democracy into a merit-based approach with publicly defined standards. In the Progressive era, professionalism and professionalization were thus emerging as major pillars to support the "search for order."

By the 1890s, the traditional professions were strongly reasserting themselves, while many new ones were arising to stake their own claims to professional authority and privilege. The leveling impulses that had run through both Jacksonianism and Populism began to recede as the Progressives bested the Populists in the battle for public opinion.[60] The revival and growth of the professions in the late nineteenth and early twentieth centuries are illustrated by table 2.1, which tracks the numbers of professional schools in the United States between 1886 and 1929. The table illustrates the rapid growth in medical and law schools in the United States between 1886 and 1909 and the relative decline of theological schools. (The decrease in the number of law schools and medical schools between 1909 and 1919 is a consequence of the publication of the Carnegie Foundation report on medical education [1910] and the first of its reports on legal education [1914], which led to the closing of low-quality medical and law schools.)[61] The table also reflects the fact that, by 1910, dentistry, pharmacy, and veterinary medicine were recognized by the U.S. Census Bureau as distinct professions.

As the numbers of professions and professionals multiplied, their associations grew in number, and many of them increasingly benefited from state

Table 2.1

Number of Professional Schools from 1886 to 1929

	Theological	Law	Medical[a]	Dentistry	Pharmacy	Veterinary
1886	142	49	89	—	—	—
1889	145	54	94	—	—	—
1899	163	96	151	—	—	—
1909	193	116	122	55	77	21
1919	105	106	78	39	51	15
1929	176	136	73	41	66	10

Source: U.S. Statistical Abstracts.
[a] Excludes medical schools classified as either homeopathic or eclectic because this distinction did not carry forward in the *Statistical Abstracts.*

protection.[62] From this position of enhanced strength, professional associations developed a focus on their particular group's societal role as opposed to merely defending its economic role. Professions themselves increasingly recognized that their nascent claims to authority had to rest on more than the perquisites of gentlemanly traditions: they needed to justify their positions through closely reasoned appeals.

As we saw in the preceding section, advances in fields such as medicine and public health in the late nineteenth century contributed to the prestige of science by demonstrating its practical benefits for society. The professions in general, in this period, were able to piggyback on progress in science to argue for their own usefulness to society. The medical profession, in particular, successfully capitalized on scientific medicine's deepening understanding of what caused, cured, or could prevent various diseases. More broadly, physicians gained in stature owing to what Paul Starr has called "the growing recognition of the inadequacy of the unaided and uneducated senses in understanding the world."[63] For most of the professions, including those still striving to establish themselves by emulating the precedent set by the medical community, the issue remained one of gaining cognitive legitimacy through claims to scientific rigor and objectivity rather than actually demonstrating efficacy.[64] With the rise of twentieth-century medicine, pharmacists, for example, sought to shape a new identity for themselves not as merchants dispensing patent medicines and quasi-magical concoctions but, rather, as professionals with expertise rooted in science (chemistry) who were capable of providing objective advice about over-the-counter medications, drug interactions, and dosage levels.[65] Yet even as the professions pursued cognitive legitimacy by making scientific claims, they also strove for sociopolitical legitimacy by distancing themselves from all that symbolized personal and professional self-interest. Abraham Flexner, writing in 1915, identified six criteria that qualified an occupation as a profession: "[P]rofessions involve essentially intellectual operations with large individual responsibility; they derive their raw material from science and learning; this material they work up to a practical and definite end; they possess an educationally communicable technique; they tend to self-organization; [and] they are becoming increasingly altruistic in motivation."[66] While it is true that the professions represented economic entities concerned with, among other things, profit making, a sense of public duty often stood counterpoised to the simple maximizing of income. Even as utilitarian a profession as engineering portrayed itself as serving the most elevated purposes, as when the president of the American Society for Mechanical Engineers proclaimed in 1911 that "as we reverently discover and apply natural laws, we find new reasons and supports for . . . fundamental ethical conceptions."[67] Indeed, by linking themselves to public and even universal purposes and professing devotion to the well-being of society as a whole, the professions were reaching back to a framework that Alexander Hamilton had used when he argued in *The Federalist Papers* that the professions—having no interests of their own in the clash between the mercantile and landowning classes of society— were properly situated to act as "an impartial arbiter" between them.[68]

Such ideas, although lying dormant in American public life through much of the nineteenth century, would be invoked by Progressives seeking to rehabilitate professionalism as part of their larger effort to restore what they saw as the nation's lost moral and civic virtue.[69] For Progressive reformers generally, one of the greatest of all virtues was "disinterestedness," as Wilfred M. McClay has explained in an essay on the Progressive writer Herbert Croly (cofounder, with Walter Lippmann, of the *New Republic*, and a leader in the movement to restructure corporate and governmental administration in America along professional lines) and his book *The Promise of American Life* (1909):

> [Croly] saw a slow, groping progress from a disorganized and decentralized form of laissez-faire individualism to an organized and socialized form of disciplined nationhood. Fueled by steady pursuit of the Promise, the movement would succeed once the virtues of pioneering independence were superseded by the virtues of social solidarity and "disinterested" knowledge. One should take note of Croly's repeated use of the word "disinterested," a word Progressive reformers could hardly have done without. It is doubtless a fact of great significance that this word's meaning is almost completely lost upon our more jaded age, in which it is nearly always used, incorrectly, as a synonym for "uninterested." For Progressives, however, the word carried strong ethical implications, pointing toward an extraordinarily high standard of unselfish, reasonable, ascetic, scientific, and impersonal judgment—a disposition that always placed the public interest above all other considerations.[70]

Such a standard of "unselfish, reasonable, ascetic, scientific, and impersonal judgment" was exactly what Progressives saw in the true professional. Professionals were supposed to place the interests of those whom they advised above their own. They were expected to actively avoid situations in which their disinterestedness could be questioned, and to refrain from activities that yielded them personal advantage. Besides disinterestedness, examples of means by which professions and professionals demonstrated their integrity and trustworthiness included transparency, signals of competence, and espousals of actions consistent with duties of care and loyalty to the client.[71] While such expectations and the means of meeting them remain characteristic of professionals today for reasons relating to the very nature of professional knowledge and work,[72] in the late nineteenth century they arose out of what were then new, very particular societal conditions revolving around the issue of trust.

Amid the profound social dislocations of the era, a particularly salient need for individuals in many different walks of life—but perhaps especially for those who presented themselves as possessing expert knowledge necessary for the performance of important social functions—was the establishment and cultivation of trust. Owing to the breakdown of the small, self-contained communities of preindustrial America—together with their traditional forms of authority, reciprocity, and face-to-face interaction—a new foundation for trust had to be created to facilitate the more impersonal, purely transactional relationships that came to dominate social life. Exchange had once been limited to an individual's local community, kinship, or ethnic groups, but this became increasingly difficult in an industrial society reflecting geographic and social mobility, immigration, and urbanization. As Mark Granovetter has pointed out, networks of trust are most often embedded in interpersonal relations, which are the channels through which emotion, common understanding, and reciprocities flow. Thus it is not a coincidence that in the transition to modernity, characterized as it was by the absence of embeddedness, more institutionalized forms of trust arose, with rationalized professions prominent among them.[73]

In an increasingly differentiated society, where it was now more and more often necessary to rely on strangers to meet basic human needs such as obtaining health care or purchasing property, the traditional professions of medicine and law assumed increasingly institutionalized forms, and occupations such as teaching and social work became professionalized for the first time. Professions, because of their norms and constraints, were ideally suited for inspiring public trust. Table 2.2 provides a sample of the various occupations that engaged in the professionalization process during this period. Many basic concerns of modern social relations could be addressed through institutions that exhibited norms of practice that were easily understood and that articulated and adhered to ethical codes. The process of establishing

Table 2.2
Professionalization Projects in Selected Professions

	First University School	First Local Professional Association	First National Professional Association	First State License Law	Formal Code of Ethics
Accounting	1881	1881	1887	1896	1917
Advertising	1909	1894	1917	None	1924
Architecture	1868	1815	1857	1897	1909
City management	1948	1914	1914	None	1924
Civil engineering	1847	1848	1852	1908	1910
Dentistry	1867	1844	1840	1868	1866
Funeral direction	1914	1864	1882	1894	1884
Hospital administration	1926	None	1933	1957	1939
Law	1817	1802	1878	1732	1908
Librarianship	1897	1885	1876	1917	1938
Medicine	1779	1735	1847	<1780	1912
Nursing	1909	1885	1896	1903	1950
Optometry	1910	1896	1897	1901	1935
Pharmacy	1868	1821	1852	1874	1850
Schoolteaching	1879	1794	1857	1781	1929
Social work	1904	1918	1874	1940	1948
Urban planning	1909	1947	1917	1963	1948
Veterinary medicine	1879	1854	1863	1886	1866

Source: Adapted from Harold Wilensky, "The Professionalization of Everyone?" *American Journal of Sociology* 70, no. 2 (September 1964): 137–158.

trust in the professions was accomplished partly via the state, through the reintroduction or strengthening of licensing as well as through judicial rulings that granted greater recognition and deference to professional opinion in legal cases (as in the case of *Muller v. Oregon* discussed above as an example of the new authority of science). Just as important in reinforcing the espoused values of the professions was the establishment of structures of professionalism such as educational credentials, accrediting institutions, and associations. The new professional schools discussed above delivered the educational credentials.

Just as science in the late nineteenth and early twentieth centuries presented itself not only as a means of solving social problems but also as a quest for fundamental truth and an intrinsically moral enterprise, the professions drew on a rich cluster of associations between professionalism and the infusion of human activity with values and meaning. Of course, none of this is meant to suggest that the professions did not face continued challenges to their legitimacy. Indeed, the legitimacy of the professions as supposed pillars of a new social order would not be fully achieved until they had aligned themselves with the third major institution emerging in the United States at this time and presenting itself as a social-ordering mechanism: the American research university.

The New American Research University

We have seen how the institutionalization of science and the revival of the professions in the late nineteenth and early twentieth centuries in America were connected with efforts to address a number of converging crises: the profound social and psychological dislocations caused by industrialization, urbanization, immigration, and the breakdown of traditional communities; rapid technological change; economic depression and labor violence; the decline of traditional religious belief; and, overall, the widespread sense that society was changing in fundamental ways that required the creation or wholesale reinvention of institutions. Whereas science and the professions both possessed powerful legitimating rationales of their own, both also received crucial assistance from the American research university, a third institution that was emerging in this period with astonishing rapidity. In many ways, its rise and development represented the most significant institutional change of the time, not only because the American research university was, and remains, one of the most vital, dynamic, and influential institutions in the modern world, but also because it enabled both science and the professions to come into their own as institutions. While science and the professions themselves lent a certain amount of legitimacy to the new American research university in its formative decades, the most powerful influences worked in the other direction. Simply put, science and the professions in the form we know them in the United States today are inconceivable apart from their relationship to the American university.

Like the institutions of science and the professions in the late nineteenth and early twentieth centuries, the university legitimized itself both by performing utilitarian functions and by appealing to widely held values. In proclaiming its mission of creating and disseminating knowledge for the public good, the American research university drew on the cognitive and normative legitimacy of its new commitment to the scientific method. By strengthening its links with the professions, it affirmed its dedication to useful knowledge and to service. Yet by virtue of an ancient lineage combined with an extremely modern flexibility and capacity to innovate, the new research university also brought its own social, cultural, and even spiritual capital to the table. As a quasi-sacred institution in an era full of longing to preserve a vanishing sense of the sacred, the university was perfectly suited to act as a vehicle for the advancement of science and the professions, and to become, as it did, an icon embodying many of society's most deeply held values and aspirations.[74]

The history of higher education in America in the nineteenth century is dominated by two closely intertwined themes—expansion of access and expansion of purpose. The story line chronicles the journey of the American university from the periphery to the center of American society. Until the early 1800s, institutions of higher education played a somewhat marginal role in the collective life of the nation, existing mostly to provide "Christian character formation" for the sons of local elites (many of whom went on to enter one of the "learned professions": the ministry, law, or medicine).[75] The first three American colleges—Harvard, William and Mary, and Yale—were all established as religious institutions. Their primary objective, summarized in Harvard's founding documents, was to "let every student be plainly instructed and earnestly pressed to consider well, the maine end of his life and studies is, *to know God and Jesus Christ which is eternal life*" (emphasis in original).[76] Young men were taught Latin, Greek, the Bible, and natural philosophy. For their instructors—many of whom were clergymen, since anyone trained for the ministry was presumed qualified to teach any and every subject the college offered—there was no such thing as an academic career. The college classroom was a kind of waiting room where "young teachers tended to view their work as temporary until something better came along, that middle-aged men sought [as] an interlude or an escape from the rigors of an active profession such as the ministry, and the elderly found [as] a berth for retirement."[77]

In the early nineteenth century, new state colleges and universities created under the terms of the Northwest Ordinance of 1787 began expanding access to higher education and giving it a more practical cast than it had theretofore possessed. This development occurred in the context of an overall growth in the number of institutions of higher learning in the young nation: whereas in 1799 only 25 colleges existed in America, by 1830 there were

Table 2.3
Institutions of Higher Learning and Ratio to Population of the United States, 1790–1930

	No. of Colleges and Universities	Population	No. per Million
1790	19	3,929,214	4.8
1800	25	5,308,483	4.7
1810	30	7,239,881	4.1
1820	40	9,638,453	4.2
1830	50	12,866,020	3.9
1840	85	17,069,453	5.0
1850	120	23,191,876	5.2
1860	250	31,443,321	8.0
1870	563	39,818,449	14.1
1880	811	50,155,783	16.2
1890	998	62,947,714	15.9
1900	977	75,994,575	12.9
1910	951	91,972,266	10.3
1920	1,041	105,710,620	9.8
1930	1,409	122,775,046	11.5

Sources: *Statistical Abstract of the United States*; *Historical Statistics of the United States*; and Randolph Collins, *The Credential Society: An Historical Sociology of Education and Stratification* (New York: Academic Press, 1979), 119.

49, and by the start of the Civil War there were 182.[78] (Table 2.3 shows the rapid growth of colleges and universities in the United States, on both an absolute and a per capita basis, between the years 1790 and 1930.)

While the establishment of these new institutions was widening access to higher education, other developments were laying the groundwork for a broadened conception of what subjects belonged in colleges and universities. At the United States Military Academy—founded in 1802 to eliminate the young nation's reliance on foreign-born and -trained military engineers—civil engineering formed the core of the curriculum under the leadership of Col. Sylvanus Thayer (superintendent of the academy from 1817 to 1833),[79] and the academic training enjoyed by West Point–educated engineers gave them considerable influence in pre–Civil War America.[80] By midcentury, the growing influence of engineering vis-à-vis the traditional professions was suggested by the fact that the University of Michigan (the first in America to grant degrees in the subject) began offering engineering courses in 1854, five years before it began teaching law.

In the midst of the Civil War, the Morrill Act of 1862—which created the mechanism for the founding of the nation's land-grant colleges—specifically designated agriculture and the "mechanical arts" as subjects for academic study in these new institutions.[81] In the ensuing decades, the growing belief that universities in a democratic society needed to provide practical benefits for the public, together with the increasing organization and prestige of science and the inspiration of the German research university, gave birth to the new institution of the American research university, of which Johns Hopkins (founded in 1876) is the classic exemplar. This new kind of American university, of which Clark University (founded in 1887) and the University of Chicago (1892) were two subsequent incarnations, emphasized research and graduate study, following the model of nineteenth-century German research universities that two generations of American scholars had by now experienced firsthand. Yet as other American universities, public and private, began to emulate these new institutions and add research to their agendas, what emerged was not a simple transplant of the German system to American soil but rather a uniquely American hybrid. In one institution, a series of unanticipated combinations now coexisted: undergraduate education along with graduate education; teaching with research; the pursuit of "pure" science with technical and vocational training; and service to society with the provision of opportunities for individual cultivation and economic advancement.[82] The result constituted much more than an academic revolution, for it generated implications for virtually the entire American population and almost all of the nation's major social institutions. While the creators of the American research university could hardly have foreseen the ultimate consequences of their institutional entrepreneurship, it is important to underscore the sense in which both Progressive social reformers and their academic counterparts conceived of higher education as an essential institution in the new social order.

With its triple mission of teaching, research, and public service, the new American research university quickly elicited enthusiastic approbation and support from both the public and the private sectors, as demonstrated by the rapid proliferation of colleges and universities in the United States and the significant increase in large private gifts to higher education. For example, the total amount of giving to universities and colleges increased fourfold between 1895 and 1915.[83] In the Progressive heartland, the "Wisconsin idea" took hold: the University of Wisconsin's School of Economics, Political Science, and History (under the direction of Richard Ely) had been founded with the objective of turning the university, in Hofstadter's words, "into an efficient practical servant of the state."[84] This idea of placing the university's research capabilities at the service of the governor and state legislature, offering its know-how in agricultural and practical sciences to support the state economy while providing continuing and widely available education to the public via satellite campuses, rapidly spread through the nation's public university system. The founding of new master's and doctoral degree programs as well as of new professional schools (or the resuscitation of older ones in universities like Harvard) became one of the most visible symbols of the university's new commitment to practical education.

Yet for all the utilitarian benefits that the new American research university conferred or was believed to be capable of conferring, there is no reason to suppose that such practical boons were the primary reason for the strong support that this new institution received from American society almost from the beginning. Just as members of many of the new and reviving professions in America began to legitimate themselves before building much of a record of verifiable achievements, the American research university quickly won legitimacy for reasons based more on faith than on works, as it were. Laurence Veysey described the prevailing attitude in terms of the American public's aspirations for its new universities: "Higher education, it was hoped, might affect the conduct of public affairs in at least three ways," Veysey wrote. "First, the university would make each of its graduates into a force for civic virtue. Second, it would train a group of political leaders who would take a knightly plunge into 'real life' and clean it up. Finally, through scientifically oriented scholarship, rational substitutes could be found for political procedures subject to personal influence."[85] A similar argument about "the ascendancy of the university" in America was developed by Edward Shils, who attributed the success of this institution in the late nineteenth century to the public's belief in the value of knowledge for its own sake, not just for its practical applications:

> What propelled the university movement was a drift of opinion toward the appreciation of knowledge, particularly knowledge of a scientific character. There was general agreement that knowledge could be accepted as knowledge only if it rested on empirical evidence, rigorously criticized and rationally analyzed, and that this kind of knowledge was worthy of all the effort and resources required to attain it. Great businessmen, leading state politicians as well as a few major national politicians, important publicists and, in a vague way,

much of the electorate joined in the appreciation of this kind of knowledge and of the university as its proper organ. The universities were supported because they performed a dual function: they infused knowledge into the young who would apply it in their professions and whose lives would be illuminated by its possession, and they contributed to the improvement of the stock of knowledge, penetrating further and further into the nature of reality.[86]

Indeed, Shils further maintained that a certain type of knowledge that the American research university pursued possessed a quasi-sacred character for the generation that witnessed this new institution's emergence:

> The knowledge that was appreciated was secular knowledge which continued the mission of sacred knowledge, complemented it, led to it, or replaced it; fundamental, systematically acquired knowledge was thought in some way to be a step toward redemption. This kind of knowledge held out the prospect of the transfiguration of life by improving man's control over the resources of nature and the powers that weaken his body; it offered the prospect of a better understanding of society that, it was felt, would lead to the improvement of society. It was thought that the progress of mankind entailed the improvement of understanding simply as a state of being and not solely as an instrument of action. The honor and the glory of a country that promoted the acquisition of such knowledge was assured; its power and influence would grow proportionately and deservedly.[87]

Remarking that the "comprehensiveness" of the modern American university provided a rationale for its dominance within the "institutionalized system of learning," Shils says that their "multitude of diverse, specialized interests enabled the universities to receive the deference that had hitherto been accorded to the churches. . . . At a time of faltering theological conviction, the university scholar or scientist assumed the role of an earnest seeker after fundamental truth."[88] In other words, the enhanced prestige of institutions of higher education in America during the last three decades of the nineteenth century also elevated the role and status of the professor in American society. Meanwhile, the founding of the American Association of University Professors in 1915 signaled that professors, independently of any particular discipline, were becoming professionalized. Paralleling the emergence of the American research university, the professionalization of academic disciplines and of the professoriat itself via professional associations meant that the lay professor could claim modern learning and expertise while capturing for his calling something of the aura that once surrounded the profession of the clergy. Indeed, the professor was now perceived as an individual devoted to the pursuit of truth in a manner that echoed the dedication of a clergyman to religious service. The scholar, like the priest or minister, lived a life oriented toward ultimate things. Albion Small expressed this sense when he wrote that the young scholar who publishes the results of his first serious research realizes that "the men who write books are no longer a superior species. They are merely elect through consecration of the same powers of which he begins to be aware. He enters their ranks feeling some of the sense of responsibility with which we like to believe other men assume holy orders."[89] This quasi-religious conception of the scholar's role was one that a whole generation of German-trained professors in American universities appropriated as their own, as Shils also observes: "They had ceased to believe in a literal Christian interpretation of the universe and of human existence, yet they were determined to repair that loss by replacing it or shoring it up with scientific and scholarly knowledge, which if it did not disclose God's design, would at least reveal the lawfulness of some of the workings of nature and society."[90]

Dedicated to the disinterested pursuit and transmission of knowledge in the service of the common good; amply endowed with resources; and led by gifted institutional entrepreneurs such as Harvard's Charles W. Eliot, Johns Hopkins's Daniel Coit Gilman, and Cornell's Andrew Dickson White (among others), the new American research university, as we have noted, evolved into not only an enormously influential institution in its own right but also a crucial source of support and legitimation for science and the professions. Through their commitment to the scientific method as a means of knowledge making, for example, universities gained legitimacy for themselves but also helped establish the moral soundness and institutional viability of the scientific enterprise.[91] A generation before the founding of the first American research universities, the publication of Darwin's *The Origin of Species* had begun to strengthen the hand of science relative to theology and Christian humanism in the college curriculum. Once the research universities were established, and research emerged as a necessary qualification for a university career and became a criterion for promotion, science finally displaced the classical subjects in the academic pecking order.[92] The natural scientists enjoyed increasing amounts of dedicated resources, in the form of laboratories and students, as well as higher salaries and more status than their colleagues in the humanities. The reasons for this reversal are not difficult to discern. Because the natural sciences relied on experimentation as well as theory, researchers in these disciplines could point to tangible results.[93] The natural sciences thus appeared superior to the humanities in their capacity to advance the university's mission of creating new knowledge. At the same time, as we have seen, they succeeded in appropriating much of the moral prestige of the older, humanistic disciplines.

A similar development occurred in the social sciences. While there was no demand from outside the university for research in the social sciences, it was believed, as we have seen, that if natural phenomena could be understood via the scientific method, then human behavior was also knowable by such means. Psychologists, economists, and sociologists, working within the university, exhibited a new fondness for the collection of data for the purpose of analyzing social phenomena.[94] Albion Small, the founder of modern American sociology, and Richard Ely, the originator of modern professional economics, viewed the city and the factory, respectively, as their newfound laboratories. Initially, the social sciences focused on establishing basic principles. However, as their disciplines grew more confident and gained legitimacy within the university, they began to address more practical and socially pressing concerns, thus bolstering their claims to authority.

Meanwhile, as Shils observed, "Science and the universities became almost identical for the broader public."[95] Yet while the university both received critical validation from, and conferred it on, the institution of science in this period, it served as an absolutely indispensable component in the revival and legitimation of the professions. In his inaugural address as first president of the University of Minnesota in 1869, William Watts Folwell—who would champion the cause of graduate and professional education at his young university in the face of strong opposition from faculty in the traditional disciplines—commented on the attraction of the professions for the sort of upwardly mobile youth drawn to the nation's public universities: "[S]o long as there is open to young men the prospect of a name and a home, of a high social position to be won with clean hands and unsoiled garments by headwork, and without capital, the learned professions, so called, will continue to absorb the best blood of the country."[96] As we have already seen, given the absence of monopolies in law and medicine (a situation that also existed in the emerging professions of teaching and civil service), aspiring professionals up into the late nineteenth century were most often trained in apprenticeships or proprietary schools with an emphasis on practical technique rather than theory. In the last three decades of the nineteenth century, however, as universities began to argue for an expanded role for higher education in preparing people for modern occupations, the rise of the research university was accompanied by rapid growth in the number of university-based professional schools, for both the traditional and the emerging—or aspiring—professions.

University-based professional schools boast an ancient lineage, inasmuch as faculties of law, medicine, and theology, along with the arts and sciences, together constituted the medieval European university. In America, as we have already noted, university-based professional schools predated the rise of the American research university, even though these early American institutions were not "professional schools" in the modern sense. In 1765, the nation's first medical school was founded at what was then called the College of Philadelphia (now the University of Pennsylvania). In 1779, Thomas Jefferson (then governor of Virginia) created the nation's first chair of law at the College of William and Mary; the College of Philadelphia began offering lectures in law in 1790, though the title of oldest continuously operating school of law in America today is claimed by Harvard Law School, founded in 1817. Separate faculties of medicine, law, and theology grew as offshoots of other American colleges during this period, although often as mere appendages to the college of arts and sciences. The training offered at such institutions was brief, relatively informal, and often downright poor; these schools employed few faculty members, and classes were taught mostly by local practitioners with what we would now call adjunct appointments.

Charles W. Eliot's reforms aimed at raising admissions and academic standards at Harvard Law School and Harvard Medical School in the 1870s signaled a key turning point for university-based education in these two professions, and by this point other occupations were establishing a presence in the university for the first time. Partly through the original Morrill Act (and its eventual successor, the second Morrill Act of 1890), the notion of vocation or "calling" was being significantly broadened beyond the traditional "learned professions" of medicine, law, and the clergy. Engineering, for example, increasingly saw itself as a learned profession, and, as we shall see in the next chapter, proponents of the professionalization project for management made the same argument for that occupation. This development prompted the rise of professional schools in increasing numbers of occupations in the second half of the nineteenth century. The emergence of an engineering school at the University of Michigan in 1854 has already been noted. The first university-based school (as opposed to a mere training institute) for dentistry was founded at Harvard in 1867 (in close affiliation with Harvard Medical School, which had been established in 1782). The following year, architecture and pharmacy gained their own first professional schools at MIT and the University of Michigan, respectively. Veterinary medicine joined the trend in 1879 (at Cornell). The University of Pennsylvania's Wharton School—the first university-based business school in the United States—appeared in 1881.

The rise of new professional schools reflected both a surge in demand for what a university education was increasingly believed to offer, and the willingness and capability of the new American university to adapt to such demand. In a nation with a weak tradition of formal social markers, the college diploma was becoming a credential enabling individuals of tenuous or threatened social status to access the respectability and economic rewards offered by the professions.[97] Meanwhile, the uniquely practical character of the American research university was manifested, in part, through its eagerness to explore the "quasi-disciplines" (Ben-David's term) that provided emerging and aspiring professions with scientific research agendas.[98] Pragmatism was also evident in the university's willingness to become a provider of credentials. Here is how Wiebe summarized the role of the university in the efforts of various occupations to legitimize themselves as professions in this period:

> The universities played a crucial role in almost all of these movements. Since the emergence of the modern graduate school in the seventies, the best universities had been serving as outposts of professional self-consciousness, frankly preparing young men for professions that as yet did not exist. By 1900 they held an unquestioned power to legitimize, for no new profession felt complete—or scientific—without its distinct academic curriculum; they provided centers for philosophizing and propagandizing; and they inculcated apprentices with the proper values and goals. Considering the potential of the universities for frustration, it was extremely important that higher education permissively, even indiscriminately, welcomed each of the new groups in turn.[99]

Through the expansion of university-based professional education, the university legitimized the authority of the professions by appealing to the Progressive belief in the value of scientific knowledge *and* the obligation of the scientifically versed expert to utilize knowledge in the service of the public good. The university, indeed, bound itself under this obligation and now committed itself to enforcing it in the professions taking shelter under its umbrella. Precisely how and why the university assumed the task of legitimating the professions remains an issue mostly beyond the scope of the present study, although it will be examined in the case of university-based business schools in chapter 3. As for why the professions turned to, and came to depend on, the university as a source of legitimation, two key factors can be identified: the nature of the knowledge underlying professional work and the difficulty of evaluating the quality of this work. Let us examine each of these considerations in turn.

Andrew Abbott's work on professional contestation emphasizes that the kind of knowledge a profession claims as its own acts as an important strategic factor in defining the exclusiveness of that profession. Thus a key prerequisite of any professionalization project is that a cognitive basis for such claims of unique knowledge be at least approximately defined before a rising profession can stake its claim to specific tools and techniques, thereby establishing its absolute superiority over competitors.[100] Education plays a critical role in the assertion of "cognitive exclusiveness" that is necessary for professionalization. In the learned professions, the most frequently used mechanisms for protecting cognitive exclusiveness are formal training in a common curriculum, educational credentials, qualifying exams, and state licensing.[101] The functions now performed by these mechanisms were initially carried out by guildlike professional associations that were often localized and operated in a manner not unlike the apprenticeship system. Beginning in the late nineteenth century, however, the provision of formal training and the conferring of educational credentials were increasingly recognized and accepted as functions of university-based professional schools.

Besides helping legitimate the claim of cognitive exclusiveness for would-be professionals, education plays an essential role in the standardization of producers that, by aiding outsiders in the evaluation of the quality of professional work, serves as a critical component of professionalization. Magali Larson argues that for a profession to exist, it must identify the distinctive "commodity" it will produce.[102] Yet the products of professional competence and skill—care for a sick patient, for example, or an argument in a courtroom—are largely intangible. Since it is not easy to standardize intangible services, professional legitimacy is attained through the standardization of those goods' producers. That is, professionals must be trained and socialized in such a way as to appear *themselves* to be the standardized products of the same training and socialization—for instance, by using the same jargon, behaving with clients in a manner that conforms to expectations, appointing their offices with similar equipment or furnishings, and so on.

There were several reasons why this task of standardizing professional producers was largely ceded by the professions themselves to the university. In a manner consistent with an increasingly rationalized and modernized society, universities were beginning to display formal structures such as large administrative staffs, formal career paths, and more specialized faculties, traits that implied both competence and efficiency. Institutions such as business and government were already adopting formalized organizational structures and hierarchies as well as formal standards and policies for hiring, evaluating, and promoting employees; as the university embraced such rational procedures (including grades for evaluating students' educational attainments), it more closely reflected the organizational attributes and values that Progressive reformers were promoting in American society generally, thereby further enhancing the university's legitimacy in the eyes of reformers, politicians, and the general public. The university was also forging links with numerous scholarly and professional associations (such as the social science associations formed in the late nineteenth and early twentieth centuries) that were *themselves* invoking a set of values and structures believed to cohere with the public interest. As a consequence of these developments, educational activities conducted under the umbrella of the university were taken more seriously and regarded as more legitimate by the professions' internal and external constituents than were those carried out either through informal structures like apprenticeship or by commercial schools—even when the educational activities within the university were identical to those offered outside it. Independent of its structure, another feature inspiring faith in educational activities conducted under the aegis of the university was that knowledge produced and diffused by universities was believed to possess a disinterested, objective quality—the same quality that enhanced the legitimacy of scientific knowledge and scientists.

With such markers of credibility, universities won the trust of both the public at large and various other resource providers, especially large individual donors. When, in 1847, Abbott Lawrence gave Harvard $50,000 to found a "scientific school," the gift made national headlines. Yet by the late nineteenth century, as Daniel Wren has demonstrated, gifts of this magnitude had become commonplace.[103] Andrew Carnegie, for example, gave $27 million to establish the Carnegie Institute of Technology. Leland Stanford, Sr., established Stanford University with $20 million. Overall, the conviction that professionals could or even should be trained in universities grew as a result of the same general process through which universities themselves came to be regarded as legitimate. By copying certain forms and activities expected by the wider culture, the new institution of the American research university created a social context that was seen to adhere to and promote norms shared by the wider culture, including the professions.

In addition to validating cognitive exclusiveness and providing a means for standardizing professional training, however, the American university offered yet another vehicle by which professional self-consciousness—another important condition that must be met before an occupational group can claim professional status—could be, and was, developed among aspiring professionals. Practitioners of an aspiring profession must at some point begin to think of themselves in collective terms and to act in concert[104]—a condition, as I argued in chapter 1, that American management was unable to satisfy as it searched for ways of establishing its authority and legitimacy. The new American university granted many existing and incipient occupational groups a locus for attaining such collective consciousness and initiating collective action. With universities and colleges increasingly serving as their training grounds, the emerging professions—or, more precisely, the groups of elites that acted as their spokesmen—began to assume a commonality, however minimal, among their members derived from the common experience of higher education. For professionals, the possession of a college degree was a source of distinction in relation to the population at large. As more children of middle-class families obtained college and university professional educations, they recognized the usefulness of this distinction for transforming occupational status.[105] Membership in the new education-based elite began to surface as a means of social categorization, determining access to elite occupations and the rewards they offered.

It is important to note, however, that, by enabling the professions to establish their legitimacy, the university did more than just facilitate the construction of boundaries of exclusivity or the carving out of expert jurisdictions. It also endowed these professionalizing occupations with the moral authority and sense of purpose inherited from the university's own founding logic. This sense of a more-than-instrumental function attends the traditional professional's performance of his or her occupational role. Among its many other notable achievements, the new American research university had quickly transformed the pursuit of secular knowledge into something very much like what America's Puritan founders would have termed a *calling* (a concept that would also become central to Weber's characterization of the Protestant ethic). For the individual following his or her calling, work was not simply a means to an end but represented, rather, a devotional act. The life and career of a university-trained professional, viewed in this light, assumed a moral significance—one less likely to have emerged had the professions been forced to find their place in society without the assistance of the university. Moreover, the new professional schools emerging toward the end of the nineteenth century explicitly considered questions about the moral purpose of their respective endeavors as they experimented with their programs for professional pedagogy and socialization—a phenomenon that we will see exemplified in the early history of the university-based business school.

Thus science, the professions, and the university all claimed, and were awarded, status as major rationalizing and order-creating institutions at a time when the occupation of management was emerging and seeking to legitimate its authority. As such, each provided crucial cognitive and normative frameworks for use by the managerial and academic vanguard engaged in the attempted professionalization of management. In the next chapter, I describe how these innovators were able to appropriate elements of the logics of each of these three existing institutions to create congruence between the emerging occupation of management and the dominant cognitive and normative standards for professional knowledge and work in late nineteenth- and early twentieth-century American society.

The Invention of the University-Based Business School   **3**

The disruption of the social order occasioned by the rise of the large corporation in America and the attempt to construct a new social order for this profoundly altered social context stand as defining events of the modern era. Industrialization, coupled with urbanization, increased mobility, and the absorption of local economies into what was increasingly a single national economy dominated by large corporations, had facilitated the deinstitutionalization of traditional authority structures. The reconstitution of the institutions of science, professions, and the university in the course of the late nineteenth century offered alternative structures and rationales that could serve as the foundation for a new social order that, its proponents argued, was more suited to changed social conditions. In particular, the structural and normative characteristics undergirding these three institutions served to bridge the gulf between the traditional and industrial orders. Amid the sometimes violent clashes of interests attending the rise of the new industrial society, science, the professions, and the university presented themselves as disinterested communities possessing both expertise and commitment to the common good. The combination made these three institutions, built on rational principles and widely shared, even quasi-sacred values, appear to be ideal instruments to address pressing social needs. In each case, a vanguard of institutional entrepreneurs led efforts to define (or redefine) their institutions, frame societal problems, and mobilize constituencies in ways that won credibility for these institutions in the nascent social order.

For the emerging managerial elite—or, more precisely, for the group of institutional entrepreneurs who assumed the task of legitimating the role and authority of management in the new industrial and social order—science, the professions, and the research university represented legitimate institutions to which management could attach itself, thereby validating its own rationality, disinterestedness, and commitment to commonly held values. As science and the professions came under the aegis of the university and, in the process, gained access to new organizational structures, resources, and prestige, the university came into focus as the logical site for management's own institution-building activities. Thus the project of legitimating modern management centered on the creation of what proved to be one of the most influential institutions in twentieth-century America: the modern, university-based business school.

When, in 1881, the University of Pennsylvania established the first university-based school of business in America with a gift from the industrialist Joseph Wharton, it did not qualify as the first "business school" per se. Throughout the nineteenth century, as business organizations became larger and more complex, increasing numbers of accountants, clerical workers, and production managers were required to keep factories running. To train this new group, private, for-profit business colleges began to spring up in the 1820s in large commercial centers such as Boston and New York. After 1850, almost every small city had at least one such school, and by 1893 more than five hundred existed in different parts of the country.

Like the industrial firms that their graduates were staffing, the commercial business schools applied concepts of scale and standardization to organizing their endeavors. For instance, the Bryant & Stratton Business College (founded in 1854 and still in existence today) maintained fifty branches spread across major industrial cities. The Eastman Schools, whose founding by the father of George Eastman, the entrepreneur behind Kodak cameras, reflected a direct link to business, operated in three upstate New York cities and in St. Louis, Missouri. E. G. Folsom's Commercial College had seven branches in the largest midwestern cities. The Packard Business College in New York claimed in 1898 "the hearts of twenty thousand men and women who during the past forty years, have been of its household."[1] Many Packard graduates would assume positions as important businessmen in the banking and finance circles of New York City. Overall, commercial business schools became a critical link between individuals and organizations in the labor market. Table 3.1 shows that by 1895 commercial schools enrolled more than 96,000 students—indeed, by then such institutions had produced several industrial titans, including John D. Rockefeller and B. F. Goodrich.

The growth and success of these schools in the latter part of the nineteenth century affirms the extent to which managers had become integral to modern organizations. Yet the substance of the training the commercial schools offered was as significant as the number of individuals they trained.

Table 3.1

Enrollments in Business Curricula in High Schools, Commercial Schools, and Colleges/Universities, 1895–1924

	Public High Schools	Private High Schools and Academies	Private Business and Commercial Schools	Colleges and Universities	Total
1895	25,539	8,819	96,135	97	130,590
1897	33,075	11,574	77,746	—	—
1899	38,134	10,609	70,186	—	—
1900	68,890	15,649	91,549	—	—
1903	73,207	15,455	137,979	1,100	233,741
1904	85,313	13,479	138,363	1,537	238,692
1905	90,309	13,394	146,086	1,710	251,499
1906	95,000	13,868	130,085	1,193	240,146
1907	—	—	137,364	—	—
1910	81,249	10,191	134,778	4,321	230,539
1911	110,925	11,956	155,244	4,194	282,319
1912	128,977	14,173	137,790	—	—
1913	154,042	15,940	160,557	—	—
1914	161,250	17,457	168,063	—	—
1915	208,605	17,706	183,268	9,323	418,902
1916	243,185	17,228	192,388	11,653	464,454
1918	278,275	23,801	289,579	17,011	608,666
1920	—	—	336,032	36,855	—
1924	430,975	18,210	188,363	47,552	685,100

Source: James H. S. Bossard and James F. Dewhurst, *University Education for Business: A Study of Existing Needs and Practices* (Philadelphia: University of Pennsylvania Press, 1931), 250.

For example, the introduction (and rapid adoption) of the Remington Model 1 typewriter and the expanding use of accounting clerks competent in double-entry bookkeeping—two key developments in the evolution of modern management[2]—can both be traced to the training offered in the commercial business colleges during the 1870s and 1880s. Meanwhile, the absolute and relative increase in the number of managers in society, and the refined skills required to administer complex communications and develop and manage financial control systems—not to mention the incipient effort to establish managerial authority and legitimate the occupation itself—all supported the notion that formal training in business was a critical step of preparation for positions of authority and responsibility in business organizations. As the president of a prominent New England trade group lamented in 1884:

> You put a man into the pulpit or at the bar or in the school room without any training, and let him undertake to preach or practice or teach, and he will prove a miserable failure. . . . Into business life, however, men rush with no certificate and nothing in the way of qualification for the calling on which a certificate could be based. Without any business talent or training or foresight they buy and sell, but get no gain. Only failure can be looked for in such cases.[3]

These circumstances, combined with the pervasive social conditions depicted in chapters 1 and 2, created not just an opportunity but even, in the minds of some, an urgent need to elevate business education from a status of vocational to professional training. This change would require grounding business instruction in science rather than mere experience, improvisation, and "rules of thumb," and would shift the venue of such instruction away from proprietary schools organized to turn a profit and into universities ostensibly dedicated to the pursuit of truth and social betterment. Indeed the creation and legitimation of the university-based business school would entail a deliberate effort to delegitimate the for-profit business colleges, which could claim neither a scientific approach to management, a professional orientation, nor the enlarged scope and purpose of the university. It is a mistake, however, to place too much emphasis (as Marxists and free-market economists have tended to do) on the monopolistic aspects of the university business schools' attempt to delegitimate the commercial colleges and establish the MBA's preeminence as a managerial credential.[4] To view the rise of modern business education as a simple result of monopoly power and coercion is to underestimate how deeply and rapidly the modern business school's authority penetrated the beliefs of organizations, and how firmly it seized, at the same time, the imagination of even some vocal critics of large business corporations. The legitimation of modern management education ultimately derived from belief rather than coercion, from cultural authority rather than power, and from the successful promulgation of cognitive and normative claims rather than the forces of either the market or the state.[5]

In the movement to found and legitimate university-based business education, the relationships between management and each of its three legitimating institutions are difficult to disentangle from one another, principally because science, the professions, and the new research university were themselves becoming so closely intertwined in the late nineteenth and early twentieth centuries (and have remained so ever since). The university, indeed, forms much of the backdrop for the stories of management in relation to science and management in relation to the professions. In rendering separate accounts of how the advocates for management attempted to appropriate the logics of science, the professions, and the university, respectively, I first show how the notion of a science of management was constructed and drawn upon to legitimate both management as a profession and the introduction of business education into the university setting. Second, I demonstrate how the traditional professions as they were being reconstructed in the late nineteenth century provided a rhetoric of social duty that framed business education as possessing a higher aim than mere "moneymaking," thus rendering it more palatable to key academics and facilitating the founding of the first university business schools. Finally, in discussing management in relation to the institution of the university per se, I outline how the advocates of business education attempted to align this new institution with two core functions of the university—the traditional one of teaching the liberal arts and the modern one of providing public service—in an effort to bolster and solidify the arguments made by analogy with science and the professions.

▙ Management as a Science

University-based business schools did not invent the science of management, if "science" it is or ever was. As I noted in chapter 1, organizational theory, of which scientific management represented the first example, arose within the profession of engineering; scientific management was adopted by business schools only after Frederick W. Taylor had developed the theory from his own studies of the factory production process and, in his consultant's role, introduced it to industry. Moreover, as we shall see, it remains a question whether university business schools, even today, have succeeded in creating a coherent, systematic, clearly bounded body of knowledge—much less one that is firmly connected with management practice—out of the individual disciplines (principally economics, applied mathematics, psychology, and sociology) in which business school curricula and research are currently grounded. Yet to understand how the institutional entrepreneurs behind the creation of the university-based business school appropriated science as a means of legitimating management, and academic training in management, it is less important to assess the validity of their claims that management had been, or could be, made into a science than to appreciate the analogies that they made between science and management, and the way they employed those analogies in defense of conclusions about managerial professionalism and business education.

The broad rationale for the strategy of presenting management as actually or potentially a science—namely, the advantage of associating management with the moral authority vested in science and the perceived objectivity of the scientific method—was presented in chapter 2. Yet one particular feature of science as it was understood in the late nineteenth century made it uniquely attractive for application in business: its capacity for resolving social problems on a rational, disinterested basis. As I noted in chapter 1, the conflict between management and labor as it was being played out in the last decades of the nineteenth century posed a major obstacle—perhaps *the* major obstacle in the eyes of the general public—to the legitimation of managerial authority. This conflict was thus one of the principal problems that the would-be science of management sought to address. With labor strife often on the cusp of violence, advocates for management attempted to remove divisive issues of rights and authority from the political domain and isolate them within the sphere of science. This is the dynamic that Yehouda Shenhav has shown to have operated in the rise of organizational theory in late nineteenth- and early twentieth-century America, as managers co-opted the rhetoric of mechanical engineers to portray themselves as coordinators rather than masters of labor—thereby grounding managerial authority in science and engineering rather than in economic, social, or political power, and dissociating management from any taint of interests in the violent struggle between capital and labor.[6]

This point must be emphasized because it is often assumed that the two broad theories that eventually (if only for a relatively short time) formed the foundation of the business school curriculum—Frederick W. Taylor's scientific management and, in the 1920s, Hugo Münsterberg's industrial psychology for managing workers—were embraced for the purpose of increasing industrial efficiency. To advocates for management, efficiency was as insufficient a rationale for the implementation of new, "scientific" theories of management as it was for the creation of the large corporation itself. The tensions in the late nineteenth and early twentieth centuries between managers and owners, on the one hand, and managers and workers, on the other, were more about power, status, and dividing up the economic spoils of corporate enterprise than they were about finding the most efficient way of producing those spoils in the first place. Victory and control were the focal objectives, not increased productivity. As Mauro Guillén has shown, the quest for efficiency was not used to justify managerial control until the advent of Taylorism in the years just before World War I. By then, however, Taylor and his supporters were framing the argument for greater efficiency and productivity in terms of their value in ameliorating labor strife and reducing the violence of strikes and the power of unions. Resolving the power struggle was the end to which efficiency was the means, not the other way around. Taylor and company justified their approach by posing these questions: What if the conflict over economic rents for owners, managers, and workers could be mitigated through an increase in the total size of the pie from which everybody took their share? Would this not make more sense than a continuing quarrel over how smaller profits would be shared among the three interested parties? Was there some way to persuade both management and labor of the benefits of cooperation as opposed to coercion?[7]

Yet linking managerial authority with science ultimately provided more than just a method for improving labor relations. As significant as that immediate objective was, connecting management with science also provided an important source of social and cultural control.[8] In the hands of its strongest advocates, the science of management gave a particular meaning to the role of the manager, thereby increasing managers' awareness of themselves as constituting a distinct occupational group, separate from labor and capital. The role of managers would be to develop "a science to replace the old rule-of-thumb knowledge of the workmen." They would systematize the workers' "traditional knowledge," by "recording it, tabulating it, and . . . finally [reducing] it to laws, rules, and even to mathematical formulae."[9] By positioning business problems in a "scientific" framework that, for instance, rationalized the division of physical from mental work in industrial labor, managerial science justified a strict hierarchy and bestowed on the manager the halo of the disinterested expert. For members of one group to dominate those of another with a clear conscience, members of the dominant group must understand themselves as superior in some capacity to members of the dominated group.[10] In this case, managers were invited to see themselves as the "brains" of the organization, in contrast to workers, who were the "brawn." The social status associated with claims to special expertise and positions of planning or coordinating the labor of others obviously influenced the ready acceptance by managers of this logic.

Taylor's own writings on scientific management, which focused on the process of production and the organization of work on the factory floor, strikingly illustrate how managerial science was employed to rationalize and justify management's authority. Taylor argued that under scientific management the harsh exercise of arbitrary power would be eliminated:

> They [management and labor] come to see when they stop pulling against one another, and instead both turn and push shoulder to shoulder in the same direction, the size of the surplus created by their joint efforts is truly astounding. . . . It is along this line of complete change in the mental attitude of both sides; of the substitution of peace for war; the substitution of hearty brotherly cooperation for contention and strife; of replacing suspicious watchfulness with mutual confidence; of becoming friends instead of enemies; it is along this line, I say, that scientific management must be developed. . . . So I think that scientific management can be justly and truthfully characterized as management in which harmony is the rule instead of discord.[11]

For Taylor, a descendent of a prominent Quaker family, scientific management consisted of more than just a series of techniques; it was also meant to serve as a means of catalyzing a "revolution" in the psychology of managers and workers. The "complete change in the mental attitude" of both workers and management that Taylor prophesied would prompt both sides to "realize that it is utterly impossible for either one to be successful without the intimate, brotherly cooperation of the other."[12] Taylor's utopian vision—an especially remarkable instance of faith in "science" as a path to moral uplift—was echoed by one of his most devoted disciples, the Progressive reformer Morris L. Cooke, who proclaimed, "[W]e shall never fully realize either the visions of Christianity or the dreams of democracy until the principles of scientific management have permeated every nook and cranny of the working world."[13]

Yet, for all these blandishments directed at both managers and workers, scientific management provided justification for managerial authority by rooting it in depersonalized, rational rules of conduct:

> Under scientific management arbitrary power, arbitrary dictation, ceases and every single subject, large and small, becomes the question for scientific investigation, for reduction to law. . . . The man at the head of the business under scientific management is governed by

rules and laws which have been developed through hundreds of experiments just as much as the workman is, and the standards which have been developed are equitable. . . . Those questions which are under other systems subject to arbitrary judgment and are therefore open to disagreement have under scientific management been the subject of the most minute and careful study in which both the workman and the management have taken part, and they have been settled to the satisfaction of both sides.[14]

Taylor's sincerity in the conviction that scientific management would establish managerial authority on a basis that workers themselves would accept as legitimate did not, of course, prevent managers from ignoring such high-minded aspirations and drawing upon scientific management as a useful means of subordinating workers.[15] Despite Taylor's lofty goals, scientific management brought about no "mental revolution" in American management—much less in American labor—along the lines envisioned by its creator. What it did help achieve was the triumph of management over labor, skilled craft workers, and foremen for control of the shop floor, providing ideological and cultural justification for that control.[16]

Along with scientific management, industrial psychology was another emerging "discipline" that enlisted the aid of science to establish managerial authority. The intellectual father of the industrial psychology movement, which began in the years just before and after World War I, was the Harvard psychologist Hugo Münsterberg. Münsterberg belonged to a small vanguard of intellectuals who sought solutions to the social and psychological problems posed by the new industrial order. Like Taylor, Münsterberg exploited the link between science and management to promote a goal that was not exclusively or even primarily economic. He believed that modern psychology could be employed to change workers' attitudes and thus resolve the problem of labor unrest. In *Psychology and Industrial Efficiency*, published in 1913, Münsterberg wrote: "[S]till more important than the naked commercial profit on both sides is the cultural gain which will come to the economic life of the nation, as soon as everyone can be brought to the place where his best energies may be unfolded and his greater personal satisfaction secured. The economic experimental psychology offers no more inspiring idea than this adjustment of work and psyche by which mental dissatisfaction in our work, mental depression and discouragement, may be replaced in our social community by overflowing joy and perfect inner harmony."[17]

Scientific management and industrial psychology (the latter soon to be succeeded by the work of Elton Mayo and the rise of the "human relations" school of organizational theory, with its contrasting of managers as "thinkers" with workers as "feelers") both acquired widespread legitimacy in the early twentieth century and remain highly influential, in their subsequent incarnations, even today. Münsterberg's ideas, for example, spawned psychological testing in the U.S. armed services during World War I, and later legitimated the personnel director as a specialist responsible for selecting workers and promoting managers. As for Taylor, his slim volume entitled *The Principles of Scientific Management* was published in 1911 and helped create the first management consultancies, such as A. T. Kearney and McKinsey. By 1915, the book had been translated into eight languages, including Japanese. Meanwhile, hundreds of articles on scientific management appeared in newspapers and magazines, many discussing the relative merits of Taylorism and its benefits to managers and workers alike, while Taylor himself continued to promote his ideas via lectures and his own writings. Capitalists, managers, and Progressive reformers all embraced Taylor and his concepts. Walter Lippmann proclaimed in the influential Progressive magazine the *New Republic* that Taylorism dovetailed with the country's interests in economic progress and industrial peace and should therefore be viewed as a means for improving society. The future Supreme Court justice Louis Brandeis characterized Taylor as "a really great man—great not only in mental capacity, but in character, and . . . his accomplishments were due to this fortunate combination of ability and character."[18] By 1918, even Vladimir Lenin had embraced Taylorism, stating, "We must organize in Russia the study and teaching of the Taylor system and systematically try it out and adapt it to our own ends."[19]

Taylor's and Münsterberg's ideas also found a receptive audience in America's new business schools. In the years just before World War I, a consensus was emerging among the leaders of the nation's new collegiate and graduate schools of business (of which there were twenty-five by 1914, at both public and private universities) that existing "scientific" schools such as Yale's Sheffield School and Harvard's Lawrence Scientific School, were inadequate for the task of training and socializing a new class of managers.[20] While such a finding may seem a self-interested inevitability, it reflected a departure from the expectation that engineers would constitute the new managerial class. Moreover, business school leaders believed that a distinct managerial science offered the best foundation on which to build management education and practice. In an essay outlining what should be taught in the University of

Michigan's newly established school of business, Dean Edward Jones asserted, "Whatever working hypothesis we may prefer with reference to scientific relationships, the great question upon which unanimity is indispensable is that business administration signifies a new frontier of science." Jones argued not only that management professors should use the model of the physical sciences for their research but also that managers should regard themselves as applied scientists: they should be trained, Jones said, to "observe the directness and care with which scientists conduct the collection and analysis of data, and they should [then] emulate the patience with which this process is carried forward year after year, before decisive results are expected." For those students intending to enter the "laboratory of industry" as business executives, the chief pedagogical goal was to be their inculcation with scientific "habits of mind."[21]

Edwin F. Gay, founding dean of the Harvard Business School (HBS), voiced a similar sentiment in a letter to a potential faculty recruit who had expressed skepticism about whether "business" could, in fact, be taught. In 1909, a year after the founding of HBS, Gay wrote:

> I am constantly being told by business men that we cannot teach
> "business." I heartily agree with them; we do not try to teach business in the sense in which business men ordinarily understand their
> routine methods, or in the sense in which you speak of teaching
> young men to be "moneymakers," or "to get the better of their competitors." We believe that there is science in business, and it is the
> task of studying and developing that science in which we are primarily interested.[22]

From the school's earliest days, Gay wrestled with the problem of formulating the "business principles" that would put the study of management on a scientific footing. At Harvard, as elsewhere, the most immediate impact of the scientific orientation was to place Taylor's burgeoning scientific management movement at the center of the curriculum. Gay made scientific management a central component of the new school's first-year curriculum, describing the discipline as "the most important advance in industry since the introduction of the factory system and power machinery."[23] Under the leadership of Harlow Person—a University of Michigan–trained engineer described by the *New York Times* as one of the nation's experts in "a field where economics, engineering, and managing merge"[24]—the Tuck School of Administration and Finance at Dartmouth had, by 1913, also adopted scientific management as the core of its curriculum.[25] Both Gay and Person tried to recruit Taylor—who was initially opposed to the idea of teaching management in business schools rather than engineering schools—to their faculties. Taylor eventually overcame his reservations and lectured annually at HBS between 1908 and 1914. While there, he and several colleagues worked with the school to establish a relationship with the city of Cambridge's Rindge Manual Training School, an institution intended to become a "laboratory in which scientific management is gradually to be introduced by the advanced [that is, second-year] students in our Business School."[26]

The approach to managerial science that Gay eventually adopted was based on the theory that business consisted of two elementary functions, manufacturing and marketing (or, alternatively stated, production and distribution), and that all other business specialties merely supported one or the other of these. By discovering the fundamental principles of these two functions, Gay believed, HBS would help create a science of management. Yet while Gay's analysis offered a functional foundation for the nascent science of management, early promoters of managerial science in the new university-based business schools were interested in accomplishing more than simply increasing the efficiency of business processes. Like Taylor, many viewed efficiency as a means to an end rather than an end in itself.

In a 1900 letter to Harvard president Charles W. Eliot, for instance, Robert Valentine (a Harvard alumnus and self-identified practitioner of a new occupation he called "industrial counselor") urged upon Eliot the necessity for Harvard to create a new school to help its graduates more effectively manage organizations for the "sake of the soundness of industrial conditions as a whole."[27] Harvard law professor (and later Supreme Court justice) Felix Frankfurter argued in a letter to Eliot six years later that "sooner or later our universities must follow the path that Valentine blazed . . . by training men for the profession of guiding the human problems raised by modern business . . . [which] must be sought for with the same relentlessly scientific spirit as the processes of production are studied."[28] Just as the case for science as a vehicle for ordering society and achieving social progress was sometimes conflated with an argument for science as an intrinsically moral activity, the language used by the academic entrepreneurs promoting managerial science sometimes implied that it, too, was essentially a moral and ethical vehicle. For example, Willard E. Hotchkiss, the founding dean of Northwestern University's School of Commerce (established in 1908) and later the first dean of Stanford Business School, asserted that the application of the scientific method to management would not only generate effective business practices but also "harmonize efficiency with considerations of public welfare."[29] Specifically, it would align the interests of capital and labor as well as those of management and society, and thus "go far toward removing the conflict between business and ethics."[30]

With the first university-based business schools focusing their efforts to formulate a science of management largely on the new disciplines of scientific management and industrial psychology, a question naturally arises as to the role of the discipline of economics in early business school curricula. Economics, not surprisingly, was one of the existing academic disciplines on which the first business school course offerings drew most heavily. Yet while it would be a required subject in most business school curricula, and was viewed by some as an essential discipline for a truly professional school of business, economics (particularly as practiced by its classical, laissez-faire school) was considered by others to be inadequate preparation for a successful business career owing to its highly abstract and theoretical nature. The eventual decision—actually reached quite early in the history of university-based business schools—to remove the study of business from economics departments stemmed from the argument that economics had no interest in one of management's most pressing concerns, namely, the internal organization of the firm. This assertion, which was true at the time, allowed advocates of university business education to point to this lack of specialized, practical knowledge within the discipline as justification for establishing management as a "science" that could stand on its own.[31]

Creating a managerial science that was both theoretically sound and susceptible to practical application, and then employing this new science to legitimate the authority of managers, was a very difficult task for the early champions of management both inside and outside the academy. It is logical to assume that innovative techniques would be controlled by their first users, for the novelty of a body of knowledge should facilitate the construction of protective boundaries around an occupation.[32] For managers, however, it was particularly challenging to define and defend their occupational jurisdiction through asserting control over new knowledge and techniques. Unlike the bodies of knowledge underlying the professions of medicine and law, for example, the knowledge base of managers evolved independently from institutions of higher learning, and in disparate, disconnected pockets at that. Practicing managers were unable to codify and transmit their knowledge beyond the boundaries of particular firms (although a consultant like Taylor could do so), and those educational establishments that claimed to be preparing managers for practice by imparting a body of codified knowledge could not point to formal affiliations with practicing managers as a way of ratifying their claim.

Until managerial knowledge and new managers were being produced within the same institution, it would be difficult to assert a foundation of common scientific knowledge for managerial authority. The vehicle that would enable management to unify production of managerial knowledge with the production of managers turned out to be the university-based business school, operating in the capacity of a *professional* school that was to be comparable in every way to schools for such established professions as medicine and law. Indeed, the founders of the modern business school had an explicit goal of creating precisely this kind of institution so as to establish management itself as not just a recognized occupation with a scientific knowledge base but, rather, as a genuine profession.

⬛ Management and the Professions

The effort to create a science of management, or at least to present management as an activity capable of being rationalized in this way, presupposed, among other things, that management entailed the application of expert knowledge and judgment to the performance of complex tasks. Since claims to scientific expertise carry with them an assertion of autonomy for those who possess and exercise such expertise (only chemists are qualified to evaluate the work of other chemists, physicists to judge the work of other physicists, and so forth), the case for management as a science also advanced an implicit claim for managerial autonomy and authority vis-à-vis potential competitors such as workers and owners. Moreover, the case for management as a science implicitly attributed a certain seriousness and even moral elevation to the work of managers. Just as scientists were engaged in a search for truth that was inherently noble and conferred concrete benefits on society as well, scientifically trained and oriented managers would also prove to be society's benefactors. Just as natural science was enabling man to gain previously unimaginable control over the physical world and thus to dramatically improve the material conditions of human existence, and social science was creating knowledge for a more balanced ordering of psychic and social life, so management in turn would harness the tremendous forces of technology, markets, and corporations to advance both material prosperity and social harmony.

Expertise, autonomy, and an ethos of service to society were viewed as distinctive features of the select number of occupations that qualified as professions.[33] Thus one of the ultimate implications of the claim that management was, or could become, a science was that management also was, or could become, a profession. At a 1901 meeting of the New England Cotton Manufacturers Association, Henry Smith Pritchett, president of MIT and a close confidant of Harvard's Charles W. Eliot, made this very point in arguing that the increasing centrality of business in American society required businessmen to take a different view of their work from that which they had held in the past. As Pritchett said, "[T]he conditions of modern life are such, the facilities of communication are so great and play such a part in success, the relations of men are so complex and upon so large a scale, that the time is near when those who are to direct great organizations, who are to control and develop manufactures between nations—in a word, the Captains of Commerce—must look upon their calling as a profession, not a business; and for this profession there is a training to be had in the schools which will not only save time for the individual, but which will develop a broader, a more efficient and a higher type of man; a training which shall bring not only a keener vision but also a wider outlook and a better perspective."[34] It is worth noting that many in Pritchett's audience of New England cotton magnates had close ties to Harvard, where President Eliot, professor and future university president Abbott Lawrence Lowell (a scion of the New England textile aristocracy), and others were beginning to contemplate offering professional education in business. Yet Pritchett, Eliot, and Lowell were not the first educators to entertain such an idea. In 1890, the American Bankers Association sent Edmund James, then the director of the University of Pennsylvania's Wharton School, to Europe to study how America's industrial competitors were deploying higher education to train their managers. James published his findings in a well-regarded book, *The Education of Business Men in Europe*, in which he detailed the history and curricula of commercial schools in the leading industrialized countries of Austria, Germany, France, Belgium, Italy, and England. James discerned the same skepticism about business education in European universities that still prevailed in the late nineteenth-century American university. He then devoted several years to lecturing all over America, telling his listeners that business education could be built on a foundation of science, and that business was as worthy of scientific study as was either law or medicine. James's views on this issue converged with a contemporary line of thought maintaining that, despite the advances brought about by the passage of the Morrill Act and the spread of public university education, American higher education remained insufficiently attentive to practical subjects. An 1885 U.S. Senate report, for instance, argued that American higher education needed to place more emphasis on preparing students for careers in business. One businessman testified:

> Our college system certainly does not train our youth in habits of
> useful industry. Its purpose is not to increase the effectiveness of
> labor, to make two blades of grass grow where only one grew before;
> it does not show the pupil how, by acquiring a manual art, he can
> double or treble the value of his labor. It does not teach a science in
> a practical form. On the contrary, college education is conducted
> with a view to imparting a knowledge of dead languages and the
> higher mathematics to the pupils, which is all well enough for the
> wealthy and leisure classes, but is not suited for bread-winners.[35]

Higher education for "bread-winners," of course, did not necessarily mean the same thing that MIT's Pritchett identified as "training which shall bring not only a keener vision but also a wider outlook and a better perspective." Yet for the vanguard of managers and academics who aimed at making management a pillar of the new social order by turning it into not only a science but a profession, the most critical component of the professionalization process was the establishment of business education on an equal footing with university-based, professional education in other occupations. In the justifications for creating university-based business schools, even the effort to portray management as a scientific discipline that could be taught in a curriculum comparable to those of existing schools of medicine and law would prove secondary to the cause of professionalizing management.

Part of the interest in professionalizing management via the university can be explained by the simple power of analogy: training for the recognized professions of law and medicine had been subsumed by the university; therefore training for management should be undertaken within the university as well. Yet another reason for the focus on establishing professional schools of management within the university arose out of an essential difference between the employment setting for managers and that of the traditional professions (as the latter were constituted at the time). Professions, or aspiring professions, whose emergence was tied to the rise of modern business—engineering, management, accounting, financial analysis, and the like—were practiced within bureaucratic or hierarchical organizations. Independent practice (that is, fee for service) as a manifestation of professional autonomy was vital to the professionalization projects of occupations that were capable of achieving it. Yet market control of the kind described by Andrew Abbott and Eliot Freidson—that is, autonomous monopoly in the provision of expert services, as in law or medicine—lay beyond the reach of managers. Few barriers stood in the way of anyone (or, at least, any white male) with a high school education or less who sought to become a manager. With market organization and control largely unattainable, this goal was subordinated to the search for, and assertion of, social status for the budding managerial profession. In the late nineteenth century, the emergence of a status order based on occupation, rather than inheritance, was beginning to create social distinctions among occupations. Education was a key route to higher status. Burton J. Bledstein has found that the identity of the new middle class derived, in part, from its attempt to achieve higher occupational status through formal education.[36] Adopting and adapting the professionalization strategies used by medicine and law, nascent occupations in structurally dissimilar contexts, including not only management but also journalism, nursing, and social work, sought professional status and prestige by connecting their occupations to the university.

Through university-based business schools, managers established an outpost in academia, thereby lending legitimacy to their assertion that a scientific and cognitive foundation existed for effective management—a foundation that likewise supported their claims to professional status. This achievement was soon reinforced by the increasing percentage of college-educated executives, a trend illustrated in table 3.2. At the dawn of the twentieth century, only a minority of the elite managerial class had passed through the university. Such managers constituted, however, a significant and cohesive minority. These individuals formed the nucleus of a nascent elite that

Table 3.2

Percent College Educated among Founders, CEOs, and Founder Successors of Large Public Corporations, 1900–1939

1900–09	1910–19	1920–29	1930–39
19	38	53	52

Source: Adapted from Anthony J. Mayo, Nitin Nohria, and Laura G. Singleton, *Paths to Power: How Insiders and Outsiders Shaped American Business Leadership* (Boston: Harvard Business School Press, 2006).

helped to legitimize the business school degree from the perspective of business itself. As wealthy businessmen saw the university playing an important role supporting business, they began extending their support to business schools. Journalists also contributed significantly in spreading and amplifying views about the importance of university-based business education for the effective management of corporate enterprises.

The foregoing analysis does not totally explain, however, why university-based professional schools, rather than the commercial schools or the existing scientific and technical institutes, became the focus of the professionalization project for management. The shift from private business education to the university-based business school was related not only to the cultural prestige of science, ideas about formal pedagogy and the development of technical competence, and the striving for status through higher education. The managerial vanguard engaged in the establishment of university-based business education was also vitally concerned with creating an effective acculturation and socialization process through which norms of business conduct could be transmitted from one generation to the next. Moreover, these institutional entrepreneurs considered business schools and universities to be part of a larger matrix of social institutions undergoing significant transformation—a development that required important adaptations on the part of business.

Historically, the organization of training for business education had reflected and reinforced the typical structure of ownership and control in business practice. Control in early business enterprises rested with the founder/entrepreneur to whom all others, including family members working in the business, would defer. The founder's authority derived from an agrarian tradition that preceded written history and rested on a patriarchal hierarchy.[37] In such traditional enterprises, whatever education was provided to implement the transfer of authority to a new generation remained rooted in the system of inheritance. Kinship was an instrument of socialization (since those in a family are presumed to be acquainted with norms of family conduct, both inside and outside of business) as well as a mechanism for the conveyance of status. The young son shaped under his father's leadership in the family business had a unique claim to legitimacy as the next leader of the enterprise.

Outside the family, the next most significant institution in vocational training for business was apprenticeship. While apprenticeship was rooted in a contractual form of exchange, it shared many elements with the broader culture of patriarchal education. As with other dependent relationships, apprentices and masters had reciprocal responsibilities. In many ways, the moral and personal character of the relationship between master and apprentice was analogous to that between father and son; for instance, in many of the New England states a master was required by law to raise an apprentice as a good Christian.[38] Yet as business enterprises began to grow larger, the apprenticeship tradition declined. It was during this transition that the commercial business colleges flourished and the first university-based business schools were founded.

Indeed the early history of university business schools shows how the idea of professionalism rapidly came to encompass the intellectual, social, and cultural aspirations of management. We can witness this process unfolding by focusing on three of the most important early business schools—the University of Pennsylvania's Wharton School, Dartmouth's Tuck School of Administration and Finance, and Harvard's Graduate School of Business Administration—to observe how each faced the difficult problem of overcoming barriers to the legitimacy of management as a profession and of management education as professional education. In surmounting these obstacles, the forerunner schools significantly reshaped the larger socioeconomic context of business and, ultimately, the nature of the university itself.

The Wharton School: Professionalism for the "Man of Affairs"

By the late 1800s, the changes in the American university outlined in the preceding chapter had increased the ideological, human, and financial resources available to aspiring elites who sought to create a profession of management. A cadre of influential actors dominated by alumni, college faculty and administrators, and enlightened practitioners had embraced the tripartite mission of teaching, research, and service to society that defined the new research university. As universities forged new alliances with the traditional professions of medicine and law, there emerged a consortium of supporters for the idea of placing business on the same footing. Even in the context of the increasing utilitarianism of the late nineteenth-century university, the imprimatur of this historic institution with its lingering mystique of sacred origins presented a dramatic statement in support of the budding managerial profession.

The first university business schools represented, among other things, an attempt to shift the traditional system of apprenticeship, with its interest in character formation as well as in the transmission of knowledge and skills, into an organizational context more amenable to the modern age. A concern with providing vocational training specifically for the sons of the local economic elite (who might, a few decades earlier, have simply clerked under their fathers to gain required skills) prompted the nineteenth-century industrialist Joseph Wharton to donate $100,000 in 1881 to the University of Pennsylvania to help establish the Wharton School—the nation's first successful collegiate school of business.[39] Wharton, a devout Pennsylvania Quaker with a robust sense of social and ethical responsibility, perceived a need for university education for wellborn youth "in the knowledge and in the arts of modern Finance and Economy." The nation's private commercial schools were, in his view, inadequate to this end. Wharton also believed that, for the purpose of developing in young men the specialized knowledge, intellectual breadth, and solid personal character that modern enterprise required of its leaders, the university-based scientific and technical schools of the day (such as Harvard's Lawrence Scientific School and Yale's Sheffield Scientific School, both founded in midcentury as separate schools for the study of the natural sciences) lacked a critical dimension. This is how Wharton described his vision for what would become the Wharton School:

> The general conviction that college education did little toward fitting
> for the actual duties of life any but those who purposed to become
> lawyers, doctors, or clergymen, brought about the creation of many
> excellent technical and scientific schools, whose work is enriching
> the country with a host of cultivated minds prepared to overcome all
> sorts of difficulties in the world of matter.
>
> Those schools, while not replacing the outgrown and obsolescent
> system of apprenticeship, accomplish a work quite beyond anything
> that system was capable of. Instead of teaching and perpetuating the
> narrow, various, and empirical routines of certain shops, they base
> their instruction upon the broad principles deduced from all human
> knowledge, and ground in science, as well as in art, pupils who are
> thereby fitted both to practice what they have learned and to become
> themselves teachers and discoverers. . . .
>
> There is, furthermore, in this country, an increasing number of
> young men possessing, by inheritance, wealth, keenness of intellect,
> and latent power of command or organization, to whom the channels of commercial education, such as it is, are, by the very felicity of
> their circumstances, partly closed, for when they leave college at the
> age of 20 to 25 years they are already too old to be desirable beginners in a counting house, or to descend readily to its drudgery.

No country can afford to have this inherited wealth and capacity wasted for want of that fundamental knowledge which would enable the possessors to employ them with advantage to themselves and to the community, yet how numerous are the instances of speedy ruin to great estates, and indolent waste of great powers for good, simply for want of such knowledge and of the tastes and self-reliance which it brings. Nor can any country long afford to have its laws made and its government administered by men who lack such training as would suffice to rid the minds of fallacies and qualify them for the solution of the social problems incident to our civilization. Evidently a great boon would be bestowed upon the nation if its young men of inherited intellect, means, and refinement could be more generally led so to manage their property as, while husbanding it to benefit the community, or could be drawn into careers of unselfish legislation and administration.[40]

This statement is notable in several respects. For one thing, Wharton's focus on young men of inherited wealth who were too old and (as he implies) too proud to begin in the "counting house," but who needed a broader education than the scientific and technical schools could offer, presents a distinction not only between social classes but also between vocational training for the routine functions of business, on the one hand, and preparation for work in the upper echelons of business organizations, on the other. While Wharton did not employ the words *profession* or *professional* here, his language clearly implies a belief that those, like himself, who toiled in the "world of matter" (Wharton had made his fortune in the steel and nickel businesses) deserved to be considered the moral equivalent of "lawyers, doctors, or clergymen" in being engaged not in the rarefied pastimes of the idle rich but in the "actual duties of life."[41] To Wharton, it seemed self-evident that those of "inherited wealth and capacity" must dedicate themselves to the needs of the community and to attacking the "social problems incident to our civilization"—if they did not discharge this responsibility via careers in the established professions, then they must do so via business or "careers of unselfish legislation and administration." He clearly desired to elevate not only the competence but also the social consciousness and moral character of those who chose to devote themselves to what the nineteenth-century gentleman called "affairs."[42]

As Steven A. Sass documents in his history of the Wharton School, Joseph Wharton was closely engaged in both civic and business affairs, and succeeded in imprinting the institution that would bear his name with an orientation toward the public good. For example, along with some of the businessmen who served on the University of Pennsylvania's board of trustees, Wharton participated in the activities of the American Social Science Association (founded in 1865), an organization that "brought the genteel community of business and professional men together for 'scientific' discussions of social problems and to formulate programs of reform."[43] When he came to conceive of a business education that would give upper-class young men the "fundamental knowledge" enabling them to employ their resources and talents "with advantage to themselves and to the community," Wharton wanted a program grounded in the liberal arts and, even more important, the social sciences. Penn had adopted the elective system as of the 1866–1867 academic year, and this, coupled with the social science courses being taught there by the polymathic Robert Ellis Thompson, "inspired Wharton," in Sass's words, "to envision a new relationship between business and higher education and the creation of a new class of university-educated businessmen."

> These men would be an amalgam of the professional and the man of
> affairs, similar to the civil service ideal that captivated so many of
> Wharton's contemporaries. . . . Wharton's college-educated business-
> man and the new civil servant would hold critical positions of power
> in society and could rely on the liberal arts education that they
> would receive at Penn as a source of prestige, perspective, and
> personal character. Both would also use the "social science" and
> vocational training offered in the new Wharton course to manage
> practical problems.[44]

Sociologists who have studied the founding of new organizations note that the social identity of the founder matters a great deal, especially when the proposed organization is of a new type that is not yet legitimate or well understood.[45] In this instance, Wharton's framing of the purpose of his new school, along with his personal reputation for integrity, enabled him to gain the support he required for establishing the Wharton School, even in the absence of evidence of a compelling need for it to exist.

Under the leadership of Edmund James, the first director of the Wharton School (and the founder of the American Academy of Political and Social Science), the Wharton School would, in the 1880s and 1890s, succeed in becoming a school of political and social science dedicated to professionalizing

a number of occupations in the area of "practical affairs" (and, not incidentally, seeking equal status with the university's schools of medicine and
law).[46] Although the Wharton School's particularly intensive focus on the social sciences would, for the most part, not be imitated by other institutions
until the post–World War II era, the goals that the school articulated for
the education of managers would become the paradigm for other business
schools founded over the next forty years.[47] Thus by the time the dean of
New York University's new School of Commerce, Accounts and Finance (established in 1890) announced to graduates in 1914 that "one of the greatest
needs of this country is for wise business men to solve fundamental economic and social questions,"[48] he was echoing a consensus among leaders of
the fledgling field of business education about the essential purpose of their
enterprise.

The Tuck School: Business Education and the Quest for Professional Status

Even while voicing these high aims, it must be emphasized, the originators of
the modern business school remained aware of the realities of business life
and of the status anxieties that attracted many aspiring managers to the idea
of a university education in business. A focus on raising the status of management to equal that of existing professions—rather than simply transforming management itself into a profession—is evident in the early history
of the Tuck School of Administration and Finance at Dartmouth College (established in 1900), the first business school to offer instruction at the graduate level. While generally accepting the distinction between business and
"affairs," on the one hand, and the professions on the other, the founders of
Dartmouth's Tuck School intended to put business education on a par with
preparation for the traditional professions. As the Dartmouth trustees' resolution inaugurating the school stated:

> This school is established in the interest of college graduates who de-
> sire to engage in affairs rather than enter the professions. It is the aim
> of the school to prepare men in those fundamental principles which
> determine the conduct of affairs. . . . The attempt will be made to
> follow the increasing number of college graduates who have in view
> administrative or financial careers, with a preparation equivalent in
> its purpose to that obtained in the professional or technical schools.

The training of the school is not designed to take the place of an apprenticeship in any given business, but it is believed the same amount of academic training is called for, under the enlarging demands of business, as for the professions or for the productive industries.[49]

Shortly thereafter, the school's bulletin for the 1900–1901 academic year elaborated on this theme: "The courses of this school are designed to prepare men for those more modern forms of business which have become so exacting as to require the same quality of academic training as the older professions." A year later, the bulletin proclaimed: "It has become evident today that business demands an increase in the number of well-trained and broad-minded men engaged in its service. The intense rivalry which characterizes industrial affairs requires the presence of men of keen insight, solid ability, and the strictest integrity." With such language, the school went on to implicitly claim that business was analogous to the traditional professions.[50]

The survival in university business schools of the apprenticeship model's emphasis on character formation as well as knowledge transmission was manifest in the Tuck School's stated goal of educating "the man first and the business man afterwards." This goal was explicit in the "3 + 2" structure of the Tuck program, one in which two years of graduate study in business, culminating in a master's degree, commenced only after a three-year undergraduate program in the liberal arts.[51] Moreover, the Tuck School's aim "to so broaden the minds and raise the ideals of its graduates that it will do something to elevate the business community above the plane of mere money-getting"[52] reflected the aim of likewise elevating business to a status resembling, or indeed equivalent to, that of the recognized professions. Higher aims, in other words, justified higher status. Dartmouth University president William Jewett Tucker affirmed this objective when, in 1906, he reported on the progress of the school to Edward Tuck, the financier who had endowed it in memory of his father (the lawyer, congressman, and cofounder of the Republican Party, Amos Tuck). "Men of information and intelligence," Tucker said, "who are concerned with education and are interested in it, and a great many businessmen are as I have before said to you, sending their sons to Dartmouth because Dartmouth has recognized and embodied the idea of giving to certain businesses professional rank, provided the requisite academic training can be given."[53]

This dual goal—of outfitting aspirants to business careers with both the "requisite academic training" and the "ideals" that would gain them recognition as the equals of traditional professionals—would become, over the next quarter of a century, the core of a full-fledged, highly focused effort to establish business education as genuine professional education, and management as a genuine profession, at the new graduate school of business to be founded at Harvard University.

The Harvard Graduate School of Business Administration: Business as a "High" Profession

As at Dartmouth, the creation of a school of business at Harvard was spurred by changes in undergraduate career paths and interests. As the proliferation of large corporations in the late nineteenth century created a need for individuals to perform the requisite administrative functions, business careers were becoming increasingly attractive to young men who might previously have entered one of the older, more traditional professions. In fact, given the explosion of undergraduate enrollments in American colleges and universities starting in the mid-1890s, openings in the older professions fell far short of the numbers of the nation's new college graduates. Moreover, the growing complexity of business made management an interesting and challenging career alternative for educated youth. The resulting change in career-choice patterns was showing itself even at Harvard. In 1897, President Eliot had reckoned that only 15 to 20 percent of Harvard College graduates went on to careers in business. Yet by 1908 Eliot was reporting that more than half of the previous year's Harvard graduating class had entered the field. With this shift, Harvard mirrored the reality of many other American colleges and universities at the time.[54]

The notion of instituting the academic study of business at Harvard had been floated as early as 1895, when alumnus George Bridge Leighton, a scion of a prominent New Hampshire family who had achieved success in the railroad business, wrote to President Eliot requesting that Harvard establish a course in railroading.[55] Eliot—who, by raising admissions and academic standards at Harvard Medical School and Harvard Law School, had begun to establish his reputation as one of the foremost educational reformers in America—had long been sympathetic to the idea that university education must be practical, but initially resisted the establishment of a school of business. Finally persuaded of the need for such a school, he explained the decision to found one thus:

> Our newest effort in Cambridge is to establish a graduate school of business administration, a graduate school requiring for admission a preliminary degree—that is, open only to persons that hold the A.B. or the S.B. What leads us to that new undertaking? In the first place, the prodigious development of many corporate businesses in our country; in the next place, the fact that more than half the recent graduates of Harvard College have gone immediately into business. . . . The explanation of that new phenomenon is that business in its upper walks has become a highly intellectual calling, requiring knowledge of languages, economics, industrial organization, and commercial law, and wide reading concerning the resources and habits of the different nations. In all these directions we propose to give professional graduate education.[56]

Unspoken, but audible in the background, lurked the wishes of not just those Harvard alumni interested in business education (and with the money to support it) but also of the Brahmin patriarchs such as those portrayed by Samuel Eliot Morison in his chronicle of his Boston youth prior to the turn of the century.[57] Brahmin fathers were perhaps chagrined by the career choices of increasing numbers of their sons but were certainly eager to have the respectability of a Harvard "professional graduate education" available to them upon graduation from the college. Indeed, of the fifty-eight men enrolled in Harvard Business School's inaugural class, forty-two held Harvard undergraduate degrees. Yet these external constituencies would have made little headway with Eliot or Abbott Lawrence Lowell (the government professor who succeeded Eliot as Harvard president the year after the so-called experiment of launching HBS began) had the university leaders not genuinely believed business education to be an enterprise worthy of a place in their institution. In a 1907 memo to F. W. Taussig, a Harvard economics professor who would become one of the first faculty members of the new business school, Lowell, for instance, had expressed reservations about the value of education in "general business." He did, however, endorse the idea of preparing students for work in particular functions and industries that might be rendered genuine professions (a notion that was explicitly being explored at the Wharton School around the same time), and evoked the paradigm of professional education in law and medicine:

Although . . . I do not believe much in the value of any special training for general business, I should like very much to see training for
particular branches of business which could be developed into professions. In that direction I should like to see Harvard a pioneer. . . .
Now, a school for any branch of business is likely to be a pretty large
one if successful. Therefore, if it is worthwhile to try the experiment
at all, it is worthwhile to try it under the best conditions for permanent success; and the more I think of it, the more I am convinced
that to do that we must have, not a department of the Graduate
School [of Arts and Sciences] or the College, but a separate professional school, with a separate faculty, whose object would be purely
to train men for their career, as the Law and Medical Schools do.

Such a school, Lowell went on to stress at some length, would be practical rather than academic in nature; his particular model for a professional
school of business at the university was Harvard Law School, which had, as
Lowell put it, "jealously kept itself free from contact with academic students
and professors."[58] The first faculty recruits at the Harvard Graduate School
of Business Administration would include several practitioners, notably
George O. May (a partner at Price Waterhouse), Thomas W. Lamont (a vice
president of Bankers Trust Company), and William J. Cunningham (a statistician for the Boston & Albany Railroad who lacked a college degree).

Although Lowell's concept of turning managerial occupations into professions was somewhat revolutionary and controversial at Harvard in 1907,
at the national level it was not. The incipient efforts at both Wharton and
Harvard actually lagged behind those under way at, for example, the University of Oregon, whose 1900–1901 course catalog stated that occupations in
the management of "civil, and consular service, banking, transportation, domestic and foreign commerce . . . are rapidly approximating the character of
professions."[59] Indeed in other places where the genteel traditions of established professions were not so firmly rooted as they were in the elite eastern
universities, there was no doubt less resistance to claims such as that advanced by a 1913–1914 course catalog at the University of Nebraska that "business [education] is now, in its higher forms, as much a learned profession as
theology, law, medicine, engineering, agriculture, and other difficult and
complicated arts, and [the profession of business] demands of those who
would rise from the ranks a thorough, scientific, and practical training."[60]
Whether at state universities in the Midwest and West or at the Ivy League

schools, however, language equating business with the professions asserted a more than merely instrumental function for professional management. In referring to business as a "calling," for example, Charles W. Eliot had chosen a word that, for his Puritan predecessors, resonated with explicitly sacred meaning; in using the term *profession*, moreover, such early advocates of professional business education invoked a secularized notion of a calling in which (as was true for the Quaker Joseph Wharton) the ethical dimension was just as important as the possession and exercise of specialized, expert knowledge.

In any event, the perceived significance of creating a business school at Harvard was well expressed by Eliot G. Mears—a Harvard College graduate, Harvard MBA (class of 1912), administrator and instructor at Harvard Business School (1912–1916), and faculty member at Stanford University's Graduate School of Business (established in 1925)—who observed in 1923 that the founding of HBS symbolized that "our oldest university recognized its inability to provide an adequate preparation for business in the other departments of the university, and at the same time accorded business the standing of a profession alongside that of the ministry, law, and medicine."[61] But what did teaching business as a profession mean in practice? In a 1915 article, "Teaching the Profession of Business at Harvard," HBS's Benjamin Baker offered an approach to this task by drawing a contrast between "the profession of business and the trades of business" (and, incidentally, spelling out the rationale for the case method that HBS had borrowed from Harvard Law School and begun adapting to its own purposes):

> A profession may be defined as the practice of applying general laws or principles to particular sets of facts which have to be investigated and verified as facts, in such a way as to secure particular desired results. The work of the business executive or manager is a profession within the terms of this definition. The work of the bookkeeper, of the stenographer, and of many others engaged in "business" is essentially as much the work of a trade as is the work of a plumber. . . .
> The trades of business can be taught from text-books.
>
>   The profession of business cannot be taught from text-books. Actual business problems, as the business executive has to meet and deal with them, are as unlike any purely text-book presentation of them as the sick person calling at the young doctor's office is unlike the "symptoms" in the medical text-book. So, just as the young

doctor must learn to know disease by service in the hospitals, the student of the profession of business must learn to recognize and deal with business facts by study of actual business undertakings.[62]

As important as the assertion of "general laws and principles" suitable for application to "particular sets of facts" was to the establishment of a new profession, the first dean of HBS, Edwin F. Gay, saw still another dimension as vital to professionalism in business—a dimension that reached beyond the expertise students acquired to the attitudes they held, determining how, in their capacity as managers, they would contribute to society. For instance, Gay surmised that placing the study of business on a firm intellectual footing would help develop "a habit of intellectual respect for business as a profession, with the social implications and heightened sense of responsibility which goes with that."[63] Such habits and attitudes appeared all the more necessary given the contemporary absence, in the case of management, of visible signs of professionalism such as associations, journals, formal requirements for entry, and ethical codes. In any event, Gay's defense of HBS's founding mission of professionalizing management—a mission that, as we shall see, drew critics both within the university and without—assumed a definition of professionalism that extended beyond knowledge and competence and a definition of business that transcended mere profit making.

Gay's successor as HBS dean in 1919, Wallace B. Donham, was equally concerned with producing business leaders who were professionals and appreciated the dignity and worth appertaining to such an occupation, not to mention the social responsibilities that accompanied it. As a lawyer and former banking executive, Donham had made a name for himself in the field of labor relations while serving as the court-appointed receiver for a Massachusetts streetcar company during World War I. Along with his strong sense of the business executive as a trustee of society's material resources, Donham exhibited a reflective, even philosophical side, influenced by his close association with the British mathematician and philosopher Alfred North Whitehead after Whitehead joined the Harvard faculty in 1924. Donham worried greatly about the effects of rapid scientific, technological, and material progress, fearing that modern industrial civilization might be outstripping society's capacity for moral self-governance, and that the professions that had traditionally provided social and moral leadership (law and the clergy) were no longer up to the task. For Donham, the professionalization of business management represented, therefore, a civilizing task of the utmost urgency.

Donham asserted his belief in the necessity of turning management into a profession, based on the model of the traditional learned professions, in an address delivered at Stanford University's business school in 1926 that was later published in *Harvard Business Review* as "The Social Significance of Business." At the outset of his speech, Donham declared: "The development, strengthening, and multiplication of socially minded business men is the central problem of business. . . . Moreover, it is one of the great problems of civilization." He continued:

> Discontent with the existing condition of things is perhaps more widespread than ever before in history. The nation is full of idealists, yet our civilization is essentially materialistic. On all sides, complicated social, political, and international questions press for solution, while the leaders who are competent to solve these problems are strangely missing. These conditions are transforming the world simultaneously for better and for worse. They compel a complete reappraisal of the significance of business in the scheme of things.[64]

"The business group," Donham went on to observe, "largely controls [the mechanisms placed in society's hands by the development of science and technology] and is therefore in a strategic position to solve [the resulting] problems. Our objective, therefore, should be the multiplication of men who will handle their current business problems in socially constructive ways." These "business problems," he said, included "the momentous labor problem"; the business cycle with its "devastating periods of alternate speculation and depression, with their corollary contribution to unemployment"; and "problems of corporate control" that pointed to a need to strengthen the "spirit of trusteeship on the part of corporate managers."[65] The responsibility of American businessmen to address such issues was all the greater, Donham held, because some of the older professions appeared incapable of securing the broader interests of society. The clergy, he argued, had seriously impaired their credibility by continuing to promote dogma that modern science had all but conclusively refuted. And to his "great personal regret as a member of the bar," Donham noted, the legal profession of his day had also failed to fulfill its highest professional obligations: "When the lawyer ceased to be advisory leader and sound counselor and, following the creation of large city business law firms, went definitely to work as the servant of the business man, mainly doing his will, he lost something and the community lost a great deal." In the process, the law had become "largely an auxiliary business rather than a learned profession."[66]

Donham's explicit objective, then, was to raise business to the status of professions such as the clergy or law so that it could fulfill the social functions that these once-revered institutions were no longer equipped to perform.[67] One of Donham's key allies at Harvard was a fervent and articulate advocate of the professionalization of management who was also one of the most influential businessmen of the 1920s, Owen D. Young. A lawyer who had served as chief counsel for the General Electric Corporation, Young was also the founding chairman of the Radio Corporation of America (RCA) and, in 1922, had become chairman of GE.[68] In 1927, he delivered the principal address at the dedication of Harvard Business School's new campus, which had been built by means of a $5 million gift from the banking magnate George F. Baker. "If I were to speak for men of business," Young declared near the opening of his speech, "it would be to express gratification that business is recognized at last as a profession, and being so recognized by Harvard, becomes a learned profession. If I were to speak for men of learning . . . it would be to express satisfaction that scholars are now to find their way to the market place, as they have heretofore to the pulpit, to the law courts, to the hospital, and to the forum."[69]

Harvard, Young remarked, had established its medical school in 1782, its law school in 1817, and its divinity school in 1819. He also pointed out that the "education of the ministry" had been a primary objective of Harvard's seventeenth-century founders, who (in their words, which Young quoted) "dreaded to leave an illiterate ministry to the Churches when our present ministers shall lie in the dust." Since 1840, Young continued, "the proportion of college graduates entering the ministry has been steadily declining, and during that period the percentage of those entering business or commercial pursuits has rapidly increased." In a sense, then, business was now thriving at the expense of religion. And yet, Young proclaimed, "I make no apology for our devotion to business." Far from being the morally suspect activity that some critics asserted it to be, business served, to Young's mind, as the new torchbearer of civilization. In language that recalled the eighteenth- and early nineteenth-century ideal of, in Richard Hofstadter's words, "the man of business as a civilized man and a civilizing agent,"[70] Young went on to recall the "dawn of trade" in the earliest exchange of goods between strangers who might otherwise have simply tried to seize each other's possessions:

A seller and a buyer have come out of the darkness of barbarism into the advancing light of civilization. The seller must now elect which article he will take. If it be not his own, a trade has been made, and the advance of human relations has begun. Trust has been substituted for suspicion; self-restraint has taken the place of uncontrolled acquisitiveness; a code of morals and of law will emerge; and last but not least, a sportsmanship, recognizing with a sense of honor the rules of the game, will come into being.[71]

After presenting his own analysis (which was similar to Wallace Donham's in many ways) of the economic and social conditions that now necessitated the professionalization of business, Young noted how important it was "that the ministers of our business, like the ministers of our churches, should appreciate their responsibility." For America's business leaders had become "in large measure the trustees of our opportunities." "We need today more than ever before," Young said, "men to administer this trust, who are not only highly skilled in the technique of business—men who have not only a broad outlook in history, politics, and economics—but men who have also that moral and religious training which tends to develop character." Harvard Business School, Young proclaimed, was to be "commended" for requiring its entering students to have a liberal education. "In no other profession," after all, "not excepting the ministry and the law, is the need for wide information, broad sympathies, and directed imagination so great. Who can say that this may not foreshadow the time when similar qualifications, evidenced by a certificate from this or like institutions, shall be required of men who desire to enter on a business career?"[72]

"I am sure we could serve Mr. Baker no better," Young concluded, "than to assure him that the Harvard Graduate School of Business Administration will do its utmost to guard against an illiterate ministry of business when our present ministers shall lie in the dust." He closed with a further flourish:

Today the profession of business at Harvard formally makes its bow to its older brothers and holds its head high with the faith of youth. . . . Today we light the fires in the temple which it is the trust of Harvard to maintain and from which may be renewed through generation after generation the high ideals, the sound principles, the glorious traditions, which make a profession. Today and here business formally assumes the obligations of a profession, which means responsible action as a group, devotion to its own ideals, the creation of its own codes, the capacity for its honors, and the responsibility for its own discipline, the awards of its own service.[73]

Characterizations of the would-be profession of business as a "ministry" sound jarring to contemporary ears but were not uncommon in the era in which Young was speaking. At a 1927 meeting of the American Association of Collegiate Schools of Business (AACSB), a professional organization formed by the founding deans of the fledgling business school movement, the dean of the University of Nebraska's School of Business Administration, J. E. Le Rossignol, delivered remarks saturated with Protestant-themed religiosity and moralism, even while deprecating, as Donham had, these same religious institutions as sources of authority in the present day:

> This seems to me to be a fine meeting. It seems to me a very remarkable occasion and I wish that Jonathan Edwards, or Cotton Mather, or any of those intellectual aristocrats of former times could come in here and see this, because we are their successors. They were talking about theological things, of which they didn't know much, I suppose, and now we are talking about ethical things, of which we do not know very much but of which we desire to know a great deal. We are in a better state of mind than they were because we really feel we do not know anything at all hardly, and so we are in a proper frame of mind and I believe this subject is much more hopeful for the progress and up building of mankind and the improvement of the world than the subjects they discussed in those days.
>
> I am almost sure that most of you gentlemen are sons of ministers—I know some of you are—and you have the proper religious attitude toward business. We say this in an age in which religion is no more, but the very fact that we are discussing this question shows we have a religious attitude, and we feel we must cultivate it, and it will be cultivated just because we have got it. A man is hopelessly religious. He has to believe something and he has to have some idealism and he has to have some worthy aims toward which to work.
>
> The idea of stewardship is a very old idea. It is in the Bible. The idea of stewardship is the idea that Adam Smith had, of not consuming all your wealth but of managing your property for the sake of other people. It is the idea of Christianity; it is the idea of economics; it is the idea of every good person.[74]

Such rhetoric, of course, would have been greeted with skepticism and even derision in many quarters of American society in the disillusioned years following the end of World War I. Nine years prior to Young's soaring address, writing in a year that also saw the United States in economic depression, Thorstein Veblen had opposed the expansion of business education within the university by denigrating the idea of business as a profession:

> The professional knowledge and skill of physicians, surgeons, dentists, pharmacists, agriculturalists, engineers of all kinds, perhaps even of journalists, is of some use to the community at large, at the same time that it may be profitable to the bearers of it. . . . But such is not the case with the training designed to give proficiency in business. No gain comes to the community at large from increasing the business proficiency of any number of its young men.[75]

In 1924—the same year that Harvard's Graduate School of Business Administration solicited and received a gift of $5 million from the financier George F. Baker, chairman of the First National Bank of New York, for the construction of the campus dedicated with Young's speech—the literary and social critic John Jay Chapman, himself a Harvard College alumnus, had been invited as a guest speaker to the annual *Harvard Business Review* dinner and openly ridiculed the business school's professionalizing aspirations:

> Do you gentlemen seriously believe that you can accept Wall Street's money and be clear of Wall Street's influence? You are idealists, indeed! It used to be thought an abuse for the plutocrat to subsidize a chair in a college and put a bit in the mouth of learning. But since business is now discovered to be a profession, such practices are perfectly all right.
>
> My friends, the truth is that business is not a profession; and no amount of rhetoric and no expenditure in circulars can make it into a profession. This fact stands like a sharp-pointed, deep-seated rock in mid-channel, and against this rock Harvard is steering her craft— or raft. . . . I can imagine a man practicing medicine or law or architecture or engineering out of sheer love for the thing. But I cannot imagine a man's running a business at a loss. It wouldn't be business. A School of Business means a school where you learn to make money.
>
> You couldn't find a man in the whole world more divested of the peculiar virtues that cause the regular professions to be revered than our American prominent business man. Then why should we "accord" him the dignity and respect due to these professions? Give him

something else! Give him a medal with a picture of himself and of his pile; give him praise for benefactions, for benevolence, for courage, mother wit, good luck. But don't play upon the accordion of his vanity and ignorance by according him the dignity and respect due to other things.[76]

Meanwhile, university business education was facing criticism from the opposite direction, as many businessmen, too, reacted scornfully to the idea of teaching business as an academic subject with a view to making business a profession. The historian Frederick Lewis Allen summarized such reactions from businessmen of the day:

> Business, a profession! What an innocent notion! Business was a rough-and-tumble battle between men whose first concern was to look out for number one, and the very idea of professors being able to prepare men for it was nonsense. As a matter of fact, many a tough-fibered tycoon of those days was dubious even about employing college graduates, whom he regarded as toplofty, impractical fellows who had to unlearn a lot before they were fit for the business arena.[77]

Yet despite the skepticism with which it was often met by contemporaries, the language of Owen Young and like-minded advocates of business schools and management's professionalization reminds us that just as science in the nineteenth century had come to represent a secular analogue of the religious seeker's quest for ultimate truth, the secular institution of the professions had grown out of the religious idea of *vocation* or *calling* that Weber perceived as intrinsic to the Protestant ethic and the "spirit of capitalism." The dominance of secular institutions in America since the late nineteenth century should not blind us to the historical and cultural roots of their authority. These remained quite evident in American colleges and universities in the era of the founding of the first business schools, with practices like mandatory chapel in private colleges, for example, surviving well into the early 1900s. Still, in the midst of the skepticism that greeted the idea of professionalizing management, what enabled its proponents to employ the religious rhetoric of a champion like Young with relative impunity was the extent to which business had, much as Veblen feared, managed to insinuate itself into another quasi-sacred institution of the late nineteenth century, the American research university.

⊫ Management and the University

The attempt to establish management as both a science and a profession, while receiving its initial impetus from outside academia, would scarcely have been feasible without the active support of the third great ordering institution to emerge in America in the last quarter of the nineteenth century. By the end of the century—with science having become increasingly dependent on the new research universities for resources, while the professions, new and old, had found it in their interests to delegate professional education and internal certification to university-based professional schools—the university was, indeed, an element essential to victory in the struggle for management's professionalization. Yet an alliance with the university represented, for the institutional entrepreneurs guiding this effort, even more than just a means of accessing the resources needed to legitimate management as a science or of mimicking those professions already admitted to the academy's precincts. In attempting to render management both a science and a profession, many members of the elite group that championed management's cause wanted it to be perceived as specifically a "learned profession," with an expectation that such learning encompassed not only science but, even more important, a broad understanding of business's role within the larger enterprise of civilization itself. Owen Young's remarks at the Harvard Business School dedication ceremony explicitly expressed this particular ambition. Even earlier, in 1913, Edward Jones of the University of Michigan had articulated the university business school's duty to elevate "industrial activity," using language clearly implying that success in the effort would entitle business education to a degree of respect equal to that of any other endeavor within the university:

> If we lament the prominence of the desire for material acquisitions
> in our civilization, we may hope to be able to form an effective coun-
> teracting force, if within the domain of industry itself we can stimu-
> late the ambition on the part of industrial leaders to realize . . .
> newer and more social ideals. Far from weakening the forces which
> make for the dominance of intellect in the world, it is our specific
> duty to raise industrial activity to the plane of an intellectual pursuit,
> governed by a high code of professional ethics, so that through the
> industrial life a new demonstration shall be given of the value of all
> which makes for the culture of the intellect.[78]

In claiming a place for business education within the American university as it was developing in the late nineteenth and early twentieth centuries, advocates for the professionalization of management not only presented it as an aspiring science and an aspiring profession but also associated management education with two core functions of the university itself, one traditional and one modern: the teaching and study of the liberal arts, and research as a vehicle for public service.

The traditional ideal of a liberal arts education with which the managerial vanguard hoped to associate itself, and to which it sincerely aspired, was articulated in the mid-nineteenth century by John Henry Newman in his discourse "Knowledge Viewed in Relation to Professional Skill" in *The Idea of a University* (1852):

> There will be this distinction as regards a professor of law, or of medicine, or of geology, or of political economy, in a university and out of it, that out of a university he is in danger of being absorbed and narrowed by his pursuit, and of giving lectures which are the lectures of nothing more than a lawyer, physician, geologist, or political economist; whereas in a university he will just know where he and his science stand, he has come to it, as it were, from a height, he has taken a survey of all knowledge, he is kept from extravagance by the very rivalry of other studies, he has gained from them a special illumination and largeness of mind and freedom and self-possession, and he treats his own in consequence with a philosophy and a resource, which belongs not to the study itself, but to his liberal education.[79]

Although, as Clark Kerr observed in *The Uses of the University*, the "beautiful world" that Cardinal Newman described (in essence, Oxford in the early nineteenth century) was being "shattered forever," even as Newman wrote, by the new model of the German research university, what Kerr labeled the "British," "German," and "American" models of the university all survived to coexist in the "multiversity" that had come into being in the United States by about 1930.[80] Indeed, as Julie Reuben argues, a decline in the old belief in the inherently moral character of the natural and social sciences and the rise of "value-free" science—first observable in the early years of the twentieth century and intensified by the scientifically enhanced savagery of World War I—produced something of a revival of the humanities in the two decades leading up to the Great Depression, as humanists began to contend, with a certain amount of success, that "science was not an adequate source of moral guidance,"[81] and that the humanities must serve as a counterweight to the sciences and preserve the university's traditional function of providing moral education. Thus throughout the decades in which the first university-based business schools were being created, the liberal arts remained available to their academic leadership as, at least in theory, tools for the production of the broadly educated, socially responsible, genuinely professional managers they aspired to fashion.

In the 1880s, meanwhile, the idea of grounding business education in the liberal arts formed an explicit part of Joseph Wharton's plan for the school that he endowed; so deeply did Wharton believe in the value of what a university could contribute to the education of future managers that he deliberately eschewed the model of the independent professional school, choosing instead to have Penn's liberal arts college serve as the locus for education in "modern Finance and Economy." Wharton's vision of the broadly educated businessman was amplified and implemented by Edmund James, a man who (like so many other leading innovators in American higher education during this period) had been greatly influenced by his experience of the German research university, and who, in Sass's words, "hoped to bring the enlightenment and dynamism of the university to all practical affairs."[82] At Dartmouth's Tuck School, the "3 + 2" structure that required students to spend their first three years in the undergraduate program of Dartmouth College built a liberal arts component into business study, while Harvard Business School, for its part, established its requirement that students already possess an undergraduate degree and would thus arrive with a thorough grounding in the liberal arts.

As the growing demand for business education at both private and public universities proved impossible to ignore, friction developed between those desiring to offer students the opportunity to take business courses as part of a curriculum otherwise devoted to the liberal arts and those who advocated the study of business as an independent field—including many who believed that the university had nothing valuable to teach aspiring business leaders. More than a few businessmen, indeed, shared Andrew Carnegie's belief that "college education as it exists seems almost fatal to [business] success":

> Nor is this surprising [Carnegie continued]. . . . While the college
> student has been learning a little about the barbarous and petty
> squabbles of a far-distant past, or trying to master the languages
> which are dead, such knowledge as seems adapted for life upon

another planet than this, as far as business affairs are concerned—
the future captain of industry is hotly engaged in the school of
experience, obtaining the very knowledge required for his future tri-
umphs. . . . The graduate has little chance, entering at twenty, against
the boy who swept the office, or who begins as shipping clerk at
fourteen.[83]

In a particularly stark example of the kind of conflict that could arise
over this issue, an argument as to whether business education ought to be offered in a separate business school took several decades to resolve at Columbia University, where Nicholas Murray Butler (who served as the university's
president from 1902 until 1945) and the Columbia College faculty held out for
many years against the creation of a school of business.

In 1880, Columbia's School of Political Science (later called the Faculty of
Political Science) had been established to offer courses in history, political science, and political economy. Under this arrangement, a course titled Practical
Political Economy was instituted to offer instruction in railroads, the "Science
of Finance," and "Fiscal and Industrial History." The next thirty years saw an
increase in the number and variety of business courses at Columbia, at both
the graduate and undergraduate levels. In 1914, Columbia's course catalog detailed a dozen business-related courses including Applied Economics, Corporation Finance, Money and Banking, Statistics, Insurance, Psychology of Advertising, Business Organization, and Principles of Accounting. These courses
were open to all upperclassmen of the college. Meanwhile, the most serious effort to offer practical courses at Columbia was mounted in Extension Teaching, Columbia's external teaching program, which was characterized as primarily concerned with "public service." In 1910, Extension Teaching presented
one course in elementary economics and one in banking. The next year's offerings included courses in bookkeeping, principles of accounting, business
organization, corporation finance, and commercial law, as well as "secretarial"
courses such as stenography and typing. Largely owing to its business offerings, the Extension Teaching program expanded rapidly, thus raising the question for the Faculty of Political Science as to whether Columbia should establish a separate school of business.

The growth of the Extension Teaching school concerned President Butler, despite his overall sympathy with the concept of offering instruction in
business. In his 1914 annual report, Butler objected to the "growing tendency
of college and university departments to vocationalize all their instruction."

While insisting on the distinction between business and the professions, Butler did, however, specifically endorse the idea of preparing Columbia undergraduates for business careers:

> It remains to provide more adequately than has yet been done for
> the large and increasing number of College students who have no in-
> tention of entering the so-called learned professions but who look
> forward to a business career. The time has come when Columbia
> College can and should offer the Senior who wishes it a well organ-
> ized group of studies that will be as effective in preparation for busi-
> ness as are the studies in the professional schools for the careers to
> which they respectively lead. Of course, it will not be possible to
> make a successful business man through the study of books, but it is
> not possible to make a successful lawyer or a successful physician by
> that method. There is no reason, however, why the future business
> man should not be trained and disciplined in those subjects of
> study which have a direct bearing upon the work in which he has
> to engage.
>
> To accomplish this it will not be necessary to increase the com-
> plexity of the University organization or to found any new school or
> department. It will only be necessary for the Faculty of Columbia
> College to select and group together those courses of instruction in
> economics, in business law, in finance, in accounting, and in allied
> subjects already established in the University, which can be so organ-
> ized and arranged as to make a strong appeal to the student who
> looks forward to business activity and to give him an excellent
> preparation for it.[84]

In response to Butler's disquiet about the place of business studies at Columbia, a committee was formed to address the issue. The committee then
produced an eight-page pamphlet entitled *Business Instruction in Columbia
College* that outlined special arrangements for cross-registration among the
Faculties of Law and Applied Science and the Extension School, to allow students to enroll in business-related courses in any of these schools. Many students found the Extension School courses to be the most useful for business
career preparation, and, within the Extension School, the number of courses
quickly proliferated. In close cooperation with the American Institute of Banking, for example, new courses were developed for the training of prospective
bank employees in the New York area.

Meanwhile, Columbia College faculty continued to object to establishing a school of business, especially as a distinct entity. As with the Faculty of Political Science, the college wanted any business education the university offered to emphasize the scholarly and theoretical as opposed to the professional and technical. Yet the Columbia trustees did approve the creation of a business school, in December 1915, in a preemptive move engineered by A. Barton Hepburn, president of the Chase National Bank. Hepburn, who had previously raised $750,000 to establish a school of commerce within the City University of New York system, only to be rebuffed, suggested to Butler that Columbia should move in this direction; in making his case for a business school at Columbia, Hepburn told Butler that other New York business leaders concurred with him in believing that management training required a more professional grounding. Butler, impressed by Hepburn's argument as well as his implicit offer to assist in securing the funds necessary for creating a separate school, finally overcame his hesitation. On July 1, 1916, despite protests from many of the Columbia faculty, the School of Business in Columbia University was granted formal recognition. In April 1917, Butler appointed Hepburn as a university trustee, thus allowing the banker to play a critical role in shaping the curriculum and direction of the nascent school. Two years of college preparation were required for admission, and a three-year curriculum was established. For its first dean, the Columbia School of Business chose the then-director of the university's Extension School, a classics professor named James G. Egbert, whose special expertise was in Latin inscriptions.[85] The dedication of a building for the new school in September 1924 affirmed "the development of business from a calling into a profession."[86]

Once university-based business schools such as Columbia's were established, even those faculty and administrators most committed to producing broadly educated businessmen continued to face skepticism from within the academic community about whether management was worthy of study in the university setting. The struggles that business education faced to justify its place in the academy, and thus to gain the full measure of legitimacy that association with the university offered, are reflected in the histories of what would become some of the nation's most prestigious institutions for the study of management.

During the first few years of the Tuck School's existence, for example, the Dartmouth trustees wrestled with the issue of what degree should be awarded to students completing the graduate portion of the Tuck program; the challenge was to find a solution that would satisfy both academic critics, who questioned whether the Tuck curriculum was scholarly enough to warrant a traditional academic degree, and businessmen, who might be suspicious of such a degree in any case. When the suggestion of giving students a mere certificate proved unacceptable to both students and faculty, a proposal that the school grant the degree of "Master of Science (Tuck School)" was introduced and defeated. In June 1902 (after Tuck had been in operation for two years), the decision was finally made to award graduates a diploma reading "Master of Commercial Science." Dartmouth economics professor Frank Haigh Dixon, who also served as secretary of the Tuck School, explained one objection to the "Master of Science (Tuck School)" degree when he posited the likelihood that graduates, "when using it, will drop the explanatory suffix." Such a circumstance, he pointed out, would subject the degree to "the criticism on the one hand of those who maintain that the granting of an academic degree by professional schools is a lowering of academic standards, and on the other of those who desire definiteness in the form of recognition granted to this kind of professional study." Dixon considered and rejected the idea of a "Master of Commerce" degree because "what would be accepted as natural in a bachelor's degree would appear presumptuous when 'master' is substituted. Furthermore, the abbreviation M.C. would lead to such possible misconception and bantering as to endanger its dignity." He preferred the eventually adopted "Master of Commercial Science" because it was "dignified and academic" and would not be "offensive" to businessmen.[87]

At Harvard, despite the strong support the business school enjoyed from two powerful university presidents, the establishment of the school also invited skepticism and even open hostility. Melvin Copeland, an HBS faculty member from 1909 to 1953, portrayed this atmosphere in his history of the school:

> The School in its early years was to find some friendly and steadfast supporters among members of the other Harvard Faculties and in other academic institutions. However, by many professors and by numerous Harvard alumni, it was deemed to be degrading for the University to offer instruction in the venal subject of Business Management. Some of the academic animosity toward the young Business School was outrightly expressed. Some of it was covert, albeit thinly concealed. Later, as an instructor in Marketing in the School, I was made especially aware of the academic animosity toward us, for with the development of the courses in Marketing some of the

sharpest barbs of the critics were directed at that subject as being particularly unworthy of academic recognition.[88]

It would be many years before such voices were stilled. For example, George F. Baker's gift of $5 million to Harvard Business School in 1924 was greeted not only with profound gratitude from the Harvard administration and the business school itself but also by this poetic effusion from a Harvard College graduate who was a partner of the architectural firm McKim, Mead & White, which would design the new HBS campus built with Baker's funds:

Fair Harvard! I hear that you've been such a fool
As to start a ridiculous Business School
Where 'Grocery 2' and 'Butchery 4'
Take the place of the classics you taught us of yore.
A Baker has given five million, it seems
To assure the success of your horrible schemes!
Great Mammon now rules where Minerva did reign
And her silly old owl has no use for its brain.
Poor Homer and Horace and Shelley and Keats
Must hang up their lyres and take the back seats.
While the youth of America rush to be taught
The germs of success without effort of thought.[89]

The charge that the study of business remained unworthy of a place within the university on account of being both anti-intellectual and concerned only with profit echoed similarly motivated critiques of the notion of business as a profession, and demanded emphatic response. To address such skepticism as well as to bolster their claims that management represented both a science and a profession, business schools not only affirmed their commitment to the humanistic traditions of the university but also aligned themselves with the modern American university's missions of research and public service.

As research emerged as an increasingly recognized function of university business schools, business educators echoed their colleagues in other parts of the university by presenting their institutions' research activity, such as it was in the early decades,[90] as an integral component of the university's mission of public service. At a dedication ceremony in 1929 for New York University's newest business school building, for instance, one speaker proclaimed that "the business future of our country will be evolved not alone in the factory, upon the highway or in the market place. It will be due even more to the patient research, systematized thought, the profound study and the wise counsels of a proper business education within these walls."[91] Columbia University's President Butler declared in 1927 that the business scholarship produced in the 1920s had achieved both intellectual and broader, public significance: "There is coming to be a philosophy of business," Butler said, "just as there has long been a philosophy of theology, of law, of medicine and of teaching, and it is through the door of that philosophy, that understanding of fundamental principles and higher standards, that the University seeks to lead men and women to prepare themselves for the capable and competent pursuit of this form of intellectual activity and public service."[92]

Meanwhile, at the University of Chicago, Dean Leon C. Marshall had been attempting to implement a research program that evoked the efforts in the 1880s and 1990s to turn the Wharton School into an institution where the study of business was integrated into a larger program for a school of political and social science. On assuming the deanship at Chicago in 1909, Marshall undertook an extensive study of American schools of commerce, civic institutions, and bureaus of municipal research in order to design a plan for the university's newest school. Later, in 1920, the University of Chicago's business school became the first in the country to offer a Ph.D. program. Viewing the social sciences as the heart of the school's intellectual endeavors, Marshall envisioned an institution that would simultaneously serve the fields of business, social work, and municipal affairs. His study concluded:

> In its relation to the community this college conceives that very considerable existing stores of scientific information in the field of the social sciences should be made more accessible for the furthering progress of society. The college will assume some responsibility for this task. In rendering this service the college has a duty to more than one section of the community. It hopes to serve by aiding commercial and industrial development; it hopes equally to serve by assisting in the solution of our pressing political and social problems. It believes that there is sufficient unity and coherence in the social sciences to justify an attempt to advance all along the line; and it has accordingly placed under one organization the functions which in some institutions are performed by schools or colleges of commerce, the functions which in other institutions are performed by schools for social workers, and the functions which in still other institutions are given

over to bureaus of municipal research. The motives actuating this tripartite alliance are more than motives concerned with economy of effort. The main motive is the belief that a conscious, cordial co-operation of all the social sciences in a sort of "social science institute" has within it greater possibilities of service for our community than can be secured by sorties, however strong, of single interests.[93]

A public service role for business school research found another advocate during this era in Wharton School economist Joseph Willits, who assumed leadership of the school's department of "geography and industry" in 1919 and transformed labor management into its strongest area by dint not only of its program's academic quality but also of Willits's own interest in promoting democracy and social justice. In 1926 Willits criticized research programs (including Wharton's own Industrial Research Department) that had been founded in the 1920s for their preoccupation with what he regarded as insignificant issues: "[J]ust as a medical school, or any other professional school worth the name, is not performing its full function unless it is contributing to thoroughgoing research on the fundamental problems in the field of medicine," Willits said, "so should a . . . school of business aim to contribute its share toward the solution of the fundamental problems of business."[94] After becoming dean of Wharton in 1933, Willits would portray the Great Depression as a summons to American business schools to direct their gaze beyond the problems of business per se to the needs of the nation. He advocated a fresh emphasis on applied economics (as opposed to the narrow specialties favored as subject matter by some members of the faculty) as part of an effort to make the school's programs more academically rigorous, the better to fashion the kind of graduates that distinguished a university from a mere professional or trade school. Willits described both the pressing need for leadership and the particular kind of leader he hoped to train: "[T]he confusions of the last two decades in our national life and in the world of affairs have stressed once more the importance of the person capable and worthy of *intellectual* leadership, whether in business, government, or academic circles."[95] With the catastrophe of the Depression, he observed, "the world demands . . . that we step up the quality of our understanding of the complex and changing phenomena with which we deal so that the basis for a more stable and better planned society may be present."[96]

Yet even as, over the course of the 1920s, university business education enjoyed impressive growth and asserted increasingly credible claims to intellectual respectability and social utility, critics continued to question whether such education belonged in the university at all. Some of the sharpest critiques came from academia's closest observers, including Abraham Flexner, who, after issuing a report on medical schools in 1910 that radically reorganized the teaching of medicine in the United States,[97] focused his attention on graduate education generally. In his book *Universities*, published in 1930, Flexner argued that business education did not constitute a legitimate academic subject, for scholars in legitimate fields, he said, embody an ideal rather than merely improving profits. "Modern business," Flexner wrote—echoing Veblen's criticism of a dozen years before—"does not satisfy the criteria of a profession; it is shrewd, energetic, and clever, rather than intellectual in character; it aims—and under our present social organization must aim—at its own advantage, rather than noble purpose within itself."[98] Like other critics of business schools, Flexner viewed business as a phenomenon, as a subject of study, not a course of study. Referring to a statement in a Harvard Business School publication that an HBS education "permits rapid progress" for its graduates, Flexner questioned both the inclusion of business within the university and its claim to be a profession, asking, "[W]hat university school of medicine would dare to define its ideals and results in such terms?"[99] Moreover, he continued, the content of business education possessed neither an ethical nor a social dimension; examining fifteen volumes of case studies published by HBS, Flexner claimed to find "not the faintest glimmer of social, ethical, philosophic, historic or cultural interest" in any of them.[100]

Such criticisms were often warranted by the evolving relationship between universities and business itself. Although universities had indeed ventured into business education with the idea that the university would improve, refine, and uplift the practice of business, influence ran in the opposite direction as well. The rise of the modern American university in the last quarter of the nineteenth century had been financed, after all, by a tremendous outpouring of private as well as public funding. The nation's industrial enterprises were producing surpluses that fueled the growth of new civic institutions such as hospitals, museums, and charitable foundations; and while colleges and universities were still often denigrated by self-made merchants and industrialists, some of the wealthiest now took an interest in higher education, with a few (including Andrew Carnegie, Johns Hopkins, Leland Stanford, and John D. Rockefeller) going so far as to underwrite entire new universities. What is significant is that no tax incentive was then offered for philanthropy; the nation's business leaders were increasingly funding educational institutions because they perceived themselves as "stewards" of wealth and likewise perceived higher education to fulfill an important societal need.[101] Nor was it just robber barons trying to launder their fortunes who became increasingly engaged in higher education. Charles Austin Beard and Mary Ritter Beard observed that "at the end of the nineteenth century the roster of trustees of higher learning read like a corporation directory."[102] Hubert Park Beck found that, by the 1930s, businessmen constituted over 40 percent of the trustees at the nation's largest public and private institutions of higher education, with the remainder coming from the professions. Most of these businessmen were senior executives in large industrial corporations and in financial service institutions such as banks and brokerages.[103] Walter Metzger noted that "[w]hereas wealth and a talent for business had once been considered virtues in trustees, now they were thought to be prerequisites."[104] This situation contrasted sharply with that of the pre–Civil War private colleges, whose boards of trustees had been dominated by clergymen and educators.[105]

Faced with the traditional liabilities of any new organization, business schools also emerged in a particularly difficult environment, lacking as they did the fundamental credibility with the public that undergirded professional schools in the more established vocations. Not surprisingly, business schools eagerly embraced the interest and support proffered by businessmen eager to advance their own status and influence.[106] The involvement of businessmen with the university was not merely symbolic or pro forma, and business schools and the disciplines affiliated with them sometimes found themselves under especially close watch from benefactors. Before the formation of the American Association of University Professors in 1915, boards dominated by business interests often forced the removal of professors and even university presidents with whose views they disagreed.[107] In 1894, the economists John R. Commons and Richard T. Ely were dismissed from Indiana University and the University of Wisconsin, respectively, for advocating such then-radical notions as free trade. Although Stanford University did not have a board of trustees until 1903, Leland Stanford's widow, Jane Stanford, prevailed on university president David Starr Jordan to fire the economist Edward A. Ross in 1901 because of Ross's opposition to the use of migrant Chinese labor for the construction of railroads. At the Wharton School, businessmen trustees dismissed economist Scott Nearing from his professorship in 1915 for campaigning for the abolition of child labor, and Philadelphia business leaders succeeded in forcing the silencing or dismissal of other faculty who proposed increased regulation of public utilities. As a result, according to Sass, Wharton was unable to attract "any first-rate, critical minds" for years afterward.[108]

For business schools, however, such direct and visible intervention in academic affairs proved less pervasive and problematic than subtler ways in which the involvement of business schools with business threatened to compromise the academic integrity and legitimacy of this new institution. Efforts to demonstrate practical utility by forging close links with business organizations for research purposes, for instance, sometimes opened up legitimate questioning of business schools' scholarly objectivity—as when a Massachusetts state legislator, in 1929, challenged payments from an electric utility to HBS professor C. O. Ruggles to finance the "overhauling" of texts on economics and public utilities.[109] Business executives unquestionably helped shape curriculum decisions. At Wharton, for example, businessmen encouraged the development of classes that would influence and improve the "personality" of students to give them more "businesslike" dispositions.[110]

Despite the alarms raised by critics like Flexner, however, it would be a mistake to suppose that the dynamics of the relationship between business schools and business represented a hostile takeover of the university by alien elements. That relationship, instead, was an example of the ongoing interaction between organizations and their social environments. As John Meyer and his colleagues have noted, because modern organizations are so dependent on both financial and social resources for their survival, they must create structures, both formal and informal, that are aligned with the expectations of the culture within which they are embedded.[111] American colleges and universities, including new professional schools, could not have survived, let alone thrived, amid the economic and social transformations of the post–Civil War era had they not acknowledged a new and broader set of societal interests and institutions that included large corporations and the new managerial class. Moreover, those who criticized the close links between business and the university failed to appreciate the ideational interests that often attracted businesspeople to universities and academics to business. Despite the scoffing in which businessmen sometimes engaged, higher education held a strong attraction for men who were often perceived by the public as concerned only with the vulgarities of profit seeking. Men such as Joseph Wharton, George F. Baker, Owen Young, A. Barton Hepburn, and scores of others who offered their organizational skills, as well as their social and financial resources, to aid the establishment of business schools represented a new kind of leader in American society. They played an important role in civic life and viewed themselves as custodians of a new social order, charged with a duty not to benefit themselves at the expense of their corporations, employees, and society, but in fact to serve them. As Owen Young stated to rousing applause from a group of American business leaders in 1930:

> We must remember that politics and economics are not the masters of men—they are their servants. The managers of both too often think and sometimes act as if human beings were merely the fodder of political and economic mills. Because I have spoken of economics and politics I would not wish you to think that I consider them in any sense ends in themselves. Back of them stand myriads of human faces, some young, some old, some prosperous, some needy, some charitable, some selfish, some generous, some envious, but all vitally affected not only in their material but in their cultural and spiritual development, by these organizations, political and economic, which they have imposed upon themselves.
>
> So long as such organizations render an uplifting service, just so long can we go forward in reaping the advantages which civilization has brought. But those faces in these days of a closely compact world can no longer be segregated into compartments, one of which shall be prosperous and the others not; one of which shall go forward and the others back. Those faces must all move together for good or ill. So politics and economics, their servants, must move together too, not in one country alone, but everywhere. That way only can the benefits of civilization be enlarged—that way only can peace ultimately come.[112]

Firmly established within the American university by the close of the 1920s, business schools—owing to the efforts of businessmen like Young as well as academic visionaries such as Edmund James, Charles W. Eliot, and many others—played a crucial role in gaining legitimacy for the new occupation of management, meanwhile elevating it to a higher social status than it had ever achieved before, almost certainly higher than it could have attained on its own. By aligning themselves with the prestigious institutions of science, the professions, and the university, the pioneers of the American business school movement articulated high aims for the new occupation of management as well as for themselves. Like all such high ideals, however, those that animated the creation of the university business school would prove difficult to realize amid pressures both from the external environment and from the internal challenges inherent in any major institution-building project. The very ambitiousness of the professionalization project in American business education required especially strong institutional foundations, and the effort to create them required business schools to turn the institutional logics they had appropriated into stable structures. This demanding undertaking is the subject of my next chapter.

"A Very Ill-Defined Institution":   **4**

The Business School as Aspiring Professional School

The once unthinkable idea of offering business education within the university did not take root and flourish all at once. For seventeen years following the founding of the Wharton School at the University of Pennsylvania in 1881, no other university established a freestanding business school. Eventually, in 1898, the University of Chicago and the University of California at Berkeley established the College of Commerce and Politics and the College of Commerce, respectively. From that point until the Great Depression university business education grew rapidly. Between 1900 and 1913, twenty-five universities established separate schools for business studies, including Dartmouth, New York University, Northwestern, Harvard, and the state universities of Wisconsin and Illinois. New business schools often appeared almost overnight, since they required neither expensive laboratories nor extensive libraries. By 1924, the U.S. Bureau of Education reported, 400 colleges and universities offered some type of business curriculum, while 132 of these schools offered business as a major.[1] By 1930, most large state-university systems offered a bachelor's or master's degree in business.

Not only did the number of schools grow, but enrollments boomed as well. Harvard Business School (HBS), which opened with just 59 MBA candidates in 1908, admitted 300 first-year students in 1922. Columbia matriculated 26 degree candidates in 1916, the year of its business school's founding, and 380 students in 1924. In American higher education generally, undergraduate and graduate business studies became the fastest-growing degree programs, and enrollments in them eventually surpassed even those in engineering (see table 4.1).[2]

According to the U.S. Bureau of Education statistics, in 1895 there were 97 students enrolled in business programs (undergraduate and graduate) in U.S. institutions of higher education; in 1903 there were 1,100; in 1910, 4,321; in 1916, 11,643; in 1920, 36,855; and in 1924, 47,552. The business historian

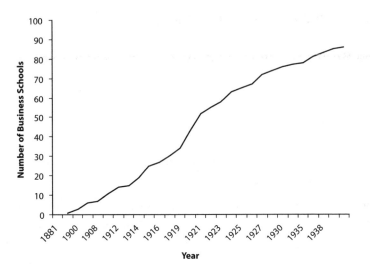

Figure 4.1

Growth in AACSB-accredited business schools, 1881–1940.

Table 4.1

Growth in Business and Engineering Degrees, 1917–1940

	Business (B.S/B.S)	Engineering	MBA
1917–1918	640	3,079	
1919–1920	1,559	4,400	110
1921–1922	3,562	6,431	192
1923–1924	4,948	7,476	267
1925–1926	5,435	7,376	390
1927–1928	6,621	7,607	460
1929–1930	6,213	7,371	578
1931–1932	10,177	10,374	1,017
1933–1934	9,591	11,409	897
1935–1936	9,869	10,629	698
1937–1938	14,652	11,039	951
1939–1940	19,036	1,348	1,139

Source: *U.S. Historical Abstracts*; Frank Cook Pierson, *The Education of American Businessmen: A study of University-College Programs in Business Administration* (New York: McGraw-Hill, 1959).

Steven A. Sass writes that "[t]he nation's business schools . . . saw their enroll-ments explode sixfold between 1915 and 1926 and include a far more demo-cratic slice of the American population than ever before."[3] A demographic analysis of business students in this era finds that between 1918 and 1927, the percentage of business degrees (undergraduate and graduate) granted to women rose from 5 percent to 17 percent. While none of the elite graduate business schools would begin admitting women until the 1960s, schools such as Dartmouth's Tuck School and Harvard's Graduate School of Business Administration enacted their own version of diversity by expanding admissions beyond graduates of their own institutions' undergraduate colleges and a handful of other feeder schools in the Northeast. Whereas only 14 colleges were represented in the Harvard class of 1908, in 1928 the students enrolled represented 203 colleges and came from 44 states and 14 foreign countries.[4]

While it is hard to characterize the typical student across all business schools, the makeup of the Northwestern University School of Commerce's class of 1913 provides a window on student demographics in many university business programs in this era. The students were by no means exclusively the sons of elites that Joseph Wharton, for example, intended as the beneficiaries of university business education. The 471 registered students at Northwestern's business school, which at the time was part of its extension school in Chicago, "consisted of 16 college graduates; 237 high school graduates; 9 with 3 years of high school; 27 with 2 years of high school; 25 with one year of high school; and 157 with less than one year in high school" (i.e., 55 percent had a high school education or better, and 34 percent had less than one year of high school). The school's dean categorized business school students as coming from the following groups: "(a) men interested in particular courses; (b) men who would like to secure a comprehensive business training; (c) men who come on the general theory that education will do them good. In the first category, by far the greatest number are those who already engaged in a particular line of business, and of these in turn much of the largest class are the accountants; next to accountants come brokers and bond men, then advertising men, bank men, railroad men, and, in the organization courses, among others, managers and heads of departments."[5] Enrollments in the business programs of Columbia University and the University of Wisconsin, programs that also originated within their university's extension schools, reflected a similarly nontraditional student population.[6]

While business schools were expanding in number and enrollments, the 1920s also saw enormous growth in the number of managerial jobs in the United States. Sass observes that "[t]he twenties . . . brought the greatest movement of labor into business employment in the eighty years between 1870 and 1950; the number of workers in banking, finance, and insurance alone grew more than 80 percent between 1920 and 1930." The proportion of managers to production workers in industrial firms also rose dramatically, increasing from 8.1 percent in 1900 to 17.9 percent in 1929.[7] As graduates of the nation's new collegiate business programs and graduate schools of business filled growing numbers of managerial jobs in these fields, the popular view that business and higher education were in diametrical opposition was also being overturned. One 1915 *New York Times* editorial trumpeted, "We are confident that the young man with a college education is better fitted for advancement in modern business than the one who begins at the foot of the ladder with small learning."[8] Business executives' attitude toward business education also took a 180-degree turn, as corporate hiring departments began to make a credentialing distinction between "graduate" managers and "uneducated" supervisors. Despite the postwar recession, 75 percent of the Harvard graduating class of 1920 had permanent positions by the time they graduated. In 1926, a report compiled by the school noted, "Roughly, four times as many requests came to the School for graduates as we had men whom we could recommend."[9] Among the twenty-four men who graduated in Tuck's first five classes, most, by the mid-1920s, held middle and senior managerial positions, and six were chief executives of significant corporations.[10]

Academic attention to, and interest in, business education also reached a new zenith during this era, as numerous books and articles about the curricula of the collegiate schools of business were written. In 1921, the University of Chicago's Leon Marshall published *Collegiate Education for Business*, which laid out a proposed curriculum for both undergraduate and graduate business programs. The following year, Washington University's L. S. Lyon published *Education for Business*, a study focusing on business education at the undergraduate and secondary-school levels. The prestigious *Journal of Political Economy* published several articles on, and devoted special issues to, the business school curriculum between 1913 and 1926. In 1931, Wharton professors James Bossard and J. Fredrick Dewhurst attempted the first comprehensive survey of business education, including a four-decade longitudinal study on the career patterns of Wharton graduates.[11] Meanwhile, it was increasingly believed that the very existence of business schools within the university was a boon for the latter, since, as one newsmagazine put it, "university ideals, and academic ways of thought and action should derive benefit from contact with the practical affairs of business life."[12]

Yet despite the strong growth and increasing acceptance they enjoyed, business schools still faced serious challenges and often found themselves in a defensive position. Business school professors, for example, continued to endure taunts from academic colleagues about the lack of "theory" or "discipline" in their field. This made business education subject to withering criticism to the effect that universities, by creating business schools, had simply sold out to commercial interests, as the Carnegie Foundation's Abraham Flexner charged.

Nor was it just outsiders or academics in the traditional disciplines who criticized business schools. Many business school deans themselves felt uneasy about what they perceived to be the directionless nature of business education. Like most such high-minded goals, the attempt to make business schools an instrument for the professionalization of management was much harder to carry out than it had been to espouse. During the 1920s, the now aging generation of pioneering business school leaders began to focus on contradictions previously ignored and environmental complexities that no one could have foreseen; business schools were supposed to become professional schools like those for medicine and (even more particularly) for law, but preparing students for a still amorphous "profession" of management was turning out to be a much more ambiguous undertaking than training for the already established professions. While continuing to publicly reaffirm the high aims to which their institutions aspired, several of the leading business school deans became concerned that existing practices were disconnected from their original ideals. Reporting the results of a study of business schools, the University of Chicago's Dean Leon Marshall confessed that "a survey of two hundred or more colleges and universities . . . demonstrates that our practices are ridiculously short of our preachments."[13]

One of the major concerns of these early business school leaders was the heterogeneity of organizational forms found in business schools generally. The haphazard way in which colleges and universities had developed their business schools certainly contributed to this heterogeneity. The decision to found a new business school was often made under the impulse of opportunism or expedience. Schools of business, for example, emerged at the graduate level during this period not because business administration was developing as a discipline but because many traditional liberal arts school faculties, such as Harvard's and Dartmouth's, opposed undergraduate business degrees. In a typical founding scenario, alumni, students, or a generous benefactor would demand a business school, and an action-oriented faculty member or business leader—often armed with only the equivalent of a cocktail-napkin plan—would take up the cause. Faculty would be gathered from various parts of the university or the business community, and would assemble courses based on their interests or career backgrounds; deans would supply faculty with such mundane stuff as students and office space.

Surveying the many types of institutions that had emerged from such improvisational beginnings by 1920, Willard E. Hotchkiss (who had helped found the business schools at Northwestern and the University of Minnesota, and served as dean at the former, before becoming dean of Stanford's new business school in 1926) saw the business school as "a very ill-defined institution. It may begin with the Freshman year; it may start only after graduation from college; or it may start anywhere in between. It may represent courses in economics regrouped and relabeled, or it may omit all so-called economic courses and center exclusively on practical courses in administration."[14] A cross-sectional sample of business schools during this period finds a mixture of many types, but three basic models are prevalent. First were those schools offering business education at the undergraduate level and starting specialized training in the first year. Their core curricula typically included Business English, Commercial Correspondence, Accounts, Office Technique, and Stenography. Such schools, which included the business schools at New York University and Northwestern in their early years, closely resembled the commercial business schools that were now being displaced by the college- or university-based business school. A second type of business school included those, like Wharton, that provided a liberal arts foundation for the first two years and then business-related courses in the final two years of undergraduate study. The third type was the graduate school of business administration, like Harvard Business School, for which an undergraduate degree was an admissions requirement.[15] The high degree of structural heterogeneity among business schools in their formative decades was to be expected in the rise of a proto-institution. Still, it meant that in most cases, university-based business education as a whole could not claim to represent much of an advance over the proprietary commercial schools.

Besides the issue of heterogeneous organizational forms, business schools in this era faced considerable operational difficulties. Many schools had to cope with overcrowded classrooms, students requiring remedial work, poorly trained teachers, and difficulty in establishing relationships with employers. Some of these weaknesses could be attributed to the rapid growth in both programs and enrollments in the early twentieth century. In this regard as well, however, the novelty of the institution of business education was a contributing factor. In any new field, fledgling organizations must create and learn new roles, develop basic administrative capabilities, establish ties to their suppliers, and generate demand for their services.[16]

Yet many business school deans, especially those heading the largest and most elite schools such as Harvard, Chicago, Michigan, and Stanford, saw even more fundamental problems than the organizational and operational ones just described. They raised questions about the essential purpose of business education in the university and sought to achieve a working consensus around ends and means so as to advance what they saw as business schools' mission. The ongoing lack of definition, meanwhile, gave rise to considerable incoherence in three areas: institutional purpose, curricula, and research. If, as Andrew Abbott contends, professional projects are successful to the extent that they are able to make certain claims about specialized knowledge and theoretical understanding, and to achieve recognition of these claims as legitimate, then the business schools of this era were substantially failing in the effort to professionalize management. Moreover, if professionalization also implies a set of shared values, business schools were failing to display a common understanding of this kind. The lack of coherence among business schools was especially problematic for advocates of the professionalization of management because this particular project was led primarily not by practitioners but by the university-based business school, which saw itself as a definer and custodian of management's professional claims. The gulf between the institution-building activity of the business schools and the life of actual working managers left room for many competing definitions of the legitimate way of preparing students for managerial work.[17] Indeed, in the first decades of business education one comes across many instances in which the incoherence of business school activities put schools at cross-purposes with one another, weakening the ability of better schools to curb the proliferation of low-quality and poorly staffed entrants to their nascent community.

While the early decades of the twentieth century produced a collection of organizations operating as university-based business schools, there was little similarity in their practices. Most business schools had devoted their early years to administrative matters—admissions policies, financial control systems, and the hiring of a teaching staff—rather than articulating standards, identifying sound methods of teaching, or developing a logical curriculum. As a result, academic coordination among schools and endeavors to formulate general standards were minimal. Each school tended its own garden, as it were, paying little attention to the commons—an approach quite antithetical to the objective of using business schools to turn management into a profession.

The primary vehicle through which the deans of the major business schools attempted to address such key challenges was an organization formed in 1916, the American Association of Collegiate Schools of Business (AACSB). To its founding members, during the period between 1916 and the eve of World War II, the AACSB was a bold organizational instrument of educational reform, one capable of creating a vanguard and a leadership for the burgeoning and unwieldy business school movement. During these years, the founding deans endeavored to transform business education into professional education, aspiring to make it truly commensurate with the emerging realities of business and the broader social transformations that business was both shaping and being shaped by. They believed that if business management were to achieve recognition as a profession, there would have to be a consensus among business schools as to what the purpose of business education should be, how this was to be reflected in the curriculum, and how faculties capable of advanced research and pedagogy should be developed. In the interest of forming such a consensus, they founded the AACSB, and to this end they attempted, sometimes successfully but often not, to direct its efforts.

Origins of the AACSB

The story of the AACSB begins in the summer of 1916, when sixteen business school deans met at Chicago's University Club to hammer out a one-page resolution creating an association dedicated to "the promotion and improvement of higher business education in North America."[18] The meeting was the result of a three-way exchange among Edwin Gay of Harvard, Leon Marshall of the University of Chicago's College of Commerce and Administration, and A. E. Swanson, the acting dean of Northwestern's School of Commerce. In the course of their communications, Gay had urged Marshall and Swanson to come up with a select list of deans who might be invited to engage in discussion of the state of business education. Gay and Marshall were particularly talented and ambitious academics, committed Progressives who saw social science and research as means to a better society. Described by his biographer as "a scholar in action," Gay had graduated from the University of Michigan in 1890 and then spent twelve years in Germany, studying under Europe's best institutional economists. After taking his doctorate in economic history in 1902, Gay was appointed a lecturer in Harvard's economics department, where he quickly became a favorite of the university's President Eliot.[19]

Recognizing Gay's entrepreneurial and administrative skills, Eliot had named him as the founding dean of Harvard's new business school in 1908. Marshall, for his part, was seen as one of the most promising scholars of his generation as a result of his work applying economic theory to the study of law and business. As one of the leading liberal economists of his time, he would later play an important role in shaping New Deal policies as a member of the National Industrial Recovery Board, which reported directly to President Franklin D. Roosevelt.[20]

When the sixteen founding deans met during that summer of 1916, there were as yet no specialized associations of either academics or practitioners dedicated exclusively to business education. There were, of course, scholars and laymen engaged in various debates about the subject, but no authoritative community was focused on imposing coherence, discipline, and structure on business schools. The deans who met in Chicago saw a need for a vehicle that would allow them to collectively tackle the challenges to business schools posed by the larger academic world, business, and society, and to bridge the gap between business education's noble aims and the practical demands of day-to-day survival. The time for emphasizing broad vision, the deans agreed, had passed. Now was the time for detailed planning, implementation, and standards. The AACSB was the first and, in the end, only meaningful attempt by deans of business schools to organize for the purpose of speaking in a coherent, collective voice and realizing their professionalization project. It was to be, for the first twenty-five years of its existence, an organization engaged in a self-conscious effort to transform business schools into genuine professional schools, and management into a genuine profession.

Following their decision to found the new association, the deans immediately got to work constructing it. Before adjourning their meeting in 1916, they set up a provisional executive committee of five deans and elected Gay as chairman.[21] Working closely with Chicago's Marshall, Gay drafted a set of minimal educational and organizational standards for the AACSB's constituent institutions and, in 1917, set a twenty-five-dollar per school membership fee. Believing that business schools needed to establish their own systems of honor and status, the provisional committee recognized the Beta Gamma Sigma society as the official scholastic honor society for business school students. To ensure the integrity of its honors system, the AACSB required that the new society's chapters be established only at member schools.[22]

Surveying the state of business education in the years just after the end of World War I, the founding deans of the AACSB saw three areas of concern that would become the primary focus of their collective activities during the interwar years: purpose and professionalism; curriculum and faculty; and research.

⊾ The Purpose of Business Schools: The AACSB's Logic of Professionalism

What set the AACSB member schools apart from other business schools was their willingness to explicitly consider the question of what was meant by professional business education. It is important to note that in the very attempt to arrive at a common definition so as to disseminate this understanding among member schools, the deans of the AACSB were themselves engaged in a process of professionalization. As sociologists studying the professions and historians of science have noted, professionalization is a function not just of the presence or absence of expertise but also of the creation of a community of interest and inquiry. By initiating an effort to define business educators themselves as a distinct group oriented toward a particular set of problems, social as well as academic, the AACSB attempted a process of professionalization within its own ranks as a means of bringing about the professionalization of management. This effort formed the core of the AACSB's agenda from its founding up until America's entry into World War II, a period in which business schools wrestled with a number of fundamental problems.

To begin with, amid the proliferation of new business schools in the early 1920s, many business school deans were appalled by a rising number of schools offering what appeared to be false and dangerous claims about the quality of their students and the education their institutions were delivering. In the view of deans of more established schools, the unconstrained growth of schools with such questionable practices undermined their project of creating a profession of management. The rapid increase in the number of business schools and programs made it all the more difficult to attain any common purpose or standards, which were a crucial part—though only a part—of the larger task of professionalizing management. The deans in the AACSB also recognized that beyond issues such as standards, curriculum, and so forth, instilling a sense of professionalism in any field—although perhaps especially in an aspiring profession like business—required enormous effort. They believed that cultivating traits such as objectivity, self-discipline, judgment, and a disinterested commitment to a larger community was among the most important goals of professional training. While deeply aware of the practical realities of business, these deans sought to develop in business school students an understanding of their own occupational activities in a larger social and moral context. They understood that this goal would require the creation within business schools of what we would now call a professional culture—something that could not be easily replicated or "scaled up" even when the best business schools had matured enough to sustain it themselves. None of the AACSB deans were under the illusion that they had, as yet, succeeded at this, and the task's daunting difficulty was sinking in.

By the mid-1920s, moreover, it was already becoming clear that while employers were increasingly enthusiastic about hiring business school students, they seemed to care very little about whether students had been inculcated with such professional attitudes as communalism, disinterestedness, and a societal orientation—norms that had been central to the rationale for creating university-based business schools in the first place. Instead, employers preferred to evaluate students on the basis of their technical skills. Discussing the reasons why employers hired business school graduates and why many business schools were not taking the notion of professionalism seriously, Columbia economist Paul Brissenden noted that several schools had raised the question of whether the goal of professionalizing management on the model of the "high" professions was attainable or even desirable:

> Many schools of business do not think they are or ought to be genuine professional schools in the sense that law schools are such. It is questioned, indeed, whether they can be professional schools in any such sense. We should have to discover an array of tools and a ritual in their use which may have as universal an application to business men as the tools and ritual put at the disposal of law students have to them in the practice of law. We shall not find anything of the sort, for the very good reasons that it does not exist. . . . But conceding the possibility . . . of making our business schools professional, there remains the question: Should it be done? Here is a very real dilemma. For the sake of putting those less fortunate non-academic groups in the non-competing category, so that we may give our students a better shot at a job, should we so shape our educational policy as to concentrate on turning out graduates who are thoroughly skilled in one or more of the more technical business disciplines? Among these disciplines are accountancy, banking practice, securities

analysis and business statistics. If we answer this question affirma-
tively we probably shall find it necessary, largely if not entirely, to
abandon our efforts to lead students to some understanding of the
nature of our modern business and industrial system and its social
significance.[23]

As Brissenden recognized, the question of whether business schools
were, or should become, genuine professional schools was, in the end, less a
matter of "tools" and "rituals" than of fundamental purpose. Harvard Business School's assistant dean, C. P. Biddle, made the centrality of purpose
in the professional logic of the AACSB quite explicit when he outlined the
choice for university business schools between training "hands" and training
"heads."[24] Both Brissenden and Biddle raised a fundamental question: did
business schools exist to give students technical skills that would help them
find employment, or to educate them about "the nature of our modern business and industrial system and its social significance"? It was a question that
might appear to juxtapose a pragmatic and an idealistic approach to business
education, and to some extent it did. Yet it would be a mistake to allow our
contemporary skepticism about the more high-minded claims of professions
to color our view of those who advocated a "social" aim for business education in these early decades. As I have argued, the idea of professionalizing
management grew from not just the economic interests and social aspirations of managers but also the ideational interests of both business leaders
and academics with a rational commitment to social reform and, in particular, to management as an institution for establishing social order. Moreover,
there appeared to be no reason in principle why business schools could not
both elevate students' conceptions of the nature and purpose of business and
give them what the University of Chicago's Leon Marshall, for example, explicitly called "vocational preparation":

> Stated in terms of subject matter and method, the collegiate school
> of business should devote itself to the study and presentation of the
> fundamental processes, conditions, and forces of business with but
> incidental attention to minor techniques. Stated in terms of voca-
> tional preparation, such a school should aim to prepare its students
> ultimately to become—(1) responsible business executives; or
> (2) professional or technical experts such as accountants, statisti-
> cians, commercial secretaries, and members of governmental
> regulatory bodies; or (3) teachers of business subjects. Stated in

terms of social outlook, a collegiate school of business should encourage students to see business tasks in the larger perspective of social values.[25]

To hold the potentially conflicting goals of producing socially minded individuals and offering vocational training in some kind of stable balance was, of course, one thing in principle and another in practice. James C. Bonbright, a faculty member at the Columbia School of Business, described the reality behind the elevated rhetoric of many early business school leaders when he complained in 1925, "Our collegiate schools of business have chosen neither a social nor a private acquisitive goal in the molding of their curricula, which are based not on philosophy but on accident. We have drifted into the convenient practice of entertaining students with what we know."[26] The AACSB, for its part, failed to adopt any detailed guidelines and policies that would have helped schools define and realize a shared professional purpose. This is evident in the different ways in which purpose and professionalism came to be defined in practice at the elite schools that largely formed the original leadership of the AACSB—schools to which others would look for models.

Columbia's Roswell C. McCrea (who had served as dean of the Wharton School from 1912 to 1916, leaving Wharton for Columbia in 1916 to become associate director of Columbia's business school and eventually its dean) was one of the AACSB deans who explicitly identified social purpose as the factor distinguishing university business schools from the trade or commercial schools that they were intended to supplant, even as he insisted that the practical realities of business must remain important in university business education. As McCrea stated in 1925, "The joining of socially motivated thinking with a knowledge of concrete, shifting reality, such as can be effected in a school of business, may well escape the puttering of the strict vocationalist on the one hand, and the futility of the closet philosopher on the other. The foundations of wise business policy can be laid in this as in no other way."[27] He also noted:

> Professional schools in other fields have faced this issue and are meeting it. Law and Medicine are noteworthy examples. Education, Dentistry, Journalism, Engineering, Architecture and Social Work are following in their train. The striking phase of the transition that is working out in these fields is a shift from the proprietary-vocational quality of earlier days to the university-professional quality of the better schools of today, with emphasis on a social goal in the education of

its practitioners. Schools of business must merge their aims and methods with this common stream of professional purpose.[28]

Perhaps the most eloquent advocate of a "social goal" for the education of
managers who would truly earn the label "professional" was Wallace Donham,
who had succeeded Edwin Gay as dean of Harvard in 1919 and who, as I
demonstrated in chapter 3, outspokenly championed the idea that management could and should become a profession comparable to the traditional
professions of medicine and law. "I have reached the conclusion," Donham
told his fellow deans in 1927, "that the greatest need of a civilization such as
ours, if it is to progress in an orderly evolution, is for socially-minded business
men. I am convinced that this social need is the sole basis which justifies our
ancient university and all of the institutions that are represented here today in
entering upon business training."[29] To call the need for "socially-minded"
business executives the "sole basis" for training managers within the university
was to say, not that business schools should not also teach technical subjects
like accounting or production, but that if conveying technical expertise were
the only purpose of business education, there would be no reason to conduct
it within the university. While Donham, as we shall see, would encounter his
share of difficulties in cultivating a socially minded orientation even for his
own school, his vision itself represented the apex of business education's aspirations for management to be accepted as not just a profession but a "learned
profession"—and one whose social mission was nothing less than redemptive.
Donham believed that the primary task of a professional school in a university
could not simply be to train students for an occupation that would gain them
a livelihood. A true professional school, he maintained, was granted special
privileges and, in turn, bound by special obligations to society. For Donham,
this meant preparing students for a career in general management and creating a distinct character for business education, which he wished to "have its
own atmosphere, its own temperament, its own standards, its own loyalties."[30]
    Donham's high-minded conception of business schools as, in effect, the
modern standard-bearers of the university's ancient civilizing mission—and of
professions as quasi-sacred callings—was, however, beginning to seem quaint
even in his own era. This is illustrated in the history of the University of Pennsylvania's Wharton School under Dean Emory R. Johnson, who served from
1919 to 1933. Wharton had initially grounded business education firmly in the
liberal arts and social sciences in its own effort to produce the kind of "socially-
minded business men" that would have pleased Donham. Subsequently, the

school had sought to create a balance among social science, general business, and specialized courses in its curriculum. During Johnson's tenure, however, Wharton began to define "professionalism" to mean technical specialization and certified expertise. "Between 1917 and 1928," as Steven Sass writes, "the detailed study of specialized business subjects flowered luxuriantly" at Wharton.[31] In 1921, the school began offering an MBA through a newly founded graduate division, although this was only, in Sass's words, "a stepped-up version of its undergraduate program of specialization."[32] Curiously, Dean Johnson had to face down opposition from alumni who saw the "social prestige" of Wharton being eroded by his program of specialization and wanted the school to return to a more generalized, liberal arts–based curriculum.[33] Sass describes the two programs in which Wharton most successfully realized Johnson's aim of specialization and professionalization:

> Johnson proposed accounting, with its rigorous discipline, practical value, and professional certification, as his model for the various specializations at the Wharton School. . . . Insurance was by far Wharton's most vigorous business specialty in the 1920s and other than accounting, was the one that advanced farthest on the road to professionalization . . . [Professor Solomon Huebner] concentrated his attention on the major analog to the public accountant in the industry—the insurance agent—and during the 1920s he led a remarkably successful movement to raise the business of life insurance sales to the level of a profession.[34]

In other business functions, however, Johnson's approach brought not crystallization of disciplines but fragmentation. As Sass also relates, Wharton's faculty in finance decided in the 1920s not to enlist in Johnson's professionalization program. The subject of marketing—which would become another staple of the functionally organized MBA curriculum once standardization of business school curricula was finally achieved in the 1950s—proved too fast-growing, because of its popularity with students, to be given a rigorous curriculum analogous to those developed for accounting and insurance, while an industry specialization like transportation, as Sass notes, "had none of that esoteric elegance or numerical clarity that distinguished accountancy or even insurance." Meanwhile, Johnson's efforts to channel undergraduates into specialized studies provoked resistance from some Wharton faculty—particularly in the social sciences and the Geography and Industry Department—who wanted to preserve the more balanced, general business curriculum that

Edmund James had originally introduced in the 1890s.[35] Indeed, as Sass points out, the whole specialization program at Wharton flew in the face of Joseph Wharton's original plan of "educating general business leaders, those who would control the major enterprises of the nation and would employ the various professionals that Johnson hoped to train."[36] Yet an effort at curricular reform in the 1920s (led by future Wharton dean Joseph Willits) largely failed, and Wharton's new specialized curriculum remained in place well into the 1950s—while Johnson's efforts "to align Wharton's various business programs with certified professions" would also (except in the cases of accounting and insurance) prove a failure in the end.[37]

Dartmouth's Tuck School of Administration and Finance also seized on particular aspects of professionalism while eschewing any particular focus on the roles and responsibilities of professionals in society. As I argued in chapter 3, the founders and early leaders of the Tuck School showed less interest in actually transforming management into a profession than in elevating the status and self-regard of managers to a level equal to that of traditional professionals. Tuck's Dean Harlow Person (a protégé of Fredrick Taylor who served in the deanship from 1906 to 1919)[38] sought to build at the school the foundations of a social network that would introduce an esprit de corps among its graduates, thus enhancing their sense of group cohesion and group identity. One of Person's ideas was that the school could further such cohesion and identity by providing Tuck students with distinct living and learning spaces:

> For the purpose of developing a group esprit, [Tuck] has its own building, and its own library. . . . In the two college courses into which it sends its students they are handled as a separate group of men; are seated as a separate group in lecture periods, and meet as a separate group for quiz purposes. This results not only in the development of group esprit but in a scholarship of better average than that of college groups. The Tuck School has built and furnished in its basement a lounging-room intended to serve the Tuck students as a distinct group in the way that College Hall serves the college as a whole.[39]

Other features of the Tuck School under Person's leadership testify to his concern with both acculturating students to practice and ensuring that the preparation they received at the school would help them to advance their careers. For example, "Every possible method is employed," Person stated, "to enable students to meet business men—lecturers—personally, and the lectures of such men are followed by a simple luncheon intended to enable the second-year men to meet the lecturers informally." Thesis work "embodying original research" and "representing [one's] work in the field of study" was to be based on fieldwork at "industrial plants" so that "our students shall see and feel such a plant in action."[40] (Tuck dropped the thesis requirement after 1946.) Finally, the Tuck School sought to create a demand for the students it educated by establishing the first business school recruiting office.[41] The need for the school to help students find employment was one of several "problems" that Person perceived as unique to graduate or professional education:

> [A] problem arising out of the relations of the School to the student is the problem of finding for students the opportunities for business service to which they are respectively adapted. We believe that one responsibility of the School is to act as a clearing-house, a labor intelligence bureau, to bring together worthy young men and concerns seeking good apprenticeship material. . . . Not only is there involved the problem of securing some position for the graduate; there is involved the problem of securing the position for which the graduate is adapted, of adjusting capacity to serve.[42]

Yet even though offering this kind of opportunity to students could have been undertaken as part of a broader professionalizing mission intended as a means of serving society, Person was unambiguous in his view of the school's chief duty: "Our judgment is that our primary obligation is to the student, and the first and largest draft which the instructor should make on his store of time and energy should be on behalf of the individual student. We attempt to develop in our instructing staff the feeling that instruction is not something formal but is a personal responsibility for the personal success of every individual student. That, we conceive, as also our largest public service."[43]

Person did go on to note that "without impairing that obligation to the individual student, we believe other forms of public service possible and obligatory." The essential public service that the school could provide, he argued, was to teach students to "develop the power to apply principles to the solution of business problems . . . which will some day be of service to all of us."[44] Person had a similar approach to the issue of professional ethics, stating: "We do not attempt any formal instruction in business ethics. We believe that the formality and artificiality of a formal course in business ethics would defeat its very purpose. But in every course it is the aim of every instructor, I know, to inspire in his students a conception of the nobility of the profession of the business man and of his responsibility to his fellow-men and to society."[45] The three paradigms of professional education in business represented by Harvard, Wharton, and Tuck—with their emphasis on general management and social responsibility, technical specialization, and career preparation and status, respectively—not only represent the dominant approaches to the all-important question of purpose among business schools generally in their formative decades. These three components have remained, ever since, in a delicate juxtaposition within business schools, with one or the other element in the triad dominating the other two at particular schools and in particular periods. As if the challenge of reconciling the tension between ideals and norms, on the one hand, and environmental realities and pressures, on the other, were not difficult enough for business schools in their fledgling phase, questions of purpose had to be resolved not only at the level of mission or aspiration but also in the thorny details of forging curricula and faculties.

Curriculum and Faculty Development

Choices about the fundamental purpose of business schools also implied choices about curriculum. If business schools were to create a profession of management with a fundamental mission of service to society, deans and faculty had to decide what particular forms of instruction and subject matter would best advance this end. How should they incorporate what Roswell McCrea called a "social goal" into the study of subjects such as accounting or transportation? Did formal ethics courses necessarily entail what Harlow Person called "formality and artificiality"? If, on the other hand, a school pursued technical specialization (in the manner of Wharton) as the avenue to the professionalization of management, or was concerned—as the early business schools obviously needed to be—about producing students who would be employable in managerial positions, how could they create a curriculum that would accomplish this end while differentiating college or university schools of business from trade or proprietary commercial schools? These were daunting questions for a generation of business school leaders with no models or precedents to guide them. Moreover, confronted with the enormous task of creating a generalized and systematic body of knowledge that was both abstract enough to have academic legitimacy and concrete enough to be useful to managers, the educators responsible for shaping

Table 4.2

Distribution of Courses across Forty-one Business Schools in 1928

Number of Distinct Subjects	Institutions
15–25	6
26–50	16
51–75	7
76–100	6
101–125	2
126–150	0
151–175	1
176–200	0
201–217	3

business education also had to find academics or practitioners who could formulate and teach it effectively.

A certain chaotic quality to the process of curriculum formation in the early days of college and university business schools can be attributed to both the newness of the enterprise and the speed with which business schools grew in the post–World War I years. Courses proliferated rapidly in the decade from 1910 to 1920 as schools attempted simply to keep pace with one another. The University of Chicago, for example, offered 16 courses in 1910 and 81 in 1921. Harvard's Graduate School of Business Administration expanded its course offerings from 31 to 47 during this same period, and Michigan moved from 23 to 36. Table 4.2 illustrates the high variance in the number of courses across the 41 largest business schools in this period.

Faculty composition was similarly uneven. For example, an AACSB survey conducted in 1920 listed "one large business school" at a private university as having eighty instructors, while another school, with a comparable enrollment, at a large state university had only two instructors teaching nineteen different courses. Ohio State's C. O. Ruggles (who would join the Harvard faculty in 1928) commented, "It is common knowledge in this group [the AACSB members] that very few if any of our schools of business are fully manned."[46] Table 4.3 shows that at a sample of original AACSB schools for which complete faculty data could be collected, more than 50 percent of the faculty were part-time lecturers and adjunct faculty. Also evident is a fair amount of variation from one school to another, suggesting that differential resources played a role in how business schools composed and organized

Table 4.3

Distribution of Faculty Degrees and Status in 1928

	Terminal Degree					Status	
	Ph.d.	A.M.	B.A./B.S	J.D.	C.P.A.	Full-time	Lecturers
Boston University	10	13	34	2	1	32	28
California, University of	8	1	1	0	1	9	2
Chicago, University of	8	4	3	2	2	7	12
Columbia University	16	4	2	2	2	17	9
Dartmouth College	2	7	1	1	1	9	3
Harvard University	10	25	4	3	1	20	23
Illinois, University of	17	28	16	4	4	23	46
Michigan, University of	3	6	0	1	0	6	4

their faculties. Of the 250 teaching faculty among this group, fewer than 30 percent had a Ph.D. The faculty teaching load was also quite high. Teaching loads averaged twelve hours in the classroom per week, with some schools reporting loads exceeding twenty.

Most full-time instructors in business, meanwhile, were graduates of the institutions that employed them, and almost all of them were trained in subjects other than business. At the 1919 AACSB meetings, Dean James Hagerty of Ohio State pointed out that "graduate students were coming out of our universities having taken almost exclusively orthodox courses in economics and . . . were going into our schools of business to teach technical courses in fields which they had no opportunity to study."[47] The dean of Boston University's business school, Everett Lord, was trained in English literature but taught business ethics.

In wrestling with the practical realities of creating courses and curricula for these faculty members to teach, business schools faced a number of problems, some of them quite mundane. One practical barrier to the development of adequate courses and curricula was the paucity of published works that could be used as textbooks. An examination of the Harvard Business School's Baker Library catalog—the largest and oldest catalog of business publications in the world—finds for 1916 few textbooks focused on management education. In the field of marketing, a limited number of government-issued pamphlets about specialized marketing were available, many of them pertaining to agriculture. A compendium of articles in the field of marketing, titled *Some Problems in Market Distribution*, was compiled in 1915 by Arch

W. Shaw, a part-time lecturer at Harvard and the publisher of *System*, the predecessor to *BusinessWeek*.[48] Shaw's book enjoyed some success, if only because it was the first usable one in the field.[49] A book called *Elements of Statistical Method*, published by W. I. King in 1912, was used in some business schools. In 1915, Wharton professor Herbert W. Hess published *Productive Advertising*, a book that managed to attract some attention and reviews. In the area of accounting, a number of company training manuals in bookkeeping were used in classes, along with a 1915 book called *Accounts*, by W. M. Cole, that outlined the basic structure of double-entry bookkeeping. In the field of management per se, many courses were linked to the subject of production and built on, or simply adopted wholesale, the principles of scientific management. Thus texts that had been developed for use by practicing managers, such as Fredrick Taylor's *Principles of Scientific Management* (1911) and Frank B. Gilbreth's *Primer of Scientific Management* (1912), were used in several business school courses.

Given the scarcity of usable classroom material, Harvard began to experiment with an alternative pedagogy using cases for classroom discussion—a method pioneered at Harvard Law School in the 1870s. The case method, or "problem-centered" teaching as it was sometimes described, as adapted for business studies involved highly interactive class discussion of a particular business problem. In a letter to Dean Gay, New York publisher Donald Scott, the chairman of Harvard Business School's visiting committee, urged the school to adopt this pedagogy:

> [T]here should be a considerable extension of what in the Law
> School is called the 'case system' to the teaching of the Business
> School. . . . The Business School should not consist simply of more
> specialized courses in economics. It should endeavor to show the
> student the business world as it is today, and to point out the funda-
> mental principles underlying all trades and commerce. . . . To do this
> means less teaching of theory and more education of principles from
> actual examples. Discussion in the class-room should be encouraged
> even more than it is at present.[50]

At a higher level of difficulty, business schools wrestled with what the basic rationale of their curricula should be, often with only the vaguest of general guiding principles. For example, the University of Chicago business school's *Announcements* for 1922 offered this explanation for a wide-ranging curriculum encompassing both the natural and social sciences: "The business executive administers his business under conditions imposed by his environment, both physical and social. The student should accordingly have an understanding of the physical environment. This justifies attention to the earth sciences. He should also have an understanding of the social environment and must accordingly give attention to civics, law, economics, social psychology, and other branches of the social sciences."[51]

While the idea that managers should have a broad education was widespread and had informed the structures and academic programs of such pioneering schools as Wharton, Tuck, and Harvard, the desire for breadth (often expressed, as we saw in chapter 3, in attempts to ground business education in the liberal arts), combined with the lack of developed subject matter in business fields per se, left many programs lacking in coherence or underlying logic. The most comprehensive and concerted attempt to create a program that would give business students an understanding of the social environment took place at Wharton, in its early experiments with the liberal arts and the social sciences, but this effort ended somewhat abruptly with Emory Johnson's accession to the deanship in 1919. At the University of Chicago's business school, the required curriculum that Leon Marshall envisioned was built on a broad foundation of the humanities and social sciences, with the objective of helping students develop an integrated perspective on business's obligations to the rest of society.[52] With the exception of economics, the behavioral sciences were in their infancy, doctoral programs in business administration (which might have produced teachers and researchers able to advance the development of the management discipline) were not widespread, and, in general, "no one had firm conclusions concerning the nature of a curriculum which would prepare students for careers in business."[53]

Despite this lack of "firm conclusions," by the 1920s a few distinct patterns were discernible in business school curricula. Certain course requirements were more or less widely shared, as illustrated by table 4.4, which shows the most frequently required courses for programs at the thirty-four AACSB member schools that provided data on this in 1928.

An analysis of the curriculum of business schools across sixty-five schools during this decade finds three fairly distinct models of curriculum design. The first involved having existing disciplines offer courses that were relevant to business students. Examples of such courses included history classes on the development of business in the United States, mathematics classes on accounting and finance, and English classes on business correspondence. An assemblage of such courses would constitute a business major

Table 4.4
Course Requirements across Thirty-four Business Schools in 1928

	No. of Schools Requiring
Accounting	34
Elementary economic theory	34
English	34
Law	31
Financial organization	24
Foreign language	19
Managerial finance	19
Mathematics	19
Statistics	19
Markets	18
Physical environment	16
Science	15
General business organization	12
Government	12
Psychology	11
Social science	9
Advanced economic theory	6
Labor	6
Social control	6
Public finance	4
Production	3
Risk	3
Personnel	2
Philosophy	2

for undergraduates or a program of graduate business study. The second model consisted of training for specific jobs or industries. Schools offered courses for particular jobs, such as clerk or banker, and on industries such as railroading and lumbering. The third model was the attempt to translate into curricular terms a "science of administration."

In 1910, Dartmouth's Harlow Person made the first systematic attempt at articulating a set of organizing principles for a business school curriculum founded on this third model. With a design based on the hierarchical structure of business firms, Person's proposal can be viewed as a rough prototype of the functionally based curriculum found in most business schools today. Dividing business activities into three "zones"—administration, management, and operations—Person detailed the knowledge and training necessary for effective performance in each. In operations (Zone 3), he reasoned, workers and clerks needed little advanced training and would learn their skills in secondary schools and on the job. The work of "administration" (Zone 1), performed by top executives and directors, required "ripe judgment" rather than technical proficiency. Since few people reach this level of authority and it is difficult to know *ex ante* who will eventually be promoted to become a senior executive, Person thought that higher education in business should be focused on "management" (Zone 2). The managers and supervisors in this crucial middle of the organization constituted the group that Person believed could benefit most from advanced business training. Training at this middle-management level would emphasize subjects such as scientific management and accounting.[54]

As Person experimented with this approach at Dartmouth, Harvard developed its curriculum, in a process of trial-and-error, to emphasize education in general management and organizational administration as opposed to job-specific training. In a memorandum he sent to the Harvard business faculty, Dean Donham outlined this general principle by declaring that the goal of the curriculum was to train students in the exercise of judgment rather than in routine procedures. Marketing professor Melvin Copeland, the author of the school's first casebook, saw this memo as the critical institutionalizing moment for the general management perspective for which Harvard Business School would become famous.[55]

A second, concurrent approach to developing a business school curriculum resting on scientific principles was to root it in economics. When the first university-based business schools were inaugurated the discipline of economics had appeared to be a logical foundation for business studies, and economics professors played key roles in the establishment of prominent business schools including Wharton, Tuck, and Harvard. Introductory economics courses were initially included in many schools' curricula. Yet a number of these same schools also made deliberate decisions, at a relatively early point, to establish their independence from their universities' economics departments, which in many instances were turning away from institutional economics—focused on history and grounded in empirical observation—toward the discipline's neoclassical school, which emphasized formal modeling and theory. Many business school faculty trained in economics, however, instinctively preferred the clean, abstract models of the discipline to the messy realities of complex systems like organizations, and the relationship between business schools and economics remained uneasy and unsettled.

To understand the tensions in this relationship, we must take note of what is sometimes called the *Methodenstreit*, or "battle of the methods," that began within the discipline of economics around 1880 in Europe and continued into the 1920s, spilling over into the United States by about 1900.[56] The main European antagonists were the Austrian economist Carl Menger and the German institutional economist Gustav von Schmoller, leaders of two intellectual traditions with contending definitions of what constituted the discipline. Menger, a brilliant economic theorist, argued for a narrowly delineated scope for economic theory and methods, with particular emphasis on developing a general theory of exchange and markets; these phenomena needed to be studied, he argued passionately, separately from society as a whole. The basic ideas of the Austrian school formed what is now called neoclassical economics, an approach to analyzing economic phenomena that relies on a small set of selective principles, theory development through deduction, and a focus on rational and self-interested individual actors. In his review of the evolution of economic thought, Richard Swedberg presents Menger and his likeminded Austrian colleagues as sharply critical of their German institutional counterparts. As Swedberg notes, Menger once compared an institutional economist to "someone who came to a building site, dumped some building material on the ground, and called himself an architect."[57] Institutional economists, who often incorporated history, political science, and sociology into their analysis of economic behavior, were no less mordant, describing neoclassical economics as an assemblage of useless "Robinson Crusoe stories."[58] In contrast to neoclassical economists—who saw institutions such as markets, contracts, trade, and property rights as examples of the outgrowths of individual behavior—institutional economists emphasized the role of power, values, belief systems, and historical contingency in their development.

The intellectual battle in Europe for the soul of economics spilled over into the United States around the turn of the century. On the one side stood preeminent American institutional economists such as Thorstein Veblen, John R. Commons, Edwin Gay, and Wesley Mitchell, all of whom were trained in the German institutional tradition. Gay, who did his doctoral work in Germany, and Mitchell, a student of Veblen's, feared that the growing popularity of the neoclassical school in American economics departments would result in the development of, in Mitchell's words, "an academic discipline, cultivated by professors and neglected by [people] of action, modest in its pretensions to practical usefulness, more conspicuous for consistency and erudition than for insight."[59]

At the Wharton School prior to the 1920s, institutional economists Edmund James (a cofounder of the American Economic Association who once described American neoclassical economics as "pure and unadulterated teaching of dogma") and Simon Patten (who held the directorship of Wharton from 1896 to 1912 and tried to lead the school into the thick of the Progressive era's battle for reform) had included institutional economics in the curriculum as part of the school's larger effort to create a socially responsible elite for the administration of both private and public institutions.[60] Yet even as Patten and his successor as head of Wharton, Roswell McCrea, attempted to hew to Patten's belief that there could be "no full discussion of economic problems without bringing political moral principles into relation with the economic,"[61] institutional economists in America were losing the battle for supremacy to the neoclassical school. By 1920, American economics had taken a sharp turn in the direction of a neoclassicism that successfully privileged deductive theory over the study of economic phenomena in relation to historical and social forces. The penetrating insights of institutional economics in its heyday from 1890 to 1920 would ultimately fail to shape the direction of the discipline in the twentieth century, and scholars who continued to work in this tradition would be marginalized, to the point where they could be described by Nobel Prize economist Ronald Coase in 1984 as producing a "mass of descriptive material waiting for a theory, or a fire."[62]

The turn toward neoclassical economics, with its combination of parsimonious theory, elegant models, and reliance on mathematics, enabled the discipline to begin cultivating an image in the academy as the most complete of the social sciences and the one closest to high-status scientific disciplines such as physics and chemistry.[63] With the aid of an effective institutional infrastructure, economics began to achieve a similarly privileged position outside the university in the formulation and implementation of public policy. In 1916, for example, the Rockefeller Foundation helped start the Institute for Government Research, the first such organization to systematically use economic research in formulating public policy.[64]

Even as the neoclassical school gained the upper hand within the discipline of economics, however, some business school leaders—still imbued with an institutional perspective on the subject—argued for the importance of economics as they conceived of it, perhaps hoping that the institutional school's "consideration of the living items," as Veblen once put it, would find a more supportive environment in business schools.[65] As dean of the Columbia School of Business in the 1920s, Roswell McCrea, another economist in the institutional mold, argued that the "permeating influence" of economics (by which he meant the institutional variety) was "the sine qua non of a 'professional' school of business." As McCrea stated:

> Economics, where ever else it may or may not belong, does belong in the school of business. Both business and economics need to be saved from themselves. Without the presence of economics in some vital form, the work of a school of business is likely to degenerate into detailed description of business organization and procedure, with no organizing principle other than the possible one of search for effective competitive devices, and with no clear vision of the social goal of business activity. And economics, divorced from business, is too likely to spend itself either in closet philosophizing by traditional modes, altogether too little affected with a present interest, or in fortifying predilections regarding public policy with broadly garnered data too remote from the intimate, work-a-day world of fresh experience to yield much more than a crop of articles, books, and book reviews. If schools of business realize their opportunities, the economic theory of the future will grow out of their researches and will be formulated by their teachers.[66]

Explicitly articulating the link between curricular choices (like whether or not to include economics) and the questions of fundamental purpose that were never far from his mind, McCrea also noted that "[s]chools of business are gradually being divorced from departments of economics in which they had their origins. A consequence is that schools of business face a choice between that type of curriculum and of an educational goal, which stresses the social purpose of business activity, and that which casually accepts the pecuniary motivation of business and confines attention to details of private practice and policy."[67] Yet because of the new dominance of theoretical economics and its disconnection from managerial problems, it seemed clear to other business school deans in the 1920s, as well as to many of their faculty, that economics could not, on its own, be the foundation upon which a new administrative science could be built. In describing economics' limitations, Donham of Harvard saw that the theoretical elegance of economics came at the cost of an unrealistic description of organizational affairs.[68] Describing the evolution of the teaching and research methods at Harvard between 1915 and 1922, Donham said:

> [T]he objective of our research changed from the collection of materials for the illustration of known principles into the ascertainment of new principles. . . . I gradually came to question whether we could continue to think of business as applied economics. We found that even though the men we sent out to gather the facts of business problems went with the definite primary errand of recording and putting on paper economic facts, facts they brought back did not stay economic. There were all sorts of things entering into the situations that were not within the concepts and the abstractions to which the economist was . . . limiting his thinking. All kinds of non-economic factors and many non-engineering and non-legal factors broke these boundaries. We made the discovery that while two and two in mathematics may always be four, two and two plus the X of human relations and other "imponderables" involved in any situation is never four . . . it gradually became obvious that a new conceptual framework was required.[69]

Stanford economics professor Eliot Mears, who would join the university's Graduate School of Business after its establishment in 1925, voiced a similar sentiment. Writing in the *American Economic Review* in 1923, Mears saw business education as "the most startling development during the twentieth century in American higher education," one with the potential to dramatically improve society. Yet the problem with it, he thought, was a tendency to emphasize economic theory in teaching the subject: "Economics is no more inclusive of commerce than is mathematics of engineering, or biology of medicine, or ethics of law. . . . Our experience of the past fifteen years has taught us that there is an entirely different spirit behind the courses in economics and those in business subjects. In the teaching of political economy, the fundamental considerations relate to questions of production, exchange, and price, viewed largely from the writings of a few individuals who have reasoned brilliantly but abstractly."

As a result, Mears concluded, the study of business "must be approached through distinct types of courses and by different types of instructors."[70] As Harvard's Melvin Copeland would recall years later, "a hypothetical world of virtually perfect foresight and complete information where all resources were freely mobile and all tastes and preferences were assumed to be God-given and fixed" was of little use to training managers who would operate in an environment "without perfect foresight and whose customers and competitors were far from static."[71] A professor of finance from Ohio State University's business school, Henry E. Hoagland, was even harsher, caricaturing theoretical economics as "point-of-view economics" and "make-believe economics," and arguing that it was more useful to its faculty devotees than to students. As Hoagland stated: "It permits finality of judgment so essential to academic complacency. It requires no laboratory test to validate its assumptions. Indeed it brooks no effort at validation of so-called economic theories, since the economists' marathon bears no definite relationship to the series of dashes experienced by the business man. It enables the poor overworked professor to conserve his energies by using the same grist for various mills."[72]

Despite criticisms such as these pointing to the shortcomings of theoretical economics for the education of managers, economists became an increasingly significant presence on business school faculties in the course of the 1920s. Among all of the existing disciplines, economics, with its focus on markets and strong quantitative orientation, was seen by some scholars as deserving of a prominent place in business school curricula. Table 4.5 shows that only accounting surpassed economics as a specialization among business school faculty members between 1925 and 1930, while the number of faculty with a specialization in economics nearly doubled over this period. Business schools in the 1920s (even those that, like Harvard, resisted the trend) drew many of their faculty members from economics departments, which had become the most reliable source for new business school faculty.[73] Especially at schools like Tuck, Wharton, Columbia, and Harvard, many faculty members were young doctoral students who had started pursuing degrees in economics but whose interests extended into business.

Given the range of curricular models among business schools, and the lack of agreement as to the purpose and means of professional graduate education in business that this implied, it is not surprising that one of the AACSB's earliest actions was to appoint a committee to examine the state of teaching in business schools and to resolve the curricular issue. The committee, assembled in 1920, consisted of an august group of business school deans, including Harvard's Donham (as chairman), Columbia's McCrea, and Chicago's Marshall. A survey of seventy-eight schools, organized by the committee, produced some rather sobering results that eventually became the basis of a report written by Tuck's Alvin Dodd in 1922. The report highlighted the considerable diversity among AACSB schools in terms of the number of faculty employed and the

Table 4.5

Faculty Fields of Specialization in 1925 and 1930 for AACSB Member Schools

1925		1930	
Faculty Fields of Specialization	Number of Faculty	Faculty Fields of Specialization	Number of Faculty
Accounting	176	Accounting	249
Advertising	43	Advertising	60
Agricultural Economics	8	Banking	93
Brokerage	3	Brokerage	4
Business Admininistration	33	Business Administration	15
Business Conditions	1	Business Cycles and Forecasting	22
Business Cycles and Forecasting	18		
Business English	20	Business Education	8
Business Education	7	Business English	45
		Business Ethics	3
Business Finance	62	Business Finance	139
Business Law	58	Business Law	79
Business Policy	6	Business Organization and Management	73
Chamber of Commerce	2		
City Planning	1	Business Policy	5
Commerce	8	Civic and Trade Association Work	4
Commercial and Economic Geography	28	Commerce	6
		Commercial and Economic Geography	50
Credits and Collections	12		
Direct Mail Sales	4	Credit	16
Economic History	19	Economic History	49
Economics	105	Economics	194
English	11	Factory Management	2
Ethics of Business	1	Foreign Trade	47
Factory Management	3	Government and Business	6
Foreign Trade	43	History of Economics	7
French	6	Industrial Relations	14
German	2	Insurance	49
Government and Business	6	International Law	4
History of Economics	2	Investments	35
Industrial Organization and Management	17	Journalism	25

Table 4.5 (Cont.)

1925		1930	
Faculty Fields of Specialization	Number of Faculty	Faculty Fields of Specialization	Number of Faculty
Industrial Relations	10	Labor	48
Insurance (Life and Property)	32	Marketing	103
Investments	22	Mathematics	12
Journalism	11	Merchandising	43
Labor (History and Problems)	26	Monopolies and Trusts	8
Manufacturing Industries	3	Office Management	14
Marketing	55	Personnel Administration and Management	31
Mathematics	8		
Merchandising	21	Political Science	13
Money and Banking	47	Psychology	21
Office Management	9	Public Finance and Financial History	62
Personnel Management	22		
Political Science	14	Public Speaking	6
Psychology	16	Public Utilities	35
Public Finance	33	Real Estate	35
Public Speaking	1	Research	23
Public Utilities	15	Risk and Risk Bearing	2
Real Estate	11	Salesmanship	25
Research	8	Statistics	72
Risk and Risk Bearing	2	Stock and Produce Exchanges	7
Salesmanship	25		
Science	2	Teaching of Commercial Subjects (Stenography and Typewriting)	9
Secretarial Training	12		
Sociology	15	Traffic Management	3
Spanish	6	Transportation	49
Statistics	31	Trusts and their Administration	9
Stenography and Typewriting	4		
Stock and Produce Exchanges	6		
Trade Associations	1		
Transportation	38		

Source: AACSB Directory of the Instructional Staffs of the Member Schools

number of courses offered. Of the schools surveyed, only twenty-eight could be said to be distinct business schools, the remainder being offshoots of existing departments. Twelve of the schools offered courses only in general business subjects, five offered highly specialized courses for specific jobs and functions, and thirty-three offered both. The remaining schools did not fit any easily definable category and had curricula consisting largely of nonmanagerial courses like geography. One member of the committee bitingly summarized the general state of business education in 1922: "Granted that business teaching of the higher order is a comparatively new factor in collegiate work; that the supply of competent instructors is but a little of the immediate need; and that the stipends of these instructors are almost invariably niggardly and unattractive; granted all of this, nothing of it appears in documents before us and nothing could surpass the cocksureness with which these high-sounding courses are dangled before expectant youth."[74]

Upon receiving the first draft of the report from Dodd, Donham immediately requested that its findings be toned down. He did not believe that it would serve business schools' interests to dwell on such issues or even to publicize such findings. About to embark on a capital campaign to fund the construction of a separate campus for the business school at Harvard, Donham likely had unstated concerns about the report's potential for discrediting business education as a whole. Writing to committee members to recommend edits, he stated:

> I am inclined to recommend a modification of your report with the
> view of reducing it to a summary of the bare facts without attempting
> to draw conclusions or to pass critical judgments. I would eliminate
> illustrative references to individual institutions, for even if the names
> of the institutions are not given, they may be identified in some cases,
> with the result that tender toes may feel that they are stepped on. . . .
> In conclusion, may I say that while the report is extremely interesting,
> it does not impress me as being primarily constructive. Your criticism
> is certainly not misplaced, but its weakness, if there is any, seems to lie
> in an assumption that well defined standards of business education
> have been established. In other words, who shall say what the yard-
> stick of comparison should be? Not only are standards lacking, but is
> it not desirable that their precise definition should be deferred until
> the institutions have had longer experience and have drawn their
> lessons from further experimentation and measurement results? The

Lord knows that here is plenty of confusion, superficiality, and need for improvement. But the fact remains that the institutions have been overwhelmed by students and are sorely handicapped by lack of qualified instructors. Many of the state institutions are doing things that they do not want to do and in ways that are distasteful to them, but they are under pressure from their constituency which seems to leave them no alternatives. All of these, [in my opinion,] are reasons for exercising patience. But at the same time, I strongly believe that they offer a splendid opportunity for such an organization as yours [AACSB] to do a constructive service.[75]

Two years later, in 1924, Donham would again describe the inchoate state of teaching in business schools as a necessary stage of experimentation, noting, "There exists in business [education] today a noticeable lack of standardization which, I believe, at this stage of development a very healthy sign . . . Widely different teaching methods are being experimented with."[76] Dartmouth's President E. M. Hopkins argued the same point in a speech to the deans of the AACSB schools in 1926, stating, "It is an extremely desirable situation which we have in the country at the present time in this the greatest educational experiment the world has ever known, now being undertaken in the United States. We have a remarkably happy situation in that education is not standardized with us and that there is little probability that it will become standardized."[77] To be sure, not everyone was as willing as were Donham and Hopkins to let a thousand flowers bloom: speaking at the AACSB meeting in 1926, the dean of New York University's business school, Wellington Taylor, questioned the fundamental intellectual quality of the business school curriculum (and of business school students) when he noted that there remained a "question [of] whether the subject matter offered is graduate work, whether business training has developed far enough to enable Graduate Schools of Business Administration to give bona fide graduate work, and whether the students who come to these schools are on the whole qualified to pursue graduate work, if such can be offered. To put it more bluntly, to consider whether Graduate Schools of Business Administration are offering graduate work, and whether they are offering work to graduate students."[78]

Overall, however, it would take the Great Depression to create a greater sense of urgency among the deans about the need for common standards to improve the quality of business education and enable business schools to achieve their original goals. Meanwhile, in addition to the challenges of recruiting faculty and fashioning a curriculum, leaders of the early business schools saw a need to create—again virtually from scratch—another function they believed critical to the establishment of business schools as genuine professional schools.

Creating a Research Function

Almost from the very beginning, the members of the AACSB felt that establishing a protocol for conducting research was critical to the eventual success of management education. As I argued in chapter 3, the leaders of the business school movement saw the establishment of a research function for business schools, tied to the new American university's own missions of research and public service as well as teaching, as critical to their quest for acceptance as a legitimate part of the university. In the early 1920s, University of Michigan president Marion Leroy Burton stated the conventional case for research as "a primary function of a true university." "Only as scholars in every field are making contributions to our knowledge of the world," Burton declared, "and only as mankind gradually but surely acquires a mastery of the universe, have we reason to hope for that progress upon which civilization ultimately rests. Moreover, it may be said with some show of truth that the teaching efficiency of a university is intimately related to its research activities." Burton also argued that most business schools would not enjoy their current level of support if research were neglected: "Schools of business cannot overlook the fact that if they are to receive support either through legislative appropriations or through endowments they must justify their existence not only by the product which they turn out but also by their attitude toward the problems of research and certain other extramural activities."[79]

The deans of the AACSB, for their part, saw that research in the field of business was critical to giving business schools their desired standing as recognized peers of professional schools in fields like medicine. An AACSB report in 1924 underscored that if business schools were to improve their academic and professional standing, research would need to become a central part of their activities as it was for professions already served by established professional and scientific associations: "The American Medical Association and certain scientific societies representing phases of agriculture and engineering have been the natural channels through which the benefits of scientific research could be incorporated into the course of study. These societies have insisted for example upon certain educational standards and upon adequate laboratory facilities before they would endorse an institution's curriculum. In business there is no organization comparable to these scientific societies."[80]

Many of the AACSB's members believed that the problems of curriculum in business schools were intimately linked to the lack of fundamental research. Ohio State's Ruggles argued that if "certain business courses are at present somewhat below standard in educational value, it may be simply because not sufficient research has been carried on in the fields which these courses represent to enable us to determine whether these new additions to our curricula are fads or are essential in business education."[81] Ruggles also opined that one reason for the poor quality of business school instructors was that only a few did any research at all. As he stated, "There is some evidence to sustain the contention that any person who hopes to become an effective teacher over a long period of years must constantly give evidence that he is not only at home in his field but is doing his part in expanding that field. . . . Consequently, research work lies at the very basis of our whole enterprise. In fact, our capacity to secure and to retain men of the very first rank upon our faculties will depend largely upon our research facilities."[82]

Business schools responded to such perceptions by trying in various ways to build up their own research capabilities. By the early 1920s, many of the largest AACSB member schools were carrying out some type of "research" program. The University of Chicago's Leon Marshall, whose program for social science research as a means of public service was described in the preceding chapter, implemented a plan allowing several members of his faculty to devote themselves entirely to research for the summer quarter. (Marshall also believed that research activities were the purview not only of faculty but of students, and decreed that all of his school's graduates would be expected to contribute in their own individual ways to increasing the general fund of knowledge in the social sciences and/or to business scholarship.) Marshall had launched the first Ph.D. program in a business school in 1920 and followed that up, in 1922, by founding the *Journal of Business* to publish academic research (by faculty and students) on business topics. In order to demonstrate that they were undertaking "research" and to disseminate the results, many other business schools began to establish magazines, business reviews, and other types of publications ranging from occasional reports to leaflets; these publications presented everything from faculty research projects to summaries of facts about certain industries or general economic conditions. By the end of 1929, sixteen AACSB member schools were publishing business magazines or reviews of some sort. Their noneconomic motives varied from what one AACSB study of business school publications called "a sincere wish to serve the business general public" to the desire for "a dignified and effective medium" for helping to establish management's credentials as a bona fide profession. For most, however, the "dominant motive of the university presidents and financial officers [in publishing business periodicals] was advertising."[83]

A review of the AACSB's proceedings also finds deans using the term *research* quite loosely. One AACSB school defined research as "the gathering of material by the faculty with the assistance of advanced students to be used either in residence classes or in extension courses, the carrying on of investigations or the study by the faculty of the actual conduct of business along given lines."[84] The word was used to describe both formal studies of a specific business or industry (such as cost studies done at Harvard on the shoe retailing industry, or a study by Northwestern's business school of meatpacking practices) and contract work for particular firms. Some AACSB member schools argued that they should be identified as research schools in AACSB materials even if their research yielded no published products: "Under such a plan for research there might be much investigation which would not necessarily emerge in published form in bulletins or books."[85]

Business school research in its early decades was carried out not primarily by faculty but by independently staffed research bureaus. The Bureau of Business Research at Harvard was the model for such research organizations. Established in 1911, the bureau was originally intended by Dean Edwin Gay to collect and compile statistical data on a variety of industries. Gay explained the inspiration for its founding:

> One afternoon in April 1911, A. W. Shaw [a lecturer at the school] and I were walking across the Harvard Yard after class. The conversation turned to the importance of scientific research in the field of distribution.
>
> "What is needed," I said, "is a quantitative measurement for the marketing side of distribution."
>
> "Why don't you get it?" asked Mr. Shaw.
>
> And thereupon the Bureau was launched. I remember that one point that was emphasized in the conversation was that such a bureau is an essential to a school that intends to be entirely a graduate school. It offers a real opportunity to gather, on a scientific basis, everyday facts about business.[86]

The bureau's first project was collecting cost data on the retail shoe industry. In 1914, it collected data on retail grocers, in 1915 on wholesale shoe firms, in 1916 on wholesale grocers, in 1917 on retail general stores. After Gay stepped down as dean, his successor, Wallace Donham, shifted the emphasis at the bureau (after a successful small-scale experiment, initiated in December of 1920) to collecting material for teaching cases on the subject of labor relations. This effort was sufficiently successful to result in a rapid increase in the scope of this activity. By the late 1920s, Harvard's Bureau of Business Research employed "20 to 30 field agents, with the necessary complement of supervisors and office staff, engaged in the collection of business cases."[87]

The establishment of the Bureau of Business Research at Harvard also led to the much-touted but ultimately disappointing *Harvard Business Reports*. Announced in 1924, the project aimed to chronicle the collective experiences of various industries so as to create a series of management precedents. (Donham's legal training had led him to believe that it was possible to create a parallel for business with the precedents-based understanding of the law in the legal profession.)[88] The first volume of the *Reports* presented 149 cases indexed according to specific principles they were intended to illustrate. The project endured for six years and eleven volumes before being abandoned after several Harvard business professors argued that the effort to identify rules and principles applying to all situations was futile.[89]

The experiment with the *Harvard Business Reports*—along with Donham's constant reiteration of the production of "socially minded business men" as the primary goal of business education—represented what was perhaps the apex of the attempt to cast business education in the mold of professional education in the "high" professions of medicine and law. Yet even such a serious and sincere attempt to establish research as an integral function of business schools was dismissed as unworthy of a true professional school by academic gatekeepers like Abraham Flexner, who caricatured the research bureau at Harvard as little more than symbolic pretension:

Research had also to be gotten under way. One can gather something as to the intelligence and sense of humour characteristic of those who out of hand contrived the School from the titles of the literature emanating from the Research Department. Here are specimens: "Operating Accounts for Retail Drug Stores," "Operating Accounts for Retail Grocer Stores," "Record Sheets for Retail Hardware Stores," "Merchandise Control in Women's Shoe Departments of Department

Stores". . . . If an educated man, a Harvard graduate, really wishes to become a retail drug or hardware merchant or a wholesale grocery salesman, does not Harvard put a low valuation on its training and his capacity when it provides him with special graduate training for the career? Cannot something be left to wit, to experience, and to the vocational "business college"?[90]

Despite such criticism, however, other schools soon followed Harvard's lead. The business schools at the University of Texas, the University of Michigan, Northwestern, and New York University all established their own bureaus of business research during the 1920s and 1930s. Like Harvard's, most of these bureaus were manned either by part-time faculty or by recently graduated business school students. The research organizations would develop close relations with regional business, and their advisory boards often included members of the local Chamber of Commerce and various associations of retailers. Particularly at publicly funded schools, the expectation was that business school research would focus on the businesses and economy of the area. For example, the stated mission of the University of Iowa business school's bureau of research was "to study and as far as possible to explain economic and industrial conditions within the State."[91] The primary objective for the University of Texas's business research bureau was "to secure and analyze the necessary data with which to plan a program for the most logical development of the natural resources and the utilization of the natural advantages of the State and to estimate business trends and current business adjustments."[92]

Whatever the particular industry or regional focus of a given research bureau, however, the work performed fell into one of two categories: either a bureau performed research *about* business or it did research *for* business. Harvard's Bureau of Business Research, for example, sought data from outside organizations but did not undertake contract work for them.[93] Research of the type the Harvard bureau collected was seen as "of broad general interest, but from a particular business' perspective, not practical."[94] From a student's perspective, it provided "a training ground in economics and statistics."[95] In contrast to research bureaus intended to gather material for teaching, others, such as those of the business schools at New York University and the University of Texas, were organized to serve businesses directly, having as their object "getting results of immediate practical value to some particular business organization or group of organizations."[96] Research of this kind, while of interest to these individual organizations that contracted for it, did not often have general implications. It was argued, however, that such research did give students "training of immediate practical value, especially in doing research of interest to business organizations."[97]

Not only did research bureaus perform work designed to advance the interests of particular firms, industries, or regions, however; they also avoided research topics that might prove offensive to business interests. As one research director summarized the situation, business school research sacrificed "independence of action" for "political expediency in the selection of subjects . . . [W]e have discovered . . . that certain subjects are just not to be mentioned. In other words, there is a very definite taboo upon certain topics that might anger certain individuals or might displease certain important business interests or some other catastrophe might occur which would imperil the university's appropriation[s] at the next legislature."[98] If a school's research bureau did approve a controversial subject, it had to handle it gingerly. Such research was structured to "treat the least controversial aspects" of sensitive topics, and each completed study was examined "very carefully" before being sent out "with a view to removing any political TNT that might be found in the pages."[99] Subjects such as taxation and labor, or challenges to the private monopolies of utilities, were simply off limits.

In an effort to create common standards in research, the AACSB's deans recommended that the various research bureaus develop some type of federation to improve research quality, disseminate ideas, and "bring order out of chaos in the collection of business problems or cases."[100] Chicago's Marshall echoed the view that such a federation would aid in the development of a critical mass of scholars dedicated to research: "The time has arrived when at least a few members of this association should accept the objective of establishing a 'community of scholars,'"[101] he proclaimed. Marshall's view on developing a community of scholars was an explicit attempt to professionalize academic research in business. He believed that it was only through collective inquiry that truth could be ascertained, and that the very existence of a community of inquiry in other professions was a guarantee against intellectual charlatanism. Yet several members of the AACSB immediately rejected the idea of a federation of research bureaus. The director of the New York University business school's research bureau, for one, said: "[I] doubt the practical advantages of any elaborate system of co-operation among bureaus of research. I doubt if the time is ripe. Let us strike root first each in our own environment and our own problems before attempting to become a forest.

I am inclined to think it wisest that each bureau should arise from the necessities of conditions in its localities."[102]

Others argued that if such a federation were to be developed, it should also include practitioners: "If there is to be a federation of bureaus of business research it should not only contain the members of this association but should have in its representation [individuals] from outstanding business organizations and industries."[103]

In the end, as in its attempts to create broadly accepted professional objectives and standards in curriculum, the membership of the AACSB was unable to reach consensus about the nature and purpose of business school research and the interests that it should serve.[104] The research bureau model for business school research would ultimately be supplanted by a more traditional model grounded in techniques and research methods more like those used by anthropologists and sociologists to study tribes and foreign cultures, and building on the earlier insights of industrial psychology. A classic example is the research in the 1930s on the interaction patterns among teams of Eastern European immigrant women working in the wiring rooms of Western Electric's Hawthorne works in Illinois—a well-known piece of work conducted by Harvard-affiliated scholars that has become known as the "Hawthorne Studies."[105] The AACSB's failure to create a stable research paradigm early in the century would come home to roost in the post–World War II era, as the varied and uneven quality of business school research provided the largest target for critics of American business schools, paving the way for externally driven reforms. Questions about both the quality and the purpose of the discipline-based research that has dominated business school scholarship for the past forty years would be raised yet again early in the twenty-first century. Even as the 1920s drew to a close, however, the catastrophe of the Great Depression transformed the sense of drift and disappointment that many business school leaders had felt at the beginning of the decade into a sense of crisis, and the professionalization project in business education got a breath of new life in the course of the 1930s.

The Great Depression, the 1930s, and the Attempt to Revive the Professionalization Project

The 1920s were heady years for the American economy, for the large American corporation, and, as a result, for the academically credentialed graduates now streaming in increasing numbers out of the nation's business schools. In the course of the decade, the growth of large corporations had fundamentally altered the nation's economic landscape. For the 100 largest U.S. corporations, the period between 1921 and 1928 brought a growth rate of 6.1 percent per year, compared to 4.4 percent for all other corporations. In 1928, the 200 largest of the 300,000 nonfinancial corporations in the country (i.e., less than seven-hundredths of 1 percent of such organizations) controlled approximately one-half of the corporate wealth.[106] Employment opportunities for business school graduates were enormous. Arthur Andersen, who founded his eponymous accounting firm in 1913, had by the late 1920s shifted away from internal training to hiring most new employees from business schools, believing that "business school training makes the average man more valuable in business than would the same time applied to practical experience alone."[107] Business school enrollment surged in response to the demand. Harvard expanded its enrollment from 400 students per year to 500 in 1928, and then to 600 in 1929. Dartmouth and Wharton deans reported that the demand for their students exceeded supply. Data from 1927 show that 57,728 students reported majoring in business across 132 colleges and universities, with growth rates for business school enrollments averaging about 10 percent per year.

These trends might have spelled good news for business schools. Yet as the 1920s drew to a close, the mood among those in the vanguard of the movement to establish business schools as peers of the existing professional schools, and thereby to establish management as a bona fide profession, was anything but self-congratulatory. In May of 1928, the deans of the AACSB gathered in New York City for their annual meeting. The opening address, given by Dean Ralph E. Heilman of the Northwestern School of Commerce, was titled "A Re-evaluation of the Objectives of Business Education." Heilman's speech reflected none of the exuberance of the age: instead of celebrating the success of business schools in creating and filling demand for their product, Heilman lamented that business schools, as he believed, had made limited strides in affecting the attitudes of professional managers. He placed the blame on member institutions as he presented the results of an AACSB-initiated study he had led on the progress of business schools. Business education, Heilman concluded, was facing a crisis. In particular, business schools were falling far short of their professional objectives, especially with respect to training students to meet their social responsibilities:

Anyone who goes to the catalogs of American collegiate schools of business expecting to get a clearly defined concept or any substantial agreement with regard to objectives is doomed to disappointment. One finds there, for the most part, glittering and general phrases, designed to command the respect of our academic colleagues, but having little reference to vocational or professional aims. . . . It is of the utmost importance in considering this subject to remember that every college and university is primarily a public service institution. All activities, whether in instruction or in research, presumably must contribute to social well-being. In that respect schools of business are to be measured by the same criteria which apply in the case of law, medical, engineering and other professional schools. The test is—Do we perform a service which is socially desirable? The existence of schools of commerce as an integral part of our system of higher education, and the expenditure of large sums of money for their maintenance, both in our public and private institutions, cannot be justified merely by virtue of the fact that we enable our students and graduates to increase their earning capacity. The justification must rest on a broader basis. It must be found in the fact that the training provided is socially desirable, that it contributes to social well-being, social progress and human welfare.[108]

Even if one did accept the preparation of students for jobs that would "increase their earning capacity" as a legitimate goal, Heilman and other deans implicitly argued, business schools were going about this in a way that was positively harmful from a social point of view. A series of assessments, presented at the same meeting where Heilman gave his speech, highlighted the fear that plagued members of the AACSB: rather than promoting social mobility by identifying and educating the best talent and enabling graduates to succeed in business careers regardless of social or class background, were business schools (especially the elite ones) contributing to the rise of a "business caste?"[109] Heilman's study of business education had concluded that it was still "not a young man's education, qualifications, or training but primarily his contacts, family, friends, and connections which count in business." Schools of business, he recommended to the AACSB, must actively mitigate these factors by "gathering and disseminating information with regard to business practices and methods, by making this information freely available to all, and by providing training for all those qualified for it." In so doing, business schools would contribute to society by creating opportunities for "latent ability and potential possibilities for business leadership . . . [thereby promoting] a large degree of equality of opportunity and a high degree of mobility from one economic group to another. From the social point of view, nothing could be more important or more desirable."[110]

Whatever the importance of this indirect effect of business education on the well-being of society, business schools, the deans believed, had a more direct and fundamental responsibility that they were failing to meet. Heilman's report criticized business schools for not teaching the normative dimensions of professionalism, thereby neglecting "the necessity for developing a strong sense of social and ethical obligation"[111] among business students—something that had been a bedrock principle of the association. Business schools, said Ohio State's H. E. Hoagland in presenting another part of the report, were "supplying better tools for young men to work with" but by no means attaining the ideal of "introducing into business an endless procession of young men who have acquired the social point of view and an understanding of the social obligations and public relations of business." The report concluded that business schools needed to improve "through research, publication and public service," and that their efforts along these lines should contribute to "the solution of important social, economic, and management problems."[112]

Commenting on the candid assessments made by the deans in their discussions of these and other findings presented at the 1928 AACSB meeting, L. S. Lyon of Washington University saw a bleak future for the professionalization project in American business schools. In his characteristically caustic fashion, Lyon stated:

> Let us consider the contents of these papers somewhat more specifically. First of all, it is clear that Professor Hoagland should be called to account before the Board of this association for pointing out to us the growing business attitudes of the profession. What is to become of an organization like this, which finds its spiritual support in such slogans as "Business a Profession," if a man like Hoagland is permitted to indulge his bad habit of trying to look beneath the names and surfaces of things, and is allowed to bring before us in public meetings evidence that the professions are in business; if one is permitted to point out that they as well as the widget manufacturers are developing the arts of obtaining and retaining customers . . . and studying the technique of collecting bills?

Lyon argued that many business deans did not want to face up to business schools' failure, to date, to turn business into a genuine profession. He then proceeded to remind his audience of words that Willard Hotchkiss had spoken at an AACSB meeting in 1920: "A school of business in a collegiate setting carries certain implications. These ideas may be indicated by the words 'public responsibility, educational sequence, scientific content, professional aim and vision.'" Lyon ended the meeting by questioning whether business schools would abandon or rededicate themselves to their professionalizing mission: "As one looks ahead, are the signs more certain or vague, which indicate that education for business will learn how to grow beyond education for management of private enterprise into education that will give us better policies, better operation and better control for the social order as a whole? Or is it better that such thought be not within the ken of the prophets of education of business?"[113]

In October of the following year, the American stock market collapsed. As the numbers of unemployed increased and capital spending came to a standstill, the self-scrutiny and even self-accusation of business school leaders like Lyon in the late 1920s only deepened. Even if some deans, as Lyon charged, preferred not to face the facts, once it became evident that the stock market collapse was not a temporary setback, and the stock-swindling activities and financial abuses of many executives (especially in the banking sector) began to come to light, businessmen themselves began to lecture business schools about their failings and plead with them to live up to their responsibilities. One prominent banker scolded business schools during the 1934 AACSB meeting for failing to fulfill their most basic duty, which he described as "to bring into the business world on the part of its graduates somewhat of a social point of view," to teach them that they had "obligations to society at large" and must not simply use their careers in business "as a means to [make] money for themselves."[114] In 1930, an AT&T executive had spoken ominously and with a dash of religious imagery in reminding the deans that their effectiveness was measured not by the employability of their graduating classes but by how well those graduates were prepared to help society confront the grave challenges it now faced:

> We want the young man coming to us, during the whole time that he is going through the grueling grind of routine and monotony and laying the foundations for his future responsibilities, to attack every problem in a thoughtful way. . . . And when he comes to that period fifteen years hence, when he has gone through his novitiate and has emerged into an executive position, he will know what to do with

these serious problems which we all know are facing us and on the solution of which rest the rise or fall of our present industrial civilization. . . . This is the plea I make to you as the outstanding one— to send your graduates into the world with a sense of responsibility for our social order, and with a consciousness that they are equipped to make a contribution to the solution of these problems which are threatening our civilization.[115]

Many business school deans and faculty, for their part, believed that these businessmen were not overstating their case. Wharton dean Joseph Willits, who had succeeded Emory Johnson in 1933, noted that many business schools had been sending their graduates "out with a social philosophy concentrated on the goal of 'a million before I'm thirty,' " thus contributing to "society's difficulties," not to their solution. He then stated that while "all of us have been guilty in greater or lesser degree of fostering this attitude," such an approach made a continuing investment in business schools "of questionable value either to the student or to society."[116] Invoking the example of the established professions, Harvard professor Clyde O. Ruggles argued that business schools needed to do more to raise standards of behavior in business:

The schools of medicine, for example, have done much to eliminate the quack in that field. The law schools have also made their contribution in making it increasingly difficult for the shyster lawyer to operate without detection and discipline. The business schools have a clear challenge to study standards of business conduct, and to furnish instruction which will give a clear perspective of the social responsibility of business men. . . . [U]niversity education in business will be incomplete in a vital respect if our studies of the field of business do not recognize the obligations of these schools to aid in raising the standards of business conduct. If the business schools do not accept this challenge, they will not only fail to justify their existence as part of modern university education but they will also fail to make the greatest possible contribution to business itself.[117]

Everett Lord, dean of Boston University's business school, boldly stated that the conduct now exposed as having given rise to the economic ills the country was facing clearly demonstrated that business had not become a profession: "If we accept the standards generally recognized that a profession is a vocation for which technical preparation is necessary and in which the motive of action is service rather than profit," Lord declared, "we may realize that our schools have done much to advance the first of these qualifications but very little towards the latter."[118] Another important feature of professions was their commitment to self-regulation, and many business school leaders feared that the ultimate failure of managers in regulating the conduct of fellow members of their presumed profession would prompt ill-conceived and heavy-handed government regulation. As Wharton's Dean Willits stated:

> It may not be unfair to say that the chances of obtaining a wise and rational policy by government . . . are increased in direct proportion to the extent to which the ethical standards and social mindedness of business men are of a kind that society can approve. In the long run, short-sightedness and unsocial practice by business will lead to political reprisals of a not very discriminating kind by those who have little understanding of business activity. All of business will continue to suffer for the conduct of a few until business learns specifically to condemn and control the practices that do not measure up.[119]

In attempting to diagnose how and why, exactly, business schools were failing to inculcate professional ideals and attitudes and thus (as Ruggles had put it) to "justify their existence as part of modern university education," many academics, both outside business schools and within, blamed the increasingly specialized and technical nature of the business school curriculum. Barnard College dean Virginia Gildersleeve, for example, argued for a return to the liberal arts in business education, declaring that it was the emphasis on narrow, technical training that was responsible for the nation's economic woes: "There is a great need for 'intellect' besides mechanical or scientific genius for men and women with a truer vision of the kind of world we should become."[120] Harvard's C. O. Ruggles made a similar analysis: "There is no blinking the fact," he stated at the 1933 AACSB meeting, "that much of the trouble in this . . . panic can be traced to our lack of understanding of our present complex industrial and business world." Ruggles lamented the fact that many of the tools with which business schools had been equipping students were being used not to create real value but to evade public accountability—at what was now obviously a steep cost to the public:

> We have seen set up within the past generation and especially within the last decade an almost hopeless maze of intercorporate

relationships in most phases of our industrial and business life . . . in the field of the public service industries, for example, the formation of numerous holding companies seemed to be in some instances for no other purpose than to evade public regulation. We have had it brought home to us in the last few years that there have been relationships between banks and their affiliates which have militated against the best interests of the public. That many corporations of all sorts have failed to get the investing public a true picture of their earnings is known only too well to many investors of very moderate means.[121]

In remarks delivered to his fellow AACSB members during the 1934 meetings in St. Louis, Joseph Willits questioned the kind of technically oriented curriculum that his Wharton predecessor, Emory Johnson, had put in place. Yet while owning up to business schools' failure to discharge their responsibilities, and lamenting, in particular, an "emphasis on turning out business technicians," Willits foreshadowed a broader, redemptive goal implied by the current failings:

It is in the common problems that we have particularly failed, the problems of a whole industry or all business, or of all society, or of the world. We have done badly in our individual management at all too many points but it is our collective management, our collective attack on common business or social problems which has been especially blind and ineffective. . . . Have we not put too much emphasis on turning out business technicians alone, and paid too little attention to the development of business men with a sense of statesmanship— men who would also be good citizens? Have we not been too much a reflection of the state of mind of the business community?[122]

If the problem with American business education was that it too accurately reflected the "state of mind" of business itself, then it was business, and not just business schools, that needed to be saved; or, as Sass puts it in his account of the Wharton School in the Depression years, the crisis in the American economy had "made it clear that business needed help from business schools, rather than vice versa, in charting the way ahead."[123] While the onset of the Depression humbled business school deans and faculty, it also stimulated an introspection that helped set the stage for a renewal of purpose. Thus the 1930s would see an attempt to revive the professionalization project that had stalled amid the growth and outward success of business schools during the preceding decade.

At the AACSB's 1931 annual meeting, the executive committee had urged that the association undertake a comprehensive survey of business education. Over the next year, the committee drafted the survey and then presented it to Dr. Henry Suzzalo, president of the Carnegie Foundation for the Advancement of Teaching, and, through him, to Dr. Frederick P. Keppel, president of the Carnegie Corporation of New York. Along with the survey, the committee proffered their request for funding for a study of business schools similar to the Flexner Report on American medical education that Carnegie had sponsored in 1910. The Carnegie Corporation proved sympathetic to the idea of such a study but, given the adverse economic conditions, was unable to fund it. Meanwhile, however, business school deans began rededicating themselves to their professionalizing mission and rethinking the means of carrying it out. Wharton's Dean Willits noted at the 1934 AACSB meeting that "the New Deal has given us all a shaking up, which causes us to re-examine the fundamental values upon which our educational planning is based."[124] Moreover, the various programs of the New Deal and, in particular, its attempts to build new institutions for a complex industrial society through such means as the National Industrial Recovery Administration, the National Labor Relations Act, and the creation of dedicated organizations to collect social and economic statistics, created opportunities for business schools to contribute to national economic recovery and stabilization. As a consequence, business school deans were determined to finally reach a working consensus about what constituted a professional business education, and to mobilize their institutions on behalf of a nation whose core political and economic institutions were being reexamined.

Over the next five years, the AACSB undertook a series of small studies and introspective dialogues aimed at fundamentally reconsidering every element of business school education. From this process a unanimous consensus emerged: business schools could no longer hope that their students would recognize the social significance and relations of business once they became managers. The schools themselves were ultimately responsible for instilling in students an understanding of the responsibilities of business for the well-being of society. University of Illinois professor Hiram T. Scovill noted that "the best way for schools of business to justify their existence in view of the apparent ills and evils in business in the past is so to train the business men of the future so that they will recognize their obligations to society. . . . Schools of business cannot afford to retain their inferiority complexes. They must push forward either with professional or graduate work and put business on a higher plane than it has heretofore experienced."[125]

Leaders at other schools—less tentative about the objective to be pursued than was Scovill with his proposal of "either . . . professional or graduate work" as the means of elevating business to a "higher plane"—stated explicitly that the professionalization of management must remain the goal for business schools. At an AACSB meeting, Boston University's Everett Lord described Columbia School of Business's new objective, set forth in 1936, of raising "to the rank of a learned profession those occupations of men which have heretofore been dominated almost exclusively by the gain-seeking instinct."[126] As in the 1920s, however, the strongest public advocate for professionalization in the most comprehensive sense of the term was Harvard's Dean Donham, who was appalled by the lack of national leadership from corporate executives in the midst of the Depression. Moreover, despite his own denials, Donham likely felt compelled to rebut Abraham Flexner's damning pronouncement (in his 1930 book, *Universities*) that "Harvard Business School raises neither ethical nor social questions; it does not put business on the defensive; it does not even take a broad view of business as business."[127] As a result, Donham in the early 1930s renewed and elaborated his previous calls for business schools to aid in transforming management into a profession—not a mere technical specialization or guild, but rather a group self-consciously dedicated to the service of society. Donham now declared that in institutions (such as his own) that called themselves schools of "business administration," too much emphasis had been placed on the first of these two words and too little on the second. Administration, he said, required managers to focus on "the human aspects of organization." Neither organization charts nor the "grossly misleading" application of economics to the management of business firms could be relied upon to give satisfactory administrative results. Drawing on the ongoing research of the eclectic collection of researchers, including Elton Mayo and Fritz Roethlisberger, that he had brought together at Harvard, Donham argued in a highly influential article that business education needed to be infused with an emphasis on the "known and discoverable characteristics of the behavior of men, both individually and in groups. It must recognize the extent to which human beings act on sentiment or prejudice rather than reason, and the importance of human routines, habits, customs, loyalties, and traditions." An understanding of this phenomenon and its accompanying theory would provide organizations of all kinds with a theoretical and empirical foundation upon which a profession of management could then be built. According to Donham:

> Administration must become a profession and assume its responsi-bilities. The principal characteristics of a profession are (1) the recog-nition of an intellectual unity based on a relevant body of experi-ence, fact, and theory; (2) the acceptance of responsibility by each member of the group to the group as a whole, which transcends re-sponsibility for mere money making and subordinates the individ-ual's profits, or success in the usual sense of the word; and (3) the development of special standards and concepts of proper conduct growing out of the relation of the group to the society of which it is a part. In many administrative fields, both public and private, the multifarious nature of the subject-matter with which administrators must deal, and the necessity of technical specialization in handling many aspects of this subject-matter, have obscured this corporate re-lation. To the great loss of society this has slowed down recognition of the responsibility of these groups to society as a whole. It is the duty of a university school to hasten the development of such con-cepts and to form a professional spirit among its students.[128]

Yet as Donham himself had long recognized, and other business school leaders now understood more clearly than ever, the task these academics were setting for themselves of educating and socializing business school students as genuine professionals would not be easy to accomplish. A particular chal-lenge, as many saw it, was posed by the motivations with which students pur-sued business studies in the first place. As one business professor stated the difficulty: "I have always felt that schools of business have a peculiarly diffi-cult problem in that the motives that actuate the students [to study business] vary so greatly. . . . Heaven knows it is hard enough in law and medicine, and we have much to learn still as to the selection of students, not merely on the academic side, but on the basis of their personal qualifications. But in the field of business it seems to me we have a peculiarly difficult problem." The dean of the University of Iowa's business school, C. Tippits, went so far as to state that in order to succeed in turning out professionals, business schools would need to attract a different kind of student, one who was motivated to enter business not because it was a means to make a living but because it was his (or her) true calling. As he remarked: "I have talked with a great many students in the past few months asking them why they came to the school of business administration. You know what the answer is from your own experiences. In nine cases out of ten they came because their fathers and mothers thought if they did come they could make more money." Moreover, Tippits continued, many students left business school believing "that business is nothing more or less than a 'racket.'"[129]

Despite such perceived obstacles, however, some deans argued that students and others with a stake in business education already were, in fact, motivated by the desire to transform management into a real profession. As Lee Bidgood, the dean of the University of Alabama's business school, opined:

> The thought underlying business education on the university level is that business is, or can become, at least in part, a profession. . . . The interested parties are at least five in number: the educators, the students, the parents, the private employers, and the government. The attitudes, the motives, and the purposes of these groups vary to a considerable extent, yet they are all moved fundamentally by the same philosophy—that business may become a profession.

The primary object of educational leaders in establishing business schools in the first place, Bidgood argued, was an altruistic one: to "broaden the service of the universities and to extend their field of usefulness." Students' motives, he claimed, were no different: "Very many students, if not an overwhelming majority of them, are sincerely desirous of rendering themselves more useful to society. Others are strongly moved by the same intellectual curiosity which urges on the professor in his researches. Almost all students are in some degree interested in raising their social status and that of their calling." The wish, on the part of parents as well as students, to improve the social status of business "had nearly or quite as much to do with the rise of professional schools of business as have the economic motives. But the social incentive has usually operated tacitly."[130]

Meanwhile, so great was the faith of the University of Michigan business school's dean, Clare Elmer Griffin, in the presence of a "social incentive" in business school students that he felt schools had merely to nurture the "naturally critical" tendencies of students in order to open their eyes to business practices that were not what they should be:

> More important than any of these aids which the schools of business can give to the maintenance of a dynamic and progressive character in business, is the process of education itself, i.e., imparting to young

men who are going into business that type of education which will
make them critical of what is, and eager for improvement. This
should not be too difficult, for youth is naturally critical . . . it is the
responsibility of universities to keep this critical spirit alive. . . . It is
the special task of the schools of business to nurture and direct this
reforming spirit not only in the broader relations of business and society but in the internal policies and methods of business. While
teaching the student how business is conducted, we must stimulate
in him a desire to find for himself how it should be conducted. In
other words, he should imitate the present business leaders not so
much in what they are now doing as in that spirit of adventure
which put them in the positions of leadership.[131]

Of course, more specific directions to business school leaders—not
just exhortations to "nurture and direct" whatever "reforming spirit" their
students might possess—would be needed if the schools were to succeed at
educating and forming students as professionals. Such aims would entail a
renewed effort to devise curricula and research agendas that would translate
aspirations into actual programs. One concern of business school deans in
the 1930s would remain a recurring question in business education long after
the professionalization project of its first half century had run its course: how
to teach business ethics. Most of the AACSB deans believed that the social
orientation they wanted to inculcate could not be imparted via a single
course on ethics but, rather, needed to be embedded in the entire business
school experience. Tuck's Dean William Gray articulated this new philosophy
in 1934 when he stated: "[T]he great social issues which permeate the whole
range of problems and measures bearing on the conduct of business deserve
to be considered and treated as integral components to be woven into the
fabric of every course dealing with the administration of business. No division of the curriculum seems to be exempt."[132] In 1939, the dean of the University of Oregon's business school, Victor P. Morris, presented a summary of
changes he would be making to his school's curriculum, most important a
turn to instructing students about the human element of work. As he stated,
"[M]ost economic wreckage today comes not from ignorance of the physical
phases of business but from ignorance of the human elements."[133]

For many of the AACSB deans, another answer to the question of how to
instill a properly social perspective in students was to give prominent attention in the business school curriculum to the social sciences, as the Wharton

School had done before Emory Johnson had steered it in the direction of specialized business courses. In arguing the need for a new science of administration, for example, Wallace Donham stated:

> If our civilization breaks down, as it well may, it will be primarily a breakdown in the administrative area. If we can make a real contribution toward preventing such a breakdown, I believe this contribution will be in the administrative area. I do not believe that we shall make any such contribution unless we study constantly the relationship of administration in our field of business administration to the various social sciences, to the structure of human society, to the behavior of human beings, in addition to the subjects which we include typically in our instruction now.[134]

Tuck's Dean Gray had earlier supported such an approach, noting that as "the depression and the New Deal have brought about a reunion of business with social sciences, so must the business school enact a re-integration of conventional branches of the curriculum with the laws and facts of economics, government, ethics, and social psychology. . . . Nothing less than social-mindedness, fortified by the scientific approach, is needed in the youngsters who look to us for a valid preparation for the practical affairs of contemporary business."[135] The University of Chicago's business school, meanwhile, rededicated itself to Leon Marshall's original vision of making the existing stores of scientific information in the social sciences accessible not just for the advancement of business but for the solving of social problems, and began to encourage research in economics in particular. In 1936, a study of forty-three of the forty-six members of the AACSB revealed significant changes in business school curricula. Harvard, for example, had launched a required course to teach a practical social philosophy emphasizing the public responsibility of business and the role of business leaders in contributing to the social order. The University of Chicago's curriculum was beginning more directly to teach students the principles of foundational social science disciplines, especially economics. Dartmouth's Tuck School was modifying its general management course to emphasize the relationship between "business and society." Seeing Wharton as a "physician for the nation's economic ills," Dean Joseph Willits had shifted the school's orientation away from clinical business training and retooled its research program in order to build an "institution of applied economics."[136] Stanford business school's dean, J. Hugh Jackson, was active in setting up the Social Science Research Council to align business school research more closely with the social sciences, including economics, sociology, and psychology.

At the same time that the social sciences were receiving renewed attention, a consensus had begun to emerge among AACSB deans about the causes of the Great Depression. From their diagnosis they began to develop a prescription for business schools beyond the general one of imparting to students a greater awareness of social responsibility and obligations. The deans traced the crisis in the American economic system to an uncritical embrace by business schools of the laissez-faire market ideology adhered to by business itself. As Harvard's C. O. Ruggles stated the case:

> Much of our laxness with regard to standards of business conduct
> has grown out of our theory that private initiative should have full
> sway and that regulation should not be substituted for management.
> Our zeal for this theory of the relationship between government and
> business has blinded us to the fact that management should be held
> responsible for misrepresentation and for mismanagement. Under a
> theory of laissez-faire and Jeffersonian philosophy that the govern-
> ment is best that governs least, we have given an opportunity for
> business practices to develop that have militated against the best in-
> terests of the public and even of business itself.[137]

In response to this concern, Harvard modified its required courses to recognize the legitimate role of regulation and the government in the economy, and, in 1934, introduced an initiative (including new courses) to incorporate into its curriculum what Donham called "public aspects of private business and the administration of public business as well."[138] In 1933, Wharton instituted the "Wharton Assembly," a periodically convened meeting bringing together the entire Wharton community to hear prominent public officials speak about the problems of the nation and what Wharton's faculty and students could do to help address them.

The renewed attention to particular social concerns sparked by the Depression was evident not only in curricular reforms in the 1930s but also in new directions for business school research, which began to move beyond the scope of studies such as "Merchandise Control in Women's Shoe Departments of Department Stores" or "Record Sheets for Retail Hardware Stores" to more policy-oriented research directed to problems such as unemployment, working conditions, and the ills of urbanization. Inside Harvard Business School, researchers like Elton Mayo who were studying blue-collar workers were deeply affected by the economic depression and their recognition of the psychological havoc it wreaked on workers.[139] At the Wharton School, Joseph Willits used the crisis of the Depression to move the school's focus from specialized business training to what Sass calls "the older academic traditions of Patten and James." As Sass describes it, "These earlier leaders had fashioned social studies into pragmatic sciences through a program of engaged academic scholarship and research. Willits hoped to do the same for the business fields by making academic research in economics 'central to our work.'"[140]

Another facet of the attempt to reform business school research in this decade was an effort to eliminate the pro-business bias that had been evident in early research initiatives. The University of Michigan's Dean Griffin argued that for too many years business schools had suppressed, and even punished, scholars who undertook research studies that were critical of business practices or emphasized social issues. In Griffin's view, such practices needed to end: "The schools of business are now turning their attention to a systematic study of internal business policies, and it is hoped that they will stimulate that analysis and self-criticism in business which is the basis of progress and the enemy of conservatism."[141] With his habitual caution, Wallace Donham expressed the fear that "to start criticizing policies before we know enough about business to give a foundation for such criticism . . . would result in half-baked unconstructive attitudes on our part . . . [and] wholly destroy any chance we might have of making constructive comments on business."[142] Yet the call had been sounded to turn business schools into objective analysts and, when necessary, critics of business rather than the apologists and boosters they had been accused of being.

In 1937, the AACSB established a committee to undertake yet another study, this one to examine how far business schools had progressed in implementing the various post-Depression initiatives they had undertaken. On the basis of this study, a detailed plan to institutionalize a new set of reforms would emerge, involving proposed changes to the curriculum, the focus of research, and the socialization of students. The results of this study were presented on the eve of World War II. The AACSB deans would continue to meet until 1941, but increasingly the meetings were focused on the shift in business and government relations occasioned by the New Deal and the potential role business schools might play should the United States enter the war in Europe and Asia. The AACSB deans would not meet again until after the war, by which time not only business schools but all of American business—and indeed all of American society, in both the public and private sectors—would be in the grip of a profound set of economic, political, cultural, and social transformations that the struggle against totalitarian aggression abroad had triggered at home. In this radically changed set of circumstances, the professionalization project that had motivated and guided, however fitfully and unevenly, the first sixty years of American business education would be not only abandoned once and for all but nearly completely forgotten. Business schools would come less and less to resemble the image upheld for them by the likes of Edmund James, Wallace Donham, and Joseph Willits. Moreover, the managerial role for which the schools attempted to prepare students would itself be transformed by epochal changes in American business, the American corporation, and the relationship of both to the surrounding society. The era of aspiring professionalism in business would die quietly, an unnoticed casualty of war, as a new era of managerialism was born.

The Institutionalization of Business Schools,
1941–1970

II

The Changing Institutional Field in the Postwar Era   5

For business schools, the years immediately following World War II were, to borrow from Dickens, the best of times and the worst of times. To all outward appearances, the beginning of the postwar era was a period of vitality and growth for college and university business education. The U.S. government had come to believe that the well-being of American society depended on the contributions of large numbers of persons with higher educational qualifications, and colleges and universities were flooded with students, many of them pursuing business studies. In 1919, a mere 110 MBAs had been granted in the United States; in 1949, 3,897 MBAs were awarded, while the country's population increased only about 50 percent over the corresponding period. Whereas in 1919, 3.2 percent of all undergraduate degrees granted in the United States were in business, by 1949 this number had climbed to 13 percent. By 1955, business degrees would come to constitute 14 percent of all higher education degrees.[1]

To keep up with the demand for business programs, the numbers of faculty and staff, as well as overall resources, devoted to business studies increased, and the number of business schools and programs likewise multiplied, rising to 587 bachelor's and 127 master's degree–granting programs by 1955. (See table 5.1.) Between 1946 and 1956, the number of AACSB member schools grew by 45 percent, roughly equaling the increase between 1925 and 1935, and the number of faculty at AACSB schools increased by 71 percent. (During this period of 1946–1956, average salaries rose 40 percent for professors, 45 percent for associate professors, and 38 percent for assistant professors, compared to about a 15 percent increase for traditional faculty salaries over the same period.[2] As a result, newly minted Ph.D.s began to command salaries far exceeding those of many renowned scholars in other academic fields.)

Remarking on this trend, Peter Drucker stated in 1950 that, after years of viewing most business schools as training grounds for narrow, functional spe-

Table 5.1

Earned Degrees in Business and Level of Degree, 1955–1956

Type of Institution	Type of Degree	No. of Institutions Conferring Business Degrees	No. of Business Degrees Granted
Colleges	Bachelor's	414	12,979
	Master's	29	255
	Doctoral	—	—
Technical institutes	Bachelor's	23	1,529
	Master's	5	96
	Doctoral	—	—
Universities	Bachelor's	150	25,862
	Master's	93	3,890
	Doctoral	21	121
All institutions	Bachelor's	587	40,370
	Master's	127	4,241
	Doctoral	21	121

Source: Robert Aaron Gordon and James Edwin Howell, *Higher Education for Business* (New York: Columbia University Press, 1959), 27.

cialists, the corporation had finally accepted the graduate business school as "its own professional school."[3] While there is a paucity of comprehensive historical placement data for business schools, Harvard Business School reported significant success in the placement of its graduating students in the years just after the war. In the academic year 1949–1950, for example, more than 200 companies, with some 900 positions to fill, vigorously recruited among Harvard Business School's 500 graduating MBA students. A Ford Foundation survey of large employers found that while a college degree had become prerequisite for entry into the management training programs of most such firms, few required advanced business degrees. Of the 587 institutions granting business degrees in 1955, only 187 offered such degrees at the graduate level, and among these, only 81 met the AACSB's modest accreditation standards, with the rest failing mainly because their faculties lacked the necessary academic credentials. As Drucker noted, it was unclear that graduate business schools knew "what to do with their victory" in gaining acceptance from corporations as legitimate professional schools.[4] Specifically, he pointed to business schools' inability to establish and clarify their own mission. Drucker cited the ongoing questions about institutional purpose being raised by influential deans such as Donald David of Harvard Business School as evidence of the "soul-searching" prevalent in business academia.

Despite the spurs to reform and innovation that arose during the Depression, most business schools, after the interruption of the war years, had reverted to practices criticized in the AACSB reports and proceedings of the 1920s. The curriculum at the majority of business schools in the 1940s and 1950s was still best described as an amalgamation of subjects, unified by little but the frayed idea of management as a distinct subject of study. With the exception of a mere handful of schools, business education also continued to be beleaguered by poorly trained faculty who lacked rudimentary preparation in basic research methods. Even elite schools like Wharton, Harvard Business School, and Stanford repeatedly granted tenure to faculty who lacked a doctorate or an academic publication record. For that matter, a survey of business school research that was published during the 1950s showed that the era's research consisted largely of superficial, anecdotal examples or broad generalizations that were rarely subjected to rigorous testing or peer review.[5] (Indeed, those business school faculty members who were regarded as notable researchers saw themselves, and were often seen by their institutions, as exceptional cases.)[6] Finally, the caliber of students in business schools was far from stellar. Growth in enrollment after the war tended to expand the proportion of students whose interests were primarily or exclusively vocational rather than academic. According to a survey published in the mid-1950s, graduate students in business at the time scored below the average for all graduate and professional students on standardized tests.[7]

What explains the extraordinary growth of business schools despite their generally poor academic quality? The answer lies in four broad, interrelated social changes that had increasing impact in the postwar years. First was the emergence of what Richard Scott has called "organizational society"—a societal order characterized by large government agencies and by the birth of a new and soon-dominant form of business corporation, the large, diversified conglomerate. Second, this new organizational society had the effect of enhancing the importance of management as a social function and of producing a more rational, technically rooted conception of professional management than had existed prior to World War II. Third, the postwar era saw a tremendous expansion in the size and scope of higher education in America, in response to postwar social, economic, and political conditions, and as a direct consequence of a revolution in the relationship between the federal government and higher education. Finally, private philanthropic foundations, prompted by the incipient Cold War to focus on ways of strengthening American democracy, became interested in promoting social science research to improve the administration of large organizations, such as those that formed the nation's industrial core. These last two developments, although they brought good news for business schools in the way of resources for expansion, also carried the seeds of less-welcome changes in the form of increasing influence within the schools by outside actors.

Indeed, these four changes helped trigger a revolution in business schools—one that, over the course of two decades, would lead American business education to a radically different conception of management and, what was just as important, of business education itself. This revolution was made possible by a basic flaw in the AACSB's organizational and governance structure that, under the external pressure exerted by the growth of business schools and the influence of both the federal government and the foundations, hastened the association's decline as an authoritative community for business educators. The AACSB's decline—with an accompanying shift in the organization's mission—created an institutional vacuum that allowed new, external authorities to step in and refashion business education. In so doing, these outside actors would advance in some respects the professionalization project that had focused the energies and efforts of the first two generations of business school leaders. In other, ultimately more important, respects, however, their actions would undermine the project's central aim.

World War II and the New Organizational Society

The nearly total mobilization of American society during World War II had critical significance for American business schools. Business schools had previously helped train members of the armed forces (between 1920 and 1939, for example, 190 active-duty officers graduated from Harvard Business School's MBA program), but as the war unfolded, the relationship became more comprehensive and formal. Immediately after the United States entered the war, many business schools required applicants for admission to sign an agreement stating that if they were admitted to school and were then offered a commission in the military, they would accept the commission. If some type of deferment prevented them from accepting this commission, students agreed to serve in a war industry or in other military-related work. In 1941,

Robert D. Calkins, dean of Columbia University's business school, reorganized its curriculum to focus on training students to help fill the numerous administrative positions that had been created to coordinate the war effort.[8] By 1943, Harvard Business School had suspended all regular admissions to focus exclusively on instructing military officers.[9]

The war also heightened the federal government's interest in techniques for management and administration. Because the war was being fought between the advanced industrial powers, it was in part a contest of organizational strength and managerial skill. The government quickly recognized the crucial role that effective organization would play in the war effort, and rapidly mobilized several of the leading business schools to focus their research and teaching activities on addressing some of the key problems of administering a war economy. These included a variety of administrative tasks, from information collection to an unprecedented level of coordinated decision making across a large number of corporations and government agencies, as well as the military. In 1942, the War Department contracted with several business schools to teach a three-month course, the Jobs Training Methods program, which trained engineers and retrained existing executives in wartime production management techniques.[10] At the Wharton School, many of the best finance and accounting faculty were diverted to the War Production Board to assist in collecting and organizing national economic statistics. It was during this time, for example, that Wharton's Simon Kuznets, working for the government, developed the first "input-output" survey of the nation's economy, mapping the process by which raw materials were transformed into industrial outputs and creating a framework for a national income-accounting system—two colossal achievements for which he would later be awarded the Nobel Prize in Economics. Harvard Business School faculty worked closely with the U.S. commissioner of education to set up a wartime training program, called the Engineering, Science, and Management War Training Program (ESMWT), to equip managers for the task of supervising armament production facilities.

In addition to the war's direct impact on business schools, effects that were less direct, but ultimately more pervasive and lasting, would arise as the postwar era began and organizations, now transformed as a result of wartime activities, assumed a new significance in American society. The intensity of America's involvement in the war, from the near total mobilization of the federal government to the expansion of America's industrial corporations to produce armaments, dramatically increased the scale and scope of American organizations, including many that had already been sizable. The war represented an unprecedented experiment in the capabilities of large bureaucracies. The War Planning Board, which coordinated national defense manufacturing, linked private enterprises such as Ford, Chrysler, General Motors (GM), General Electric, and Borg-Warner to government units including the War and Navy departments, the Aircraft Scheduling Unit, the Board of Economic Warfare, and the Office of Civilian Supply.[11] Unlike the aftermath of World War I, when many of the government agencies that had been created during the war were quickly demobilized, and industries that had retooled for the war effort resumed peacetime production, institutional changes in government and private business that took place during World War II persisted after its end. Many government entities set up during the war evolved into permanent agencies and departments—the Office of Strategic Services, for example, would ultimately become the Central Intelligence Agency—and many corporations that had diversified for wartime production remained in their new lines of business. GM, for instance, was one of the largest federal contractors in the postwar period, supplying everything from tanks to airplane parts, products that GM had either created or produced in significantly larger numbers during the war. Several factors contributed to the persistence of these institutional innovations—the most significant, perhaps, was the Cold War, which kept the nation in a continued state of military readiness. Another factor in preserving the changes, closely related to American experience in the war and to the geopolitical challenges of the postwar age, was a fundamental shift in Americans' attitudes toward large organizations of all types.

World War II generally softened Americans' historically suspicious attitudes toward large organizations and their management. The organizational scholar Charles Lindbloom has remarked that the postwar growth of organizations was "never much agitated, never even much resisted, a revolution for which no flags were raised," even though it was fundamentally transforming the nature of American society.[12] Millions of men and women who served in the military or worked in America's wartime factories were exposed to the productive features of a large-scale bureaucracy, with its defined authority structures, administrative rules, and predictable career paths. This exposure profoundly affected public assumptions about the nature of large organizations, as it left citizens with a favorable impression of what could be accomplished through collective action. The Allied victory itself, indeed, was framed by observers like Peter Drucker as a demonstration of America's organizational and managerial prowess. Drucker noted that the technology, logistics, and management of the war effort made clear what was possible when large organizations planned and coordinated their operations.[13]

In addition to the wartime achievements of large organizations, another factor influencing Americans' new acceptance of them was the connection perceived by policy makers and educators between large organizations and the achievement of broad societal goals such as strengthening democracy and national security. In contrast to early twentieth-century fears that large organizations represented a threat to America's social order, Americans were increasingly enchanted by claims that the same organizational technologies that had won the war could now be used to strengthen society. As a result, large organizations came to be seen not only as tools by which certain immediate objectives could be achieved but also as the means by which problems like "social" and "political tensions" could be rectified.[14] Large corporations, Dean Calkins of the Columbia School of Business believed, could no longer be neatly categorized as either "public" or "private."[15] Writing in 1957, sociologist Philip Selznick did not hesitate to mention industry, along with politics and education, in a list of institutions that "have become increasingly *public* in nature" (emphasis in original) and were "attached to such interests and dealing with such problems as affect the welfare of the entire community."[16] Corporate leaders were increasingly described as "statesmen," responsible not only for a firm's economic performance but also for its political and social legitimacy. The executive class, in other words, was now considered part of the political leadership of the country.

▌ The Rise of the Rational Manager

The elevated conception of corporate leaders reflected the critical role managers were now understood to play in realizing the possibilities of large organizations. Indeed, if the war was a vindication of sorts for large organizations, it was also a vindication of the managers who rendered these organizations so effective. Indeed, memories of the Great Depression, fears of a postwar recession, and the threat of communism at home and abroad led some observers to link the survival of liberty and democracy to the nation's ability to coordinate and plan the activities of organizations. The health of American democracy, some argued, would therefore partly depend on the health of management as an institution.

In a 1948 speech to business executives titled "Business Leadership and the War of Ideas," Wallace Donham's successor as HBS dean, Donald K. David, described effective managers as essential to capitalism's victory in the contest with communism: "We face a long continuing struggle throughout the world for men's minds and indeed for men's souls. . . . In this conflict of systems, the best way to preserve our system is to make it work. To me the brightest ray of hope in these troubled times is my firm belief that the business men can and will measure up to the task."[17] Harvard University president James Conant (who had succeeded Abbott Lawrence Lowell in 1933) voiced a similar theme—and evoked the old idea that management needed to be elevated to the plane of the high professions of law and medicine—when he linked American freedom to the free enterprise system and the mission of the Harvard Business School:

> The United States has developed its greatness as a nation in a period in which a highly fluid society overran a rich and empty continent; one of the highly significant ideals of the American nation has long been equality of opportunity. Our educational system, our political institutions, and our social ideals form a closely interwoven pattern. Equality of opportunity could be realized only in a political democracy; it would have meaning only in a competitive society in which private ownership and the profit motive were accepted as basic principles.
>
> As never before business needs men who appreciate the responsibilities of business to itself and to that unique society of free men which has been developed on this continent. Such men must understand not only the practical workings of business organizations, but also the economic and social climate in which business operates; they must be as well trained as our professional men in law and medicine.[18]

Such views of the importance of business education for American freedom and democracy became increasingly commonplace as the nation steeled itself for its new task of containing the spread of communism around the world. In 1948, the Wharton School linked its $2 million capital campaign to winning the Cold War; Wharton's fund-raising prospectus emphasized that the money would be spent on efforts to help the nation produce managers who could effectively administer the world's dominant economic institutions and enable corporations to advance the military and security needs of the United States.[19] Some of the nation's major philanthropic institutions—particularly the Ford Foundation, as we shall see in chapter 6—also now saw the effective training of managers as one of the primary means by which America would meet its postwar challenges.

To address the threat of communism by means of organization and management, many believed, a new, more rational conception of management and the managerial role was critical. Military leaders, managers, and organizational experts had created an arsenal of quantitative tools such as linear programming, systems analysis, computer simulations, network analysis, queuing theory, and cost accounting systems to control and administer the war machine. Progress in statistics and statistical sampling had come about through quality-assurance efforts in the production of armaments. Survey methods, such as focus groups, had originally been developed to gauge the morale of the armed forces and civilian support for the war. When the thousands of experts and administrators who had developed these tools moved back into their offices and factories, they brought with them not only wartime-generated knowledge and techniques but also a changed conception of organizations and management spawned during the same period. Much as scientific management, at the turn of the century, had utilized tools like time-motion studies to rationalize production, management consulting firms like Arthur D. Little now created ways of applying the new techniques developed during the war to a host of organizational problems.[20]

The importation of these technical innovations into business gave rise to a different conception of what it meant to be a professional manager. Prior to the war, management practice had been increasingly influenced by the so-called human relations school, a theoretical perspective that emerged in large part from the famous 1930s Harvard Business School studies of Western Electric's Hawthorne factory. This perspective conceived of management as a task that drew on the combined insights of social psychology, anthropology, sociology, and psychoanalysis. The postwar conception of management, however, was built neither on these disciplines nor on the normative ideals that had animated the idea of "professional management" for prewar business educators. It was grounded, instead, in a technical outlook often described as "management science" that emphasized analytical training, especially in systems dynamics and cybernetics. This new definition of management reflected a general trend in postwar social science, which, in an effort to raise its status in the eyes of the federal government, now sought to appear more "scientific"— meaning that most of the effort in the social sciences was being put into improving research techniques and constructing theories rather than conducting the deep empirical investigations that had characterized most social science research in the 1920s and 1930s. What would now make management "scientific" was not social science per se but rather the new methods of social science research that had gained prominence during the war. Thus even promising fields like industrial sociology, which had begun to diffuse before the war, declined in its aftermath.[21] One consequence of the new emphasis on scientific research techniques in the social sciences was the final severance of fields such as economics, sociology, and psychology from their roots in the humanities.

Stephen R. Barley and Gideon Kunda describe how the growing emphasis on scientific techniques brought about a merger of the managerial role itself with the tools that managers now employed:

> As OR [operations research] and management science grew more prominent, the general tenor of managerial discourse began to change. Theorists again began to search for an "orderly body of knowledge" to guide the manager. . . . Process theorists equated management with setting objectives and designing systems for meeting those objectives. Planning, forecasting, and controlling were to be the manager's watchwords . . . thereby [providing] management with a definition of itself consistent with the tools of OR and management science.[22]

Managers were described as "systems designers," "information processors," and "programmers" involved in regulating the interfaces between the organization and its environment. The key to improving firm performance was an expert manager able to bring rational analysis and a body of sophisticated technical knowledge to bear on a firm's problems, whatever they might be. Another important aspect of this new wave of rational thinking was that it emphasized managerial expertise not with respect to a functional job, as Taylorism had done, but rather as a general skill that could be applied independently of function or context. A 1952 *BusinessWeek* article describing these innovative managerial technologies, and the newly christened Sloan School at MIT, proclaimed: "The day of the truly professional general management man isn't here yet, but it is not far away. That man will be trained for management in general, rather than in any one phase of business. He'll learn his technique in school, rather than on the job."[23] Armed with these new tools, proponents suggested, managers could work in an organization without knowing the details of its operations because what mattered was the structure and process of management decision making rather than the specific details of a business.

Postwar America also saw the rise of a new social contract between the manager and the corporation, one that reflected, in social terms, the subordination of particularized experience and individual judgment to the impersonal logic of the new tools of management. William Whyte famously captured the changed relationship in his description of what he called the organization man: the "professional" manager whose profile melded the characteristics of a career civil servant with those of a businessman. Paradoxically—in view of how the new conception of management created a zone of detachment between managerial work and the particular business of any one organization—the organization man was a loyal lieutenant in the corporate army, singularly committed to the organization whatever its product or service and willing to subordinate his individual identity to the pursuit of organizational goals. The social contract between the organization man and his company was a complex one, rooted in the structure, culture, and practices of organizations now aspiring to the machinelike precision and efficiency that, in an earlier era, scientific management had tried to bring to the factory. But in essence it was a type of exchange: in return for loyally pursuing the development of firm-specific skills, an individual received a middle-class wage and lifestyle. In this system, companies engaged in intensive efforts to socialize individuals for lifetime careers. For example, General Electric, which hired 1,000 college and business school graduates every year during the 1950s, exposed all of its new hires to training programs lasting, in some cases, close to four years and administered by a group of 250 full-time General Electric employees. New recruits knew that many people were watching them, and learned that they must "[n]ever say anything controversial"; they generally recognized that fitting in mattered more than anything else.[24]

Some individuals, like Harvard Business School's Donald David, worried about the implications of this new type of manager for American corporations and American society (David faulted his own institution for having "turned out far too many men who have sought the shelter and security of positions in large corporations"),[25] but the organization man, particularly in the largest corporations, remained a fixture well into the 1970s. It is easy today to ridicule this model of the corporate executive, but many of that era's most successful corporations, including Procter and Gamble, IBM, Colgate-Palmolive, and General Electric, attained their outstanding results via this management model. It was also a model that reflected and depended upon a particular external environment created by a new social contract between business and other institutions—including labor and capital but also, especially, government—that was another feature of the postwar era.

At the top of the corporate hierarchy in the era of the organization man stood a type of CEO who was often described as an industrial statesman, an executive known for his courtly manners, poise, involvement in organizations such as the Business Roundtable or the Council on Foreign Relations, and an ability to work closely with outside parties, including government regulators and elected politicians. The new industrial statesman was at least partly a creation of a postwar industrial consensus in which business and government (as well as labor and providers of financial capital) worked together in a de facto partnership that University of Chicago economists Raghuram Rajan and Luigi Zingales have called "relationship capitalism," a system of managed competition enforced through a mixture of government policy and informal cartelization.[26] Relationship capitalism was distinct from managerialism in that it not only featured the separation of ownership and control that Berle and Means had identified in 1932 but also took place within a highly regulated economic structure in which competition, especially within industries, was restrained to a considerable degree. Regulatory bodies established and enforced barriers to entry; legislative controls dictated prices; and firms, unions, and regulatory bodies commonly submitted to mediated, economywide agreements. For example, the Interstate Commerce Commission regulated the trucking industry (as well as substitute forms of transportation such as railroads) by requiring all interstate motor carriers to adhere to minimum rates that the commission itself set. In another example of the managed national economy of the era, pattern bargaining in the largest industries, such as the automotive, ensured that companies all paid similar wages and provided similar benefits, while workplace rules had to be formally negotiated between companies and their unions. (Under the terms of the National Labor Relations Act of 1935, nearly two-thirds of all manufacturing employees in the country were now covered by collective bargaining agreements.)

Relationship capitalism, and the managed economy it constructed, reinforced the trends in management set in motion by the organizational demands of World War II. This effect is particularly visible in the rise of a new form of corporate organization—the conglomerate—in the postwar era, and in the impact that this new organizational form had on managerial roles and work. Following Congress's passage of the Cellar-Kefauver Act of 1950, firms were prohibited from using vertical or horizontal mergers to dominate a single industry.[27] An aberration amid the generally positive postwar attitudes toward large organizations, the act reflected continuing national concern about the potentially harmful influence of concentrated economic power on

American democracy. This concern had been validated through observation of the role played by market-dominating firms in fostering European fascism.[28] If the public emerged from the war with a new respect for the positive capabilities of large organizations, it also now had new evidence of the threat they could pose. The act did not, however, prevent the emergence of large industrial concerns—it only constrained their growth to a diversified model. Firms initially pursued mergers with firms in related, and then in completely unrelated, industries.[29] Postwar economic conditions of rapid expansion, rising stock valuations, and strong corporate cash flow allowed corporate executives to react to Cellar-Kefauver by shifting their focus to growing sales rather than market share and by spreading market risks across unrelated product and service lines. Another factor contributing to the rise of conglomerates was the fickle nature of what investors valued in determining a firm's stock price. During this period, Wall Street analysts emphasized growth in earnings per share rather than return on current capital investments as the key indicator of a firm's prospects. To put it more simply, investors relied primarily on a firm's revenue growth rates when deciding its value.[30] As one chief executive of a conglomerate said of this development: "We have to be concerned with increasing our earnings per share . . . because that seems to be the way the game is scored in the stock market. The market seems to value increasing earnings per share more than a high return on corporate net worth, so just maintaining a high return on net worth is not enough. In fact, our additions to equity each year from retained earnings mean that we have to keep increasing our absolute level of earnings considerably just to stand still."[31]

Diversification offered a solution to this dilemma by allowing firms to seek out new sources of profit. The conglomerate approach conceived of firms as mere collections of financial assets, and conglomeration offered the possibility of reallocating those assets to growing industries while leaving stagnant ones behind. The multidivisional form of organization, pioneered at General Motors and DuPont, facilitated the model by allowing multiproduct firms to be controlled by a central headquarters; return on investment, in turn, became the preferred way of allocating a firm's capital. By deploying personnel and resources in these ways, managers began to acquire firms in industries where they had little production or marketing expertise. By the early 1960s, for example, General Electric consisted of 190 distinct departments, each with its own budget, and 43 strategic business units. Gulf & Western, one of the many multibusiness firms that emerged during the era of

Table 5.2

Evolution of U.S. Economy and the Largest U.S. Corporations

	1920	1929	1950	1960	1970
Ratio of administrative to production employees (%)	15.6	17.9	23.6	28.9	30.3
Industrial employment (%)	32.3	29.2	32.9	30.8	28.2
Services employment (%)	39.5	44.7	54.4	59.5	66.8
Union membership (as % of total employment)	12.9	7.2	24.3	25.9	24.6
Diversified firms (%)*	11.0	15.0	38.0	60.0	76.0
Multi-divisional firm (%)*	0.0	2.0	20.0	57.0	73.0

Source: Adapted from Mauro Guillén, *Models of Management: Work, Authority and Organization in a Comparative Perspective* (Chicago: University of Chicago Press, 1994), 306–307, table B1.
*100 largest US corporations

conglomerates, owned Paramount Pictures (a film studio), Kayser-Roth (an apparel maker), Simon & Schuster (a publisher), Simmons (a mattress manufacturer), and the Miss U.S.A. and Miss Universe beauty contests, as well as one of the world's largest zinc mines. As a result of the perceived advantages of the diversification strategy, the number of conglomerates increased dramatically. Table 5.2 shows that, by 1960, 60 percent of the one hundred largest American companies were diversified, versus 15 percent in 1929. The table also shows that conglomeration increased the managerial intensity of firms (as measured by the ratio of managers to employees), because larger numbers of managers were now required to plan, budget, and control activities across a wide variety of businesses. Also evident is the onset of a shift toward a service economy that would render certain kinds of operational skills and knowledge on the part of managers (especially skills related to manufacturing and to management of a blue-collar workforce) increasingly obsolete.

The rise of the conglomerate form of organization, with its multiplicity of managers increasingly removed from hands-on operations, thus reinforced the rational, scientific conception of management—the conception for which the plethora of new analytical tools now formed a foundation.[32] Conglomerates had a profound impact not only on the sheer number of managers employed but also on the kinds of activities in which managers engaged and the techniques they used to do their jobs. Textron, one of the first of the new breed of conglomerates, was described by its chairman as "a pure conglomerate. . . . We have no part of our original business. We have no principal division. We have no principal product."[33] One executive described the activities of this "new organizational form": "This new group of enterprises has been classified under many different names such as multimarket, free-form conglomerate, acquisition type, diversified, and other semantic variations of these. But call them what you may—there is a common theme which may vary in execution from one management to another but, nevertheless, it is still there. The common element of this new management technique is a complete orientation toward total profit as compared with a product or industry orientation."[34]

As a result of this profit-maximizing orientation—and because, in conglomerates such as Textron or Litton, a single executive was often responsible for ten or twelve different businesses—concrete, industry- or firm-specific knowledge and skills were devalued. The newer, more abstract and analytical tools and techniques of rational management offered an approach to success that operated without regard to industry distinctions. For example, the common method for evaluating a division's products and services now employed financial metrics. Financial metrics had already been at the heart of the control system of the multidivisional form of organization, because they determined the allocation of capital and other resources to individual businesses. Now they were quickly and easily applied to the management of divisions even in unrelated businesses. The human relations model of management from the 1930s, with its emphasis on interpersonal skills and motivation, felt less and less suited to the conglomerate environment. The rational model, by contrast, fit like a glove, given its conception of management as analytics, planning, and control, an approach that organizational scholars have sometimes called "systems rationalism" or the "Carnegie perspective" (reflecting the central role played in its development and diffusion by the Carnegie Institute of Technology's Graduate School of Industrial Administration, to be discussed in chapter 6). The perceived value of a human relations perspective on the corporation—akin to what today falls under the rubric of "organizational behavior"—was dramatically reduced by the organizational design of the new, diversified corporation, where the corporate center was rigidly segregated from the divisions, and the divisions from one another. The organizational structure and promotion policies of Textron illustrate the insular attitude cultivated among managers under this strict division of labor: "One of the keys to our success has been our approach to organization. We have no promotion up to the corporate level from the division ranks; all of our corporate men have come into the company from the outside . . . [I]f we are going to manage the capital entrusted to us most efficiently, it is essential to maintain the independent review of an outside corporate group. . . . We don't have any committees of division managers voting on each other's projects, either; that would just end up with everybody doing favors for each other."[35]

The adoption and intensive use of techniques of rational management by conglomerates strengthened in organizations of all kinds the now growing belief that management was, at its core, a technical activity. The ultimate importance of these techniques would lie not only in their use for administering large, complex enterprises but also in how the techniques shaped managers' understanding and analysis of organizational issues, and, further, shaped the ways in which managers communicated about them. The development and diffusion of the new techniques of rational management in the postwar American corporation would be significantly facilitated by changes in the business school curriculum in the late 1950s and 1960s. In turn, the conception of rational management that took hold in corporations after the war would leave a deep imprint on business education from the 1950s well into the 1970s.

▙ Growing Involvement of the Federal Government with Higher Education

Meanwhile, business schools and their parent institutions were being directly, and profoundly, influenced by a second major change in American society that stemmed from the Depression era's New Deal programs and from World War II: increasingly, the federal government was taking a role in areas of national life where it had previously played little or no part. The professions, private business, and other private institutions had become larger and more powerful in the postwar period, but their significance paled in comparison with the expanded powers of the government.[36] One of the most important of the areas in which the federal government exerted new influence was higher education.

Aside from the passage in the nineteenth century of the two Morrill acts, which had made federal resources available to finance the founding of "land grant" colleges and universities run by the states, the federal government had played virtually no role in the creation of the American research university. It had been under the auspices primarily of private philanthropy and state governments that the university had become a dynamic center of teaching, research, and public service. After the end of World War II, however, amid widespread concern both to avoid a postwar recession and to win the emerging political contest with Soviet communism, the U.S. government turned its attention to higher education. The goals of the nation now appeared to justify a federal interest in institutions of higher learning and in academic research. Numerous books and articles have described the development of the postwar American research university, linking it to a number of conditions: unprecedented demand for higher education; a comprehensive array of new financial aid programs; the large endowments of private universities; funding for research from a variety of federal agencies and national research institutes; and the institutionalized support and stability provided by large-scale, publicly funded state university systems.[37] My purpose is not to review all these factors but, rather, briefly to describe two federal policies that had particular implications for the development of business schools: the GI Bill and extensive support for university research.

The GI Bill and the Boom in Business School Enrollments

Often described as one of the most important factors in the creation of the large and prosperous American middle class of the post–World War II era, the GI Bill—or the Servicemen's Readjustment Act of 1944, as it was officially known—was enacted with the intention of heading off a potential unemployment crisis following the demobilization of millions of soldiers at the end of the war. As the tensions that had beset the wartime alliance between the United States and the Soviet Union grew and began to harden into the conflict known as the Cold War, the government saw an educated citizenry and a secure and prosperous middle class as necessities for defending democracy and other basic American values. With their modern history as instruments of meritocracy in the United States, the nation's colleges and universities seemed to offer an obvious mechanism for creating economic opportunity and social mobility for ordinary Americans. Policy analysts of all types promoted the belief that higher education should be enlisted in this task.

By offering returning veterans the opportunity to attend colleges and universities (as well as by providing other benefits including low-interest home loans), the GI Bill created the conditions necessary for the emergence of a significant middle class. When universities began responding to the needs of veterans, the institution of higher education in the United States changed forever. During the eight years that the original act was in force (the "Korean GI Bill," passed in 1952, included benefits for Korean War veterans), the government distributed vouchers to some eight million veterans, enabling them to attend whatever educational institutions accepted them. In fact, the GI Bill represented the most widespread, comprehensive educational entitlement in American history. The influx of nearly 1.5 million veterans to colleges and universities immediately after the war meant that higher education was no longer seen as simply a training ground for the nation's elite.

That business schools and undergraduate business programs were greatly affected by the GI Bill in the postwar era should come as no surprise. Business was among the most popular areas of study for the returning GIs, with the number of individuals enrolled in business programs jumping from about 19,000 (accounting for 3 percent of all bachelor's degrees awarded) in 1939 to 72,000 (accounting for 17 percent of degrees awarded) in 1950.[38] The increase in enrollments in business schools and programs, and the proliferation of new schools and programs that it brought about, exerted an overall downward pull on quality and standards that, as we shall see, made business education highly vulnerable to attack from outside forces. At the same time, by inviting higher levels of government involvement in academia, the GI Bill and other forms of federal aid to higher education had the effect, in the long run, of limiting business schools' ability to solve these problems on their own. For colleges and universities generally, as well as for business programs and schools in particular, the implementation of the GI Bill contributed to a subtle but unmistakable erosion of autonomy in relation to the federal government and, ultimately, to other powerful outside actors.

Because the government was now providing a significant amount of the funding that colleges and universities received from tuition, Congress naturally took an interest in how the money was being spent. The original version of the GI Bill lacked any clear articulation of what actually constituted a college or university—an omission that gave rise to massive corruption and abuses by the "fly-by-night" universities, for-profit educational institutions, and "diploma mills" that arose and attempted to benefit from this new source of federal largesse. Alarmed by congressional proposals that would have placed the government in charge of determining which institutions were qualified to receive funds from student loans and tuition grants under the GI Bill, colleges and universities banded together to placate Congress while preserving their access to federal resources. In this highly politicized context, university administrators' primary strategy was to urge Congress to recognize the role of accrediting bodies for setting educational standards and certifying the quality of educational institutions.[39] Educators sought to limit governmental involvement in higher education solely to making decisions about funding, and to maintain their own authority over decisions about appropriate content and methods for academic programs.[40] Accreditation as a requirement for federal funding was, therefore, the result of a political compromise between Congress, which sought accountability for the use of government resources, and educators, who sought to limit the government's interference in higher education.

When the GI Bill was reauthorized in 1952, the new version gave the U.S. commissioner of education the legal authority to publish a list of federally approved educational accrediting agencies. Soon after President Harry S. Truman signed the 1952 GI Bill, the U.S. Office of Education published a list of federally recognized agencies using the criteria recommended by the newly established National Commission on Accrediting. Thus the GI Bill played an important part in dramatically changing the nature of the relationship between the federal government and institutions of higher education, ultimately enhancing the power of the government and reducing the place for self-regulation and -certification of the kind that accrediting or visiting bodies had been exercising since the 1920s in colleges, universities, and professional schools.[41] For business schools, the new accrediting mechanism transformed a process that had been rooted in values of voluntarism and self-improvement—the grounding philosophy of the AACSB—into a quasi-governmental function through which business schools, along with other institutions of higher education, established their eligibility for federal funding.[42] As a result of this change, business schools found themselves in a much more organized, complex, and interdependent environment than they had previously inhabited. The complexities of this new environment would eventually cause business schools to cede control of their destiny to outside actors—and effectively, as a result, to abandon the professionalization project that had animated the schools since their founding. Yet we cannot fully understand these complexities without taking account of a second factor, besides the implementation of the GI Bill, that served to increase federal involvement in higher education after the war, forever altering the relationship between the government and the university, and thus also the nature of the university and its constituent parts.

Federal Support for University Research

While the GI Bill occasioned the indirect involvement of the federal government in evaluating and accrediting institutions of higher learning, the government became directly involved in activity within the university through greatly increased support for university-based research—a phenomenon that originated with the government's heavy reliance on such research during World War II. Even prior to the United States' entry into the war the government, for the first time, began to mobilize scholars for projects and systematically shape academic research. In the summer of 1941, President Franklin D. Roosevelt established the Office of Scientific Research and Development (OSRD) to mobilize civilian research and development activities in service of national defense. Led by Vannevar Bush, a former dean of engineering at MIT and president of the Carnegie Institution of Washington, this agency enlisted the cooperation of many of the most influential figures in science and technology in the United States, including the presidents of Harvard University and MIT and the chairman of Bell Telephone Laboratories. The projects ultimately overseen by the OSRD, including the development of radar, the computer, and the atomic bomb, would make clear the importance of organized science to the nation's defense. Because these developments had resulted from a cooperative effort among the institutions of government, universities, and corporations, they also helped solidify a conflation of interests that would have been unthinkable in the 1920s or 1930s.[43]

In 1945, Bush published his famous report *Science, the Endless Frontier*, which called for a postwar federal science policy. Its principal recommendations offered a road map for the creation of scientific research programs and policies by individual federal agencies.[44] By the end of the war, the federal government had become the center of basic research in the United States. Most federal agencies, such as the Department of Agriculture and the Department of Defense, initiated intra-agency programs to support basic research that was consistent with their broad missions. The National Institute of Health, which had been part of the OSRD, gained permanent status and became the chief supporter of basic research in the health sciences, establishing an elaborate grant and contracting system with the nation's medical schools. The U.S. Navy, seeking to initiate a research program as formidable as the one created by the army's atomic monopoly, founded the Office of Naval Research in 1946. That same year, Congress established the Atomic Energy Commission to develop nuclear power, independent of military interests; the commission introduced a model for contractual agreements between the government and private sector organizations, including universities and corporations. In 1950, Congress, acting on one of the key recommendations of the Bush report, set up the National Science Foundation (NSF), a government-funded but essentially civilian-controlled system for funding research and development across the various natural and social sciences. Meanwhile, the establishment of institutions such as the Bureau of Applied Research at Columbia, numerous defense-related institutes located near universities such as MIT and the California Institute of Technology, as well as national laboratories like that at Los Alamos—all supported by income from contracts with both government and private corporations—helped change the face of research and the university. Whereas, prior to World War II, the federal government had funded a negligible amount of university research, by 1953 more than half of the support for basic research on university campuses came from federal grants. By 1963, that proportion had reached 76 percent.[45]

While initially the bulk of federal funding went to support the basic sciences and health care, social scientists felt that they, too, offered expertise worthy of federal support. During the war, social scientists, like their counterparts in the physical and natural sciences, had carried out numerous federally funded studies to support the war effort. Sociologists conducted the first large-scale attitude studies on the factors affecting the commitment of American soldiers. Psychologists had studied the behavior of bomber crews and created psychological tests for matching individuals to particular jobs. Within the Foreign Broadcast Intelligence Service (originally established as the Foreign Broadcast Monitoring Service in 1941), sociologists were employed to examine the content of both enemy and U.S. propaganda and suggest how the latter could best be used to advance U.S. interests. Social scientists argued that such studies, utilizing rigorous scientific methods, had proven the usefulness of social science and could be applied to many important postwar problems. Moreover, new scientific techniques such as surveys, psychological tests, statistical analysis, and computer modeling would require significant financial resources—not as large as the amounts needed by the natural sciences, but far larger than the social sciences had ever needed before. For instance, the sample-survey technique that had become widely used during the war, especially by the Department of Labor and the Department of Agriculture, required the employment of large numbers of economists, demographers, and statisticians to collect usable data.[46]

The dramatic increase in federal funding for university-based research affected the economic model of the major American research university by creating a substantial new source of revenue, but the impact was more than monetary. Federal funding programs also produced changes in the university's basic structure. Given this large financial stake in higher education, the government had a correspondingly large interest in how such funds were administered and spent. As a result, a plethora of government guidelines and requirements specified practices that universities had to follow in order to qualify for federal grants. In response to these requirements, universities increasingly grew to resemble one another in their basic structures and practices. For example, NSF grants enforced common protocols for policing how research money was being spent, reviewing studies that used human or animal subjects, establishing environmental protection measures, and record keeping. The administrative structures and practices introduced by universities to comply with these requirements contributed to a narrowing conception of what constituted appropriate research methods. The new structures also altered the composition of university workforces. While we often think of the heart of an American university as being its full-time faculty, the administrative requirements entailed by federal research grants gave rise to a burgeoning contingent of what Clark Kerr called the "unfaculty"— researchers who did not hold regular faculty appointments.[47] These included non–tenure track faculty; administrative staff to both secure and account for federal grants; postdoctoral fellows; research associates; and technicians to maintain the complex laboratories, computers, and other facilities required for advanced research.

As was the case with the accrediting process that arose in the wake of the GI Bill, the entry of the federal government into the funding of university-based research entailed a considerable loss of autonomy for the university. For business schools—which engaged in very little research at this point and received little federal research funding—the impact of the new federal support for research was negligible. However, the dynamic that operated between universities and the federal government would eventually make itself felt in business schools, as federal support for university-based research had the effect of making research a criterion for educational legitimacy in the eyes of another set of outside actors who began to exert a decisive influence on the American university.

📖 Foundations and Higher Education

While the GI Bill and federal funding for basic research introduced a powerful new actor—the federal government—into the arena of higher education, these initiatives also strengthened the role of other intermediate authorities focused on education, chief among them the nation's large philanthropic foundations. Two large foundations in particular—the Carnegie Corporation and the Ford Foundation—would take a keen interest in university business education in the postwar era. Whereas many smaller foundations, along with almost all charities established prior to the advent of the modern foundation, had focused on almsgiving, the large foundations funded by the great fortunes of individuals such as Andrew Carnegie, John D. Rockefeller, and Henry Ford saw themselves not as providers of alms but as catalysts of scientific and social progress. This meant that when wealthy foundations such as Carnegie and Ford turned their attention to a field like business education, significant, large-scale change could be expected. To appreciate the postwar impact this shift would cause, we need to review the earlier steps that solidified the prominent role of these foundations in influencing American colleges and universities.

By the 1920s, foundations constituted the most powerful institution shaping the general policies of U.S. higher education. Foundation executives such as Rockefeller's Frederick T. Gates or Carnegie's Frederick P. Keppel ("philanthropoids," as they were self-described by Keppel) became some of the most prominent and visible supporters of higher education.[48] One survey carried out just before the outbreak of World War II concluded that between 1880 and 1939, foundations and similar charitable trusts had given $680 million to higher education.[49] For the Rockefeller and Carnegie foundations, the mandate of solving social problems became virtually synonymous with supporting higher education, especially large private research universities.

Given the rich vein of foundation money available, universities adapted their structures and practices to attract foundation monies. At the Carnegie Foundation for the Advancement of Teaching, Henry S. Pritchett (who, while still president of MIT, had organized the foundation in 1906, and then served as its president from that year until 1930) stated in 1906 that the foundation's definition of a college "would go far to resolve the confusion that then existed in American higher education."[50] Pritchett was referring to the fact that many self-described "colleges" often lacked even such rudiments of an institution of higher education as a permanent faculty or permanent buildings; the prospect of foundation funding, however, would create powerful incentives for conformity to standards that a foundation like Carnegie might impose as a condition of making grants. John D. Rockefeller's General Education Board, established in 1903 to provide aid for education at all levels, also exercised significant influence on the educational policies and programs of the colleges and universities to which it provided funds.[51] As one scholar notes, "The Board might 'suggest' that a college reduce an over-expanded program, modify its endowment policies, install an adequate system of book-keeping, or better articulate [in the foundation's vernacular, this might mean a merger] with related or near-by colleges."[52] Colleges and universities, in turn, would restructure their activities to take these requirements into account. In this way, foundations, for example, helped universities establish social science departments and essentially developed the position of post-doctoral research fellow. Universities also sometimes hired faculty who had received prior research funding from a particular foundation, hoping thereby to forge closer ties between the university's administration, or the department chair, and the foundation executives. Moreover, even if they had not yet received grants, many colleges and universities voluntarily conformed to the foundations' requirements, both to remain in the running for future grants and to adopt what were increasingly regarded as best practices.

Foundations would exercise a powerful effect on business schools, along with the academic institutions of which they were a part, in the post–World War II era by helping to emphasize research as a criterion of academic legitimacy. In the case of business schools, however, foundation support for research would take a particular form, rooted in what was already, by the end of World War II, a long-standing commitment by some of the most important American foundations to research in the social sciences.

Prior to World War I, the large foundations such as Carnegie and Rockefeller had focused their patronage primarily on two activities: supporting natural scientists, especially those in the physical and biological sciences, and facilitating the growth of the American research university.[53] The Carnegie Institution of Washington focused on the physical sciences and undertook the development of the solar telescope, marine biology stations, and a physics laboratory. The Rockefeller Institute for Medical Research was organized as a freestanding research laboratory in which the best available researchers were hired to investigate whatever topics or subjects interested them most. Both Carnegie and Rockefeller also seeded the development of new institutions of higher education. Rockefeller monies, for example, funded the University of Chicago while also endowing a number of technical institutes and teaching colleges that served black Americans. The Carnegie Foundation, in turn, undertook an extensive effort to reform American professional schools, the most famous example being the 1910 Flexner report on medical education, discussed in chapter 2.

After World War I, both the Rockefeller and Carnegie foundations expanded their research activities to address broader social problems such as crime, poverty, race relations, and industrial unrest. James Rowland Angell (son of University of Michigan president James B. Angell, a psychologist at the University of Michigan and then the University of Chicago, and briefly the president of the Carnegie Corporation before he left to assume the presidency of Yale in 1921) broadened Carnegie's activities to include support for research on "those forces in the social order that promise to be significant and fruitful," by which he meant work in the emerging social sciences.[54] During the interwar years, the Carnegie and Rockefeller foundations were the most significant sources of funding for social science research, showering disciplines such as economics, sociology, and psychology with resources to expand departments, hire faculty, and conduct research. The foundations' interest in using the social sciences to solve social problems can be traced, in part, to an increasing belief that the social sciences were at the edge of a paradigm breakthrough akin to that which had occurred in medicine and the physical sciences a few decades earlier. The hope was that, for the first time, important social problems could be addressed in a systematic and scientific manner. Foundation leaders such as Carnegie's Angell or the Laura Spelman Rockefeller Memorial Foundation's Beardsley Ruml believed that the social sciences, by demonstrating their usefulness in this way, would finally achieve equal status with the natural sciences.

The strategy for foundation support of the social sciences, however, took a different form from the one for support for the physical and biological sciences. Part of the challenge faced by social science disciplines in their formative decades was that the work of social scientists was always considered more "political" than "scientific." Dismissals of social science faculty, typically on political grounds, played a large part in triggering the 1915 founding of the American Association of University Professors to establish and defend the principle of academic freedom. The focus of sociologists and psychologists on phenomena such as alienation and anomie in urban, industrial society attracted the suspicion and hostility of conservative apologists for the new industrial order, as did the tone of Protestant moralizing that characterized many of the social scientists' pronouncements.[55] Skepticism about social science arose in liberal circles as well, as when the Rockefeller Foundation was accused of bias for using a Rockefeller family adviser (who did have a Ph.D. in political economy from Harvard) to assess the state of American industrial relations and evaluate the role of unions in American society.[56]

Recognizing the potentially sensitive nature of social science theories and research, the heads of Carnegie and Rockefeller believed that a formal and effective separation would have to be made between the foundations and their researchers and, what was just as important, that foundation support should be directed primarily toward empirical work rather than theoretical research. As a result, most foundation support for the social sciences, during the interwar years, took the form of either establishing arm's-length relationships with research institutes, such as the National Bureau of Economic Research and the Brookings Institution, that conducted policy-oriented research, or directly underwriting the research projects of individual social scientists in universities. The Carnegie Corporation, for example, underwrote several important social science studies during the 1920s based on survey and field research, including *The Negro in Chicago*, one of the first surveys of race relations, and funded a number of studies concerning the Americanization of different ethnic groups. Other similarly significant inquiries conducted in this era with the support of foundation monies included Yale anthropologist John Dollard's *Caste and Class in a Southern Town* (published in 1937) and Duke University sociologist Hornell Hart's *The Techniques of Social Progress* (1931).

By supporting this type of survey- and field-based research, foundations contributed to a distinctly American form of social science research. Foundations simultaneously discouraged scholarly research projects that aimed at developing overly broad or polemical theories of the type that characterized the European social sciences.[57] Edward Shils noted that, by the late 1930s, it was widely understood in social science circles that the key to winning a foundation research grant was to propose a practical, empirical project that would be grounded in facts and close observations.[58]

By the end of the 1930s, this approach to research had become institutionalized, so that most social scientists had come to take it for granted that collecting data was the primary way to advance a science of society or the mind, and that the best evidence was quantitative and statistically reliable. If such data were not available, then the next best data were based on deep field study, interviews, and primary documents. By pressing social science researchers in the direction of empirical studies focused on hard data, the foundations helped ensure that the results of studies in the social sciences could contribute to important policy decisions. In her history of the Carnegie Corporation, Ellen Condliffe Lagemann asserts: "Without the assistance of the Corporation and a few other philanthropies, economics and the social sciences generally might well have remained on a par with the classics, Egyptology, and other branches of the humanities; that is, they might have remained interesting to many able people, but not bases for public policy-making." She further notes that it was the foundations—particularly Carnegie and the Laura Spelman Rockefeller Memorial Foundation—that strategically placed social scientists, especially economists, in positions where they could influence policy.[59]

With respect to business schools, the role of the Laura Spelman Rocke-feller Memorial Foundation is of particular note, insofar as it sponsored the first significant research to demonstrate the potential of the social sciences for management education. The foundation's head, Beardsley Ruml, believed that the key contribution of social science was its ability to address social problems that accompanied the development of an industrial society. Ruml was particularly concerned with the industrial workforce and its associated phenomena—urbanization, social anomie, and mass society—as subjects of study. In 1922, he set aside $20 million to fund scholars in the fields of sociology, psychology, and anthropology whose work was directed at solving the most significant societal problems of the day. Ruml's focus on industrial problems allowed him to distinguish the Spelman Foundation's activities from the other Rockefeller research programs. During his tenure, the foundation secretly funded the development of the fifteen-volume *Encyclopedia of the Social Sciences*, which "took shape at the nexus of private philanthropy, scientific social reform, and the quest for professional prestige."[60] It was also Ruml who discovered Elton Mayo, the man who would become the moving spirit behind the famous Hawthorne studies, perhaps the most influential management research of all time.

For much of the early 1920s, Elton Mayo was an itinerant scholar, moving from school to school without a permanent academic position. While, as he would later describe it, "wandering aimlessly through the streets of San Francisco" and planning to return to his native Australia because of his inability to secure lecture bookings or an academic position, Mayo received an invitation and a train ticket to come east and meet with Ruml to discuss his musings about the psychology of industrial workers. In a letter to his wife, Mayo would describe his meeting with Ruml as "the best thing that ever happened to us."[61] Ruml subsequently secured an appointment for Mayo in Wharton's Department of Industrial Research and helped finance Mayo's research on industrial plant workers in the Philadelphia area. At Wharton, Mayo very quickly became a close confidant of the dean, Joseph Willits; the two shared a conviction that industrial work as it was then organized and managed was causing workers to become increasingly alienated both from their employers and from the larger society. This disaffection of the workforce, Mayo believed, was bringing American society closer to the precipice of radicalism and large-scale rebellion. A flamboyant lecturer and a popular writer, Mayo quickly became known in the Philadelphia business community. A series of articles he published in *Harper's* magazine about modern industrial problems brought him to the attention of Harvard Business School's Wallace Donham, who then invited Mayo to a dinner in New York City. Over the next few months, Donham and Mayo communicated regularly, having found a common bond in their similar ideas about the malaise affecting modern society. Donham subsequently secured funding from Ruml for a professorship for Mayo. In 1926, Donham appointed Mayo, then forty-six, as an associate professor of the Harvard Business School, with a salary and a research budget significantly in excess of those commanded by any other HBS faculty member. In an unprecedented move, Donham relieved Mayo of all teaching duties so that Mayo could devote his full attention to studying the motivations of workers.

Over the next several years, Mayo would become one of the most prominent members of the Harvard Business School faculty. His contributions to interpreting the initially anomalous findings in the study of the effects of environmental and physiological conditions on worker productivity at Western Electric's Hawthorne plant laid the foundation for the human relations conception of management. The conception emphasized that organizations are not just technical and production systems but social systems as well. The manager's role, in this light, was reinterpreted to include the oversight of a complex social system in which "soft" factors such as status, informal communication, norms, and roles powerfully affected organizational behavior. Managerial effectiveness thus depended on expertise in managing interpersonal relations and group dynamics.

When the United States entered World War II at the end of 1941, however, interest in the human relations approach to management took a backseat as American society focused on the practicalities of mobilizing the nation's factories to win the war. When the war ended, the boom in business school enrollments and the ensuing expansion of business programs in the nation's colleges and universities masked underlying weaknesses in American business education. These weaknesses, with which business school leaders had been unsuccessfully wrestling for quite some time, became glaring in view of the requirements of a new organizational society. As the influence of the federal

government and the philanthropic foundations on American higher education increased, business schools seemed unable to put their own houses
in order. Their failure to maintain control of their own destiny—which resulted in a failure to complete the professionalization project of the early
twentieth century—would be a product, not just of influence by powerful external institutions (the government and foundations) over American colleges
and universities, but also of the weakening of the one institutional mechanism
business schools themselves possessed for initiating a shared strategy and program of action.

The Decline of the AACSB

As we saw in chapter 4, throughout the 1920s and 1930s, the deans and leading
faculty members of AACSB member business schools had struggled with the
most fundamental kinds of issues—issues of purpose, curriculum, and research agendas—in their effort to establish their institutions as bona fide professional schools, and to turn management itself into a bona fide profession.
For leaders of these schools, the rapid growth that business education began
to experience almost immediately after the end of World War II failed to obscure the problems it still faced. As enrollments in business schools and undergraduate business programs expanded, creating demand for new schools
and programs, the problems previously identified during the Great Depression remained unaddressed; the war had simply postponed an inevitable reck-
oning. A postwar AACSB study found, for example, that few business schools
had adopted the curricular changes recommended by reform-minded deans
shortly before World War II began.[62] This failure was related not only to the
upheaval of the war itself but also to the changing of the guard in business
school leadership across the country, as deans who had been preeminent in
the drive to professionalize business education and management began to
leave the scene. Columbia's Roswell McCrea retired in 1941, Harvard Business
School's Wallace Donham at the end of the 1942–1943 academic year, and
NYU's Wellington Taylor in the fall of 1943. In the words of Robert Calkins
(who had been dean of Berkeley's College of Commerce, then of the Columbia School of Business, and later president of the Brookings Institution) as he
addressed an audience of business school deans in 1955, the pioneers "who established and directed the first business schools had to fight every principle,
prejudice, and preconception of academic life to introduce such a mundane

subject as business administration." These warriors were being replaced by a new generation of deans who saw themselves as custodians charged with the task of "consolidating the gains, of putting more intellectual body into the product."[63]

Given the state of the institutions inherited by the new generation of business school deans, combined with the expectations being placed on business education and management in the new organizational society, this custodial approach virtually guaranteed that business schools would accomplish little over the next few years beyond simply accommodating rapidly increasing numbers of students. A focus on "putting more intellectual body into the product," for example, tacitly assumed that the product had achieved more coherence than it actually had. Business schools remained related to one another more by a common name than by a common theory, pedagogy, or academic content. Not only was there, as yet, no common intellectual tradition or normative ethos on which the business curriculum could be centered; there was no reason to believe that one was developing. Even many of the original AACSB member schools continued to emphasize vocational and job-specific training in their curricula. New York University, for example, offered courses like Advertising Typography and Printing. Columbia's and Michigan's business schools offered classes in "secretarial science," elementary bookkeeping, and other routine office work. Functional courses in fields such as marketing or production were not substantively linked to any type of foundational knowledge such as might have been provided by psychology or engineering, respectively.

The lack of progress was difficult to justify, even allowing for the disruption due to World War II. Business schools could no longer claim the ignorance of youth. By 1946, the Wharton School was sixty-five years old, and nearly fifty years had passed since business schools at the University of Chicago, New York University, and Dartmouth had opened their doors. Several observers including Clark Kerr, chancellor of the University of California, now questioned whether the field of business could even be distilled into a coherent body of knowledge. He noted that other professions and academic disciplines that had arisen in the late nineteenth century, such as law, sociology, and psychology, exhibited, after a half century's development, well-recognized journals, professional associations, ongoing research sponsors, and academic publishing arms. Why had business education been such a laggard?

Internal AACSB studies undertaken in the 1930s had emphasized two possible explanations for the dismal state of business education: the students and the faculty. One set of studies criticized the quality and preparation of students. Some members believed that, in an effort to maintain or increase enrollment, many schools had failed to screen applicants adequately or to impose rigorous standards for graduation. These AACSB studies also found that the students going into graduate business schools, as measured by grades or standardized exams, were not as academically accomplished as those going into other fields of study.[64] A second set of AACSB studies suggested that the basic problem with business schools was the faculty, who were described, for example, as unfamiliar with even rudimentary research methods. Doctoral training for future business school faculty was relatively poor. In most business schools that offered it, doctoral education was marginal and not closely linked to training in either theory or systematic research methods. Harvard Business School's doctoral program, which was relatively well regarded, was said to consist of candidates spending

> most of their time collecting cases as research assistants for particular professors. After a few years of this training in case research (as it was understood by the professor for whom they worked), they often collected a half dozen or more cases of their own about some particular problem or topic. They added a final chapter about the administrative implications of the cases, and this constituted a thesis. Thus a graduate of the early program usually had training in only one method of research and one method of teaching. If he wanted to go into teaching as a career, he had to stay at the School or go to one which used the same methods.[65]

Even the most interesting research projects launched by business schools—the Hawthorne experiments, for example, which captured the attention and imaginations of both business managers and the public in the 1930s—failed to inspire other business academics to embrace the best practices these projects embodied. As Berkeley economist Robert A. Gordon would state in 1958, after having interviewed a large cross-section of business school faculty during the early 1950s, "I should be surprised if five per cent of the faculty members in graduate business school programs could provide a reasonably coherent account of basic research methodology (of the relationship between theory development and empirical investigation, hypothesis formulation and careful measurement and testing through observation)."[66]

In any case, academic standards at business schools failed to rise, and even deteriorated, during the early postwar years, while the federal government and the philanthropic foundations increasingly made their influence felt in the sphere of higher education. The AACSB remained the one hope that business education had for enforcing higher standards on itself and defending the autonomy of business schools against external encroachments. Yet just as it had failed, in the years between the two world wars, to foster a coherent approach to business education among its member schools, the organization would prove inadequate to the tasks of raising and enforcing standards in the post–World War II era. The impotence of the AACSB became apparent first in its unwillingness to sanction schools of marginal quality, and second in its transformation, after the passage of the two GI bills in 1944 and 1952, from a professional association into an accrediting agency acting essentially on behalf of third parties.

Unwillingness to Sanction Marginal Schools

The steady increase in the number of American business schools over the first half of the twentieth century constituted, by itself, an important influence on the evolution of the AACSB from its founding in 1916 to the beginning of its decline in the post–World War II era. Between 1916 and 1941, the association had grown from its original membership of 16 schools to 55 member institutions. Between 1946 and 1951, membership increased from 56 to 70 schools[67]— about half the total number of U.S. business schools. Recall that the original AACSB had been characterized by a high degree of homogeneity and strong agreement among its core members. As a result, deans from the more prominent schools (Harvard, Chicago, Dartmouth, Columbia, Northwestern, Pennsylvania, and Stanford) had been able to put the weaker schools (NYU, Nebraska, Texas, Tulane) at a disadvantage. In the postwar period, by contrast, the substantial (and uncontrolled) growth in business schools led to greater heterogeneity of interests within the association and a corresponding level of disagreement over what criteria would be used to define the components of a proper professional education in business. Even though many business schools founded in the postwar years did not qualify for membership in the AACSB even by its minimal standards, the expansion of membership overall allowed the lower-quality schools among its membership to exert greater influence and to resist more exacting standards or explicit stratification among schools.

The AACSB's inability to control even its weaker members was due, in part, to an inability to finance a permanent administrative function. There was little support among the general membership for creating a strong, centralized organizational structure. As late as 1941, when the AACSB had fifty-five members, each school paid annual dues of twenty-five dollars (the same amount as when the organization had been founded), most of which was spent to organize and administer the association's annual meeting. The problem, however, went deeper than finances. It lay in the basic organizational and governance structure of the AACSB, whose constitution ensured that "no act of the Association shall be held to control the policy or action of any member institution." This provision, originally intended by the AACSB's founders as a way to encourage experimentation, had become an impediment to creating any membership standards beyond the stipulation that member schools require at least two years of high school for admission to undergraduate programs and at least one year's study prior to the awarding of a master's degree. The association's weak enforcement of its minimal standards in the quarter century between its founding and 1941 is self-evident—it had never dropped a member school, even when violations were known to be occurring. This laxity stands in contrast to the strict standards of the accreditation activities of the American Bar Association, which, during this same era, frequently placed members on probation or dropped them from membership.

The inherent weaknesses of the AACSB—an inability to develop meaningful standards for what constituted a minimally acceptable curriculum or level of faculty qualifications, and the inability or unwillingness to discipline poor-quality business schools—became especially acute during the postwar business school boom. As business school programs expanded and enrollments soared between 1941 and 1952, lower-quality schools had strong incentives to resist attempts by higher-quality schools to modify the bylaws to introduce reforms, like minimal faculty credentials or research support, so as to make some schools ineligible for membership. An examination of AACSB "Proceedings" from the years immediately before and after the war reveals little discussion of creating more formal standards. Even powerful members of the association were pressured by colleagues to temper their desire for reform. A 1952 letter to Harvard Business School's dean, Donald David, from Lee Bidgood, dean of the University of Alabama's School of Business and newly elected president of the AACSB, cautioned David against pushing for enforceable standards at the next meeting. Acknowledging that most of the faculties at American business schools "do not average better than those of junior colleges," Bidgood warned that while "we may succeed in keeping a small accredited group on a high level of quality instruction," drawing attention to the "huge unaccredited output" would end up "reflecting unfavorably upon our profession."[68]

Active suppression of any criticism of business education thus became the informal policy of the AACSB. More stringent standards than those already entailed by the AACSB membership process, it was argued, would deny the lesser schools the spoils of tuition and federal financial aid. As a result, no serious attempts were made either to stem the unrestricted access of marginal business schools to the AACSB's mantle of presumed academic legitimacy, or to restructure the organization to recognize the divergent interests of research-oriented business schools and those that were more vocationally focused. Even the supposedly better schools were willing, when expedience demanded it, to ignore the AACSB's standards, low as they were. For example, at Wharton during the mid-1950s, half of the faculty taught more courses than the limit established by the AACSB.[69] One observer noted that the association "has not been noteworthy for bold and vigorous action or imaginative and progressive leadership." In general, he added, the association's "voice carries no weight at all in the best schools," with "some member schools seek[ing] to keep it weak."[70]

The AACSB's inability to keep out weaker schools, or to discipline schools for a lapse in standards, impeded progress of the professionalization project in business education, for reasons that are easily understandable. Eliot Freidson has noted that a credible professional association must be able to exercise control over the entry and exit of its members. Moreover, the criteria for membership must be clearly defined so as to prevent erroneous claims of association. All of this requires an ability to exercise legitimate control over marginal members of a group. The AACSB's inability to exercise that control when confronted with the unprecedented growth of American business schools would eventually consign it to a marginal role in affecting the course of business education. The marginalization of the AACSB within the constellation of forces that would determine the future direction of business schools is reflected, in turn, by the association's evolution in the postwar years into an accrediting agency acting not to support its own interests but essentially only for the benefit of powerful outsiders.

The Shift from Professional Association to Accrediting Association

The marginalization of the AACSB within the institutional field of business schools is best represented by the drift of the association away from its original dual mission of improving business education—through accrediting, among other means—and professionalizing management. Gradually, the AACSB assumed the much more limited role of being simply an accrediting body. This transformation began during World War II and accelerated in the wake of the Korean GI Bill with the creation of a list of federally approved accrediting agencies charged with certifying schools as eligible for federal funding. The change was foreshadowed by discussions among AACSB members toward the end of the world war about the availability of federal resources for business schools. After the war's end, having discovered the enormous financial resources of the federal government, these AACSB members, originally part of a wartime curriculum committee charged with developing courses to meet military needs, now assembled as a lobbying group focused on shaping postwar educational policy to "insure that the interests of schools of business would be considered when the educational program for persons returning to school after the war was being developed." The group stated that it would thereafter work with the government "in order to help member schools cooperate with various governmental agencies and to keep posted on current legislation so that it can inform congressmen of the interests of schools of business in proposed legislation."[71]

Following the passage of the second GI Bill, business schools responded to the government's creation of a system of nationally recognized accrediting agencies by turning the AACSB from a voluntaristic association of business educators into an accrediting agency, pure and simple. Moreover, the nature of the accrediting process itself changed for the association: whereas accrediting had once been part of the AACSB's overarching mission of improving business education, with the ultimate goal of turning management into a bona fide profession, accrediting now meant certifying that business programs and business schools met the minimal standards for enrolling students under the terms of the GI Bill. An AACSB report summarizes the steps leading up to this transformation:

> Throughout the war period and immediately thereafter the Association undertook a complete review of the total resources available for the improvement of business education and a serious re-evaluation of its own function in this process. In this review it became immediately obvious that whether the Association wished it or not, the increase in membership was causing it to be looked upon more and more as an accrediting agency and not merely a consultative association. This change in the view . . . became even more pronounced

with the enactment of the GI Bill, and the listing in public documents of member schools as accredited by the Association. Thus,
this recognition came on the part of the public before the Association itself acknowledged that it was in fact an accrediting agency.[72]

   In this fundamental transformation of its character and role, the AACSB—
while weakened by the internal structural flaws discussed above—was also
strongly influenced by a series of unforeseen consequences of the federal government's new interest in certifying the integrity and competence of institutions of higher education. While the purpose of the initial federal legislation on
accreditation was to prevent the abuse and fraudulent use of government
grants, accreditation was seen, at least by the time of a 1970 report compiled by
the U.S. Office of Education, to be the "single most reliable indicator of institutional quality in higher education."[73] Over time, accreditation became a strategic route by which other objectives could be met: it soon worked as a screening
criterion, for example, for those in the corporate sector who were looking to
hire qualified university graduates. Likewise, when private citizens planned donations to universities, or when state licensing boards evaluated them, whether
or not an institution was accredited became of the utmost concern.
   Whether utilized for the benefit of the government or for that of private
interests, however, the accreditation process became yet another factor undermining the overall quality of business schools. The downward pressure on
standards exerted by accreditation was partly due to the fact that the
AACSB—in contrast to the accrediting bodies for medical, legal, and other
professional schools—was not an arm of a functioning profession but, rather,
an assembly of academic institutions. Accrediting bodies for other professional schools generally included practicing members of the related profession.[74] When practitioners are actively linked to accrediting agencies for
professional schools, some degree of balance between intra-academic and
professional interests is maintained, and concerns of practitioners can shape
curricula. The AACSB, by contrast, having little connection to practicing
managers, was oriented toward the interests of its member institutions rather
than to those of practicing professionals. The fact that the AACSB had
no formal links with practitioners meant that curricular decisions, and the
accreditation process that certified them, were dominated by university administrators concerned with buffering their institutions from economic uncertainty, and were insulated from the interests of practicing managers in
screening and training prospective practitioners. As a consequence, AACSB

standards for accreditation were minimal compared to those in any other major field of "professional" study.

Without any strong orientation toward practice, moreover, the structure and activities of the AACSB bore less and less resemblance to those of a group self-consciously engaged in a professionalization project. To be sure, it is difficult to imagine how a system originally designed to accommodate a small number of schools collectively producing two or three thousand practitioners a year could have been adapted to accommodate hundreds of schools with conflicting interests and tens of thousands of students of greatly varying goals and academic abilities. In any event, after the passage of the renewed GI Bill in 1952, the AACSB could no longer be described as a true association or community. In 1966, an AACSB publication would describe business schools as "still unable to speak with a united voice."[75]

Organized society abhors an organizational vacuum, so the vacuum created by the decline of the AACSB as an effective instrument of self-governance for business schools was quickly filled, in the years following the end of World War II, by one set of outside actors in particular—the large philanthropic foundations. The foundations stepped in, ostensibly to save college and university business education from itself and turn it into a purposeful educational and social force. While resources contributed by foundations would offer an enormous source of stability for business schools in the late 1950s and early 1960s, this would come about only after a transition period during which the involvement of foundations in business education created a particularly unstable context for business schools. In the aftermath of World War II, business schools found themselves in the enviable position of being considered vital to the economic, social, and political interests of the nation; at this critical moment of recognition, however, the schools were unable to initiate reform from within. Lacking the organizational capacity to answer the challenges of a fragmenting mission and declining academic standards, they would be forced, in the course of the 1950s and 1960s, to adopt a new set of organizational prescriptions to reassure external constituents about the viability of business education. These prescriptions would be handed down by two entities in particular: the Ford Foundation and, to a lesser extent, the Carnegie Corporation. But the story of how these foundations, in the postwar era, exercised a decisive influence on the future of business education merits telling in a chapter of its own.

Disciplining the Business School Faculty: **6**

The Impact of the Foundations

The first sixty years of university-based business education—from the founding of the Wharton School up until the eve of World War II—had been a period of diversity, experimentation, and, for the leaders of the business school movement, mounting frustration. In the 1920s and 1930s, the high aims with which the first business schools had been launched were increasingly thwarted by the challenges of creating a new variety of professional school—and indeed a whole new profession—virtually from scratch. The outbreak of the war brought the AACSB's attempted revival of the professionalization project in the 1930s to an abrupt halt, and the influx of new students and new funds after the war exacerbated the very problems that had threatened this project at the outset. The transcendent idea of professionalization that had animated the creation of the first business schools—to the extent that anyone remembered it at all—now seemed somehow beside the point.

The postwar environment, to be sure, created a very different context for business schools from the one that existed during the institution's early decades. Surging enrollments spurred by the GI Bill encouraged improvised solutions as opposed to purposeful experimentation and innovation. The availability of large amounts of federal funding (in the form of student aid, not research grants, for business schools at the time), combined with the pressures for external accountability that this funding entailed, created a demand for coarse-grained forms of quality assessment that could be applied across the board to a wide range of institutions. In terms of pedagogy, the labor-intensive process of instilling in future managers a strong sense of their social responsibilities as businesspeople (the perceived need for which had occasioned the strong consensus among AACSB deans in the 1930s about the future direction for business education) was impractical in light of the postwar expansion; a more mechanized, capital-intensive process for training large numbers of managers appeared to be required instead. Moreover, the moral introspection about the nature of the American economic system that had been induced by the Depression had given way—when the victory over fascism was followed swiftly by the rise of a new adversary in the form of Soviet communism—to a pragmatic desire to make the system *work*. Indeed, in the McCarthy era, anything that looked like criticism of business aroused suspicion. Under the pressure of these forces, the old problem of creating and imposing a definition of quality in business education was approached, in the postwar era, with a new solution: standardization.

While being desirable for ease in accreditation and efficiency in instruction, standardization in business education received enormous impetus from another factor: the increasing influence of large philanthropic foundations—the Carnegie and Ford foundations in particular—in the postwar years. In some ways, the impact of the foundations on business schools in this era continued the process of standardization that large foundations, such as the Rockefeller Foundation and the Carnegie Foundation for the Advancement of Teaching, had been effecting for most of the century in American higher education generally, as discussed in the previous chapter.

The standardizing effect of foundation funding for higher education was intensified by the concentration of resources that came about as large foundations such as Carnegie and Rockefeller (and eventually Ford) became increasingly important players in American higher education, first during the interwar years, and then after World War II. The Rockefeller and Carnegie foundations, for example, accounted for 64 percent of all philanthropic giving to universities between 1900 and 1935.[1] This concentration was in marked contrast to the situation that had existed throughout the nineteenth and even into the early twentieth century, when support for higher education came from widely disparate sources. Until the large national foundations arrived on the scene and eventually became influential players, private universities gathered resources by approaching individuals and organizations in their local areas, while public universities lobbied their respective state legislatures. The emergence of large, national-profile foundations, as well as the federal government, as major financial supporters of higher education after World War II concentrated the sources of higher education funding to an unprecedented degree. Moreover, foundation priorities in the funding of higher education changed after World War II in ways that reinforced the trend toward increased homogeneity and standardization. Prior to the war, foundations had placed equal emphasis on making grants to individuals, seeding new organizations, and giving to established ones; in the postwar period, by contrast, the proportion of foundation dollars allocated to already-established institutions of higher education steadily increased, and giving to individual grantees and to new institutions declined proportionately.[2]

The story of foundation funding for business schools and its effects follows this same overall pattern of increasing concentration and homogeneity, although one must allow for the fact that, even in established universities, business schools were relatively young institutions, and business schools overall (for the reasons outlined in chapters 4 and 5) were often more vulnerable to outside influence than were other parts of the university. Before World War II, the various Rockefeller philanthropies (including the General Education Board and the Laura Spelman Rockefeller Memorial Foundation) exerted the greatest impact on business education. The General Education board provided one-half of the unrestricted $125,000 subscription fund that enabled the Harvard Graduate School of Business Administration to be launched in 1908. The Laura Spelman Rockefeller Memorial Foundation, as we saw in chapter 5, had supported the psychologist Elton Mayo's research, first at Wharton and then at Harvard. In the postwar period, foundations supported business education with the explicit goal of changing the institution. The Carnegie and Ford foundations' interest in business education derived from a shared perception that the poor quality of many American business schools threatened American business institutions and, ultimately, the health of the economy and of American democracy. As business schools proliferated and enrollments increased, this expansion imperiled the meager academic legitimacy of business education by multiplying the number of weak institutions; to retain whatever legitimacy they had, schools needed to be judged not only on the basis of the number of students passing through them but on the basis of well-defined, consensus-driven expectations for the quality of students, faculty, and research. Whereas the AACSB, as we have seen, had been unable to establish such expectations from within, the foundations would impose them from without.

The process of standardization engineered by the foundations worked in subtle ways. For example, foundations gained influence over business schools partly through the advantages that foundation support offered over existing funding mechanisms for business schools (mechanisms that were, of course, the same ones relied on by colleges and universities in general). Public funding depended on the political climate, and gifts from individuals depended on the whims of benefactors. Because foundation grants were often doled out over several years, they offered the significant benefit of bringing predictability to at least a portion of a school's otherwise unpredictable revenue stream. Over time, several business schools favored by the Ford Foundation (the ones that would be categorized as "centers of excellence") came to count on regular contributions, even incorporating foundation grants into their budgetary expectations. In the process, curricula, faculty composition, and research were all profoundly affected, as we shall see.

Paradoxically, the standardization that foundation support for business school education was intended to promote also resulted in the kind of formal stratification that, before the war, it had been the deliberate policy of the AACSB to prevent. As standardization became the path to legitimacy, the existence of a large number of business schools with increasingly similar needs became the dominant reality, as did the importance of competing for funds from increasingly concentrated sources. In the more diffuse and localized funding environment that existed before the war—one that fostered the high degree of variance in business school education models that it had been the policy of the AACSB to promote—business schools (like other institutions of higher education) viewed themselves as essentially incommensurable with one another. In an environment of competition for concentrated resources, on the other hand, the foundations attempted to create commensurability so as to have a rational basis for awarding grants to some schools and not others. As certain schools were singled out for significant foundation support, a self-reinforcing stratification process began to set in: the best faculty and doctoral students were attracted to those institutions that offered the stability and prestige bestowed by foundation grants. Thus the foundations exerted both centripetal and centrifugal force on business schools, creating incentives for standardization while simultaneously helping the favored schools to distinguish themselves from the majority. That most business schools apparently fell short of the standards being promulgated by the foundations helped fuel a growing perception among educators and the broader public that business schools as a group had become, in Herbert Simon's words, "a wasteland of vocationalism" attracting the university's least intellectual faculty and lowest-quality students.[3] This perception, in turn, created a rationale for the continued involvement of the foundations in improving the quality of American business education.

The large foundations' power to allot resources ultimately meant that they were able to determine whether schools were "legitimate." Yet the foundations gained their considerable influence over business schools not only by dispensing money but by presenting themselves as neutral arbiters advocating on behalf of society. The largest foundations came to be characterized as organized collectivities of expertise, and Carnegie and Ford were seen as (and believed themselves to be) disinterested judges of what business education should look like in the future. Given their confidence in this vision, taking action to realize it was a natural next step, so the judges also became builders—architects of a new order among the business schools. The reality behind these foundations' stance of detachment and disinterestedness vis-à-vis business schools was, however, a bit more complex—particularly, as we shall see, in the case of the Ford Foundation.[4]

The broad-based reforms in business education initiated by the Carnegie and Ford foundations began in the early 1950s. Carnegie's impact would be restricted mostly to undergraduate business education, where the foundation pursued a goal of incorporating more liberal arts courses and fewer vocational ones into the curriculum for undergraduate business majors. The Ford Foundation, by contrast, would leave a deep imprint on graduate business education. For a period of nearly fifteen years, Ford used its enormous financial resources as both carrot and stick to reform not only MBA curricula but also the entire structure of graduate business education.

The lesser influence exercised by the Carnegie Corporation on graduate business education was a function of its historical approach of relying on the issuance of reports to catalyze professional school reform. This strategy centered on commissioning extensive surveys and studies and then broadly disseminating their findings and recommendations; the intention was to affect the direction of professional education by providing what Clark Kerr, who had been chairman of two Carnegie-sponsored educational programs, called "blueprints for action."[5] Up until the 1950s, the Carnegie foundations had been undisputed leaders in shaping the direction of university-based professional schools,[6] while in the 1930s business school leaders had actively but unsuccessfully sought Carnegie's support for their efforts to reform business education.[7] By the time Carnegie was in a position to act on its interest in business education after the end of World War II, its efforts would be overshadowed by the much more assertive approach of the Ford Foundation.

In contrast to Carnegie, Ford had no historical legacy in the area of higher education. Yet also in contrast to Carnegie, the Ford Foundation had adopted an explicit policy of not limiting its activities to the drafting of reports and administration of research grants. Because of its broad mission to "improve human welfare," and the enormous riches that had flowed into the foundation's coffers following the deaths of Henry Ford and his son Edsel in the 1940s, the Ford trustees earmarked $500 million in 1955 to be spent on the implementation of programs in all of its various fields of interest. By the time the Ford Foundation concluded its program in business education in the early 1960s, it would have spent over $35 million (approximately $175 million in 2005 dollars). Thus, although I will discuss elements of the 1959 Carnegie report on business education in this chapter, my focus will be on the activities of the Ford Foundation, whose trustees regarded its business school project as one of its most important undertakings throughout the 1950s.

Overall, the changes in business education that occurred in the 1950s and 1960s had their origins in specific agendas developed by the Carnegie and Ford foundations, and were driven by individuals who had both foundation and business school affiliations. Notable among them were Dean Donald K. David of the Harvard Business School (HBS), who served on the board of the Ford Foundation and would become chairman of the executive committee of the foundation's board of trustees, and George Leland ("Lee") Bach, founding dean of the Carnegie Institute of Technology's Graduate School of Industrial Administration (GSIA), who was an adviser to and confidant of Thomas H. Carroll, the Ford Foundation vice president who oversaw and administered Ford's business school activities throughout their most intensive phase. Bach, through his connections with the Ford Foundation, would help ensure that his own fledgling business school's model of discipline-trained faculty and disciplinary research served as the exemplar for business education as a whole, while David would advocate, with mixed success, for Harvard's general management approach to business education and for the case method of teaching. The interconnections between the Ford Foundation and these two business schools would help shape the content of the foundation's recommendations for business education reform—recommendations that were presented as if they had emerged independently from systematic research. Indeed, as I will show, the "crisis" in business education that would be proclaimed by the Carnegie and Ford foundations in 1959 was in fact engineered by parties such as David and Bach, whose roles as business school deans were intertwined with—and also, to a degree, in conflict with—their roles as agents of the foundations, and whose specific ideas for reshaping business education were initially developed as early as 1949. By 1953, at which point the Ford Foundation was well on its way to transforming itself from a small foundation of virtually no national significance into a major player on both the national and the international scenes, forward-looking business school deans such as David and Bach were able to yoke their causes to the intensifying conflict of the Cold

War, in which context the most serious questions facing business schools appeared to overlap with the most pressing issues facing the United States itself.

⌐ The Ford Foundation in the Postwar Environment

The interest of both the Carnegie and the Ford foundations in business education in the postwar years was, in part, a response to the growth of business schools and to the heightened public interest in higher education that followed upon the federal government's new involvement in this area. It was also linked closely to Cold War anxieties about the strength of American democracy and of the economic system that was held to underpin it. Leaders at both Carnegie and Ford believed that strengthening democracy in the face of the communist threat was integral to the post–World War II missions of their respective foundations. Support for democracy, in turn, was seen as inextricably linked to support for corporations and management. For example, given both the growing tensions between the United States and the Soviet Union and the lessons of World War II about the importance of mobilizing industry for winning modern wars, research on the nature and administration of organizations was believed to be critical. Postwar economists believed that "if war should break out again . . . the United States would need to remobilize its economy almost overnight. Research was needed to determine how to do this better than it had been done between 1941 and 1944."[8]

Along with the pragmatic rationale of preparing for a potential war, the relationship posited by the foundations between democracy and the management of business organizations had an ideological basis. Maintaining a strong and growing American economy was considered critical to success in the battle with communism for the hearts and minds of people all over the world. In 1953, H. Rowan Gaither, Jr., the newly appointed president of the Ford Foundation, stated, "If we are to achieve a better realization of democratic goals within the United States and for the peoples of the world, our domestic economy must stand as an example before the world as a strong and growing economy characterized by high output, the highest possible level of constructive employment and a minimum of destructive instability."[9] In a speech in the late 1950s to Stanford Business School faculty, Gaither would make a more direct connection between the struggle against communism and the need to strengthen management, saying, "The Soviet challenge requires that we seek out and utilize the best intelligence of American management—and in turn puts on management a national responsibility of unparalleled dimensions."[10] Thomas Carroll, the vice president in charge of the bulk of the Ford Foundation's business school activities, was particularly concerned about keeping up economically with the Soviet Union, which in the early 1950s appeared to be making enormous strides in improving its economy.[11] In his public speeches about the foundation's activities, Carroll—a former Harvard Business School professor and assistant dean, as well as a former dean of the business schools at Syracuse University and the University of North Carolina—justified the science-oriented overhaul of American business education by pointing to Soviet successes in using science to achieve economic growth. In the wake of the Sputnik launches in 1957, Carroll (paraphrasing remarks of CIA chief Allen Dulles about the integral role of science in waging the Cold War) would state that America's greatest peacetime challenge was "very largely based on the economic and industrial growth of the Soviet Union, [a challenge] which concerns very directly the business leaders in our country . . . and the business, engineering and science educators of our country."[12] Thus the reform of business education became nearly synonymous with patriotism, a conflation that helped mobilize resources but also created an atmosphere of suspicion and insecurity, putting business school academics "who critiqued several of the recommended reforms as well as those criticizing the foundations' role 'on the defensive.' "[13]

One of the Ford Foundation's trustees during the years when its program for business education was being formulated and implemented was, significantly, the man who had been named in 1942 to succeed Wallace Donham as dean of Harvard Business School, Donald K. David. David had been appointed dean by Harvard University president James Bryant Conant, who had succeeded Abbott Lawrence Lowell in 1933. Conant, a chemist, was closely involved with the development of the atomic bomb and supported Vannevar Bush's successful effort to mobilize American universities as a research arm of the federal government. A staunch anticommunist, Conant admired David greatly and often echoed his thinking when writing about business.[14] Just as Conant differed significantly in background and outlook from Lowell, David differed in important ways from his predecessor. Donham, a lawyer by training, had broad intellectual interests and a reverence for scholarship. Though he had never earned a doctoral degree, Donham was a member of the Elton Mayo research group, which included some of Harvard's best minds (such as the biochemist L. J. Henderson, Abbott Lawrence Lowell, sociologist George Homans, and Fritz Roethlisberger) and had contributed to the construction of the human relations school of management described in the previous chapter. During the Depression years, Donham became an outspoken critic of American business culture. David, on the other hand, was much more a businessman than an academic. A graduate of the University of Idaho, he had worked in his family's retail store before attending Harvard Business School. He wrote cases in the school's research bureau after graduation and, despite his lack of a doctoral degree, was appointed to the marketing faculty, leaving in 1927 to take a job as vice president of the Royal Baking Powder Company. David became president of the American Maize Company in 1932 but returned to Harvard in 1941 to be groomed as Donham's successor.

David was a member of several federal commissions and corporate boards, including that of the Ford Motor Company; when he joined the automaker's board in 1950, he was the first nonstockholding outside director in the company's history. Since 1948, he had also been a member of the Ford Foundation's board of trustees, and this interlocking appointment was a sore point with some members of the Ford Foundation staff, according to one account.[15] In 1955, when David resigned as dean of HBS, he would leave the Ford Motor Company board and move to New York City to intensify his involvement in the Ford Foundation, taking up the invitation of Henry Ford II to become chairman of the executive committee for the foundation's board of trustees. David's wide-ranging activities made him a prototypical member of America's new postwar elite, equally at ease within the halls of government, the administrative centers of academia, and the boardrooms of America's mightiest corporations. He was also a strong anticommunist and a staunchly pro-business conservative who criticized government regulation of the private sector. Following his 1942 appointment as dean of HBS, David became a darling of the nation's business elite and a coveted speaker for the economic clubs of major cities and Harvard alumni clubs around the country. At such engagements, he often warned that government regulation of business was a manifestation of creeping socialism in the United States. David's view of business was not just a contrast to but, seemingly, a deliberate repudiation of the views of a previous generation of business school deans. Wallace Donham, for example, had cited the conduct of American businessmen as a principal cause of the Depression. At a 1948 meeting of Harvard alumni, David, taking a very different tone, called on businessmen to enlist in the "war of ideals against communism," declaring, "Morals of businessmen are better today than they have ever been, and they are vastly better than in most other segments of the community."[16]

David's statement highlights how the critical examination of the leadership and operation of the American economic system prevalent during the Depression had now been replaced by an urgent sense of the need to keep the engines of commerce running. David wrote to James B. Conant in 1954: "[E]xecutive ability is needed in many places. . . . Here is a quality the world much requires, for the economy of nations and of the free world cannot long proceed without the participation of professional administrators. Perpetuation of a free society depends upon prompt and equitable industrialization of undeveloped countries, upon freer trade, and upon the extension of American productivity to the world in which America has risen to leadership."[17] Such sentiments were welcomed by the nation's business community. They also undergirded a broad national effort to strengthen American economic institutions, an effort in which the Ford Foundation's program in business education would play a significant role. The foundation's activities in business education, in fact, formed only one arm of a hugely ambitious initiative by Ford to enlist the social sciences in service of stability and progress in the postwar world.

Although it had been established in 1936, for the first twelve years of its existence the Ford Foundation had operated almost exclusively on the local level from the Ford family's center of operations in Detroit, making grants to Michigan-based organizations such as the Henry Ford Hospital and the Henry Ford Museum. The death of Henry Ford's son Edsel in 1943, followed by the death of the family patriarch four years later, suddenly made Ford the largest philanthropic foundation in the world.[18] Its newfound wealth and stature seemed to call for a fundamental reassessment of its scope and mission, and in the fall of 1948 the board of trustees—now chaired by Henry Ford's grandson and successor as president of Ford Motor Company, Henry Ford II—appointed a Study Committee "to take stock of our existing knowledge, institutions, and techniques in order to locate the areas where the problems are most important and where additional efforts toward their solution are most needed."[19] The committee was chaired by H. Rowan Gaither, a San Francisco lawyer who was then serving as chairman of the RAND Corporation; Gaither had developed the social science division at RAND and was then leading the organization through its transition from an air force research and development arm under contract to the Douglas Aircraft Company to an independent, nonprofit think tank. The Study Committee's report, presented in 1950, identified five broad areas of foundation concern: the establishment of peace; the strengthening of democracy; the strengthening of the economy; education in a democratic society; and individual behavior and human relations. This agenda reflected a decision to avoid fields, such as the natural sciences and medicine, that were already heavily supported by foundations such as Rockefeller and the Commonwealth Fund. The third area on the Study Committee's list, "strengthening of the economy," would at first be tagged with the nondescript identification "Area III" in foundation activities. Later, however, activities in support of this goal would be termed the Program in Economic Development and Administration, abbreviated as EDA. It was under the auspices of EDA that foundation efforts to shape business education would be conducted.

Also in 1950, Henry Ford II turned the day-to-day operation of the Ford Foundation over to a new president of his own choosing, Paul Gray Hoffman. An Illinois native who had attended the University of Chicago for a year before financial hardship forced him to leave and take a job as a car salesman, Hoffman had been president of the Studebaker Corporation from 1935 to 1948. He had also acquired philanthropic experience, of a sort, as head of the Economic Coordination Administration (ECA), which administered the Marshall Plan's programs from Washington. Leonard Silk, an economist for the federal government in the early 1950s who would have a lengthy career writing for *Business-Week*, later characterized Hoffman as one of the few American businessmen who (like such business academics as former HBS dean Donham) believed that the irresponsibility of American business had helped cause the Depression. He was, Silk wrote, someone who "hoped to bring the American business community back into the position of leadership and respect it had abdicated in the 1920s."[20] Hoffman believed that American business had things to learn from economists and other scholars; to help put this knowledge to work in planning for a postwar economy, he had founded the Committee for Economic Development (CED) in 1942, serving as its chairman until 1948, when he left Studebaker and took charge of the ECA.[21]

Hoffman was also a trustee of the University of Chicago, and when he assumed the presidency of the Ford Foundation he brought along as his right-hand man the brilliant but mercurial Robert Maynard Hutchins, who had been president of the University of Chicago from 1929 until 1945 and was still its chancellor at the time of his appointment at Ford.[22] In a multipart profile of the Ford Foundation published in the *New Yorker* in 1954–1955 and subsequently as a book called *The Ford Foundation* (1955), journalist Dwight Macdonald described Hutchins's cantankerous ways: "Tall, dark and almost alarmingly handsome, he is as dramatic in behavior as he is in appearance. . . . Not only is he a 'controversial' figure of maximum visibility but he also rather obviously enjoys being one. He likes to tread on dignified toes, he rarely produces the soft answer that turneth away wrath, and his formula for troubled waters does not include oil." As for Hoffman, he was, in Macdonald's words "the glittering ringmaster of a philanthropic circus," "a crusader," "the enthusiastic amateur who rushed in where the trustees feared to tread."[23] Between the two of them, Hoffman and Hutchins managed to create turmoil within the foundation and to make it into a lightning rod for outside criticism.

The criticism came from the (paradoxically) both anticommunist and isolationist American Right, which amid the mounting tensions of the Cold War saw men such as Hoffman, Hutchins, and their ilk at the Ford Foundation (and others of the era's new establishment institutions) as a fifth column of socialists and internationalists.[24] In response to accusations such as (to quote from a newspaper headline of the time) "Ford Foundation Is Front for Dangerous Communists,"[25] a congressional investigation was launched in April 1952 by Georgia Democrat Eugene Cox to consider "the question of whether the foundations have used their resources to weaken, undermine, or discredit the American system of free enterprise . . . while at the same time extolling the virtues of the Socialist state." The Cox Committee's final report, while asserting that "[h]ere and there a foundation board included a Communist or a Communist sympathizer," for the most part affirmed the positive contributions made by foundations to American society.[26] In discussing how suspicions of foundation activity had risen to a level that appeared to warrant investigation, the report helpfully noted, "Many of our citizens confuse the term 'social,' as applied to the discipline [sic] of the social sciences, with the term 'Socialism.' "[27] Though the point now seems amusing, it illustrates the connection already being made by the public between foundations and the social sciences, disciplines that would be at the heart of postwar efforts to reform business education.

Despite the Cox Committee's rather mild conclusions, Henry Ford II—though angered by charges that the foundation was somehow "un-American"—had decided that the combination of the internal strife and external criticism brought about by Hoffman and Hutchins's rule was more than he wished to tolerate, and Hoffman resigned as president and trustee of the foundation in March 1953.[28] Ford replaced Hoffman with Rowan Gaither, whose "low-keyed" manner, as Dwight Macdonald observed, made for a sharp contrast with the "high-powered salesman" Hoffman.[29] Along with Hutchins, associate directors Chester Davis and Milton Katz left their posts, and a new set of vice presidents—Dyke Brown, Thomas H. Carroll, William McPeak, and Don K. Price, all of whom had been involved with the Study Committee of 1948–1950—completed the transition of the Ford Foundation to a more staid leadership of longtime foundation executives.

With this new leadership in place and its headquarters returned to New York from Pasadena (where Hoffman had maintained them during his tenure), the foundation saw fit to revisit its broader mission. Despite his displeasure with Hoffman and Hutchins, Henry Ford II, for one, saw no need to distance the foundation from the philanthropic programs they had established. Not surprisingly, given that the new leadership included so many former Study Committee members, the foundation's "Annual Report" for 1953 proclaimed that the trustees had "re-examined and reaffirmed the philosophy and program objectives announced by them in September, 1950." To help outline areas of potential focus for the renewed EDA initiative, Rowan Gaither assembled an outside advisory group of twelve distinguished economists and experts in business administration.

Shortly after assuming the presidency of Ford Motor Company in 1945, Henry Ford II had hired the group of brainy Army Air Force officers who would become known as the "Whiz Kids" to resuscitate his grandfather's company. In similar fashion, Gaither brought in for his advisory group a collection of individuals who believed that a rational, analytical approach to management would shape the organization of the future. Among the group of twelve advisers was Lee Bach, the economist and dean of the four-year-old Carnegie Tech GSIA. Bach had been recommended to Gaither by Theodore Schultz, a Study Committee member and University of Chicago economist who had become Bach's mentor during his years of doctoral study there. Another adviser was Berkeley economist Robert A. Gordon, who would in 1959 coauthor the foundation's major report on business education.[30] Gaither's expert advisory group recommended four key objectives as focal points for the foundation's economic development efforts: "improving the organization, administration and performance of economic units"; "achieving growth, development and economic opportunity without undue instability"; "clarifying the appropriate role of government in economic life"; and "improving economic relations among nations."

Given the perceived centrality of competent management in the achievement of such goals—as well as, perhaps, the academic affiliations of several members of the advisory group—business schools became an initial target for EDA programs. In 1953, the foundation began purposively wading into the murky waters of postwar business education. Ford's trustees gave Thomas Carroll, the vice president heading up EDA's efforts, approval to initiate a pilot program distributing research grants of between $15,000 and $250,000 to various universities' economics departments and business schools for "problem-oriented research in economics and business administration."[31] Among its numerous activities in the area of economic development and administration, the foundation's sponsorship of research in business schools would take on special importance. Gaither and the Ford trustees hoped that investing in business schools would, among other things, help the foundation to further separate itself from the controversial Hoffman years.

Meanwhile, both Donald David and Lee Bach—the business school deans positioned in this process as Ford Foundation trustee and key advisory group member, respectively—had their own reasons for interest in the foundation's program for business education reform. Even though David headed Harvard, one of the nation's most well-established business schools, and Bach led GSIA, one of its newest and most innovative, both men were concerned that an erosion of quality in lower-tier business schools (the kind they termed "intellectual backwaters") could eventually undermine the credibility of their own institutions.[32] They saw potential benefit to their schools from the Ford Foundation's project, not just in the form of grants, but also through the enhanced legitimacy the reform initiative could generate for the field of business education as a whole. These leading business educators were thus motivated to join forces with foundation leaders in spearheading what was essentially an externally driven reform of their field. In the postwar context of rationalist managerial ideologies, the new paradigm that emerged for business education would reinforce one key aspect of the pre–World War II professionalization project: the attempt to create a body of expert knowledge and a pathway for acquiring it. At the same time, however, the foundation-led reforms would ignore or repudiate other aims of professionalization, such as the development of a professional mission, identity, and association for the occupation of management.

The Strategy for Business Education

Creating systematic expert knowledge with a sound theoretical foundation was an unquestioned requirement for those who addressed business education reform in the postwar era, whether from the inside or the outside.

Reflecting later on the state of undergraduate and graduate business schools in the early 1950s, James Howell (coauthor, with Robert Gordon, of the Ford Foundation's 1959 report on business education), remarked, "[C]ollegiate schools of business, with a few notable exceptions, were regarded as the slums of the educational community."[33] As the Ford Foundation and its expert advisory committee administered the first round of grants to business schools in 1953, low intellectual standards and an apparent lack of direction were among the most notable features of business education. With a new sense of urgency, the Ford Foundation significantly stepped up its program on business education, focusing more closely on what people inside the foundation referred to as this "uncertain giant."[34] Beginning in 1954 and for a decade thereafter, the foundation would take several steps to raise the quality of business school faculty, curricula, students, and research, and, in so doing, would point business education in a very specific intellectual direction. Meanwhile, in a move that symbolized the importance that business education had assumed in the Ford Foundation's overall program, in 1955, just as this effort was moving into high gear, Donald David left Harvard Business School, tendering his resignation as dean to become chairman of the foundation's executive committee and a "trustee-in-residence" at its headquarters in New York City.

This concerted effort to transform American business schools was driven by a two-part premise about how best to increase the intellectual quality of business education and to make the field truly "professional": first, the reasoning went, business schools must increase the proportion of faculty with doctorates; second, business school faculty and MBA students must be extensively trained in quantitative analysis and the behavioral sciences. These two objectives would determine the character not only of Ford's program but of American business schools themselves for the remainder of the twentieth century. At first, the strategy took the form of encouraging discipline-oriented students to undertake doctoral studies in business. At the same time, business school deans and senior faculty were encouraged to adopt a disciplinary orientation when recruiting new faculty and evaluating research. For example, in 1955 the foundation created two types of doctoral fellowships, one to stimulate postdoctoral students from scientific and quantitative disciplines to conduct research on business problems, and another to attract MBA students to doctoral studies in business.

Also in 1955, the foundation committed $3.3 million to launch a program aimed at improving doctoral studies in business and economics; the first grants for this purpose were also awarded that year. Four schools received the bulk of the funding: Harvard Business School, Carnegie Tech's GSIA, Columbia University's business school, and Yale University (which, though it had no business school, was granted funds for use in its economics department). The lion's share—$2 million—went to Harvard Business School for an expansion of its doctoral program, which up to that point, according to Fritz Roethlisberger, "had been a side show . . . to produce more locals for the faculty of our own MBA program."[35] A few years later, Thomas Carroll would describe to an audience of academics at the University of Michigan the changes taking place in the doctoral program at HBS as a result of the grant: "While the present doctoral program [at Harvard] continues to emphasize the case approach, this is being supplemented by a new emphasis on application of the behavioral sciences, statistics, and mathematics to business administration for research training."[36] GSIA received $250,000, and Carroll's later comments highlighted how, at this "comparative newcomer to the field," emphasis was being placed "on the application of the underlying disciplines, principally the behavioral sciences and mathematics, to problems of administration."[37] Yale University's economics department was awarded funds to revamp its ailing doctoral program in the discipline. Columbia's grant was relatively modest, intended to strengthen the international component of graduate education and to fund an experimental research program for developing a philosophy of business. Even this latter effort, which alone among the programs singled out for Ford Foundation support appeared to have a humanities component, had a strong social sciences bent. The grant, according to Columbia's Dean Courtney Brown, would aid in "the development of study materials dealing with the sociological development of American business institutions and an inquiry into why these institutions have evolved differently in various parts of the world."[38]

In the fall of 1955, the Ford Foundation and the AACSB jointly sponsored a national conference to, as Carroll wrote three years later, "consider means for improving and expanding the supply of college and university teachers in business administration." For foundation staff, the conference confirmed not only that business schools needed to be reformed but also that neither the schools nor the AACSB would reform on their own: if major change was to take place, it would have to be "externally initiated." Carroll, in 1958, also recounted how the foundation's attitude had evolved: "As the scope of the Foundation's activities in business education expanded, it became increasingly evident that the problems were not only important but acute. . . . It also became evident that a comprehensive and rather formal re-examination of business education as a whole was desirable."[39] An internal memorandum from the early 1950s makes the foundation's assessment of the problems confronting business schools clear:

> The Foundation's interest in undertaking a major effort in the field of business education can be stated bluntly in two propositions: (1) Departments and schools of business are currently attracting an enormous number of students (approximately one out of every seven enrolled in colleges); (2) the quality of business education is generally inferior, a fact admitted by many responsible individuals in the field of business education. Indeed, to put the matter in its harshest light . . . the problem consists of unimaginative, nontheoretical faculties teaching from descriptive, practice-oriented texts to classes of second-rate, vocationally-minded students.
>
> Any significant impact on the field of business education will probably come only through a major improvement in the *substance* of business education itself . . . [since the schools have thus far] been chiefly systematizers of current business methods, rather than . . . pioneers in advancing business knowledge.[40]

Foundation officials, James Howell would later write, saw at this point three changes that would have to be made to rectify the situation: raising the quality of business school faculty and students; making their education more intellectual and relevant to management; and reducing (if not actually eliminating) undergraduate business education.[41]

With the foundation having made this diagnosis of what ailed business education and what had to be done to fix it, Thomas Carroll asked Lee Bach, a member of the 1953 EDA advisory committee assembled by Gaither and, of course, also the dean of grant-recipient GSIA, to work closely with him on a strategy for achieving the needed reforms. The strategy outlined by Carroll and Bach was relatively straightforward: invest considerable resources in "good or promising schools of business which would then be the instruments of change for the rest of the field."[42] Given the amount of funding the foundation was prepared to provide to a small group of select institutions,[43] its leaders expected to encounter no trouble having recommendations accepted and implemented. By focusing on a small group of deans, who had the formal authority to hire junior faculty and appoint senior faculty trained in disciplinary methods, Carroll and his colleagues believed they could have an immediate impact on the quality of business school faculty and research.

The years between 1956 and 1958 marked the start of what Ford insiders referred to as "The Big Push." Harvard Business School, Carnegie Tech's GSIA, and the business schools of Columbia, Chicago, and Stanford were designated as "centers of excellence" whose well-financed examples would give American business schools a "New Look," a phrase coined by the foundation and repeatedly used in connection with its efforts. Endorsement of the centers of excellence by the Ford Foundation, which presented itself as a neutral intermediary, obliquely created a formal differentiation process distinguishing "excellent" schools from the rest. Within short order, the foundation hoped, these five exemplary institutions would inspire anxious alumni, university officials, or other constituents to exert pressure on lower-tier schools to adopt the new standards. One foundation memorandum, using an awkward metaphor, described the strategy as a "trickle down from peaks of excellence to the grass roots."[44] In theory, the trickle-down dynamic would operate on various pressure points, both external and internal. Internal pressure would come from "propaganda and even direct aid to strengthen the hands of dissidents within faculties" and "propaganda to university administrators and trustees." One example of strengthening the hands of dissidents—those faculty in elite business schools outside the centers of excellence—was a program of flexible research grants of $150,000 to support "problem oriented research" that was rooted in quantitative analysis and social sciences.[45] External pressure would come from "direct grants to schools who would break ranks to endorse" the new program and "propaganda to the business community," the latter to be brought about through the allocation of $1 million in 1956 for a two-year study of business education that would culminate in the famous Ford Foundation report.[46]

Over the period 1953–1964, during which most of the Ford grants for business education were distributed, Harvard Business School would receive $5.2 million—more than any other institution.[47] From the Ford Foundation's perspective, there were many reasons why HBS was an obvious choice as a center of excellence, and why it would be given the most money. First, by virtue of its sheer size and a storied history, "it dominated business education to the extent any one school could."[48] Second, "its standing in the business community was unequalled." Third, it had a clear mission, expressed in its commitment to a general management approach to business education. Fourth, "although the nonscholars on the right bank of the Charles far outnumbered the few genuine scholars who had taken up residence [at the business school]," as James Howell noted in an internal Ford memorandum, the Hawthorne experiments had made a name for the school as a research institution.[49] For all these reasons, HBS commanded enough status to enhance the legitimacy of the entire Ford project, as James Howell would observe when he noted that "the Harvard gift legitimated the smaller gift to the less well-known Carnegie Tech, and subsequently to other institutions, where reputation may have even more greatly outdistanced productivity."[50] Finally, of course, both Carroll, who headed up the foundation's activities in business education, and David, chairman of the foundation's executive committee, had significant past and present ties to HBS.[51]

Despite receiving the lion's share of grant monies, however, HBS did not receive Ford's first large publicly announced grant. In a highly symbolic gesture, the first such grant went to Carnegie Tech's GSIA—a school that had then been in operation for a mere five years. The GSIA model was one to which the foundation hoped all other business schools, even HBS, would aspire, although this came as news to the wider business education community. "To all but a few insiders, the inclusion of Carnegie in the list of primary centers was a surprise," James Howell observed.[52] Carnegie did not even meet two of the five official qualifying criteria in Ford's initial business school grant announcement: "it was a small school" and "a minor technical institute" rather than part of a major university.[53] But Lee Bach had greatly influenced Thomas Carroll's and Donald David's thinking as to the trajectory that research by business school faculty needed to take. Tracing the history of GSIA and the diffusion of its research philosophy and methods under the sponsorship of the Ford Foundation offers a critical vantage point on the emergence of a new institutional order in graduate business education.

Fomenting the Revolution: Carnegie Tech's Graduate School of Industrial Administration

Founded in 1949 with a $6 million gift from William Larimer Mellon, a member of the powerful Mellon family and founder of the Gulf Oil Company, the Carnegie Institute of Technology's Graduate School of Industrial Administration had a mandate to "help meet the growing need in American industry for potential executives *trained in both engineering and management*" (emphasis in original).[54] Lee Bach, a member of Carnegie Tech's economics department and a close confidant of W. L. Mellon, was appointed as the school's first dean. A graduate of Grinnell College in Iowa who had received his Ph.D. in economics from the University of Chicago, Bach had been deeply affected by the Depression—his father's small-town bank failed, and his family was forced to move back in with his grandparents. This experience profoundly shaped his view of the social sciences and their uses. In an interview, Bach described a memorable incident in an economics class at Grinnell in which "the professor was explaining that theoretically there couldn't be a lasting depression in a competitive, capitalist-type economy. I looked out the window at a long line of unemployed men, waiting to apply for two WPA jobs the town government had managed to get. There must be a better way for either the economists or the 'practical' men who ran the system, I thought."[55]

After a teaching stint at Iowa State University and a job as special assistant to a member of the Federal Reserve Board in Washington, Bach received a U.S. Navy commission and spent most of World War II working on postwar economic reconstruction planning. At the end of the war, he accepted an appointment as chairman of the economics department at Carnegie Tech, where he eventually succeeded in convincing W. L. Mellon to underwrite a new type of business school. As dean-elect of a school that was still under construction, Bach spent a year talking to businessmen, observing on-the-job training in various settings, visiting business, law, engineering, and medical schools, and sitting in on both undergraduate and graduate classes as well as interviewing the deans of the leading business schools. He recorded dismay at the quality of the business schools he saw (except for Harvard's) but was impressed with how some of the top engineering schools in the country, like MIT, were integrating engineering's underlying disciplines into a professional school curriculum focused on problem solving. From his observations, he formulated a model of business education reflected in a description that he later gave of how GSIA built its first faculty. Besides "very smart people with imagination—really first-rate minds," Bach said, he and his colleagues in the new GSIA administration "wanted a block of faculty members to provide the disciplinary foundations for the applied fields to business. For this group, we preferred people from the disciplines (economics, political science, the behavioral sciences, operations research) and the quantitative methods (mathematics, computers, statistics, accounting)." While faculty members from such fields would have to be "interested in the managerial use of discipline-based knowledge," faculty hired from "other business schools and actual operating businesses" in such "applied fields" as finance, marketing, and the other functional areas would be required to meet "the general qualifications laid out for all faculty members." "In brief," Bach continued,

> what we wanted was a faculty, including a substantial group of discipline-based but applied teachers and researchers who were interested in developing the disciplines as a foundation for the applied courses in the business school curriculum. We were also especially interested in people who were willing to be interdisciplinary where necessary—to solve real, complex problems rather than making each problem fit an existing discipline—to work at the boundaries of the disciplines. And we wanted people who were interested in the real world. Theory has a powerful role to play in education for management, but the real work of an MBA program is using that theory to help solve business problems. We didn't want people who just wanted to sit and spin off theory.[56]

Bach's vision for GSIA, grounded in discipline-based scholarship and quantitative methods, reflected a radical departure from existing practices, and his hope, from the outset, was that GSIA's model would serve as a template to be adopted, eventually, by all the elite business schools in the country. In a 1954 letter to HBS professor Stanley Teele (who would succeed Donald David as dean at Harvard the following year), Bach remarked that GSIA was founded on "an underlying faith—perhaps born of inexperience—that a real integration of social scientists and business school men can produce much greater things research wise than the business school faculties can reasonably hope to produce themselves. I am not here drawing a distinction between 'pure' and 'applied' research, but rather emphasizing that in either type of research, a joint effort is likely to be more fruitful than the two separate efforts."[57] One of Bach's earliest faculty hires was Herbert Simon, a University of Chicago–trained political scientist and eventual winner of the Nobel Prize in economics, who was focused on developing a formal theory of organizational behavior grounded in the behavioral sciences. Another of Bach's earliest faculty recruits, William W. Cooper (also from the University of Chicago economics department), shared Bach's interest in the new management science methods that had emerged since the war, particularly linear programming and system dynamics, which both Bach and Cooper believed were quite applicable to organizational problems. As Herbert Simon later recalled, he, Bach, and Cooper formed a "revolutionary cell that would forever reshape business education," which they saw as "a wasteland of vocationalism that needed to be transformed into science-based professionalism."[58]

The radicalism of Bach and his GSIA colleagues was expressed in the way they set themselves against not only the "vocationalism" of the mediocre majority of American business schools but also the comparatively genteel, noblesse oblige version of "professionalism" represented by Harvard Business School—an institution that the GSIA founders admired but of which they intended GSIA to be the antithesis. In contrast to Harvard's stately McKim, Mead & White buildings, Bach and company eschewed luxury of any kind in their physical surroundings. (When the final plans for GSIA's building came in at an estimated cost of $600,000 over the original $1 million budget, Bach and the others decided to forgo air-conditioning and an elevator. "A few years later, needing more space, we installed an office for an associate dean in the elevator shaft," Herbert Simon recalled.)[59] More significantly, GSIA reshaped the paradigm for business school research that, to the extent one existed at all, had been created at Harvard.

The GSIA curriculum, too, would be different, although it is notable that GSIA's "science-based professionalism" carried within it certain elements familiar from the pre–World War II programs for professionalization at Wharton, HBS, and various AACSB schools that attempted to incorporate a social perspective. A new wrinkle for GSIA, however, was that advanced training in quantitative analysis and a background in engineering would be prerequisites.[60] The master's degree curriculum was built around four pillars: organizational behavior, economic analysis, quantitative management science, and business and society. None of them would lack for analytical emphasis. In organizational behavior, for example, the focus was to be on "analytical tools designed to help understand and influence processes, motivation, communication processes, and so on, in the organization,"[61] as opposed to the descriptive methods used in most existing business school pedagogy. The curriculum in economic analysis would have two dimensions; Bach described this portion of the GSIA curriculum:

> The first [dimension] is the traditional liberal arts, public-policy-oriented role of economics. It is essential for the businessman, as citizen and as civic leader, to understand the broad mechanism of the economic system in which his firm operates and to be able to think intelligently and independently in arriving at positions on major public policy issues. Second, economics can provide some

tools, but only a modest part of the necessary tools, for making managerial decisions about the conduct of the firm.[62]

The third pillar of the curriculum, quantitative management science, emphasized the use of accounting, simulation, and statistics for making decisions. Finally, the study of business and society linked the subjects of corporations, management, and democratic society. The focus would be on the relationship between government and business, "not in the narrow sense of how to beat the anti-trust laws, but in the broader sense of trying to understand the reasons for government intervention in and regulation of business. . . . It would try to force students to think through deeply problems of business ethics and social responsibility, and their own systems of social values."[63]

Bach and his colleagues knew that their experiment at GSIA was fraught with risk, but they believed that the risk lay not in their approach to business education per se but rather in what sociologists call the "liability of newness" confronting fledgling organizations—especially those trying to differentiate themselves from an existing group. While GSIA had been able to attract some human and financial capital and enjoyed a significant degree of autonomy to experiment and innovate, it lacked the type of social recognition that was critical for attracting more faculty and students of the quality desired. At the time of GSIA's founding, any perceived differentiation among business schools was mainly an inherited effect of the age, size, and prestige of each school's parent university. Lacking a venerable parent institution (Carnegie Tech, which first offered bachelor's degrees in 1912, was younger than most major East Coast schools by a century or more), GSIA sought to raise its status by gaining the favor of a prominent outside organization. By developing a strong relationship with the Ford Foundation, beginning at least as early as Bach's 1953 membership in Rowan Gaither's advisory group, GSIA succeeded in propelling itself into the inner circle of business schools, thus legitimating its pedagogical and research models as well as its faculty. Inside the Ford Foundation, as James Howell later revealed, GSIA was regarded by 1954 as "the advanced projects laboratory, the R&D group that [the foundation] had to find or create; fortunately, it already existed."[64] In the early 1970s, Kermit Gordon, a director in the EDA program at Ford who replaced Thomas Carroll in 1961, recalled this process of discovery, so advantageous to both the foundation and the school:

Today, it is widely recognized that one of the most important, and certainly the most influential graduate schools of business administration in America is Carnegie Tech Graduate School of Industrial Administration. It has done more, I think, to influence the strategy and structure and general level of intellectual respectability of graduate business education than any school; more so than Harvard and I think the people of Harvard would concede this. Tom [Carroll] wasn't capable of providing the leadership himself, but he saw [sic] Lee Bach, who was then the dean of GSIA Carnegie Tech, a man who impressed him as having the insight and the intellectual quality and the core staff, to provide this leadership. And Tom buried the man in money. All it took was a telephone call from Lee Bach and the check was heading his way by return mail.[65]

While GSIA may have taken the lead over Harvard in Ford's program for the reform of business schools, Harvard was given an important role of its own, one that was grounded in its tradition of educating general managers so as to groom them as "professionals." Yet the tensions that arose around Ford's attempt to retain this place for HBS within its overall business education program show that the notion of professionalism—inasmuch as it remained a goal for the leaders of the reform movement—still entailed a balancing act between differing approaches to business education that would not be easily reconciled amid the forces at play in postwar business schools.

Teaching the Teachers: The Role of Harvard Business School

For reasons already stated—prestige among both business schools and the business community, possession of a clear mission, pioneering efforts in social science–based research, and the roles of Donald David and Thomas Carroll inside the Ford Foundation—Harvard Business School was, as James Howell later noted, an "obviously" correct choice to receive funding from the foundation.[66] Yet there was another reason why HBS, along with GSIA, became not just a participant but a standard-bearer in Ford's reformation of American business education. The foundation recognized that raising the overall quality of business schools depended not just on developing and supporting a faculty research agenda. Business schools had a teaching mission as well, and HBS, by virtue of its case method, was considered to be the leader among business schools as a teaching institution. Writing in 1954 to HBS assistant dean Teele, Thomas Carroll explained that Harvard's participation in

Ford's effort was crucial to the legitimation of the reform program because "[f]or many years the Harvard Business School has been the recognized leader in the development and use of the case method of instruction in business education." Harvard had also taken measures to bring its doctoral program in line with the Ford program for increasing the academic rigor of business education, as Carroll went on to note: "Without diminishing its interest in that [case] approach at the MBA level, the School is demonstrating its continuing vitality by adding a strong theoretical emphasis to its program for the DBA [doctorate in business administration] degree. It is our judgment, in which many respected observers of the business school concur, that such a theoretical emphasis is necessary to improve the quality of professional preparation for teaching business."[67]

As we have seen, the $2 million that HBS received from the Ford Foundation in 1955 for the expansion of its doctoral program would be used, along with subsequent grants, to "supplement" the program's existing orientation to the case method in business research and pedagogy with "a new emphasis on application of the behavioral sciences, statistics, and mathematics to business administration for research training." Adoption by HBS of this direction would, Ford hoped, not only legitimate the foundation's support of the GSIA model but also transform the HBS doctoral program from a farm system for the school itself into a source of faculty for business schools generally. Moreover, by training existing faculty at other business schools in the use of its case method, HBS—also well known for a general management perspective that emphasized an integrated rather than a functional approach to managerial decision making—would help to balance the emphasis on theory and the disciplines in Ford's reform program. The complementary components would together transform business education into the genuinely professional institution that the foundation envisioned.

Despite the way in which Harvard's approach dovetailed, in theory, with that of GSIA to form a seemingly coherent whole, the possibility that HBS might play any role but the starring one in Ford's overall program for business schools apparently caused some conflict between the program officers and Donald David. Bernard Berelson, an influential behavioral scientist who joined the foundation's staff in 1951, recalled that David opposed the initial social science emphasis in the business school reform program because he believed that it would limit Harvard Business School's access to foundation resources. In the wake of the consolidation of the departments of sociology, social anthropology, social psychology, and clinical psychology at Harvard University into a new department of "social relations" in 1946, Berelson said, "Don David was afraid that with the definition of the [Ford] Program . . . the Social Relations Department at Harvard was going to get all the play and the Business School was going to get pushed out, and [he said] that if we were to define behavioral science so that all of the case study type of stuff would get equal billing with the more 'scientific stuff' that [Samuel A.] Stouffer did over in the Social Relations Department, then he would join up."[68] Berelson added:

> [T]hat first year and a half or so [spanning 1955–1957] was a continu-
> ing sort of running skirmish between Don and the Program where
> Don was pushing the Program—where, in effect, I think it's fair to
> say that Don was saying to Rowan [Gaither] and to me, "Look, we
> can easily make a deal here. Just deal us in and I'm your friend. If
> you deal us out, I'm going to oppose you at every turn." And we were
> trying to compromise that out by my saying that properly qualified
> stuff at the Business School, of course, was in. The old [Lawrence J.]
> Henderson studies would have been in, and certainly the Hawthorne
> study would have been in, and some of the new people there were
> certainly qualified, like [Abraham] Zaleznik, then a young fellow. But
> not everything at the Business School. That wasn't quite enough for
> Don. He was a very influential figure in the first years of the Founda-
> tion, very influential, partly strategizing what some of us came to
> think of as the Chicago-Harvard war.[69]

Yet even if David had to wield his influence at the top of the foundation to see that HBS continued to get its share of funds from the business school program, the foundation regarded HBS and GSIA as poles of a neatly fused axis around which the new model for business education would revolve. As one Ford Foundation docket on HBS noted, "[Harvard] puts primary emphasis on the 'clinical approach' in business education, while [GSIA] places primary emphasis on the 'scientific' contributions to the art of business administration through mathematics and the social sciences."[70] Both GSIA and HBS concentrated on graduate education, and both offered doctoral programs that were not centered solely on economics or narrow functional fields. HBS successfully positioned itself as bringing a practical focus to busi-ness education; GSIA pioneered disciplinary research in quantitative analysis and the behavioral sciences. Finally, HBS was seen as the best place to train business school faculty in teaching techniques, and GSIA as the best place for developing research-based pedagogy.

As the Ford Foundation embraced training business school teachers for their roles in the classroom in addition to grounding them in science-based research, its first tactic was to affirm the value of the case method. As the authors of a 1987 study of the creation and implementation of Ford's New Look program point out, "the obvious parallels with the cases used in medicine and law were themselves strong arguments for making the case method central to the task of academic uplift." The foundation also harbored a "strong belief that the case method would help reshape the way economics was taught by offering a more realistic content in addition to the theoretical concerns that dominated the discipline."[71] This point reflected an awareness of the potential excesses of the disciplinary approach that would prove warranted, as we shall see, by later developments. In all, Ford would spend nearly $1 million to facilitate diffusion of the case method, with 80 percent of the money going to Harvard for, as Howell described it, "the preparation of cases and proselytizing for the case method."[72] The foundation also spent more than $250,000 on grants to other business schools to send their faculty to a series of Harvard seminars on case teaching held between 1957 and 1959.[73]

Despite the idea that Ford's support for HBS would offer a counterbalance to the GSIA element within the foundation's entire program for business education, David's anxiety regarding Harvard's role was not unjustified. Indeed, of the two schools, HBS would end up more influenced by GSIA than vice versa. Through the late 1950s and 1960s, HBS would move away from what had been a strong clinical training focus and emphasis on "management as art" in its DBA and MBA programs—with consequences for business education generally that we will consider in part 3.

Diffusing the New Look

As we have noted, the Ford Foundation's strategy for remaking American business education involved designating a handful of schools—dubbed "centers of excellence"—as models to be emulated by others, with change expected to "trickle down" from these peaks to the lower-quality schools that were most in need of reform. Yet rather than allow this process of diffusion to occur on its own, the foundation actively sought to spread the revolution in business education for which it had designated GSIA as the standard-bearer, and HBS as the high-status adopter, by pushing reforms out beyond these two schools. This was accomplished, first of all, by grants to the other three centers of excellence, then by second-tier awards to particular schools under-taking efforts that the foundation wanted to recognize, and, finally, by a series of even more widely diffused grants and seminars designed specifically to propagate the ideas and approaches at the heart of the reform program.

Although Columbia University's business school was chosen along with GSIA and Harvard as one of the first three centers of excellence, this honor had more to do with the school's proximity to the Ford Foundation's head-quarters in New York City than with any excellence exhibited by the program in Ford's eyes. Yet the foundation had a more substantial reason for investing in Columbia, which was that the school had already signaled its willingness to reform. Shortly after the war, Columbia had eliminated its undergraduate business program. In 1954, the school's newly appointed dean, Courtney Brown, assured Ford's representatives of his willingness to expend political capital in order to reform the curriculum and faculty around the GSIA model. Yet James Howell would later assess the changes at Columbia as rela-tively modest: "No business school received as much money from the Foun-dation and did so little with it," he said.[74]

The foundation's choice of the University of Chicago's School of Busi-ness as a fourth center of excellence would have much more significant con-sequences for the reshaping of business education in the postwar era. In contrast to Columbia's professed willingness to change direction, Chicago's grant application promised a return to its roots, reaffirming the school's original intent of making the social sciences part of the foundation of both its research and its curriculum. Under the leadership of Dean Leon Marshall in the 1920s, Chicago's business school had begun incorporating the social sciences as the basis for its doctoral and MBA programs, until the appoint-ment of Robert Maynard Hutchins—famous for his disdain for vocational education generally and Chicago's business school in particular—as presi-dent of the university in 1929 effectively derailed Marshall's plan.[75] Yet under the leadership of chancellor Lawrence Kimpton, who succeeded Hutchins in 1951,[76] and new business school dean W. Allen Wallis, who would be ap-pointed in 1956, the shift to a social science–based faculty was accelerated.[77] Kimpton authorized a $32 million capital fund drive for the business school in 1956, contingent on the understanding that Wallis would push the school to a full social science orientation. Even before the fund drive, Chicago's busi-ness school had significantly strengthened its relationship with many of the university's social science departments: by the early 1950s it was not uncom-mon, for example, for MBA and doctoral students in business to take courses in both the sociology and economics departments. The significant flow of Chicago-trained faculty into GSIA during the 1950s also reflected a kinship between the two schools' discipline-oriented approaches to business education. Chicago's commitment to equipping business school students with the theories and methods of the social sciences was reflected in the description of goals for its MBA program provided in its Ford grant application:

> The optimum function of a graduate school of business is to equip the student to add to the stock of our total knowledge or to give new meaning to individual business experience when it is achieved. Graduate education in business cannot be a substitute for liberal education and can only be an inefficient substitute for on-the-job training. . . . Graduate education for business can most usefully build upon a liberal education by providing specialized training in the social sciences as well as in the more traditional subject matter of business education such as accounting, statistics, law, finance, marketing, production, and personnel administration.[78]

The fifth and last school named by the Ford Foundation as a "center of excellence" was the Stanford Graduate School of Business (GSB), which, as the second-oldest strictly graduate school of business in the United States, had been modeled on its predecessor institution, Harvard Business School. After Stanford's founding dean Willard Hotchkiss stepped down in 1932, the school was led by former HBS accounting professor J. Hugh Jackson. Faced with rapidly declining enrollments during the Depression, Jackson had dramatically lowered admissions standards and adopted an increasingly narrow, vocationally oriented MBA curriculum in an attempt to expand enrollments and stabilize the school's financial situation.[79] After the war, despite several attempts by Stanford University's new president, J. E. Wallace Sterling, to encourage Jackson to raise academic standards and foster the development of a more research-oriented faculty, the business school's curriculum remained narrow, and no support for faculty research materialized. After Jackson retired as dean in 1955, an acting dean was appointed and Stanford University's trustees, led by former president Herbert Hoover, crafted a plan to seek a new dean for the GSB who would reshape the program and raise its intellectual standards.

It was only in 1958, when Stanford appointed Ernest Arbuckle as GSB dean, that Ford declared its unqualified support for the school's new strategic direction. Arbuckle, a former executive of W. R. Grace and Company and the Standard Oil Company of California, and a Stanford University trustee who had served on the search committee for the new dean, fully embraced the Ford Foundation's recommendations for business schools. In its 1959 application to Ford, the school described its willingness to recruit from the disciplines, significantly raise its entrance requirements, and embark on an "implicit downgrading of the case method model hitherto central to [its] curriculum."[80] Thomas Carroll and the other Ford Foundation executives were duly impressed. Carroll described Stanford's GSB as "showing vigorous forward movement" and as having the potential for linking with "other relevant sections of the university, most notably economics and law but sociology and psychology as well."[81] In a clear demonstration of his school's commitment to reform, Arbuckle took the unprecedented step of actively encouraging MBA applicants with social science and natural science backgrounds and discouraging those with undergraduate degrees in business.[82] In its admissions brochure, the newly rejuvenated MBA program was described as being "especially suited to students who have had their academic backgrounds in the various fields within liberal arts. . . . Undergraduate business majors should not apply without consulting with the Admissions Committee."[83]

Stanford's embarkation on this new course of action was generously rewarded. The Ford Foundation offered Stanford's GSB its second-largest individual grant, in the amount of $1.5 million, and recognized the school as a center of excellence. Of the $1.5 million, $750,000 was specified for senior-level faculty appointments of candidates fitting the GSIA mold, $250,000 for visiting professors from other schools, and $500,000 for faculty research support. In 1959, Ford granted Stanford an additional $1.5 million to improve the research skills of its faculty and doctoral students. Then in 1960, Stanford received a $3.5 million separate earmark to establish the International Center for the Advancement of Management Education (ICAME), a program dedicated to training future business school faculty from developing countries.[84] (These last funds came from outside the Ford Foundation's official business school grant program, in which HBS still commanded the largest amount of grant money, but the total award of $6.5 million to Stanford's GSB exceeded the total amount of Ford grants to any other business school.) Further evidence of Stanford's commitment to Ford's reforms came in the 1960s with the appointments of James Howell and Lee Bach to the Stanford faculty. At Stanford, Bach would become a close adviser to President Sterling and to a succession of Stanford business school deans, including Arbuckle's successor, Arjay Miller, who had been one of the Ford Motor Company Whiz Kids.

As reform-related efforts at the centers of excellence percolated between 1956 and 1959, the Ford Foundation also initiated a set of programs to prod a "second tier" of schools toward adopting the recommended reforms. Within this three-year period, several million dollars were spent on what the foundation staff called "trickle-down grants." The business schools at UC Berkeley, UCLA, and MIT received the three largest of these grants. By 1960, the structure and faculty composition of these three institutions bore the salient marks of the post-Ford business school: a functional curriculum with a strong quantitative bent, taught by a discipline-trained faculty with economists at the core. As James Howell reported of these schools: "Their faculties contained a large proportion of respectable economists operating either as economists or as specialists in marketing, finance, accounting, etc. They viewed business administration more or less as applied economics, had significantly more rigorous degree programs than the bulk of business schools (MIT even required calculus!), and produced a disproportionately large share of the field's research."[85]

In the end, the New Look model began to take hold even in such grassroots institutions as the large state university-based business schools, as well as in private schools such as Wharton and Northwestern that had initially resisted the foundation's program for reform.[86] Ford aided this process of diffusion through four major activities: grants for producing and disseminating new subject matter for classroom use; direct research support to centers of excellence to enlarge their doctoral programs and model them after GSIA's; a faculty fellowship program that, via direct grants, gave money to schools hiring newly minted doctoral graduates from the centers of excellence;[87] and a variety of seminars, workshops, and conferences.

Among these varied approaches to shaping business school faculties, the Ford-sponsored workshops and faculty seminars are particularly noteworthy. Figure 6.1 highlights the disciplinary and technical focus of these workshops. In 1957, for example, Ford launched a faculty seminar administered by GSIA and entitled "Business Administration: Marketing and Quantitative Controls." The faculty members heading seminar sessions were leading scholars in quantitative methods and strong advocates of discipline-based research. Ford strongly encouraged other elite schools to send their senior faculty to the seminar, which was designed, as Lee Bach wrote to HBS dean Stanley Teele that year, to give business school professors "the time and opportunity to reexamine . . . some of the major developments of the past decade or two in major fields of business administration."[88]

3/19/62

SEMINARS ON NEW DEVELOPMENTS IN BUSINESS ADMINISTRATION

INSTITUTION	DATE	LOCATION	SUBJECT OF SEMINAR
1957			
Carnegie Tech	Aug 4-30	Williamstown	Business Administration: Marketing and Quantitative Controls
1958			
Carnegie Tech	Aug 4-29	Williamstown	Quantitative Methods (accounting and statistics); Industrial Management and Production
1959			
Carnegie Tech	Aug 2-28	University of Denver	Quantitative Methods; Personnel Management and Human Relations; Electronic Computers and the Management Game
Chicago	Aug 2-28	Williamstown	Business Finance; Business Economics
1960			
Carnegie Tech	Aug 7-Sept 2	Cornell	Production; Personnel Management and Human Relations; Research Methods, Electronic Computers, and the Management Game
Chicago	Aug 1-26	Williamstown	Industrial Relations; Business Statistics
University of California, Berkeley	Aug 1-26	Berkeley	Managerial Accounting; Marketing
1961			
Carnegie Tech	July 30-Sept 1	Pittsburgh	Simulation and Management Games
Chicago	July 31-Aug 25	Williamstown	Accounting; Marketing
UC-B	Aug 6-Sept 1	Berkeley	Industrial Relations; Managerial Economics; Organization Theory
1962			
Carnegie Tech	July 29-Aug 31	Pittsburgh	Management Games, Mathematics, and Simulation
Chicago	July 30-Aug 24	Williamstown	Application of Behavioral Sciences to Industrial Relations and Personnel Administration, Financial Management, Marketing and Production
UC-B	July 31-Aug 28	Berkeley	Accounting; Private Finance

Figure 6.1

"Seminars on New Developments in Business Administration."

Many of the Ford Foundation seminars were scheduled during the summer, when most business school faculty were not teaching, on the idyllic campus of Williams College in western Massachusetts. Lasting anywhere from two to eight weeks, the seminars emphasized economics, finance, quantitative analysis, game theory, and decision theory. Ford also established a one-year program at a new entity called the Institute of Basic Mathematics for Application to Business that was jointly administered by HBS and MIT's School of Industrial Management. The program was led by the mathematician Howard Raiffa, who had recently been lured to HBS from Columbia's mathematics department specifically for this purpose. According to a later Ford Foundation assessment, the institute "probably had more impact than any other single seminar" in affecting the research and methodological orientation of those who attended its programs.[89] The overarching goal of Ford's training activities, according to Carroll himself, was to "raise teachers' and students' receptivity for quantitative methods to such a point that these methods will be incorporated, wherever appropriate, into the teaching of production, marketing, accounting, finance, and the other recognized areas in business."[90]

As figure 6.2 highlights, many of the Ford seminars were run by GSIA and Chicago faculty under separately negotiated grants. This arrangement enabled Lee Bach, in particular, to closely shape the format, content, logistics, and lists of faculty and other participants for the programs. According to James Howell, it was during these workshops that concerns first surfaced, on the part of some participating faculty, about the dominant role of economics within the emerging template for discipline-oriented business education. "The Foundation [was] vigorously criticized," Howell wrote, "but not always openly, for letting economics and economists dominate its business education effort. . . . [F]or many [deans] the commissioning of economists for the study of business education was going too far."[91] The dominant role of economists in shaping the implementation of its reforms would later be privately regarded by the Ford Foundation as representing a serious "tactical error."[92]

Between 1957 and 1960, nearly fifteen hundred faculty members from three hundred institutions (about one-fourth of the full-time business school faculty in the United States) attended a Ford-sponsored program. Yet the most profound and long-term impact of the Ford Foundation's effort to transform American business education would come not from the direct training or retraining of business school faculty but from the publication, in 1959, of the

3/19/62

SEMINAR LEADERS: NEW DEVELOPMENTS IN BUSINESS ADMINISTRATION

Carnegie Tech

1957
  Melvin Anshen (CIT), Frederick Balderston (UC-B), Richard Cyert (CIT), Harold Leavitt (Chicago), John Wheeler (UC-B)

1958
  Anshen, Cyert, Leavitt, James G. March (CIT), Robert Fetter (Yale), Wheeler

1959
  Quantitative Methods: Cyert, Wheeler
  Personnel Management and Human Relations: Leavitt, Donald W. Taylor (Yale)
  Electronic Computers and the Management Game: Kalman J. Cohen (CIT), Austin Hoggatt (UC-B)

1960
  Production: Fetter, Peter R. Winters (CIT)
  Personnel Management and Human Relations: Leavitt, Taylor
  Research Methods, Electronic Computers, and the Management Game: Cohen, William Dill (CIT)
  Visiting Staff: William W. Cooper (CIT), Daniel Katz (Michigan), Herbert A. Simon (CIT), William F. Whyte (Cornell)

1961
  Seminar Leaders: Cohen, Cyert, Dill, Merton H. Miller (CIT), Fred M. Tonge (RAND)
  Visiting Staff: Harold Guetzkow (Northwestern), James Jackson (UCLA), Guy Orcutt (Wisconsin)
1962
  Seminar Leaders: Cohen, Alfred A. Kuehn (CIT), March, Gerald L. Thompson (CIT), Tonge, Winters
  Visiting Staff: James S. Coleman (Johns Hopkins), Cyert, Harry M. Markowitz (RAND), Simon

Chicago

1959
  Director: John E. Jeuck (Chicago)
  Business Economics: Joel E. Segall (Chicago), Robert M. Solow (MIT), Kenneth Boulding (Michigan)
  Business Finance: Sidney Davidson (Chicago), John V. Lintner (Harvard), Ezra Solomon (Chicago), George H. Sorter (Chicago)

1960
  Director: Alex Orden (Chicago)
  Statistics: Harry V. Roberts (Chicago), Robert Schlaifer (Harvard)
  Industrial Relations: Howard W. Johnson (MIT), Bernard D. Meltzer (Chicago Law), Paul Pigors (MIT), George P. Shultz (Chicago)

1961
  Director: Sidney Davidson
  Accounting: Robert N. Anthony (Harvard), Charles T. Horngren (Chicago), Maurice Moonitz (UC-B, American Institute of CPA's), William Andrew Paton (Michigan)
  Marketing: Kuehn, B. Peter Pashigian (Northwestern), Roberts, Gary A. Steiner (Chicago), Hans B. Thorelli (Chicago)

Figure 6.2
Seminar Leaders: New Developments in Business Administration.

-2-

(cont.)

1962
Director: James H. Lorie (Chicago)
Seminar Leaders: Leonard R. Sayles (Columbia), Steiner
Visiting Staff: Frank Barron (Institute of Personality Assessment and Research, UC-B),
Morris Janowitz (Chicago), Walter R. Reitman (CIT), Renato Tagiuri
(Harvard), Gerald Thompson (CIT)

University of California, Berkeley

1960
Managerial Accounting: William J. Vatter (UC-B), John T. Wheeler (UC-B)
Marketing: Reavis Cox (Wharton), E. T. Grether (UC-B), Richard Holton (UC-B)
Afternoon Sessions: C. West Churchman (UC-B), Thomas A. Cowan (Rutgers Law), Philburn
Ratoosh (UC-B)

1961
Industrial Relations: Robert Dubin (Oregon), Joseph W. Garbarino (UC-B), George Strauss
(UC-B)
Managerial Economics: Robert Dorfman (Harvard), Julius Margolis (UC-B)
Organization Theory: James G. March (CIT), Wheeler

1962
Coordinator: J. W. Garbarino
Seminar Leaders: Austin C. Hoggatt (UC-B), Franco Modigliani (Northwestern), Maurice
Moonitz (UC-B), Fredric P. Morrissey (UC-B), Vatter, J. Frederick
Weston (UCLA)

Gordon-Howell report on the state of the nation's business schools, a document that provided a road map for those business schools around the country aspiring to academic legitimacy.

▙ Institutionalizing the Revolution: The Ford Foundation Report and Its Immediate Impact

In 1959, both the Ford Foundation and the Carnegie Corporation issued book-length, highly critical reports on the state of American business education. The Carnegie Corporation released *The Education of American Businessmen: A Study of University-College Programs in Business Administration*, written by Swarthmore College economist Frank C. Pierson. While greeted with less fanfare than the Ford report, the Carnegie report was to have a major impact on undergraduate business education, which was in fact the focus of Pierson's analysis. He decried the narrowness of the undergraduate business curriculum, especially its excessive specialization, illustrating his argument with such memorable examples as these courses offered at a major Southern university business school: Principles of Baking: Bread and Rolls; Principles of Baking: Cakes and Variety Products; and Bread and Roll Production: Practical Shop Operation.[93]

The Ford Foundation's report of the same year, *Higher Education for Business*, was written by Robert Gordon, who had been part of Gaither's 1953 expert advisory group and was a longtime member of the economics faculty at UC Berkeley, and James Howell, a younger, Yale-trained economist who had served on the Ford Foundation staff and was now teaching at Stanford. Dense, detailed, and closely reasoned, the 490-page document represented the most comprehensive collection of data on American business education ever assembled. These data, covering subjects ranging from faculty credentials to student enrollments in various courses, were presented in numerous figures and tables, along with a rich array of qualitative observations and interviews with business educators from around the country. The report examined issues including the nature of postwar business careers, the role of education in developing business skills, and what the broader goals of a university-based business education should be. As Howell himself later observed, the Gordon-Howell report would end up establishing "the educational paradigm that has guided the nation's business schools" to this day.[94]

Among its other findings, the Gordon-Howell report stated that "what passes as the going standard of acceptability among business schools is embarrassingly low, and many schools of business do not meet even these low standards."[95] Here, in black and white, was evidence that many business schools blatantly violated the minimal standards set forth by the AACSB. For example, even the number of hours required by the AACSB for basic instruction in nonvocational courses was routinely ignored by member schools: "We visited every one of the institutions included in our sample of Association schools, and there is no doubt that many member deans are aware that member schools often violate with apparent immunity both the letter and the spirit of the Association's Curriculum Standards."[96] The report described the present state of business education as indefensible. In all the essential elements of an institution of higher education—caliber of students, training of faculty, coherence of curriculum, and quality of research—business schools, the report asserted, failed to meet even rudimentary standards. Students studying business were among the least intellectual on campus; faculty had little understanding of basic research methods and were often most productive at exploiting their positions for gains from private consulting. While this situation might have been excusable when business schools were in their infancy, it was no longer tolerable, the authors stated, in light of the tremendous progress that had been made in assembling the building blocks of a true science of management during World War II and subsequently at places like Carnegie Tech's GSIA.

The data for both the Ford and Carnegie reports had been collected mostly via foundation-administered surveys, national educational statistics, and visits by the reports' respective authors to the nation's business schools. The authors interviewed deans and collected data on faculty composition, curricula, and faculty research. Both reports openly lamented the state of American business education and rendered a much harsher judgment on the quality of business school faculty and students than the AACSB had ever allowed to be publicly voiced (although many of the reports' recommendations mirrored ones made by several AACSB deans during the 1930s). Indeed, the reports suggested that many business school professors were disingenuous in presenting themselves as academics and business education as an academic program. Frank Pierson declared that graduate business school programs "should be represented for what they are—vocational training in trade techniques to prepare students for specific job openings. . . . [They] certainly should not qualify for the MBA degree or for an advanced degree of any sort."[97] "[W]ell documented," wrote Gordon and Howell, "is the failure of most business schools to develop in their students the qualities of mind and character and the kinds of professional-type skills for which business and society have the greatest need."[98] The Ford and Carnegie authors also harshly criticized business school administrators and faculties for dragging their feet in addressing the schools' glaring problems.

The goal of both the Ford and Carnegie reports was not simply to present a set of findings but, rather, to shake business schools out of their complacency and instigate change. The Carnegie Corporation's five decades of experience in reforming medical and legal education had convinced the organization that exposing faculties to intense public scrutiny was a powerful means of shaming otherwise recalcitrant institutions into acting. According to James Howell, those at the Ford Foundation hoped its report would become "a major instrument of pressure on business schools," especially the most prominent public university business schools. Thousands of complimentary copies of the Ford and Carnegie reports, along with summaries of their major findings, were sent by the foundations to college and university presidents, as well as to national business leaders and hundreds of business journalists. Popular business magazines offered extensive coverage of the reports and their recommendations. The Ford Foundation even hired *Business-Week*'s senior editor, Leonard Silk, to write *The Education of Businessmen*, a condensed and less technical version of the original Ford report for corporate executives who did not have time to read the full version.

Although many business educators were surprised at the harsh tone of the published reports, the authors' major findings and recommendations did not come as a surprise to most business school deans. As early as 1955, the Carnegie Corporation had begun to circulate early drafts of Pierson's report to the deans of the better business schools. Ford had done the same with drafts of its report, starting in 1957. Additionally, Ford's Thomas Carroll and Robert Gordon had spoken to business school academics at numerous conferences prior to the publication of the foundation's report, presenting summaries of the principal findings. The Gordon-Howell report, as one internal Ford memo noted, "made very few program suggestions that had not already been put into effect by the Foundation by the time the book came out."[99] Bringing the material into full public view, however, still served to turn up the heat on schools that had been slow to heed prior calls for reform.

The reports also resurrected the issue of professionalism for business educators. "We speak of 'professional education' for business, but in what sense is business a profession?" asked Gordon and Howell. They noted that a profession rests on the pillars of "a systematic body of knowledge of substantial intellectual content"; "standards of professional conduct, which take precedence over the goal of personal gain"; an "association of members, among whose functions are the enforcement of standards, the advancement and dissemination of knowledge"; and "the enforcement of minimum standards and competence" often by requiring education at a "professional school" and "a qualifying examination."[100] Pierson devoted a whole chapter to examining the development of professional education in American universities and argued that, by the measure of possessing a coherent knowledge base and an ethos of service, business education was woefully inadequate. Not surprisingly, given the direction already supported by foundation monies, both reports emphasized the redefinition of business school curriculum and research on a rigorous, scientific basis as the primary mechanism through which a profession of management could be created.

Both the Ford and Carnegie reports also argued that, after half a century of false starts, there now finally existed a "management science" that could be taught to students as a methodology for managerial decision making. While the oldest business schools had drifted from their original intention of developing a managerial science, the decision-making tools developed during the war, such as decision analysis and game theory, combined with the theoretical insights from the behavioral sciences, constituted the basic elements of this new management science—or so the business school reformers believed. In contrast to the old model of business training, this new science would allow managers to make decisions solely on analytical and rational grounds, without recourse to fuzzy notions such as intuition or judgment (the latter being a quality that Harvard Business School explicitly tried to cultivate in its students). Grounded in the behavioral sciences (particularly economics), the new management science could best be taught to students, both reports maintained, through a rigorous immersion in quantitative analysis and concepts from decision theory. Like Frederick Taylor, who saw in scientific management the possibility of controlling organizations as if they were fine-tuned machines, the foundation reformers placed great faith in management science and the prospects for a technocratic leadership. To teach and research this new science of administration, both reports concluded, a new type of business school faculty was needed—one focused more on fundamental research than on descriptive analysis, and deriving decision-making principles more from theory than from existing practice. Embedded within this view, though not explicitly discussed, was a vision of a new type of manager and a new managerial orientation quite distinct from the human relations tradition. The hoped-for result was a more dispassionate and rational manager whose decision making was not clouded by experience or sentiment, but driven by hard facts and cold logic. In an essay about managerial decision making that was included in Pierson's report, Lee Bach predicted that the rational manager represented the future of American business leadership:

> Over the quarter-century ahead, management will almost certainly become persistently more analytical, more rational. The role of "hunch" and even of "informed judgment" will become smaller as the years go by. At the extreme, this will mean increasing use of such fairly elaborate analytical approaches as mathematical programming. . . . The critical change will be the increase in the clarification of variables that need to be considered in the making of decisions, the increase in the use of carefully obtained quantitative information concerning these variables, and the increase in rigorous analysis weighting and combining the variables involved. We all know that in some vague, intuitive way this is what we must be doing when we make decisions now. The change I am predicting is, therefore one of clarifying and of bringing to the surface the variables and implicit logical models our minds must be using now in decision making, and of persistently improving the logic of these models.[101]

Both the Ford and Carnegie reports, finally, expressed a conviction that, among the various types of business school programs (undergraduate, graduate, and executive education) only graduate business education could be made truly worthy of academic status. Most undergraduate programs, both reports stated, were of poor quality and should eventually evolve toward becoming exclusively graduate programs. If schools insisted on keeping their undergraduate programs, it was suggested, most of the curriculum should consist of deep immersion in the liberal arts and social sciences. Executive education programs, meanwhile, should be revamped and kept to a manageable size so as not to overwhelm faculty or distort a school's primary mission of serving full-time students. It was graduate education—at both master's and doctoral levels—that was considered the leverage point for transforming business education and that was, in fact, the arena that would ultimately be most affected by the recommendations of the foundation reports, especially Ford's.

The recommendations summarized in the Ford and Carnegie reports fell into three broad areas: (1) increasing the proportion of research-oriented faculty; (2) standardizing the required MBA curriculum around a basic set of courses with a strong emphasis on quantitative analysis and the incorporation of the social sciences; and (3) improving the doctoral programs that would train future generations of business school faculty. Examining the extent to which each of these three objectives was attained provides a revealing look at the enduring impact of the Ford Foundation's efforts, in particular, on postwar business education.

▙ Creating Research-Oriented Business School Faculties

To improve the academic quality of business schools, which was the major overall thrust of the Ford Foundation's program, raising the intellectual caliber of the faculty appeared essential. The way to accomplish this, from the foundation's perspective, was to increase the level of faculty training in what were regarded as the core disciplines of quantitative analysis and the behavioral sciences—especially economics—and, on this basis, to increase the amount of faculty research drawing on such disciplines. A 1964 examination of the impact of the 1959 Gordon-Howell report noted several changes that portray the foundation's success in building a more research-oriented faculty. First, business schools had significantly increased the number of faculty with doctoral degrees, and many had moved toward adopting academic hiring and promotion processes similar to those found in disciplinary departments. Second, the next generation of business school professors was now being educated in doctoral programs that emphasized disciplinary foundations and quantitative methods. Third, the greater emphasis on published research by schools had led to an increased number of academic outlets for the publication of business school research, which in turn helped promote research activity.[102]

In an illustration of the first of these trends, between 1954 and 1964 the proportion of full-time faculty with doctoral degrees at the twenty-five largest business schools rose from about 69 percent to 83 percent. As a result, the percentage of the twenty-five largest schools that met AACSB accreditation standards jumped from about 50 percent in 1954 to 100 percent by 1965.[103] The search for research-trained faculty led, in turn, to the development of an active external labor market for star researchers. Business schools began not only to hire faculty members from other business schools but also to actively recruit research-oriented, discipline-trained faculty from math, economics, and statistics departments. Such faculty would not have been attracted to business schools prior to the Ford-led reforms, because they would have found few genuine peers in these institutions. For example, Stanford's Graduate School of Business in the early 1950s was a place, according to one observer, where "the amount of time devoted to research was left entirely to individual proclivities" while "[m]ost faculty members devoted their surplus time to consulting."[104] Nor did the school consider an individual's research output in decisions about promotion and tenure. Between 1959 and 1969, however, Stanford began aggressively implementing the Ford Foundation reforms by recruiting faculty, not only from GSIA, but from the nation's top economics and psychology departments. By 1969, Stanford's business school enjoyed an academic reputation as one of the premier business school research institutions. Similar changes could be found at the University of Chicago's business school, where in 1963 Dean George Schultz launched a three-year study of the impact of economic conditions and technological change on labor relations, using this program to create within the business school an economics department that rivaled the top graduate economics departments in the United States. By the 1960s, even "trickle-down" schools such as Northwestern, Wharton, and MIT deliberately avoided hiring their own doctoral students for faculty positions: "[T]he filling of any new post is now viewed as a sacred opportunity and approached with the greatest of care," wrote Joseph Willits about Wharton's post-1959 reforms.[105]

The period between 1954 and 1964 also saw a significant increase in the number of journals, scholarly and otherwise, publishing business school research, as compared with the situation that had existed in 1954 (when the Ford Foundation had identified all of three "scholarly" academic business journals). Some of the new journals, like MIT's *Sloan Management Review* (established in 1959), were modeled on *Harvard Business Review* and oriented toward practitioners. Other publications, such as *Management Science* (est. 1954), *Administrative Science Quarterly* (1956), and the *Journal of the Academy of Management* (1958; renamed the *Academy of Management Journal* in 1963), modeled themselves on scholarly journals in the social sciences, featuring blind reviews and theoretical and empirical articles that would fall under the Kuhnian category of "normal science."

Coincident with the growing number of scholarly journals that published business-related research, the type of research being published also changed in ways that reflected the Ford Foundation's agenda of bringing quantitative analysis to the center of business school research and pedagogy. In 1965, a Ford Foundation–commissioned study that "examined the leading business journals plus a sampling of books written by business school faculty" found that "significant developments in research have occurred in business administration in the last ten years." The major change was that published research from faculty in the twenty-five largest schools demonstrated "an increased use of quantitative analysis and model building."[106] The same report also found that business school faculty were more frequently publishing in disciplinary journals, especially in fields such as "economics, psychology and statistics," where "[journal] contributions by authors in business schools were greater in 1960–64 than they were in 1950–54."[107] About two-thirds of these publications in disciplinary journals by business school faculty were authored by those teaching at the five centers of excellence.

In sum, just five years after the publication of the Ford and Carnegie reports, business school faculty had become increasingly professionalized along the lines expected in the traditional academic disciplines. By the mid-1960s, the average business school faculty member in any of the twenty-five largest schools was more rigorously trained and quantitatively oriented, and produced more high-quality, "publishable" research, than his counterpart prior to 1954. The orientation of faculty toward academic disciplines and quantitative methods would be reflected, in turn, by a quantitative emphasis in the new MBA curriculum.

Standardizing the Core Curriculum

When the AACSB convened its first regular annual meeting in 1917, one of the sessions was titled "What Are the Basic Elements and Their Proper Balance in a Business School Curriculum?" Despite posing this question at the outset and then repeatedly for more than thirty years afterward, the AACSB had always left the decision of what to teach up to individual business schools. Over this period, the association issued only one significant guideline with respect to curriculum. In 1938, it revised its standards and membership requirements to state that members' curricula should "approximate quantitatively and qualitatively the standards in effect in recognized professional schools of business, [with] due allowance being made for the meeting of proper regional objectives."[108] Given the wide latitude granted even in this pronouncement, it is not surprising that, as the foundation reports chronicled, most business school curricula were characterized well into the 1950s by specialized, vocational courses, resulting in an education that was narrowing rather than broadening. By 1964, however, the situation had changed dramatically. The course catalogs from that year for the twenty-five largest MBA programs show significant homogeneity in curricula characterized by three salient features: a decrease in the number of specialized, vocational courses geared to prepare students for first jobs; an increase in functional courses as the basis of a required curriculum; and more course content from the behavioral sciences, with particular emphasis on economics and quantitative analysis (with some courses even entailing the use of computers).

Part of the reason for the greater homogeneity was that many graduate business programs were founded during the era of postwar reform. Two-thirds of all MBA programs in 1964 were less than ten years old at the time, meaning that the emergent model of MBA education had arrived just in time to shape their curricula in their formative years. In 1964, as a consequence of the Ford Foundation's recommendations for a functional curriculum with a strong quantitative foundation, all sixty-four AACSB-accredited MBA programs required one or more courses in accounting and finance. All the AACSB-accredited schools had also instituted an economics requirement, offering courses that fell under the headings of microeconomics, managerial economics, macroeconomics, or forecasting. Most programs required at least three quantitative courses in their core curriculum, all of which drew on mathematical concepts beyond those of high school algebra. All of the twenty-five largest MBA programs offered elective courses that made extensive use of statistics, differential calculus, and linear programming. With respect to nonquantitative courses, forty of the sixty-four programs had an explicit behavioral science component to their curricula, whether under the category of "human relations" or "organizations and administration." Courses in these areas increasingly incorporated concepts developed in psychology, economics, and sociology.

Putting its stamp on what was, on this evidence, essentially a fait accompli, the AACSB affirmed in 1965–1966 the Ford Foundation's recommendations for a core curriculum. With its own professionalization project by now a distant memory, eclipsed in significance by the foundation-led initiatives, the AACSB asserted that "without an agreed, recognized discipline, there is no basis for the professional label as applied to business."[109] The association's 1965–1966 accreditation standards stipulated that as part of "the foundation for training in business administration, instruction shall be offered in the fields of economics, accounting, statistics, business law or legal environment of business, business finance, marketing and management."[110]

While the main emphasis of the Ford Foundation's business school reform effort had been on the content of faculty research and of graduate education in business, the foundation had, as we have noted, paid some attention to educational methods as well. Yet while a significant goal of the Ford program had been to increase the adoption of the case method as the basic pedagogy of business education, the foundation had mixed results in this area, for reasons that can be traced directly to the success of its efforts in promoting a greater research and disciplinary orientation among business school faculty.

Outside of HBS and the University of Virginia's business school, which had been modeled closely on Harvard's, most research-oriented faculty did not regard case writing as a legitimate form of scholarly output.[111] At the University of Chicago, for example, cases were increasingly considered to be time-consuming activities, focused on narrow examples, that did little to contribute to the development of management as a science. Ford's John Wheeler, who wrote the foundation's assessment of its own impact on business education five years after the Gordon-Howell report, noted that, despite the enormous sums Ford had spent on sending faculty to seminars at Harvard to promote case-based teaching, there was little evidence of broad acceptance of the case method, especially among the elite schools. "The major trend," Wheeler stated, "has been towards increased use of cases [as part of course materials] although the exclusive use of case courses has declined. Cases are used in advanced courses as a major part of the course but they are supplements to assigned readings and class discussion, projects, lectures, and small group seminars."[112] At most schools, cases were not used to facilitate an inductive and interactive class discussion about how best to handle a particular managerial situation. Rather, faculty members would use cases in their lectures as examples of how to apply a research method or conceptual framework to deduce a particular solution. How a business problem was actually resolved by the managers portrayed in a case was not of interest to most faculty because, "it was assumed, [the solutions derived from academic theory] would be superior to those commonly used by businessmen."[113]

In sum, a student graduating from business school with an MBA in 1966 had experienced a qualitatively different education from that undergone by a student who graduated in 1956. The best MBA programs now had a strong quantitative core with an emphasis on analytical skills. At Stanford, Carnegie Tech's GSIA, and the University of Chicago, many MBA courses were based on the theory and methods being taught in doctoral programs; the kinds of electives that had once reflected a faculty member's particular experiences or an adjunct lecturer's industry background had largely vanished, replaced by others shaped by a professor's discipline-focused research interests. Yet if the nature of business school programs had changed significantly, so had the type of students enrolling in them. The more stringent quantitative requirements, and higher academic standards generally, in business schools demanded a more academically oriented student than these schools had attracted in the past. In particular, the schools now expected students to have a facility with numbers. To measure the academic quality of their students along the lines believed to be most desirable, business educators approached the Educational Testing Service (ETS) in the early 1950s about the feasibility of creating an examination similar to those used by law schools and medical schools for admissions. (The intended parallel was not perfect, however, as the other professional school exams were administered not by ETS but, significantly, by profession-specific organizations—the Law School Admission Council and the Association of American Medical Colleges.) In 1954, the ETS administered the first Admissions Test for Graduate Study in Business (renamed the Graduate Management Admissions Test [GMAT] in 1976) to seven thousand business school applicants. The first admissions test, in other words, predated the issuance of the foundation reports on business education. By the mid-1960s, however, the test was more broadly accepted and had become a standard requirement for applicants at the largest university-based MBA programs. In the early 1970s, in an indication of a growing professional identity within business education, the Graduate Business Admissions Council (renamed the Graduate Management Admissions Council around 1976) took sole responsibility for developing and administering the admissions test.[114]

Transforming Doctoral Programs

The Ford Foundation recognized that, if its reforms in master's level business education were to be sustained, doctoral education would have to be transformed to produce faculty equipped to support the new vision. Those leading the foundation's efforts in business education believed that, although the social sciences had attracted high-caliber academics during the 1920s and

1930s, in the postwar period the best minds were increasingly going into the physical sciences. "This problem," reported a Ford Foundation committee in 1954, "seems to us especially acute in business administration because of the small number of first-class men who go on to the doctorate and thence to university teaching or basic research in this field."[115]

As a result of the Ford reforms, doctoral programs in business and the types of students going into them changed significantly. First, doctoral program admissions criteria were broadened to attract students who otherwise would have been drawn to traditional disciplinary doctoral programs. The Ford Foundation then provided substantial financial aid and research support to students in business doctoral programs, support that exceeded the type of aid available in disciplinary departments. For example, to encourage students to spend more time in doctoral programs so as to pursue their dissertation research in greater depth, twenty predoctoral fellowships of four thousand dollars per year were introduced in 1956–1957; this amount essentially matched what an assistant professor or instructor would make at one of the top five business schools. Ford also invested in creating a postdoctoral program that targeted recent recipients of social science doctorates who were interested in pursuing the implications of their research in business settings; this program offered an annual stipend considerably in excess of typical starting salaries for faculty in the social sciences. Moreover, Ford introduced rotating research professorships, hoping to attract prominent disciplinary faculty to help train business doctoral students. For example, Columbia sociologist Paul Lazarsfeld, Berkeley psychologist Mason Haire, and Yale political scientist Robert Dahl were each given a rotating professorship to instruct doctoral students and existing faculty members at different business schools in "how the techniques and theoretical structure of the basic discipline [*sic*] of sociology, psychology, and political science can apply to such traditional business areas as marketing, organization, administration, and industrial relations."[116]

Remedying the deficiencies the Ford Foundation perceived in business school doctoral programs, however, would require more than money. The foundation believed that existing business doctoral programs in places such as Harvard Business School, Columbia, and the University of Chicago needed to be restructured along the lines of the program at GSIA. HBS's doctorate in business administration (DBA) program, by far the largest business school doctoral program and one that had historically emphasized general management and qualitative methods (especially detailed case studies as a standard foundation for doctoral dissertations), was no longer universally acknowledged as the best of breed. Instead, by the late 1950s, GSIA's Ph.D. program had displaced Harvard's DBA as "the acknowledged leader" in the minds of many deans.[117] (Lee Bach later revealed that making GSIA's Ph.D. program—not the MBA program—second to none had been the primary aim of the Ford Foundation's support for the school.)[118] The GSIA doctoral program was organized around quantitative analysis. Indeed, it was "the language of mathematics [that] allowed the various factions [among faculty] at GSIA to communicate together," write business historians Robert Gleeson and Steven Schlossman.[119] GSIA's vision of a quantitatively oriented Ph.D. program was opposed in almost every way to the then-dominant model of doctoral education as defined by the HBS doctoral program, notwithstanding the key role the Ford Foundation had assigned to HBS as a center for training teachers in case-method instruction.[120] When it came to training researchers, the GSIA doctoral program was the preferred model, as its organization matched much more closely the lines of a traditional disciplinary Ph.D. program.

This last point needs to be understood in light of the emergence during this period of a growing sense, among business educators, of a qualitative difference between DBA and Ph.D. programs. In 1954, Robert Gordon had held that the distinction between DBA and Ph.D. programs was primarily one of name. Ten years later, however, many people perceived significant differences between the training of students in DBA programs and that in Ph.D. programs. While DBA programs had become more rigorous and quantitatively oriented, there was a belief that they were still too focused on practice and not as intellectually rigorous as Ph.D. programs. Graduates of DBA programs, it was thought, were more knowledgeable about business but less well trained as scholars than graduates of Ph.D. programs. This perception was influenced partly by the different requirements of the two kinds of programs. DBA programs, for example, did not have a foreign-language requirement, whereas even in the mid-1960s most Ph.D. programs did. The DBA curriculum tended to be based upon the MBA program and to "require the completion of the required courses in the MBA program and/or the passing of tests covering the material."[121] Most Ph.D. programs in business schools did not require familiarity with MBA course work.

The topics and methods of dissertations in DBA and Ph.D. programs also varied one from the other. Students in DBA programs often collected their dissertation data through fieldwork in actual firms; as a result, most DBA dissertations were built around a small number of case studies rather than the large-sample studies more suitable for statistical analysis. Some business schools dominated by discipline-trained academics dismissed the DBA as a "bigger and better MBA graduate."[122] Between 1954 and 1964, of thirteen new business doctoral programs created at the twenty-five largest business schools, only three offered the DBA degree, while the rest were Ph.D. programs. By 1969, most faculty members holding a DBA were concentrated in schools that awarded such degrees.

As a result of these changes, by the early 1960s the number of doctoral students in business being trained according to the principles of the New Look increased dramatically. In 1960, GSIA's New Look doctoral program had an enrollment of 75, up from zero ten years earlier. That same year, the HBS doctoral program, the nation's largest, had more than doubled in size from a decade earlier to a little over 130 students. Although still granting a DBA, the program at HBS had been pushed by Ford initiatives in the direction of the New Look and had taken on a more quantitative emphasis. By the mid-1960s, the five largest business school doctoral programs were graduating about 40 doctoral students per year, versus 15 in 1954. Yet despite these advances, Lee Bach still saw the small number of high-quality faculty as the most significant problem facing business schools. As he stated in 1960:

> The first and central fact is that there simply is not today enough highly-trained, imaginative manpower available in and around the field of business administration to make a major assault on the vast research problems involved. In the United States today, I suspect there are no more than two-dozen men in the category of distinguished, intellectual research *leaders*. . . . This is not to belittle the research efforts or abilities of the large number of people in business administration who are doing essentially descriptive research or who are competent to carry on useful research within the general framework of ideas developed by others. But it is not from these roots that the fundamental research most needed is likely to come. (Emphasis in original)[123]

Bach went on to note that, despite the enormous investments made in existing doctoral programs, and with the exception of places like GSIA, "new analytical concepts and approaches for use in research on business is [*sic*] more likely to come from the related disciplines than from the field of business administration itself." In reviewing the important innovations in the various functional fields, Bach concluded, "The major advances in organization theory, analysis of consumer behavior, and production and inventory control, have all come directly from research workers trained in the disciplines but interested in business problems," not from the business schools themselves.[124] Bach arguably exaggerated his case by failing to mention the insights of individuals such as Elton Mayo and Fritz Roethlisberger at HBS or Simon Patten at Wharton, but his conviction that the research destined to shape the future of business education would come from those with disciplinary, quantitative training is thereby all the more evident.

Because of such perceptions by key figures like Bach, the pressure on business schools to recruit from disciplinary departments only increased throughout the late 1960s. The nation was also in the midst of a major boom in higher education enrollment, and the AACSB estimated in 1960 that, even operating at full capacity, the ten strongest business school doctoral programs would produce fewer than one-fourth of the new business school faculty projected to be needed over the next twenty years. Despite the significant growth in the total number of doctoral programs, the number of students graduating with business doctorates was still relatively small compared to the growth in demand for faculty. Even if business school administrators were not being pushed to make hires from the disciplines, they needed to look outside their own doctoral programs to fill faculty slots. As a result, by the mid-1960s, business schools had become one of the major recruiters for economists, psychologists, and sociologists doing empirical work on business organizations.

Shades of Things to Come: The Unwinding of the Ford Program

In the early 1960s, having brought about a revolution in business education whose effects still reverberate today, the Ford Foundation began withdrawing from the field. Thomas Carroll resigned from the foundation in 1960 to become president of George Washington University. Shortly afterward, Lee Bach was offered Carroll's position in the Ford Foundation but declined it. A year later, Ford began moving to end its business school program. In the winter of 1961, an internal report recommended that the program be terminated: Ford's "investment in business education appears to have made a real difference in the level of education acquired by large numbers of present and future students. . . . We believe that the era of heavy expenditures for this purpose is probably past," the memo concluded.[125] In the spring of 1962, the

Ford trustees approved $11 million in terminal support funds to extend existing doctoral and faculty fellowships for another three years so as not to disrupt existing research.

The Ford Foundation's impact on business schools, especially the twenty-five or so top-tier schools in major research universities, was profound. Lee Bach wrote that the foundation had been "by far the single most powerful force" in bringing about the dramatic changes seen in business schools over the course of the 1950s.[126] However, the abruptness with which Ford terminated the program left important issues unresolved and concerns about some of the reforms' unanticipated consequences lingering in the air.

To begin with, while several elements of the Ford reforms had taken firm hold among the largest MBA programs, even by the mid-1960s Harvard Business School was still resisting some aspects of those reforms. While Harvard had moved to revamp its DBA program and hired several discipline-trained faculty members, it still had a large contingent of faculty who quietly rebuffed the changes. Lee Bach noted in 1960 that, unlike the University of Chicago, Stanford, or Columbia, Harvard was moving "cautiously," and that "the bulk of the faculty is not yet convinced" about the superiority of the reforms "to the more traditional Harvard approach."[127] These faculty members remained skeptical as to whether signing on wholeheartedly to the Ford program would actually improve the training of students as general managers, something they believed Harvard had been doing quite effectively for nearly half a century. As a result, while Harvard Business School's doctoral program did significantly increase the number of quantitative methods courses, the general thrust of the program continued to be managerial practice, and HBS continued to produce doctoral students with a strong administrative and managerial point of view.

Meanwhile, an important unanticipated consequence of the Ford reforms was the creation of warring factions inside many business schools. The orientation toward research had fostered a situation in which individual faculty members were more concerned with building a reputation in their respective disciplines than with making contributions to multidisciplinary team projects. "As more and more faculty members became enmeshed in—and famous for—revolutionizing their own disciplines with mathematical rigor, they became less interested in group projects that required them to cross disciplinary boundaries," notes one history of Carnegie's GSIA.[128] Slowly, as the proportion of faculty members from distinct disciplines increased across a number of business schools such as Northwestern, Stanford, and Chicago, what emerged was not a flowering of ideas or a critical exchange of perspectives, but rather a set of factions forcefully making and defending their claims over certain classes of problems.

Not surprisingly, the first school to experience such a schism was Carnegie's GSIA, where the new model of business education had originated and had, by 1956, been in place for six years. Although the fact was not widely known outside of GSIA itself, by around 1956 two identifiable factions had emerged within the faculty. On one side were economists, led by Franco Modigliani, who were deeply immersed in neoclassical theory and whose primary focus was on the development of economic theory built around the neoclassical model. On the other side was a loose coalition of organizational scholars, operations researchers, and cross-disciplinary-oriented faculty with broad and general interests, led by Herbert Simon. Through the force of his will and the strength of his vision for GSIA, Lee Bach had, for a time, sustained an environment of creative tension between the two camps; in his autobiography, Simon noted that GSIA's unique culture was held together by "the complete dedication and strong leadership of Lee Bach."[129] Because they greatly respected Bach, Modigliani and Simon maintained a cordial and collegial atmosphere within the faculty. By the late 1950s, however, "the common language of quantification and mathematics" was no longer enough to sustain the dialogue, sense of common purpose, and cohesion between the two opposing camps.[130]

Despite Bach's efforts, the hoped-for intellectual synthesis arising from the various disciplinary sciences was not realized at GSIA. This failure eventually led to a rejection of Bach's entire vision of a business school where interdisciplinary social scientists, working side by side, would build an integrated body of management theory and practice. Simon noted bitingly that his economist colleagues had "made almost a positive virtue of avoiding direct, systematic observations of individual human beings while valuing the casual empiricism of the economist's armchair introspections."[131] Economists in turn believed that Simon was bullying them to move their research in "directions relevant to a school of business."[132] With tensions between the two camps mounting, Modigliani left for Northwestern in 1960 and, shortly afterward, moved to MIT's School of Industrial Management. Around this time, Bach was diagnosed with early-stage Parkinson's disease. In 1962, Bach resigned as dean of GSIA and moved to Stanford where, first as an informal adviser to the dean and later as a full-time faculty member, he would to help implement many elements of the New Look program there. After Bach's

departure, GSIA lost its sense of common purpose, and the relationship between the two sides rapidly deteriorated. Simon and others who challenged
neoclassical economic orthodoxy found themselves intellectually isolated as
the number and power of the economists within GSIA increased. Andrea
Gabor, who interviewed Simon shortly before his death in 2001, summarized
the situation: "[The] economists won the war—to the long-term detriment
of GSIA. He [Simon] found it increasingly difficult to get appointments for
his doctoral students. It didn't help that he refused to temper his arguments
or veil his contempt for mainstream neoclassical economics. 'I was prepared
to preach the heresies of bounded rationality to economists . . . in season and
out,' he said." "In the end," Gabor concludes, "GSIA became inhospitable to
all views but those of the neoclassical economists, a legacy the school would
come to rue as age, ill health, and new pre-occupations diminished the role of
behaviorists, leaving a vacuum at the school."[133]

Similar divisions would occur at other schools, though sometimes over
different issues. At Northwestern, for instance, which had been an active producer of cases, the proliferation of faculty in the quantitative disciplines that
followed Northwestern's implementation of the Ford Foundation reforms in
the 1960s led to a sharp division among faculty about whether case writing
constituted a legitimate scholarly activity. By 1970, those faculty members
who were still teaching and writing cases had become marginalized and were
held in "low esteem" by colleagues.[134] Within a few years, as the number of
faculty in the quantitative disciplines being recruited from Chicago, GSIA,
and MIT increased, the dean, who had until then maintained support for
case teaching, relented; Northwestern moved away from its case orientation
and ceased to regard cases as legitimate scholarly output.

In addition to the growing schisms between various disciplinary groups
inside business schools and the reduced status of case writing and teaching,
another unintended consequence of the New Look was an emerging divergence between the concerns of research-oriented faculty and those of their
MBA students. Should business schools be fundamentally "research and doc-
torally oriented or should we maximize a pedagogy designed to produce managers in our economy?" asked one Northwestern administrator involved in the
debate about whether the school should maintain its commitment to the case
method.[135] MBA students also increasingly sensed that their business school
educations had been designed not around their own academic and professional interests but rather around the research interests of the faculty. One
of the first graduates of the GSIA program observed: "I don't think I learned

anything [at GSIA] that was particularly useful to me in any of my jobs. But then again, I didn't learn anything that was harmful. We were a group of bright, intelligent people, eager to learn whatever we were taught."[136] Another student described his experience of the wide gap between the theory taught in the classroom and the realities confronted in management: "In a relatively short time after returning to the world of private enterprise, you are made general manager and substantial stockholder in a very small corporation. . . . At first you try in vain to convince yourself of the economic necessity of a punched-card system in your two-man bookkeeping department. You look around wildly for something to program linearly, or perhaps a game theory situation. You know that the cat on the hot tin roof has nothing on you!"[137]

The schism opening between faculty and students gave rise to a corresponding divergence between the concerns of business school faculty and alumni. Participants in a GSIA alumni association meeting in 1958, having gathered to learn about faculty research taking place at the school, found that most faculty members were too busy to receive them. The association then issued a memo to Lee Bach with a damning assessment of what faculty research they had seen: "Some of the older graduates viewed with skepticism and dismay we commonly attribute to rank outsiders the reports on current research that were presented at the conference. The program itself apparently reinforced the attitudes of some graduates that the faculty of GSIA is 'learning more and more about less and less.' "[138] By the late 1960s there was growing doubt about the claims and usefulness of management science, as Steven Sass notes in his history of Wharton: "Errors in modeling, measurement, or computation had led to serious blunders, and in some cases the results were unequivocally disastrous." The mounting casualties in Vietnam, combined with the hubris shown by former Ford Motor Company Whiz Kid and HBS accounting professor Robert McNamara, eventually offered a "nagging public symbol" of management science's human cost and seemed to indict the notion that cold, rational calculus was productive of good judgment.[139]

The growing gulf between the research interests and disciplinary orientation of business school faculty, on the one hand, and the practical and multidisciplinary interests of students and alumni, on the other, reflected not just the success of the Ford Foundation's program in imbuing business schools with an academic, discipline-based, and abstract intellectual orientation. It also represented a neglect by the foundation of what the leaders of the pre–World War II professionalization project had seen as a necessary complement to the aspect of "professionalism" represented by expert knowledge.

More than just having the tools for the job, an earlier generation of business school architects had believed, a professional manager should possess a normative orientation, reinforced through management education, that ensured managers would act to strengthen and not harm American society and its democratic institutions. Lee Bach and his colleagues at GSIA had intended the study of business and society to form one of four pillars of the school's MBA curriculum, so that students would be forced "to think through deeply problems of business ethics and social responsibility, and their own systems of social values."[140] Even at GSIA, however, such intentions appeared to have amounted to little by 1958, when economist Martin Bronfenbrenner visited the school from Michigan State University. Bronfenbrenner was taken aback at the students' lack of interest in connecting what they were learning in business school with the larger concerns of society. He found a program that, rather than educating enlightened future business leaders, was turning out technically skilled individuals who were steeped in quantitative abstraction and largely indifferent to social problems. He relayed his concerns in a letter to Lee Bach:

> The students seem disinterested [*sic*] in public policy issues. . . . They are not, like most commerce students, aggressively pro-business; rather, like most engineering students, they don't seem to give a damn. Perhaps it is a matter of "this brain for hire"—if you have enough technical training, and if your nose is clean, you can be equally indispensable for Joe McCarthy today and Adlai Stevenson tomorrow. Or perhaps the students are just too occupied with other work for idle curiosity about the social implications of economics and business.[141]

In 1969, Lee Bach, now in his third year as a full-time faculty member at Stanford's business school, began to recognize the consequences of this particular failure of the movement for business school reform when the Stanford business school was attacked by student protesters. The protesters' outrage was directed at military contracts administered by the Stanford Research Institute, an entity that would eventually be severed from the university and with which the business school had no relationship. This event, however, appears to have rekindled Bach's old ardor about the need for business schools "to solve real, complex problems" in the "real world," for, even in failing health, he helped organize seminars at Stanford highlighting the relationship between business and society, and initiated a new, public management concentration at Stanford's GSB. Over the next three decades, despite initiatives like Bach's, the insulation of business students from public concerns would generally increase as the Ford Foundation reforms took hold and an older generation of faculty members retired.

By the end of the 1960s, it was apparent that the Ford Foundation had, indeed, dramatically transformed American business education. With the exception of Harvard, all of the major business schools now conformed closely to the model advocated by Ford. At the leading schools, faculty had little reason for concern about the intellectual legitimacy of their institutions. They ceased to fret about the status of business education vis-à-vis the rest of the university, especially as they gained greater respect from their disciplinary brethren. While the Ford reforms had been intended to produce a new type of manager, they had also produced a new type of business school faculty member. The attempt to professionalize management along the lines that the foundation envisioned had resulted in the professionalization of the faculty in the manner of the traditional academic disciplines. Business academia now boasted a precisely defined system of self-regulation based on research degrees oriented toward the social and quantitative sciences, specialized areas of study, numerous journals actively determining the boundaries of legitimate scholarship and validating what constituted legitimate managerial knowledge, and a faculty hiring and promotion system mirroring the approach of traditional arts and sciences departments. The Ford-initiated reforms created a faculty whose knowledge domain and scholarly identity would increasingly develop along disciplinary lines; of the disciplines, economics would become the center of gravity in business education. These developments would leave what remained of the professionalization project in American business schools just enough off center that it would be toppled by the turbulent events that followed the consolidation of the Ford reforms, as we shall see in part 3.

The Triumph of the Market and the Abandonment of the Professionalization Project, 1970–the Present

Unintended Consequences: The Post-Ford   **7**

Business School and the Fall of Managerialism

The Ford Foundation reforms had brought about sweeping changes in business schools that had the effect of institutionalizing managerialism as the governing rationale for "professional" business education. In the process, as we saw in chapter 6, the concept of professionalism that had provided the original rationale for university-based business education had been stripped of much of its original content. The ideal of professionalism had always rested on combining mastery of specific knowledge with adherence to certain formal or informal codes of conduct and, even more fundamental, to an ideal of service. The notion of "science-based professionalism" that had motivated the founders of the Carnegie Institute's GSIA, however, made short shrift of ideas like the social obligations of professionals while focusing, instead, on improving expertise through such means as the creation of a science of rational decision making. As we shall see, even the managerialist philosophy that came to dominate business schools in the wake of the Ford reforms made room for a certain notion of stewardship in its definition of the manager's role. Yet almost no sooner had managerialism been enshrined as the justification for both managerial authority and the existence of university business education than it began to be swept away by new forces that would result in the abandonment of managerialism—along with any meaningful concept of professionalism—altogether. This repudiation of the logic that had sustained university business education from its formative period in the late nineteenth and early twentieth centuries through the growth and maturation of the post–World War II era came about in a convergence of changes internal to business schools in the wake of the Ford reforms, and external events in the 1970s that severely undermined the legitimacy of managerialism and managerial authority.

In discussing this transformation, we must recognize that while the Ford reforms had effected profound changes in the larger, more prominent business schools in the country, they did not—contrary to the expectations of the Ford reformers—affect the vast majority of schools. Nor did the Ford reforms slow down the proliferation of business schools or of narrow, vocationally oriented programs designed to train specialists for particular industries. If anything, the foundation reforms may have had the opposite effect. Endeavoring to raise standards while controlling the establishment of new business schools in an employment market characterized by a significant credential inflation for many jobs that had previously required only an undergraduate degree, the reforms contributed to a resurgence of commercial trade schools, business-operated training programs, and further mushrooming of business degree programs in American education. By the 1980s, fewer than one-third of MBA programs were AACSB accredited, with many schools, Berkeley's Dean Raymond Miles noted, coming "very close to selling the degree."[1] The combination of continuing economic growth in the 1960s and the widespread diffusion, throughout the 1960s and 1970s, of the managerially intensive conglomerate form of organization resulted in even greater demand for MBA graduates, thereby increasing the incentives for colleges and universities to expand into business education. Between 1965 and 1980, as GMAT registrations ballooned from about 36,000 annually to more than 300,000, an average of 26 business schools were established each year. In 1972, about 32,000 MBA students graduated from around 400 MBA programs—nearly twice as many such programs as had existed in 1964, when the Ford Foundation terminated its business education project. By 1980, more than 57,000 MBA students were graduating from more than 600 U.S. MBA programs, accounting for one in five of the total number of master's degrees granted.[2]

As the better schools shifted away from turning out functional specialists or students trained for particular industries, three stratified categories of business schools emerged during the late 1960s. The first two categories arose from the competition among business schools to raise their academic reputations and reorganize their curricula along the functional, technical, and quantitative lines recommended by the Ford Foundation.

The first group of business schools consisted of those inside the leading American research universities—the Ivy League universities and the flagship private and public schools of the Midwest and West. Following the broad acceptance of the Ford Foundation reforms, these schools successfully leveraged the reputations, traditions, and existing research and fund-raising platforms of their parent institutions to quickly adapt their faculty and curriculum along the lines suggested by the foundation. By the early 1970s, those business schools that enjoyed national reputations and had the most sought-after MBAs—as measured by dean and faculty surveys and the starting salaries of MBAs—were those at the most prestigious of the nation's universities. One consequence of this new order was that by the mid-1970s, Carnegie Mellon's[3] GSIA—the Ford Foundation's prototype par excellence of the future business school—was no longer considered a top school. The conditions that had given GSIA the freedom to experiment and innovate during its formative years (specifically, its being a newly founded school inside a small technical institute in Pittsburgh) had become a strategic liability; for example, because the school was so young and not part of an established, elite university, it lacked a wealthy and powerful alumni base from which to raise a significant endowment. Meanwhile, business schools located in prominent American universities such as Chicago, Stanford, MIT, and Texas succeeded in recruiting GSIA's strongest faculty and best doctoral students, with the result that the school's national reputation slowly faded and its MBA program took on a more specialized character. By contrast, business schools such as those at the University of Michigan, Berkeley, Texas, Cornell, and MIT lost any residue of regional character and emerged as first-tier national schools when the first business school rankings were published in the mid-1970s.

Next in rank after the establishment schools were those large regional business schools that offered a specialized but AACSB-accredited MBA program. These schools often excelled in one or two functional areas, such as accounting, marketing, production, and finance; or offered a hybrid MBA program linked to a particular industry, such as health care or information technology; or were geared to a particular demographic group, like midlevel managers. For example, while it offers a regular, full-time MBA, Northeastern University's College of Business Administration also seeks to distinguish itself by offering a "High Tech MBA" that has a strong information technology focus. It also offers a part-time, eighteen-month MBA program targeting middle managers.

The last group, representing by far the largest segment of MBA programs, consisted of schools offering vocational programs in which academic requirements were modest and obtaining a degree fairly painless. These schools, which tended to have a regional flavor, could be found mostly in small public and private universities and colleges; often the business education program existed as a department within a college rather than as a distinct school. The curricula of these third-tier programs were organized to provide students with sound entry-level skills for a particular department within a business.

The MBA program was often ancillary to the larger college or university, and many of the students were nontraditional or part-time, with most courses taught by part-time instructors who either worked in business or had private consulting practices. The continued growth and heterogeneity of MBA programs like these demonstrated the weakness of the AACSB even as an accrediting body. While the AACSB continued to set standards in areas such as student-faculty ratios, percentage of faculty with doctoral degrees, teaching loads, and the availability of a functional curriculum, only about one-third of the nation's MBA programs were accredited as of 1980.

While the proliferation of such programs also reflected a more general weakening of the boundaries by which business schools could be recognized as legitimate professional schools (a problem also affecting education in the much more established professions of law and medicine), my focus in this chapter will be on elite or first-tier schools. Here, in the course of the 1970s and early 1980s, the combined effects of the Ford reforms and the turbulence experienced by American capitalism in this period were manifested in significant changes in how business schools conceived of the purpose of business, of management, and of business education itself; in the composition and organization of business school faculties; in the role and nature of research in business schools; and in the kinds of students who enrolled in them and the career goals these students pursued. Naturally all of these factors are interrelated. But any account of how the professionalization project in American business education finally came to be abandoned must begin with an examination of how elite business schools approached questions of their purpose in the relatively brief interval between the final implementation of the Ford reforms and the upending of the logic of managerialism amid the economic and academic storms unleashed in the 1970s.

The Idea of General Management

In the 1970s, elite business schools such as those at Columbia, Stanford, Harvard, Michigan, and Berkeley were still very much organized around the goal of producing general managers. The teaching of general management, as defined and practiced at these schools, was the pedagogical expression of the ideology of managerialism. Lawrence Fouraker, who served on the faculty of Harvard Business School from 1961 to 1970, and as dean from 1970 to 1980, described the general manager as "the sovereign" of America's economic system and the singular focus of management education. Of these corporate sovereigns, Fouraker went on to say (in a variation on the Chandler thesis on the origins of the visible hand):

> Their organizations are large, producing many different products which are offered in a variety of different national and international markets. Each of these intersections of product and market requires the attention of a general manager, acting in the capacity of a problem solver. . . . The fundamental advantage of this system over [free market] capitalism is that the fate of the organization has been divorced from the finite life cycle of a proprietor or a single product. Thus it is possible for the well managed diversified organization to function without limit of time.[4]

As we saw in examining the emphasis on rational decision making in business school research and curricula under the influence of the Ford Foundation reforms, the idea of the manager as what Fouraker called a "problem solver" implied that the expertise and skills of a general manager were independent of particular firms or even industries—a conception that dovetailed completely with the conglomerate form of organization. In pedagogical terms, the needed expertise and skills were to be imparted not only through the quantitative methodologies that Ford had championed but also in the organization of the basic MBA curriculum into functional areas. All the elite schools devoted a major portion of their core program to general administration, with required courses in accounting, economics, finance, production, statistics, and principles of general management. The functional program was designed to prepare students to enter corporate management development programs that would eventually lead to broad managerial responsibilities. The MBA curriculum was intended to give students a wide-ranging exposure to many forms of knowledge and discourage a narrowing of focus—the notion being that as graduates moved higher in their organizations and into positions of greater responsibility, they would require familiarity with a broad array of corporate functions and find themselves managing people from a variety of corporate functions.

At Harvard, which took a practical, action-oriented approach to the teaching of general management via the case method, the functional courses were integrated by means of a general management course, titled Business Policy, and treated as the capstone of the MBA curriculum. Harvard University's then-president, Derek Bok, summarized Harvard Business School's approach: "In its basic two-year master's program, Harvard does teach basic courses in the major functional specialties, such as production, marketing, control, and finance. But all these courses are taught from the standpoint of the general manager, and all are eventually tied together in the required second-year course on Business Policy, which emphasizes the crucial role of the chief executive in defining corporate goals and creating a strategy to which each of the units and functions of the corporation must relate."[5] Only a relatively small percentage of schools adopted the Harvard perspective (Dartmouth's Tuck School and the Darden School of Business at the University of Virginia were the most prominent among them), as countervailing trends in business education came to dominate. In the 1970s, these trends were best exemplified by the Stanford Graduate School of Business, where the approach to general management tended to be more detached and focused on diagnosis, explanation, theory, and quantitative analysis rather than case studies and an emphasis on implementation, with little or no attempt to explicitly integrate the various functional areas or disciplines within a single capstone course.[6] An AACSB-commissioned examination of MBA curricula in the period found an "insufficient emphasis on integration across functional areas."[7] This lack of intellectual cement would make business schools vulnerable as the idea of managerialism came under assault from the outside world beginning in the late 1970s.[8]

At many of the better business schools—whether they taught general management in the style of Harvard or of Stanford—faculty did not altogether abandon concern for the social role of management. Harvard's Dean Fouraker said that "[t]he avoidance of disorganization and the social costs associated with disorganization is the dominant philosophical consideration in the managerial system,"[9] and other deans of the era spoke of a role for management beyond the corporation itself. Stanford's Arjay Miller, for example, stated that the manager "must take a broader-than-business view of his environment and of the effects of his business actions upon it. He must be prepared to bring to the solution of industry-related social problems comprehensive, rational and sound approaches before the pressures reach a boiling point. . . . This is a fundamental responsibility of management."[10] As may be suggested by the language of such statements—reminiscent of the fear of social disorder that had haunted enlightened business school leaders like Harvard's Wallace Donham in the 1920s—business schools were hardly the province of social progressives during this era, but they were not unconcerned about the responsibilities of business to society.[11] Views about managerial responsibility were rooted less in notions of professional obligation than in "stakeholder" models of corporate responsibility, which were presented explicitly in general management or business policy courses. The stakeholder model did hark back to the views of early advocates of professionalization, however, by describing the CEO as a mediator balancing the claims of various individual interests both within and without the corporation.

Yet the notion of the CEO as enlightened corporate statesman—one of the pillars of managerialism and a key feature of the relationship capitalism in which the managerial model flourished for thirty years after the end of World War II—would, beginning in the late 1970s, become one of the major casualties in yet another of the periodic contests for control of the American corporation such as that which, in the early decades of the twentieth century, had established managerial authority in the first place.[12] This development would have dramatic consequences for American business schools with their embrace of managerialism.

The Emergence of Investor Capitalism

Beginning in the early 1970s, the United States experienced an extended period of intense economic distress. This period represented an inflection point for the American economy *and* American society as the postwar industrial system began to unravel. A perfect storm of external economic shocks, compounded by a drop in productivity growth, cost-of-living adjustments built into union contracts, and an economy shifting toward services, dealt the final blows to the postwar managerialism described in chapters 5 and 6. The Bretton Woods international monetary agreements, which had fixed foreign exchange rates to the U.S. dollar since the end of World War II, were abandoned at the same time that there was a significant rise in foreign competition in manufactured goods, from automobiles, steel, and televisions, to raw materials including copper, aluminum, and oil. The postwar prosperity of the 1950s and 1960s, argued by some to be a permanent part of the American economy, first slowed and then reversed direction for a significant number of Americans. For only the second time in the twentieth century, the poverty rate rose over the course of a decade, from 8.8 percent in 1973 to 12.3 percent by 1983. The recession of 1981–1982 was so deep and cut across so many sectors that a fifth of America's workforce was unemployed at some point. These changes reflected seismic shifts in the global economic order. Even Alan

Greenspan (who in 1975 was chairman of the President's Council of Economic Advisors), although not known for plain speaking, testified to Congress, "Capitalism is in crisis."[13]

During the mid-1970s, the percentage of GDP accounted for by manufacturing dropped from 23.7 percent to 17.1 percent.[14] Whereas only 3.5 percent of the labor force had been jobless in 1965, by 1980 unemployment had reached 10 percent. Overall U.S. productivity growth dropped from 2.8 percent a year during the postwar era to approximately 1.4 percent in the mid-1970s. Real wages began a slow and sustained fall, as did overall U.S. corporate profitability, which dropped from about 12 percent in 1965 to 6 percent in 1980. The old industrial winners—including the chemical, steel, and auto industries—became the new losers. The region containing once-great American cities such as Buffalo, Pittsburgh, Cleveland, and Detroit was rechristened the Rust Belt, its empty factories and surrounding urban squalor symbols of America's industrial decline. While some believed that the nation's change in economic fortunes could be blamed on the oil embargoes of the early 1970s, the energy crisis actually accelerated a previously unnoticed trend. Nitin Nohria and his colleagues described the shift:

> In retrospect, it seems clear that the energy crisis of 1973 and 1974
> accentuated trends adversely affecting the big industrials. But it also
> ushered in an era that the industrials perceived and experienced as
> new, qualitatively different, and mostly hostile. U.S. economic growth
> stagnated for a decade, and when it resumed, prosperity did not come
> from the traditional drivers, the big industrials, but rather from recent
> entrants in high technology, as well as the service sector. The big industrials continued their drift from the center toward the periphery of
> the economy. The direction and pace of change became painfully evident to owners, managers, employees, and other stakeholders.[15]

One casualty of the era was Americans' faith in their institutions, starting with the government and its ability to improve economic conditions and impose constructive order on business through either regulation or national industrial policies. Government agencies such as the Interstate Commerce Commission, the Occupational Health and Safety Administration, and the Environmental Protection Agency were seen to have devolved into byzantine, ineffectual bureaucracies incapable of achieving the objectives for which they had been established. Senator Daniel Patrick Moynihan laid some of the blame for the growth of these bureaucracies on the hubris of academics and policy makers, who believed they could engineer organizational or bureaucratic solutions to complex economic and social problems: "We constantly underestimate difficulties, over promise results, and avoid any evidence of incompatibility and conflict, thus repeatedly creating the conditions of failure out of a desperate desire for success," Moynihan complained. "I believe that this danger has been compounded by the increasing introduction into politics and government of ideas originating in the social sciences which promise to bring about social change through the manipulation of what might be termed the hidden processes of society."[16]

A second casualty was the trust in American corporations that had characterized the organizational society of the postwar years. The new distrust of corporations was especially evident among American workers. Sociologists Richard Sennett and Jonathan Cobb found that workers had become disillusioned with the large American corporation and the meritocracy it allegedly represented.[17] At General Motors, for example, 10 percent of the workforce failed to arrive for work on most Mondays or Fridays. In other cases at GM, one business magazine reported, "screws have been left in brake drums, tool handles welded into fender compartments (to cause mysterious, unfindable and eternal rattles), paint scratched, and upholstery cut."[18] Autoworkers, the reporter went on to note, took special pride in damaging the most expensive cars.

Rightly concerned with the trajectory of the American economy, a variety of groups from all points on the political spectrum—including corporate executives, shareholders, union leaders, and elected politicians—began to lobby the Carter administration to disassemble the postwar relationship capitalism that now seemed to have hobbled the economy. Harvard Business School professor George C. Lodge described the breakdown of the postwar consensus and the competing forces now pulling the corporation in different directions: "Large corporations, the backbone of the nation's economy and the mainstay of its employment, are in the grip of a many-sided squeeze," he wrote. "These organizations feel the scarcity of resources, the pressures for environmental protection, the imposition of many new and sometimes contradictory definitions of community needs."[19] Deregulation took place in a variety of industries such as airlines, communications, trucking, and financial services, within a political and economic climate that was unfavorable toward organized labor.

Yet while many talked about the American corporation's being squeezed by high oil prices, new foreign competition, or excessive regulation, other

Americans were becoming more skeptical about attributing all of the problems affecting the nation's corporations to such exogenous factors. Thus began an active reassessment of postwar managerialism in the 1970s and early 1980s. Amid the search for explanations for the woes of American business, Reagan administration official Admiral Hyman G. Rickover lambasted the nation's business schools for producing ineffectual managers, arguing that "many who teach 'management' in our universities do their students and society a disservice." Management schools, Rickover said, were graduating students who "almost without exception . . . are fluent in the jargon of systems analysis, financial manipulation, and quantitative management. They graduate convinced they have learned management techniques that will enable them to administer any job. Yet most seem to have an unrealistic perception of what is actually involved with little appreciation of the importance of technical knowledge, experience, and hard work."[20]

This was the critique that Harvard Business School professors Robert Hayes and William J. Abernathy made in a famous *Harvard Business Review* article published in July 1980 and titled "Managing Our Way to Economic Decline." In their article, Hayes and Abernathy laid the blame for America's economic troubles squarely on the shoulders of American managers and, ironically, on many of the management techniques put in place as a consequence of the business education reforms of the 1950s and 1960s. "American managers," they wrote, "have increasingly relied on principles which prize analytical detachment and methodological elegance over insight, based on experience, into the subtleties and complexities of strategic decisions. As a result, maximum short-term financial returns have become the overriding criteria for many companies." Strategic planning offices had created "structural distance between those entrusted with exploiting actual competitive opportunities and those who must judge the quality of their work." Portfolio techniques originally used to manage stock and bond portfolios were being transferred to the management of the corporation, they argued, resulting in management by "remote control" in the nation's conglomerates. Abernathy and Hayes called for managers to develop a longer-range focus and to voluntarily divest themselves of unrelated businesses—to adopt, in effect, a type of "back to basics" action plan.[21] Meanwhile, prominent business school researchers including William G. Ouchi, Richard T. Pascale, and Anthony G. Athos were studying the Japanese economic miracle and arguing in their books and articles that the solution to the problems of America's corporations lay in reforming the American managerialist model more along Japanese lines. These scholars advocated the adoption of such features of the Japanese corporate system as progressive human resource policies emphasizing lifelong employment, quality circles, lean manufacturing techniques, and a more cooperative labor-management relations system—all under the broad umbrella of a national industrial policy.[22]

In opposition to this reformist approach to the problems posed by American managerialism stood a second camp that also implicated American managers as the source of many of the nation's economic woes, but did so in the context of a sweeping critique of relationship capitalism itself. This group—consisting mostly of economists and policy makers, many trained in the free-market tradition of the University of Chicago—argued that managers would not voluntarily reform. They were also skeptical that the problems facing American corporations could be solved either through voluntary restructuring or through the adoption of the industrial planning and industrial welfare policies of Japan or Germany. National industrial planning policies like Japan's, this group argued, would only exacerbate the economy's woes. The imperatives of government conflicted with the imperatives of competition; the government, for example, would not close down an outmoded plant. The government, in fact, was to be regarded as another interest group, focused on expanding its reach and financed by increased taxation, and would only suppress competition and entrepreneurship. Indeed, most government policies (even those prohibiting insider trading, as some of the more extreme members of this group argued) typically destroyed incentives for sound economic and social behavior. Thus the solution to the problems of American competitiveness entailed minimizing the government's role in the national economy. Moreover—in an argument that upended the Chandler thesis about the "managerial revolution"—it was not only the government but management that stood in the way of the efficient operation of competitive markets. In particular, business school academics like economists Michael C. Jensen and William H. Meckling—who would become the most prominent architects of the theoretical justifications for takeovers and the maximization of corporate value, measured by share price, as the overriding objective for firms—argued that the lack of an active market for corporate control had contributed to a lack of corporate discipline and managerial accountability. Ultimately, then, the answer was to rely more on markets both for the regulation of the overall economy and for corporate governance.

Throughout most of the postwar era, when Keynesianism was the reigning economic orthodoxy, this market logic had been considered extremist and marginal. Increasingly, however, the American polity sided with the free-market or neoliberal economists in their belief that institutional investors and other shareholders were more trustworthy than managers as custodians of the American corporation. The 1980 election of Ronald Reagan as president was the symbolic and political watershed of this transformation. Rightly or wrongly, Americans had come to believe not only that "government was the problem" but that corporate executives had prospered—often at the expense of employees, communities, and shareholders—even while their firms' performance faltered.[23] Corporate raiders like T. Boone Pickens portrayed corporate executives as primarily concerned with only their own hides; as he charged: "U.S. executives aren't looking at takeovers as a means of enhancing shareholder value. They only look at takeovers as a threat to their salaries and perks. And the reason they perceive it this way is that they generally own very little stock in their own companies. They don't relate to the shareholders' interests because they aren't substantial shareholders themselves."[24]

In countless profiles of executive excess, the business media provided an image of corporate managers as unaccountable plutocrats who were mismanaging corporate assets.[25] Society's growing acceptance of the need for a market for corporate control was thus partly a response to a perceived breakdown in the social contract between corporations and society. The social and political context that had favored managerialism since the Progressive era, and was institutionalized in a variety of regulatory policies and normative practices that had virtually guaranteed managerial autonomy since then, was rapidly dismantled during the 1980s.[26]

The wave of deregulation that took place during this decade created the active market for corporate control that critics of managerialism were calling for. The creation of this market quickly delegitimized the conglomerate form of the corporation; moreover, it tilted the balance of power between corporate executives and financial actors—including not only institutional investors and mutual fund companies but also financial analysts, investment bankers, and takeover firms—in favor of the latter. This resulted in many firms' either being forcibly broken up, voluntarily shedding unrelated businesses, or borrowing money to engage in stock buybacks, all in an attempt to improve their stock prices and stave off corporate raiders.[27] University of Chicago economist Steven N. Kaplan has noted that of the 150 largest public corporations in the United States in 1980, 22 percent had been merged with or acquired by other public companies by 1988, while another 5 percent had been taken private.[28] And while hostile takeovers did not affect the majority of America's largest corporations, managerial behavior in these organizations was still influenced by them.[29] Just as making an example of one unprepared student can sober up an entire classroom, a few hostile takeovers of companies like RJR Nabisco sent shudders through CEOs and clubby boardrooms throughout corporate America.

With the creation of shareholder value positioned as the key criterion for business success and the only way to maintain independence from corporate raiders, companies not only divested unrelated businesses but sought to lower costs by cutting out layers of management, improving processes, and outsourcing noncore functions. Corporations downsized, dramatically reducing the middle management ranks that had been one of the defining characteristics of postwar corporate America.[30] The new corporate order, declared the *New York Times*, "eschews loyalty to workers, products, corporate structures, businesses, factories, communities, even the nation. All such allegiances are viewed as expendable under the new rules. With survival at stake, only market leadership, strong profits and a high stock price can be allowed to matter."[31]

The new logic of shareholder primacy absolved managers and corporate executives of responsibility for anything other than obtaining the desired financial results. As in the era of the conglomerates, firms were seen as aggregations of financial assets, only now they were to be sorted in value by the market rather than prudently tended by senior managers. They were certainly not institutions to be built and preserved in perpetuity, as Harvard's Lawrence Fouraker had opined.

Many positive changes resulted from this shift. Old, inefficient firms and uncompetitive industries were allowed to die, thereby enabling new firms and new industries to emerge, the most spectacular of which involved the convergence of communications and information technology. Popular media accounts—building on ideas that Daniel Bell had anticipated in the early 1970s when he foretold the coming of "Post-Industrial Society"[32]—heralded the birth of a new Knowledge Economy. Michael Jensen called the transformation the "Third Industrial Revolution."[33] Whatever one calls it, what is certain is that a new type of American capitalism had emerged, with profound effects both on firms (whose very boundaries were blurred by phenomena including strategic alliances, interorganizational teams, outsourcing, and just-in-time delivery) and on the relationship between economy and society.[34]

By the end of the 1980s, even after new state legislation had made it significantly more difficult for corporate raiders to execute a hostile takeover, the trend toward greater shareholder power continued unimpeded.[35] Private and public pension funds, mutual funds, and other investors and financial intermediaries, buoyed by the retirement savings of Americans through pension fund contributions and 401K plans and in search of high stock returns, continued to exert pressure on corporations and chip away at corporate and managerial autonomy. These large shareholders began to actively press for more control over decisions about mergers and acquisitions, cost containment, executive compensation, and even who should occupy the CEO position. The twenty-year restructuring that was largely completed by the early 1990s marked the overthrow of managerialism as both the defining logic of American capitalism and the arbiter of its actual practices.

If the movement to establish and legitimate managerial authority that had led to the creation of American business schools and motivated the professionalization project in American business education could be described as the successful definition of the tasks and decisions that were to be the exclusive domain of management—and the defense of this domain against other interests such as labor, the state, and shareholders—this latest transformation in American capitalism represented the deprofessionalization of management. Even as the grip of labor and the state had been relaxed, managerial control of the firm vis-à-vis shareholders was sharply eroded. External forces, especially in the form of activist shareholders and their intermediaries, interpenetrated the internal activities of the corporations, reducing managerial autonomy.[36] By the early 1990s, for the first time in nearly a century, owners or their investor proxies, such as institutional investors, had successfully asserted meaningful control over the large corporation.

Under the sway of the new economic orthodoxy, any suggestion that the corporation was subordinate to any societal institution other than shareholders was increasingly regarded as soft-minded and suspect. With neoliberal market ideology providing the cognitive template, the core idea that the relationship among managers, boards of directors, and equities markets should be mediated and evaluated primarily through the lens of a firm's share price became institutionalized throughout the corporate and financial worlds.[37] Progressive ideology and post–World War II American policy, holding that corporate interests were subordinate to the public interest, had seen concentrated wealth and power as threats to American democracy; in sharp contrast, restraints on the corporation's pursuit of the purely financial interests of shareholders were now widely construed (as they had long been by the American Right) as threats to Americans' liberty. Markets and corporations were no longer seen as part of a nexus of complementary institutions but were, instead, elevated as the most important institutions in society. The objective of managerial work—especially at the uppermost strata of the corporation—was increasingly framed as serving shareholders and shareholders alone. In a crowning irony, this Copernican revolution in the definition of corporate and managerial purpose was accomplished with the unstinting assistance of American business schools as they had been refashioned in the era of managerialism.

The Disciplinary Model and the Eclipse of General Management

In the 1970s, even as the shifting economic and political climate started to undermine the foundations of managerialism on which postwar American business education rested, the Ford Foundation reforms of the 1950s and 1960s continued to determine the underlying intellectual structure of business schools. This fundamental intellectual structure—which privileged the academic disciplines and quantitative techniques that Ford had imposed through its grant program—would turn out to be far more decisive for the mission of business schools as the turbulent events of the 1970s unfolded than would any formal declarations of allegiance to principles such as "professionalism" or "general management."

Beginning in the 1960s, as we saw in chapter 6, the Ford reforms had a profound impact on the composition of business school faculties and their research and pedagogy. Originally motivated by the Ford Foundation's goal of increasing the proportion of discipline-oriented faculty in business schools, the trend toward hiring faculty with backgrounds in the academic disciplines rather than in business studies per se (i.e., Ph.D.'s rather than DBAs) continued in the 1970s and 1980s. Two large-scale surveys of deans in the 1980s found that among those business schools located in research universities, the "potential for high-quality research" had become the number one criterion in the selection of new tenure-track faculty, and that research productivity was the number one criterion for promotion and tenure.[38] At the top twenty-five business schools, the proportion of faculty with doctorates jumped from about 40 percent in the mid-1950s to more than 75 percent by the 1980s, including a significant increase in the number of faculty trained in the social science disciplines. It was also during this time that business schools began to reduce the production of new business doctorates, with most AACSB-accredited schools shrinking their business doctoral programs.[39] For elite business schools like Stanford, MIT, and the University of Chicago, academic pedigree became the dominant factor in faculty selection and promotion. Given the perennial shortfall in the number of well-trained graduates from business school doctoral programs, the top business schools began to regularly recruit from the best social science departments in the country, often competing with these departments for the best graduates. Moreover, most of the elite schools—which had historically recruited the majority of their new faculty members from their own doctoral programs— adopted policies discouraging this practice.

The growth in research-oriented faculty was also accompanied by a new set of norms and incentives that shaped how business school faculty spent their time. Catalyzed by the original funds provided by the Ford Foundation, elite business school administrators reorganized their programs, decreasing faculty teaching loads to allow faculty more time to conduct research.[40] Business school deans also established the first permanent research funds to support faculty research, and faculty promotion processes significantly increased the weight of a faculty member's research productivity and quality in promotion decisions.[41]

As also noted previously, the growing emphasis on research in business schools encouraged by the Ford Foundation led to the creation of a number of new journals in which management faculty could publish. During the 1960s and 1970s, the rate at which new academic business journals were established significantly increased (see table 7.1), while existing journals expanded the number of articles published per year. By 1978, *The Directory of Publishing Opportunity in Business Administration* listed more than two

Table 7.1

Foundings of Scholarly Academic Business Journals, 1950–2006

	Number of Journals
1950–1959	8
1960–1969	126
1970–1979	111
1980–1989	120
1990–1999	861
2000–2006	540

Source: EBSCO Publishing Business Source Title List. Source lists includes disciplinary journals that appear relevant to management scholars.

hundred business journals, in contrast to the twenty identified in the Ford Foundation report.[42] (Today, EBSCO Publishing includes more than sixteen hundred titles in its database of scholarly journals relevant to business research. Included in this number are the scores of disciplinary journals in economics, psychology, and sociology.)

Amid such developments, the culture of business school faculties came to resemble the larger academic culture with its social structure built around regular research seminars, decreased emphasis on teaching, strong loyalty toward disciplines rather than institutions, and a status order that placed what James March and Robert Sutton have called "the priests of research purity" at the top.[43] In making promotion and hiring decisions, many business schools began to attach greater weight to the number of publications in leading journals and the number of times an individual's work was cited by other academics. Claims that teaching counted for as much as research productivity were belied by the reality that research was emphasized at the expense of teaching or the development of classroom materials, as was also the case in the university at large.

During the 1970s, with the aid of relatively light teaching loads, high pay compared with that in faculties of arts and sciences, modern classrooms, and generous research budgets, the better business schools began to regularly attract an array of high-caliber, discipline-trained and -oriented psychologists, sociologists, and economists who would not have been the least bit attracted to business schools only a few years earlier. As the faculty research output at these schools soared, so did the academic respectability of business schools, creating a self-reinforcing cycle that continues to this day.

So powerful, in fact, was the overall trend toward disciplinary orientation and discipline-based research that even Harvard Business School—once considered a laggard in implementing the Ford reforms—eventually succumbed to its pull. Harvard had long seen itself as, "first and foremost, a teaching school . . . aimed at preparing general managers" and sought "to produce top executives for corporations everywhere," as Derek Bok noted in an assessment of the business school in the late 1970s;[44] Dean Lawrence Fouraker described the school as pursuing a "distinctive" strategy. Yet Harvard's uniqueness, as Fouraker himself noted, was not without its cost. The model required a faculty that was willing to invest a significant amount of time in teaching, thereby acquiring skills that had little marketability outside of Harvard. Moreover, by the now-dominant measures of academic productivity, such as publication in scholarly journals and social science citation counts, Harvard did not measure up well. Specifically, Harvard Business School's faculty, if denied tenure there, could not get tenure at most other establishment business schools; as Fouraker observed: "There is no large number of comparable institutions providing employment opportunities—and therefore employment security—for junior Faculty. There is an inescapable conflict between the School's purpose and the self-interest of non-tenured Faculty."[45]

In the earliest rankings of U.S. business schools, *MBA Magazine*—which in 1976 began the first annual poll of deans of the country's leading business schools—consistently ranked Stanford's number one, with Harvard Business School a distant second and the University of Chicago's Graduate School of Business and MIT's Sloan School (so renamed in 1964) a close number three and four, respectively. Asked in 1978 to explain why Stanford ranked number one and Harvard continued to lag behind it, the chairman of Harvard Business School's MBA program, James L. Heskett, replied that the ratings heavily weighted published research, and Harvard had historically emphasized teaching over research.[46] Later that same year, Derek Bok issued a report criticizing Harvard Business School's approach to business education, raising fundamental questions about the school's exclusive focus on the case method and the faculty's low level of scholarly research. In his report, Bok noted that while the case method had important strengths in helping students acquire the skills for addressing the practical problems facing managers, it also had some significant limitations; in particular, the use of cases as the primary teaching vehicle came at the expense of instruction about general principles and concepts. Moreover, Bok noted, teaching and case writing were so time-intensive that they left faculty with little opportunity to conduct research.

While the business school initially rebuffed the president's report and responded with one of its own, documenting the success of its strategy over the years, Bok's criticism actually created much consternation within the faculty. The academic legitimacy of Stanford's research model proved to be too powerful a force and began to interpenetrate even Harvard Business School, which slowly began to adopt many of Stanford's practices, shifting its curricular orientation away from general management (or the "administrative point of view," as it was sometimes called), increasingly hiring discipline-trained Ph.D.'s, and weighting research output much more heavily than previously in the faculty promotion process. The Ford Foundation's Gordon and Howell report had criticized Harvard for hiring faculty mostly from its own doctoral program (a practice that Gordon and Howell called "inbreeding"), but by 1979 the number of new faculty with Harvard doctoral degrees had declined to 44 percent, from 63 percent in 1963.[47] The school not only began recruiting more faculty from other business schools' doctoral programs but also started regularly hiring individuals with nonbusiness doctorates (23 percent of the Harvard faculty in 1959, up to 47 percent in 1983).[48]

As Harvard and the other elite business schools discovered, there were several positive consequences—some of them unanticipated—of hiring a discipline-trained faculty. The new disciplinary scholars, trained in psychology, economics, and sociology, began to develop a corpus of theory and research methods that could be used to study business. As a result, several new subfields in management studies—including strategy, negotiations, human resources management, and entrepreneurship—emerged as distinct fields of study. At the same time, in already-established fields such as organizational behavior, corporate finance, accounting, and marketing, research became more firmly grounded in the basic social science disciplines.

It is difficult to describe in detail the full range of research that emerged during this time, but it is worth highlighting two areas that underwent rapid development as they became increasingly populated with academics trained in economics, attaining significant new relevance for practitioners and, indeed, affecting managerial practice. The first of these areas was strategic management, as it was developed by Harvard Business School's Michael Porter. Porter's influence was the result of both deep theoretical work in industrial organization economics and empirical field research on a variety of industries. His book *Competitive Strategy* (1980), which summarized Porter's theoretical and empirical insights, became one of the best-selling management books of all time. The essential findings of the book became widely diffused and contributed to the process by which strategic management—once a subfield of general management—became a business discipline of its own. Porter's identification of "five basic competitive forces" and notions of competing on "cost" versus "differentiation" became part of the intellectual framework of many management consulting practices and were used to help restructure firms.[49]

Meanwhile the field of finance, which had centered on strategies for firms to attract and allocate capital, was developing a new focus on capital markets, especially on how financial decisions affected the market value of firms. Michael Jensen and a colleague described the shift in the field that took place from the 1950s to the 1980s:

> The analytical methods and techniques traditional to economics
> began to be applied to problems in finance, and the resulting

transformation has been significant. This evolution was accompanied by a change in the focus of the literature from normative questions such as "What should investment, financing, or dividend policies be?" to positive theories addressing questions such as "What are the effects of alternative investment, financing, or dividend policies on the value of the firm?" This shift in research emphasis was necessary to provide the scientific basis for the formation and analysis of corporate policy decisions.[50]

These changes in the field of corporate finance, combined with the introduction of a variety of ideas developed in econometrics and accounting, eventually resulted in the positing of the Efficient Market Hypothesis, a theory that came to represent "the cornerstone of modern academic finance."[51] The theory is built on the assumption of John Stuart Mill's *homo economicus*, a rational economic man "characterized by perfect self-interest, perfect rationality and free access to perfect information regarding a specific condition."[52] According to this theory, if markets are efficient it is not possible for investors to make profits by trading on already-available information. In other words, it is not possible for investors to consistently earn above-market returns on the basis of publicly available information. As a result, market prices—the price someone is willing to pay to take over a firm, or the firm's stock price—are the best reflectors of the fundamental economic value of the firm. The idea was extended to the responsibilities of managers:

> If capital markets are efficient, then the market value of the firm reflects the present value of the firm's expected future net cash flows, including cash flows from future investment opportunities. Thus the efficient market hypothesis has several important implications for corporate finance. First, there is no ambiguity about the firm's objective function: managers should maximize the current market value of the firm. Hence management does not have to choose between maximizing the firm's current value or its future value, and there is no reason for management to have a time horizon that is too short . . . This allows scholars to use security returns to estimate the effects of various corporate policies and events on the market value of the corporation.[53]

These ideas, as we shall see shortly, revolutionized finance and transformed many business schools from training grounds for general managers to institutions that trained professional investors and financial engineers, especially in the areas of investment banking, private equity, and hedge funds. A powerful theory of the firm that would come to be known as agency theory—rooted in the school of neoliberal economic philosophy at the University of Chicago—would consolidate these ideas and contribute to a fundamental reconsideration of the purpose of corporations and the role of managers in realizing that purpose.

While the turn toward the disciplines during the 1970s energized fields like strategy and finance, in other areas the results were more mixed. Fields such as organizational behavior and organizational theory, in particular, became much more diversified and fragmented during the 1970s. Stanford's Jeffrey Pfeffer has noted that a proliferation of theoretical perspectives, each drawing from its own unique discipline or theoretical paradigm, has led to a field without any cohesion, unable to identify even one or two conceptual frameworks that could aid managers in improving organizational practice.[54] While others saw the diversity of organizational theory and the range of perspectives as an overall positive, even they acknowledged that "more integration of these varied ideas would help move the field forward."[55]

A growing divergence between an academic field like organizational behavior and the exigencies of practice was caused not only by a lack of theoretical integration but also by the fact that many of the discipline-trained scholars joining business school faculties were not intrinsically interested in business. One result was that, unlike earlier generations of business school professors, few younger faculty members now had regular contact with practicing managers outside of executive education classes. Few were motivated in their research by a desire to examine the real problems that managers faced. Instead, to the extent that business school faculty were problem-driven, it was increasingly with respect to the theoretical and conceptual problems of the disciplines in which they were trained.

Lacking a general manager's perspective or an integrative administrative point of view about how the functions in which they specialized related to other parts of a business, most business school faculty members also restricted their research to a single functional domain. The narrow, specialized work that was produced by an ever more narrow and specialized faculty— while often of very high quality—was of little value for practitioners or even for researchers in other fields for the same reason that academic research generally was increasingly addressed only to other specialists in a particular field or subfield, for academic career structures and rewards in business school had come to mirror those found in the more traditional academic disciplines. As Lyman W. Porter and Lawrence E. McKibben have noted:

> The reason for specialization is obvious: This is how one acquires expertise in a given area. This expertise, insofar as university faculty members in general and business professors in particular are concerned, is what can facilitate not only teaching in a disciplinary area, but also high quality research. It is rare to encounter a generalist who has made specific research contributions. Thus doctoral students, with the assistance of their faculty mentors, are motivated to narrow their focus so that they can be better prepared to do research, which, in turn, will help them get hired and promoted.[56]

With business school faculties having little experience or understanding of business, business schools themselves seemed in obvious danger of forgetting their ostensible purpose. The goal of producing deep knowledge about organizations for improving managerial practice was displaced as a greater proportion of business school faculty saw other academics, rather than practicing managers, as their constituency. Moreover, as Peter Drucker had warned back in 1968, business schools' newfound academic respectability had come at a cost with respect to their extra-academic purpose and responsibilities: "The business schools no longer see themselves as social instruments. They want to be 'respectable' as, say, mathematics departments are respectable. But this is wrong. Professional schools are not intellectual institutions but social institutions. Old-timers at the business school had one great strength; they knew what they were talking about."[57]

Business schools' increasing intellectual involvement with, and dependence on, the disciplines also exposed business school academics to intellectual currents in the social sciences in the late 1960s and 1970s that sought to level all traditions of authority and reduce value systems to human social constructions. Business academics were free (or obliged, if they wanted to get published) to drift where their disciplines drifted, which not only pushed them further away from the concerns of business practice but also involved them in the delegitimation of such original pillars of their institutions as science, the professions, and the university. The discipline of economics was not immune to such influences, and the major push to delegitimate the traditions of authority and narratives of purpose that had guided business schools, in one form or another, since their invention at the end of the nineteenth century came from this now revolutionary quarter.

⬛ The Revolution in Economics

Economics had historically played a significant role in business schools, but its relationship to the study of management had long been awkward and ill-defined. In the era when university business schools were being invented from scratch, institutional and historical economists like Edmund James and Simon Patten at the Wharton School had attempted to use economics as part of a broad-based effort to ground business education in the social sciences, and thereby to produce business leaders with a thorough understanding of the social dimensions of their enterprises and their callings. There had been a widespread assumption that the more theoretical and mathematical school of economics to which the institutional and historical economists stood opposed (and vice versa) offered the most readily available basis for rooting the business school curriculum in "science"; nonetheless, this branch of the discipline failed to gain a foothold in business schools owing to its lack of interest in the internal workings of firms. In their 1931 study *University Education for Business*, conducted for the Wharton School, Wharton professors James H. S. Bossard and J. Frederic Dewhurst described the uneasy relationship between business schools and economics departments:

> If the liberal arts college is the grandmother [of business schools], then the department of economics has served in the dual capacity of father, and midwife to the collegiate school of business. The attitude of the economists has constituted a second factor of primary importance in the evolution of the business curriculum, and the relation of the business school to the department of economics is one of the outstanding problems in the development of collegiate education for business. . . . To the extent that there is anything like a common or typical attitude, it may be likened to that of a petulant father who is partly proud of, partly envious of, partly skeptical of, or even antagonistic toward his offspring, who has outgrown him or is threatening to do so.[58]

As I showed in chapter 6, one unintended consequence of the Ford Foundation reforms in the 1950s and 1960s was that economists came increasingly to dominate business school faculties, to the consternation of many traditionally minded business academics as well as mavericks like GSIA's Herbert Simon. During the 1960s and 1970s, large numbers of business school academics who had specialized training in economics came to be

employed in business schools and to engage in business research. The impact
on business education of scholars trained in, and primarily oriented toward,
the discipline of economics went beyond the particular effects of the perspective they brought to the business school curriculum and business school
research; it also signified the growing acceptance of the legitimacy of economics as the foundational discipline of business education.[59]

At almost all the elite business schools, the ideas of economists came to
dominate not only finance but also accounting, international business, production, negotiations, and strategy. Even courses on human resources increasingly addressed issues of motivation, race and gender discrimination,
and incentives with neoclassical formulations. Surveying three decades of
management research, Jeffrey Pfeffer and his colleagues have recently concluded, "There is little doubt that economics has won the battle for theoretical hegemony in academia and society as a whole, and that such dominance
becomes stronger every year." Surveying academic citation patterns in business schools and research on organizations, Pfeffer states that "one is hard
pressed to think of many substantive areas in which economic models are not
cited, even if only as providing an alternative hypothesis."[60] The ideas of
economists, as we shall shortly see, also proved decisive in shaping how organizational problems are perceived and the nature and purpose of the corporation and of management are understood in the contemporary business
school.

Despite its prominence in the fields of economic history and institutional
economics, the managerialism that took root in the 1950s and early 1960s did
not have a major impact on neoclassical economics, which had long since won
the battle with institutional economics that raged in the early decades of
university business education. In his highly influential book *The Nature and
Significance of Economic Science* (1935), Lionel Robbins had argued that economics should concern itself with "high theory" and that institutions were
largely irrelevant. One consequence of the success of this argument was that
the firm came to be regarded as merely a production function that should be
treated as a lone actor responding to market forces much as individuals do.
Whereas much of nineteenth-century economics had studied economic phenomena historically and *then* developed an accompanying theory and model,
neoclassical economics constructed its theories primarily through deductive
reasoning. Thus because it was assumed in the neoclassical view, for example,
that market processes ensure unanimity of responses, the issue of ownership
and control (which had provided a critical underpinning of managerialism)

was deemed irrelevant. Competition in the marketplace was assumed to solve any and all problems arising from, say, the separation of ownership and control. Despite the assertions of economists such as Berle and Means that profit maximization was no longer necessarily a goal of firms, which could now focus on other factors, economists exhibited little interest in testing this assertion empirically, and most simply ignored such ideas.

Beginning in the late 1960s and early 1970s, however, some economists began to seriously consider the behavioral implications of managerialism. Building on the theoretical insights of individuals like Herbert Simon and such institutional economists of the 1930s as Ronald H. Coase and Berle and Means, these economists started to explore the idea that the firm was not simply a production function. This new interest manifested itself in two economic perspectives that took the firm seriously: transaction-cost economics and agency theory, both of which were founded on neoclassical assumptions about individuals pursuing their self-interest. Transaction-cost economics and agency theory had a significant impact on business school research insofar as they provided a new logic of the firm that was both theoretically powerful and reflective of changing attitudes in the external environment toward managers and managerialism.

Transaction-cost economics actually traces its roots to a paper published in 1937 by London School of Economics (later University of Chicago) economist Ronald Coase, wherein he asked the question "Why are there firms?" Coase's article begins with the assumption of market exchange as the natural condition for human exchange. If every economic transaction could be negotiated in the marketplace, firms would be unnecessary; thus the very existence of the firm, Coase deduced, was an example of market failure. In some imperfect markets, creating firms proved a less costly way of organizing particular exchanges. In lay terms, there would be no need to create firms if one could contract for everything in the marketplace and if markets were costless. Coase argued, indeed, that firms and markets were *alternative* mechanisms for ordering the very same transactions. "The main reason why it is profitable to establish a firm," as he wrote, "would seem to be that there is a cost of using the price mechanism."[61]

Despite its theoretical novelty, Coase's original article "had little or no influence for thirty or forty years after it was published" owing to most economists' lack of interest in institutions like firms. It was not until economist Oliver E. Williamson—who earned his Ph.D. from Carnegie Mellon in 1963—elaborated on the contingencies of particular transactions and how they would affect a transaction's "cost" that Coase's original idea gained significant academic attention (eventually garnering Coase the Nobel Prize for economics in 1991).[62] Incorporating the assumption of bounded rationality developed by Carnegie Mellon's Herbert Simon,[63] Williamson created a model of managerial discretion in which stockholders' decision to hire managers as opposed to contract employees could be understood as an efficient means of lowering transaction costs. Williamson then reinterpreted Alfred Chandler's historical analysis of large corporations to show the importance of managerial decision making, particularly in "make-or-buy" decisions. The decision whether to internalize production and/or distribution or to rely on markets rests with managers assumed to possess discretion and expertise. In other words, managers exercise authority that is independent of market forces.[64]

While transaction-cost economics examined managerial discretion over what activities firms perform internally and what they contract for or buy in the market, agency theory sought to explain not why there are managers or a need for managerial autonomy but, rather, why managers and managerial autonomy are actually problematic from the perspective of shareholders. More than any branch of economic theory since Berle and Means's discussion of the implications of the separation of ownership and control, agency theory focused on the complexities and difficulties of monitoring managers when ownership is widely dispersed. It essentially recast management as an agent of shareholders and shareholders as the principal authority to whom managers are responsible. Thus the principal (i.e., the shareholder) uses the agent (i.e., management) to realize the former's interest in maximizing the share price of the company. Because, as agency theory holds, "both parties to the relationship are utility maximizers," the interests of the two can never be perfectly aligned.

Quite apart from their validity as economic theories or their usefulness in explaining phenomena that constitute the proper subjects of business education—neither of which I would dispute, but which simply fall outside the purview of my argument here—both transaction-cost and agency theory are important for the assumptions they make and the arguments they develop about the role and identity of managers and the relationship of managers to the corporation. Transaction-cost economics, viewing organizations and markets as merely alternative mechanisms for organizing economic transactions, has normative implications for organizational design and managerial identity, since it postulates that bringing transactions inside the firm creates the possibility of managers' behaving opportunistically.[65] Yet the tenets of agency theory are, if anything, even more revolutionary in their reconceptualization of the role and identity of managers.

▙ Agency Theory and the Delegitimation of Managerial Authority

The rise of agency theory and its dissemination in business schools reflected, among other things, the revolution in ideas about management and the purpose of the corporation that came with the emergence of investor capitalism in the 1970s. It is difficult to pinpoint exactly when the debate about the sources of America's economic malaise, and what could be done about it, began to penetrate mainstream business schools, but Michael Jensen has suggested that it happened in the early 1970s, when the postwar order of relationship capitalism showed its first signs of impending collapse. Jensen pointed to the publication in the *New York Times Magazine* in 1970 of an article on the purpose of the corporation by University of Chicago economist Milton Friedman as both a sign of growing academic skepticism about managerialism and an important cultural event in its own right. In his article, Friedman argued that that the sole concern of American business should be the maximization of profit, since the existing system, in his view, was one of accommodation to a host of conflicting interests, an arrangement that damaged society's economic well-being. Friedman's article spoke for a school of economic doctrine that would become strongly associated with the University of Chicago. It rested upon neoclassical economics, albeit within a more general framework that transcended mere economic policy to privilege the market as the most desirable institution for addressing problems of social order.[66]

Agency theory itself, meanwhile, was in many respects an attack on the legitimacy of managerial authority as it had been constructed during the founding era of business schools and then revised in the post–World War II period. In a series of seminal papers published between 1976 and 1996, a core group of University of Chicago–trained economists—Michael Jensen, William Meckling, and Eugene Fama—propounded a theory forcefully asserting that the sole purpose of the corporation is to maximize value, and argued that since managers, who serve as the agents of shareholders, have self-interested motives that differ from those of the latter, monitoring managers under conditions of widely dispersed stock ownership is a major practical challenge. Jensen,

Meckling, and Fama asserted that because managers' work is not easily observable, they will fail to pursue actions that maximize the value of the firm. The challenge, these scholars concluded, is to create an "alignment of incentives" in which managers' personal financial interests will come into close correspondence with those of owners.

Much of the discussion in the foundational papers by Jensen, Meckling, Fama, and their colleagues focuses on the means by which owners can effectively create such alignment.[67] Their research emphasizes three mechanisms: monitoring managerial performance, providing comprehensive economic incentives, and promoting an active market for corporate control. Monitoring managerial behavior involves the deployment of complex accounting practices, sophisticated internal control systems, and the appointment of a professional board of directors whose members operate in the stockholders' interest by virtue of their need to maintain their personal reputations. The alignment of incentives entails remunerating management with company stock and stock options, so that managers and owners possess exactly the same incentives, and self-interested managers will maximize shareholder value as a by-product of maximizing their own material gain. The market for corporate control, finally, is said to lead to stock prices reflecting firm fundamentals, and ensures that poorly performing "insiders" will be threatened and ultimately replaced by efficiency- and profit-oriented "outsiders."

Agency theory quickly created a unified approach to organizations and corporate governance in American business schools, catalyzing academic revolutions in the study of corporate finance, organizational behavior, accounting, corporate governance, and the market for corporate control.[68] In contrast to earlier business school scholarship grounded in inductive observation, and with no overarching conceptual framework, agency theory brought a deductive and generalizable approach to business school research—the lack of which had haunted business education from the start, and had particularly concerned the Ford Foundation—and progressively applied it to a widening variety of corporate phenomena. Drawing on the legitimacy of the economics discipline, agency theory in the business school had the academic authority to classify managerial action and managerial character in decisive ways.

What gave particular power to Jensen and his colleagues (and the strong advocates they soon gained) was that unlike many of their disciplinary brethren, they made considerable effort to disseminate their ideas and findings not only through traditional academic channels, such as journals and professional meetings, but also into the wider world of practice. For example,

Jensen authored or coauthored several articles and editorials in such highly authoritative and influential outlets as the *Harvard Business Review* and the *Wall Street Journal*.[69] Using dramatic examples to animate the dry mathematical formulations of modern economic theory, such writings offered to explain the changing corporate environment and provided a prescriptive set of approaches to improved corporate profitability.[70] In particular, Jensen and the others provided economic justification for the takeover movement, arguing that leveraging corporations with debt was the best way to discipline supposedly wasteful managers.[71] Framing the market for corporate control as one in which managerial teams compete for the right to manage corporate resources, they argued that the deregulation that enabled hostile takeovers had made this market more efficient. They stated that managers who were unable to run their companies efficiently, as measured primarily by the firm's stock price, should suffer the consequences in the form of a takeover, and predicted that takeover entrepreneurs and imaginative investment bankers would continue to prosper.[72] Jensen himself, indeed, described takeover artists like T. Boone Pickens not as financial speculators but as "inventors."[73] Meanwhile, a 1985 article in *Institutional Investor* remarked on Jensen's work in relation to the hostile takeover movement, writing that Jensen "has come out in favor of corporate raiders and greenmailers to the point of developing an economic rationale for takeovers."[74] Frank Dobbin and Dirk Zorn suggest that Jensen's published articles on the takeover movement helped legitimize takeover activity by "convinc[ing] the world that what [takeover artists] did for a living, far from threatening the corporation, was efficient: that it was in the interest of the shareholder and the broader public interest."[75] F. M. Scherer writes that the impact of agency theory was how it altered the language and understanding of corporate control. Jensen and Meckling "transformed the discourse by changing the semantics—from the 'separation of ownership and control' of Berle and Means, with its ominous negative ring, to the much better sounding challenge of securing the optimal relationship between principals (stockholders) and agents (managers)."[76] Invoking expert authority to explain ambiguous, uncertain, and contested events like hostile takeovers, advocates of agency theory exerted a powerful influence over how members of the public framed and interpreted them.

The agency theorists also had a broad impact on corporate policy and, in particular, on a fundamental redefinition of the purpose of the corporation by executives themselves. Consider, for example, the shift that occurred in the course of the 1990s in public statements about the nature and purpose of the corporation by the Business Roundtable, recognized within the corporate world as an authoritative body on matters affecting large corporations. In 1990, an official Business Roundtable policy statement declared:

> Corporations are chartered to serve both their shareholders and society as a whole. The interests of the shareholders are primarily measured in terms of economic return over time. The interests of others in society (other stakeholders) are defined by their relationship to the corporation.
>
> The other stakeholders in the corporation are its employees, customers, suppliers, creditors, the communities where the corporation does business, and society as a whole. The duties and responsibilities of the corporation to the stakeholders are expressed in various laws, regulations, contracts, and custom and practice.
>
> For instance, OSHA, civil rights laws, wage and hour laws, ERISA regulations and so forth determine many of the formal conditions of employment. Beyond these laws, the desire of responsible corporations to have loyal and motivated employees determines the kinds of relationships that corporations seek to achieve with and among their employees.
>
> Similarly, zoning laws, environmental regulations, the tax code and related laws and regulations define the corporation's legal obligations to its communities and society as a whole. As with employees, many corporations go far beyond mere legal requirements in supporting the communities in which they do business. The reasons range from wanting their employees to enjoy a good quality of life to a strong sense of responsibility, as an influential citizen, to help address urgent social problems.
>
> The central corporate governance point to be made about a corporation's stakeholders beyond the shareholder is that they are vital to the long-term successful economic performance of the corporation. Some argue that only the interests of the shareholders should be considered by directors. The thrust of history and law strongly supports the broader view of the directors' responsibility to carefully weigh the interests of all stakeholders as part of their responsibility to the corporation or to the long-term interests of its shareholders.
>
> Resolving the potentially differing interests of various stakeholders and the best long-term interest of the corporation and its

shareholders involves compromises and tradeoffs which often must be made rapidly. It is important that all stakeholder interests be considered but impossible to assure that all will be satisfied because competing claims may be mutually exclusive.[77]

By 1997, however, the Business Roundtable had abandoned the objections to the notion of shareholder primacy that it had expressed in its earlier statement. The new statement adopted by the Roundtable clearly shows the influence of Jensen and his colleagues, who argued that

> the weakness of the stakeholder model is the absence of an overall objective function which implicitly or explicitly specifies the tradeoffs from expenditures on various items, including each of the firm's stakeholders. This in turn implies that the top managers of such organizations cannot be held accountable for their decisions because without an overall objective function, there is no way to measure and evaluate their performance. Managers are then left free to exercise their own preferences and prejudices in the allocation of the firm's resources with no logical way to hold them accountable.[78]

The Business Roundtable's statement includes the following:

> In the Business Roundtable's view, the paramount duty of management and of boards of directors is to the corporation's stockholders; the interests of other stakeholders are relevant as a derivative of the duty to the stockholders. The notion that the board must somehow balance the interests of other stakeholders fundamentally misconstrues the role of directors. It is, moreover, an unworkable notion because it would leave the board with no criterion for resolving conflicts between interests of stockholders and of other stakeholders or among different groups of stakeholders.[79]

Inside the classroom, meanwhile, a course grounded in agency theory that Jensen and several colleagues had developed at Harvard Business School—called The Coordination and Control of Markets and Organizations, or CCMO, for short—became one of the most popular elective courses at the school, regularly attracting more than two-thirds of the MBA students. The goal of the course was "[t]o provide a general framework for analyzing organizational problems, and a better understanding of how the internal rules of the game affect organizational performance." The types of problems the course focused on included "issues of motivation, information and decision-making, the allocation of decision rights, performance measurement systems, organizational and personal rewards and punishments, corporate financial policy, and governance." These problems were examined in settings such as organizational "restructuring, leveraged recapitalizations, leveraged buyouts, takeovers, downsizing, exit, and reengineering."[80]

"Students," Jensen and his Harvard colleagues wrote, "were hungry for a general framework that they could use to structure the vast store of knowledge, including implicit theories, that they had accumulated in the case-oriented first year of the program. . . . The students find it useful to have CCMO's explicitly articulated theory in which to store, organize, and generalize the implicit theories they learn in the first year of the program."[81] At the University of Rochester, where Michael Jensen and William Meckling had first developed agency theory and integrated it into the MBA curriculum, the perspective became part of the core curriculum. Similar courses were taught at the University of Chicago, the University of Southern California, and other schools whose faculties were soon populated by Jensen's students and the wider community of agency theorists.

According to Jensen and his colleagues, students exposed to agency theory increasingly used this approach as their primary way of framing managerial, organizational, and social issues. They began, Jensen writes, to "apply it to their environment—including all the other classrooms in which they are spending time thinking and learning." So powerful was the course in creating a particular point of view, Jensen said, that students found that the logic and outlook of CCMO challenged "some of their deeply felt beliefs." The course helped students, Jensen argued, to become more "tough-minded" and shifted them away from the "stakeholder model" of organizational purpose, which was "dear to the hearts of many of our students." Jensen's distinction between such "tough-minded" ideas as shareholder primacy and "dear to the heart" notions like the stakeholder model is notable not only for its own subtly emotive (not to say values-laden) language but also for the way in which this language usefully shifts focus away from the objective content of the two competing theories and on to the subjective attitudes and frames of mind of those (i.e., students) whom he sought to persuade of the rightness of agency theory.[82] In so doing, Jensen's formulation enacts the elusive transformation—not subject to direct observation but issuing in observable phenomena—through which agency theory ceases being a theory and becomes, instead, a catalyst in a phenomenological process by which certain understandings and ideas come to be taken for granted in a type of shared cognition that assumes a "rulelike status in social thought and action."[83]

Writing about how managers are affected by the discourse that describes their practices, Nitin Nohria, Robert G. Eccles, and James Berkley have noted that *"the way people talk about the world has everything to do with the way the world is ultimately understood and acted in, and . . . the concept of revolutionary change depends to a great extent on how the world is framed by our language"* (emphasis in original).[84] Jeffrey Pfeffer and his Stanford colleagues writing about the impact of economics on how students understand organizations have argued that "the assumptions on which theories are built and the language in which they are presented can exert a substantial influence on individual and collective behavior, separate from the theories' conceptual structures and degree of empirical truth." They have also found that in professional education, the identity and ideal types created for students have a normative status that takes on validity independent of their empirical validity.[85] Offered a powerful theory about how the world works in the context of the formal systems of higher education, students become socialized into a belief system and then act according to those beliefs. In other words, theories about, for example, managers as inevitably self-interested "utility maximizers" can become self-fulfilling prophecies.[86]

The set of tenets inculcated in students by agency theory explicitly rejected such basic precepts of managerialism as that managerial work had a social function (e.g., upholding the legitimacy of American capitalism and democracy in the Cold War struggle against communism) beyond its purely economic one. Agency theory dissolved the idea that executives should be held—on the basis of notions such as stewardship, stakeholder interests, or promotion of the common good—to any standard stricter than sheer self-interest. How could they be if they were incapable of adhering to such a standard in the first place? Students were now taught that managers, as a matter of *economic principle,* could not be trusted: in the words of Oliver Williamson, they were "opportunistic with guile."[87] Jensen and Meckling, in a 1994 paper in the *Journal of Applied Finance* modestly titled "The Nature of Man," took such an indictment of managers further by applying it to the entire human race; they quoted an amusing anecdote about George Bernard Shaw offering an actress money for sex in order to make the point that (in Jensen and Meckling's own words) "pushed to the limit, every woman—and every man—is a willing prostitute."[88] Needless to say, all organizational life presents opportunities for purely self-interested behavior, because an organization's overarching goals do not always provide guidelines for conduct in specific instances. Moreover, it is naive to think that managers never behave opportunistically. However, to admit to such organizational realities is different from legitimating opportunism as the dominant mode of managerial behavior.[89]

In rejecting the managerialist ideology that had become the central justifying rationale for the existence of business schools in the years since the end of World War II, agency theory also served to delegitimate managerial authority itself.[90] This was a striking development to have occurred in university business schools, which owed their original raison d'être to their ascribed role of legitimating managerial authority in the late nineteenth and early twentieth centuries, and which had also been given an enormous infusion of private and public resources in the decades after World War II in order to carry out a managerialist agenda. It represented, within the confines of a "professional school," a thorough repudiation of professionalism as that notion had been understood in the founding era of American business schools. This act of repudiation deserves to be examined in some detail, as it represents a remarkable instance of elements within an institution mounting a concerted, unrestrained attack on the institution's traditions and conceptual foundations.

At the center of the idea of professionalism that shaped the founding principles of American business education was, as we have seen, the notion of a calling, a concept as old as Calvinism and deeply ingrained in the heirs of the American Protestant tradition who established the modern American university as well as the university business school. In this conception, an individual's sense of obligation to work steadily and reliably at a calling, to subject all of his activity to a rationalized discipline in the service of a higher end than self-interest, is the sine qua non of professionalism. As I showed in part 1, it was precisely the promise that business schools would socialize managers into a culture of professionalism—thereby legitimating managerial authority in the face of competing claims to corporate control from the socially disruptive forces of capital and labor—that gave rise to the university business school in the first place. The autonomy and authority of professional managers would be rooted not only in expert knowledge but in their obligation not to represent the interests of either owners or workers—much less of themselves—but to see that the corporation contributed to the general welfare. Agency theorists, however, dismiss any such framing of managerial work as tenderhearted do-gooding. Agency theory also excludes from consideration any notion of collective identity—a fundamental attribute of professions in any sociological framing of the phenomenon—let alone collective responsibility. On the contrary, it frames managerial agents as distinct and dissociated from one another, defining an organization as simply a nexus of contracts among individual agents.[91]

In keeping with the concept of the corporation as a mere nexus of contracts, and in contrast to the notion that the interests of the professional manager would be aligned with the interests of those institutions they were charged with leading, agency theory defined the interests of managers as separate and distinct not only from shareholders' but also from the organization's. Thus managers were no longer fiduciaries or custodians of the corporation and its values. Instead, they were hired hands, free agents who, undertaking no permament commitment to any collective interests or norms, represented the antithesis of the professional. The mechanism agency theory used to break the connection between the manager and any notion that he or she owed an obligation to the firm was to argue that the firm itself was a legal fiction, a ghost of the mind. The organization, according to early agency theorists Armen A. Alchian and Harold Demsetz, was merely "the centralized contractual agent in a team productive process—not some superior authoritarian directive or disciplinary power."[92] By treating the organization (or any institution, for that matter) as a legal fiction, the theory implied that the manager had no obligation to any collective entity, including the organization itself. Thus managers brought to their organizations no a priori values other than those any individual brings to a typical market exchange. Once a firm is seen for the legal fiction that it is, agency theorists argued, the relationship between, say, a manager and an employee is different in content but not in form from any transactional relationship in the market.

Once a contract is concluded between the parties to such a relationship, agency theory thus suggests, the parties have no further obligations toward each other and slip immediately back into being strangers. This sudden, two-way transfiguration is problematic, for the theory that postulates it has nothing to say about the stubborn, unavoidable fact that agents remain in touch with one another within an organization, and that this contact—like other sustained human contact—becomes layered with affect, content, and meaning. Moreover, by framing the organization as a nexus of contracts, agency theory conveniently dispenses with issues of power, coercion, and exploitation. It denies any unique relationship between an organizational leader and other constituents. Such a perspective is at odds with extensive empirical research on actual workplace relations.[93] Yet because such a framing of the relationship between individuals and the organization relieves a manager of any meaningful responsibility to other members of the organization, it easy to see its appeal to business school students once they began to be pulled loose, by the educational and socialization process undergone in the post-Ford business school, from any countervailing intellectual moorings they might have brought from past experience and education.

Notwithstanding the existence of evidence that directly contradicts some of the tenets of agency theory (and the fact that behavioral economics, a new and growing subfield within the discipline of economics, calls into question most of its core assumptions), my own argument here, again, is not intended to challenge the empirical validity of agency theory but only to consider how the theory began to shape the discourse, identity, and behavior of students exposed to its core ideas. Stanford's Harold Leavitt has described how the influence of an agent view of managers began to affect the type of product his school was producing once agency theory became established within business schools: "The new, professional MBA-type manager [in the 1980s] began to look more and more like the professional mercenary soldier—ready and willing to fight any war and to do so coolly and systematically, but without ever asking the tough pathfinding questions: Is this war worth fighting? Is it the right war? Is the cause just? Do I believe in it?"[94] The point Leavitt makes deserves attention in light of evidence that among the many other transformations that the Ford Foundation reforms effected in business schools in the 1960s and 1970s was a discernible change in the type of student enrolling in the elite business schools and the types of careers to which these new students were attracted.

MBAs and the Flight from Management

Not surprisingly, in view of the continued expansion of business schools in the wake of the Ford Foundation reforms, the quality of students entering MBA programs across the whole range of them in the late 1960s and the 1970s was highly variable. This was not true, however, for the first-tier, "establishment" schools, for the absolute growth in the number of students seeking an MBA enabled the top MBA programs to become more selective. For example, in 1960 the acceptance rate for applicants to the University of Chicago's MBA program was above 80 percent; by 1980, it had dropped

below 40 percent. By the late 1970s, the intellectual gap (as measured by standardized test scores) between students entering an elite business school and
those matriculating at an elite law school or a doctoral program in the social
sciences—a gap that had persisted more than eight decades—was rapidly
closing.[95] The typical student in the elite MBA programs in the 1970s was
much more academically oriented than earlier business school students had
been, owing not just to increased competition for slots in these programs but
also to qualitatively different admissions standards reflecting the new analytical orientation of the curriculum and the values of research-oriented faculty. Admissions offices at the elite schools now placed greater weight on
criteria such as the academic reputation of an applicant's undergraduate
institution, grades, and standardized test scores, and less emphasis than formerly on considerations such as how committed students were to a long-
term career in business or to pursuing a career as a general manager. As early
as 1971, indeed, Harvard Business School dean Lawrence Fouraker noted that
fewer students among the approximately twenty-five hundred enrolled in
Harvard's MBA program in 1970–1971 seemed interested in careers as general
managers than had once been the case.[96]

Yet while the elite business schools attracted a more academically qualified student during the 1970s than they had among earlier generations, this
new breed of business school student also tended to be uncertain about his
or her long-term career objectives. Products of the postwar meritocratic system of sorting young people for admission to higher education (and for as-
signment to the higher, middle, or lower echelons of an increasingly stratified
college and university system) by means of standardized tests of academic
"aptitude" (primarily the SAT), students who qualified for admission to elite
business schools under the new set of admissions criteria had also embraced
the assumption that such aptitude entitled one to a rapid climb up the American status hierarchy.[97] MBA career office surveys and numerous anecdotes
from corporate executives suggest that students were no longer willing to
climb twenty- to forty-year job ladders as administrators. The desire for
rapid promotion and flexibility had replaced the desire for job security. Students, indeed, were increasingly seeing the MBA as a versatile degree, a two-
year opportunity for self-discovery, and a pathway to a variety of potential
careers beyond business management. Almost half the MBA students entering business school in the late 1970s had not planned on obtaining an MBA
degree when they graduated from college.[98] In his annual report on the state
of the university in 1978, Harvard president Derek Bok noted that business

schools had begun to compete with law schools for those highly ambitious, achievement-oriented students who did not know exactly what they wanted from their careers other than that they wanted to "take charge" and "run something."[99]

Many of these students who entered business school without definite career goals, however, quickly began heading down a particular set of career paths. While the Ford Foundation reforms had been directed toward training students for managerial and executive careers, beginning around the mid-1960s a noticeable change in the job choices of newly minted MBAs became evident. Advisory businesses such as consulting firms and investment banks, which offered considerably higher salaries and greater career flexibility than most corporate positions, increasingly became the first-choice jobs for students graduating from elite business schools. Table 7.2 shows that between 1965 and 1985, Harvard Business School—which had always defined its core mission as educating the nation's general managers—saw the number of its students going into positions in fields such as financial services and consulting

Table 7.2

First Job for Graduating Harvard Business School Students, 1965–1985 (percent)

	1985	1980	1975	1970	1965
Service/Non-Manufacturing	70	66	62	68	51
Consulting	22	23	12	12	4
Entertainment/Media	2	4	0	0	0
Advertising/Marketing/PR	0	1			
Entertainment/Media	1	3			
Food Service/Lodging	0				
Financial Services					
Commercial Banking	4	7	15	9	7
Investment Banking / S & T	19	11	8	8	8
Investment Banking	19	11	8	8	8
S & T	0				
Venture Capital (01-03 includes PE)	2	0	0	0	0
Other Fin. Services	7	2	6	6	4
Accounting	1	1	5	3	4
Diversified Fin. Svcs.	2				
Insurance	0	1	1		
Investment Mgmt.	4			3	

rather than pursuing careers as corporate managers rise from 23 percent to 52 percent. (As consultants and investment bankers, indeed, these business school graduates would play a significant role in downsizing traditional manufacturing and product firms.) Other elite schools, such as Wharton and the business schools at Stanford and the University of Chicago, began seeing similar shifts in student job preferences around this time. Moreover, even those students entering large corporations often typically went into staff positions in areas such as strategic planning, business development, or corporate finance, not into line positions.[100]

By the late 1970s, moreover, after research had begun to document that students in higher education generally were becoming increasingly interested in reaping large financial rewards from their educations,[101] it was not unnoticed that the MBA itself was garnering holders of the degree some impressive financial returns. A Graduate Management Admissions Council study that examined the starting salaries of MBA students from the University of Chicago, Columbia University, Harvard, and Stanford between 1972 and 1980 found that graduates of these elite schools received higher median starting salaries than graduates of advanced degree programs in almost any other field.[102] The 750 members of Harvard Business School's graduating class in 1978 received more than 3,000 job offers.[103] Throughout the 1970s, a period of high inflation and general wage stagnation, the increases in the starting salary levels for MBAs from elite schools not only exceeded the inflation rate but rose at a time when real wages for the average American worker were declining. Moreover, it was a greater demand for MBAs in particular, not simply for students trained in business, that was driving the higher financial returns to the MBA degree. Between 1965 and 1980, the difference between the starting salaries for MBAs and holders of undergraduate business degrees increased from about 27 percent to 50 percent.[104] By 1980, the starting salary for an elite MBA student was almost double the U.S. median pay level.[105] In 1977, *Fortune* magazine noted that whether students were interested in manufacturing, investment banking, consulting, or any other aspect of business, it was becoming clear that the elite MBA had become "the ticket required for the executive suite."[106] In 1978, the *New York Times* described a Harvard MBA as a "golden passport" to financial well-being.[107]

The changes in priorities and attitudes among the students now lining up for access to such rewards came as a shock to faculty in Harvard Business School's MBA program, which over the years had created a culture that simulated American corporate culture. In classrooms where instruction revolved around cases thick with descriptions of actual business situations, students had been expected to come in business dress, and classroom norms dictated that students and faculty adhere to a strict hierarchy that modeled faculty-student relations after "corporate rather than academic patterns."[108] The entire educational process was designed to impart skills and a sense of professional identity to students "eager" for general management responsibility. Now those students were no longer much in evidence, and the school was forced to adapt.

It was not just dress codes and standards of classroom decorum that were now changing at Harvard Business School. A *Fortune* magazine article in 1987 described how the new environment affected what had once been the core management course in the HBS curriculum:

> For as long as anyone can remember Harvard's courses have mostly bubbled up from its faculty's interests: A professor would become intrigued by something and do research on it. . . . What MBA candidates have wanted of late are financial formulas, mathematical models, and analytical tools—the kind of stuff consultants and investment bankers use. In the past ten years such materials have made their way into the classroom and altered the curriculum. Consider, for example, how Business Policy I turned into Competition and Strategy. Ten years ago BP I, as it was known, was the only required course in the first semester of the second year. It treated corporate strategy, in the genteel tradition of those days, not as a set of formulas but as the mission of the company, its distinctive competence, reflecting the values of its managers. The course was not particularly popular.

The article went on to describe how, by 1983, the Business Policy course had evolved into one on corporate strategy, strongly rooted in industrial economics, with all "the material on the general manager, and on the values of society and the manager" eliminated. "It became a course in strategy, not in general management."[109] One of the last links to the general management tradition at HBS had fallen prey to the combined forces of the Ford Foundation's recasting of American business education and the demands of a new generation of students, who as consultants advising firms on how to streamline and restructure themselves, or investment bankers and buyout artists carrying out the actual restructurings, would take up arms of their own in the effort to roll back the last vestiges of the managerial revolution in American business.

Even as late as 1987, however, many business school deans were dismissive of what was by then a long-standing trend among their graduates away from managerial employment, believing that students would eventually be returning to the ranks of management. Harvard Business School's dean at the time, John H. McArthur, compared the rush into consulting and financial services to a stock market bubble, stating, "I think it's crazy where they're going, but we ought to just relax and enjoy it; it won't last long."[110] Underlying the trend toward investment banking and consulting as avenues of employment for graduates of the elite schools, however, were larger changes in the national economy that were still only beginning to be understood in business schools.

One reason why business school deans and administrators may have been reluctant to face up to the reality of the changes unfolding before their eyes is that these changes, examined closely, can be seen to carry implications that severely undermine the intellectual and social foundations of the university-based business school itself, calling into question its very reason for continued existence. The ideas of shareholder primacy and managers as the agents of shareholders stripped the occupation of management of any last vestiges of the professional identity, self-respect, or responsibility that had been attached to it through the efforts of business school founders, leaders, and faculty going back over a century to the birth of the university business school. This raised the question, among others, of whether business schools were actually "professional schools" if business management itself was not actually a profession. And if they were not—if, instead, business schools were highly sophisticated trade schools that existed to prepare students, by and large, for careers dedicated to the sole purpose of creating private wealth, for themselves as "agents" as well as for shareholders as "principals"—another question that arose was whether business schools remained aligned with the mission of the university to preserve, create, and transmit knowledge to advance the public good.

Such questions would begin to force themselves on both business schools and the public with increasing insistence as the economic boom years of the 1990s gave way, at the beginning of a new century, to a wave of corporate scandals in which shareholders, employees, and the public generally reaped some of the more bitter fruits of the intellectual and social revolution in business schools in the 1970s and 1980s. Business schools, in the meantime, attempting to respond to public concern about their role in promoting or helping to prevent managerial malfeasance, would find themselves hampered by their own lack of a frame of reference within which even to consider the questions now being asked about them. For it was not only in the corporate, financial, and political spheres that the marketplace had been elevated as the ultimate arbiter of essential questions of authority and value. Business schools themselves had now adopted this market logic not just in the classroom but in their very definitions of institutional identity and purpose, as we shall see in my concluding chapter.

Business Schools in the Marketplace 8

Although, as I argued in the previous chapter, intellectual developments within the discipline of economics such as transaction-cost economics, agency theory, and the efficient-market hypothesis played a central role in overthrowing the managerial paradigm that had governed business education throughout the post–World War II era, what I have called the "disciplining" of business school faculties encompassed more than just the ascendancy of economics. Inside business schools, quantitative analysis increasingly came to be seen as the most legitimate form of research. In fields from organizational behavior to marketing to operations, sociology and psychology also claimed many adherents oriented more to their disciplines than to the study of business per se, further weakening the claim that either scholarship or teaching in these institutions represented any genuine engagement with the realm of "professional" practice. As the research and instruction taking place in business schools came to have less and less to do with practice, these core activities came to be more and more loosely coupled with the ostensible purposes for which business schools existed.[1]

Yet even if economics was only one discipline among many that played a part in decoupling business schools from their mission of professional education, it supplied the ideology that would fill the vacuum created by the discrediting and eventual abandonment of managerialism. Intellectual constructs such as agency theory and the efficient-market hypothesis provided no rationale—and indeed directly contradicted the previously existing rationale—for trusting managers, rather than incentives and markets, to ensure the fair and efficient deployment of corporate resources. These same concepts, however, even as they discredited the idea of training managers to exercise judgment and responsibility, ironically offered business schools a new lease on life, albeit in a significantly redefined role. For just as managerial discretion, to say nothing of the notion of professionalism in which it had once been embedded, was subjected to the laws of the market, managerial education itself turned out to be susceptible to the same treatment. That is, business education as a form of *paideia*, as a process of induction into a calling—or even as the cultivation of expert knowledge and judgment—could be discarded for the cleaner, simpler idea of business education as a marketable commodity.

This logic of the all-encompassing market, though its intellectual underpinnings rested in theoretical work done by economics and business school professors, had become so broadly diffused in the course of the 1980s and 1990s as to be part of the American zeitgeist. It was the same logic that disgruntled shareholders and corporate raiders had brought to bear on American management during the takeover craze of the 1980s. It was the logic by which politicians like Ronald Reagan had convinced large numbers of Americans that an untrammeled private sector could be trusted to advance, and the public sector to oppose, their own best interests. Moreover, the assumptions of market logic had begun during the 1980s to infuse the language not just of finance professors and business school deans but also of their colleagues in schools of law, medicine, and arts and sciences, not to mention university presidents and their teams of central administrators.[2] Thus it is hardly surprising that university business schools—despite early efforts to ground themselves in what were once held to be the transcendent values of science (that is, truth), the professions (service), and the nineteenth-century research university (knowledge and culture), and even despite a midcentury revival of something like this original vision—now willingly adopted the concept of higher education as a purely instrumental system of production and consumption.

In the 1950s, as we saw in part 2, the failure of the AACSB to enforce meaningful standards on its own members had caused business schools to lose control of their destinies in the face of interventions by outside actors including the federal government and the foundations. By the end of the 1980s, in turn, business schools' adoption of the disciplinary orientation promoted by the Ford Foundation had left business education itself at the mercy of institutional influences incompatible with, if not downright hostile to, its very purpose. While it is true that a sustained critique of the managerial and professional conceptions of the purpose of business education was mounted from within business schools themselves, this palace revolt occurred at a time when many forces were assembled in opposition to the schools' pursuit of their historical mission. In the late 1980s, the persistent weakness of business schools vis-à-vis such interested external actors was exploited to their detriment by a hitherto unfelt influence: the commercial business press.

⬛ The Tyranny of the Rankings

The decades-long effort to establish business schools as legitimate professional schools had always, and quite necessarily, involved the creation of a status hierarchy among these institutions. An informal hierarchy among business schools is evident as far back as 1916, when the deans of the self-identified "better" business schools came together to found the AACSB. In subsequent years, many factors—among them, a business school's size, the reputation of its parent university, whether it had a doctoral program, and whether it was a member of the AACSB—all contributed to creating a de facto stratification system. During the 1950s and 1960s, the federalization of the accrediting process and the Ford Foundation's designation of specific schools as "centers of excellence" introduced even finer distinctions among business schools.

The decade and a half that followed the publication of the 1959 Ford and Carnegie reports on business education saw a number of attempts to assess the scholarly caliber of individual departments within business schools. A typical study would involve sending a cover letter to department chairs at various business schools asking them to rank-order the top five or ten schools in their particular fields. The results of most such surveys were published in academic journals.[3] By the late 1960s, methods for ranking departments had become more innovative and elaborate, including, for example, annual counts of the number of scholarly articles published by faculty members in a particular department, with the journals in which they were published weighted for prestige. Whatever the specific method used, the defining characteristic of these published rankings was that they centered on scholarly achievement as assessed by peers.

In 1974, an independent monthly magazine, *MBA*, published the first media-constructed national ranking of MBA programs. The magazine, aimed at readers who held the MBA degree, surveyed deans from AACSB-accredited schools and asked them to rank-order the "best" business schools in the United States. Because most deans, in constructing their rankings, focused on the scholarly reputations of individual schools, research-oriented business schools usually ranked highest—a fact that caused some angst among faculty and alumni from more teaching-oriented business schools like Harvard, which consistently found itself ranked behind Stanford's business school during the period when *MBA* published its lists.[4] Overall, however, the impact of the *MBA* rankings on business schools was limited.

In 1988, the process by which business school reputations were constructed and diffused underwent a significant transformation when *Business-Week,* one of the highest-circulation business magazines in the United States, published a cover story that rank-ordered U.S. MBA programs. The ranking, based mostly on the opinions of corporate recruiters and second-year MBA students, challenged the self-perceptions and claims of many supposedly "top" schools. Equally important, it certified evaluative criteria largely outside of traditional academic concerns as appropriate for rating the quality of business schools.

In contrast to earlier rankings emphasizing the research productivity and the scholarly reputation of faculties, *BusinessWeek*'s ranking system focused on factors such as quality of teaching, number of job offers received by graduates, and starting salaries of graduates. This new lens produced results that were often quite different from those to which business schools had become accustomed. The number-one school in the 1988, 1990, and 1992 *BusinessWeek* rankings, for example, was the hitherto little-known Kellogg School of Management at Northwestern University—a choice that stunned the Ivy League business schools and such elite research institutions as the business schools at Chicago and Carnegie Mellon. In the 1992 *BusinessWeek* survey, three schools with strong research reputations—Cornell, Carnegie Mellon, and UC Berkeley—found themselves ranked fourteenth, seventeenth, and eighteenth, respectively, out of twenty top schools. *BusinessWeek,* in other words, overturned the status order that had emerged out of the foundation reforms, generating what business school faculty and administrators recognized as a threat to the established order. In their 1996 study of the impact of *BusinessWeek* rankings on business school deans and administrators, Kimberly D. Elsbach and Roderick M. Kramer provided direct quotations illustrating the efforts of staff to make sense of their school's identity in light of ranking changes. At Stanford, many complained that the rankings "end up measuring things that aren't important." Berkeley's low ranking in the initial *BusinessWeek* surveys raised a great deal of anxiety and even cognitive dissonance among faculty and administrators: "I look at some of the schools," said one respondent, "and I have a hard time believing, from what I know of colleagues and what I know of the schools, that they really belong ahead of us. So in that sense I'm in denial."[5]

John Byrne, the enterprising journalist behind the creation of *Business-Week*'s rankings, described their purpose by stating, "With a few exceptions, the schools didn't seem to care about the perceptions of their customers, the people who actually buy their product." Ranking, Byrne argued, would help "create a market" for business education where schools would be focused on their two primary "customers," "students and the corporations."[6] Byrne's intuition that the rankings would affect business school behavior proved correct. Within months of the first appearance of the *BusinessWeek* rankings, top-ranked schools found themselves with increased numbers of applications and greater recruiter interest, while low-ranked schools confronted unhappy alumni and students and tried to take action to raise their schools' rankings.[7] Over the next several years, other major publications including *Forbes*, the *Financial Times*, *U.S. News & World Report*, and the *Wall Street Journal* began to publish their own business school rankings. The methodologies used and factors weighted most heavily varied considerably from one publication to another, although they all tended to reinforce the biases introduced by the first *BusinessWeek* rankings. *Forbes*'s rankings, for example, focused on the financial return on an MBA education, a figure the magazine calculated by totaling the cumulative salary earned by alumni in the first five years after graduation and dividing this sum by the cost of obtaining a degree at the particular school. The *Financial Times* emphasized the average salary increase from just prior to a student's enrollment in an MBA program to three years after graduation.[8] The *Wall Street Journal* heavily weighted the opinions of recruiters and the general reputation of each school.

One factor contributing to the emergence of media rankings was the continuing proliferation of MBA programs, making what was already a large and fragmented institution only larger and more fragmented. Between 1990 and 2000, the number of MBA degrees granted jumped from 80,000 to more than 111,000. Over this same period, the number of MBA programs grew from about 640 to 900, while AACSB-accredited business schools represented a declining percentage (from about 33 percent to 25 percent) of institutions offering management education. (Table 8.1 compares the increase in the number of business schools between 1956 and 2004 against the increases for law and medical schools during these years.) Increasing specialization, another form of response to market forces, also multiplied the number of programs offered by any single school. In 2000, the AACSB surveyed 228 schools and found 878 different types of business education programs, including offerings in executive education, a new area that had become a major source of revenue for

Table 8.1

Number of U.S. Institutions Awarding Advanced Degrees, 1955–2004

	Business (MBA)	Law (JD/LLB)	Medicine (MD)
1955–1956	138	131	73
1960–1961	207	134	79
1975–1976	428	166	107
1980–1981	539	176	116
1988–1989	669	182	124
2003–2004	955*	195	118

Source: MBA: Leadership and Learning, cited in Dianna Magnani under David Collis and Cynthia Montgomery, "Harvard Graduate School of Business Adminstration," HBS case No. 2-793-066, p. 16. 2003–2004 data; source: U.S. Department of Education Statistics.
*U.S. business schools accredited by the AACSB, the governing body, numbered 393 in 1998. AACSB is the Association to Advance Collegiate Schools of Business. For a list see www.aacsb.edu/General/InstLists.asp?lid=2.

business schools. Another important change during this period was the reappearance of for-profit commercial schools as significant players in business education, though these schools now offered not just technical training, in the manner of their nineteenth-and early twentieth-century counterparts, but advanced "college" and "university" business degrees. In 1992, about 1 percent of the 104,618 U.S. master's degrees in business were granted by for-profit institutions; in 1999 that number had risen to 6 percent.[9] The for-profit University of Phoenix granted about 4,800 MBA degrees in 1999, of which approximately 3,400 originated from its eleven campuses and 1,400 from its online program.[10]

In sum, by the year 2000, the continued, uncontrolled growth in MBA programs had seriously undermined the orderly academic galaxy envisioned by the Ford Foundation, in which elite "centers of excellence" would be orbited by numerous smaller and less prestigious, but still research-driven, satellite schools. In 1998, a former dean of the University of Michigan's business school, B. Joseph White, described the contemporary situation when he observed: "Thirty years ago there was a degree of uniformity to what stood behind the three letters 'MBA.' That's no longer true. All kinds of things occur under that rubric, and we all know they range from correspondence courses for which no degree or credit should be given to really fantastic educational-development experiences, with everything else in between."[11]

As the tremendous heterogeneity among MBA programs made evaluation and comparison ever more difficult, employers and prospective students increasingly relied upon the rankings to provide order amid the proliferating chaos. Even if the measures used were debatable, the involvement of presumably disinterested third parties in establishing and administering the evaluations raised the credibility of the rankings by lending them an air of objectivity. While some business school administrators criticized the rankings and the methodologies employed in them—complaining, for instance, that they often privileged a single dimension of business schools at the expense of other important ones, or that they constructed a false hierarchy based on differences that were sometimes minuscule—their objections had little impact on students or recruiters, and most schools chose to not to buck the system. As one dean remarked, "The reality is that, independent of whether you believe rankings accurately reflect quality, the perception of the outside world is [that] it [sic] does and consequently resources flow to schools who are highly ranked."[12] An associate dean, in turn, noted the power of the rankings to shape student perceptions, stating, "Students think there's truth in those numbers."[13] Cornell business school professor Robert H. Frank described how the rankings affected the choices of prospective students: "MBA applicants focus much less on the particular mix of courses and specialties that a school has to offer, or on the particular nature of the school's microenvironment and how that might mesh with their own interests and needs. Instead, they zero in on that bottom-line summary number from the rankings."[14] An annual Graduate Management Admissions Council (GMAC) Survey lends strong support to these views; the survey of five thousand graduates of MBA programs in 2001 found that 95 percent cited rankings as the most influential media source informing their perceptions of business schools.[15]

Under the external pressure exerted by the rankings, business schools began to change their administrative attention, resource allocations, and cultures to better respond to recruiter and student needs. In 2001, an associate dean at the University of North Carolina's Kenan-Flagler Business School noted that the rankings had led business schools to pay more attention to feedback from the business community, especially from those firms that hired many of their students.[16] In other schools, low rankings led to efforts to improve student satisfaction. For example, when MIT's Sloan School of Management dropped in *BusinessWeek*'s ranking from ninth place in 1996 to fifteenth in 1998, the school made a significant investment in its career office in an effort to improve students' recruiting experience. As Rod Garcia, Sloan's director of MBA admissions, described the decision, "[W]hen we slipped in the rankings, we decided to look at the services we offered to see how we could make our current students happier. It was an issue of internal student satisfaction."[17] In 2005, one dean summarized how *BusinessWeek*'s judgments had affected the culture of business schools over the preceding two decades:

> Few people can remember what it was like before 1987—what I call the year before the storm. It was a time when business school deans could actually focus on improving the quality of their schools' educational offerings. Discussions about strategic marketing were confined mostly to the marketing curriculum. PR firms were hired by businesses, not business schools. Many business schools had sufficient facilities, but few buildings had marble floors, soaring atriums, or plush carpeting. Public university tuition was affordable for most students, and even top MBA programs were accessible to students with high potential but low GMAT scores.[18]

This characterization of the arrival of the *BusinessWeek* rankings as a "storm" highlights a subtle but important point: the media-driven ranking system exercised a sudden and dominant power over business schools for much the same reason that outside actors could take the lead in the post–World War II reform of business education. Business schools had yet to develop and sustain an internal driving purpose that was strong enough to prevent periods of institutional weakness and drift when the winds of change in the external environment became particularly strong. The media-constructed rankings were able to move the institution in a new direction at least in part because business schools themselves had failed to establish evaluative criteria and processes of their own that constituents would accept as legitimate. Like the active intervention of the Ford Foundation in the 1950s, the emergence of an external authority in the form of media rankings highlighted the inability or unwillingness of business schools to engage in self-regulation—a critical element in any process of professionalization.[19]

The media rankings, in fact, gained credibility with business education stakeholders because of the dissatisfaction many harbored with the institution. Corporate employers, for example, were becoming frustrated with the attitudes and skills of MBAs recruited from elite schools, as documented in the AACSB-commissioned study by Lyman W. Porter and Lawrence E. McKibbin published in the late 1980s. As this study reported, employers were criticizing elite business schools for graduating students who lacked "knowledge of how the business world operates in practice as well as in theory" and exhibited "relatively low levels of so-called soft, or people, skills—e.g. leader-ship and interpersonal relations."[20] The report also revealed that most corpo-rate managers did not find business school research useful,[21] and described an attitude of "self-satisfaction" and "complacency" among business school administrators and faculty. Meanwhile, MBA students, too, were becoming dissatisfied with MBA education, expressing what John Byrne described as "severe concerns about the quality of the teaching and the lack of attention to detail in these institutions that affected both the learning and the environ-ment for the student . . . [and about] professors who would speak with deri-sion about their obligation to communicate knowledge."[22]

Despite the harshness of such critiques, however, most elite business schools paid little attention to them prior to the institutionalization of the ranking system. Indeed, similar concerns about business education had been expressed in assessments leading up to the Porter-McKibbin report, but were routinely discounted even after the report appeared, as a former dean of Carnegie Mellon's GSIA, Robert Sullivan, has noted. "Many people began to rationalize [the findings of the Porter-McKibbin report]," Sullivan writes. "They said industry was in no position to judge, the critics were not scholars and were not qualified. All of this was very self-serving, very defensive, cir-cling the wagons."[23] Stanford's James G. March has pointed out that business schools had been able to ignore their critics while they still held sway over the evaluation system: "As long as the business school community could control the way schools were ranked, there was a stable social order. Everybody knew where everyone stood. While it was possible to argue about the details, dra-matic changes were unlikely."[24] Yet once the media rankings began to appear (in the same year that the AACSB published the Porter-McKibbin report), the stable order March described was upended and business schools found—or imagined—themselves at the mercy of their external evaluators.

Even as they pursued higher rankings for their schools, some business school administrators and faculty now began suggesting that the rankings were leading to the same kinds of dysfunctional behaviors that quarterly-earnings deadlines had imposed on corporations, making them increasingly willing to sacrifice long-term organizational health for short-term gains. Jerold Zimmerman, an accounting professor at the William E. Simon Gradu-ate School of Business Administration at the University of Rochester, ob-served in 2001 that American business schools were "locked in a dysfunctional competition for rankings—notably in the *BusinessWeek* surveys. This ratings race has caused schools to divert resources from investment in knowledge creation, including doctoral education and research, to short-term strategies aimed at improving rankings." American business schools, Zimmerman warned, "are mortgaging their future."[25] In 1998, one of the journalists responsible for *BusinessWeek*'s ranking found administrators and student groups at several schools trying to manipulate student responses to the magazine's biannual survey.[26] Business schools now also attempt to influence perceptions of themselves on the part of deans at other institutions. For example, just before *U.S. News & World Report* mails its annual business school survey (one that incorporates deans' rankings of other schools), many deans mail "glossy brochures, fancy announcement cards, and sometimes even gifts" to their colleagues at other business schools. "Schools are spending a great deal of money not to improve their infrastructures and curricula, but to curry favor with other deans," one business school dean laments.[27] The relationship between magazine rankings and the tenure of business school deans further confirms the power of rankings to affect administrators' behavior; one recent study has found that a school's decline in the *BusinessWeek* rankings increases the likelihood of the dean's departure.[28]

Donald Jacobs, legendary for his twenty-six-year tenure (1975–2001) as dean of the Kellogg School of Management at Northwestern University, and for having led his school from relative obscurity to the top of the *BusinessWeek* rankings three times between 1988 and 1992, argues that the media rankings have brought needed improvements to American business schools. As Jacobs states: "The rankings that have become highly visible in recent years have had a very beneficial effect on MBA education. They force us to be concerned about the classroom experience of our students. Today, every school is saying it wants to produce something called quality, whatever that means and however they interpret it. Before, many of these schools just didn't care. Because of the public rankings, they must now."[29]

It is undoubtedly true that, as I have argued, business schools had been paying insufficient attention to their stated mission of preparing students for the practice of management, and in light of that fact the rankings have played a salutary role by focusing them on their external environment. If the emergence of media-based rankings had been the only consequence of the directionlessness of American business education by the end of the 1980s, this development would have been important but not transformative. As it happened, however, the emergence of the media-generated business school rankings coincided with a broader change in how business schools conceptualized and communicated their purpose.

▙ The Commercialization of the MBA

When *BusinessWeek*'s John Byrne described wanting to "create a market" for business schools and identified students and corporations as their primary "customers," he was doing more than simply using a business writer's terminology. He was both reflecting and helping to shape a changing conception of business education, one that has become part of the institutional character of business schools and indeed, as many have recently argued, of the American university itself. When B. Joseph White, formerly dean of the University of Michigan's Ross School of Business and now president of the University of Illinois, remarked in 1998 that "MBA education is a proliferated industry today, with many market segments and niches,"[30] one could not assume that he was speaking metaphorically. Twenty-five years after finance professors Michael Jensen, William Meckling, and Eugene Fama began to argue that a business firm was not an organization in any traditional sense but a mere legal fiction or "nexus of contracts" carrying out the ineluctable laws of the market, business schools had begun defining themselves, as well, as market institutions. Instead of the professional logic that had defined them at their inception or the managerial logic that had animated them during their maturation period after the Second World War, business schools had now embraced—for all practical purposes even if not in their proclamations of mission—a market logic that, as William Sullivan and his coauthors have remarked, rests on a unique normative structure in which "the only moral obligation of any enterprise is to maximize its economic well-being."[31]

Over the past decade, the apparent dominance of market logic in how business educators think about their enterprise has become evident in their discourse. Business schools make a "value proposition" to students, who are now commonly described as "customers." A 2002 AACSB report titled "Management Education at Risk," heavily laced with business jargon, described the increased "segmentation of consumer markets" for business education and explored its implications for "strategies to deliver educational and research services" on the part of business schools.[32] Nowhere in this report, authored by a committee consisting mostly of business educators, was there any discussion of education as a mission, management as a profession, or the risk to the integrity of university business schools from an uncritical adoption of a commercial self-conception. An article in the AACSB publication *Biz Ed* recently advocated applying CRM (customer relationship management) principles to both relationships with students and the administrative structures of business schools themselves. "While some administrators find it difficult to accept the idea of students as consumers," the author stated, "in reality, that's what they are. In today's competitive marketplace, schools are sellers offering courses, a degree, and a rich alumni life. Students are buyers who register for courses, apply for graduation and make donations as alumni. The longer these ongoing transactions are satisfactory to both parties, the longer the relationship will endure, to the benefit of everyone."

The article then described how business schools could adopt the CRM processes used by for-profit enterprises to retain customers, employing these techniques not just to change the ways they deal with students but also to "restructure the management team at a university."[33] Another article in the same publication, titled "The Zen of B-School Branding," urged business schools to see themselves as market brands. ("At a cost of $60,000 to $100,000, an MBA is a very carefully considered purchase," states a public relations executive quoted in the article. "It's not a $60 pair of shoes or a $1,000 computer. . . . The selection of a business school becomes a part of a student's personal branding process.") One GMAC publication called on administrators to see business schools as analogous to Hollywood feature films,[34] while similar publications offered extensive advice on how to boost a school's visibility to the media through the adoption of modern marketing techniques, including attention to "the importance of packaging." As the director of communications for one business school stated bluntly: "We are a business, and we realized that we needed to structure our spending on marketing like a business. . . . The market is becoming more consumer-oriented. Therefore, we need to make a stronger appeal to consumers through retail or product advertising, rather than try to reach them through brand advertising alone."[35]

In the logic exhibited here, the MBA degree itself is a "product" that business schools simply sell to consumers. By this same logic, it is not a way of certifying to outside parties that students have mastered any particular body of knowledge, any more than the purchase of a textbook in a college bookstore certifies that the buyer has mastered the knowledge within. It does not attest that an individual has been socialized to assume a particular identity and set of attendant obligations, any more than buying a ticket to a charity event attests to a virtuous character.[36] In other words, whatever else the MBA may be once it has been subjected to such commercialization, it is a professional degree only in the loosest, most popular sense of the term. That business schools no longer have a basis to claim that they offer professional education in any traditional sense has not, however, reduced the monetary value of the MBA (arguably, rather, the degree's value has increased). Though it fulfills no formal requirement for entry into any occupation and, as I argued in chapters 6 and 7, imparts knowledge with increasingly questionable relevance to the practice of management, the average full-time, accredited two-year MBA degree comes at a cost of approximately $60,000. Moreover, university-based business schools, especially the elite ones, have so far retained this pricing power in the face of increasing competition from providers such as corporations and management consulting firms, and cheaper as well as shorter programs from both nonprofit and for-profit universities. The way that university-based business schools have continued to differentiate their "product" from those of their nonacademic competitors in the field of business education, however, seems quite far removed from the original professional, scientific, and academic purposes that situated the institution in universities in the first place.

The MBA "Value Proposition"

Faced with the challenges of an increasingly competitive marketplace for business education, the authors of the AACSB report "Management Education at Risk" sought to identify the competitive advantage enjoyed by traditional business schools by invoking two of the institutional pillars on which these schools had been founded: science and the university. In the words of the report: "Although other types of business education providers may deliver effective business teaching, none can serve as a business knowledge creator, steeped in the scientific method, as can business schools. This role is critical for business school faculty as a professional differentiator that protects market value. Even more important, the scholarship role of business faculty is an essential and irreplaceable function because societies and markets turn to business schools for knowledge advances that reflect academic traditions of theory and method."[37]

The first point to notice about this statement is that its appeal to the quasi-sacred institutions on which the first business schools founded their claims to legitimacy is couched in market language that describes "business teaching" as something that schools "deliver" and knowledge-creation as an activity that "protects market value." As for its argumentation, the claim that no other type of business education provider can equal the university-based business school "as a business knowledge creator" might be disputed through a comparison of business schools with some of the more prestigious management consulting firms, which tend to have permeable boundaries with university business schools and can plausibly claim, moreover, to be closer to the day-to-day realities of business practice than are business schools. The AACSB authors hinge their argument on a characterization of university business schools as "steeped in the scientific method," a description on which they subsequently elaborate when—in their lone nod to service to society as a function of business schools—they assert that "societies and markets turn to business schools for knowledge advances that reflect academic traditions of theory and method." Yet in so doing, the authors fail to address persistent questions about the relevance of business school research to the practice of management. Their claimed point of differentiation between business schools and their rivals thus hangs on a premise that seems, at the very least, open to dispute.

Meanwhile, a closer examination of the way business schools currently market themselves, and how faculty and students talk about the contemporary business school experience, suggests that a more accurate picture of the advantages accruing to such institutions in the marketplace is presented by a business school dean (author of the article on customer relationship management for business schools cited above) who describes business schools as "sellers offering courses, a degree, and a rich alumni life."

A top business school recently took out a full-page ad in an airline magazine that posed the question "Want a hard-working investment?" The ad then described the value of the school's MBA in financial terms: "We don't just teach you how to make and manage solid investments, we'll be one. We're proud to say our program was recently named one of the top 10 'MBAs for your buck' by *Forbes* magazine. This distinction was earned through a combination of criteria, including tuition and pre- and post-MBA salaries. It's nice to know that when you make an investment in a————MBA, you are getting an investment that works as hard as you do."[38] In another advertisement, a Columbia School of Business associate dean described the "high ROI [return on investment] associated" with the school's executive MBA program.[39] By marketing themselves in this way, business schools mimic and indirectly validate the media's use of starting salaries and "before and after" salary differentials as a way of assessing the quality of schools.

As we saw in chapter 4, in the days when an aspiration of professionalizing management provided the template for American business education, business school leaders attempted to balance their efforts to gain status for management as an occupation and prepare students for employment against an offsetting acknowledgment of the larger intellectual and social obligations attendant on professional privileges. Yet with little or nothing to be gained in the marketplace from reputations for intellectual rigor or educating students in the social responsibilities of management, business school administrators are now challenged primarily to demonstrate that their schools provide access to high-paying jobs; in the case of the elite schools, the challenge is to demonstrate an ability to place students in fields such as investment banking, hedge funds, and private equity, where the economic rewards available to new MBAs dwarf those offered by traditional management positions. As Jeffrey Pfeffer and Christina T. Fong have stated the case, "[I]n return for the ability to obtain huge and growing enrollments, schools have presented themselves and their value proposition primarily, although certainly not exclusively, as a path to career security and financial riches."[40]

At the elite American business schools, where intense competition for admission prescreens students for certain select characteristics such as stellar GMAT scores and precociously accomplished careers in industries such as consulting and financial services, the task of furnishing these students with access to their desired employment opportunities has become increasingly disconnected from what takes place in the classroom during two years of full-time course work leading to an MBA. The organizational scholar James March, now a professor emeritus at the Stanford Graduate School of Business, was asked in 1998 why someone should go to a prestigious, high-cost business school like Stanford. March replied with a list of "things a student should want from a business school," and suggested that what differentiated the elite schools from the rest had nothing to do with the core content of the MBA curriculum:

> One [reason for attending an elite school] is to learn something about business disciplines like organization, accounting, finance, production, and marketing. The second is to deepen an intellectual understanding of the relation between activities in business and the major issues of human existence. The third is to be able to signal that you're the kind of person who goes to a certain kind of business school. . . .
>
> If your primary interest is in learning about business disciplines, you don't need to spend money on a first-class business school, because its comparative advantage lies in the other [areas]. I think that's a fairly open secret. There are any number of places that do a

pretty good job of teaching organization, accounting, finance, production and marketing. They don't, however, do nearly as good a job of establishing that you're one of the very smart folks.[41]

In his description of how the elite business schools enable their students to claim membership in a select group merely by virtue of admission, March points to a phenomenon that the Nobel Prize–winning economist Michael Spence has called "market signaling."[42] The concept of market signaling explains how difficult-to-observe information about individuals, such as their productivity or commitment to a particular career, can be conveyed and obtained via proxy measures. Employers, for example, face uncertainty when hiring an employee without any preliminary, direct observation of his or her productivity or commitment. To overcome this uncertainty, they use proxy measures such as educational attainment. If a student has decided to invest in an MBA degree, for example, this investment signals to employers something about the student's commitment to a business career. If the student has gained admission to an elite school, this signals something about his or her innate ability. While the idea of market signaling allows for the possibility that useful or relevant skills will be gained through education, Spence argues that this is not necessary in order for an investment in education to function as a market signal. Instead, a student invests in higher education simply to purchase a signal that is received by prospective employers as an indication of the likelihood that he or she is committed to a business career and will perform productively.[43]

Employers, in turn, read and use these market signals to streamline their recruiting processes and reduce hiring mistakes. As a result, as Robert Frank has explained, student perceptions of a correlation between graduating from a top business school and gaining access to the best-paying jobs, especially in the elite, high-paying reaches of financial services and management consulting, are essentially accurate. "The high-profile jobs, the big-winner jobs in society pay ever-larger salaries," Frank notes,

> and more and more people want those jobs. If you're a gatekeeper
> for an entry-level position in one of those fields [e.g., investment
> banking or elite consulting], you get mail sack after mail sack of ap-
> plications. You can't even begin to think of interviewing all the appli-
> cants who might be qualified for the position. You've got to screen
> them some way, and credentials have become increasingly important
> for that first cut. If you're not from a top school, an employer knows

you might be qualified but just doesn't have time to talk to you. So the pressure to get into a top school is enormous now.[44]

While administrators at the elite business schools undoubtedly chafe at the notion that diplomas are merely market signals for employers, the same administrators have nevertheless continued to promote their schools as a means of access to benefits one would expect educators to consider ancillary to education. In his list of reasons for attending an elite business school, James March says that the fourth and final reason is "to lay the basis for a set of personal connections." Not only do average-quality business schools, he noted, fail to brand an individual as "one of the very smart folks"; they also do not succeed as well as do the "first-class" schools in "putting you in contact with other smart folks to build a national or international network of personal contacts."[45] An elite MBA is now, indeed, seen as critical to gaining access to two overlapping networks: the peer group of one's own business school class, and a school's entire body of alumni.

Becoming an alumnus or alumna of a high-status business school ties an individual to a vast network of high-status individuals occupying positions at or near the top of organizations all over the world; the magazine advertisement for Columbia School of Business quoted above notes, for example, that a degree from Columbia offers access to "a global network of more than 35,000 alumni around the world [sic]."[46] In hyperlucrative occupations such as investment banking or private equity, an MBA from one of the elite institutions, like Harvard Business School or the University of Chicago's business school, is virtually a prerequisite for gaining access to the networks that lead to a position with a top firm; the same holds true for gaining entry into the best consulting and financial services firms. While it is difficult to get accurate data about the backgrounds of executives in unregulated fields such as hedge funds, having an elite MBA and access to its associated network appears, at least from anecdotal evidence, to be critical for breaking into these industries. Among the 180 principals and managing directors in the 20 largest private equity/venture capital firms in 2005, 73 individuals possessed an MBA from one of six elite schools: Harvard (51), Chicago (7), Columbia (6), Stanford (5), Dartmouth's Tuck (3), or Northwestern (1).[47] Ed Diffendal, a 2000 Tuck MBA, describes in an online alumni interview the critical role of the Tuck network in obtaining a coveted job in private equity:

> [M]y strategy was to identify connections (either a Tuck connection or a personal connection) to specific funds and evaluate whether

I would be interested in joining these funds. If I was interested, I tried to leverage my connection into an informational interview. There were two or three funds where that connection was pretty strong; Broadview Capital was one of them (a couple of Tuck guys were at Broadview at that time). . . .

The Tuck network effect was very strong. My peers graduating around that same time from larger MBA programs had alumni networks that were broader in terms of who they might be able to contact at a given fund, but narrower in terms of who might be willing to take a meeting. There were a lot of guys looking for the same type of job I was who could pick a fund and say, "I know there is someone from my school there," but it was really a shot in the dark whether the person was going to take that meeting. In those cases, there often had to be an additional connection for them to get a meeting, whereas the Tuck connection was enough to get me in the door.[48]

Students recognize and acknowledge—after the fact if not in their admissions applications—that attending business school is a means of developing and accessing social networks. In 2005, Harvard Business School's annual survey of graduating MBA students found for the first time that students regarded developing a social network as the number-one benefit of attending business school.[49] Schools, for their part, emphasize this benefit in their value proposition to students. The Web site for the University of Chicago's business school stresses the program's powerful alumni network: "When you join Chicago GSB, you gain access to an influential alumni network of nearly 40,000 graduates in 90 countries worldwide—5,400 of whom are business owners, CEOs or top company officers. Forever connected to Chicago GSB, they give our students access to top companies, and create a vast networking base for students and alumni around the world."[50]

Business education, in other words, can be understood as providing social capital, a resource that students see as something to be acquired and invested with the prospect of return to themselves, much like financial capital. Needless to say, this idea is fundamentally different from the notion of cultivating a sense of collective identity and responsibility with fellow practitioners of a profession. An elite MBA program comes instead to resemble an exclusive fraternity or country club that confers social advantage in the labor market.

The role of business schools as a repository of social rather than academic assets, functioning as a gatekeeper for networks of access to society's most lucrative employment opportunities, points to a tacit social compact among business schools, employers, and students. As sources inside many of the nation's most prestigious business schools now report, such a pact can also increasingly be discerned in the classroom, where it operates between faculty members lacking credibility with their students to speak authoritatively about their subjects, and students who want to obtain their degrees without the rigor associated with other graduate programs.[51] Part of the pact is a grading system that does not make fine distinctions in student performance, reducing both the pressure on students to work for grades and the necessity for professors to defend assessments that students might find unsatisfactory. As Jeffrey Pfeffer and Christina Fong have found, the probability of a student's failing out of an elite business school is very low.[52] Some of these schools have developed elaborate grading systems to ensure that even the most apathetic students are able to graduate. In 2005, significant tension between students and administrators erupted at both Harvard Business School and Wharton when administrators proposed allowing students—whose grades, as a matter of policy, had hitherto been withheld from recruiters—the option of disclosing them. Administrators hoped that such a policy would improve student performance, which had begun a slow but noticeable decline over recent years. The vice dean of Wharton articulated the reason for the proposed change:

> In recent years, a number of our faculty have reported a gradual but discernible shift away from academics in the students' priorities. Some have kept careful records to document the trend. We have heard, from some of our most sought-after faculty, that not only is the MBAs' performance lower in our cross listed courses than undergrads', but that the trend over time shows a widening gap between the performance of the two subpopulations. (One faculty member speculated that the widening gap could be caused by the undergrads getting smarter at a faster rate than the MBAs, but thought that the more plausible explanation lies in changing effort levels!). Another faculty member, the winner of countless teaching awards, reports that on exams that are psychometrically calibrated to have similar levels of difficulty, he has found a clear decline in performance in recent years. A few other frequent winners of teaching awards have stopped teaching MBA classes.[53]

The response of students at both Harvard and Wharton was overwhelmingly against the proposed policy change. Some suggested that it would inhibit cooperation among students (thus undercutting the education in teamwork that business schools are supposed to provide). Others suggested that it was faculty members who had been implicitly conveying the message that class preparation did not count. One second-year MBA student at Harvard, responding to the administration's stated view that grade disclosure would motivate students to better prepare for class, declared: "[W]hen talking to [students in their second year], where the lack of focus on academics is most prevalent, they appear to believe that faculty do not mind them not studying and that there is an underlying understanding that it is 'alright' not to study. It would appear to me that the most obvious and immediate course of action is to promptly inform the students that is NOT alright to let the academics be the lowest priority."[54]

The diminished role of education as a source of value in the MBA degree, not surprisingly, has in turn tended to diminish the perceived importance of its educational requirements—not only to students but, as the students themselves perceive it in this case, possibly to faculty as well. Indeed, if the analyses of veteran business school academicians such as Pfeffer and March are correct, fundamental questions exist as to whether business schools retain any genuine academic or societal mission and whether they are discharging any institutional responsibilities beyond helping their students find employment. If academic credentialing and providing a social network are now the primary functions of business schools, then the role of the institution is that of a gatekeeper rather than a transmitter of knowledge and values. Understandably unwilling to accept such a marginal role—one that hardly justifies the status that business school faculty, after decades of struggle, have attained within the university, and largely fails to furnish meaning and purpose for the activity of teaching—business schools have had to find new ways of conceiving and describing their institutional purpose. With the option of managerialism as a guiding rationale for business education effectively trumped by the rise of agency theory and associated economic concepts, the idea that business schools have seized upon since the early 1990s for a renewed definition of purpose goes by the name of *leadership*.

The "Leadership" Nostrum

Having participated, inadvertently or not, in the wholesale discrediting of American management that flowered during the rise of investor capitalism in the 1970s, by the late 1980s business schools had effectively been taken to the

woodshed through the advent of the media rankings—a public pronouncement that insufficient attention by schools to the needs of their student and
corporate "customers" could not be corrected from within. By the beginning
of the 1990s, business schools—particularly those elite schools that had
staked their reputations on academic superiority—faced a full-blown crisis
of identity and purpose. It was no longer possible for business schools to tout
a mission of educating managers according to the canons of postwar managerialism, for traditional managers had been successfully portrayed by the
takeover artists and shareholder activists of the 1970s and 1980s, as well as by
business school professors influenced by the work of scholars such as Oliver
Williamson and Michael Jensen, as incompetent at best, and venal and un-
trustworthy at worst. Moreover, increasing numbers of students at the most
prestigious schools now shunned traditional management careers altogether
in favor of fields like consulting and investment banking. Faculty at the elite
business schools were thus educating fewer future managers, which left
them increasingly ambivalent and uncertain about what they *were* educating
students for.

As in the 1920s, a proliferation of business schools and growth in business
school enrollments in the 1990s provided a veneer of success that concealed a
mounting existential crisis. Many faculty and business school administrators
recognized that in the new era of corporate downsizing and shareholder sov-
ereignty, business education needed to reorient itself. Lyman Porter noted that
in the context of these changes, the model put in place by the Ford Foundation reforms "needs to be reconsidered and modified," and that "management
education needs to do a lot of serious self-examination to determine what
should be retained and what should be changed."[55] Others noted that it was
not clear in what direction business education should go. Whereas during the
1950s the Ford Foundation offered a clear and largely unchallenged vision for
business education (i.e., that it required more analytical tools and an emphasis on disciplinary research), in the 1990s there was, as one dean put it, "disagreement among many faculty about the role of business schools." William
Ouchi, who had been involved in several study committees examining business education, noted the dearth of foresight and direction among business
educators when he observed, "[T]here isn't yet any kind of new vision, a new
point of view, a new model that one can lean on for support in seeking a new
direction."[56] It was thus in a pervasive atmosphere of drift and uncertainty
that business schools turned to the notion of *leadership* as a way to redefine
their identity and mission.

Academic concern with the subject of leadership began in 1945 with a research program at Ohio State University, under the aegis of the federal government's War Manpower Commission and the Department of Labor, known as the Ohio State Leadership Studies.[57] The program grew out of an interest in using the social sciences to help improve the quality of military leadership should the nation again have to mobilize for war. The perceived success of business schools' involvement in training both military officers and civilian managers in war-related industries during World War II made this kind of investment a natural extension of such programs. It was an early instance of the postwar trends (discussed in chapter 5) of significant new spending by the federal government in support of university research and advocacy of social science as a tool for strengthening the American economy. Ohio State's program produced the first systematic studies attempting to quantify the factors behind effective leadership, using a statistical technique called factor analysis that allowed for examination of the relations among different variables. Much of the initial research examined military units.

The Ohio State researchers, who were mostly psychologists, sought to identify and catalog the traits affecting individual leadership ability. Much of this research focused on individual leaders, with most early work paying little attention to either the situational or group context for leadership. Eventually, by using increasingly sophisticated statistical techniques, the researchers identified two dimensions or "factors" said to account for variations across leadership style and group performance. One factor, called "initiation of structure," emphasized the leader's and subordinates' formal roles and the organization of tasks. A leader who scored high in this area would be focused on the goals of the group and on planning how to achieve them. The second factor, "consideration," emphasized the socioemotional aspects of leadership. A leader who scored high on this measure would be focused on reducing interpersonal tensions, and fostering cooperation and trust, within the group.[58]

The distinction made by the Ohio State researchers between "initiation of structure" and "consideration" would be echoed and recast, in the mid-1970s, by a seminal article in business-related leadership studies, a piece in the May–June 1977 issue of *Harvard Business Review* by Harvard Business School professor Abraham Zaleznik, titled "Managers and Leaders: Are They Different?" "[M]anagers and leaders are very different kinds of people," Zaleznik wrote, giving rise to a conceptual distinction that has proven both popular and enduring. "They differ in motivation, in personal history, and in how they think and act." Characterizing a "managerial culture" as one that "emphasizes rationality and control," Zaleznik described the manager as essentially a "problem solver."[59] "To get people to accept solutions to problems," he stated, "managers continually need to coordinate and balance opposing views. . . . Managers aim to shift balances of power toward solutions acceptable as compromises among conflicting values." However, according to Zaleznik, "Leaders work in the opposite direction. Where managers act to limit choices, leaders develop fresh approaches to long-standing problems and open issues to new options."[60] In an updated version of the article that ran in 1992, Zaleznik qualified further how these "fresh approaches" are introduced by leaders: "To be effective, leaders must project their ideas onto images that excite people and only then develop choices that give those images substance."[61]

In essence, Zaleznik's distinction between managers and leaders is a variant of Max Weber's description of three types of leadership—traditional, rational, and charismatic—with Zaleznik's concept of the "manager" corresponding to Weber's rational leader, and his notion of the "leader" standing for Weber's *charismatic* leader.[62] Although Zaleznik recognized that organizations cannot simply dispense with managers, his association of managers with "bureaucratic culture," "tactical" approaches to problems, and the preservation of "an existing order of affairs" makes it clear that a reliance on management at the expense of leadership represents a potentially fatal flaw in an organization. Zaleznik's resuscitation of the Weberian notion of charismatic leadership—an idea that was taken up not only by other business school academics but also by management consultants, motivational speakers, and corporate trainers—found a receptive audience in the economic environment of the late 1970s, when managerialism had come to be blamed for the poor performance of American corporations, while the rise of investor capitalism was paving the way for the appearance of a new type of corporate leader, the charismatic CEO à la Chrysler's Lee Iacocca and his progeny.[63] Corporate America, many of its critics now contended, had become "overmanaged" and "underled." Eventually business schools began responding to the clarion call for developing leaders, not managers.

In the early 1990s, for example, Harvard Business School formally shifted its focus from its traditional concern with general management, issuing a new mission statement that described its purpose as "to educate leaders who make a difference in the world."[64] Dartmouth's Tuck School of Business came to define its primary educational goal as preparing "students for leadership positions in the world's foremost organizations."[65] Stanford's business school now aims to "develop innovative, principled, and insightful leaders who change the world,"[66] and MIT's Sloan School of Management "to develop principled, innovative leaders who improve the world."[67] Nonelite schools like Michigan State's Eli Broad Graduate School of Management, which defines itself as being "in the business of developing leaders for the global, multicultural marketplace,"[68] and Thunderbird's MBA program, which focuses "on educating global leaders who create sustainable prosperity worldwide,"[69] delineate their missions in terms that echo those of the elite institutions.

A crucial question raised by business schools' substitution of the leadership paradigm for the managerial one is whether the former constitutes an adequate foundation for a university-based professional school. One of the central features of a bona fide profession, as I have repeatedly emphasized, is possession of a coherent body of expert knowledge erected on a well-developed theoretical foundation. The function of a university professional school includes transmitting such knowledge to aspiring practitioners and creating new and better knowledge for the improvement of professional practice. The history of the decades-long attempt, within business schools, to erect a science of management on the foundation of disciplines such as economics, sociology, and psychology testifies to the difficulty of creating such a knowledge base in the absence of broad agreement as to foundations. Although it is still too early to render definitive judgment, the history of leadership scholarship and pedagogy within business schools to date suggests that, at the very least, business schools will find the task of creating a professional knowledge base around leadership no easier than previous efforts to establish firm intellectual foundations for the study and teaching of management.

Despite tens of thousands of studies and writings on leadership since the days of the Ohio State Leadership Studies, several scholarly reviews of the literature on leadership have found little progress in the field since Chester Barnard observed in the 1930s that leadership in general, and particularly the "Great Man" view of the topic popular in his day, was "the subject of an extraordinary amount of dogmatically stated nonsense."[70] For example, Ralph Stodgill in 1974, and Bernard Bass in an independent study conducted in 1981, examined more than 4,700 separate studies of leadership and found little in the way of a conceptual framework or frameworks for this field. Stodgill stated that an "endless accumulation of empirical data has not produced an integrated understanding of leadership."[71] Bernard Bass found a surprising lack of clarity for a subject that was supposedly being examined in a scholarly manner, noting that most studies failed to even define the terms *leader* and *leadership*. In 1988, after reviewing more than 450 leadership stud-ies, D. Brent Smith and Randall Peterson lamented having found little in the way of usable knowledge about leadership: "Cumulatively, the chapters delin-eate the impasse which many researchers of leadership have diagnosed in recent years, and which has led quite a few practitioners to conclude that re-search into leadership has little to offer."[72] In his book about the state of aca-demic scholarship on leaders and leadership, Joseph Rost noted in 1991 that "most of what is written about leadership has to do with its peripheral ele-ments and content rather than with the essential nature of leadership."[73] Leadership as a subject of study, Rost noted, was "anything anyone wants to say it is," and a leader was "anyone who is so designated."[74] As a result, in Rost's view, the subject of leadership "does not add up because leadership scholars and practitioners have no definition of leadership to hold on to. The scholars do not know what it is they are studying and the practitioners do not know what it is they are doing."[75]

From a scholarly perspective, then, leadership as a body of knowledge, after decades of scholarly attention under the social science research lens that the Ford Foundation viewed as so eminently promising, remains without ei-ther a widely accepted theoretical framework or a cumulative empirical un-derstanding leading to a usable body of knowledge. Moreover, the probability that leadership studies will make significant strides in developing a funda-mental knowledge base is fairly low. The reality is that inside universities and research-based business schools, leadership research has relatively low status. In elite business schools, for example, there are no "leadership" departments.[76] Those studying leadership are dispersed across departments including strat-egy, organizational behavior, entrepreneurship, finance, and accounting, and tend to lack status within their departments. Indeed, the dominant paradigm in organizational behavior, the field most closely associated with leadership study in business schools, regards leadership as an epiphenomenon, empha-sizing the role of the external environment and organizational bureaucracy in constraining the ability of individuals to affect organizational outcomes.[77] Young business school faculty and doctoral students are discouraged from studying the subject and directed, instead, toward examining less elusive phe-nomena that lend themselves better to quantitative analysis. Even established scholars who study the subject later in their careers risk academic marginal-ization and cynical accusations of having "sold out." Within the Academy of Management, the largest professional association for business school scholars, leadership is not even recognized as a distinct interest group or subfield of management research. As Joseph Rost observes: "The reality is that there are very few leadership studies scholars. Rather, there are anthropologists, educators, historians, management scientists, organizational behaviorists, political scientists, social psychologists, and sociologists who have developed an expertise in leadership."[78]

Not surprisingly, the lack of coherence in leadership research is reflected in the pedagogy of leadership as well. Courses in leadership at most business schools cover a wide range of topics including negotiations, team management, conflict resolution, incentives, organizational behavior, communication, employee motivation, power and influence, and change management, although this disparate subject matter is not, by itself, an indication of weakness in the underlying pedagogical structure of the subject. More significant is the fact that in business schools leadership is taught, for the most part, via any of three distinctly different approaches, each of which possesses a certain validity but no one of which lends substance to the claim that leadership instruction constitutes, in whole or in part, an element of a genuinely professional education.

The first approach to teaching leadership that one finds in American business schools focuses on content and the transmission of explicit knowledge. Leadership teaching in this vein emphasizes academic theories, drawn largely from psychology, sociology, and economics, with a strong focus on specialized content.[79] Yale's School of Management, for example, exposes students in its Strategic Environment of Management course to a broad set of contextual issues through a general survey of "governmental, civil, and economic institutions that shape the major opportunities and risks available to senior management."[80] These institutions are defined to include "national governments, central banks, regulatory agencies, the joint stock corporation, equity markets, labor unions, non-profits, and international regimes," while "[r]eadings and discussions on capitalism and mass affluence, demographics, failed states and the construct of ownership, and the rise of the managerial class afford an informed perspective on modern economies, corporations, and the management profession itself." The University of North Carolina's Kenan-Flagler Business School draws heavily on the disciplines to teach leadership by "covering a variety of core concepts and theories from sociology, psychology and organizational science which form the knowledge base for leadership and management skills. The course teaches students to apply scientific, research-based knowledge to management challenges in order to diagnose organizational and professional problems and decide on the best course of action." Kenan-Flagler's approach to teaching leadership recalls the disciplinary approach to creating a science of decision making pioneered at Carnegie Tech's GSIA in the 1950s and 1960s, while Yale's attention to the social and political environment of business looks back to the early attempt by Edmund James and his colleagues at the Wharton School in the late nineteenth and early twentieth centuries to center the Wharton curriculum on social and political science and an institutional approach to the economic role of the corporation.

A second approach to teaching leadership in business schools focuses on the development of interpersonal skills and their application to small-group situations. Leadership here is conceptualized not as a matter of explicit knowledge or content but rather as tacit knowledge that must be mastered through hands-on practice. For example, Wharton's MBA program focuses on exposing students to a wide variety of situations in which they must lead small groups. Kellogg's MBA program also emphasizes leadership as an experiential exercise: "In the student-initiated Learning through Experience and Action Program, Kellogg students are matched with outside organizations that have specific management questions or problems. The students form groups and spend about 90 hours per quarter, including eight hours a week on-site, on the project. Students have worked on activity-based cost accounting for a hospital, business process reengineering for a packaging company and a marketing segmentation study for a telecommunications company."[81]

The University of Chicago's Graduate School of Business places a similar emphasis on teaching "leadership" through practice in applying techniques. The school's Web site describes Chicago's leadership program:

Chicago GSB's unique Leadership Effectiveness and Development (LEAD) Program is about maximizing success in business. LEAD is a laboratory class where students practice and perfect key communication skills such as negotiation, team-building, and giving feedback. We consider these skills so critical to success in business that we require all full-time campus and International MBA students to complete the class.

LEAD builds these skills through role playing, team building, and a host of other creative activities and experiences. Students are grouped in cohorts of about 50 students and participate in all activities together. Cohorts offer the camaraderie of shared experiences and a lasting network of friends and contacts. LEAD begins during

CORE, our orientation program, and continues over a student's
entire first year.

LEAD also offers a tremendous learning opportunity for a select
group of second-year students who serve as course facilitators. After
intensive training, they present course material and coach and
mentor first-year participants.[82]

A third approach to leadership pedagogy, which may incorporate aspects
of the first two approaches of decision-making and interpersonal skills, associates leadership with personal growth and self-discovery and focuses on giving students opportunities for personal development. Programs taking this
tack give students a great deal of freedom to explore "personal" values and use
a variety of exercises and self-assessments, such as the Meyers-Brigg (Personality) Type Indicator or the Hay Group's Personal Values Questionnaire, in
an attempt to help students integrate discoveries about themselves into their
career choices and professional lives. Case Western Reserve University's
Weatherhead School of Management, for example, uses such an approach in a
course titled Leadership Assessment and Development. The course "requires
students to develop their leadership through an examination of their values,
purpose and ideals. It encourages them to see themselves as agents for positive
change in the world. In their term reports about their personal leadership values, students must include their approach [to] both social and environmental
responsibility as future leaders." Harvard Business School's required leadership course centers case discussions on leadership frames consistent with
those of Zaleznik and John P. Kotter. Leadership development is conceived of
as a personal journey, and leading change is a central activity of interest:

> The course helps you develop an understanding of what it takes to
> be an effective leader. . . . Leadership is about coping with change by
> developing a vision of the future for the organization, aligning the
> organization behind that vision, and motivating people to achieve
> the vision. . . . To build a successful and satisfying leadership career,
> one must understand how to make appropriate career choices and
> become a self-directed learner. One also has to understand how to
> identify and capitalize on developmental opportunities, thereby
> updating and broadening one's expertise. Learning to lead is a
> process of learning primarily from on-the-job experience, by doing,
> observing, and interacting with others. . . . By analyzing common
> dilemmas managers encounter, you will learn how to anticipate

and avoid problems and take advantage of missed opportunities. Throughout the course we will engage in role-plays, simulations, and self-assessment exercises. These activities allow you to see how you personally interpret and behave in different situations. Supplementing the classroom materials are readings that refine and integrate concepts and lessons that emerge in discussions.

While reflecting distinct sets of assumptions about what constitutes leadership, the three approaches to teaching leadership in business schools outlined here—treating leadership as a formal body of knowledge, a set of skills, and a mode of personal mastery, respectively—correspond to the elements of an integrated approach to leadership seen in a profession that I have not previously discussed but that bears all the hallmarks of the "high" professions of the clergy, medicine, and law—namely, the military. The United States Military Academy at West Point describes its mission as "[t]o educate, train, and inspire the Corps of Cadets so that each graduate is a commissioned leader of character committed to the values of Duty, Honor, Country; professional growth throughout a career as an officer in the United States Army; and a lifetime of selfless service to the Nation."[83] The correspondence between the triad *educate, train, and inspire* and the three approaches to business school leadership education that I have identified is suggested by the elaboration of West Point's mission statement in the army's *Cadet Leader Development System* handbook:

A mission analysis revealed two central elements in this statement. First, there is an objective, the target of our [West Point's] efforts— a "commissioned leader of character." To become a commissioned leader of character requires adopting a unique identity or self-concept, one that is consistent with our Nation's expectations of what it means to be an army officer. Second, there are the verbs— "educate, train, and inspire." Taken together, these three verbs define development—the holistic means by which USMA accomplishes its mission, the process by which cadets internalize the defining fundamentals of officership.

The army defines officership, in turn, as "[t]he practice of being a commissioned Army leader, inspired by a unique professional identity, that is shaped by what an officer must KNOW and DO, but most importantly, by a deeply held understanding and acceptance of what an officer must BE."[84]

Expert knowledge, skill in its application, and an acquired identity in which individual interest is subordinated to group norms revolving around the service of a greater good—these three elements, as I have argued in this book, virtually constitute the institution we call the professions, at least in the sense understood by the originators and proponents of the professionalization project in the twentieth-century American business school. By the beginning of the twenty-first century, as I have also argued, business schools had largely set aside the demanding, relatively constraining notion of professionalism for the looser, more protean idea of leadership. Yet the ways in which the cry of "leadership" in the American business school of today echoes, however faintly and disconnectedly, the institution's nearly century-long effort to define itself in terms of professionalism suggest, perhaps, that business schools have not severed themselves so completely from their historical roots and inherited identity as recent developments might seem to indicate.

As Max Weber observed a century ago in trying to define the essence of capitalism, "the idea of duty in one's calling prowls about in our lives like the ghost of dead religious beliefs."[85] As long as the ghost of professionalism continues to prowl about in the life of the American business school, the future of the institution cannot be fully extricated from its past.

Ideas of Order Revisited: Markets, Hierarchies,

and Communities

This book has traced an arc through the history of university business education showing that an institution created to legitimate management
has become, through the abandonment of the professionalization project that
provided its initial direction and impetus, a vehicle for the *de*legitimation of
management. This 180-degree turn in the fundamental orientation of business
education has come about via the substitution of market logic for the professional and managerial logics that successively dominated business schools
from their beginnings in the late nineteenth century up until the end of managerial capitalism in the 1970s and 1980s. The dramatic transformation in the
nature of American capitalism that unfolded at that time was one in which
business schools were influenced by developments in the external business environment but also, to an extent that has not been sufficiently understood and
appreciated, actively reshaped that environment. They did this by providing
both the ideological justification and the revolutionary cadres for the overthrow of the old managerialist order, with its preference for consensus, compromise, and stability, and its replacement by a neoliberal utopianism that
valued what were taken to be historically ineluctable market processes over the
contingent concerns and decisions of human actors, including managers and
their constituents other than shareholders.

The revolution that overthrew the system of managerial capitalism and
replaced it with the current system of investor capitalism restored necessary
balance to a corporate governance system that had tilted too far in favor of
managers. During the 1960s and 1970s, without large shareholders on corporate boards or the threat of a takeover to restrain them, many corporate
executives had felt free to sacrifice profit in favor of creating large, diversified
corporations that often destroyed economic value. During the 1980s, leveraged buyout firms and corporate raiders improved many such firms by selling off unrelated assets and actively managing their acquisitions. They held

management accountable for meeting financial and strategic objectives and aligned compensation plans with improved cash flow and share price. In so doing, they exemplified the process of "creative destruction" that the economist Joseph Schumpeter called "the essential fact about capitalism."[1]

One less salutary legacy of the investor revolution, however, was a changed conception of the purpose of the corporation and the role of managers. Inside business schools, economists on finance faculties used principal-agent theory to recast the role of management. Instead of being responsible to multiple stakeholders for the long-term well-being of the corporation, managers were now said to be responsible only to shareholders, a group whose composition changed continually and that was focused entirely on short-term gains. Meanwhile, business school professors instructed thousands of students and executives on how to use financial engineering tools, like leverage and stock options, to align corporate actions with the goal of maximizing shareholder value.

For a while, investors and academics alike believed that pay-for-performance schemes such as stock option grants, an active market for corporate control, and the fiscal discipline of leverage would succeed in focusing managers on creating value for shareholders. Unforeseen by the intellectual architects of the revolution in economics and finance was that by delegitimating the old managerialist order and turning executives, in theory and practice, into free agents who owed their primary loyalty to a group who assumed no reciprocal obligations to them, they had cut managers loose from any moorings not just to the organizations they led or the communities in which those organizations were embedded but even, in the end, to shareholders themselves. The resulting corporate oligarchy had no role-defined obligation other than to self-interest. The unintended consequences of this revolution, first evident in the anomalies of executive pay in relation to individual and corporate performance first noticed in the late 1990s, have since the beginning of the current decade come to include the long string of corporate scandals involving misstated earnings, backdated stock options,[2] and various exotic variations on such themes that have as their common thread the enrichment of individual executives at the expense of shareholders, employees, and the public trust in the essential integrity and fairness of the system on which democratic capitalism itself depends.

The effect of these corporate scandals on business schools has been confined mostly to debate and, to some degree, action with respect to the subject of business ethics. In the wake of Enron and Tyco, some business school deans argued that the scandals reflected the presence in the corporate world of a few "bad apples," not any systemic problems that reflected in any way on business schools, which, they maintained, should not be held accountable for the moral failings of their graduates. At other schools, deans recycled their talking points about business ethics from the insider trading scandals of the 1980s, describing what their schools were doing to strengthen the ethics component of their curricula, which in some cases entailed the creation of new centers or programs on business ethics. Debates about ethics in the business school curriculum centered on whether instruction in ethics should be provided in a single, freestanding course or integrated into the entire MBA curriculum. One dean made the case for treating ethics in the context of the existing curriculum by noting that the most intelligent MBA students would not get much out of an ethics course because the subject could not be reduced to equations: "unless the student is really interested in the issue [ethics], it's not effective because it's too easy to blow off. It's not like there's a formula that you absolutely have to learn. If you're not interested in a required course of this kind, you don't have to spend much time on it if you're a smart student, and you don't get anything out of it and the whole thing is lost."[3] Other schools have a more optimistic view about their ability to educate students on ethics and have incorporated ethics courses either throughout the curriculum or through required courses.[4]

Such debates have been waged in business schools almost from their beginnings. What has been missing from the most recent discussions of how to teach ethics in business schools is any attempt to put the subject within any holistic, institutional context. Putting the debate into such a framework would require business schools to examine, first of all, whether and how the fundamental rationale, structure, and content of business education might need to be revised or even overhauled to bring business education into alignment with the environment of investor capitalism not simply by echoing and reproducing the dominant market logic, or challenging it only at and from the margins, but rather by systematically interrogating it from the standpoint of alternative models. As things stand, there is little sustained discussion among business school faculty and administrators about whether new technologies, the globalization of trade, demographic trends, the growing inequality between rich and poor, and shifting social norms may be rendering the investor capitalism model unsustainable, if not actually obsolete. Yet these and other developments in the world since the rise of investor capitalism suggest that a new model—one akin to the stakeholder model that reigned in

American capitalism during the era of managerialism, one that recognizes the legitimate economic and social interests of many members of society other than shareholders—may well be called for. If university business schools, in turn, are to continue to play any role in the education of managers that could not be filled equally well by corporate training programs or for-profit, purely vocational business schools, they belong in the forefront of the discussions now taking place among informed and thoughtful citizens all around the globe about the shape that capitalism should take in the twenty-first century.

Yet it is not just alternative models of the purpose of the corporation or the relationship of the corporation and society that university business schools must seek to develop if they are to continue to justify their claims to be anything but sophisticated trade schools or efficient credentials factories. For to raise the kinds of questions I have outlined above about the role and purpose of the corporation in the contemporary world is also to raise fundamental questions about who and what a manager is and the very purpose of corporate leadership. In a world increasingly characterized by collaborative systems rather than rigid hierarchies, where public attention to the consequences of corporate activity now focuses on issues such as global labor standards and environmental degradation, and where a vacuum in global political leadership has left the world rudderless in a period of enormous economic and social upheaval, the purpose of management and corporate leadership necessarily goes beyond "maximizing shareholder value." It is not hyperbole to suggest that business is at a unique inflection point calling for a fundamental reconsideration of the meaning of corporate leadership. Such a reconsideration of what exactly business schools exist to prepare their students for would necessarily take into account that business education, like university education generally in most of its traditional forms, is a matter not just of imparting knowledge or preparing students for roles as economic and social actors. For educating leaders, if that is what business schools are truly about, is also a matter of socializing individuals into a particular conception of themselves, of the peer group to which they belong, and even of the meaning of their "higher" education itself, thus helping to develop informed, reflective, integrated individuals fully able to engage with ultimate questions about the meaning and purpose of their lives and their work.

Viewed from this perspective, university education itself in America today exhibits many symptoms of crisis, from the march toward an ever greater emphasis on vocationalism that has remained virtually unchecked since the rise of the post–World War II research university, to the commercialization that

critics such as Derek Bok and others have warned against, to the fragmentation, careerism, and lack of collective purpose that afflict faculties at even the
nation's most prestigious institutions.[5] In the view, for example, of Harry
Lewis, formerly dean of Harvard College, "In the absence of any credible
educational principles, money is increasingly the driving force of decisions in
universities."[6] A former dean of the University of Chicago, Donald Levine,
laments: "*the scandal of higher education in our time is that so little attention gets
paid, in institutions that claim to provide an education, to what it is that college
educators claim to be providing.*"[7] Such criticisms from within the American
university strike at its heart and indicate the enormity of the task of achieving
a genuine reorientation of either the whole or its constituent parts.

At its founding, as we have seen, the American research university—
successor to the religiously affiliated college as the expression of the nation's
aspirations for the education of its leading citizens—attempted to maintain a
delicate balance between the goals of instilling future elites with the character, values, knowledge, and skills that would contribute to the common good,
and providing individuals with the means of economic and social advancement. Yet the attempted synthesis, to the extent that it was realized at all,
proved as difficult to maintain as all such institutional balancing acts invariably are, and the American university of today bears few traces of the pedagogical ambitions for it harbored by educators such as Charles W. Eliot,
Daniel Coit Gilman, Andrew Dickson White, and others who saw the university as nothing less than society's best hope for achieving a humane and progressive social order in the modern world. While today's college presidents,
faculties, and administrators express dismay at the utilitarian and careerist
outlooks of their students, their institutions offer no effective counterforce.
As Harvard's Lewis observes, "Students become customers to be placated
rather than whole beings challenged to stand on their own."[8]

As for business schools, having entered the university as supplicants a
century or so ago, they now, along with the natural sciences, occupy the com-
manding heights of higher education, their contributions to university rev-
enues giving them unchallengeable status in the institutional hierarchy, and
the kinds of knowledge and skills they purvey now seemingly more essential
to the tasks of university—and indeed societal—leadership than anything
taught elsewhere on campus. Universities increasingly look to their business
schools to develop the enlightened and responsible business leadership that
can help address the major challenges of our global age. Johns Hopkins University, the original American research university, recently announced the

establishment of its first undergraduate and graduate business school, whose mission will be "producing leaders armed with both specialized business skills and cross-disciplinary knowledge from other top-ranked Johns Hopkins programs" such as those in medicine and public health.[9] In numerous other American universities, graduate schools in law, medicine, education, and public policy are now partnering with business schools to offer joint degrees and joint executive education programs, all in an effort to meet the challenges in these sectors. In the light of the prestige and influence business schools now enjoy both within the university and in the world at large, however, it is not at all obvious to outsiders, although increasingly clear to many within business education, that the university-based business school of today is a troubled institution, one that has become unmoored from its original purpose and whose contemporary state is in many ways antithetical to the goals of professional education itself.

The downfall of managerialism, in the business world and in business schools, and its replacement by the ideologies of shareholder primacy and managers as the fallible, indeed eminently corruptible, agents of shareholders, have not only severely eroded the cultural authority of managers that the creators of the university business school sought to establish and uphold.[10] These changes have also posed what I believe to be the most profound challenge faced by business schools since their appearance on America's university campuses a century ago. During the 1980s, while the goal of management as a profession was never explicitly renounced by business schools, the essential concept was allowed to fall into desuetude, first through neglect and then through displacement by the emerging logic of investor capitalism. I should make it clear that my intention in highlighting this shift is not to call for a turning back of the economic clock in an effort to re-create the era of managerialism, a time when too many business leaders took advantage of lax monitoring to build corporate empires with little strategic coherence, producing commensurately lackadaisical results. I do believe, however, that with the abandonment of the professionalization project and the idea that managers—not shareholders, labor, the state, or the market—should exercise ultimate control over the corporation, university business education lost the grand narrative that had sustained it from its beginnings. The loss of this historical metanarrative of management as a profession—a narrative that had placed managers at the center of the corporation and made them the primary link between the narrower concerns of business and the broader ones of society—is, I believe, the root cause of the inchoateness and drift that, more than 125 years after the establishment of the Wharton School and nearly 100 years after the founding of Harvard Business School, characterizes much contemporary business education. The effects of this loss, in turn, are visible all around those of us who teach in business schools today.

Consider, for example, how external signs of success or failure, approval or condemnation—signs such as the *BusinessWeek* rankings and the starting salaries of our students—have replaced internal markers that might serve to measure the quality of business schools against the high aims that many faculty members and administrators still have for them. The absence of an organizing narrative has also left the elite business schools in a condition of institutional fragmentation. A major function of an institutional narrative, in the form of a mission, vision, or articulation of overarching and noninstrumental goals, is to protect inherently delicate ideals and values from being overwhelmed by expediency, to act as a counterforce to the organizational tendency to select quantitative measures as the indicators of an institution's worth. Such a narrative motivates and guides action on the part of institutional leaders. Yet whereas identifiable, organized, and coordinated efforts could be found pushing first for the professionalization of business education and of business management in the first sixty years of business schools' existence, and then for significant reform in the era of the Ford Foundation report, today there is no single central actor—whether it be a particular organization or a group of reform-oriented deans—leading business education. This is not for lack of dedicated and thoughtful leaders at individual schools but, rather, because of a lack of a common, explicitly articulated understanding of what business schools stand for as institutions.

Anyone who spends time in an elite business school today knows that it is a place riddled with contradictions. Faculty are hired and promoted on the basis of discipline-oriented research that, as critics such as Warren Bennis and James O'Toole have noted of late, often has little or no bearing on the practice of management. Inside the classroom, as Henry Mintzberg has observed, faculty and their students have little in common in terms of shared experience and interests;[11] in contrast to such milieus as law and medical schools, many business school faculty members no longer identify with their MBA students, and, not surprisingly, their students no longer identify with them. As a result, many business school faculty members are losing what Paul Starr called their "cultural authority" as experts in the very jurisdiction within which their students intend to work. The undermining of faculty authority is exacerbated by everything from lax grading policies, to the dramatic growth in the number of practitioners employed as lecturers and adjunct faculty in order to compensate for the diminished credibility of the full-time faculty, to the lavish facilities with which the more affluent business schools try to lure students, as if they were already potentates rather than apprentices. That such criticisms might be applied to other parts of the contemporary American university does not detract from their pertinence to the situation of business schools today.

A loss of authority for business school faculty translates, in turn, into a loss of ability to introduce normative or ethical standards of conduct in business education. The best business ethics courses in the world can have little or no impact in the absence of the cultural authority that can actually impart their message to students in ways that will call forth response and commitment on their part. If students do not regard their faculty as legitimate authorities on business practice, or see business schools as the custodians of high business ideals, or if they believe that ethics gets in the way of progressing in business, they will regard their ethics courses as peripheral to managerial practice or a cynical attempt by business schools to placate external critics during periods of business scandals. Of course there are those who dismiss the very notion that "ethics can be taught," and if by teaching ethics is meant simply adding another item to an already wide-ranging curriculum, these critics are probably right. Yet does this mean that business schools should simply abandon the idea of trying to influence their students' values and conduct, and concentrate instead on imparting the instrumental knowledge necessary for successful practice, whatever that might mean? Or that a curriculum more focused on the exigencies of practice would, of itself, restore to business school faculty the cultural authority that would enable them to speak credibly about subjects like ethics?

My first response to these questions would be to point out that, as business school teachers, we inevitably do teach values, whether we are aware of so doing or not. For example: a 2003 Aspen Institute survey that followed a large contingent of MBA students from the time they entered business school to the time they graduated found that students' values changed during the process. In the course of their two years of study in an MBA program, students' views of the legitimate claims on the corporation of shareholders and other constituents such as employees, customers, and the larger community shifted toward a higher valuation of the rights and claims of shareholders relative to those of others. Such views have a direct bearing on questions of ethics and values in business, because any meaningful discussion of the ethical responsibilities of business requires prior agreement about to what or to whom business is "responsible" in the first place. However, too many business schools persist in the illusion that, just because a subject is presented in the "value-free" language of social science, the instruction given is, indeed, value-free. Such an illusion could arise only after business schools had abandoned the idea that they were preparing students for such a normatively bound occupational category as a profession.

A second, related point is that if the MBA curriculum were more like that of a genuine professional school in being geared to what students need to know for practice, it is possible that the gain in cultural authority for business school faculty would aid in teaching ethics in the classroom.[12] Such a model, however, would still be subject to the criticism that ethics and values, being highly "personal" matters with respect to which students have already been formed (or not) over the course of normal development into young adulthood, are beyond the purview of postgraduate education. The idea that business schools—or universities, for that matter—are responsible for developing the character of their students often generates the heated objection that it is inappropriate for schools to try to shape students' moral identity. My answer to this objection is that undergoing preparation for a profession (in the understanding of the term I have presented in this book) is always and necessarily a matter of personal transformation that affects individuals at much more than just a cognitive level. Becoming a professional involves the adoption, as I have indicated, not just of a role but also of an identity. Institutions charged with educating and developing professionals (or leaders, for that matter) need to actively shape professional identity—that is, how one conceives of oneself and one's relationship to work. For professions, at their core, involve a complex sense of identity rooted not only in expert knowledge and prescribed forms of practice but also in commitment to a set of collectively held norms that elevates an occupation to what Weber described as a *calling*, and that ultimately distinguishes a professional from others who simply employ technical knowledge in particular ways.

Yet the arguments I am making here require me, in the final analysis, to say why, more than a hundred years after the invention of the university business school, one should continue to regard professionalism and professionalization as lodestars. After all, business schools have remained professional schools in name, even while abandoning the professionalization project in substance. If society continues to recognize them as "professional schools," why should they hold themselves to any higher standard? Moreover, at a time when such traditional professions as medicine and law are coming less and less to resemble professions in the traditional sense, with market-based conceptions of their nature and purpose becoming increasingly dominant and their own cultural authority diminishing steadily, why should their earlier avatars be cynosures for management? In short, why does the professionalization project in business schools now matter as anything but a topic of historical interest, and why shouldn't it be left to die in peace?

My answer to such questions is rooted in the idea of institutions as mechanisms for the establishment and maintenance of social order, and in a conception of the utility of particular types of institutions for particular forms of order making in the contemporary world. Professions, I believe, are a vital but underrecognized part of the social and economic order. They have inherent qualities that are distinct from those of other order-creating institutions such as markets and bureaucracy, and when they are compromised or corrupted, society as a whole is harmed.

An influential stream of twentieth-century economic thought gave rise to a distinction between what have come to be considered the two primary mechanisms for the ordering of economic activity: markets and hierarchies. In his 1937 essay "The Nature of the Firm," the Nobel Prize–winning economist Ronald Coase noted that while classical economics assumed that the market governed all economic exchange, the modern economy was in fact dominated by both markets and the hierarchies created by and within organizations. In a market system, exchanges between buyers and sellers depend on negotiated contracts and the price mechanism. Contracts and the price system are, in effect, the two digits of the invisible hand. As Coase pointed out, however, many economic exchanges take place not in the market but, rather, within the boundaries of firms. Because not all economic exchange takes place in the market, the existence of the firm, Coase deduced, was evidence that there are market exchanges that are not costless. For example, it can be difficult to specify the obligations of each party to a contract in the face of significant uncertainty. Under such circumstances, organizations are likely to be viewed as attractive alternatives to the market. In the hierarchical systems of organizations, managers are in a position to use their authority over employees to lower transactions costs below what they would be in a market. The Coasian framework was extended by the institutional economist Douglass North, who argued that government offered yet another example of a hierarchical organization. In this instance, transaction costs were reduced by the mechanism of authority to enforce rules, such as property rights, that would be costly to enforce in a pure market mechanism.

Over the past few decades, considerable effort has gone into the study of the conditions under which organizations and hierarchies are superior to markets for managing particular types of transactions, and of the state's role in specifying and enforcing rules determining where and how transactions occur. However, the categorization of economic ordering regimes into markets and hierarchies overlooks a third mechanism for ordering economic activities: communities, the institution from which professions derive their basic structure and logic.

One influential thinker on the nature of social order in the late nineteenth and early twentieth centuries was the German sociologist Ferdinand Tonnies, who distinguished between the type of order provided by institutions like markets or certain types of hierarchies, which he called *Gesellschaft*, and the type of social order created by communities, which he called *Gemeinschaft*. *Gesellschaft* denotes an abstract, impersonal, and formalized system of social rules, roles, and institutions marked by selective affinities, rational calculation, and negotiated interests: that is, markets and the kind of hierarchy represented by rational administration and bureaucracy. In contrast, *Gemeinschaft* relations are based on traditional beliefs, forms of status based on such beliefs, and deep affective relationships rooted in norms of reciprocity, loyalty, and commitment to the group. Tonnies argued that the increasing number of formal organizations, the expanding size and role of the state, the increase in specialized occupations, the rise of formal education systems, and the proliferation of market transactions were all evidence of nineteenth-century *Gemeinschaft* relations giving way to a twentieth-century social order dominated by *Gesellschaft* relations.

The history of late nineteenth- and early twentieth-century social science can be understood partly as an attempt to discover how to achieve social continuity, solidarity, and engagement in the face of a new social order based on markets and bureaucracy. Many of the founders of the modern social sciences recognized that while modernity and its ordering institutions of markets and bureaucracy promised much in the way of human progress, they exacted a social and psychological price that was manifested in phenomena such as increased crime and divorce rates and high degrees of social isolation, alienation, and anomie. In traditional societies, community represented the totality of life. One's family, place in the community, and status among one's neighbors offered predictability, order, a sense of place and belonging. To be expelled from the community was the symbolic equivalent of death. The pioneers of social science also understood that none of the rewards offered by large-scale organizations or markets could easily substitute for the social and psychic benefits provided by membership in a well-functioning community. In the *Gemeinschaft*-based society from which the United States was born, the framers of our Declaration of Independence and Constitution put the voice of the community at the center of the idea of America. ("We hold these truths to be self-evident . . ." "We the people . . .") In the *Gesellschaft*-based America of today, as in any modern society, neither organizations nor markets offer those who participate in them the sense of purpose afforded by communities sharing common values, rituals, and meanings.

The significance of the triad markets-hierarchies-community for my subject is that, as sociologists such as Durkheim, Weber, Merton, and, more recently, C. Everett Hughes and Eliot Freidson have understood, the essence of professions lies in their status as communities with shared knowledge, standards of practice, and norms of conduct. The standards and norms that professional communities enforce upon themselves are intended to compensate for the shortcomings of markets and hierarchies in situations where, for example, information asymmetries make it difficult for either purchasers of a service or outside regulators to evaluate the competence of a practitioner or the quality of service he or she renders. Self-regulation in the form of ethical codes and disciplinary procedures, however, can be an imperfect mechanism for ensuring the integrity of professionals and the quality of their work. This reality—coupled with the fact that professions often work in areas where society has a considerable stake in the quality of practice and the success of outcomes (i.e., health, justice, knowledge)—makes it essential that professions not only evolve systems for disciplining errant practitioners but instill in them from the beginning the values and commitments that allow *individuals* to govern themselves. The internalization of such values and commitments distinguishes professionals from others for whom the employment of expert knowledge and technical skill may be simply a market exchange and a way to earn a living. For the professional, work is more than a market exchange; it is, rather, a source of meaning and identity within a community of like-minded practitioners. In sum, discipline, self-restraint, and a willingness to renounce individual self-interest to preserve the good name of the professional community and advance the greater good are hallmarks of professionals in the sense that the original advocates for the professionalization of management understood the term. In light of this fact, one way to describe the deprofessionalization of American management in the post–World War II era and beyond is to say that managers, having successfully claimed specialized knowledge and skills, have succeeded in retaining and, indeed, enlarging the privileges of membership in a profession while throwing off the attendant restraints and responsibilities.

In the wake of the recent corporate scandals, debate about how to respond to them has moved between the poles of calls for greater regulation—answered, in part, by the passage of the Sarbanes-Oxley Act of 2002—and defense of the status quo ante on the grounds that the malfeasance revealed, however widespread, was attributable to errant individuals rather than to systemic flaws in incentive structures or governance systems. That business schools might bear responsibility for not instilling values such as honesty and integrity in their students was duly noted by several observers, including many in business schools themselves. That business schools might have actively fostered misconduct by instilling in their students, over the course of a generation, the idea that markets provide an adequate mechanism for motivating, monitoring, and disciplining managers and boards of directors who are not susceptible, in any case, to appeals to anything beyond self-interest was a distinctly minority view,[13] but one that appears compelling in the context of the abandonment of the professionalization project in business education. The tactic of "incentivizing" managers with stock options, for example, followed from a market logic—inculcated in directors and managers alike by business schools beginning in the 1970s—that assumes that managers are both purely self-interested and motivated only by the prospect of lavish material rewards. By demoting managers from professional stewards of the corporation's resources to hired hands bound only by contractual requirements and relationships, business schools thus helped create the conditions and standards of behavior through which the market-based mechanism of stock options was turned into an instrument for defrauding investors, jeopardizing the livelihoods of employees, and undermining public trust in managers and corporations. Given the failure of the market, in this case, to deliver on the promise that market incentives and controls would be sufficient to restrain the greed and self-indulgence of managers, it is hardly surprising or deplorable that the body politic responded with calls for greater regulation.

Regulation, to be sure, is a costly and ham-handed way of monitoring the complex affairs of the modern corporation, and runs the risk of stifling the innovation and risk taking that have contributed so much to the success of American capitalism. Yet to decry the hierarchical solution of regulation, as many on Wall Street and in Washington have done, without addressing the manifest deficiencies of markets for restraining antisocial behavior is to evade an honest accounting for what has transpired in our business culture and a realistic assessment of what might be done to correct it. Moreover, to juxtapose hierarchy (in the form of law and regulation) and markets as the only two ways of ensuring that our capitalist system retains the confidence and trust necessary for its optimal functioning is to overlook a third possibility, as one of the most distinguished American business leaders of the twentieth century recognized eighty years ago.

Praised in his day by the muckraking journalist Ida Tarbell, who called him a "new type of industrial leader," and more recently by the communications scholar Robert W. McChesney, who describes him as a "visionary capitalist" who believed that his industry (broadcasting) "had a public service obligation that went beyond what could be expected from simply pursuing profit maximization,"[14] Owen Young was neither a freebooting 1920s industrialist nor an anticorporate moralizer. The chairman of two powerful American corporations (RCA and General Electric), Young believed that such organizations needed to maintain their social legitimacy in order to function effectively in a democratic society. In drawing his analogy, in his speech at the Harvard Business School dedication ceremony in 1927, between the Puritan ministry that established Harvard College and the "ministry of business" that it was the mission of HBS to prepare, Young noted that in seventeenth-century New England, when business could be called more of an "art" than a science, the ethical constraints imposed on a businessman by "the law of the land and the moral restraints existing in the community in which he lived" were enough to keep business conduct within acceptable bounds. Yet as American business had increased in scope and complexity, with giant corporations now serving national and even international markets via operations in many different locales, modern enterprise had "outstripped all local sanctions," leaving businessmen "free from restraints except those of the law." Young continued:

> Now the law is not a satisfactory censor. It functions in the clear light of wrong doing—things so wrong that the community must protect itself against them. Set over against the law on the opposite side is the clear light of right doing—things which are so generally appealing to the conscience of all that no mistake could be made no matter how complicated the business. The area of difficulty for business lies in the penumbra between the two. When business was simple and local, it was fairly easy for local public opinion to penetrate the

shadowed area. When business became complicated and widespread, it was in this area that all restraints were removed. It was in this shadowed space that troublesome practices were born. It was from acts here that suspicions of business arose. It was the loss of these normal restraints which caused business to suffer.[15]

In these new circumstances, Young said, "Men of character began to realize that the success of their business depended not alone upon what they did, but, in some measure, upon what others in the same line of business did."

They began to form trade associations, first, merely to promote acquaintance and to create morale in the organization which would, in a sense, be a substitute for the public opinion of the local community in the earlier days. Gradually through these organizations codes of conduct are being developed, and rules are emerging to enforce standards both as to character of goods and methods of trading, which are designed to afford proper protection to the members of the organization and for the better service of society. It is these self-imposed rules designed to enforce standards on the entire group engaged in similar business that are the distinguishing mark of the new profession. In fact, products have become so highly technical and the rules of business so complicated, that it is difficult, if not impossible, for anyone other than business men, and for the most part only those in the same line of business, to sit in judgment on unfair practices which the law cannot well reach and which the church cannot well understand. Indeed, as a disciplinary force in the complexities of modern society, a profession of business with many specialized subdivisions should be welcome to all.[16]

Yet despite the steps that some businessmen had taken to begin regulating their own collective conduct, Young noted, "so far as the public is concerned, organized business has been quick to take advantages of group action, but has been slow to assume group responsibilities. Too frequently business men have acquiesced, even if they did not participate, in objectionable practices until an outraged society compelled amateurs to interfere."[17] These "amateurs" included legislators who passed "unwise" or even counterproductive laws because they simply did not understand the matters about which they attempted to legislate. A truly professional business class, however, could both help regulate itself and furnish legislators and policy makers with the information required for wise and effective laws and regulations. In proposing this idea, Young located management within a broader American tradition of self-regulation in a social system that seeks to promote responsible action through a sense of shared purpose rather than through the atomized interactions of the marketplace or the centralized direction of the state.

Although Young's analysis of public perceptions of business sounds strikingly contemporary, his idea of business as a profession with "self-imposed rules designed to enforce standards on the entire group" is now easily taken as naive. This is not just because the idea of executives as free agents has come to be taken for granted but because—as the growing encroachment of both markets and hierarchies on the traditional professions of law and medicine illustrates—professions, like all human institutions, can and do fall short of their promise. Just as there are numerous examples of market failure or bureaucratic failure, a profession can fail when, for example, the professional community loses the will or authority to regulate itself, or when market incentives or rigid rules crowd out professionals' commitment to act in the best interests of clients or society. Granted, however, that professions are not infallible means of achieving the goals that they exist to advance, is the idea of collective self-regulation by managers any more naive than the position—taken by many of the relative handful of American business leaders who have been willing to speak out forcefully about the business scandals of the first decade of the present century—that the answer to the widespread misconduct that has so tarnished the reputation of businesspersons lies in greater "personal integrity" among executives and board members?

A cynical response would be to suggest that the advantage of pointing to personal integrity as a solution is that business leaders can do little to increase the supply of it on any meaningful scale. A more generous and realistic response would be to recognize that, eighty years after the chairman of General Electric drew upon the historical past to envision a collective response from American management to a shifting of the moral ground beneath American capitalism, we no longer have much in the way of concepts or vocabulary to even discuss such things. Moreover, as William M. Sullivan has pointed out, "The prevalence of the notion that the market is self-regulating and morally self-sufficient has cast doubt on the public value of an individual's lengthy and expensive induction into a professional guild." The related idea that "the only moral obligation of any enterprise is to maximize its economic well-being" also "denigrates the importance of a specifically professional perspective, deeply tied to educational and regulatory institutions, in providing expert services."[18] The market logic that has taken over business schools and American business itself has prevented us from even seeing that there might be an alternative to either markets or regulation as a way of preserving the integrity of our capitalist system.

This self-inflicted blindness is symptomatic of an even deeper malady. Lacking either the religious framework invoked by the founders of the modern university and the university-based business school, or shared agreement about basic societal values, we have no meaningful language for civic discourse about the ultimate purpose of our secular institutions.[19] Thus we have been left only with empty rhetoric about "excellence" or "leadership" with which to discuss the educational mission of the university. As a result, our universities are now apt to turn out what the late Robert Nisbet called "loose individuals." The loose individual Nisbet described is someone who does not feel constrained by norms arising from social values such as fairness or equity, or by allegiance to social institutions such as nations, firms, or even jobs. Such individuals lack any sense of "moral responsibility," often playing "fast and loose with the other individuals in relationships of trust and responsibility."[20] Their relationships with those who are not their intimates are anchored only in utilitarian self-interest. Loose individuals thrive in amoral environments in which ideas such as duty and reciprocity seem alien or are ridiculed as old-fashioned and naive. They respond only to the invisible hand, reflexively following market signals as though they were road signs indicating the appropriate direction for their actions. Nisbet's account of the "loose individual" echoes John Dewey's description of what he called the "lost individual"; as Dewey observed:

[T]he loyalties which once held individuals, which gave them support, direction, and unity of outlook on life, have well-nigh disappeared. In consequence, individuals are confused and bewildered. It would be difficult to find in history an epoch as lacking in solid and assured objects of belief and approved ends of action as is the present. Stability of individuality is dependent upon stable objects to which allegiance firmly attaches itself. There are, of course, those who are still militantly fundamentalist in religious and social creed. But their very clamor is evidence that the tide is set against them. For the others, traditional objects of loyalty have become hollow or are openly repudiated, and they drift without sure anchorage. Individuals vibrate between a past that is intellectually too empty to give stability and a present that is too diversely crowded and chaotic to afford balance or direction to ideas and motion.[21]

Nisbet's "loose" individual and Dewey's "lost" individual are by no means unfamiliar figures in either business schools or actual business environments today. In the elite business schools, the delegitimation of management accomplished through the hegemony of economics and the propounding of doctrine from agency theory has coincided, not surprisingly, with a decline in their traditional function of supplying managers to corporations. That function is clearly in tension with the career choices being made by MBA students at the elite schools, who have long preferred consulting and investment banking to managerial work and now increasingly seek entry to the lucrative world of hedge funds and private equity. The enormous sums of money being made in these fields, combined with fears that the cycle will run out soon, have bred an anxiety-driven frenzy to get in now or miss the chance to retire by the age of forty. Notions of sustained effort to build companies that create useful products and services, provide employment, and contribute to their communities are less and less a part of the aspirations of American business school students.

In the corporate world, meanwhile, the doctrines of the firm as a mere nexus of contracts, of the creation of shareholder value as the primary task of the firm, and of managers as loose individuals who must essentially be bribed into attending to the interests of shareholders have helped underpin a system in which stock prices are the measure of all value and managers have become increasingly preoccupied with what Joseph Schumpeter called "evaporated property"—shares and other forms of intangible property held by "[d]ematerialized, defunctionalized and absentee ownership."[22] Managers, whose empowerment was the purpose for which university business schools were created, are now subservient to an extraordinarily powerful group of financial intermediaries such as hedge funds and private equity firms. The backbone of the system is no longer the executive or manager with a lifetime career but, rather, a number of hired hands who buy and sell corporate assets. The CEO—himself now merely a hired hand—is loaded with stock options and golden parachutes that essentially ensure that whatever loyalty he has for sale is transferred from the firm and its employees, customers, and community to shareholders. Severance packages running into the tens or even hundreds of millions ensure a soft landing if and when the CEO violates the covenant that requires putting personal gain ahead of fiduciary duty to the institution, including its shareholders, thus undercutting the basic imperatives of fairness and trustworthiness that are so essential to a well-functioning free enterprise system.

In *Capitalism, Socialism, and Democracy*, Schumpeter described the ultimate consequences of an economic system built around evaporated property:

> The capitalist process, by substituting a mere parcel of shares for the walls of and machines in a factory, takes the life out of property. . . . And this evaporation of what we may term the material substance of property—its visible and touchable reality—affects not only the attitudes of holders but also of the workmen and the public generally. Dematerialized, defunctionalized and absentee ownership does not impress and call forth moral allegiance as the vital form of property did. Eventually there will be nobody left who really cares to stand for it—nobody within and nobody without the precincts of the big concerns.[23]

If Schumpeter was right about these effects of the system of investor capitalism of which business schools have become a mainstay, and instilling a sense of "moral allegiance" and stewardship is vital to the healthy functioning of our society's economic institutions, business schools could help create a group of stakeholders who possess these qualities by reconsidering the proposition of management as a profession. The reinvention of management itself along the lines envisioned for it by our predecessors—not just the content of the MBA curriculum but the fundamental assumptions about the purpose of managerial work embedded in both the curriculum and the whole ethos to which students are introduced in the course of their experience on a business school campus—would have obvious benefits for society if it helped foster such virtues as custodianship, duty, and responsibility. A recovery of the higher aims once held to be intrinsic to the professions would have considerable benefits for students as well. Commenting on the impact of agency theory on business school students, the behavioral economist Robert Frank makes this observation:

> There are obviously many economists who still believe that self-interest is the dominant human motive. There's no doubt that it's a very important human motive . . . but I think most people who aren't in that narrow tradition realize that other motives are important, too. We try to get ahead of our rivals, but we also care about

other people and wish them well. We don't take advantage of every conceivable opportunity to gain at the expense of others. Students exposed to the narrow self-interest model often don't like it; they often feel alienated by it.[24]

Ultimately, from the viewpoint of an aspiring manager, the most pernicious effect of agency theory's perspective on management has been to drive out any possibility of managers' deriving meaning from their work or creating meaning for others, for that matter. As sociologists, anthropologists, and psychologists all recognize, human beings seek meaning; it is as fundamental to human existence as the search for material sustenance. In traditional societies, religion, family, and community satisfied this need for meaning. These structures provided a framework for understanding one's life and its significance. They offered guidance for answering such ultimate questions as: Who am I? What is the good life? What are my responsibilities? To what moral order should I commit myself? As the rise of modern industrial capitalism tore at the fabric of society's sustaining institutions and awakened a new hunger for meaning, the modern professions—which, among their other innovations, adapted the old religious concept of *calling* to offer individuals in the modern world a sense of intrinsic meaning from work—were created in an attempt to repair some of the damage and offer individuals, both professionals and their clients, guidance and anchorage in a world from which transparency and trust appeared to have fled. I cannot see that we have since invented any better means of accomplishing certain important social purposes when markets and hierarchies show their limitations as promoters of the common good.

The delegitimation of managerial authority and the abandonment of the professionalization project in business schools have created conditions in which the ultimate purposes of management and of business schools as institutions are now up for grabs. As institutional theory shows us, to propose opening up debate about the fundamental questions I have tried to raise here is to work against the grain of established institutions themselves. New institutions, as business schools were a century ago, have the luxury, from a certain standpoint, of choosing their purposes rather than having them thrust upon them by institutional history and inertia, including the inertia of success. Yet several developments today—declines in applications and the pre-to-post-MBA salary differential at the elite schools, dissatisfaction with the quality of MBAs at employers such as elite consulting firms, and the rise of for-profit MBA programs, for example—suggest that, as successful as they have been in the past, business schools cannot, perhaps, take their future success for granted. History, in the meantime, tells us that when institutions lose their legitimacy or find it called into question, the times are ripe for their reinvention. It is more than possible that we live in such times now.

Acknowledgments

Numerous people have supported me throughout the research and writing of this book.

I would like first to acknowledge my intellectual debt to Sumantra Ghoshal (deceased), Michael Jensen, Rosabeth Moss Kanter, Jay Lorsch, Nitin Nohria, Jeff Pfeffer, Scott Snook, and Richard Tedlow, whose ideas have profoundly shaped my thinking about business education and its relationship to society. I know they will not all agree with what I have written, but without their guidance, the coherence and explanatory interpretation of the events and relationships I describe in this book would have been greatly diminished.

A number of colleagues have read and commented on the book or parts of it, or have generously given their time to discuss various aspects of business education: Michael Beer, Warren Bennis, Joseph Bower, Kim Clark, Dwight Crane, Srikant Datar, Thomas Delong, Mihir Desai, Frank Dobbin, Robin Ely, Ben Esty, David Garvin, Bill George, Jack Gabarro, Boris Groysberg, Ray Fisman, Monica Higgins, Linda Hill, Geoff Jones, Rajiv Lal, Paul Lawrence, Jay Light, Chris Marquis, Joshua Margolis, Lynn Paine, Krishna Palepu, Leslie Perlow, Tom Piper, Bill Pounds, Jeff Polzer, John Quelch, Julio Rotemberg, Bruce Scott, David Scharfstein, Toby Stuart, David Thomas, Michael Tushman, and Scott Snook all provided thoughtful suggestions and valuable advice.

I appreciate the generous financial support, resources, guidance, and advice I've received from Harvard Business School. Jean Cunningham helped me gain access to Harvard Business School's archives. Baker Library's Laura Linnard and Tim Driscoll diligently helped me find what I needed once I was in the archives. The Ford Foundation's Alan Divack and Anthony Mahoney tirelessly worked to locate materials related to the Ford Foundation's activities in business education. Laura Singleton reviewed and ordered the endnotes, as well as providing numerous editorial suggestions. My assistant Emily Hall skillfully prepared the manuscript and the tables. As I typed away in a hidden corner of McArthur Hall, Gaby Borghoul kindly attended to my comfort with food, drink, and encouragement. Scores of colleagues at Cornell, MIT, Stanford, the Academy of Management, and the American Sociological Association provided very important, constructive feedback during presentations of various elements of this book. The Center for Public Leadership at Harvard's Kennedy School of Government graciously supported my initial exploration of this subject.

I'd like to thank everyone at Princeton University Press: Ian Malcolm, who stewarded this book from conception to completion, even after relocating from New Jersey to England; Peter Dougherty, whose enthusiasm for the project provided a significant boost in helping me reach the finish line; and Lauren Lepow, for her skillful and careful editing of the manuscript.

Most of all, I am grateful to Daniel Penrice. This book could not have been written without him. Over the past five years, Dan has been a research associate, taskmaster, motivator, skillful editor, and confidant. In addition to helping me sort through the data, he zeroed in on flaws in logic and evidence, discriminated between ideas that should be further developed and those that should be discarded, clarified my prose, and insisted that I not hide behind the foggy abstractions of sociology but instead present readable, evidence-based ideas. Thank you, Dan.

I would like to thank my family: Ram and Anjana Khurana for their unconditional love; my brothers, Pradeep and Hareesh, for their sarcasm and wit about academic life; and my wonderful extended family, Marisa, Catlin, Arjun, Asha, Amita, Trent, and Rita.

And, finally, the generative force of my life's meaning—Stephanie, Sonia, Nalini, and Jai. All of you are my calling.

Bibliographic and Methods Note

This note describes the strengths and weaknesses of my primary research methodology and provides an accurate description of the resultant data. First, however, I want to place this book in context vis-à-vis the spate of recent writings on business education, much of which is soul-searching or polemical critique. Although this work informs elements of this book, I want to make clear that my goal is not to offer a critique of business education. Instead, this book attempts to contribute to the organizational and sociological research on institutions and professions by offering a historically grounded account of the development of a little understood but important source of our society's business leadership—American business schools. To the extent that there are normative implications of this research, I believe they derive from the fact that one cannot study a significant social institution like American business education without raising questions about sensitive topics such as the fundamental nature and purpose of business education, the place of professions in twenty-first-century America, and the current state of higher education.

Primary and Secondary Sources

I began this research by reading as many published sources as I could on the beginnings of business education. These included books, magazine articles written by scholars, public addresses delivered by college presidents and deans that appeared in newspapers, school periodicals, academic conference proceedings, and edited volumes. Two books were especially useful in illuminating the beginning of American business schools: Carter Daniel's *MBA: The First Century* (Lewisburg, PA: Bucknell University Press, 1998), which chronicled the early debates about the place of business education in university and business school curricula; and Benjamin Haynes and Harry Jackson's monograph, *A History of Business Education in the United States* (Cincinnati: Southwestern Pub. Co., 1935), which explored nineteenth- and twentieth-century commercial and vocational schools. I also benefited from reading a number of histories of individual business schools, including Jeff Cruikshank's *A Delicate Experiment: The Harvard Business School, 1908–1945* (Boston: Harvard Business School Press, 1978), on the first fifty years of Harvard Business School; Steve Sass's *The Pragmatic Imagination: A History of the Wharton School, 1881–1981* (Philadelphia: University of Pennsylvania Press, 1982), on the first century of Wharton; Wayne Broehl's *Tuck and Tucker: The Origin of the Graduate Business School* (Hanover: University Press of New England, 1999), on the first century of the nation's oldest graduate business school; Thurman Van Metre's *History of the Graduate School of Business, Columbia University* (New York: Columbia University Press, 1954), on the first fifty years of Columbia's business school; Melvin Copeland's *And Mark an Era: The Story of Harvard Business School* (Boston: Little, Brown, 1958), published on the fiftieth anniversary of Harvard Business School; Michael Sedlak and Harold Williamson's *The Evolution of Management Education: A History of the Northwestern University J. L. Kellogg Graduate School of Management, 1908–1983* (Illinois: University of Illinois Press, 1983); Abraham Gitlow's *New York University's Stern School of Business: A Centennial Retrospective* (New York: New York University Press, 1995); and Steven Schlossman, Michael Sedlak, and Harold Wechsler's *The "New Look:" The Ford Foundation and the Revolution in Business Education* (Los Angeles: Graduate Management Admissions Council, 1987), which provided useful information about the early history of many business schools. I should note that all of the books about individual schools were, to some extent, "authorized histories" and thus manifested the weaknesses common to such material. However, notable exceptions included the work of Cruikshank, Sass, Sedlak and Williamson, and Schlossman, Sedlak, and Wechsler, which had a strong scholarly foundation, relied on both primary and secondary data, and presented a lively and balanced narrative of the early days of business education.

To amplify my understanding of business education's early years, I made extensive use of primary archival material. While collecting this data, I was surprised to learn from the archivists that few people had ever looked at this treasure trove of material for reasons other than occasional fact checking. Indeed, during the summer of 2001 in the Harvard Business School archives' restricted materials, I was doing some fact checking of my own for my earlier

book on the CEO labor market when I discovered that business schools had
evolved in a way that was quite distinct from the intentions of their founders.
As I smoothed the almost translucent, yellowing pages detailing Dean Edwin
Gay's aspirations for the Harvard Business School and paged through the
bright yellow carbon copies of the meticulous correspondence among business school deans reflecting the dark mood of the 1930s and then the heady
optimism of the 1950s and 1960s, I felt that I had entered a different world of
both ideas and *ideals*.

Between 2001 and 2005, I worked closely with Harvard Business School's
historical archivists and the archivists at the Ford Foundation to identify as
much material as possible related to the founding of business education in the
United States. The materials were of five types: correspondence files, both official and personal; unpublished speeches, minutes, and proceedings; published
articles and essays; public communications; and published and unpublished
research reports. At HBS, the largest and most comprehensive collection of
primary business material in the world, I went through tens of thousands of
pages of material not only about the Harvard Business School, but also about
the development of the AACSB, the Ford and Carnegie foundations, and other
schools. In addition, I pored over extensive professional correspondence between deans and academics related to the organization of numerous business
schools. I supplemented this material with visits to other university archives
and a wealth of microfilms and newly digitized archival material from around
the country, all of which gave me access to academic journals, databases, magazines, grant proposals, grant requests, and Department of Education reports
that documented and commented on this development in higher education.
The most important of these data sources were the following:

- American Association of Collegiate Schools of Business (AACSB).
  The minutes, proceedings, and founding documents related to the
  American Association of Collegiate Schools of Business (AACSB),
  the professional association of business educators founded in 1916,
  provided invaluable information on the resource and legitimacy
  challenges facing the first business schools. In particular, the proceedings and earliest studies undertaken by the AACSB inform my
  discussions of the debates about the purpose of business education,
  the curriculum, and business school research.
- Annual reports and letters of business school deans. The annual reports of business school deans to university presidents, such as those

found in the archives of Harvard Business School and Columbia University's business school, are important sources of statistical information on the students and faculty of business schools, and the types of employers that recruited from them.

- Annual reports of the Carnegie and Rockefeller foundations. These reports provided data on foundation activities in a number of areas, especially those related to scholarly research, and to raising the status of graduate education, and of the social sciences.
- Academic journals. I draw heavily upon special issues of scholarly journals, such as the *Journal of Political Economy* and the *Journal of Business* that chronicled curriculum debates, summarized syllabi, and provided the earliest descriptions of business schools as academic organizations.

To supplement the aforementioned sources, I also relied on a number of biographies and autobiographies of individuals who either critically affected the trajectory of business education or were involved in its founding. Of particular relevance were George Homan's *Coming to My Senses* (New Brunswick, NJ: Transaction, 1984), which describes the early days of social science at Harvard Business School and Harvard University; Wallace Donham's *Education for Responsible Living: The Opportunity for Liberal Arts Colleges* (Cambridge: Harvard University Press, 1944), about the relationship between business education and society; Sheridan Logan's book *George F. Baker and his Bank, 1840–1955* (self-published, 1981), recounting the life of a significant donor to Harvard Business School; John Jordan's *Machine Age Ideology: Social Engineering and American Liberalism, 1911–1939* (Chapel Hill: University of North Carolina Press, 1994), which describes the activities of Progressive era reformers such as Walter Lippmann, Louis Brandeis, and Herbert Croly in trying to create a public theory about professional management and professional civil service; Leon Marshall's *Business Administration* (Chicago: University of Chicago Press, 1921) and *Modern Business: The Business Man in Society* (New York: Macmillan, 1926) on the development of the University of Chicago's curriculum and Marshall's philosophy of business education, respectively; David Riesman's *Thorstein Veblen* (New Brunswick, NJ: Transaction, 1995), on an economist who was quite critical of business education; Fritz Roethlisberger's *The Elusive Phenomena* (Cambridge: Division of Research, Graduate School of Business Administration, Harvard University, 1977), an autobiographical account of the development of research at the Harvard Business

School; William G. Scott's *Chester Barnard and the Guardians of the Managerial State* (Kansas: University Press of Kansas, 1992), the story of an influential AT&T executive turned scholar who developed the first theoretical challenge to the mechanistic view of management popularized by Frederick Taylor, and who would later become the internationally influential president of the Rockefeller Foundation; Herbert Simon's autobiography *Models of My Life* (New York: Basic Books, 1991); Ida Tarbell's *Owen D. Young, a New Type of Industrial Leader* (New York: Macmillan, 1932); Frank B. Copley's *Fredrick W. Taylor: Father of Scientific Management* (New York: Harper and Bros., 1923) on the early history of Taylor and his personal background; Joseph Frazier Wall's *Andrew Carnegie* (New York: Oxford University Press, 1970); and Andrea Gabor's *The Capitalist Philosophers: The Geniuses of Modern Business, Their Lives, Times, and Ideas* (New York: Times Business, 2000), which provided cogent accounts of the personal lives and professional contributions of several of the twentieth century's most influential business thinkers.

I also had an opportunity to speak with several former business school administrators and faculty who were participants or observers during the postwar events recounted in the book. While I do not cite most of these discussions in the book, I'd like to acknowledge these individuals, the documents and reports they provided me from their own personal files, and their significant contributions to my understanding of the significance of these events as well as their pointing me to other factors I missed in my initial analysis.

My understanding of the activities that shaped post–World War II business education was informed by numerous reports and commissions that examined business education. The most important sources were the Ford and Carnegie foundation reports on business education and the material used to generate those reports; the Ford Foundation archives; AACSB reports and studies; and the Graduate Management Admissions Council (GMAC), which administers the Graduate Management Admissions Test (GMAT) and publishes detailed statistics, occasional research papers, and survey data about business school students. From 1984 to 2004, GMAC also published an excellent professional journal, for a primary audience of business school faculty and administrators, titled *Selections*. The journal, no longer published, was a wonderful source of insights on business education and regularly featured extended interviews with leading business school educators and administrators. I especially benefited from reading a historical series written by Steven Schlossman, Michael Sedlak, and Harold Wechsler that chronicled the postwar activities of individual business schools after the publication of the Ford Foundation reports.

In researching the postwar business context and changes in the capital markets I depended on a number of secondary sources. In particular, I relied heavily on Neil Fligstein's *The Transformation of Corporate Control* (Cambridge: Harvard University Press, 1990); Michael Useem's *Executive Defense: Shareholder Power and Corporate Reorganization* (Cambridge: Harvard University Press, 1993); Raghuram Rajan and Luigi Zingales's *Saving Capitalism from the Capitalists: Unleashing the Power of Financial Markets to Create Wealth and Spread Opportunity* (Princeton: Princeton University Press, 2004); and Nitin Nohria, Davis Dyer, and Frederick Dalzell's *Changing Fortunes: Remaking the Industrial Corporation* (New York: Wiley, 2002).

For discussions of postwar higher education and philanthropic foundations, I found the following sources invaluable in shaping my understanding of how government policies and philanthropic foundations affected higher education: Roger Geiger's *To Advance Knowledge: The Growth of American Research Universities, 1900–1940* (Oxford: Oxford University Press, 1986); Geiger's *Knowledge and Money: Research Universities and the Paradox of the Marketplace* (Stanford: Stanford University Press, 2004); Dwight MacDonald's *The Ford Foundation: The Men and the Millions* (New York: Reynal, 1956); and Ellen Condliffe Lagemann's *Private Power for the Public Good: A History of the Carnegie Foundation for the Advancement of Teaching* (Middletown, CT: Wesleyan University Press, 1983) and *The Politics of Knowledge: The Carnegie Corporation, Philanthropy, and Public Policy* (Chicago: University of Chicago Press, 1992).

▲ Methods and Analysis

As many institutional researchers know, a comprehensive institutional analysis is difficult, if not impossible. I was mindful of William Stubbs's remarks:

> The History of Institutions cannot be mastered,—can scarcely be approached,—without an effort. It affords little of the romantic incident or of the picturesque grouping which constitute the charm of History in general, and holds out small temptation to the mind that requires to be tempted to the study of Truth. But it has a deep value and an abiding interest to those who have courage to work upon it.

It presents, in every branch, a regularly developed series of causes
and consequences, and abounds in examples of that continuity of
life, the realization of which is necessary to give the reader a personal
hold on the past and a right judgment of the present. For the roots
of the present lie deep in the past, and nothing in the past is dead to
the man who would learn how the present comes to be what it is.
(*The Constitutional History of England* (1874), 1:v)

To analyze the data, I used a grounded theory approach common to institutional theory that iterated between the primary data, secondary sources,
and extant sociological and organizational theory. I began my analysis by
looking at how business education, business schools, and the relevant business
context for business schools (e.g., the nature of the corporation, intermediaries trying to shape business schools, the composition of the faculty, the
composition of the students) changed over time. Next, working inductively,
I generated propositions that sought to examine whether that variation could
be accounted for by extant theory. The weaknesses of this methodological approach are, of course, well known. For example, in contrast to projects that
begin with large sample studies and extant theories, and then test a series of
hypotheses deductively generated from existing theory on the data set, this approach does not test hypotheses. Instead, it indicates a general direction for
the formation of testable propositions and hypotheses.

The strength of this approach is its emphasis on contingency and speci-
ficity in place of broad, general theory. A qualitative approach rarely invokes a
singular social force as the catalyst for change—the material conditions of society or the "invisible hand," for example. Another potential criticism is that
the speeches and public communications I relied upon did not reflect the true
views of business school leaders. They were instead deceptive forms of impression management meant to fool the public. In response to this concern,
I sought to complement any public communication with *private* communications, such as the correspondence between deans and internal reports and
notes. Second, even if these individuals were engaged in impression management, the fact that they felt a need to link business education to broader societal concerns is an important indicator of the prevailing beliefs of the time
and the importance of social legitimacy, points that are central to my argument as to how new institutions are successfully formed.

Because much of the information I used was historical, fine-grained, and
qualitative, I relied heavily on the sociological method of *Verstehen* (social

understanding) in interpreting the data. This analytical approach is rooted in the methods and procedures laid out by Max Weber, one of the founders of modern sociology. Weber argues that the interpretative method should be utilized in the endeavor to understand the development of new social institutions and their evolution. This method requires the researcher to identify with the relevant social actor (individual or group) and the motives of this actor. It typically involves two steps. The first step is "observational understanding," which involves gathering the relevant facts and establishing their sequence. The second step—which distinguishes this approach from historical research—is "explanatory understanding."

Explanatory understanding asks the researcher to view the world through the actors' eyes rather than his or her own. The objective is to discover why actors followed a certain path of conduct by reconstructing the situational choices and constraints present at the time. The scholar, Weber argues, is capable of putting him- or herself in the shoes of social actors, particularly when that scholar has paid attention to the context within which the actors made their choices. As Weber pithily put it, "one need not have been Caesar in order to understand Caesar." We can understand the actions of Caesar or any other social actor by seeing them as the working out of a series of problems linked to a set of motivations and ideas.

It is important to underscore that *Verstehen* is not an alternative to positivism but rather an attempt to balance out mechanistic observations of action with a theory of action. Conduct, to repeat, is not a function of a single overriding force, like Marx's "material conditions of a society" or Adam Smith's "invisible hand." Instead it emerges out of the intersection of numerous social forces and interests, including power, status, economics, beliefs, and legitimacy. Thus the method requires researchers to understand the alternative lines of conduct confronted by actors, how particular choices were weighed and deliberated, and why one approach was selected over another. The researcher achieves explanatory understanding by placing the observed action in an intelligible sequence of motivations, which can be treated as an explanation for the behavior.

Sociologists and organizational theorists favor this approach to understanding institutions over the "materialist determination" approach. The latter is common to economic analyses and routinely emphasizes efficiency as the primary catalyst to institutional development and change. In contrast, the Weberian approach argues that the future is wide open. History, in other words, has not already been written. *Verstehen*, sociologists have contended, is what distinguishes the institutional approach of sociology from other disciplines. It is a method that seeks to clothe the bare facts with the flesh and blood of social significance, interpretation, and meaning.

Finally, I'd like to note that many of the ideas that inform my analysis and many of the arguments I make are not original to me but emanate from concepts developed in the sociology of institutions (both classical and new institutional theory) and the sociology of professions. From classical institutional theory, I followed the research approaches of Alvin Gouldner, Robert Merton, and Philip Selznick to describe the pragmatic aspects of constructing a new organization; new institutional theory as reconceptualized by Paul DiMaggio, Frank Dobbin, Mauro Guillén, John Meyer, Walter Powell, Haygreeva Rao, and Richard Scott provides most of the specific concepts I use to describe the relationship between external organizations and a focal organization; the professions literature, especially the work of Andrew Abbott, Eliot Freidson, Magali Larson, and Paul Starr, guides my understanding of the creation and evolution of professional boundaries; and the economic sociology of Roberto Fernandez, Kieran Healy, Marion Fourcade-Gourinchas, Charles Perrow, Jeff Pfeffer, Joel Podolny, Martin Ruef, Richard Swedberg, Ezra Zuckerman, and Viviana Zelizer is the source of ideas about the relationship between economics and the other social sciences.

Notes

Introduction

1. C. Wright Mills, *White Collar: The American Middle Classes* (New York: Oxford University Press, 1951).

2. Gordon Donaldson, *Corporate Restructuring: Managing the Change Process from Within* (Boston: Harvard Business School Press, 1994).

3. Rakesh Khurana, *Searching for a Corporate Savior: The Irrational Quest for Charismatic CEOs* (Princeton, NJ: Princeton University Press, 2002), 61–67.

4. Michael Jensen, "The Modern Industrial Revolution, Exit, and the Failure of Internal Control Systems," *Journal of Finance* 48, no. 3 (1993).

5. The U.S. government reports that in 2004 the top three master's degrees granted were in education (162,345), business (139,347), and health professions and clinical sciences (44,939); see U.S. National Center for Education, Statistical Abstracts. The number of chief executives with MBAs at the NYSE-listed companies is more than 33 percent; Aron A. Gottesman and Matthew R. Morey, *Does a Better Education Make for Better Managers? An Empirical Examination of CEO Educational Quality and Firm Performance* (SSRN, 2006). Moreover, the MBA degree has been exported and is now one of the fastest-growing graduate degrees around the world; Hyeyoung Moon, "The Worldwide Diffusion of Business Schools, 1881–1999: The Historical Trajectory and Mechanism of Expansion," University of Washington, Working Paper, 2004.

6. There has been a spate of recent criticisms from inside business schools about MBA education, which I will discuss in part 3.

7. C. P. Biddle, "Eighth Annual Meeting of the AACSB" (Eighth Annual Meeting of the AACSB, Hanover, NH, 1926).

8. Heather Haveman and Hayagreeva Rao describe this blending of the structures of institutions with one another as a coevolutionary process; Heather A. Haveman and Hayagreeva Rao, "Structuring a Theory of Moral Sentiments: Institutional and Organizational Coevolution in the Early Thrift Industry," *American Journal of Sociology* 102, no. 6 (1997); Heather Haveman and Hayagreeva Rao, "Hybrid Forms and the Evolution of Thrifts," *American Behavioral Scientist* 49, no. 7 (2006).

9. Derek Curtis Bok, *The Cost of Talent: How Executives and Professionals Are Paid and How It Affects America* (New York: Free Press 1993); Derek Curtis Bok, *Universities in the Marketplace: The Commercialization of Higher Education* (Princeton, NJ: Princeton University Press, 2003); Robert A. Nisbet, *The Degradation of the Academic Dogma*, Foundations of Higher Education (New Brunswick, NJ: Transaction, 1997); Bill Readings, *The University in Ruins* (Cambridge: Harvard University Press, 1996); Steven Shapin, "University-Industry Relations: Getting Perspective" (Boston Colloquium for Philosophy of Science, Boston University, November 3, 2005).

10. Haveman and Rao, "Structuring a Theory of Moral Sentiments"; Haveman and Rao, "Hybrid Forms and the Evolution of Thrifts."

11. Magali Sarfatti Larson, *The Rise of Professionalism: A Sociological Analysis* (Berkeley and Los Angeles: University of California Press, 1977).

12. Robert K. Merton, "Bureaucratic Structure and Personality," *Social Forces* 18, no. 4 (1940); Talcott Parsons, "The Professions and Social Structure," *Social Forces* 17, no. 4 (1939).

13. Kevin T. Leicht and Mary L. Fennell, *Professional Work: A Sociological Approach* (Malden, MA: Blackwell Publishers, 2001).

14. Harold L. Wilensky, "The Professionalization of Everyone?" *American Journal of Sociology* 70, no. 2 (1964): 138.

15. William J. Goode, "Community within a Community: The Professions: Psychology, Sociology and Medicine," *American Sociological Review* 25 (1957); Wilensky, "The Professionalization of Everyone?"

16. Wilensky, "The Professionalization of Everyone?" 138.

17. Professional training, for example, was seen not as a matter of offering meaningful skills or knowledge but as largely a disingenuous credentialing and persuasion process aimed at defrauding "the potential public or publics and the political authorities." Professional associations, which functionalists interpreted as means of ensuring the quality of a profession's members, were viewed as mechanisms for insulating professionals from public scrutiny and preserving their privileges. "If professions obtain extended powers of self-evaluation and self-control they can become almost immune to external regulation." Larson, *The Rise of Professionalism*, xii.

18. Randall Collins, *The Credential Society: An Historical Sociology of Education and Stratification* (New York: Academic Press, 1979); Larson, *The Rise of Professionalism.*

19. The traditional "high" professions of law and medicine, for example, both lay claim to a codified body of knowledge. The study of law in America today remains rooted in the centuries-old traditions of Roman and Anglo-American law as systematized and interpreted by the discipline of legal philosophy or jurisprudence. Law students now learn "the law" not as a collection of statutes but rather as a set of principles, doctrines, and rules that have evolved over the course of centuries and are said to constitute legal reasoning itself. The study of medicine, for its part, has been continually transformed since the Middle Ages by the rise and ongoing progress of

modern science, with the development of the germ theory of disease in the nineteenth century, for example, and of the science of genetics in the twentieth having gone into the formation of a theoretical structure that undergirds the body of knowledge every medical student is now required to master. The medical school curriculum proceeds from the premise that in order to diagnose and treat disease, the would-be physician must have a firm grounding in what science (or, perhaps more accurately, what is generally accepted as science) currently understands to be its causes. While the validity of this knowledge shifts and changes over time, Andrew Abbott notes that the need to lay claim to some body of abstract knowledge is key: "what matters is abstraction effective enough to compete in a particular historical and social context, not abstraction relative to some supposed absolute standard." Andrew Delano Abbott, *The System of Professions: An Essay on the Division of Expert Labor* (Chicago: University of Chicago Press, 1988), 9.

20. "Professional autonomy allows the experts to select almost at will the inputs they will receive from the laity. Their autonomy thus tends to insulate them: in part, professionals live within ideologies of their own creation, which they present to the outside as the most valid definitions of specific spheres of society." Larson, *The Rise of Professionalism*, xiii.

21. The contrast between the functionalist approach with which sociologists like Larson take issue and the approach taken by Larson herself is an example of two lines of thought in sociological explanations of social hierarchies. One of these calls attention to differences in the functional importance of individuals in different parts of a hierarchy. In this functional theory of stratification, those roles that are most important to society as a whole are ranked higher than those that are of lesser importance. A second perspective emphasizes variations in the power of individuals in different structural positions in a society. The functionalist perspective tends to emphasize the needs of society and to link them to positions in hierarchical status. The power position tends to emphasize the position and an ability to command economic rents.

Each of these two views has its own strengths and weaknesses. The functionalist approach tends to recognize that skills vary among different people, but underestimates the role of structural inhibitors to mobility, such as race, gender, or class. In contrast, the power approach overestimates the power of groups to coordinate and exercise closure over access to certain positions. Neither is easily reconciled with the other. The limitations of these two points of view are apparent when one tries to use them to interpret the rise of the MBA to the status of a quasi-professional degree. The functionalist approach would ascribe this rise to the growing importance of business skills to society. A power theorist would cite the MBA's value as a credential as evidence of the monopolistic tendencies of the managerial "profession." Both approaches illuminate important aspects of the phenomenon, but neither does justice to the overlapping area in which social needs and private interests are blended or reconciled.

22. Everett C. Hughes, "Professions," in *The Professions in America*, ed. Kenneth S. Lynn (Boston: Houghton Mifflin, 1963).

23. Eliot Freidson, *Professionalism: The Third Logic* (Chicago: University of Chicago Press, 2001). Also see n. 12 in this chapter.

24. Arthur L. Stinchcombe, *Constructing Social Theories* (Chicago: University of Chicago Press, 1987).

25. Walter W. Powell and Paul J. DiMaggio, eds., *The New Institutionalism in Organizational Analysis* (Chicago: University of Chicago Press, 1983), 16–20.

26. For a review of the key works on institutions in economics, political science, and sociology, see Mary C. Brinton and Victor Nee, *The New Institutionalism in Sociology* (Stanford: Stanford University Press, 2001); Powell and DiMaggio, *The New Institutionalism in Organizational Analysis*; W. Richard Scott, *Institutions and Organizations*, Foundations for Organizational Science (Thousand Oaks, CA: Sage, 1995).

27. Scott, *Institutions and Organizations*, 33.

28. Roger Friedland and Robert R. Alford, "Bringing Society Back In: Symbols, Practices, and Institutional Contradictions," in *The New Institutionalism in Organizational Analysis*, ed. Walter W. Powell and Paul J. DiMaggio (Chicago: University of Chicago Press, 1983), 248, 251.

29. R. Horn, "An Overview of Trialectics within an Application of Psychology and Public Policy," in *Trialectics: Toward a Practical Logic of Unity*, ed. R. Horn (Lexington, MA: Information Resources, 1983), 1.

30. Mary Douglas, *How Institutions Think*, The Frank W. Abrams Lectures (Syracuse, NY: Syracuse University Press, 1986).

31. Friedland and Alford, "Bringing Society Back In," 250–251. In their study of the publishing industry, Patricia Thornton and William Ocasio show how the functional background of publishing executives shifted as the industry moved away from an editorial logic to a market logic; Patricia H. Thornton and William Ocasio, "Institutional Logics and the Historical Contingency of Power in Organizations: Executive Succession in the Higher Education Publishing Industry, 1958–1990," *American Journal of Sociology* 105 (1999). For an elaboration of this phenomenon in medicine, see W. Richard Scott, *Institutional Change and Healthcare Organizations: From Professional Dominance to Managed Care* (Chicago: University of Chicago Press, 2000).

32. Talcott Parsons, *Structure and Process in Modern Societies* (Glencoe, IL: Free Press, 1960), 175.

33. John Dowling and Jeffrey Pfeffer, "Organizational Legitimacy: Social Values and Organizational Behavior," *Pacific Sociological Review* 18, no. 1 (1975): 122.

34. Powell and DiMaggio, *The New Institutionalism in Organizational Analysis*.

35. Paul Starr, *The Social Transformation of American Medicine* (New York: Basic Books, 1982).

36. Paul DiMaggio and Walter W. Powell, "Institutional Isomorphism and Collective Rationality," in *The New Institutionalism in Organizational Analysis*, ed. Walter W. Powell and Paul DiMaggio (Chicago: University of Chicago Press, 1991).

37. The institutionalization of a new organizational form, particularly such a significant one as the university-based business school, requires ongoing efforts to articulate what Paul DiMaggio calls the organization's "public theory." Specifically, organizations of an innovative type need to put forth legitimate reasons as to why they should exist, why they should be given access to scarce resources, and what distinct benefits they will be capable of providing that are not already being provided by existing types of organizations. In the absence of such plausible claims to legitimacy, an organization will be unstable and its practices will be continually called into question. Paul J. DiMaggio, "Interest and Agency in Institutional Theory," in *Institutional Patterns and Organizations: Culture and Environment*, ed. Lynne G. Zucker (Cambridge, MA: Ballinger Publishing, 1988).

38. Quoted in Peter L. Berger, *A Rumor of Angels: Modern Society and the Rediscovery of the Supernatural* (Garden City, NY: Doubleday, 1970), 53.

39. Philip Selznick, *Leadership in Administration: A Sociological Interpretation* (Evanston, IL: Row Peterson, 1957), 17.

40. Abbott, *The System of Professions*, 59.

41. Starr, *The Social Transformation of American Medicine*.

42. An important recent exception is Scott, *Institutional Change and Healthcare Organizations: From Professional Dominance to Managed Care*.

43. By the same token, I believe that the explanation for the renewed interest in institutions in recent times is not just academic, but may partly be caused by our current age of great economic and social change. My hypothesis is that when the failings of existing institutions are more visible than usual, people start paying attention to those institutions. Social change makes existing institutions less taken for granted because the customary meanings attached to them and their taken-for-granted nature no longer seem beyond question.

44. Robert H. Wiebe, *The Search for Order, 1877–1920* (New York: Hill and Wang, 1967).

Chapter 1
An Occupation in Search of Legitimacy

1. Bureau of the Census (1938); Burton J. Bledstein, *The Culture of Professionalism: The Middle Class and the Development of Higher Education in America* (New York: Norton, 1976), 37.

2. Edward D. Jones, "Some Propositions concerning University Instruction in Business Administration," *Journal of Political Economy* 21, no. 3 (1913): 187.

3. James H. S. Bossard and James F. Dewhurst, *University Education for Business: A Study of Existing Needs and Practices* (Philadelphia: University of Pennsylvania Press, 1931), 30–32.

4. Adolf A. Berle and G. Means, *The Modern Corporation and Private Property* (New York: Macmillan Press, 1932).

5. The subject of the emergence of the large corporations has been studied extensively. There are essentially two accounts. The first is the economic efficiency account represented by Alfred D. Chandler, Jr., *The Visible Hand: The Managerial Revolution in American Business* (Cambridge: Harvard University Press, Belknap Press, 1977). Chandler's thesis focuses on the role of communication and transportation technologies in creating national markets, and posits that the administrative coordination of the firm was more efficient than the market in serving these markets. Ronald Coase argued that firms arise as a consequence of the high cost of relying on markets for certain kinds of transactions. Oliver Williamson elaborates on this argument in his work on transaction-cost economics describing the scope of conditions under which a transaction would be more likely to take place within a firm than in a market. (For Coase's and Williamson's work, respectively, see Ronald H. Coase, "The New Institutional Economics," *Journal of Institutional and Theoretical Economics* 140 [1984], and Oliver E. Williamson, *Markets and Hierarchies* [New York: Free Press, 1975].)

The second dominant account of the rise of the large corporation is found in institutional accounts in sociology and organizational behavior that challenge the fundamental idea of large corporate efficiency. Writers with this perspective emphasize the high level of variation in size of firms that characterizes similar industries across different countries. This group also underscores the role of the legal, political, and social contingencies that created conditions either favorable or unfavorable to the growth of large corporations. The classic work in this area is Neil Fligstein, *The Transformation of Corporate Control* (Cambridge: Harvard University Press, 1990).

6. Chandler, *The Visible Hand*, 1.

7. Ibid., 7.

8. Berle and Means, *The Modern Corporation and Private Property*.

9. Frank Dobbin, "The Sociological View of the Economy," in *The New Economic Sociology: A Reader*, ed. Frank Dobbin (Princeton, NJ: Princeton University Press, 2004), 11.

10. Fligstein, *The Transformation of Corporate Control*; Mauro F. Guillén, *Models of Management: Work, Authority, and Organization in a Comparative Perspective* (Chicago: University of Chicago Press, 1994); Roland Marchand, *Creating the Corporate Soul: The Rise of Public Relations and Corporate Imagery in American Big Business* (Berkeley and Los Angeles: University of California Press, 1998); Mark J. Roe, *Strong Managers, Weak Owners: The Political Roots of American Corporate Finance* (Princeton, NJ: Princeton University Press, 1994).

11. John W. Meyer and Brian Rowan, "Institutionalized Organizations: Formal Structure as Myth and Ceremony," *American Journal of Sociology* 83, no. 2 (1977).

12. Mark Granovetter, "Economic Action and Social Structure: The Problem of Embeddedness," *American Journal of Sociology* 91, no. 3 (1985).

13. For an excellent review of this literature, see the introductory chapter of Frank Dobbin, *The New Economic Sociology: A Reader* (Princeton, NJ: Princeton University Press, 2004).

14. Meyer and Rowan, "Institutionalized Organizations."

15. After the public education system began to take shape in 1860, America rapidly evolved into a more literate society. By 1880, approximately 90 percent of whites were literate. Between 1870 and 1900, the overall illiteracy rate dropped from 20 percent of the nation to 10.7 percent (figures compiled by the U.S. Bureau of the Census and given in *The World Almanac,* 1955). Figures before the Civil War are not available, but there was a steady increase in the number of pupils attending public elementary and secondary schools in the United States. The Morrill Land Grant Act of 1862 marked the start of one of the most powerful trends affecting the social landscape: the broad availability of higher education. This law, which reconceptualized the relationship between government and education, made higher education accessible to a significant percentage of society while also helping to shift it away from a primarily religious orientation to a more scientific and practical one. See chapter 2, p. 75.

16. This was not just a matter of organizations' requiring individuals capable of performing particular tasks. Indeed, some scholars have argued that the retention of written records and files and the subsequent carrying out of activities through explicit, written forms of communication represent some of the defining characteristics of any modern corporation. Whereas oral communication is, by its very nature, imbued with mutual acknowledgment and affect, written communications allow for abstraction and impersonality. In addition, because written instructions are not restricted to face-to-face interaction, a literate managerial workforce is less constrained by the limits of time and space. Written instructions and communications can thus knit together dispersed localities to create national markets. The modern emphasis on written communication, written instructions, and numerical competence then enables individuals to regard the complex activities of firms and people as abstract and impersonal systems of cause and effect.

17. Richard S. Tedlow, Courtney Purrington, and Kim Eric Bettcher, "The American CEO in the Twentieth Century: Demography and Career Path," HBS Working Paper, no. 03-097, 2003. Tedlow and his coauthors argue that even within business history there is a clear trend away from considering the role of individual agents in the development of corporations.

18. Paul J. DiMaggio, "Interest and Agency in Institutional Theory," in *Institutional Patterns and Organizations: Culture and Environment,* ed. Lynne G. Zucker (Cambridge, MA: Ballinger Publishing, 1988). See especially pp. 14 and 15 regarding institutional entrepreneurs and the creation of institutions.

19. Alvin W. Gouldner, *Patterns of Industrial Bureaucracy* (Glencoe, IL: Free Press, 1954), 237, as cited in DiMaggio, "Interest and Agency in Institutional Theory," 12.

20. Guillén, *Models of Management*.

21. For an example of previous work from this same point of view, see Yehouda Shenhav, *Manufacturing Rationality: The Engineering Foundations of the Managerial Revolution* (New York: Oxford University Press, 2001). Note especially the introduction, which argues that the efficiency account is not sufficient to explain the rise of management. A predecessor to this ideological tradition is Reinhard Bendix, *Work and Authority in Industry: Managerial Ideologies in the Course of Industrialization* (New Brunswick, NJ: Transaction, 2001, orig. publ. 1956).

22. Roe, *Strong Managers, Weak Owners*.

23. Ibid., also Mark S. Mizruchi, "What Do Interlocks Do? An Analysis, Critique, and Assessment of Research on Interlocking Directorates," *Annual Review of Sociology* 22 (1996); Charles Perrow, *Organizing America: Wealth, Power, and the Origins of Corporate Capitalism* (Princeton, NJ: Princeton University Press, 2002). Management would be the ultimate victor in the legal battle against shareholders when Progressive reformers argued that through effective, professional administration, a more just and peaceful society could be created, run by a group of experts with strong technical knowledge. The tide fully turned in favor of managers during the 1930s, when New Deal administrators sought to repair the corporate economy through further regulation by creating a large administrative state, thus giving management the potent structural autonomy vis-à-vis owners that it enjoyed until the shareholder rights movement that arose during the 1980s; see Roe, *Strong Managers, Weak Owners*.

24. Fligstein, *The Transformation of Corporate Control*.

25. William G. Roy, *Socializing Capital: The Rise of the Large Industrial Corporation in America* (Princeton, NJ: Princeton University Press, 1997). That large corporations were not necessarily efficient would seem to have been known at the time—for example, Olivier Zunz discusses Louis Brandeis's successful argument before the Interstate Commerce Commission in 1910 against rate increases for railroads, an instance in which, Zunz says, "Brandeis showed that the corporations' claim to efficiency was unsubstantiated." Olivier Zunz, *Making America Corporate, 1870–1920* (Chicago: University of Chicago Press, 1990), 34–36.

26. Perrow, *Organizing America*.

27. Ibid., 47.

28. Yehouda Shenhav, "From Chaos to Systems: The Engineering Foundations of Organization Theory, 1879–1932," *Administrative Science Quarterly* 40, no. 4 (1995).

29. Scholars who describe engineers as the original prototypes for managers, include Guillén, *Models of Management*; John M. Jordan, *Machine-Age Ideology: Social Engineering and American Liberalism, 1911–1939* (Chapel Hill: University of North Carolina Press, 1994); Shenhav, "From Chaos to Systems." Martin Ruef has shown that early management texts also cited slave overseers manuals in the industrialized

North. Martin Ruef, "The Myth of Modern Management: Agrarian Origins of Administrative Theory," Princeton University, Department of Sociology, Working Paper, 2007.

30. For a description of the labor system and job structures in the nineteenth century steel industry, see Katherine Stone, "The Origins of Job Structures in the Steel Industry," in *Labor Market Segmentation: Papers from Conference on Labor Market Segmentation at Harvard University, 1973*, ed. Richard Edwards, Michael Reich, and David M. Gordon (Lexington, MA: D. C. Heath, 1975). C. Wright Mills wrote: "Of all occupational strata, in fact, none has been so grievously affected by the rationalization of equipment and organization as the industrial foreman. With the coming of the big industry, the foreman's functions have been diminished from above by the new technical and human agents and dictates of higher management." C. Wright Mills, *White Collar: The American Middle Classes* (New York: Oxford University Press, 1951), 87.

31. Sudhir Kakar, *Frederick Taylor: A Study in Personality and Innovation* (Cambridge: MIT Press, 1970).

32. Guillén, *Models of Management*. See also Bendix, *Work and Authority in Industry*. Bendix describes how management turned Taylorism into a means of subordinating workers even though Taylor himself might not have intended such an outcome.

33. Shenhav, "From Chaos to Systems," 566–567.

34. See David Montgomery, *Workers' Control in America: Studies in the History of Work, Technology, and Labor Struggles* (Cambridge: Cambridge University Press, 1979). For a discussion of the breakdown of social order that accompanies rapid economic growth, see Mancur Olson, Jr., "Rapid Growth as a Destabilizing Force," *Journal of Economic History* 23, no. 4 (1963).

35. Guillén, *Models of Management*, 39.

36. For example, see Zunz, *Making America Corporate*, 61–64. He discusses how, in the wake of the violent railroad strikes that occurred in 1877, middle managers in the railroads were conflated with owners, and consequently vilified, by increasing numbers of the middle class, and how being "embattled" in this way helped managers form a collective identity.

37. Populists, who were more closely aligned with nativism and xenophobic impulses, blamed factors like immigration and socialist ideology for the labor strife, and chastised business for encouraging massive immigration into the country.

38. Roe, *Strong Managers, Weak Owners*.

39. Marchand, *Creating the Corporate Soul*.

40. Max Weber, *The Protestant Ethic and the Spirit of Capitalism*, trans. Talcott Parsons (London: Allen & Unwin, 1930; reprint, with foreword by R. H. Tawney).

41. C. Wright Mills, *The Power Elite* (New York: Oxford University Press, 1967).

42. James Samuel Coleman, *The Asymmetric Society*, The Frank W. Abrams Lectures (Syracuse, NY: Syracuse University Press, 1982).

43. Mills, *White Collar*, 108–111.

44. Richard Hofstadter, *The Age of Reform: From Bryan to F.D.R.* (New York: Knopf, 1955).

45. Charles Perrow, *Complex Organizations: A Critical Essay*, 2d ed. (Glenview, IL: Scott Foresman, 1979).

46. See Christopher Lasch, *The Revolt of the Elites and the Betrayal of Democracy* (New York: W. W. Norton, 1996), 81–82.

47. Jordan, *Machine-Age Ideology*.

48. Henry Adams, *The Education of Henry Adams* (New York: The Modern Library, 1931; reprint, with introduction by James Truslow Adams), 500.

49. Quotation from Charles W. Eliot in *American Contributions to Civilization* (1907), cited by Hofstadter, *The Age of Reform*, 231 n. 5.

50. Walter Lippmann, *Drift and Mastery: An Attempt to Diagnose the Current Unrest*, A Spectrum Book: Classics in History Series (Englewood Cliffs, NJ: Prentice-Hall, 1961; reprint, with introduction and notes by William E. Leuchtenberg), 23–24.

51. Marchand, *Creating the Corporate Soul*.

52. Ibid., 9.

53. Hofstadter, *The Age of Reform*, 227.

54. Marchand, *Creating the Corporate Soul*, 2–3. He writes: "At question was not primarily their legal legitimacy. Although antitrust and litigation abounded, the legal form of the corporation had stood unchallenged for decades. . . . [T]he crisis of legitimacy that major American corporations began to face in the 1890s had everything to do with their size, with the startling disparities of scale."

55. Roe, *Strong Managers, Weak Owners*; Roy, *Socializing Capital*. Sheldon Wolin accurately summarizes the basic intellectual consensus regarding the role of the corporation and the emerging role for managers: "Whatever differences there were in diagnosis and prescription, most of the major writers were agreed on the general formula—*organization*: organization *of a socialist commonwealth* where competition and private ownership of the instruments of production were abolished and work was administered along more rational lines; organization of society *into a vast hierarchy of authority* where . . . king and pope, assisted by a public-spirited aristocracy, would reinstitute stability and peace . . .; organization of society *on the basis of professional and producing groups*, as Durkheim suggested: or, as many recent writers have urged, organization of society *under the control of managerial elites* who alone possessed the requisite knowledge for maintaining social equilibrium in an age of successive technological revolutions. The primacy assumed by the idea of organization was not the achievement of any one school, but of many. Each of us, as members of societies dominated by organized units, is part socialist, part reactionary, part managerialist, part sociologist. Organizational man is a composite." Sheldon S. Wolin, *Politics and Vision: Continuity and Innovation in Western Political Thought*, expanded ed. (Princeton, NJ: Princeton University Press, 2004), 327 (emphases added).

56. An increased rate of incorporations under "general law" as opposed to "special acts" of the legislature was the result of a series of Supreme Court rulings (beginning with its landmark decision in *Dartmouth College v. Woodward* in 1819) that found that corporations of all sorts possessed rights as private entities, so that state legislatures could not easily revoke their charters. As a result, legislatures began to loosen their restrictions on what corporations could do. For example, in 1830, the Massachusetts legislature eliminated the requirement that a corporation be engaged in public works to be given the status of limited liability. Connecticut did the same in 1837. By 1850, many states were competing with one another to define corporate rights as broadly as possible, with New Jersey and Ohio (where Standard Oil exerted significant influence) offering some of the most liberal terms.

57. On the legal origins of the doctrine of corporate personhood, see Coleman, *The Asymmetric Society*, 37–77. On the race to strengthen the hands of managers versus owners among states, see Roe, *Strong Managers, Weak Owners*, 163–167.

58. Herbert David Croly, *The Promise of American Life* (New York: Macmillan Company, 1910); Louis D. Brandeis, *Business: A Profession*, 2d ed. (Boston: Hale, Cushman, and Flint, 1933, orig. publ. 1914).

59. Robert H. Wiebe, *The Search for Order, 1877–1920* (New York: Hill and Wang, 1967), 165–166.

60. Progressives expected more from government as well. They looked to government to provide greater protection for the public against economic tyranny and unscrupulous corporations, and to dispense with political machines. See Jordan, *Machine-Age Ideology*.

61. Hofstadter, *The Age of Reform*, 215.

62. Lippmann, *Drift and Mastery*, 42–43.

63. See Zunz, *Making America Corporate*, 59–61. Zunz argues that "managers who were responsible for implementing bureaucratic structures in the United States were also profit-conscious businessmen whose concerns reflected the dual imperative of order and gain."

64. Marchand, *Creating the Corporate Soul*.

65. Lynne G. Zucker, "Production of Trust: Institutional Sources of Economic Structure, 1840–1920," in *Research in Organizational Behavior*, vol. 8, ed. Barry Staw and L. L. Cummings (Greenwich, CT: JAI Press, 1986), 53–111.

66. Guillén, *Models of Management*.

67. Chandler, *The Visible Hand*.

68. The self-help ideology that had granted some legitimation to robber barons and other "self-made" men, by invoking rugged individualism and character as the means toward success, was of little help to managers whose positions were not based on romantic notions of entrepreneurship, on having put their own capital at risk, or on deep knowledge of the work itself.

69. Andrew Delano Abbott, *The System of Professions: An Essay on the Division of Expert Labor* (Chicago: University of Chicago Press, 1988).

70. Magali Sarfatti Larson, *The Rise of Professionalism: A Sociological Analysis* (Berkeley and Los Angeles: University of California Press, 1977).

71. Zunz, *Making America Corporate*, 61 and 64. In his treatment of railroad managers as the "first executives," Zunz says that "drawing the line between management and labor," as these managers did in effectively siding with owners against labor, was one way for contemporaries to "identify the new managerial class," and that opposition from workers and the middle class alike to the antilabor views of many early managers "reinforced their sense that they belonged to a new class."

72. The 1890 census, which was the first to examine the distribution of U.S. income, found that 71 percent of the nation's wealth was controlled by just 9 percent of its families.

73. Hofstadter, *The Age of Reform*, 136.

74. Exact estimates are difficult to obtain, but some rough comparisons are available. The typical factory worker earned roughly $700 annually in 1910; by the 1920s, workers were earning approximately $1,200 per year. These wages were identified in relation to the first income tax laws, which were passed in 1909. The tax was 1 percent on incomes over $2,500 (by 1913 the base jumped to $3,000 for single tax filers and $4,000 for married couples), and it impacted about 1 percent of the U.S. population (roughly 500,000 individuals); see Steven R. Weisman, *The Great Tax Wars: Lincoln to Wilson. The Fierce Battles over Money and Power That Transformed the Nation* (New York: Simon & Schuster, 2002). We do have some anecdotal evidence of CEO pay; for instance, the CEO of Coca-Cola, Robert Woodruff, was offered $36,000 when he took over the company in 1923, roughly thirty times average manufacturing salaries during that time.

75. Ida M. Tarbell, *Owen D. Young, a New Type of Industrial Leader* (New York: Macmillan, 1932).

76. Lippmann, *Drift and Mastery*, 35.

77. DiMaggio, "Interest and Agency in Institutional Theory," 14.

78. E. Digby Baltzell, *Puritan Boston and Quaker Philadelphia: Two Protestant Ethics and the Spirit of Class Authority and Leadership* (New York: Free Press, 1979); E. Digby Baltzell, *The Protestant Establishment: Aristocracy and Caste in America* (New Haven: Yale University Press, 1987).

79. "The economic and social transformations of the late nineteenth century, however, threatened their position, and catalyzed the establishment elites," sociologist Jerome Karabel writes, to try to create a new set of unifying institutions that "bridged the cultural and social divide among the old patricians and the nouveaux riches of the Gilded Age." Their bridging activities, carried out mostly in the late nineteenth and early twentieth centuries, included expanding the reach of boarding schools, developing identifiable social groupings like the *Social Register* to include the best of

the new rich, intermarriage between the old patrician families and the "new men," and opening the institutions of higher education to the sons of this new group. Jerome Karabel, *The Chosen: The Hidden History of Admission and Exclusion at Harvard, Yale, and Princeton* (Boston: Houghton Mifflin, 2005), 24–25.

80. Hofstadter, *The Age of Reform*. See chapter 4, "The Status Revolution and Progressive Leaders," particularly the sections titled "The Plutocracy and the Mugwump Type" and "The Alienation of the Professionals" (131–164). Elsewhere, Hofstadter wrote of the displaced patrician class of this period: "Wherever men of cultivation looked, they found themselves facing hostile forces and an alien mentality. They resented the new plutocracy which overshadowed them in business and in public affairs—a plutocracy they considered as dangerous socially as it was personally vulgar and ostentatious; for it consisted of those tycoons about whom Charles Francis Adams, Jr., said that after years of association he had not met one that he would ever care to meet again, or one that could be 'associated in my mind with the idea of humor, thought or refinement.'" Richard Hofstadter, *Anti-Intellectualism in American Life* (New York: Knopf, 1963), 176.

81. Hofstadter, *Anti-Intellectualism in American Life*, 245. See pp. 244–249 for Hofstadter's whole discussion of this social type.

82. Samuel Eliot Morison, *One Boy's Boston, 1887–1901* (Boston: Houghton Mifflin, 1962), 68. This passage was called to my attention by Jeffrey L. Cruikshank, *A Delicate Experiment: The Harvard Business School, 1908–1945* (Boston: Harvard Business School Press, 1987). The historian Peter Dobkin Hall explains the significance of the Boston elite described by Morison for forms of Progressive social change in the nation at large when he notes that "although Boston would be eclipsed by New York as the nation's financial center, the pattern it set for elite philanthropy would not only profoundly affect the wealth in other metropolitan areas, but would lead to the creation of a new national elite based on educational and professional credentials. This 'new middle class' of experts, serving in corporations; in government; and institutions of culture, health care, and social welfare would lead the nation into the twentieth century." Peter Dobkin Hall, "What the Merchants Did with Their Money: Charitable and Testamentary Trusts in Massachusetts, 1780–1880," in *Entrepreneurs: The Boston Business Community, 1700–1850*, ed. Conrad Edick Wright and Katheryn P. Viens (Boston: Massachusetts Historical Society, distributed by Northeastern University Press, 1997), 414.

83. Carter Daniel writes: "Although some prominent alumni had urged the establishment of studies in business areas . . . Harvard's revered president, Charles W. Eliot, was not enthusiastic about the idea. . . . Even as late as 1905, in the thirty-sixth year of his presidency, he was holding the line by arguing that the object of education should be not to teach students how to earn a living but to show them how to live happy and worthwhile lives inspired by ideals that exalt both labor and pleasure." Carter A. Daniel, *MBA: The First Century* (Lewisburg, PA: Bucknell University Press, 1998), 39.

84. Cruikshank, *A Delicate Experiment.* The "overlap" can be seen in the increased correlation between higher education and corporate leadership over the course of the twentieth century. For a review of the paths to corporate power over the twentieth century, see Anthony J. Mayo, Nitin Nohria, and Laura G. Singleton, *Paths to Power: How Insiders and Outsiders Shaped American Business Leadership* (Boston: Harvard Business School Press, 2006).

85. Wallace B. Donham, "The Social Significance of Business," reprinted from the *Harvard Business Review* (July 1927), in the printed document *Dedication Addresses*, HBS Archives, CAC 1927 17.1. 24.

86. Wayne G. Broehl, *Tuck and Tucker: The Origin of the Graduate Business School* (Hanover: University Press of New England, 1999).

87. Daniel A. Wren, "American Business Philanthropy and Higher Education in the Nineteenth Century," *Business History Review* 57, no. 3 (1983).

88. Ibid., 343.

89. Max Weber, *The Theory of Social and Economic Organization,* ed. Talcott Parsons, trans. A. M. Henderson (New York: Free Press, 1964; reprint, with introduction by Talcott Parsons, orig. publ. 1947), 115.

90. Ibid.

91. Ibid.

92. Edward Shils, "Charisma, Order, and Status," *American Sociological Review* 30, no. 2 (1965).

93. Richard H. Brown, "Bureaucracy as Praxis: Toward a Phenomenology of Formal Organizations," *Administrative Science Quarterly* 23 (1979), 375. Brown begins this article on the social construction of bureaucracy by quoting Kafka's *Great Wall of China*: "Leopards break into the temple and drink the sacrificial chalices dry; this occurs repeatedly, again and again; finally it can be reckoned on beforehand and becomes part of the ceremony."

94. James N. Baron and William T. Bielby, "Bringing the Firms Back In: Stratification, Segmentation, and the Organization of Work," *American Sociological Review* 45, no. 5 (1980); Otis Dudley Duncan, "Social Origins of Salaried and Self-Employed Professional Workers," *Social Forces* 44, no. 2 (1965).

Chapter 2
Ideas of Order: Science, the Professions, and the University
in Late Nineteenth-Century America

1. Robert H. Wiebe, *The Search for Order, 1877–1920* (New York: Hill and Wang, 1967), 12.

2. By the end of World War II, the United States would overtake Germany, which until then had been the undisputed leader in the sciences. See Joseph Ben-David, *The Scientist's Role in Society: A Comparative Study,* Foundations of Modern Sociology (Englewood Cliffs, NJ: Prentice-Hall, 1971).

3. John Cotton, "A Briefe Exposition . . . Upon . . . Ecclesiastes," in *The Puritans*, ed. Perry Miller and Thomas H. Johnson (New York: Harper Torchbooks, 1963), 731. See pp. 729–738 in Miller and Johnson for an overview of the attitudes toward science and the variety of scientific activities in seventeenth-century New England.

4. Joseph Ben-David and Gad Freudenthal, *Scientific Growth: Essays on the Social Organization and Ethos of Science* (Berkeley and Los Angeles: University of California Press, 1991), 125–147. Ben-David suggests that although science enjoyed state sponsorship in France (for purposes strictly limited by the government) in the eighteenth century, "bureaucratic, organized" scientific activity cannot be said to have really begun before 1825, when it started to take shape in Germany.

5. Hofstadter lists several such proposals Adams made during his first annual message to Congress in 1825, and which show him to have been ahead of his times in many ways: "a national university at Washington, a professional naval academy, a national observatory, a voyage of discovery to the Northwest to follow upon the expedition of Lewis and Clark, an efficient patent office, federal aid to the sciences through a new executive department." (The U.S. Naval Observatory would be founded as the Depot of Charts and Instruments in 1830; the U.S. Naval Academy would be established in 1845; and American University would be chartered by Congress in 1893.) Adams was also, Hofstadter observes, "the last nineteenth-century occupant of the White House who had a knowledgeable sympathy with the aims and aspirations of science." See Richard Hofstadter, *Anti-Intellectualism in American Life* (New York: Knopf, 1963), 157–158.

6. Simon Newcomb, "Abstract Science in America, 1776–1876," *North American Review* 122, no. 250 (1876): 91. The observation here on attitudes toward science in the Jacksonian period is made by Paul Starr, *The Social Transformation of American Medicine* (New York: Basic Books, 1982), 140.

7. Newcomb, "Abstract Science in America, 1776–1876," 103.

8. Ben-David, *The Scientist's Role in Society*, 171.

9. Newcomb, "Abstract Science in America, 1776–1876," 122. Newcomb contrasted this reality with the attitude that he found prevalent among the nation's government officials when he wrote, "The fact that there are any operations, the conduct of which requires special skill and special training, is one which our administrators generally are very slow to recognize, unless compelled by the force of circumstances" (ibid., 103).

10. See Ben-David, *The Scientist's Role in Society*, 142–143.

11. John Dewey, *Freedom and Culture* (New York: Putnam, 1939), 153; and "Authority and Social Change" (1936), reprinted in *The Philosophy of John Dewey*, ed. Joseph Ratner (New York: Random House, 1939), 352. Quoted in Sheldon S. Wolin, *Politics and Vision: Continuity and Innovation in Western Political Thought*, expanded ed. (Princeton, NJ: Princeton University Press, 2004), 510.

12. Ben-David, *The Scientist's Role in Society*; Thomas L. Haskell, *The Emergence of Professional Social Science: The American Social Science Association and the Nineteenth-Century Crisis of Authority* (Urbana: University of Illinois Press, 1977); John M. Jordan,

Machine-Age Ideology: Social Engineering and American Liberalism, 1911–1939 (Chapel Hill: University of North Carolina Press, 1994).

13. Steven Shapin, *The Scientific Revolution* (Chicago: University of Chicago Press, 1996), 124.

14. Karl Marx and Friedrich Engels, *The Communist Manifesto* (Harmondsworth, England: Penguin Books, 1985), 85.

15. Marion Cecile Fourcade-Gourinchas, "The National Trajectories of Economic Knowledge: Discipline and Profession in the United States, Great Britain and France" (Ph.D. diss., Harvard University, 2000).

16. Ben-David, *The Scientist's Role in Society*, 142–143.

17. Starr, *The Social Transformation of American Medicine*, 19. Starr argues that the growing prestige of science and technology generally benefited the field of medicine even before medicine itself had much to show for it: "Technological change was revolutionizing daily life; it seemed entirely plausible to believe that science would do the same for healing, and eventually it did . . . once people began to regard science as a superior and legitimately complex way of explaining . . . reality, they wanted physicians' interpretations . . . regardless of whether the doctors had remedies to offer."

18. Ibid. For example, the New York Department of Health developed a renowned laboratory and staffed it with researchers who were able to develop and successfully administer practices for quarantining devastating water-borne illnesses and other highly communicable diseases. Public health departments around the country soon imitated New York's practices for managing sewage and collecting health and disease statistics, and worked alongside civil engineers to improve water treatment so as to increase life expectancy and reduce infant mortality rates.

19. Yehouda Shenhav, "From Chaos to Systems: The Engineering Foundations of Organization Theory, 1879–1932," *Administrative Science Quarterly* 40, no. 4 (1995).

20. As quoted in Jordan, *Machine-Age Ideology*, 76.

21. Steven Shapin has written about the differences (and similarities) between science as a knowledge-making activity strongly influenced by the norms of gentlemanly society (in early modern England) for creating collective knowledge and the more rationalized, bureaucratized ways of generating and disseminating such knowledge more familiar to sociologists of science today. See Shapin, *A Social History of Truth* (Chicago: University of Chicago Press, 1994).

22. Between 1910 and 1925, the various Carnegie foundations and the Rockefeller Foundation made "scholarly influences" and "scientific research" preconditions for their awarding of grants relating to public problems such as public health, poverty, and elementary education; see Ellen Condliffe Lagemann, *The Politics of Knowledge: The Carnegie Corporation, Philanthropy, and Public Policy* (Chicago: University of Chicago Press, 1989).

23. For an excellent review of this early history, see Haskell, *The Emergence of Professional Social Science*. Haskell's rich history describes the origins of the predecessor organizations for the major associations in political science, economics, sociology, and

history. For an outstanding examination of the emergence of the modern economics profession and the debates surrounding it, see Michael A. Bernstein, *A Perilous Progress: Economists and Public Purpose in Twentieth-Century America* (Princeton, NJ: Princeton University Press, 2001).

24. The prototype for the enlistment of social science in the tasks of legislation and public policy making was created in Wisconsin in the Progressive era with the development of the "Wisconsin idea," a term that encompasses both the ideal of public service articulated and implemented at the University of Wisconsin—under the leadership of academics and administrators including Richard Ely, Frederick Jackson Turner, John R. Commons, Edward A. Ross, and Charles Van Hise (president of the university from 1903 to 1918)—and many of the governmental reforms instituted by Robert LaFollette during his term as governor (1901–1906). See Hofstadter, *Anti-Intellectualism in American Life*, 199–204.

25. The term *political science* itself can be traced to Thomas Hobbes, who argued that the study of politics should be undertaken not as a branch of philosophy but, rather, as a branch of the natural sciences.

26. Jesse Macy, "The Scientific Spirit in Politics," *American Political Science Review* 11, no. 1 (1917) 13–4.

27. G. Stanley Hall, "Mental Science," *Science* 20, no. 511 (1904): 481.

28. G. Stanley Hall, "The Unity of Mental Science," in *Congress of Arts and Sciences, Universal Exposition*, vol. 5, ed. Howard J. Rogers (St. Louis: 1906), 578.

29. Julie A. Reuben, *The Making of the Modern University: Intellectual Transformation and the Marginalization of Morality* (Chicago: University of Chicago Press, 1996), 5–6.

30. Ibid., 11, 138.

31. The sociologists Robert K. Merton and Joseph Ben-David have separately documented that this ethos represents a secularized version of early Protestant thinking that by gaining knowledge of the natural world one could gain "a fuller appreciation of [God's] works" and "ascend to a grasp of the essence of the world" (Robert K. Merton, "Puritanism, Pietism, and Science," in *Social Theory and Social Structure* [New York: Free Press, 1968], 634). Because God did not fully reveal Nature's truths in religious texts, the practitioners of science believed, the truth could be uncovered not through philosophical introspection but only through active engagement with the empirical world (Ben-David, *The Scientist's Role in Society*). "In the systems of scientific thought . . . the testimony of experiment is the ultimate criterion of truth, but the very notion of experiment is ruled out without the prior assumption that Nature constitutes an intelligible order, so that when appropriate questions are asked, she will answer, so to speak" (Merton, "Puritanism, Pietism, and Science," 636). Edward Shills has, in turn, noted, institutions that link themselves to what are viewed as the central elements of society, connected to ultimate reality, achieve a sacred status that commands deference; see Edward Shils, "Charisma, Order, and Status," *American Sociological Review* 30, no. 2 (1965).

32. Haskell, *The Emergence of Professional Social Science*, 44–45.

33. Ibid., 47.

34. Edward Shils, "The Order of Learning in the United States: The Ascendancy of the University," in *The Organization of Knowledge in Modern America, 1860–1920*, ed. Alexandra Oleson and John Voss (Baltimore: Johns Hopkins University Press, 1979), 35.

35. Dorothy Ross, "The Development of the Social Sciences," in *The Organization of Knowledge in Modern America, 1860–1920*, ed. Alexandra Oleson and John Voss (Baltimore: Johns Hopkins University Press, 1979), 115.

36. Haskell, *The Emergence of Professional Social Science*, 175, 179. Ross also describes the quasi-prophetic role in which American social scientists of the 1870s and 1880s cast themselves: "The men . . . who sought to develop in the colleges a more worldly and effective kind of knowledge were particularly sensitive to the need for intelligent leadership and social order. Like many of their contemporaries in various fields, . . . the social scientists thought of themselves as members of a social and cultural elite who represented the dominant line of American development; as the heirs of the republican tradition, they sought to assume the moral authority befitting their station. Generally the sons of native Protestant families, they had been taught in college that they constituted an elite of learning and virtue whose leadership American society should follow. They regarded themselves, often quite explicitly, as a natural aristocracy generated by and in some ways identified with the 'people,' but yet a class apart. In the general social crisis, the authority of their class was seen as synonymous with intellectual order in the society at large—the assertion of the one being a guarantee of the other" (Ross, "The Development of the Social Sciences," 112). The idea of an "elite of learning and virtue" evokes not only Thomas Jefferson's idea of a "natural aristocracy" in America but also the late nineteenth-century model for the traditional professions of the clergy, medicine, and law—an ideal to which, as we shall see, many of the emerging professions of the era aspired or claimed to aspire.

37. A. W. Small, "The Era of Sociology," *American Journal of Sociology* 1, no. 1 (1895): 15.

38. Albert E. Moyer, *A Scientist's Voice in American Culture: Simon Newcomb and the Rhetoric of Scientific Method* (Berkeley and Los Angeles: University of California Press, 1992), 208.

39. Ross, "The Development of the Social Sciences," 117.

40. Ellen Condliffe Lagemann, *Private Power for the Public Good: A History of the Carnegie Foundation for the Advancement of Teaching* (Middletown, CT: Wesleyan University Press, 1983), 34–35.

41. David A. Hollinger, "The Problem of Pragmatism in American History," *Journal of American History* 67 (1980): 99–100. As quoted in Moyer, *A Scientist's Voice in American Culture*, 209.

42. Robert K. Merton, "Science and the Social Order," in *Social Theory and Social Structure* (New York: Free Press, 1968).

43. John W. Meyer, "Ontology and Rationalization in the Western Cultural Account," in *Institutional Environments and Organizations*, ed. W. Richard Scott and John W. Meyer (Thousand Oaks, CA: Sage, 1994), 46.

44. There is a strong parallel here with what Steven Shapin says about science in seventeenth-century England, where knowing whose testimony to trust—and basing decisions about that on where a person stood in the social hierarchy and how interested or disinterested he could therefore be presumed to be—were key to the creation of reliable scientific knowledge (Shapin, *A Social History of Truth*). Moreover, Shapin argues, science remains an activity based more than most modern observers realize on interpersonal as opposed to institutionalized forms of trust, which is another way of saying that it remains a community-based activity, not a bureaucratic, totally rationalized one. This organizational structure also links scientists with professionals generally in terms of how they order their activities.

45. Again, American science in this period can be seen to have replicated a phenomenon familiar from the rise of science itself in early modern Europe. Ben-David, for example, links the "reverence" for Baconian science widely extant in seventeenth-century England (and the support for it that "became part of the official policy of the Commonwealth") with the extreme contentiousness surrounding questions of religion and politics during the English Civil War: "empirical science," he notes, was seen as a route not only "to innovation, but also to social peace, as it made possible agreement concerning research procedures to specific problems without requiring agreement about anything else." See Ben-David, *The Scientist's Role in Society*, 72–73.

46. Ben-David and Freudenthal, *Scientific Growth*, 357.

47. Edward Shils, "The Intellectuals and the Powers: Some Perspectives for Comparative Analysis," *Comparative Studies in Society and History* 1, no. 1 (1958).

48. Reuben, *The Making of the Modern University*, 138. As Reuben also notes, faith in the inherently moral nature of science and the beneficial nature of its products would be shattered in the trenches of World War I, after which the idea of "value-free science" began to gain ground in university circles. Like the concept of science as an intrinsically moral activity, this notion would eventually have an impact on the development of professional education in general and business education in particular—although, as we shall see in part 2 of the book, with a significant time lag.

49. Ben-David and Freudenthal, *Scientific Growth*, 143–145.

50. Some of the occupations that claimed professional status, but with little in the way of demonstrable efficacy, included education, social work, and urban and town planning. See Eliot Freidson, *Professional Dominance: The Social Structure of Medical Care* (Chicago: Aldine Publishing, 1970). Paul Starr's description of colonial-age medicine makes a similar observation.

51. Starr, *The Social Transformation of American Medicine*, 140.

52. Hofstadter, *Anti-Intellectualism in American Life*, 155–156.

53. The first medical school was established by the University of Pennsylvania in 1765; then King's College (later Columbia University) in 1767; then Harvard University in 1783; and Dartmouth College in 1797.

54. Abraham Flexner, *Medical Education in the United States and Canada* (New York: Carnegie Foundation for the Advancement of Teaching, 1910), 6.

55. Ibid., 7.

56. James Willard Hurst, *The Growth of American Law: The Law Makers* (Boston: Little, Brown, 1950).

57. Starr, *The Social Transformation of American Medicine*, 56–59. Starr describes the rapid rescinding of licensure laws in the United States in the early nineteenth century. Politicians saw licensure as an example of monopoly rather than a signal of competence, a framing that would be reversed in the Progressive era.

58. Wiebe, *The Search for Order*, 13–14.

59. Morris Janowitz, *The Professional Soldier, a Social and Political Portrait* (Glencoe, IL: Free Press, 1960).

60. In examining changing attitudes toward professionalism, one must be careful not to overstate the contrast between the Jacksonian and Progressive eras. Both periods saw sustained and powerful attacks on concentrated economic power amid increasing corporate and bureaucratic organization. Yet whereas the Jacksonians tended to equate business monopolies with professional ones, Progressives were more apt to see professional monopolies (like the complexity and relative inaccessibility of expert knowledge) as inevitable.

61. The decrease in numbers of medical schools between 1899 and 1909 was also partly caused by the American Medical Association's establishment of the Council on Medical Education in 1904, which quietly began to grade medical school quality.

62. Hurst, *The Growth of American Law*. Hurst summarizes the diffusion of licensing requirements across the states in the late nineteenth and early twentieth centuries. During the 1890s, various states adopted teacher licensing requirements and set up teachers colleges within their state university systems.

63. Starr, *The Social Transformation of American Medicine*, 134–135.

64. Andrew Delano Abbott, *The System of Professions: An Essay on the Division of Expert Labor* (Chicago: University of Chicago Press, 1988).

65. Donald C. Brodie and Frederick H. Meyers, "Role of the Pharmacist as Drug Consultant," *American Journal of Hospital Pharmacy* 18 (1961); Don E. Francke, "The Expanding Role of the Hospital Pharmacist in Drug Information Services," *American Journal of Hospital Pharmacy* 22 (1965).

66. Abraham Flexner, "Is Social Work a Profession?" *Research on Social Work Practice* 11, no. 2 (2001): 156. (The article reprints a 1915 conference presentation by Flexner.)

67. Jordan, *Machine-Age Ideology*, 34.

68. Hamilton assumed that merchants, landowners, and professionals would constitute the governing classes of the new American society. In *The Federalist*, No. 35, he outlined the interests that each of these classes could be expected to represent in the national legislature. Merchants, he suggested, were "the natural representatives" of artisans and manufacturers; while since the "landed interest" comprised everyone "from the wealthiest landlord to the poorest tenant," landowners of any degree of wealth could adequately represent the interests of all other proprietors. Yet the "learned professions," in Hamilton's view, were unique, for "they truly form no distinct interest in society; and according to their situation and talents will be indiscriminately the objects of confidence and choice of each other and of other parts of the community. . . . Will not the man of the learned profession, who will feel a neutrality to the rivalships between the different branches of industry, be likely to prove an impartial arbiter between them, ready to promote either, so far as it shall appear to him conducive to the general interests of the society?" See Alexander Hamilton, "The Federalist, No. 35—the Same Subject Continued (Concerning the General Power of Taxation)," in *The Federalist*, ed. J. R. Pole (Indianapolis: Hackett Publishing, 2005), 184–185.

Thomas Jefferson—who undertook to elevate the legal profession in Virginia when, shortly after his election as governor in 1779, he persuaded the Board of Visitors of the College of William and Mary to make that institution "the first college in America to offer a formal course of study in law"—embraced a vision of lawyers as "public citizens," defined by one scholar of legal education as "those who would place public interest ahead of private interest and exercise leadership in preserving republicanism." See Davison M. Douglas, "The Jeffersonian Vision of Legal Education," *Journal of Legal Education* 51, no. 2 (2001): 197, 193. Douglas's article contains valuable background on the history of university legal education and the intellectual and civic values promulgated by Jefferson and others in contrast to the trade-school approach of most of the proprietary law schools—a tension, Douglas argues, that significantly influenced the direction that legal education took in the nineteenth century and that lies behind debates about the state of legal education and of the legal profession still raging today.

69. This is the view of Progressivism favored by Hofstadter, in contrast to Wiebe's emphasis on order and efficiency as Progressive virtues. See, for example, the introduction in Richard Hofstadter, *The Age of Reform: From Bryan to F.D.R.* (New York: Knopf, 1955), 3–22.

70. Wilfred M. McClay, "Croly's Progressive America," *Public Interest*, no. 137 (1999): 62–63.

71. For examples of such descriptions of professions, see Eliot Freidson, *Professionalism: The Third Logic* (Chicago: University of Chicago Press, 2001); Magali Sarfatti Larson, *The Rise of Professionalism: A Sociological Analysis* (Berkeley and Los Angeles: University of California Press, 1977); Talcott Parsons, "The Professions and Social Structure," *Social Forces* 17, no. 4 (1939).

72. Whatever idealizations may be inherent in this portrait of who professionals are and what they do—an issue of some importance in the sociology of professions—it was, and remains, efficacious for established and aspiring professions to present themselves in this light for the sake of establishing their legitimacy because of what sociologists of the professions have recognized as particular features of the relationship between the professional or "expert" and his or her client. Magali Larson astutely recognized that because what the professional offers the client is intangible (often referred to as a "soft commodity") and not amenable to standardization—and perhaps even more because of the asymmetry between the client's knowledge and that of the professional—the relationship between professional and client requires a high level of trust on the part of the latter. For variations of this argument, see Parsons, "The Professions and Social Structure"; Lynne G. Zucker, "Production of Trust: Institutional Sources of Economic Structure, 1840–1920," in *Research in Organizational Behavior*, ed. Barry Staw and L. L. Cummings (Greenwich, CT: JAI Press, 1986), 8.

73. For an extensive discussion of nonembedded, institutionalized forms of trust, see Susan P. Shapiro, "The Social Control of Impersonal Trust," *American Journal of Sociology* 93, no. 3 (1987). Shapiro draws her starting point from Mark Granovetter, "Economic Action and Social Structure: The Problem of Embeddedness," *American Journal of Sociology* 91, no. 3 (1985).

74. Shils, "Charisma, Order, and Status."

75. Richard Hofstadter and C. De Witt Hardy, *The Development and Scope of Higher Education in the United States* (New York: Columbia University Press for the Commission on Financing Higher Education, 1952); Richard Hofstadter and Walter P. Metzger, *The Development of Academic Freedom in the United States* (New York: Columbia University Press, 1955).

76. Samuel Eliot Morison, *The Founding of Harvard College* (Cambridge: Harvard University Press, 1935), 434.

77. Burton J. Bledstein, *The Culture of Professionalism: The Middle Class and the Development of Higher Education in America* (New York: Norton, 1976), 269.

78. These figures, it should be noted, include only institutions that have survived into the present day; one study has found that 516 colleges had been established in the United States before the Civil War. See Hofstadter and Metzger, *The Development of Academic Freedom in the United States*, 211.

79. http://www.usma.edu/bicentennial/history/ (accessed November 18, 2003).

80. John Rae, "The Application of Science to Industry," in *The Organization of Knowledge in Modern America, 1860–1920*, ed. Alexandra Oleson and John Voss (Baltimore: Johns Hopkins University Press, 1979), 251–252.

81. J. B. Edmond, *The Magnificent Charter: The Origin and Role of the Morrill Land-Grant Colleges and Universities* (Hicksville, NY: Exposition Press, 1978).

82. On the influence of the German research university on the creation of its American counterpart, see Alexandra Oleson and John Voss, eds., *The Organization of*

Knowledge in Modern America, 1860–1920 (Baltimore: Johns Hopkins University Press, 1979), x–xiv. See also Hofstadter and Metzger, *The Development of Academic Freedom in the United States*; Laurence R. Veysey, *The Emergence of the American University* (Chicago: University of Chicago Press, 1965).

83. Roger L. Geiger, *To Advance Knowledge: The Growth of American Research Universities, 1900–1940* (New York: Oxford University Press, 1986); Daniel A. Wren, "American Business Philanthropy and Higher Education in the Nineteenth Century," *Business History Review* 57, no. 3 (1983).

84. Hofstadter, *Anti-Intellectualism in American Life*, 199–200.

85. Veysey, *The Emergence of the American University*.

86. Edward Shils and Philip G. Altbach, *The Order of Learning: Essays on the Contemporary University* (New Brunswick, N.J.: Transaction, 1997), 37.

87. Ibid.

88. Shils, "The Order of Learning," 7–8.

89. "The Doctor's Dissertation: Selection of Subject, Preparation, Acceptance, Publication," *AAU Journal* 9 (1908): [50, 54] cited in Hugh Hawkins, "University Identity: The Teaching and Research Functions," in *The Organization of Knowledge in Modern America, 1860–1920*, ed. Alexandra Oleson and John Voss (Baltimore: Johns Hopkins University Press, 1979), 295.

90. Shils and Altbach, *The Order of Learning*, 17.

91. Hofstadter and Metzger, *The Development of Academic Freedom in the United States*; Thorstein Veblen, *The Higher Learning in America: A Memorandum on the Conduct of Universities by Business Men* (New York: A. M. Kelley, 1965, orig. publ. 1918); Veysey, *The Emergence of the American University*.

92. Shils and Altbach, "The Order of Learning."

93. Ibid.

94. Andrew Delano Abbott, *Department and Discipline: Chicago Sociology at One Hundred* (Chicago: University of Chicago Press, 1999).

95. Shils and Altbach, *The Order of Learning*, 12.

96. William Watts Folwell, *University Addresses* (Minneapolis: H. W. Wilson, 1909), 10–11.

97. Veysey, *The Emergence of the American University*. Veysey suggests that one of the reasons for the growth in enrollments in the modern American university was the concern of the newly emerging middle class for the social status of their children. Amid the highly fluid class structure of late nineteenth-century America, the college degree in business was becoming a distinction that could establish a measure of social distance between the native-born middle class and newly arrived immigrants, like the Eastern European Jews, who were engaging, and succeeding, in commerce.

98. Ben-David, *The Scientist's Role in Society*, 142.

99. Wiebe, *The Search for Order*, 121.

100. Abbott, *The System of Professions*.

101. Larson, *The Rise of Professionalism*; Martin Ruef, "The Construction of a Professional Monopoly: Medical Education in the U.S., 1765–1930," Princeton University, Department of Sociology, Working Paper, 2006.

102. Larson, *The Rise of Professionalism*, 14.

103. Wren, "American Business Philanthropy and Higher Education in the Nineteenth Century."

104. Eliot Freidson, "The Changing Nature of Professional Control," *Annual Review of Sociology* 10 (1984); Everett C. Hughes, "Institutional Office and the Person," *American Journal of Sociology* 43, no. 3 (1937).

105. Medical schools, for example, demonstrated that a professional school could assist in rehabilitating a profession by carefully screening aspiring applicants. See Starr, *The Social Transformation of American Medicine*, 224, 360.

Chapter 3
The Invention of the University-Based Business School

1. Benjamin Rudolph Haynes and Harry P. Jackson, *A History of Business Education in the United States* (Cincinnati: Southwestern Pub. Co., 1935), 126.

2. Max Weber suggested that "standardized practices," such as those made possible by written communication, were integral to the administration of large enterprises. For Joseph Schumpeter, it was accounting that "turns the unit of money into a tool of rational cost-profit calculations, of which the towering monument is double-entry bookkeeping." Joseph Alois Schumpeter, *Capitalism, Socialism, and Democracy* (New York: Harper & Brothers, 1942), 123.

3. Quoted in Carter A. Daniel, *MBA: The First Century* (Lewisburg, PA: Bucknell University Press, 1998), 23.

4. For examples of scholarship treating the antagonism between the university and proprietary business schools as a contest for monopoly privileges, see Paul Starr, *The Social Transformation of American Medicine* (New York: Basic Books, 1982), especially chapter 2. The repression of competing systems of management education by the proponents of the university business school, although it actually occurred, was only a minor and relatively unsuccessful means of advancing the legitimation of management by casting it as a profession.

5. This idea of cultural authority is most closely captured in Starr, *The Social Transformation of American Medicine*.

6. See Reinhard Bendix, *Work and Authority in Industry: Managerial Ideologies in the Course of Industrialization* (New Brunswick, NJ: Transaction, 2001, orig. publ. 1956); Yehouda Shenhav, "From Chaos to Systems: The Engineering Foundations of Organization Theory, 1879–1932," *Administrative Science Quarterly* 40, no. 4 (1995).

7. Mauro F. Guillén, *Models of Management: Work, Authority, and Organization in a Comparative Perspective* (Chicago: University of Chicago Press, 1994). Also see

Samuel Haber, *Efficiency and Uplift: Scientific Management in the Progressive Era, 1890–1920* (Chicago: University of Chicago Press, 1964). Haber shows that Taylorism's emphasis on efficiency provided a key element of the new corporate capitalist ideology as presented by Progressive business managers. He argues that the core notion of efficiency appealed to the public mind. "It incorporated, at once, the personal virtues of the Puritan ethic in terms of hard and disciplined work; the belief in the scientific revolution in terms of rational order to improve productivity; and social efficiency with respect to its implementation that would result in a state of social harmony" (59).

8. Guillén, *Models of Management*, 41–45.

9. Frederick W. Taylor, "Testimony to the House of Representatives Committee," in *Organization Theory*, ed. D. S. Pugh (London: Penguin Books, 1912), 158.

10. Max Weber, *Economy and Society*, ed. Guenther Roth and Claus Wittich, trans. Ephraim Fischoff et al., 2 vols. (Berkeley and Los Angeles: University of California Press, 1978), 1:941–948.

11. Quoted in Sudhir Kakar, *Frederick Taylor: A Study in Personality and Innovation* (Cambridge: MIT Press, 1970), 21.

12. Fredrick Winslow Taylor, *The Principles of Scientific Management* (New York: Harper, 1947), 100. Taylor's influence among engineers preceded his national fame. For several years, managers and engineers, among them Dartmouth's Harlow Persons, made pilgrimages to Taylor's Philadelphia estate where he lectured them on the methods and virtues of scientific management. The esteem in which engineers held Taylor reached its apex when the American Society of Mechanical Engineers elected him president in 1905, giving him further influence on the emerging engineering subfield of operations research.

13. Morris L. Cooke, "The Spirit and Social Significance of Scientific Management," *Journal of Political Economy* 21, no. 6 (1913): 493.

14. As quoted in Bendix, *Work and Authority in Industry*, 278.

15. Ibid. Bendix suggests that management turned Taylorism into a means of subordinating workers even though Taylor himself intended no such thing.

16. In his history of the Wharton School, Steven A. Sass discusses the place of science in a set of curricular reforms proposed at the school in the early 1920s by a committee chaired by future Wharton dean Joseph Willits, who championed science and research as core elements of business schools. And yet, as Sass notes, "Wharton's professors of the 1920s had a somewhat different understanding of science from the one we have today. The science that they championed had little regard for deductive theory, hypothesis falsification, or mathematical subtlety; it recognized 'naught save the suzerainty of fact' and emphasized the collection and correlation of data. This definition of science came in part from engineers like Frederick Taylor and his 'scientific' management movement; in part it reflected the stripped-down pragmatism that was then so much in vogue. Coming under these

influences, it is not surprising that science became a search for control, not for knowledge per se." See Sass, *The Pragmatic Imagination* (Philadelphia: University of Pennsylvania Press, 1982), 193–194.

17. Hugo Münsterberg, *Psychology and Industrial Efficiency* (Boston: Mifflin, 1913), 308. The idea about work as "joy," etc., in the context of teaching managers how to manipulate workers sounds very contemporary and has resonance in the recently revived positive psychology movement; see Kim S. Cameron, Jane E. Dutton, and Robert E. Quinn, *Positive Organizational Scholarship: Foundations of a New Discipline* (San Francisco: Berrett-Koehler, 2003).

18. Quoted in Kakar, *Frederick Taylor*, 2.

19. Quoted in ibid., 2.

20. The Sheffield School at Yale emphasized engineering, while Harvard's Lawrence School focused on the basic natural sciences of biology, chemistry, and physics. Schools like MIT and Stevens Institute focused on engineering and emphasized the physical sciences such as physics, astronomy, and chemistry.

21. Edward D. Jones, "Some Propositions concerning University Instruction in Business Administration," *Journal of Political Economy* 21, no. 3 (1913): 190–191.

22. Letter from Edwin Gay to W. E. Rappard, HBS Archives, Dean's files, 1908–1910, June 6, 1909.

23. Quoted in Ray Stannard Baker's "The Gospel of Efficiency," *American Magazine* 71 (1911): 563.

24. Quoted in Daniel, *MBA*, 36.

25. In October 1911, Person and the Tuck School faculty invited Frederick W. Taylor, his disciple Lillian Gilbreth, and three hundred leading industrialists to a conference on scientific management that launched Taylorism as an international movement; see Wayne G. Broehl, *Tuck and Tucker: The Origin of the Graduate Business School* (Hanover: University Press of New England, 1999), 38.

26. Baker Library, Historical Collections Department, Notes: 1900–1909, ADE Box 1 of 2.

27. Ibid.

28. Ibid.

29. Willard E. Hotchkiss, "The Northwestern University School of Commerce," *Journal of Political Economy* 21, no. 3 (1913): 207.

30. Ibid., 208.

31. For a discussion of the competing schools of economics at the time of the founding of the first business schools and of debates about the role of economics in the business school curriculum, see chapter 4, pp. 160–165.

32. Shenhav, "From Chaos to Systems."

33. Eliot Freidson, *Professionalism: The Third Logic* (Chicago: University of Chicago Press, 2001), 18–32.

34. Henry Smith Pritchett, "Is There a Place for a Profession in Commerce?" *Engineering News* 435 (1901). This article was the speech that Pritchett gave to the New England Cotton Manufacturers' Association in Boston, Massachusetts, on April 24, 1901.

35. Senate Committee on Education and Labor, *Report of the Committee of the Senate upon the Relations between Labor and Capital* (1885). Quoted in Daniel, *MBA*.

36. Burton J. Bledstein, *The Culture of Professionalism: The Middle Class and the Development of Higher Education in America* (New York: Norton, 1976).

37. For a more general statement of this argument describing the link between patriarchy and education, see Bernard Bailyn, *Education in the Forming of American Society*, Needs and Opportunities for Study (Chapel Hill: University of North Carolina Press, 1960), 15–20.

38. Ibid., 31.

39. The first attempt to organize a collegiate school of business was by the southern editor, publisher, and statistician James Dunwoody Brownson De Bow (1820–1867), who, after much cajoling, succeeded in having the University of Louisiana incorporate a business school in 1851. The program met with little success and support and closed in 1857. See Haynes and Jackson, *A History of Business Education in the United States*, for a description.

40. Quoted in Sass, *The Pragmatic Imagination*, 21–23.

41. Wharton would appear to have had in mind what Wallace Donham of Harvard Business School would later label the "inferior sons" of genteel families—that is, those disposed to choose business over the "learned" professions of law, medicine, and the clergy—as being in need of the education and character development that would render them better able to conduct themselves in their chosen occupations while accruing further credit for their social class (which was heavily identified with the traditional professions) as a whole.

42. The same concern with the moral condition of America's hereditary industrial aristocracy would be expressed in 1913 by Edward Jones, the dean of the University of Michigan's business school, when he explained the need for the university to begin seeing to the training of business leaders for the nation: "The first generation of great 'captains of industry' in this country was composed of men of exceptional native powers who fought their way upward and gained eminence through a process of survival of the fittest. . . . Since the ranks of these pioneers have begun to be seriously thinned by death, a notable change has been taking place in the character of our industrial leadership. The sons of the pioneers, reared in self-indulgence, do not as a rule show either the ability or the desire to take the places of their fathers as leaders" (Jones, "Some Propositions concerning University Instruction in Business Administration," 187).

43. Sass, *The Pragmatic Imagination*, 29.

44. Ibid., 35.

45. John Freeman and Audia Pino, "The Creation of Local Banks: Social Sponsorship and Embeddedness," University of California-Berkeley, Working Paper, 2005.

46. On James's plans for the Wharton School, and their eventual fate, see chapter 3, "The School of Practical Affairs: The College of Political and Social Science," in Sass, *The Pragmatic Imagination*. After being dismissed from his post by a new Penn provost in 1895, James went on to help establish the University of Chicago's undergraduate School of Commerce and Industry (founded in 1898), where, as we shall see, his idea of business education as a means of bringing about social and economic progress would prove influential.

47. The University of Chicago was one place where, under the influence of Leon Marshall, something like the Wharton approach would be tried, as I relay in chapter 4.

48. Quoted in Daniel, *MBA*, 47.

49. Quoted in Broehl, *Tuck and Tucker*, 36. That the Tuck School did not commit itself to the goal of professionalizing management in the same sense as did most of the other early business schools at the nation's elite universities was in keeping with a deliberate decision made by Dartmouth under the leadership of President William Jewett Tucker (who served from 1893 to 1909) to remain a primarily undergraduate institution in the face of "widening demands" on the college accompanying the rise of the American research university. Dartmouth, at the time of Tucker's accession to the presidency, already had both a medical school (founded in 1797) and a school of engineering (founded in 1867 as a postgraduate institution, the first such in the field in the United States). Yet as Tucker stated in 1893, "Dartmouth College belongs to a group of foundations, now of historic dignity, which have retained the name, and which continue to exercise the functions of the college, in distinction from the school of technology or the university." The solution that Tucker and the Dartmouth trustees settled on as a means of responding to the demand for practical education was to retain the college's existing character and structure while offering a certain amount of supplementary education for students not going into professions—e.g., in the programs of the Tuck School (Broehl, *Tuck and Tucker*, 33).

50. Ibid., 45.

51. Ibid., 42–44. The awarding of master's degrees was not part of the original plan for the Tuck School, although the school began awarding a "Master of Commercial Science" degree after 1902. The school required above-average undergraduate grades for admission to the two-year program, which rested upon a prerequisite of several undergraduate economics courses. An oral exam and a thesis were part of the original requirements for the master's degree.

52. From the Tuck announcement for 1901–1902, quoted in ibid., 44–45.

53. Quoted in ibid., 65.

54. Laurence R. Veysey, *The Emergence of the American University* (Chicago: University of Chicago Press, 1965), 57–120.

55. Baker Library, Historical Collections Department, Notes: 1900–1909, ADE Box 1 of 2. Shortly thereafter, in February 1897, Charles Eliot received a letter from Oscar Ely of Holyoke, Massachusetts, inquiring as to the percentage of Harvard graduates pursuing careers in business. Eliot, guessing, replied, "I have no adequate statistics about the success of our graduates in business. From fifteen to twenty percent of every graduating class go into business, including under the term business is the service of business corporations." He noted in his reply that in his own class of eighty-nine graduates, fifteen men had succeeded "eminently in business"—"a larger proportion of decided success than my classmates obtained in any other calling."

56. Address to the Harvard Club of Connecticut, February 1908, Baker Library, Historical Collections Department, Notes: 1900–1909, ADE Box 1 of 2. Also quoted in Jeffrey L. Cruikshank, *A Delicate Experiment: The Harvard Business School, 1908–1945* (Boston: Harvard Business School Press, 1987).

57. See chapter 1, p. 45.

58. Quoted in Cruikshank, *A Delicate Experiment,* 34.

59. Daniel, *MBA,* 41.

60. Ibid.

61. Eliot G. Mears, "The Teaching of Commerce and Economics," *American Economic Review* 13, no. 4 (1923): 648.

62. Benjamin Baker, "Teaching the Profession of Business at Harvard," Supplement to Official Register of Harvard University, vol. 12, no. 1, pt. 6 (February 27, 1915), pp. 9–10.

63. Quoted in Cruikshank, *A Delicate Experiment,* 44.

64. Wallace B. Donham, "The Social Significance of Business," reprinted from the *Harvard Business Review* (July 1927), in the printed document *Dedication Addresses,* HBS Archives, AC 1927 17.1, p. 24.

65. Ibid., pp. 25, 27.

66. Ibid., pp. 28–29.

67. Donham was clearly aware of the difficulties of the task he was proposing that university business education undertake. In an exchange with Charles W. Eliot in 1922, as he contemplated Harvard Business School's need for physical facilities adequate to the ambitious professionalizing mission it had set for itself, Donham stressed the importance of providing dormitories for HBS students, which he saw as necessary for the kind of professional socialization that schools of law and medicine performed: "I attach much importance to a dormitory or dormitories for men in this School. Without this, particularly with our lack of centralized administrative and teaching space, the faculty feel the great difficulty of developing the professional spirit without which we are hardly justified in having such a school. I am sure you recognize how much harder it is to build up a professional attitude toward business than it is to build

up a knowledge of the ethics and practices of law or medicine." Quoted in Cruikshank, *A Delicate Experiment*, 99.

Both Donham's concern with addressing fundamental social problems and his appeal to the traditional professions as models for the new profession of business were reiterated by another influential business educator of the post–World War I era, Dean Leon C. Marshall of the University of Chicago's business school. The University of Chicago's undergraduate School of Commerce and Industry was founded in 1898. In 1902, the faculty approved a proposal allowing the newly established school to hire its own faculty and administrators. It was not until 1910, after receiving the final gift of $10 million from the university's original benefactor, John D. Rockefeller, that the school became legitimately established. There is some ambiguity about the exact founding date, which might be related to the difference between the approval date and the date of the inaugural class. In his own book, *Business Administration* (Chicago: University of Chicago Press, 1921), Marshall refers to it as the "The School of Commerce and Administration."

Marshall, who assumed the deanship at Chicago in 1909 and served until 1924, led an institution that already bore the imprint of Edmund James, who, after being dismissed as director of the Wharton School in 1895, became the president of Northwestern University and then the University of Illinois, where his geographical proximity to Chicago enabled him to encourage the incorporation of the social sciences into the school's curricular foundations. Marshall, insisting that Chicago's entire business curriculum be grounded in the ideal of "service to society," concentrated on making the school's stock of knowledge in the social sciences available not only for assisting commercial and industrial development but also for helping to solve the most pressing social and political problems of the day. Arguing that any activity undertaken by a university requires a social purpose and a social justification, Marshall invoked the example of professional education in medicine and law: "However important it may be to turn out business men who can make money, social workers who can command good salaries, civic workers who can rise to positions of influence and affluence, the most important task of all is to aid in promoting the progress and welfare of society. Our medical schools are demanded not primarily that physicians may command good fees but that society may be served. Our law schools may aid in making lawyers who will be wealthy, but the mere fact that we impose a bar examination shows that the interest of society, not that of the individual, is dominant" (Leon C. Marshall, "The College of Commerce and Administration of the University of Chicago," *Journal of Political Economy* 21, no. 2 [1913]: 101).

68. It is important to note that Young was not unknown to the Boston business and legal community, who considered him one of their own. Before ascending to the chairmanship of General Electric, Young was a prominent and well-respected lawyer in Boston, where he specialized in public utilities. See Ida M. Tarbell, *Owen D. Young, a New Type of Industrial Leader* (New York: Macmillan, 1932), 91–114.

69. Owen D. Young, "Dedication Addresses," in *Dedication Addresses*, 3.

70. Richard Hofstadter, *Anti-Intellectualism in American Life* (New York: Knopf, 1963), 245. For Hofstadter's whole discussion of this cultural artifact, see pp. 243–252.

71. Young, "Dedication Addresses," 4–5.

72. Ibid., 11–12.

73. Ibid., 12.

74. American Association of Collegiate Schools of Business, "Proceedings of the Ninth Annual Meeting" (Ninth Annual Meeting of the AACSB, Cambridge, MA, May 5, 6, and 7, 1927), 19–22.

75. Thorstein Veblen, *The Higher Learning in America,* 152. Quoted in Cruikshank, *A Delicate Experiment,* 25.

76. John Jay Chapman, "Harvard and Education," *Harvard Graduates' Magazine* 33 (1924). Three years later, presiding over a ceremony held in 1927 to dedicate the Harvard Business School campus that had been built with Baker's gift, Abbott Lawrence Lowell would answer critics like Chapman by elaborating on the parallel between business and the traditional professions:

> Some of our good friends whose prejudices are stronger than their imagination were inclined to say that business could not be made a profession, because the only object of business was money-making, and that money-making could not be made a profession. I do not know with which of their tradesmen they had had difficulty, or what was the cause of this unfortunate feeling, but if it is true that business cannot be made into something of the nature of a profession, if it be true that business is nothing but the selfish pursuit of money-making, then there is only one wise course for the people of this country to pursue, and that is to get the whole group together on the Aquitania and pray for a new flood.
>
> Whatever may have been true of the past there is no doubt at the present time that the business man has a position in the community not unlike that of the lawyer, the doctor, the architect or anyone else. The lawyer has a series of duties. Of course he enters upon his profession to support himself primarily. His main object in work of course is to secure for himself and his family the comforts of life. But no lawyer thinks that his duties end there. He has duties to another set of people called clients, and then again to the courts, and finally to the public.
>
> The quality of a lawyer may be roughly judged by the order in which he arranges those duties in his own mind, and it is the same way with a businessman. The manager of a corporation owes a duty to stockholders corresponding to that which a lawyer owes to his clients; he owes duties to his Board of Directors, to government boards that control his actions, and finally he owes duties to the public. And if we cannot teach businessmen how to manage successfully their own business with due regard to all those various responsibilities we have undertaken a fruitless task; which we have not. ("Dedication of New Buildings under the George F. Baker Foundation for the Graduate School of Business Administration, Harvard University" [June 4, 1927], HBS Archives Collection, AC 1927 17.6, pp. 5–6)

77. Frederick Lewis Allen, *The Big Change: America Transforms Itself, 1900–1950* (New York: Harper, 1952). Quoted by Stanley F. Teele in his foreword to Melvin Thomas Copeland, *And Mark an Era: The Story of the Harvard Business School* (Boston: Little Brown, 1958), viii.

78. Jones, "Some Propositions concerning University Instruction in Business Administration," 195.

79. John Henry Newman, *The Idea of a University* (Notre Dame: University of Notre Dame Press, 1982; reprint, with introduction and notes by Martin Svaglic), 126.

80. Clark Kerr, *The Uses of the University*, 5th ed. (Cambridge: Harvard University Press, 2001), 3, 13–14.

81. Julie A. Reuben, *The Making of the Modern University: Intellectual Transformation and the Marginalization of Morality* (Chicago: University of Chicago Press, 1996), 217. On the new assertiveness on the part of scholars of the humanities in these decades, see pp. 6–7, and chapter 7, "From Truth to Beauty," passim.

82. Sass, *The Pragmatic Imagination*, 66.

83. Andrew Carnegie, *The Empire of Business* (New York: Doubleday Page & Co., 1902), 109–111; quoted in Daniel, *MBA*, 25. On the widespread hostility of businessmen of the era to formal education generally, and liberal education in particular, see Hofstadter, *Anti-Intellectualism in American Life*, 257–260.

84. Quoted in Thurman William Van Metre, *A History of the Graduate School of Business, Columbia University*, The Bicentennial History of Columbia University (New York: Columbia University Press, 1954), 17–18.

85. Ibid., 24.

86. "Butler Lays Stone for New School; Men Prominent in Finance and Commerce Attend Ceremonies at Columbia. Meets Needs of Business. Building Will Cost $1,000,000—355 Students in Institution Last Year, Says Director," *New York Times*, December 19, 1923.

87. Broehl, *Tuck and Tucker*, 42–44.

88. Copeland, *And Mark an Era*, 17.

89. Lawrence Grant White, "Thoughts on the Business School," quoted in Sheridan A. Logan, *George F. Baker and His Bank, 1840–1955: A Double Biography* (St. Joseph, MO: S. A. Logan, 1981), 244. The *Harvard Lampoon* dedicated an entire issue to satirizing the Harvard Business School. Unmoved by declarations of "service," "ethics," etc., the *Lampoon* said the true message of the school was "the world judges a businessman by the money he makes." The issue included a cartoon of Dean Donham posing as Harvard's next president and showed a lion cub named HBS eating Johnny Harvard.

90. For a discussion of the early research programs of key business schools, see chapter 4, pp. 170–176.

91. Quoted in Daniel, *MBA*, 102.

92. Ibid., 103.

93. Marshall, "The College of Commerce and Administration of the University of Chicago," 100.

94. Sass, *The Pragmatic Imagination*, 209.

95. Ibid., 206. Emphasis in original.

96. Ibid., 204.

97. Abraham Flexner, *Medical Education in the United States and Canada* (New York: Carnegie Foundation for the Advancement of Teaching, 1910).

98. Abraham Flexner, *Universities: American, English, German* (New Brunswick, NJ: Transaction, 1994; reprint, with an introduction by Clark Kerr), 164.

99. Ibid., 166.

100. Ibid., 169.

101. Daniel A. Wren, "American Business Philanthropy and Higher Education in the Nineteenth Century," *Business History Review* 57, no. 3 (1983): 321 and 342–343.

102. Charles Austin Beard and Mary Ritter Beard, *The Rise of American Civilization* (New York: Macmillan, 1927), 470.

103. Hubert Park Beck, *Men Who Control Our Universities: The Economic and Social Composition of Governing Boards of Thirty Leading American Universities* (Morningside Heights, NY: King's Crown Press, 1947).

104. Metzger, *Academic Freedom in the Age of the University*, 141.

105. In 1860, nearly 40 percent of the members of the boards of the nation's fifteen largest private colleges were clergymen; by 1930, the number was about 7 percent. See ibid., 78.

106. In 1930, a group made up of prominent East Coast executives, which came to be known as "The Two Hundred Fifty Associates of the Harvard Business School," was formed to bolster the school's shaky finances during the Depression.

107. Metzger, *Academic Freedom in the Age of the University*, 146.

108. Sass, *The Pragmatic Imagination*, 126.

109. Ruggles, who taught Public Utility Management and Regulation at the school, was receiving $15,000 a year—twice his Harvard salary—from the New England Electric Light Association. "I want to know and I believe the people of this State want to know what is the relation between the Harvard Business School and the power interests," a Massachusetts legislator declared ("Ask Bay State Inquiry into Power Financing," *New York Times*, April 23, 1929, 54).

110. Sass, *The Pragmatic Imagination*, 195.

111. John W. Meyer and Brian Rowan, "Institutionalized Organizations: Formal Structure as Myth and Ceremony," *American Journal of Sociology* 83, no. 2 (1977).

112. Tarbell, *Owen D. Young, a New Type of Industrial Leader*, 261.

Chapter 4
"A Very Ill-Defined Institution": The Business School
as Aspiring Professional School

1. Department of Education, "Bulletin, 1929" (Washington, DC: Department of Education, 1929).

2. Unless otherwise noted, the statistics on the number of schools and student enrollment data come from either the United States Statistical Abstracts or James H. S. Bossard and James F. Dewhurst, *University Education for Business: A Study of Existing Needs and Practices* (Philadelphia: University of Pennsylvania Press, 1931).

3. Steven A. Sass, *The Pragmatic Imagination: A History of the Wharton School, 1881–1981* (Philadelphia: University of Pennsylvania Press, 1982), 164.

4. Wallace B. Donham, "The Graduate School of Business Administration, Dean's Report" (Boston: Harvard University, 1929), 135.

5. Willard E. Hotchkiss, "The Northwestern University School of Commerce," *Journal of Political Economy* 21, no. 3 (1913): 201.

6. William A. Scott, "Training for Business at the University of Wisconsin," *Journal of Political Economy* 21, no. 2 (1913); Thurman William Van Metre, *A History of the Graduate School of Business, Columbia University*, The Bicentennial History of Columbia University (New York: Columbia University Press, 1954). A 1928 report by the Bureau of Education found fifty-one colleges and universities offering 384 extension classes in business subjects; see James H. S. Bossard, "University Education for Business: A Survey," *Journal of Business of the University of Chicago* 4, no. 3, pt. 2: Proceedings of the Thirteenth Annual Meeting of the American Association of Collegiate Schools of Business (1931).

7. Mauro F. Guillén, *Models of Management: Work, Authority, and Organization in a Comparative Perspective* (Chicago: University of Chicago Press, 1994), 308.

8. "College Men in Business," *New York Times*, May 4, 1915.

9. Wallace B. Donham, "Annual Report to the President and Fellows of Harvard College" (Cambridge: Graduate School of Business Administration, 1926), 122.

10. Wayne G. Broehl, *Tuck and Tucker: The Origin of the Graduate Business School* (Hanover: University Press of New England, 1999), 74.

11. Bossard and Dewhurst, "University Education for Business."

12. "University Training for Business," *Weekly Review* 2, no. 57 (June 1920).

13. Leon C. Marshall, "A New Objective: A University School of Business" (paper presented at the Tenth Annual Meeting of the AACSB, Chicago, IL, 1928), 8.

14. Willard E. Hotchkiss, "The Basic Elements and Their Proper Balance in the Curriculum of a Collegiate Business School," *Journal of Political Economy* 28, no. 2 (1920): 92.

15. As noted in chapter 3, Tuck was constituted as a 3+2 program in which a student would have to complete a three-year undergraduate program in liberal arts

before being admitted to the master's program. Thus the Tuck program fell midway between Wharton's and Harvard's in terms of its basic academic model.

16. Arthur L. Stinchcombe, "Social Structure and Organizations," in *Handbook of Organizations*, ed. James G. March (Chicago: Rand McNally, 1965).

17. In other professions in America, associations of practitioners played key roles in the formation of university professional schools. The American Society of Mechanical Engineers, for example, used its powerful position as a professional association to encourage business leaders and politicians to fund engineering schools and technical institutes within many colleges and universities.

18. AACSB Notes, HBS Archives, AACSB folder, Box 9. Unless otherwise noted, the primary material about the AACSB comes from the proceedings and summaries of its annual meetings and correspondence among business school deans about the AACSB.

19. Herbert Heaton, *A Scholar in Action, Edwin F. Gay* (Cambridge: Harvard University Press, 1952).

20. "President's Order on NRA," *New York Times*, September 28, 1934. Leon Marshall's work on regulation and industrial relations was of great interest to those individuals crafting the New Deal; see Leon C. Marshall, *Unemployment Relief and Public Works*, The National Crisis Series (New York: Bureau of Publications, Teachers College, Columbia university, 1933); Leon C. Marshall and Mildred J. Wiese, *Modern Business; the Business Man in Society* (New York: Macmillan, 1926).

21. Despite having been elected as chair of the association's executive committee, Gay did not attend the AACSB's first official meeting in 1919. (The 1917 and 1918 meetings of the association were canceled because of World War I.) Harvard's new president, Abbott Lawrence Lowell, had not taken to the independent-minded Gay the way his predecessor Charles Eliot had, and, in 1918, Gay resigned as dean of the business school and left Harvard. He would go on to become one of the great social entrepreneurs of the Progressive era, cofounding (with Wesley Mitchell) the National Bureau of Economic Research, an independent institution for the study of economic policy, and becoming a founding director of the Council on Foreign Relations. In 1919, Harvard President Lowell appointed his former law student, Wallace Donham, who was a trustee of the Boston Railway Company, as the new dean of the Harvard Business School.

Despite his numerous achievements as an institutional entrepreneur outside of academe, Gay would believe for the rest of his life that his decision to leave the academic field of economics to engage with the larger world had been a Faustian bargain that prevented him from realizing his scholarly ambitions. Given the success of Gay's other institutional ventures, the AACSB's subsequent weaknesses could be partly attributed to his absence from the organization after 1918.

22. Beta Gamma Sigma had been established in 1907 at the University of Wisconsin, then became a national organization in 1913 after a merger with similar honor societies that had been founded at the University of Illinois and the University of California. It would appear not to have undertaken any significant activities until tapped by the association in 1919 (see "History of Beta Gamma Sigma," at http://www.betagammasigma.org/history.htm [accessed January 19, 2005]).

23. American Association of Collegiate Schools of Business, "Proceedings of the Eighth Annual Meeting" (Eighth Annual Meeting of the AACSB, Hanover, NH, 1926), 28.

24. See introduction, pp. 4–5.

25. American Association of Collegiate Schools of Business, "Proceedings of the Tenth Annual Meeting" (Tenth Annual Meeting of the AACSB, Chicago, IL, May 3, 4, and 5, 1928), 7.

26. American Association of Collegiate Schools of Business, "Proceedings of the Seventh Annual Meeting" (Seventh Annual Meeting of the AACSB, Columbus, OH, May 7, 8, and 9, 1925), 12.

27. Roswell C. McCrea, "The Place of Economics in the Curriculum of a School of Business" (paper presented at the Seventh Annual Meeting of the AACSB, Columbus, OH, May 7, 8, and 9, 1925).

28. Ibid. Despite McCrea's socially oriented definition of "professional purpose" here, however, Columbia under his leadership would implement a working definition of professionalism in business more akin to that pursued at Wharton in the 1920s, as described in Sass, *The Pragmatic Imagination*, 63–75.

29. American Association of Collegiate Schools of Business, "Proceedings of the Ninth Annual Meeting" (Ninth Annual Meeting of the AACSB, Cambridge, MA, May 5, 6 and 7, 1927), 1.

30. Steven Sass has stated that Harvard Business School, led by Donham, was the only business school in this period to develop a "successful management program," which it did by forging its own path: "Rather than hoping to develop management as a technology, as a procedural science, or to promote the various functional areas as independent specialties, Harvard wanted to cultivate skills of integrated executive judgment, decision, and leadership. . . . Equipped with good family connections, an undergraduate liberal arts education, and a 'Masters [*sic*] of Business Administration' degree, many of Harvard's graduates became 'gentleman' leaders of America's established corporations and financial institutions"(Sass, *The Pragmatic Imagination*, 157).

31. Ibid., 163.

32. Ibid., 187.

33. Ibid., 167.

34. Ibid., 168–169. It is worth noting that Sass himself defines professionalism in the terms adopted by Wharton in this period, describing professionals as specialists

"relying on ideas and expertise rather than corporate office or the ownership of property, as a basis of income and economic authority" (158).

35. On James at Wharton, see ibid., 63–75. Emory Johnson's program at Wharton for the professionalization of management emphasized technical and formal aspects of professionalism—specialized knowledge and certification for practice, respectively—while giving short shrift to the normative and social components of professionalism that figured so prominently in Wallace Donham's vision for Harvard Business School.

36. Ibid., 175. Technical mastery also seemed demonstrably irrelevant to business success, based on a survey of 1,670 Wharton alumni from the classes of 1885 to 1928 that revealed those who had been most successful in business based on "power and income" were also those "who had done most poorly in their work at Wharton"—a finding that opponents of the specialized curriculum tried to use to bolster their case for more of a general business orientation (194–195).

37. On Johnson's introduction of his program of specialization at Wharton and the efforts to roll it back, see ibid., chapter 6 ("Cranking Up the Professional Machine"), passim.

38. Person assumed leadership of the school in 1904, but with the title of "Secretary." President Tucker appointed him dean in 1906; see Broehl, *Tuck and Tucker*, 58.

39. Harlow S. Person, "The Amos Tuck School of Dartmouth College," *Journal of Political Economy* 21, no. 2 (1913): 124.

40. Broehl, *Tuck and Tucker*, 41; Person, "The Amos Tuck School of Dartmouth College," 124.

41. Person, "The Amos Tuck School of Dartmouth College," 124.

42. Ibid., 125.

43. Ibid. This was not an uncommon approach among schools, given that only a handful of them had the prestige of institutions like Harvard to confer on the study of business, while many others had to think about catering to students with a very practical orientation for whom a place like Harvard was probably never on the radar screen. An example is Northwestern, which was scarcely fifty years old as a university when it started its business school, and where the latter started out as an evening school for working people (as did Columbia's and other relatively prestigious ones such as the University of Wisconsin's).

44. Ibid., 126.

45. Ibid.

46. American Association of Collegiate Schools of Business, "Proceedings of the Seventh Annual Meeting," 13.

47. As recalled by C. O. Ruggles during the 1924 AACSB meetings; American Association of Collegiate Schools of Business, "Proceedings of the Sixth Annual Meeting" (Sixth Annual Proceedings of the AACSB, New York, NY, May 1, 2, and 3, 1924), 11.

48. These same books were also identified by Carter Daniel using an unidentified approach; see Carter A. Daniel, *MBA: The First Century* (Lewisburg, PA: Bucknell University Press, 1998).

49. Ibid.

50. Jeffrey L. Cruikshank, *A Delicate Experiment: The Harvard Business School, 1908–1945* (Boston: Harvard Business School Press, 1987), 76. While the case method would eventually become a defining characteristic of a Harvard Business School education, the idea that the case method could be seamlessly transferred from the law school was greeted with some skepticism by critics like Abraham Flexner, who wrote: "Faced suddenly with the problem of training for business a thousand students—graduate students—the School had to manufacture a literature. Texts and reference books existed in the field of economics, which was, of course, already cultivated on the campus of the University. But the School of Business had to do something that was not already being done by the economists and statisticians of the University—some of whom it lured into the new adventure—or by an ordinary school of accounting. The head of the institution had an inspiration. The great [Harvard Law School Dean Christopher Columbus] Langdell had conceived the idea of using case books for instruction in law; why not case books in business? Of the fact that the case book in law had developed unexpected shortcomings from the University point of view he was perhaps not cognizant; anyway the Harvard Graduate School of Business has in short order ground out a series of case books in business." Abraham Flexner, *Universities: American, English, German* (New Brunswick, NJ: Transaction, 1994; reprint, with an introduction by Clark Kerr), 168–169.

51. Ford Foundation, University of Chicago file, File No. 58-140, p. 6.

52. Marshall saw society as consisting of three groups: the business group (i.e., business executives), the civic group (i.e., government administrators, university personnel), and the charitable/philanthropic group (i.e., foundations). After completing the required curriculum, students would specialize in the study of one of these fundamental groups. Marshall wrote that the student who graduated from this program "should go out with some idea of social needs, with some zeal for serving those needs, with some appreciation of the rights, the privileges, and the obligations of the other members of society, and with some training to enable him to be of real usefulness. . . . In brief, the college assumes that, at the last analysis, its justification must be a social justification" (Leon C. Marshall, "The College of Commerce and Administration of the University of Chicago," *Journal of Political Economy* 21, no. 2 [1913]: 101). Unfortunately, Marshall's experiment would be short-lived: Robert Maynard Hutchins, who became president of the University of Chicago in 1929 (a year after Marshall's departure from the deanship), made no attempt to hide his disdain for business education and gave little support, financial or otherwise, to the business school.

53. American Association of Collegiate Schools of Business, *The American Association of Collegiate Schools of Business, 1916–1966* (Homewood, IL: R. D. Irwin, 1966), 2.

54. Person's model and responses to it are discussed in Roswell C. McCrea, "The Basic Elements and Their Proper Balance in the Curriculum of a Collegiate Business School," *Journal of Political Economy* 28, no. 2 (1920). For a comprehensive description of early business school curricula, see chapter 2 in Daniel, *MBA*.

55. Melvin Thomas Copeland, *And Mark an Era: The Story of the Harvard Business School* (Boston: Little Brown, 1958), 150–152.

56. Richard Swedberg, *Max Weber and the Idea of Economic Sociology* (Princeton, NJ: Princeton University Press, 1998), 174.

57. As quoted in ibid., 176.

58. As quoted in ibid., 175.

59. As quoted in Michael A. Bernstein, *A Perilous Progress: Economists and Public Purpose in Twentieth-Century America* (Princeton, NJ: Princeton University Press, 2001), 47.

60. On Patten's leadership of Wharton, see chapter 4 ("On the Firing Line of Civilization") in Sass, *The Pragmatic Imagination*.

61. Quoted in ibid., 100.

62. Ronald H. Coase, "The New Institutional Economics," *Journal of Institutional and Theoretical Economics* 140 (1984): 230.

63. The leading neoclassical economists of the time included the University of Chicago's Frank Knight, and Tjalling C. Koopmans. For a history of how neoclassical economics came to dominate professional economics in America, see Bernstein, *A Perilous Progress*.

64. In 1920, Edwin Gay and Wesley Mitchell would undertake one final institutional effort to make economics more empirical and relevant to policy by starting the National Bureau of Economic Research (NBER). The goal was to create a new type of research organization that would occupy a unique space at the intersection of academia, private foundations, and public policy making. Over time, the NBER would take on a more neoclassical character as well; see ibid.

65. Ibid., 45.

66. Roswell C. McCrea, "The Place of Economics in the Curriculum of a School of Business," *Journal of Political Economy* 34, no. 2 (1926): 221–222.

67. American Association of Collegiate Schools of Business, "Proceedings of the Seventh Annual Meeting," 12.

68. The disconnect between economics and business administration also appeared in the performance of students at Harvard after the business school, at the start of the 1920s, began to consider requiring applicants to have taken a Principles of Economics course. The requirement never went into effect, for it was quickly discovered that "students who had taken a course in economic theory in college generally showed no extra proficiency in the Business School." Copeland, *And Mark an Era*, 173.

69. Wallace B. Donham, *Administration and Blind Spots: The Biography of an Adventurous Idea*, George H. Weatherbee Lectures (Boston: Harvard University, Graduate School of Business Administration, 1952), 13–14.

70. Eliot G. Mears, "The Teaching of Commerce and Economics," *American Economic Review* 13, no. 4 (1923): 648–649.

71. Copeland, *And Mark an Era*, 176.

72. American Association of Collegiate Schools of Business, "Proceedings of the Tenth Annual Meeting," 19.

73. By the 1920s, there were only two reasonably viable business doctoral programs, the University of Chicago's and Harvard's, both of which were relatively small and produced faculty mostly for their own schools.

74. American Association of Collegiate Schools of Business, "Program of the Third General Meeting" (Program of the Third General Meeting of the AACSB, Pittsburgh, PA, May 5, 6, and 7, 1921). The author of this comment is not identified in the source.

75. Letter from Wallace Donham to Alvin E. Dodd, HBS Archives, Gay files, July 23, 1922.

76. American Association of Collegiate Schools of Business, "Proceedings of the Sixth Annual Meeting," 9.

77. American Association of Collegiate Schools of Business, "Proceedings of the Eighth Annual Meeting." April 30, 1926—Evening Session, Address by President E. M. Hopkins, Dartmouth College.

78. Ibid., 12.

79. As quoted by C. O. Ruggles, "The Significance of Research in Business Education" (paper presented at the Sixth Annual Meeting of the AACSB, New York, 1924).

80. American Association of Collegiate Schools of Business, "Proceedings of the Sixth Annual Meeting."

81. Ibid., 11.

82. Ibid., 12.

83. Lewis Haney, "Organized Research" (paper presented at the Sixth Annual Meeting of the AACSB, New York, NY, 1924).

84. American Association of Collegiate Schools of Business, "Proceedings of the Sixth Annual Meeting," 11.

85. Ibid.

86. Quoted in Copeland, *And Mark an Era*, 209.

87. American Association of Collegiate Schools of Business, "Proceedings of the Sixth Annual Meeting," 14.

88. Daniel, *MBA*, 95–96.

89. In one important way, the project cannot be considered entirely futile, for it marked an inflection in the history of business education when Harvard recognized that framing business education as a branch of "applied economics" was inadequate for creating a profession of management.

90. Flexner, *Universities*, 169.

91. American Association of Collegiate Schools of Business, "Proceedings of the Twelfth Annual Meeting" (Twelfth Annual Meeting of the AACSB, Iowa City, IA, May 1930), 108.

92. American Association of Collegiate Schools of Business, "Proceedings of the Sixth Annual Meeting."

93. Copeland, *And Mark an Era*, 209–220.

94. American Association of Collegiate Schools of Business, "Proceedings of the Sixth Annual Meeting," 17.

95. Ibid.

96. Ibid.

97. Ibid.

98. Ibid., 110.

99. Ibid.

100. Ibid.

101. American Association of Collegiate Schools of Business, "Proceedings of the Tenth Annual Meeting," 8.

102. American Association of Collegiate Schools of Business, "Proceedings of the Sixth Annual Meeting," 108.

103. Ibid., 13.

104. The AACSB schools' inability to reach consensus on this matter owed much to the conflicting demands placed upon them by the academic world and the business world. Their dependency on the university pulled them in one direction, while their dependency on business (for benefactors as well as for the hiring of their graduates) pulled them in another. The AACSB's failure to reconcile these competing interests through development of its own institutional strength ultimately left business education highly susceptible to outside influences that took it further and further from its original mission, as we will see in parts 2 and 3.

105. The researchers involved—an eclectic bunch of psychologists, sociologists, medical doctors, and anthropologists led by the academic impresario Elton Mayo—were brought to Harvard by Wallace Donham as a part of his determined attempt to move the business school away from applied economics and toward a consideration of the relationships among individuals, work, and society. This group of researchers shared with Donham an intense belief that the most significant problems of society involved the relations between individuals and industrial work. Like Donham, they saw business education as a means of addressing the most vexing problems of industrialization through "socializing the results of science" so as to create a new type of manager. Their research findings, when eventually published at the nadir of the Great Depression, would single-handedly transform the prevalent ideas of what constituted "real" management scholarship, and would subsequently be

codified into what became the most important managerial idea since scientific management, the human relations movement. I discuss the enduring significance of the Hawthorne Studies for management theory and business schools more fully in chapters 5 and 6.

106. Adolf A. Berle and G. Means, *The Modern Corporation and Private Property* (New York: Macmillan Press, 1932), 32, 35.

107. American Association of Collegiate Schools of Business, "Proceedings of the Tenth Annual Meeting," 44.

108. Ibid., 1–2.

109. Ibid., 2.

110. Ibid., 3.

111. Ibid.

112. Ibid., 5.

113. Ibid., 33–37.

114. American Association of Collegiate Schools of Business, "Proceedings of the Sixteenth Annual Meeting" (Sixteenth Annual Meeting of the AACSB, St. Louis, MO, April 26, 27, and 28, 1934), 9.

115. American Association of Collegiate Schools of Business, "Proceedings of the Twelfth Annual Meeting," 34, 35.

116. American Association of Collegiate Schools of Business, "Proceedings of the Eighteenth Annual Meeting" (Eighteenth Annual Meeting of the AACSB, Boston, MA, April 22, 23, 24, and 25, 1936), 13.

117. American Association of Collegiate Schools of Business, "Proceedings of the Fifteenth Annual Meeting" (Fifteenth Annual Meeting of the AACSB, Lexington, KY, Summer 1933), 255–256.

118. American Association of Collegiate Schools of Business, "Proceedings of the Eighteenth Annual Meeting," 25.

119. Ibid., 12–13.

120. Quoted in "Sees Great Need Now of Liberal Education," *New York Times*, December 27, 1931.

121. American Association of Collegiate Schools of Business, "Proceedings of the Fifteenth Annual Meeting," 245, 253.

122. American Association of Collegiate Schools of Business, "Proceedings of the Sixteenth Annual Meeting," 37.

123. Sass, *The Pragmatic Imagination*, 201.

124. American Association of Collegiate Schools of Business, "Proceedings of the Sixteenth Annual Meeting," 37.

125. Ibid., 82.

126. As iterated by Everett Lord in describing Columbia's rededication to this mission. American Association of Collegiate Schools of Business, "Proceedings of the Eighteenth Annual Meeting."

127. Flexner, *Universities*, 166–167. As related in Jeffrey Cruikshank's history of Harvard Business School, Donham told an HBS supporter who asked for his reaction to Flexner's criticism that the latter's views were "so far away from my own conception of our philosophical job that I was not even annoyed by it." Cruikshank, *A Delicate Experiment*, 185.

128. American Association of Collegiate Schools of Business, "Proceedings of the Eighteenth Annual Meeting," 120.

129. Ibid., 33.

130. American Association of Collegiate Schools of Business, "Proceedings of the Nineteenth Annual Meeting" (Nineteenth Annual Meeting of the AACSB, Baton Rouge, LA, March 22, 23, and 24, 1937), 65, 66, 67.

131. American Association of Collegiate Schools of Business, "Proceedings of the Twentieth Annual Meeting" (Twentieth Annual Meeting of the AACSB, Urbana, IL, April 21, 22, and 23, 1938).

132. American Association of Collegiate Schools of Business, "Proceedings of the Sixteenth Annual Meeting," 53–54.

133. American Association of Collegiate Schools of Business, "Proceedings of the Twenty-first Annual Meeting" (Twenty-first Annual Meeting of the AACSB, Stanford, CA, April 20, 21, and 22, 1939), 146.

134. American Association of Collegiate Schools of Business, "Proceedings of the Eighteenth Annual Meeting," 120–121.

135. American Association of Collegiate Schools of Business, "Proceedings of the Sixteenth Annual Meeting," 54.

136. Sass, *The Pragmatic Imagination*, 201–202.

137. American Association of Collegiate Schools of Business, "Proceedings of the Fifteenth Annual Meeting," 253.

138. Wallace B. Donham, "Business and the Public: Harvard School's New Training to Stress an Understanding of Social Forces," *New York Times*, December 16, 1934, XX6.

139. Elton Mayo, *The Human Problems of an Industrial Civilization* (New York: Macmillan, 1933). Mayo's book is one example of how the Great Depression catalyzed a period of deep introspection among business educators and other social scientists about whether capitalism could survive if it did not address fundamental needs of society and workers.

140. Sass, *The Pragmatic Imagination*, 201. Sass adds: "As the leader of Wharton's 1920s reformers, Willits had championed the place of science in the business curriculum, and he not surprisingly thought that academic economic science now held the key to solving the nation's crisis. Willits's brand of scientific economics held prewar, progressive moral zeal at arm's length, and took a hard-boiled, matter-of-fact attitude toward affairs" (203).

141. American Association of Collegiate Schools of Business, "Proceedings of the Twentieth Annual Meeting"; C. E. Griffin, "Education Looks at Business" 1938.

142. Cruikshank, *A Delicate Experiment*, 185–187. Donham's letter was a response to a Harvard Business School supporter who had asked him to comment on Flexner's criticism of the school in *Universities*.

Chapter 5
The Changing Institutional Field in the Postwar Era

1. U.S. Census, Statistical Abstracts.

2. "National Conference on Doctoral Training in Business Administration," White Paper, Ford Foundation Archives, 1955.

3. Peter Drucker, "The Graduate Business School," *Fortune* 42 (August 1950): 92.

4. Ibid.

5. "Conference on Professional Education for Business: Faculty Requirements and Standards" (Arden House, New York, October 27–29, 1955).

6. F. J. Roethlisberger, *The Elusive Phenomena: An Autobiographical Account of My Work in the Field of Organizational Behavior at the Harvard Business School*, ed. George F. F. Lombard (Cambridge: Division of Research, Graduate School of Business Administration, Harvard University [distributed by Harvard University Press], 1977).

7. The question of whether undergraduate business majors were academically inferior to students studying other fields was carefully considered by several researchers in the postwar years. Data gathered by a government-sponsored study group, the Commission on Human Resources and Advanced Training, as well as a study done by the Educational Testing Service of 500,000 male college students, found that undergraduate business schools enrolled the weakest students. See Commission on Human Resources and Advanced Training and Dael Lee Wolfle, *America's Resources of Specialized Talent: A Current Appraisal and a Look Ahead* (New York: Harper, 1954). For the ETS study results, see Educational Testing Service, *Statistical Studies of Selective Service Testing* (Princeton, NJ: Educational Testing Service, 1955).

8. Thurman William Van Metre, *A History of the Graduate School of Business, Columbia University*, The Bicentennial History of Columbia University (New York: Columbia University Press, 1954), 83.

9. The HBS programs, lasting from five weeks to more than a year, would form the foundation for the school's executive education program after the war. HBS faculty also did contract research for the government during this period. Working closely with the Army Air Forces (the predecessor to the modern air force), several HBS faculty— including a brilliant, newly appointed accounting professor named Robert McNamara—helped develop the logistics and statistical systems necessary to orchestrate the development of systems that managed everything from the manufacturing of military planes to the deployment of troops and equipment; see Melvin Thomas Copeland, *And Mark an Era: The Story of the Harvard Business School* (Boston: Little Brown, 1958), 117–146; Andrea Gabor, *The Capitalist Philosophers: The Geniuses of Modern Business, Their Lives, Times and Ideas* (New York: Times Business, 2000), 131–151.

General Charles de Gaulle noted that the American military had the benefit of links to American business schools, including Harvard's, in what he described as the "Army Industrial College" model for training officers "in the technical services" to contribute to the mobilization of the economy. Translated from Charles de Gaulle, *Trois études, suivies du memorandum du 26 janvier 1940* (Paris: Éditions Berger-Levrault, 1945); Robert Locke, "Postwar Management Education Reconsidered," in *Management Education in Historical Perspective*, ed. Lars Engwall and Vera Zamagni (Manchester, England: Manchester University Press, 1998).

10. L. F. Urwick, *Management Education in American Business* (New York: American Management Association Publications, 1953).

11. Robert Cuff, "Organizational Capabilities and U.S. War Production: The Controlled Materials Plan of World War II," *Business and Economic History* 19 (1990).

12. As quoted in W. Richard Scott, *Organizations: Rational, Natural, and Open Systems*, 3d ed. (Englewood Cliffs, NJ: Prentice Hall, 1992), 4.

13. As a freelance writer and consultant for both *Time* and *Fortune* magazines, Drucker had become well known outside of management circles by the late 1940s; see Gabor, *The Capitalist Philosophers*, 291–324.

14. Sheldon S. Wolin, *Politics and Vision: Continuity and Innovation in Western Political Thought*, expanded ed. (Princeton, NJ: Princeton University Press, 2004), 315–389.

15. Van Metre, *A History of the Graduate School of Business, Columbia University*, 83–85.

16. Philip Selznick, *Leadership in Administration: A Sociological Interpretation* (Evanston, IL: Row Peterson, 1957), 1–2.

17. Donald K. David, "Business Leadership and the War of Ideas" (paper presented at the Magazine Forum, April 27, 1948). In a 1947 article, the *New York Times* applauded Harvard Business School's brief pamphlet *Education for Business Responsibility* as an intellectual turning point for the development of a free-market retort to those academics calling for greater governmental involvement in the economy. Russell Porter, "Stress Social Responsibility as Factor in American Life," *New York Times*, September 7, 1947, F1.

18. James B. Conant (paper presented at the National Retail Dry Goods Association, February 12, 1950).

19. Carter A. Daniel, *MBA: The First Century* (Lewisburg, PA: Bucknell University Press, 1998), 139.

20. In 1949, USTAP (U.S. Technical Assistance and Productivity Program), a federal program that was part of the Marshall Plan, contracted with many American universities and colleges to teach the new management techniques to European business managers to help their countries rebuild their economies. More than five hundred European executives annually enrolled in this program, taught at universities like MIT and Stanford's business school. See Jacqueline McGlade, "The Big Push: The

Export of American Business Education to Western Europe after the Second World War," in *Management Education in Historical Perspective*, ed. Lars Engwall and Vera Zamagni (Manchester, England: Manchester University Press, 1998).

21. Edward Shils, *The Calling of Sociology and Other Essays on the Pursuit of Learning*, vol. 3 of *Selected Papers of Edward Shils* (Chicago: University of Chicago Press, 1980), 320.

22. Steven R. Barley and Gideon Kunda, "Design and Devotion: Surges of Rational and Normative Ideologies of Control in Managerial Discourse," *Administrative Science Quarterly* 37, no. 3 (1992): 377.

23. "Can You Teach Management?" *BusinessWeek*, April 19, 1952, 126.

24. C. Wright Mills, *The Power Elite* (New York: Oxford University Press, 1967).

25. As quoted in Jeffrey L. Cruikshank, *A Delicate Experiment: The Harvard Business School, 1908–1945* (Boston: Harvard Business School Press, 1987), 264.

26. See Raghuram Rajan and Luigi Zingales, *Saving Capitalism from the Capitalists: Unleashing the Power of Financial Markets to Create Wealth and Spread Opportunity* (Princeton, NJ: Princeton University Press, 2004), 238–243.

27. Neil Fligstein, *The Transformation of Corporate Control* (Cambridge: Harvard University Press, 1990), 192–225.

28. Historians Allan Kaufman and Ernest Englander note that "when Congress enacted the Cellar-Kefauver bill, it did so to ensure that the economic conditions conducive to political dictatorship would not emerge in the United States. Such postwar sentiments contributed to the stringent antitrust enforcement of the 1950s and 1960s." Allen Kaufman and Ernest J. Englander, "Kohlberg Kravis Roberts & Co. and the Restructuring of American Capitalism," *Business History Review* 67, no. 1 (1993): 60.

29. Fligstein, *The Transformation of Corporate Control*, 177–190.

30. When a new organizational form or new organizational strategy like conglomerates first emerges, investors struggle with how to value the entity. For example, during the Internet boom, analysts and investors set aside conventional valuation methods like price-earnings ratio for a variety of nonconventional measures such as number of Web page "hits," "eyeballs," Web site "stickiness," and revenue growth as a percentage of marketing expenses. See Ezra W. Zuckerman, "Internet Valuations: Surveying the Landscape" (Palo Alto, CA: Stanford University, Graduate School of Business, 1999).

31. Norm Berg, "Textron, Inc.," Case No. 37337, *Harvard Business School Case* (Boston: Harvard Business School Publishing, 1973), 9.

32. Herbert Simon would wryly note in 1960 that the new "management science" was in fact the old "scientific management." Aside from the reversal of words, the primary difference was that the new management science used mathematics rather than the stopwatch to exert control.

33. Berg, "Textron, Inc.," 3.

34. Ibid.

35. Ibid., 16. This new conception of management can be interpreted as one in a series of recurring oscillations in management theory between the rational conception of managerial work originally embodied in scientific management and the more human-relations-oriented conception first championed by the researchers involved in the Hawthorne studies. In the variant of scientific management that flourished in the postwar conglomerate, strategic management (often associated with the top executives) operated in a centralized headquarters, staffed by nonoperating executives, and those being managed were the operating managers.

36. After World War II, the reach of the federal government extended into many areas that had historically been beyond its purview. For example, as Richard Scott et al. have pointed out, Medicare (federal health insurance for the elderly) and Medicaid (state insurance for the poor) gave rise to a number of regulatory bodies that challenged the control of the AMA over the medical profession. James N. Baron and his colleagues have described the role of federal contracting policy in the diffusion of human resource departments across large corporations, as well as in the diffusion of specific human resource practices. Once in place, these scholars note, organizations such as the AMA or human resource departments increasingly incorporate the needs of the state into their strategies, organizational structures, and practices. See W. Richard Scott et al., *Institutional Change and Healthcare Organizations: From Professional Dominance to Managed Care* (Chicago: University of Chicago Press, 2000); James N. Baron, P. Devereaux Jennings, and Frank R. Dobbin, "Mission Control? The Development of Personnel Systems in U.S. Industry," *American Sociological Review* 53, no. 4 (1988). For a strong social constructionist view of this phenomenon, see Frank Dobbin et al., "Equal Opportunity Law and the Construction of Internal Labor Markets," *American Journal of Sociology* 99, no. 2 (1993).

37. Two excellent books about the rise of the postwar university are Roger L. Geiger, *To Advance Knowledge: The Growth of American Research Universities, 1900–1940* (New York: Oxford University Press, 1986), and Clark Kerr, *The Uses of the University*, 5th ed. (Cambridge: Harvard University Press, 2001).

38. Frank Cook Pierson, *The Education of American Businessmen: A Study of University-College Programs in Business Administration* (New York: McGraw-Hill, 1959), 7. The large number of GIs entering business programs exerted two pulls on the intellectual quality of students: their large numbers led to a downward pull on overall business school student quality but an improvement in student quality in the better business schools, which had the luxury, as a consequence of a higher absolute number of applications, of becoming more selective in admissions.

39. To provide a review process for unaccredited schools and to manage specific programs within schools, higher education administrators convinced Congress to fund a system of state agencies for determining the eligibility of schools and programs for enrolling students under the GI Bill.

40. John R. Proffitt, "The Federal Connection for Accreditation," *Journal of Higher Education* 50, no. 2 (1979).

41. William K. Selden and Harry V. Porter, "Accreditation, Its Purposes and Uses" (occasional paper, Council on Post-secondary Accreditation, Washington, DC: Council on Post-Secondary Accreditation, 1977), 2.

42. The impact of the GI Bill on the development of a government-influenced accrediting system has been extensively analyzed, but the analysis has been provided primarily by education scholars and historians; see, for example, Kenneth E. Young, ed., *Understanding Accreditation* (San Francisco: Jossey-Bass, 1983). I would suggest that developments in accreditation can and should be viewed not simply in relation to the process of formal accreditation in education but also in terms of the rise of informal accrediting of both educational institutions (e.g., through the *U.S. News and World Report* rankings of colleges, universities, and professional schools) and large institutions, including corporations (e.g., through ratings of corporate governance by institutional shareholders) and hospitals (e.g., the *U.S. News and World Report* annual ratings). This subject will be examined in part 3, where I discuss how both business schools in particular, and institutions of higher education in general, became more market-oriented as a result of historical developments in the mid-1970s and early 1980s.

43. Christopher Jencks and David Riesman, *The Academic Revolution* (Garden City, NY: Doubleday, 1968); Kerr, *The Uses of the University*.

44. United States Office of Scientific Research and Development and Vannevar Bush, *Science, the Endless Frontier* (Washington, DC: Government Printing Office, 1945).

45. Geiger, *To Advance Knowledge*, 264–266.

46. Michael A. Bernstein, *A Perilous Progress: Economists and Public Purpose in Twentieth-Century America* (Princeton, NJ: Princeton University Press, 2001).

47. Kerr, *The Uses of the University*, 49–50.

48. The large foundations established by tycoons such as Carnegie and Rockefeller eventually underwent a separation of ownership and control (paralleling that which had led to the rise of modern management in private, for-profit corporations) that shifted the direction of their activities from the founders to trustees and, especially, chief executives and their staffs. In the case of many foundations, full control would pass to the administrators following the founder's death, which usually coincided with the final, and usually most significant, bequest. Frederick P. Keppel, president of the Carnegie Corporation from 1923 to 1941, only half-jokingly described himself as an example of a new type of organizational executive, the "philanthropoid," whose "profession is the giving away of other people's money," and who was "the key figure in most of today's great foundations, now that the original donors are safely dead." See Dwight Macdonald, *The Ford Foundation: The Men and the Millions* (New York: Reynal, 1956), 95–96. The fact that foundation trustees and executives

were disproportionately drawn from academia may partly explain their deep interest in higher education. The Carnegie Coroporation's original board of trustees, for example, was made up almost exclusively of university presidents.

49. Ernest Victor Hollis, *Philanthropic Foundations and Higher Education* (New York: Columbia University Press, 1938). Cited in Carter V. Good, "Organized Research in Education: Foundations, Commissions, and Committees," *Review of Educational Research* 9, no. 5, *Methods of Research in Education* (1939): 569. This funding was directed to a range of activities including the establishment of new universities, the creation of specific schools—including schools of business—underwriting research, buildings, and endowing faculty chairs.

50. Quoted in Ernest Victor Hollis, "The Foundations and the Universities," *Journal of Higher Education* 11, no. 4 (1940): 177.

51. The General Education Board (GEB) was one of several Rockefeller philanthropies that focused on higher education. To put the GEB's size in perspective, in 1907 the foundation gave away $32 million, the equivalent of about $500 million today.

52. Hollis, "The Foundations and the Universities," 177.

53. Geiger, *To Advance Knowledge*, 141–162. The foundations supported these activities by funding university initiatives and through the support of activities outside the university, such as creating nonteaching research institutes.

54. Ellen Condliffe Lagemann, *The Politics of Knowledge: The Carnegie Corporation, Philanthropy, and Public Policy* (Chicago: University of Chicago Press, 1989), 61.

55. For example, Richard T. Ely—an institutional economist who was a co-founder of the American Economic Association—once wrote: "We regard the state as an educational and ethical agency whose positive aid is an indispensable condition of human progress. While we recognize the necessity of individual initiative in industrial life, we hold that the doctrine of *laissez-faire* is unsafe in politics and unsound in morals. . . . We hold that the conflict of labor and capital has brought to the front a vast number of social problems whose solution is impossible without the united efforts of Church, State and Science." Richard T. Ely, "Report of the Organization of the American Economic Association," *Publications of the American Economic Association* 1 (1886): 6.

56. Geiger, *To Advance Knowledge*, 144–145.

57. European social science tended toward the development of broad overarching conceptions of categories like class, status, and power as determining social outcomes and was often too abstract to allow for grounded descriptions of particular empirical outcomes. In contrast, American social science developed more along the lines of what Robert K. Merton called middle-range theory, which emphasized empirically testable propositions and concepts over broad conceptual categories and ideas.

58. Edward Shils, *The Calling of Education: The Academic Ethic and Other Essays on Higher Education* (Chicago: University of Chicago Press, 1997).

59. Lagemann, *The Politics of Knowledge*, 70.

60. John M. Jordan, *Machine-Age Ideology: Social Engineering and American Liberalism, 1911–1939* (Chapel Hill: University of North Carolina Press, 1994), 165. The reason for the "secret" funding was continued suspicion about whether the Rockefeller foundation was biasing social scientists toward the view that it was workers, not employers, who were contributing to the problems of industrial society.

61. Gabor, *The Capitalist Philosophers*, 99.

62. Richard L. Kozelka, chairman of the study, presented the preliminary findings at the 1951 AACSB meeting. A similar theme was reiterated at the Arden House Conference in 1955, which brought together deans and administrators of AACSB member schools.

63. Robert Calkins, 1955, AACSB Address, HBS Archives, Donald K. David papers, 1955. This new generation also faced a radically different educational and disciplinary context from that of their predecessors: "Both broad and specific developments in the behavioral sciences, in organizational theory, and in mechanical facilities for data processing and computation are having an impact on business school faculties and curricula. The pressure of college enrollments, while burdensome, also offers opportunities for raising admissions standards and quality of instruction in the business schools. The present is thus a particularly strategic time for thinking about the objectives and techniques of education for management responsibilities."

64. *Preliminary Statistical Summary of the Survey of Higher Education in Business Administration*, AACSB, pamphlet, HBS Archives, Donald K. David papers, 1951.

65. In his autobiography, Harvard Business School's Fritz Roethlisberger described the doctoral program's second-class status: "The [doctoral] program had been a small show; the big show was the MBA program, of which the School was justifiably proud. The doctoral program had been a side show . . . Its most important function . . . was to produce more locals for the Faculty of our own MBA program; there was no other place to get them." Roethlisberger, *The Elusive Phenomena*, 287.

66. Robert A. Gordon, "Some Current Issues in Business Education" (paper presented at the Annual Meeting of the AACSB, Gatlinburg, TN, May 2, 1958).

67. See table 5.1, p. 196.

68. Lee Bidgood, Personal Correspondence to Donald K. David, HBS Archives, Donald K. David papers.

69. Steven A. Sass, *The Pragmatic Imagination: A History of the Wharton School, 1881–1981* (Philadelphia: University of Pennsylvania Press, 1982), 237.

70. Robert A. Gordon, "Business Education at the Undergraduate Level" (Convocation Commemorating the Fiftieth Anniversary of the Founding of the College of Business Administration, The University of Denver, April 25, 1958), Ford Foundation Archives, Robert Aaron Gordon files, 445.

71. American Association of Collegiate Schools of Business, *The American Association of Collegiate Schools of Business, 1916–1966* (Homewood, IL: R. D. Irwin, 1966), 16.

72. American Association of Collegiate Schools of Business, "The AACSB Bulletin" (St. Louis, MO, April 1966), 9.

73. Office of Education, "Working Paper on Congress' Power to Rely upon Determinations of Private Accrediting Agencies as Basis of Eligibility for Federal Educational Assistance" (unpublished manuscript, Washington, DC: Office of Education, Division of Eligibility and Agency Evaluation, June 1970). Cited in Proffitt, "The Federal Connection for Accreditation," 153.

74. In medicine, for example, the American Medical Association is actively involved in setting educational standards, as what was originally the mandate of a temporary AMA committee became a permanent function when the Council on Medical Education was created in 1906. In the field of dentistry, the American Dental Association is designated by its membership to fulfill an accrediting role. Similarly, the American Bar Association started the Association of American Law Schools as a means to influence and improve legal education in the United States. Other accrediting agencies in the professions and semiprofessions, such as the Accreditation Board for Engineering and Technology, the American Council on Education for Journalism, or the American Board of Funeral Service Education, are supported by several professional societies in each of their respective fields. Robert Glidden, "Specialized Accreditation," in *Understanding Accreditation*, ed. Kenneth E. Young, Charles Chambers, and H. R. Kells (San Francisco: Jossey-Bass, 1983), 192–193.

75. American Association of Collegiate Schools of Business, "The AACSB Bulletin," 10.

Chapter 6
Disciplining the Business School Faculty: The Impact of the Foundations

1. Ernest Victor Hollis, *Philanthropic Foundations and Higher Education* (New York: Columbia University Press, 1938), 254–272.

2. Richard E. Bjork, "Foundations, Universities, and Government: A Pattern of Interaction," *Journal of Higher Education* 33, no. 5 (1962).

3. Herbert Alexander Simon, *Models of My Life* (New York: Basic Books, 1991), 139.

4. Ellen Condliffe Lagemann notes that characterizing themselves as societal trustees was an attractive strategy for foundation executives to pursue, as it suggested responsibility and a sense of civic obligation while also deflecting some of the criticism directed at the concentration of vast amounts of wealth in private hands that foundations represented. Foundation executives such as Rockefeller's Frederick Gates or Carnegie's Henry Smith Pritchett presented themselves as "disinterested" observers focused on the common good rather than motivated by personal gain or institutional self-interest. By extension, foundations themselves were trustworthy institutions. They were seen as formalized systems whose actions and decisions were impersonal and, thus, neutral. Lagemann's institutional analysis of the Carnegie Corporation, however, highlights a different reality that underlay this appearance of neutrality. In

her analysis of the Carnegie foundations' sponsored research and higher education activities, Lagemann notes that how problems were framed and how data were interpreted was very much colored by the political context within which foundations operated and the political leanings of foundation executives. See Ellen Condliffe Lagemann, *The Politics of Knowledge: The Carnegie Corporation, Philanthropy, and Public Policy* (Chicago: University of Chicago Press, 1989).

5. Mary Clark Stuart, "Clark Kerr: Biography of an Action Intellectual" (Ph.D. diss., University of Michigan, 1980). Ellen Condliffe Lagemann, *Private Power for the Public Good of the Carnegie Foundation for the Advancement of Teaching* (Middletown, CT: Wesleyan University Press, 1983), 58.

6. The strategy of commissioning studies and disseminating their findings as a means of effecting reform in professional schools had first been used by the Carnegie Foundation for the Advancement of Teaching in 1910, when it issued its *Bulletin 4* (better known as the Flexner report on medical education), which introduced and institutionalized a science-based paradigm for medical education. Later, Carnegie would do the same for the legal, teaching, and engineering professions. Schools of dentistry, forestry, and library science are also among the institutions that benefited from Carnegie's support for professional education. For an analysis of Carnegie's activities in higher education, see Lagemann, *Private Power for the Public Good*.

7. On this approach to the Carnegie Corporation in the 1930s, see chapter 4, p. 184.

8. Robert E. Gleeson and Steven L. Schlossman, "George Leland Bach and the Rebirth of Graduate Management Education in the United States, 1945–1975," *Selections* 11, no. 3 (1995).

9. Andrea Gabor, *The Capitalist Philosophers: The Geniuses of Modern Business, Their Lives, Times and Ideas* (New York: Times Business, 2000), 242.

10. H. Rowan Gaither, "Freedom and the Challenge to Management," Speech at Stanford University, Ford Foundation Archives, Gaither Papers, box no. 47, July 23, 1958.

11. In addition to the management education program, the EDA initiative focused on supporting research oriented toward solving large-scale economic problems, including improving the training of engineers, international economics and improving labor productivity.

12. As quoted in Steven L. Schlossman, Michael W. Sedlak, and Harold S. Wechsler, *The "New Look": The Ford Foundation and the Revolution in Business Education* (Los Angeles: Graduate Management Admission Council, 1987).

13. Ibid.

14. For a brief account of Conant's influence on the postwar American university, see "The Long Shadow of James B. Conant" in Louis Menand, *American Studies* (New York: Farrar, Straus and Giroux, 2002), 91–111.

15. Ford Foundation Archives, Oral History Project, Interview by Charles T. Morrissey, 1972.

16. Quoted in "Business Is Rallied to Fight Communism," *New York Times*, September 11, 1949.

17. Donald K. David, "Personal Correspondence," to James B. Conant, HBS Archives, box no. 11, June 13, 1953.

18. Unlike the Carnegie Foundation, which Andrew Carnegie founded and generously endowed in order to carry out the mandate of his "Gospel of Wealth," the Ford Foundation owed its existence not to any philanthropic motivation per se but rather to Henry Ford's desire to keep his fortune from falling into the hands of Franklin Roosevelt and the administrators of the New Deal. An increase in the federal estate tax, enacted by Congress at FDR's urging in 1935 (when Ford was seventy-two years old), faced the automobile tycoon with the prospect of having his personal fortune help finance the New Deal programs that he despised; according to Ford family biographer Robert Lacey, this prospect apparently worried Ford even more than did a second likely consequence of the new estate tax, which was that either Ford's own death or that of his son Edsel—not to mention the deaths of both—would present their heirs with a tax bill requiring them to sell off large amounts of stock and relinquish family control of the company. Ford's lawyers thus devised a scheme to split the company's stock into Class A and Class B shares, with the latter having all the votes; by converting 95 percent of the stock to Class A, nonvoting shares and keeping the Class B stock in family hands, Henry and Edsel would be able to will up to 95 percent of the company's stock for charitable purposes (thus avoiding what would have turned out to be approximately $321 million in estate taxes) and keep the company 100 percent under family control. Thus even though Henry Ford had little use for philanthropy, the Ford Foundation was established in 1936 by Henry and Edsel, with Edsel becoming its first president; the Fords' initial gift to the foundation of $25,000 was followed, the next year, by a gift from both Henry and Edsel of 125,000 shares of nonvoting stock in the Ford Motor Company. Edsel Ford died in 1943 at the age of forty-nine, and Henry Ford followed his son to the grave four years later. In 1948, the foundation received more than a million shares of class A stock from Edsel's estate; having received an additional 26,000 shares from the Henry Ford estate in 1950, the Ford Foundation suddenly found itself the largest private philanthropic foundation in the world—larger, indeed, than the Rockefeller and Carnegie foundations combined. On the history of the establishment of the Ford Foundation, see Robert Lacey, *Ford: The Men and the Machine* (Boston: Little, Brown, 1986), 471–473.

19. Ford Foundation, "Annual Report" (New York: Ford Foundation, 1950), 4.

20. Leonard Silk and Mark Silk, *The American Establishment* (New York: Basic Books, 1980), 240.

21. The CED would be involved in the Marshall Plan as well as in bucking postwar isolationism to get the United States into the IMF, the World Bank, and the General Agreement on Tariffs and Trade. Another individual involved in the establishment of the CED was Beardsley Ruml—the Rockefeller philanthropoid who had poured Rockefeller money into research in the social sciences in the 1920s and

launched Elton Mayo's academic career, and had since gone on to become, in succession, dean of social sciences at the University of Chicago, treasurer of Macy's, and chairman of the New York Federal Reserve Board.

22. Although Hoffman and Hutchins are described as having run the foundation together, technically Hutchins was one of four associate directors at Ford under Hoffman, the others being Gaither; Chester C. Davis, president of the Federal Reserve Board of St. Louis; and Milton Katz, who had been Averell Harriman's successor as the chief administrator of the Marshall Plan in Europe.

23. Dwight Macdonald, "Foundations: IV—Next Winter or by Plane," *New Yorker*, December 17, 1955.

24. As if Hoffman's association with enterprises such as the Marshall Plan and the Committee on Economic Development were not damning enough, Hutchins— along with the ubiquitous Beardsley Ruml, among others—had been involved with the mostly University of Chicago–based Committee to Frame a World Constitution in the immediate aftermath of World War II.

25. By the famous McCarthyite journalist Westbrook Pegler, as quoted in Dwight Macdonald, *The Ford Foundation: The Men and the Millions* (New York: Reynal, 1956), 26.

26. As quoted in "No Red Grip Found on Foundation Aid," *New York Times*, January 3, 1953. Cox died in December 1952, and the following July Tennessee Republican Congressman Brazilla Carroll Reece launched a second set of hearings to investigate the foundations. The Reece hearings were one of the major low points of the McCarthy era, equating the experimentation with ideas or concerns about economic, social, or political conditions in the United States with sedition. Before issuing its final report in December 1954, the Reece Committee discussed a wide range of issues affecting foundations, from their tax-exempt status to the supposed hostility of empirical research in the social sciences to fundamental American values. For example, Reece asked why the Ford Foundation did not sponsor studies demonstrating the "excellence of the American Constitution . . . and the profundity of the philosophy of the Founding Fathers" (Macdonald, *The Ford Foundation*, 32). The irony behind the right-wing criticism of the Ford Foundation in the early years of the Cold War is that—as many scholars have since documented—the foundation, in its international programs, actually worked closely with the CIA in the 1950s and early 1960s in what has been called the "cultural Cold War," using covert CIA funding of literary journals, arts organizations, and the like in an attempt to counter what was thought to be the dangerous allure of Soviet communism in Western Europe. See Edward H. Berman, "The Extension of Ideology: Foundation Support for Intermediate Organizations and Forums," *Comparative Education Review* 26, no. 1 (1982).

27. As quoted in Macdonald, *The Ford Foundation*, 29. See Cox Committee Report from the Special Committee to Investigate Tax-Exempt Foundations, United States Congress, 1952.

28. The fates of Hoffman and Hutchins as leaders of the Ford Foundation may have been sealed by the personal sensitivity of Henry Ford II and his first wife, Anne McDonnell Ford, to criticism of the foundation, and by Hutchins's impolitic treatment of the impressionable Mrs. Ford. According to Ford family biographer Robert Lacey, W. "Ping" Ferry, Henry Ford II's liaison between the Ford Motor Company and the Ford Foundation, had formed the impression that, prior to a visit by the Fords late in 1952 to foundation headquarters in Pasadena, California, Anne Ford—a devout Catholic—"had been fed an awful lot of stuff by the parish priest or somebody about what an awful place the Foundation was," and had even been told that Hoffman and Hutchins were communist sympathizers. Upon meeting Hutchins, in any event, Mrs. Ford told him of her hopes that the foundation would pay attention to "the problems of Catholic education, mainly in the city of Detroit." As Lacey describes Hutchins's response: " 'I told her . . .,' Hutchins would later recount with glee, 'to hell with it—no business of ours.' And for good measure he treated the young Catholic mother to a lecture on the virtues of birth control" (Lacey, *Ford*, 481–482). Both Hoffman and Hutchins (who was no longer listed as an associate director of the foundation by 1954) remained affiliated with Ford after being forced out of their posts at the foundation proper. Hoffman became chairman, and Hutchins president, of the foundation's Fund for the Republic. Hoffman also remained active in Ford's Fund for the Advancement of Education, and Hutchins, in 1957, proposed what would eventually become a Ford Foundation study on the corporation and the freedom of the individual.

29. Macdonald, "Foundations." Reference taken from offprint, HBS Archives, Donald K. David papers. Owing to his previous association with the RAND Corporation, however, Gaither, no less than Hoffman, was an object of right-wing suspicion.

30. The group was chaired by Robert D. Calkins, president of the Brookings Institution and the former dean of the Columbia University School of Business. Besides Bach and Gordon, its membership consisted of Kenneth E. Boulding, professor of economics at the University of Michigan; J. M. Clark, professor emeritus of economics at Columbia University; Walter E. Hoadley, an economist with Armstrong Cork Company, Inc.; John Lintner, an associate professor at Harvard's Graduate School of Business Administration; Howard B. Myers, director of research for the Committee for Economic Development; Lloyd G. Reynolds, professor of economics at Yale University; Edward S. Shaw, professor of economics at Stanford University; C. Gordon Siefkin, dean of the School of Business Administration at Emory University; and R. Miller Upton, dean of the School of Business and Public Administration at Washington University.

31. Thomas Carroll, "Memo to the Program Committee—April 1953," Memorandum to Ford Foundation Program Committee, Ford Foundation Archives, no. 47, Gaither Papers, April 29, 1953. Other universities that received these funds included Columbia (business); Duke (economics and business); Harvard (economics and

business); Indiana (business); Stanford (economics); Vanderbilt (economics and business); Yale (economics); MIT (economics); UCLA (business); Michigan (economics); Minnesota (economics and business); Rochester (economics); Washington (economics); and Wisconsin (economics).

32. In the case of GSIA, Bach was particularly concerned that Carnegie's fledgling program not be lumped in with other business school programs. In a biographical sketch of Lee Bach, historians Robert Gleeson and Steven Schlossman write: "Perhaps more than anyone else, Bach saw the tremendous opportunity that could come from blending together a Chicago-style academic department—with its emphasis on advanced graduate training and faculty research—and a practically oriented professional school of management. Such a school would respond directly to the nation's needs as defined by Gaither: tackling the political challenges of the Cold War by creating a new social science of administration, and applying that science directly to vital problems of public and private management." See Gleeson and Schlossman, "George Leland Bach and the Rebirth of Graduate Management Education in the United States, 1945–1975," 10.

33. James Edwin Howell, "A Terminal Program in Business Education: GCT," Discussion Paper, Ford Foundation Archives, GCT, box no. 366, March 23, 1962.

34. Robert A. Gordon and James Edwin Howell, *Higher Education for Business* (New York: Columbia University Press, 1959), 4.

35. F. J. Roethlisberger, *The Elusive Phenomena: An Autobiographical Account of My Work in the Field of Organizational Behavior at the Harvard Business School*, ed. George F. F. Lombard (Cambridge: Division of Research, Graduate School of Business Administration, Harvard University [distributed by Harvard University Press], 1977), 287.

36. Thomas Carroll, Sixth Annual Conference on the Economic Outlook, Ann Arbor, MI, November 3, 1958. A 1954 Ford document describing how the money for the Harvard Business School doctoral program would be spent gives some sense of Ford's impact on one school: "The doctoral program will be expanded and revised to provide for more teachers of business administration, to achieve a level of 40 candidates per year versus three per year in the recent past. As most candidates have been trained in 'commerce' schools, their first year will be spent learning 'administration.' During the second year they will be case assistants, and during the last year they will work on dissertations. It is planned to provide fellowships for the dissertation work so this may be done before undertaking research responsibilities. A year of economics is no longer required of DBA candidates, although almost all of them do take Professor Lintner's Economic Analysis course. Candidates are examined, however, on the economics, public policy and business historical implications of their special fields." President and Fellows of Harvard College, "Research and Advanced Training Activities of the Graduate School of Business Administration," Grant Proposal to Ford Foundation, Ford Foundation Archives, September 10, 1954.

37. Thomas Carroll, "Ford Foundation Activities in Economics and Business Administration" (speech made at Sixth Annual Conference on the Economic Outlook, University of Michigan, November 3, 1958). Thomas Carroll, "Sixth Annual Conference on the Economic Outlook," Ford Foundation Archives, Papers of Thomas Carroll, November 3, 1958.

38. Courtney Brown, "Presentation of the Graduate School of Business of Columbia University to the Ford Foundation," Ford Foundation Archives, box no. 55-228, June 1955.

39. Thomas Carroll, "Ford Foundation Activities in the Field of Business Education," Ford Foundation Archives, no. 002970, December 27, 1958.

40. The internal memorandum was cited in James Howell's 1966 report to Ford Foundation executives summarizing the foundation's business education activities; see James Edwin Howell, "The Ford Foundation and the Revolution in Business Education: A Case Study in Philanthropy," Report, Ford Foundation Archives, no. 006353, September 1966. I believe that the undated memorandum was written in 1952 or 1953, since that was the date on the file folder it was referenced to.

41. Ibid., 4. One hope among Ford Foundation executives and individuals such as Lee Bach, Robert Gordon, and James Howell was that undergraduate business education would be replaced by graduate programs. In a 1958 speech, Robert Gordon suggested that such a trend was beginning: "Doubt about the value of undergraduate business education extends into the business schools themselves. All across the country, schools of business administration are coming to put increasing emphasis on their graduate programs. . . . The faculties of several business schools that I have visited during the past two years are giving serious thought to whether they should look ultimately to the dropping of their undergraduate business programs and to an exclusive concentration on work for the master's and doctoral degrees." Robert A. Gordon, "Business Education at the Undergraduate Level" (Convocation Commemorating the Fiftieth Anniversary of the Founding of the College of Business Administration, The University of Denver, April 25, 1958), Ford Foundation Archives, Robert Aaron Gordon files.

42. Howell, "The Ford Foundation and the Revolution in Business Education," 5–6.

43. My reading of the program memoranda and correspondence is that even by 1954, the foundation was prepared to spend at least $10 to $15 million on the program, primarily because it needed to give away large amounts of money and was therefore considering only very large-scale projects.

44. Howell, "The Ford Foundation and the Revolution in Business Education," 6.

45. Ibid.

46. Ibid. "Propaganda" directed at the business community included commissioned articles about the ongoing reforms in business education, such as one written by *BusinessWeek*'s Leonard Silk, and a commissioned placement in the December 1964 issue of *Fortune* titled "New Report Card on the Business Schools."

47. Stanford would eventually receive more than $6.5 million, but $3 million of that was for a program that was technically outside the auspices of Ford's original business school initiatives. This additional $3 million was used for an international program aimed at influencing foreign business schools and foreign doctoral students to adopt the Ford Foundation model in their home institutions.

48. Howell, "The Ford Foundation and the Revolution in Business Education," 8.

49. Ibid. In his autobiography, Harvard Business School professor Fritz Roethlisberger described the two types of faculty in the business school: "The first kind was composed of professors who were more institutionally than disciplinary or subject-matter oriented. For them the institution, that is, the Business School with its values regarding the administrative point of view and the case method, was the chief reference. They were willing to forsake any allegiance they may have had to a discipline of specialization for the development of the nonspecialized administrator. . . . The second class of professors . . . was composed of those who could neither wholly accept the sacred cows of the institution nor wholly forsake their disciplinary or specialist leanings." Roethlisberger, *The Elusive Phenomena*, 263.

50. Quoted in Schlossman, Sedlak, and Wechsler, *The "New Look"*, 21.

51. In its 1954 grant application to the foundation, Harvard Business School made several claims regarding its contributions to business education generally. For example, the school stated that 500 of its graduates were teaching or serving in administrative capacities at 178 colleges and universities. The school also said that it was providing teaching materials to 300 other American colleges and universities (and to 30 schools in other countries), having distributed 25,569 cases to these schools and permitted reproduction of more than 50,000 copies of the cases for use in more than 800 individual business school courses other than its own. It described a program, given once a year, for deans and faculty from 80 business schools on teaching with the case method. Moreover, the application stated, Dean David had helped fill deanships at 9 other schools. "To the Trustees of the Ford Foundation: A Proposal of the Harvard Graduate School of Business Administration," Ford Foundation Archives, no. 55-02, November 16, 1953.

52. Howell, "The Ford Foundation and the Revolution in Business Education," 9.

53. Ibid.

54. Carnegie Institute of Technology Graduate School of Industrial Administration, "Fact Sheet: Official Dedication, Carnegie," October 2 and 3, 1952. Donald K. David papers, HBS Archives.

55. Gleeson and Schlossman, "George Leland Bach and the Rebirth of Graduate Management Education in the United States, 1945–1975." Originally quoted in James G. March (chair), Charles Bonini, James Howell, Harold Leavitt, Arjay Miller, and Ezra Solomon, "Memorial Resolution: George Leland Bach (1915–1995)" (Campus Report, Stanford University, April 26, 1995). See also History of the Graduate School of Business, Stanford University, at http://www.gsb.stanford.edu/history/timeline/faculty_bach.html (accessed June 30, 2006).

56. Quoted at http://www.gsb.stanford.edu/history/timeline/faculty_bach.html (accessed June 30, 2006).

57. George Leland (Lee) Bach, "Proposal to the Ford Foundation for Partial Support of a Pioneering Center for Graduate Study and Research in Industrial Administration—Economics," Ford Foundation Archives, no. 55-10, Section I, September 7, 1954. The proposal was sent as part of a letter to Stanley Teele.

58. Simon, *Models of My Life*, 139.

59. Ibid.

60. The notion of linking engineering to the social sciences was developed in the Carnegie Plan for Professional Education that was initiated in 1939 by the Carnegie Institute of Technology's third president, Robert Doherty. Doherty was focused on reforming Carnegie's engineering program, which had never been as prominent as others in the field. The idea was that engineers who were not only given technical training but also educated in the humanities and social sciences (from which engineering students were required to choose one-quarter of their courses) would be better prepared to take on larger responsibilities in society. See http://www.cmu.edu/home/about/about_history.html (accessed June 30, 2006). Economics, which was seen as the most "advanced" of the social sciences, was given a central role in this plan to recast business education. See Gleeson and Schlossman, "George Leland Bach and the Rebirth of Graduate Management Education in the United States, 1945–1975."

61. George Leland (Lee) Bach, "Some Observations on the Business School of Tomorrow," *Management Science* 4, no. 4 (1958): 354.

62. George Leland (Lee) Bach et al., "Economics in the Curricula of Schools of Business: Discussion," *American Economic Review* 46, no. 2, Papers and Proceedings of the Sixty-eighth Annual Meeting of the American Economic Association (1956): 563.

63. Bach, "Some Observations on the Business School of Tomorrow," 357.

64. Howell, "The Ford Foundation and the Revolution in Business Education" 9; Schlossman, Sedlak, and Wechsler, *The "New Look"*, 19.

65. Charles T. Morrissey, "Kermit Gordon Interview with Charles Morrissey," Ford Foundation Archives, no. 18, December 19, 1972. GSIA's consecration by the Ford Foundation as an elite institution was cause for chagrin at many older schools (including Wharton, Northwestern, New York University, and the University of Michigan) that did not know what to make of this upstart. Although they were unaware of their declining reputations, schools such as Wharton and Northwestern were regarded by the Ford Foundation as having "sunk very much into the second level of business education." James Howell described "Wharton, the grande dame of them all," as "embarrassingly mediocre." Howell, "The Ford Foundation and the Revolution in Business Education," 14. These schools would later fall over themselves trying to recruit Carnegie's doctoral students and over the years would successfully lure Carnegie faculty as either faculty members or deans.

66. Howell, "The Ford Foundation and the Revolution in Business Education" 7.

67. Thomas Carroll, "Letter to Stanley Teele," Ford Foundation Archives, Thomas Carroll papers, sec. 57-224, 1954.

68. Ford Foundation Oral History Project: Bernard Berelson, 6–7, Ford Foundation Archives, 1972. Stouffer, a Harvard sociologist, was an expert in statistical analysis of public opinion research. The Social Relations Department was a Rockefeller-funded experiment at Harvard during the 1950s that attempted to unify the social sciences. It would eventually encompass the major social sciences of psychology, sociology, economics, and anthropology. Harvard's economics department chose to remain independent from this experiment, and the social relations department was dismantled in the late 1960s.

69. Ford Foundation Oral History Project: Berelson, 7–8, Ford Foundation Archives, 1972. L. J. Henderson was a university professor at Harvard. Trained as a physician, Henderson played an instrumental integrative role in developing the systems perspective of organizational behavior associated with Harvard Business School. Zaleznik's contributions to research on leadership will be discussed in chapter 8. On how the Ford reforms affected the University of Chicago's business school, see 260–261.

70. Quoted in Howell, "The Ford Foundation and the Revolution in Business Education," 25.

71. Ibid., 11.

72. Ibid., 11–12.

73. The seminars, held on the campus of Harvard Business School, were structured to mirror case discussion methods and also involved teaching participants to write cases.

74. Quoted in Schlossman, Sedlak, and Wechsler, The "New Look", 37–38.

75. In his The University of Utopia, Hutchins outlined his basic philosophy of education and its responsibility to society: "The object of the educational system, taken as a whole, is not to produce hands for industry or to teach the young how to make a living. It is to produce responsible citizens." Robert E. Gleeson, "Stalemate at Stanford, 1945–1958: The Long Prelude to the New Look at Stanford," Selections 13, no. 3 (1997).

76. The head of the University of Chicago was called the chancellor from 1945, when Hutchins took the title, until 1961, the year after Lawrence Kimpton, his successor, resigned from the chancellorship.

77. Wallis was an economist with close intellectual affinities with Chicago colleagues Milton Friedman and George Stigler. Wallis went on from the deanship at Chicago to become chancellor and president of the University of Rochester, where he appointed William Meckling dean of the business school; Rochester's business school, in turn, became the intellectual center for the development of agency theory, which would subsequently be used to legitimate the idea of an active market for corporate control as a way to impose discipline on corporate management. During his

distinguished career, Wallis also served as a special assistant to President Eisenhower, advised Presidents Nixon, Ford, and Reagan, served (under Reagan) as under secretary of state for economic affairs in George Shultz's State Department, and was a resident scholar at the American Enterprise Institute.

78. Quoted in Schlossman, Sedlak, and Wechsler, *The "New Look"*, 48.

79. Ibid.

80. Gleeson, "Stalemate at Stanford, 1945–1958."

81. Quoted in Gordon and Howell, *Higher Education for Business*, 255.

82. Howell, "The Ford Foundation and the Revolution in Business Education," 14.

83. Schlossman, Sedlak, and Wechsler, *The "New Look."*

84. http://www.gsb.stanford.edu/history/timeline/international.html(accessed June 30, 2006) describes ICAME thus: "The International Center for the Advancement of Management Education (ICAME) was established at the Graduate School of Business under a $3,500,000 grant from the Ford Foundation in 1960. The purpose of the grant was to offer a flexible program of advanced training for faculty members from business schools in emerging countries and to make available a wide range of resources to meet the varying needs of the schools. The program as it was originally established provided fellowships to foreign professors of business for a nine-month program of study with emphasis on a different functional area each year. Its first course of study began June 1963. ICAME was the first school-within-a-school in the world where the students were faculty at foreign institutions."

85. Quoted in John Wheeler, "Changes in Collegiate Business Education in the United States 1954–64 and the Role of the Ford Foundation in These Changes," Draft Report, Ford Foundation Archives, no. 004933, 1965, 142.

86. Although Ford focused on graduate education and had hoped that its efforts would bring an end to undergraduate business education, by 1959 the foundation recognized that many business schools would continue to have large undergraduate programs in business. Wharton and Northwestern, for example, were given grants to improve their undergraduate curricula. Wharton radically changed its undergraduate curriculum in the late 1960s to emphasize management science and quantitative analysis; for a detailed description of this change, see ibid., 167. Northwestern eventually eliminated its undergraduate business program in 1966 and began to adopt Ford's social science research model.

87. In 1958, Ford granted $1.2 million per year for five years for "a program to Improve Teaching and Encourage Research in Less Prominent Schools of Departments of Business Administration" through development seminars, summer fellowships to allow faculty to complete doctorates, and grants to less prominent schools to support research. That same year, Ford launched a multiphase program designed to improve business education through increased application of the social sciences, mathematics, and statistics to business problems. This program included summer seminars, on-campus programs, and fellowships to permit faculty

to retool; visiting research professorships on various campuses; and encourage-ment of faculty and doctoral students in the social sciences to do research on busi-ness-related problems. As part of this effort, Ford provided fellowships for faculty members already in business schools who wanted further training in quantitative analysis and the social sciences. From about 1959 to 1962, the foundation funded one-year sabbaticals for faculty to improve their competence in these areas. Of the thirty-three faculty fellowship winners during these years, "about half . . . studied mathematics and statistics and the others concentrated on some aspect of the behavioral sciences." Thomas Carroll, "Memo to AACSB Deans," Memorandum to Deans of Member Schools of AACSB, Ford Foundation Archives, no. 002970, December 24, 1958.

88. Bach letter to Stanley F. Teele, January 28, 1957; Carnegie, Summer Program Box 18, f.8, HBS Archives, Stanley Teele papers.

89. Howell, "The Ford Foundation and the Revolution in Business Education," 29.

90. Quoted in ibid.

91. Ibid.

92. James W. Schmotter, "An Interview with Professor James E. Howell," *Selections* 1, no. 1 (1984): 9.

93. Frank Cook Pierson, *The Education of American Businessman: A Study of University-College Programs in Business Education* (New York: McGraw-Hill, 1959).

94. Schmotter, "An Interview with Professor James Howell," 9.

95. Gordon and Howell, *Higher Education for Business*, 6.

96. "Research and Advanced Training in Business," Ford Foundation Archives, Activities of Program in Economic Development and Administration, 1950–1961.

97. Pierson, *The Education of American Businessmen.*

98. Gordon and Howell, *Higher Education for Business*, 70–71.

99. Wheeler, "Changes in Collegiate Business Education in the United States 1954–64 and the Role of the Ford Foundation in These Changes."

100. Gordon and Howell, *Higher Education for Business*, 69–70.

101. George Leland Bach, "Managerial Decision Making as an Organizing Con-cept," in Pierson, *The Education of American Businessmen*, 321–322.

102. In the wake of the issuance of the Gordon-Howell report, the foundation undertook an effort to ensure that its recommendations would be implemented be-yond the "centers of excellence" and second-tier schools that had formed the focus of its program to date; it did this by sponsoring a series of regional conferences for busi-ness school faculty and deans to discuss the report's findings and guidelines for im-plementing its recommendations. In 1959, alone, Ford-sponsored conferences were held at Oklahoma State University and the universities of Michigan, Pennsylvania, North Carolina, and Minnesota. New York University was given $500,000 to train its faculty in how to conduct research. The Wharton School was granted $700,000 to move its program away from its heavily vocational curriculum and to reenergize

faculty research. These efforts were all directed toward making a faculty's foundation in the social sciences and quantitative analysis the norm in virtually every competent business school across the United States.

103. Wheeler, "Changes in Collegiate Business Education in the United States 1954–64 and the Role of the Ford Foundation in These Changes."

104. Ibid.

105. Sass, 259. Moreover, Sass notes, procedures for faculty hiring and promotion at Wharton began to resemble the methods used in the disciplinary departments of the University of Pennsylvania.

106. Wheeler, "Changes in Collegiate Business Education in the United States 1954–64 and the Role of the Ford Foundatiion in These Changes."

107. Ibid.

108. American Association of Collegiate Schools of Business, "The AACSB Bulletin" (St. Louis, MO, April 1966), 147. Consistent with the AACSB's tradition of providing little guidance on how such guidelines should be interpreted, no explanation of how this stipulation should be translated into practice appears in any AACSB document that I could find.

109. American Association of Collegiate Schools of Business, *The American Association of Collegiate Schools of Business, 1916–1966* (Homewood, IL: R. D. Irwin, 1966), 151.

110. Ibid., 153.

111. Herbert Simon was one influential business school professor who questioned the pedagogical value of the case method. As he once noted: "I observed the case method several times during seminars I helped teach at the Bureau of the Budget. I would teach a class, and I would be followed by a Harvard Business School professor. He could run an entire case discussion by standing up in front of the room and saying nothing more than 'Oh,' 'Um,' and 'Uh-huh,' with a thousand different inflections of his voice. This type of teaching relied on the students to figure out what they were supposed to learn. I could cite a thousand different psychology articles that say you need to tell people explicitly what you want them to learn, or else they won't learn it." Quoted in Robert E. Gleeson and Steven L. Schlossman, "The Many Faces of the New Look: The University of Virginia, Carnegie Tech, and the Reform of American Management Education in the Postwar Era (Part II)," *Selections* 8, no. 4 (1992): 4.

112. Wheeler, "Changes in Collegiate Business Education in the United States 1954–64 and the Role of the Ford Foundation in These Changes," 101.

113. Advisory Group to the Ford Foundation, "Program for Area III on Economic Development and Administration," Report, Ford Foundation Archives, no. 005047, 1954, 32. In many courses, cases were not used at all. For example, in 1964, thirty of the sixty-four MBA programs at AACSB-accredited schools used a textbook rather than cases to teach subjects like accounting and finance.

114. James W. Schmotter, "The Graduate Management Admissions Council: A Brief History, 1953–1992," *Selections* 9, no. 2 (1993). For a background on the GMAC, see Carroll, "Memo to AACSB Deans," 5.

115. Wheeler, "Changes in Collegiate Business Education in the United States 1954–64 and the Role of the Ford Foundation in These Changes."

116. Additional disciplinary faculty receiving rotating professorships were sociologists Peter Blau (Chicago), Robert Dubin (Oregon), Morris Janowitz (Michigan), and William F. Whyte (Cornell); psychologists Harold Guetzkow and Harold Kelley (Minnesota); and political scientist David Truman (Columbia).

117. Gleeson and Schlossman, "The Many Faces of the New Look," 12–13; Wheeler, "Changes in Collegiate Business Education in the United States 1954–64 and the Role of the Ford Foundation in These Changes."

118. As Bach explained: "We were too small to produce enough current managers to make a difference. MBAs were not the main product. We wanted just enough for credibility. Research was our main product." During the 1950s, it was the Ph.D. program that "grew to become the jewel in the school's crown." See Wheeler, "Changes in Collegiate Business Education in the United States 1954–64 and the Role of the Ford Foundation in These Changes," 84.

119. Gleeson and Schlossman, "The Many Faces of the New Look," 11.

120. Roethlisberger, *The Elusive Phenomena*, 293.

121. Wheeler, "Changes in Collegiate Business Education in the United States 1954–64 and the Role of the Ford Foundation in These Changes."

122. The type of graduate who received a doctorate of business administration or doctorate of commercial science in the mid-1950s, as termed by George Leland (Lee) Bach, "Foundation Policy toward Basic Research in Business," Memorandum to Thomas Carroll and Robert Aaron Gordon, Ford Foundation Archives, no. 002592, December 14, 1960.

123. George Leland (Lee) Bach, "The Ford Foundation and the Revolution in Business Education," Ford Foundation Archives, no. 002591, September 20, 1960.

124. Bach, "Foundation Policy toward Basic Research in Business," 3.

125. Bach, "The Ford Foundation and the Revolution in Business Education," 4.

126. Ibid.

127. Ibid.

128. Gabor, *The Capitalist Philosophers*, 230; Gleeson and Schlossman, "George Leland Bach and the Rebirth of Graduate Management Education in the United States, 1945–1975," 13.

129. Simon, *Models of My Life*, 143.

130. Gleeson and Schlossman, "George Leland Bach and the Rebirth of Graduate Management Education in the United States, 1945–1975," 24.

131. Quoted in Gabor, *The Capitalist Philosophers*, 230.

132. Quoted in ibid., 252.

133. Ibid.

134. Michael W. Sedlak and Steven L. Schlossman, "The Case Method and Business Education at Northwestern University, 1906–1971," *Selections 7*, no. 3 (1991): 33.

135. Ibid., 35.

136. Gleeson and Schlossman, "The Many Faces of the New Look," 20.

137. Ibid.

138. Ibid., 21.

139. Sass, *The Pragmatic Imagination*, 312.

140. Bach, "Some Observations on the Business School of Tomorrow," 357.

141. Bronfenbrenner quoted in Gleeson and Schlossman, "The Many Faces of the New Look," 21.

Chapter 7
Unintended Consequences: The Post-Ford Business School and the Fall of Managerialism

1. John A. Byrne, "The Battle of the B-Schools Is Getting Bloodier," *BusinessWeek*, March 24, 1986, 61.

2. Part of the growth in number of MBA students can also be accounted for by the changing demographic composition of the group receiving MBAs. As a result of the Bakke decision (legalizing affirmative action in university admissions) and changing societal values, the number of MBAs awarded to women and minorities increased dramatically during the 1970s. The percentage of women receiving MBAs rose from about 1 percent in 1965 to about 4 percent in 1970 and then to 30 percent by 1980. It was also during this period that the percentage of minority students pursuing an MBA increased beyond token levels to about 10 percent in 1980. Ellen Ruben, "Trends in Minority Enrollment," *Selections* (Special Issue, 1986).

3. In 1967, the Carnegie Institute of Technology merged with the Mellon Institute of Industrial Research in Pittsburgh to form Carnegie Mellon University.

4. Lawrence Fouraker, "Graduate School of Business Administration" (Boston: Harvard Business School, 1974), 372.

5. Derek Bok, "The President's Report" (Cambridge: Harvard University, 1978), 5.

6. Pamphlet, Graduate School of Business, Stanford University, 1978.

7. Lyman W. Porter, Lawrence E. McKibbin, and American Assembly of Collegiate Schools of Business, *Management Education and Development: Drift or Thrust into the 21st Century?* (New York: McGraw-Hill Book Co., 1988), 65. See pp. 47–87 for a full summary of the state of business school curricula in the 1970s and early 1980s.

8. Gerald F. Davis, Kristina Diekmann, and Catherine H. Tinsley, "The Decline and Fall of the Conglomerate Firm in the 1980s: The Deinstitutionalization of an Organizational Form," *American Sociological Review* 59, no. 4 (1994); Gerald F. Davis and Douglas McAdam, "Corporations, Classes, and Social Movements after

Managerialism," in *Research in Organizational Behavior*, vol. 22, ed. Barry Staw and John R. Sutton (New York: Elsevier, 2000), 195–238.

9. Fouraker, "Graduate School of Business Administration," 372.

10. Arjay Miller, "Business' Social Responsibility," *New York Certified Public Accountant* 36, no. 6 (1966): 456.

11. During the late 1960s and early 1970s, student protests had a discernible impact on the elective curriculum at several prominent business schools. MIT, NYU, and Stanford, for example, all offered urban studies courses. Stanford's Arjay Miller and Lee Bach were particularly committed to urban causes, and the Stanford catalog came to feature several courses in public-sector decision making, black economic development, small business development, and the management of new firms, as well as the new concentration in public management mentioned in the discussion of Bach at Stanford in chapter 6.

12. Mark J. Roe, *Strong Managers, Weak Owners: The Political Roots of American Corporate Finance* (Princeton, NJ: Princeton University Press, 1994).

13. As quoted in David Frum, *How We Got Here: The 70's, the Decade That Brought You Modern Life, for Better or Worse* (New York: Basic Books, 2000), 302.

14. Nitin Nohria, Davis Dyer, and Frederick Dalzell, *Changing Fortunes: Remaking the Industrial Corporation* (New York: Wiley, 2002).

15. Ibid., 43

16. Daniel P. Moynihan, *Maximum Feasible Misunderstanding: Community Action in the War on Poverty*, The Clarke A. Sanford Lectures on Local Government and Community Life, 1967 (New York: Free Press, 1969), xii–xiii

17. Richard Sennett and Jonathan Cobb, *The Hidden Injuries of Class* (New York: Vintage Books, 1973).

18. Judson Gooding, "Blue-Collar Blues in the Assembly Line," *Fortune* 82 (July 1970). As quoted in Frum, *How We Got Here*, p. 21.

19. George C. Lodge, *The New American Ideology: How the Ideological Basis of Legitimate Authority in America Is Being Radically Transformed, the Profound Implications for Our Society in General and the Great Corporations in Particular* (New York: Knopf, 1975), 4.

20. Adm. Hyman Rickover, "Getting the Job Done Right," *New York Times*, November 25, 1981.

21. William J. Abernathy and Robert Hayes, "Managing Our Way to Economic Decline," *Harvard Business Review*, July–August 1980, 70.

22. William G. Ouchi, *Theory Z: How American Business Can Meet the Japanese Challenge* (Reading, MA: Addison-Wesley, 1981); Richard T. Pascale and Anthony G. Athos, *The Art of Japanese Management: Applications for American Executives* (New York: Simon and Schuster, 1981).

23. For another discussion of the dethronement of corporate management in response to the economic crisis of the 1970s and the ideological shifts it ushered in, see

my *Searching for a Corporate Savior: The Irrational Quest for Charismatic CEOs* (Princeton, NJ: Princeton University Press, 2002), 52–61.

24. T. Boone Pickens, "Shareholders: The Forgotten People," *Journal of Business Strategy* 6, no. 1 (1985): 4

25. For a particularly unflattering portrayal of takeover artists and corporate executives, see Bryan Burrough and John Helyar, *Barbarians at the Gate: The Fall of RJR Nabisco* (New York: Harper & Row, 1990). For a discussion of how this gave rise to a new model of CEO, see chapter 2 of Khurana, *Searching for a Corporate Savior*.

26. Davis, Diekmann, and Tinsley, "The Decline and Fall of the Conglomerate Firm in the 1980s"; Davis and McAdam, "Corporations, Classes, and Social Movements after Managerialism"; Michael Useem, *Executive Defense: Shareholder Power and Corporate Reorganization* (Cambridge: Harvard University Press, 1993).

27. Nohria, Dyer, and Dalzell, *Changing Fortunes*.

28. Steven N. Kaplan, "The Effects of Management Buyouts on Operating Performance and Value," *Journal of Financial Economics* 24 (1989); Steven N. Kaplan, "The Staying Power of Leveraged Buyouts," *Journal of Financial Economics* 29 (1991).

29. Bengt Holmstrom and Steven N. Kaplan, "Corporate Governance and Merger Activity in the United States: Making Sense of the 1980s and 1990s," *Journal of Economic Perspectives* 15, no. 2 (2001); Useem, *Executive Defense*.

30. Nohria, Dyer, and Dalzell, *Changing Fortunes*, 104–109.

31. Steven Prokesch, "Remaking the American CEO," *New York Times*, January 25, 1987.

32. Daniel Bell, *The Coming of Post-industrial Society: A Venture in Social Forecasting* (New York: Basic Books, 1976).

33. Michael Jensen, "The Modern Industrial Revolution, Exit, and the Failure of Internal Control Systems," *Journal of Finance* 48, no. 3 (1993).

34. Gerald F. Davis, "New Directions in Corporate Governance," *Annual Review of Sociology* 31 (2005); Nohria, Dyer, and Dalzell, *Changing Fortunes*.

35. Holmstrom and Kaplan, "Corporate Governance and Merger Activity in the United States."

36. Useem, *Executive Defense*.

37. Holmstrom and Kaplan, "Corporate Governance and Merger Activity in the United States."

38. Porter, McKibbin, and American Assembly of Collegiate Schools of Business, *Management Education and Development*, 133.

39. American Assembly of Collegiate Schools of Business, *Sustaining Scholarship in Business Schools* (St. Louis: AACSB, International, 2003).

40. Porter, McKibbin, and American Assembly of Collegiate Schools of Business, *Management Education and Development*, 161–169.

41. James W. Schmotter, "Interview with Dean Robert Jaedicke," *Selections* 6, no. 2 (1989); James W. Schmotter, "An Interview with Professor James E. Howell," *Selections* 1, no. 1 (1984).

42. David W. E. Cabell, *Cabell's Directory of Publishing Opportunities in Business, Administration, and Economics* (Beaumont, TX: Cabell Pub. Co., 1978).

43. James G. March and Robert I. Sutton, "Organizational Performance as a Dependent Variable," *Organization Science* 8, no. 6 (1997): 703.

44. Bok, "The President's Report," 5.

45. Lawrence Fouraker, "Graduate School of Business Administration," (Boston: Harvard Business School 1976), 330.

46. Nancy L. Ross, "B-School Ratings: Name of the Game; Rating Game Played at U.S. B-Schools," *Washington Post*, January 4, 1978.

47. Nancy F. Koehn et al., "Historical Perspective. Making Choices: Aspects of the History of the Harvard Business School MBA Program" (Boston: Harvard Business School, 1992), 26.

48. Ibid., 56. These changes in Harvard's hiring practices were partly a response to the Ford Foundation reforms and partly a pragmatic response to the inability of the school to produce enough high-quality faculty, adequately immersed in the new disciplinary and quantitative orientation, from its own doctoral program.

49. Alexander T. Nicolai, "The Bridge to the 'Real World': Applied Science or a 'Schizophrenic Tour De Force'?" *Journal of Management Studies* 41, no. 6 (2004).

50. Michael C. Jensen and Clifford W. Smith, "The Theory of Corporate Finance: A Historical Overview," in *The Modern Theory of Corporate Finance*, ed. Michael C. Jensen and Clifford W. Smith (New York: McGraw-Hill, 1984), 2.

51. Panagiotis Andrikopoulos, "Modern Finance vs. Behavioural Finance: An Overview of Key Concepts and Major Arguments," SSRN Working Paper, 2005.

52. Ibid., 2.

53. Jensen and Smith, "The Theory of Corporate Finance," 5.

54. Jeffrey Pfeffer, "Barriers to the Advance of Organization Science: Paradigm Development as a Dependent Variable," *Academy of Management Review* 18 (1993).

55. Kimberly D. Elsbach, Robert I. Sutton, and D. A. Whetten, "Perspectives on Developing Management Theory, circa 1999: Moving from Shrill Monologues to (Relatively) Tame Dialogues," *Academy of Management Review* 24 (1999): 627.

56. Porter, McKibbin, and American Assembly of Collegiate Schools of Business, *Management Education and Development*, 142.

57. Sheldon Zalaznick, "The MBA, the Man, the Myth, and the Method," *Fortune*, May 1968, 202.

58. James H. S. Bossard and J. Frederick Dewhurst, *University Education for Business: A Study of Existing Needs and Practices* (Philadelphia: University of Pennsylvania Press, 1931), 319.

59. For discussions of the role of economic theory in changing the paradigm of management education and management research, see Fabrizio Ferraro, Jeffrey Pfeffer, and Robert I. Sutton, "Economics Language and Assumptions: How Theories Can Become Self-Fulfilling," *Academy of Management Review* 30, no. 1 (2005); Sumantra Ghoshal and Peter Moran, "Bad for Practice: A Critique of the Transaction Cost Theory," *Academy of Management Review* 21, no. 1 (1996); Jeffrey Pfeffer, *New Directions for Organization Theory: Problems and Prospects* (New York: Oxford University Press, 1997).

60. Pfeffer, *New Directions for Organization Theory*, 44. In a lecture on organizational theory, Pfeffer notes that the asymmetric influence of economics goes beyond management research: "Citation patterns in academia show the growing importance of economics in political science (Green and Shapiro, 1994), law (Posner, 2003), and organization science (Pfeffer, 1997). Economics is cited more by other social sciences even as economics cites those other social sciences much less frequently (Pieters and Baumgartner, 2002: Baron and Hannan, 1994), which provides evidence of the status advantage enjoyed by economics" (ibid.).

61. Ronald H. Coase, "The Nature of the Firm," *Economica* 4, no. 16 (1937): 390.

62. Oliver E. Williamson, Sidney G. Winter, and R. H. Coase, *The Nature of the Firm: Origins, Evolution, and Development* (New York: Oxford University Press, 1991), 61.

63. Herbert Alexander Simon, *Administrative Behavior: A Study of Decision-Making Processes in Administrative Organization*, 2d ed. (New York: Macmillan, 1957).

64. Oliver E. Williamson, *The Economics of Discretionary Behavior: Managerial Objectives in a Theory of the Firm*, Ford Foundation Doctoral Dissertation Series (Englewood Cliffs, NJ: Prentice-Hall [published thesis from Carnegie Institute of Technology], 1964).

65. Ghoshal and Moran, "Bad for Practice." A related critique of transaction-cost theory was discussed by Granovetter in his groundbreaking article on social networks and markets. Granovetter argued that that transaction-cost theory substantially misspecified the mediating role of relationships and trust in governing economic relations; see Mark Granovetter, "Economic Action and Social Structure: The Problem of Embeddedness," *American Journal of Sociology* 91, no. 3 (1985).

66. Milton Friedman, "The Social Responsibility of Business Is to Increase Its Profits," *New York Times Magazine*, September 13, 1970. Historian Steven Schlossman notes that in the 1970s, "a business community mired in recession . . . outpaced by foreign competition," "a skeptical public," and "assertive and more powerful students" raised questions about what was being taught in business school classrooms. Steven L. Schlossman, Michael W. Sedlak, and Harold S. Wechsler, *The "New Look": The Ford Foundation and the Revolution in Business Education* (Los Angeles: Graduate Management Admission Council, 1987). The views of Michael Jensen referred to here were spoken to the author in a personal communication.

67. *Institutional Investor* described this group: "Jensen, Jarrell, Ruback, and a co-terie of other researchers, mostly like-minded Chicago or Rochester alums, have a new tune for the pundits and pear-shaped executives who agitate for a return to the days of genteel board luncheons and smaller block trades. They sing loud, and Jensen the loudest. Their stage is Jensen's research center, which funds conferences and such studies as 'Antimerger Policy and Stockholder Returns: A Re-Examination of the Market Power Hypothesis,' 'Take-Over Defenses via Corporate Charter Amendments and Their Effects on Stockholder Welfare' and 'Raiders or Saviors?: The Evidence on Six Controversial Investors.' Their fan-club newsletter is Jensen's *Journal of Financial Economics*, which then publishes much of this research." Michael VerMeulen, "Mergers and Acquisitions: Economist Michael Jensen Defends Corporate Raiders and Greenmailers and Has Developed an Economic Rationale for Takeovers," *Institutional Investor*, August 1985, 75. Some of the core papers are Eugene F. Fama, "Agency Problems and the Theory of the Firm," *Journal of Political Economy* 88, no. 2 (1980); Eugene F. Fama and Michael C. Jensen, "Separation of Ownership and Control," *Journal of Law and Economics* 26, no. 2 (1983); Michael C. Jensen and William H. Meckling, "Theory of the Firm: Managerial Behavior, Agency Costs, and Ownership Structure," *Journal of Financial Economics* 3 (1976).

68. For a summary of these contributions, see Kathleen M. Eisenhardt, "Agency Theory: An Assessment and Review," *Academy of Management Review* 14, no. 1 (1989); Kathleen M. Eisenhardt, "Control: Organizational and Economic Approaches," *Management Science* 31, no. 2 (1985); John W. Pratt and Richard Zeckhauser, "Principals and Agents: An Overview," in *Principals and Agents: The Structure of Business*, ed. John W. Pratt, Richard Zeckhauser, and Kenneth Joseph Arrow (Boston: Harvard Business School Press, 1991).

69. Michael C. Jensen, "CEO Incentives: It's Not How Much You Pay, but How," *Harvard Business Review*, May–June 1990; Michael C. Jensen, "Is Leverage an Invitation to Bankruptcy?," *Wall Street Journal*, February 1, 1989; Michael C. Jensen and Perry Fagan, "Capitalism Isn't Broken," *Wall Street Journal*, March 29, 1996.

70. An *Institutional Investor* profile depicts Michael Jensen as not only creating an idea but creating his "own aesthetic in violent opposition to the status quo. Jensen, in a sense, is making a kind of punk statement by rejecting the axioms that even financial conservatives accept and instead advocating efficient-market remedies in their absolute extreme." VerMeulen, "Mergers and Acquisitions," 72.

71. Jensen, "Is Leverage an Invitation to Bankruptcy?" The use of high levels of debt to finance "leveraged buyouts" also received crucial theoretical support from the work of economists Merton Miller and Franco Modigliani on corporate finance. Their seminal paper, titled "The Cost of Capital, Corporate Finance and the Theory of Investment" (1958), as was noted by the Nobel Prize committee in its announcement for Miller's prize, demonstrated that leverage did not affect a firm's market value: "Using this basic model, Miller and Modigliani derived two so-called invariance theorems,

now known as the MM theorems. The first invariance theorem states that (i) the choice between equity financing and borrowing does not affect a firm's market value and average costs of capital, and (ii) the expected return on a firm's shares (and hence the cost of equity capital) increases linearly with the ratio between the firm's liabilities and equity, *i.e.*, the well-known leverage effect. The second invariance theorem states that under the same assumptions, a firm's dividend policy does not affect its market value." Royal Swedish Academy of Sciences, "This Year's Laureates Are Pioneers in the Theory of Financial Economics and Corporate Finance," *The Bank of Sweden Prize in Economic Sciences in Memory of Alfred Nobel* (October 16, 1990).

72. Michael Jensen, "Takeovers: Folklore and Science," *Harvard Business Review*, November–December 1984. This article was described by the editor of *Harvard Business Review* as one of the most controversial it ever published, generating numerous angry responses and reactions that took up seven pages in the subsequent issue. The Harvard Business School Publishing Web site summarized the article thus: "Shareholders, who are the most important constituency of the modern corporation because they bear its residual risk, benefit most directly from acquisitions because of the increase in the value of target company shares. Many current criticisms directed at takeover activity are wrong or based on faulty logic. Takeovers protect shareholders from mismanagement of a corporation as they allow alternative management teams to compete for the right to manage the corporation's assets. The takeover market provides a unique, powerful, and impersonal mechanism to accomplish the major restructuring and redeployment of assets continually required by changes in technology and consumer preferences." http://harvardbusinessonline.hbsp.harvard.edu/b02/en/common/item_detail.jhtml?id=84609 (accessed May 30, 2006).

73. Michael C. Jensen, "A Helping Hand for Entrenched Managers," *Wall Street Journal* (Eastern edition), November 4, 1987, 1. Pickens reportedly handed out copies of Jensen's famous *Harvard Business Review* article defending takeovers. Part of Jensen's argument in this article was that those who were against takeovers believed in "folklore," whereas his views were grounded in "science."

74. Michael VerMeulen, "The Iconoclast of M&A," *Institutional Investor* 19, no. 8 (1985): 71. The reporter summarized Jensen's views on takeovers: "Jensen focuses on three benefits of takeovers, stating that they do not harm shareholders. They are an efficient use of a company's resources. And, that golden parachutes which guarantee multi-million dollar payouts to CEOs in the event of a takeover are defensible since shareholders still benefit when a firm is taken over."

75. Frank Dobbin and Dirk Zorn, "Corporate Malfeasance and the Myth of Shareholder Value," in *Political Power and Social Theory*, ed. Diane E. Davis (Greenwich, CT: JAI Press, 2005), 187.

76. F. M. Scherer, "Corporate Ownership and Control," in *The U.S. Business Corporation: An Institution in Transition*, ed. John R. Meyer and James M. Gustafson (New York: Ballinger Publishing Company, 1988), 53–54.

77. Corporate Governance and American Competitiveness, March 1990: *Statement of the Business Roundtable,* The Business Roundtable: An Association of Chief Executive Officers Committed to Improving Public Policy.

78. Michael Jensen et al., *Organizations and Markets: History and Development of the Course and the Field* (1997), 15.

79. The Business Roundtable: An Association of Chief Executive Officers Committed to Improving Public Policy, "Statement on Corporate Governance," September, 1997, 3–4. Bengt Holmstrom and Steven N. Kaplan write that by the 1990s, the shareholder perspective, particularly the one rooted in legitimating hostile takeovers, had become institutionalized inside the culture and structure of American corporations. They write: "[C]orporations in the 1990s began to emulate many of the beneficial attributes of leveraged buyouts. This could explain why hostility declined: hostile takeovers were no longer needed, as companies voluntarily restructured and adopted a shareholder value perspective with the prodding from time to time of institutional shareholders. The fear of the 1980s hostile takeovers likely played a part in this development. Also important (and perhaps more so) is that managers became aware of the potential benefits of pursuing shareholder value by observing the success of LBOs and takeovers in the 1980s. Helped along by generous stock option programs, management came to endorse shareholder value in the 1990s and to pursue it with vigor." Holmstrom and Kaplan, "Corporate Governance and Merger Activity in the United States," 132–133.

80. Michael Jensen and Karen Hopper Wruck, "Coordination, Control, and the Management of Organizations: Course Content and Materials (3rd of 4 CCMO Documents)," *SSRN* (2001), 1–3.

81. Jensen et al., *Organizations and Markets,* 14.

82. Students taking the course were told, for example, that "[a]t times the material may be extraordinarily frustrating, at others deceptively easy. Frustration often results from material that adopts a position radically different from students' current views." Jensen and Wruck, "Coordination, Control, and the Management of Organizations," 1.

83. John W. Meyer, "The Effects of Education as an Institution," *American Journal of Sociology* 83, no. 1 (1977).

84. Robert G. Eccles, Nitin Nohria, and James D. Berkley, *Beyond the Hype: Rediscovering the Essence of Management* (Boston: Harvard Business School Press, 1992), 29.

85. Ferraro, Pfeffer, and Sutton, "Economics Language and Assumptions."

86. Ghoshal and Moran, "Bad for Practice."

87. Quoted in ibid.

88. M. C. Jensen and W. H. Meckling, "The Nature of Man," *Journal of Applied Finance* 7, no. 2 (1994) (revised July 1997). Commenting on this passage in Jensen and Meckling's paper, Henry Mintzberg, Robert Simons, and Kunal Basu, in a 2002 *MIT Sloan Management Review* article titled "Beyond Selfishness," somewhat understatedly

call Jensen and Meckling's use of the Shaw story "startling." Henry Mintzberg, Robert Simons, and Kunal Basu, "Beyond Selfishness," *MIT Sloan Management Review*, Fall 2002, 68. Recently, Jensen has revisited this cost-benefit approach as it applies to integrity. He now suggests that a trade-off approach can lead to a utilitarian logic that undermines individual and organizational effectiveness.

89. Ghoshal and Moran, "Bad for Practice."

90. Addressing the changing rhetoric about management in business schools during the late 1980s, Harvard Business School professor Gordon Donaldson noted, "The sinister phrase 'management entrenchment' became popular in academic research, even in schools of business administration—a startling reminder of how far we had come from the days when the excellence of American professional management was widely proclaimed as a unique competitive advantage." Gordon Donaldson, *Corporate Restructuring: Managing the Change Process from Within* (Boston: Harvard Business School Press, 1994), 18.

91. By contrast with this atomistic conception of managers, many agency theorists conceptualize shareholders as a single interest group, then argue that this group represents the only interest with a legitimate claim to influence managerial decision making. Lucian A. Bebchuk and Jesse M. Fried, for example, write: "The separation of ownership and control creates what financial economists call an 'agency relationship': a company's managers act as agents of its shareholders. The principals (the shareholders) cannot directly ensure that the agents (the managers) will always act in the principals' best interests. As a result, the manager-agents, whose interests do not fully overlap those of the shareholder-principals, may deviate from the best course of action for shareholders." Lucian A. Bebchuk and Jesse M. Fried, *Pay without Performance: The Unfulfilled Promise of Executive Compensation* (Cambridge: Harvard University Press, 2004), 15–16. For an example of how agency theory's ideas of maximizing firm value are linked to shareholder value, see Sundaram and Inkpen, "The Corporate Objective Revisited," SSRN, 2001.

92. Armen A. Alchian and Harold Demsetz, "Production, Information Costs, and Economic Organization," *American Economic Review* 62 (1972): 778.

93. The notion that organizations are social systems is one of the most fundamental to have been established in modern sociology, political science, anthropology, and psychology. Through numerous ethnographies (for example, see Gideon Kunda, *Engineering Culture: Control and Commitment in a High-Tech Corporation*, Labor and Social Change [Philadelphia: Temple University Press, 1992]; Leslie A. Perlow, *When You Say Yes but Mean No: How Silencing Conflict Wrecks Relationships and Companies, and What You Can Do about It* [New York: Crown Business, 2003]), and detailed field studies (e.g., Alvin W. Gouldner, *Patterns of Industrial Bureaucracy* [Glencoe, IL: Free Press, 1954]; Philip Selznick, *TVA and the Grass Roots: A Study in the Sociology of Formal Organization* [Berkeley and Los Angeles: University of California Press, 1949]), one of the core ideas that has been established is that when people come together in collectivities, a normative structure develops, and that this normative structure subsequently creates a

commonality among people in the forms of behaviors and patterned interactions, as well as feelings and sentiments, among the group and those outside of the group. For an overview of this research, see W. Richard Scott, *Organizations: Rational, Natural, and Open Systems*, 3d ed. (Englewood Cliffs, NJ: Prentice Hall, 1992). For a legal criticism of the nexus of contracts view, see Robert C. Clark, "Agency Costs versus Fiduciary Duties," in *Principals and Agents: The Structure of Business*, ed. John W. Pratt, Richard Zeckhauser, and Kenneth Joseph Arrow (Boston: Harvard Business School Press, 1991).

94. As quoted in "The MBA," *Selections*, Special Issue (1990): 46.

95. Derek Curtis Bok, *The Cost of Talent: How Executives and Professionals Are Paid and How It Affects America* (New York: Free Press 1993).

96. Lawrence Fouraker, "Graduate School of Business Administration" (Boston: Harvard Business School 1971), 305–308.

97. Nicholas Lemann, *The Big Test: The Secret History of the American Meritocracy* (New York: Farrar, Straus and Giroux, 1999).

98. For an interesting summary of elite MBA students, employers, and business schools, see *Business Week Guide to the Best Business Schools*, 6th ed. (New York: McGraw-Hill, 1999); Monica Higgins and Christine Teebagy, "Recent Facts about MBA Job Searches," *Harvard Business School Case* 9-404-013 (2004). For specific examples of how MBA students have avoided traditional career paths, see the Building Career Foundations video cases developed by Monica Higgins: Monica Higgins, "Building Career Foundations," in *Building Career Foundations* (Boston: Harvard Business School Publishing, 2000).

99. Bok, "The President's Report," 5. It is worth noting that the vocational uncertainty of their new student bodies led business schools in the 1970s to make significant investments in strengthening their placement and career offices as well as career counseling services, so they could offer students an expanded array of choices that met their individual lifestyle goals.

100. These industries (consulting and financial services) also became important feeders into the applicant pool for the elite business schools. For example, among the eight hundred students admitted to the Harvard Business School class of 1989, nearly 25 percent entered from investment banking and management consulting.

101. At UCLA, the Graduate School of Education's long-running annual survey of college students showed that, beginning in 1972, there was a significant increase in the proportion of college and university students rating being "very well off" as "very important" or "essential" to them. *The American Freshman: Thirty-five-Year Trends*, Higher Education Research Institute, UCLA.

102. GMAC, *Global Graduate Survey* (2000).

103. Michael Knight, "Harvard M.B.A.: A Golden Passport," *New York Times*, May 23, 1978, D1.

104. This difference does not control for the effects of "elite" schools.

105. Ross M. Stolzenberg, "The Changing Demand for Graduate Management Education," *Selections* 2, no. 1 (1985).

106. "My Son, the MBA," *Fortune*, June 1977, 160.

107. Knight, "Harvard M.B.A.."

108. Fouraker, "Graduate School of Business Administration," 304.

109. Walter Kiechel III, "New Debate about Harvard Business School," *Fortune*, November 9, 1987, 48.

110. Ibid.

Chapter 8
Business Schools in the Marketplace

1. There have been numerous discussions in recent years about the growing gap between management theories and managerial practice. In a speech to management scholars, the President of the Academy of Management exhorted members to confront their growing irrelevance to management practice. (See Donald C. Hambrick, "1993 Presidential Address: What If the Academy Actually Mattered?" *Academy of Management Review* 19, no. 1 [1994]: 11–16.) For a discussion of the implicit antimanagerial stance in contemporary management theory, see Lex Donaldson, "Damned by Our Own Theories: Contradictions between Theories and Management Education," *Academy of Management Learning and Education* 1, no. 1 (2002).

2. Several books have sought to address this complex topic in recent years, and no brief, comprehensive survey of them is possible. Three persistent themes emerge in these books: the increased number of commercial activities undertaken by universities and colleges, and the dilemma these pose for institutions built on the principle of open inquiry and a historic aversion to privatizing the benefits of publicly funded research; how professional marketing has become an element of university administration, especially in positioning schools vis-à-vis the numerous media rankings and attracting donors; the poor quality of undergraduate education. For an interesting discussion of the dilemmas that commercializing university research presents for the university as an academic institution, see Derek Curtis Bok, *Universities in the Marketplace: The Commercialization of Higher Education* (Princeton, NJ: Princeton University Press, 2003); Robert A. Nisbet, *The Degradation of the Academic Dogma*, Foundations of Higher Education (New Brunswick, NJ: Transaction, 1997). For a discussion of the increased role of marketing and branding in universities, see Bill Readings, *The University in Ruins* (Cambridge: Harvard University Press, 1996).

3. For examples, see George Brooker and Philip Shinoda, "Peer Ratings of Graduate Programs for Business," *Journal of Business* 49, no. 2 (1976); Allan Murray Cartter, *An Assessment of Quality in Graduate Education* (Washington, DC: American Council on Education, 1966); Kenneth D. Roose and Charles J. Andersen, *A Rating of*

Graduate Programs (Washington, DC: American Council on Education, 1970); Guy W. Trump et al., "A Ranking of Accounting Programs," *Journal of Accountancy* 130, no. 1 (1970).

4. With the exception of the first year the rankings were published, when Harvard Business School was rated number one, Stanford's Graduate School of Business came in first by a "wide margin" in the *MBA* rankings until the magazine ceased publication in the early 1980s. Harvard Business School, the University of Chicago, and MIT's Sloan School jostled with one another for second through fourth place during these same years.

5. Kimberly D. Elsbach and Roderick M. Kramer, "Members' Responses to Organizational Identity Threats: Encountering and Countering the *Business Week* Rankings," *Administrative Science Quarterly* 41, no. 3 (1996): 456.

6. Quoted in Carlotta Mast, "The People behind the Rankings," *Selections* 1, no. 2 (2001): 19.

7. Two studies suggest that highly ranked as well as low-ranked schools viewed the *BusinessWeek* rankings as a threat to their academic status and identity. Even if their own schools were highly ranked, most academics and administrators saw the rankings as a threat because they focused on criteria like recruiter opinions and student ratings, rather than the criteria academics value, such as scholarly reputation; see Elsbach and Kramer, "Members' Responses to Organizational Identity Threats"; Jerold L. Zimmerman, "Can American Business Schools Survive?" *SSRN Working Paper no. FR 01-16, 2001.* For a more recent view of how rankings have led schools to allocate resources and focus on activities marginal to their educational mission, see Dennis A. Gioia and Kevin G. Corley, "Being Good versus Looking Good: Business School Rankings and the Circean Transformation from Substance to Image," *Academy of Management Learning and Education* 1, no. 1 (2002).

8. For an example of how the *Financial Times* ranking affects business schools, see Timothy Devinney, Grahame Dowling, and Nidthida Perm-Ajchariyawong. "The MBA Rankings Game," Australian Graduate School of Management, Working Paper, 2006.

9. Data on the number of MBA degrees and accreditation status were collected from American Association of Collegiate Schools of Business, "Management Education at Risk" (St. Louis, MO: AACSB International, August 2002), 8.

10. Ibid., 7.

11. James W. Schmotter, "An Interview with Dean B. Joseph White," *Selections* 14, no. 2 (1998): 25.

12. Kevin G. Corley and Dennis A. Gioia, "The Rankings Game: Managing Business School Reputation," *Corporate Reputation Review* 3, no. 3 (2000), as cited in Harry DeAngelo, Linda DeAngelo, and Jerold L. Zimmerman, "What's Really Wrong with U.S. Business Schools," University of Southern California, Working Paper, 2005.

13. Jeff Wuorio, "The Impact of the Rankings: Multiple Perspectives," *Selections* 1, no. 2 (2001): 37.

14. James W. Schmotter, "An Interview with Robert H. Frank," *Selections* 15, no. 1 (1998): 18. While some guides to American colleges and universities like Barron's did examine business schools, they did not rank schools or survey students and employers. Instead, they used externally available data (e.g., average entrance exam scores, student-faculty ratios) to construct different categories of business schools.

15. Wuorio, "The Impact of the Rankings," 29.

16. Ibid., 32.

17. Ibid., 31. One significant example of how important career services has become was the formation of the MBACSC, a professional association for MBA career service officers.

18. Andrew J. Policano, "What Price Rankings?" *Biz Ed, an AACSB Publication*, September/October 2005, 26.

19. Theodore Porter notes that in professions whose authority is deemed legitimate, quantitative measures of quality are less used than in others whose authority is subject to challenge. See Theodore M. Porter, *Trust in Numbers: The Pursuit of Objectivity in Science and Public Life* (Princeton, NJ: Princeton University Press, 1995).

20. Lyman W. Porter, Lawrence E. McKibbin, and American Assembly of Collegiate Schools of Business, *Management Education and Development: Drift or Thrust into the 21st Century?* (New York: McGraw-Hill Book Co., 1988), 122–123.

21. Porter and McKibbin appear not to have interviewed finance executives, who could have testified that ideas from the field of finance including the efficient markets hypothesis, agency theory, and activity-based accounting have all led to significant changes in business practice.

22. "*Selections* Interview with John Byrne, Senior Writer at *Business Week*," 2001 at http://www.gmac.com/selections/fall2001/byrne/index.html (accessed October 9, 2006). The disconnect between students and faculty research is also discussed in Porter, McKibbin, and American Assembly of Collegiate Schools of Business, *Management Education and Development*, 161–192.

23. "Research Relevancy Remains a Challenge for Business Schools," *Biz Ed, an AACSB Publication*, Spring 1997.

24. James W. Schmotter, "An Interview with Professor James G. March," *Selections* 14, no. 3 (1998): 56.

25. Zimmerman, "Can American Business Schools Survive?" 1.

26. Mast, "The People behind the Rankings," 21.

27. Policano, "What Price Rankings?" 31 (emphasis in original).

28. Edward C. Fee, Charles J. Hadlock, and Joshua R. Pierce, "Business School Rankings and Business School Deans: A Study of Nonprofit Governance," *Financial Management* 34, no. 1 (2005).

29. James W. Schmotter, "Interview with Dean Don Jacobs," *Selections* 8, no. 3 (1992): 5.

30. Schmotter, "An Interview with Dean B. Joseph White," 23.

31. William Sullivan, "Markets vs. Professions: Value Added?" *Daedalus* 134, no. 3 (Summer 2005): 19–26.

32. "Management Education at Risk," report of the Management Education Task Force to the AACSB—International Board of Directors, 2002, 28.

33. David Bejou, "Treating Students Like Customers," *Biz Ed, an AACSB Publication*, March–April 2005, 44.

34. See Gail Tyson, "A Look behind the Numbers," *Selections*, Fall 2001, 9–15.

35. Tracy Bisoux, "A Matter of Reputation," *Biz Ed, an AACSB Publication*, March–April 2003, 48.

36. In the wake of the corporate scandals, several business schools have made efforts to strengthen the ethics elements of their curricula. These efforts generally take one of three forms: consequentialist, deontological, or virtue approaches. The consequentialist approach focuses on the costs and benefits of managerial decision making. The deontological approach encourages the incorporation of notions like duties, justice, and rights into managerial decision making. Virtue approaches encourage students to focus on character and personal integrity in managerial decision making. The pedagogical method underlying this last approach encourages students to reflect on their own personal values and then decide on a framework of ethical decision making consistent with these personal values. Without intending to demean these efforts to address a complex issue, I wish to point out that such an approach to ethics is qualitatively different from that of professional ethics. Unlike ethical systems that deal with individual decision making and individual conscience, professional ethics operate at an institutional level. Professional ethics are animated by a moral concern for the specific discipline and the set of obligations that practitioners owe to the larger society and to their fellow practitioners. The ideology underlying professional ethics is that the behavior of the professional must be guided by a devotion to using his or her knowledge and skills to further the public good. It is against this public good that the professional's actions and decisions must be evaluated.

37. "Management Education at Risk," 13. The third institutional pillar on which traditional business schools were founded is, of course, the professions. It is not easy to say precisely what the word *professional* is intended to mean in the phrase "as a professional differentiator that protects market value," but it seems clear that it does not refer to any differentiation between university-based business schools as "professional" institutions and their nonacademic competitors as something less. As I have previously asserted, the whole notion of *professionalism*, as I have used the term, forms no part of the conceptual framework of the authors of the AACSB report.

38. *US Airways*, March 2006, 195.

39. "Columbia University School of Business, Columbia University," *US Airways*, March 2006. At Harvard Business School, starting salaries and number of job offers per MBA student are regularly highlighted to the faculty as the primary measure of the success of the school in educating "leaders who will contribute to society's wellbeing."

40. Jeffrey Pfeffer and Christina T. Fong, "The Business School 'Business': Some Lessons from the US Experience," *Journal of Management Studies* 41, no. 8 (2004): 1503.

41. Schmotter, "An Interview with Professor James G. March," 59. March's subsequent statements in the same interview imply that business schools are not necessarily performing well with regard to "deepen[ing] an intellectual understanding of the relation between activities in business and the major issues of human existence." As he puts it, the "general acceptance of the consequentialist language of economics in business schools tends to inhibit other voices—voices that proclaim, for example, that action is justified not by its consequences but by the way it fulfills our aspirations for being human or our conception of what is important in life" (60).

42. See, for example, Michael Spence, "Job Market Signaling," *Quarterly Journal of Economics* 87, no. 3 (1973).

43. Harvard Business School uses its application process as a way of screening for whether students are serious about attending business school. For example, in 1980 more than twenty-five thousand people requested MBA applications, but only about sixty-six hundred applied. "By design," noted Thomas McCraw and Jeffrey Cruikshank, applications are "extremely long and laborious to complete" so as to screen for serious students. Thomas K. McCraw and J. L. Cruikshank, eds., *The Intellectual Venture Capitalist: John H. McArthur and the Work of the Harvard Business School* (Boston: Harvard Business School Press, 1999), 7.

44. Schmotter, "An Interview with Robert H. Frank," 18.

45. Schmotter, "An Interview with Professor James G. March," 59.

46. "Columbia University School of Business, Columbia University."

47. Compiled from "Capital I-Q," electronic database (Standard & Poor's, 2006); *Galante's Venture Capital and Private Equity Directory* (Wellesley, MA: Asset Alternatives, 2006).

48. Center for Private Equity and Entrepreneurship, Tuck School of Business at Dartmouth, "Interviews—Ed Diffendal, Vice President, Broadview Capital," at http://mba.tuck.dartmouth.edu/pecenter/resources/interview_diffendal.html (accessed October 9, 2006).

49. Personal conversation with administrator.

50. University of Chicago Graduate School of Business, "Full-Time MBA Program," at http://chicagogsb.edu/fulltime/index.aspx (accessed October 9, 2006).

51. Part of the trend away from relevance can be traced to changes in business school promotion policies that actively or subtly dissuade faculty from spending too much time writing business cases and instead push them to focus on more "serious" academic work associated with journal publications and research. At Northwestern's business school, much of the faculty interpreted the Ford Foundation recommendations "and the general direction of curriculum changes to be toward a more substantive approach. In the minds of those sharing this opinion, cases are considered to be

somewhat superficial teaching vehicles, and case research is given a very minor role in terms of academic effort." Michael Sedlak and Steven Schlossman, "The Northwestern University, 1906–1971," *Selections*, Winter 1991, 31. A similar push to have faculty devote more time to publishing in academic journals can be observed at Harvard Business School, where, during the late 1990s, faculty promotion processes increasingly relied on scholarly contributions and external letters rather than on the school's historical approach to promoting faculty based on its own unique, internal criteria, which privileged course development and management impact over scholarly audiences.

52. Pfeffer and Fong, "The Business School 'Business.' "

53. Anjani Jain, "Proposed Honors Expansion: Content and Rationale," *Wharton Journal*, April 18, 2005, www://media.whartonjournal.com/media/storage/paper201/ news/205/04/18/Perspectives/ProposedHonors.Expansion.Conetext.AndRationale-928 074.shtml (accessed January 15, 2007). In a letter to the editor of the *Wall Street Journal* responding to the publication of that paper's 2004 business school rankings, Wharton marketing professor J. Scott Armstrong described asking his students to provide "written descriptions of techniques" learned in business school, only to obtain responses such as "I learned that advertising is important" and "I learned to think out of the box." Armstrong added: "I have long taught a capstone course in which students are asked to apply what they learned. From this, I have concluded that they do not have skills for making persuasive management presentations, writing management reports, calculating net present value, or managing a group—the list is endless. More troubling is that they resist learning about useful management techniques. On the other hand, they love jargon." J. Scott Armstrong, "Are MBAs Really Learning How to Do Things?" *Wall Street Journal*, October 11, 2004, A19.

54. Dylan Bourguignon, "Student Voices Displeasure Regarding Proposed Changes to Non-Disclosure Policy," *The Harbus*, December 12, 2005. Both Harvard and Wharton eventually allowed for grade disclosure, despite continued student protests.

55. "The Members of the Commission on Admission to Graduate Management Education," *Selections*, Spring 1990, 34–35.

56. Ibid., 37.

57. In 1946, Ohio State University received a research contract from the federal government to undertake leadership research under the auspices of its new Personnel Research Board, a university-wide committee of deans and representatives of departments and research bureaus. The university had created the board to coordinate the activity of the social science departments that, as was typical of land-grant universities like Ohio State, were spread throughout various schools. (For example, in 1946 the psychology department at Ohio State was located in the College of Education; anthropology, sociology, and economics were located in the College of Commerce and Administration; and the department of political science, which pursued the study of public administration, was in the College of Arts and Sciences.) Supported by various

federal government departments, including the Office of Naval Research, as well as by foundations, corporations, and individual research grants, the Leadership Studies program became one of the largest systematic research efforts undertaken in the postwar period.

58. Having started out with a trait-based approach to leadership that tried to locate the factors behind successful leadership in individual qualities that good leaders seemed to possess, the Ohio State researchers later began paying greater attention to how followers perceived the leader's effectiveness. Using an extensive questionnaire, the researchers asked soldiers and sailors to describe the frequency with which their officers exhibited particular behaviors. It was from analyzing the patterns of behavior described that the researchers came to identify the two main factors of "initiation of structure" and "consideration." In the decades following the Ohio State Leadership Studies, much of the research on the subject concluded that there was no "one best way to lead." The view that emerged from this work was that the effect of leadership on group performance is complex and "contingent" on variables such as the task and the situational context within which the group is operating. Sociologists who studied the effect of leaders on organizational performance were coming to similar conclusions, arguing that outside the extremes of outstanding or poor leaders, the relationship between leadership and organizational performance was marginal at best. Instead, they concluded, organizational performance, as measured by economic return or survival, was much more dependent on factors outside the control of organizational leaders, such as the industry in which a firm competed, the rate of environmental change, and general economic conditions. For a brief summary and discussion of this research, see Rakesh Khurana, *Searching for a Corporate Savior: The Irrational Quest for Charismatic CEOs* (Princeton, NJ: Princeton University Press, 2002), 21–23.

59. Abraham Zaleznik, "Managers and Leaders: Are They Different?" *Harvard Business Review* 55, no. 3 (1977): 68.

60. Ibid., 72.

61. Abraham Zaleznik, "Managers and Leaders: Are They Different?" *Harvard Business Review* 70, no. 2 (1992): 129.

62. On Weber's distinction among traditional, rational, and charismatic leadership, see Khurana, *Searching for a Corporate Savior*, 156–158. The manager-leader dichotomy has been developed by subsequent leadership scholars including John P. Kotter, who shifted away from Zaleznik's focus on personal disposition to leadership behaviors; see John P. Kotter, *A Force for Change: How Leadership Differs from Management* (New York: Free Press, 1990). Other scholars have continued to emphasize the role of "crucible events" in shaping leaders' attitudes and values, along with the Jamesian metaphor of leaders as "twice-born" used by Zaleznik in his 1977 article; see Warren G. Bennis, *On Becoming a Leader* (Reading, MA: Addison-Wesley Publishing, 1989); Warren G. Bennis and Robert J. Thomas, *Geeks and Geezers: How Era, Values, and Defining Moments Shape Leaders* (Boston: Harvard Business School Press, 2002).

63. See chapter 3, "The Rise of the Charismatic CEO," in Khurana, *Searching for a Corporate Savior.*

64. Harvard Business School, "Who We Are," at http://www.hbs.edu/about/index.html (accessed October 9, 2006).

65. Tuck School of Business at Dartmouth, "Our Strategy," at http://www.tuck.dartmouth.edu/about/strategy.html (accessed October 9, 2006).

66. Stanford Graduate School of Business, "About the Stanford Graduate School of Business," at http://www.gsb.stanford.edu/about/ (accessed October 9, 2006).

67. MIT Sloan School of Management, "About MIT Sloan—Background: Mission," at http://mitsloan.mit.edu/about/b-mission.php (accessed October 9, 2006).

68. Broad School MBA, "Examine Broad's Difference," at http://mba.msu.edu/benefit/ (accessed October 9, 2006).

69. Thunderbird—The Garvin School of International Management, "Mission Statement," at http://www.thunderbird.edu/about_thunderbird/inside_tbird/mission_statement.htm (accessed October 9, 2006).

70. As quoted in Joseph C. Rost, *Leadership for the Twenty-first Century* (New York: Praeger, 1991), 8.

71. As quoted in ibid., 14. I draw heavily on Rost's comprehensive review of leadership scholarship, and on my own extensive personal discussions with Scott Snook, a leadership researcher at Harvard Business School who helped shape the United States Military Academy's approach to cadet development, to summarize the state of leadership scholarship in this section.

72. Ibid., 15.

73. Quoted in Joel Podolny, Rakesh Khurana, and Marya Hill-Popper, "Revisiting the Meaning of Leadership," *Research in Organizational Behavior* 26 (2005).

74. Rost, *Leadership for the Twenty-first Century*, 14.

75. Ibid., 8.

76. The only major university I am aware of that regards leadership as a legitimate subject of study is the University of Richmond, whose Jepson School of Leadership was established in 1992. Businessman Robert Jepson gave the University of Richmond $20 million to create a cross-disciplinary undergraduate program that stresses moral leadership and service to society.

77. See, for example, James R. Meindl, Sanford B. Ehrlich, and Janet M. Dukerich, "The Romance of Leadership," *Administrative Science Quarterly* 30, no. 1 (1985).

78. Rost, *Leadership for the Twenty-first Century*, 15.

79. Podolny, Khurana, and Hill-Popper, "Revisiting the Meaning of Leadership."

80. Unless otherwise noted, the source for the course descriptions is the Aspen Institute's Business and Society Program Web site, beyondgreypinstripes.com. Aspen's Business and Society Program aims to improve the ethical development of MBA students.

81. Kellogg School of Management, "Learning by Doing," at http://www.kellogg.northwestern.edu/difference/academics/doing.htm (accessed October 9, 2006).

82. University of Chicago Graduate School of Business, "Leadership Effectiveness and Development," at http://www.chicagogsb.edu/fulltime/academics/experiential/lead.aspx (accessed October 9, 2006).

83. United States Military Academy at West Point, "USMA Mission," at http://www.usma.edu/mission.asp (accessed October 9, 2006).

84. Ibid., 3, 8.

85. Max Weber, *The Protestant Ethic and the Spirit of Capitalism*, trans. Talcott Parsons (London: Allen & Unwin, 1930; reprint, with foreword by R. H. Tawney), 182.

Epilogue
Ideas of Order Revisited: Markets, Hierarchies, and Communities

1. Joseph A. Schumpeter, *Capitalism, Socialism, and Democracy* (New York: Harper, 1975, orig. publ. 1942), 82.

2. Michael Jensen and colleagues have recently proposed a more contingent view of how stock options could destroy economic value in a situation of "overvalued" equity; see Michael Jensen, Kevin J. Murphy, and Eric G. Wruck, "Remuneration: Where We've Been, How We Got to Here, What are the Problems, and How to Fix Them," Harvard NOM Working Paper No. 04-28; ECGI—Finance Working Paper No. 44/2004.

3. http://mitsloan.mit.edu/newsroom/v-dean.php (accessed January 1, 2007).

4. Harvard Business School now requires that all its first-year students take a graded course titled Leadership and Corporate Accountability. Yale University's School of Management has restructured its curriculum to incorporate an ethics module in all of its required courses.

5. See, for example, Derek Bok, *Universities in the Marketplace: The Commercialization of Higher Education* (Princeton: Princeton University Press, 2004); William G. Bowen, Martin A. Kurzweil, and Eugene M. Tobin, in collaboration with Susanne C. Pichler, *Equity and Excellence in American Higher Education* (Charlottesville: University of Virginia Press, 2005); William Readings, *The University in Ruins* (Cambridge: Harvard University Press, 1997).

6. Harry R. Lewis, *Excellence without Soul: How a Great University Forgot Education* (New York: PublicAffairs, 2006), 195.

7. Quoted in Andrew Delbanco, "Scandals of Higher Education," *New York Review of Books* 54, no. 5 (March 29, 2007), italics in original.

8. Lewis, *Excellence without a Soul*, 268.

9. http://www.jhu.edu/news_info/news/univ06/dec06/schools.html (accessed April 2, 2007).

10. As evidence of this erosion of the cultural authority of managers, consider that a Gallup poll conducted in 2003 found that business leaders were less trusted by Americans than were Washington politicians. See Joseph Carroll, *Gallup Organization Poll Analysis: Gallup's Annual Survey on the Honesty and Ethics of Various Professions* (December 1, 2003).

11. Warren G. Bennis and James O'Toole, "How Business Schools Lost Their Way," *Harvard Business Review* 83, no. 5 (2005): 84; Henry Mintzberg, *Managers Not MBAs: A Hard Look at the Soft Practice of Managing and Management Development* (London: Financial Times; New York: Prentice Hall, 2004).

12. With regard to a subject like agency theory, while a preference for an elegant and parsimonious model is necessary for the development of theory, in professional schools that are training students for practice such models need to be presented with great care. Legal scholars Margaret Blair and Lynn Stout have argued that agency theory became a dominant paradigm, in the Kuhnian sense, in legal scholarship. They write, "The principal-agent literature was the primary intellectual tool available to business law scholars in the 1980s and 1990s, and they naturally tended to apply it liberally to many aspects of the corporate form. As the saying goes, when your only tool is a hammer, every problem tends to look like a nail." Margaret M. Blair and Lynn A. Stout, "Specific Investment and Corporate Law," *European Business Organization Law Review* 7 (2006): 477. Robert Clark writes that agency theory represents an extreme contractualist view that "is almost perverse." Robert C. Clark, "Agency Costs versus Fiduciary Duties," in *Principals and Agents: The Structure of Business*, ed. John W. Pratt, Richard Zeckhauser, and Kenneth Joseph Arrow (Boston: Harvard Business School Press, 1991), 60. It is particularly perverse when it is taught in a "professional" school not as part of a simplified model or derived from simplified assumptions but as empirically grounded. With the ascendancy of the discipline of economics in business schools, the realism of the concepts and propositions that had characterized organizational and managerial research—what Paul Hirsch and his colleagues call the "dirty hands" approach to empirical research—was replaced by a "clean" but simplistic model. (Paul Hirsch, Stuart Michaels, and Ray Friedman, "Dirty Hands versus Clean Models," *Theory and Society* 16 [1987]: 317–336). That the simplified models of academic economists have been imported into business school curricula without being explained as such to MBA students represents yet another perverse effect of what I have called the "disciplining" of business school faculties.

13. An important exception here is the late Sumantra Ghoshal's work on managerial theory and managerial identity. As I noted in chapter 7, many of my ideas about agency theory and transaction theory are deeply informed by Ghoshal, who recognized the normative aspects of management education as shaping managerial identity. Ghoshal argued that managerial education had a lot to do with language, both in the sense of how language is used to shape MBA students' ideas about organizations and in the sense that the theoretical language of economics informed students' understanding of the role of management in organizations. Managerial theory, Ghoshal argued, was not a neutral construct but a mechanism to persuade students of the legitimate role of management.

14. Robert W. McChesney, *Rich Media, Poor Democracy: Communications Politics in Dubious Times* (New York: New Press, 2000), 206.

15. Owen D. Young, "Dedication Address," in *Dedication Addresses*, a compilation of transcripts of speeches and related documents from the dedication of the Harvard Business School campus on June 4, 1927, reprinted from the July 1927 issue of *Harvard Business Review* and now in the HBS Archives Collection (AC 1927 17.1), 6–7.

16. Ibid., 7–8.

17. Ibid., 8.

18. William M. Sullivan, "Markets vs. Professions: Value Added?" *Dædalus* 134, no. 3 (2005): 19, 20.

19. Here I have drawn heavily on Robert A. Nisbet's discussion of the breakdown of social institutions in the United States during the 1980s, as well as his analysis of the role of the American university in shaping American culture; see Robert A. Nisbet, *The Degradation of the Academic Dogma*, Foundations of Higher Education (New Brunswick, NJ: Transaction, 1997); Robert A. Nisbet, *The Present Age: Progress and Anarchy in Modern America* (New York: Harper & Row, 1988).

20. Nisbet, *The Present Age*, 84.

21. John Dewey, *Individualism—Old and New* (New York: Capricorn Books, 1962), 52.

22. As quoted in Nisbet, *The Present Age*, 87.

23. Quoted in ibid., 89.

24. James W. Schmotter, "An Interview with Robert H. Frank," *Selections* 15, no. 1 (1998): 15.

Selected Bibliography

Abbott, Andrew Delano. *The System of Professions: An Essay on the Division of Expert Labor*. Chicago: University of Chicago Press, 1988.

———. *Department and Discipline: Chicago Sociology at One Hundred*. Chicago: University of Chicago Press, 1999.

Abernathy, William J., and Robert Hayes. "Managing Our Way to Economic Decline." *Harvard Business Review*, July–August, 1980, 67–77.

Adams, Henry. *The Education of Henry Adams*. New York: Modern Library, 1931. Reprint, with introduction by James Truslow Adams.

Advisory Group to the Ford Foundation. "Program for Area III on Economic Development and Administration." Report, Ford Foundation Archives, no. 005047, 1954.

Alchian, Armen A., and Harold Demsetz. "Production, Information Costs, and Economic Organization." *American Economic Review* 62 (1972): 777–795.

Allen, Frederick Lewis. *The Big Change: America Transforms Itself, 1900–1950*. New York: Harper, 1952.

American Assembly of Collegiate Schools of Business. *Sustaining Scholarship in Business Schools*. St. Louis: AACSB, International, 2003.

American Association of Collegiate Schools of Business. "Program of the Third General Meeting." Program of the Third General Meeting of the AACSB, Pittsburgh, PA, May 5, 6, and 7, 1921.

———. "Proceedings of the Sixth Annual Meeting." Sixth Annual Proceedings of the AACSB, New York, NY, May 1, 2, and 3, 1924.

———. "Proceedings of the Seventh Annual Meeting." Seventh Annual Meeting of the AACSB, Columbus, OH, May 7, 8, and 9, 1925.

———. "Proceedings of the Eighth Annual Meeting." Eighth Annual Meeting of the AACSB, Hanover, NH, 1926.

———. "Proceedings of the Ninth Annual Meeting." Ninth Annual Meeting of the AACSB, Cambridge, MA, May 5, 6 and 7, 1927.

———. "Proceedings of the Tenth Annual Meeting." Tenth Annual Meeting of the AACSB, Chicago, IL, May 3, 4, and 5, 1928.

American Association of Collegiate Schools of Business. "Proceedings of the Twelfth Annual Meeting." Twelfth Annual Meeting of the AACSB, Iowa City, IA, May 1930.

———. "Proceedings of the Fifteenth Annual Meeting." Fifteenth Annual Meeting of the AACSB, Lexington, KY, Summer 1933.

———. "Proceedings of the Sixteenth Annual Meeting." Sixteenth Annual Meeting of the AACSB, St. Louis, MO, April 26, 27, and 28, 1934.

———. "Proceedings of the Eighteenth Annual Meeting." Eighteenth Annual Meeting of the AACSB, Boston, MA, April 22, 23, 24, and 25, 1936.

———. "Proceedings of the Nineteenth Annual Meeting." Nineteenth Annual Meeting of the AACSB, Baton Rouge, LA, March 22, 23, and 24, 1937.

———. "Proceedings of the Twentieth Annual Meeting." Twentieth Annual Meeting of the AACSB, Urbana, IL, April 21, 22, and 23, 1938.

———. "Proceedings of the Twenty-first Annual Meeting." Twenty-first Annual Meeting of the AACSB, Stanford, CA, April 20, 21, and 22, 1939.

———. *The American Association of Collegiate Schools of Business, 1916–1966*. Homewood, IL: R. D. Irwin, 1966.

———. "The AACSB Bulletin." St. Louis, MO, April 1966.

———. "Management Education at Risk." St. Louis, MO: AACSB International, August 2002.

Andrikopoulos, Panagiotis. "Modern Finance vs. Behavioural Finance: An Overview of Key Concepts and Major Arguments." SSRN Working Paper, June, 2005.

Armstrong, J. Scott. "Are MBAs Really Learning How to Do Things?" *Wall Street Journal*, October 11, 2004.

"Ask Bay State Inquiry into Power Financing." *New York Times*, April 23, 1929, 54.

Bach, George Leland (Lee). "Proposal to the Ford Foundation for Partial Support of a Pioneering Center for Graduate Study and Research in Industrial Administration—Economics." Ford Foundation Archives, no. 55-10, Section I, September 7, 1954.

———. "Some Observations on the Business School of Tomorrow." *Management Science* 4, no. 4 (July 1958): 351–364.

———. "Foundation Policy toward Basic Research in Business." Memorandum to Thomas Carroll and Robert Aaron Gordon, Ford Foundation Archives, no. 002592, December 14, 1960.

———. "The Ford Foundation and the Revolution in Business Education." Ford Foundation Archives, no. 002591, September 20, 1960.

Bach, George Leland (Lee), Melvin G. de Chazeau, Donald W. O'Connell, and Arthur M. Weimer. "Economics in the Curricula of Schools of Business: Discussion." *American Economic Review* 46, no. 2, Papers and Proceedings of the Sixty-eighth Annual Meeting of the American Economic Association (May 1956): 563–577.

Bailyn, Bernard. *Education in the Forming of American Society*. Needs and Opportunities for Study. Chapel Hill: University of North Carolina Press, 1960.

Baltzell, E. Digby. *Puritan Boston and Quaker Philadelphia: Two Protestant Ethics and the Spirit of Class Authority and Leadership*. New York: Free Press, 1979.

———. *The Protestant Establishment: Aristocracy and Caste in America*. New Haven: Yale University Press, 1987.

Barley, Steven R., and Gideon Kunda. "Design and Devotion: Surges of Rational and Normative Ideologies of Control in Managerial Discourse." *Administrative Science Quarterly* 37, no. 3 (September 1992): 363–399.

Baron, James N., and William T. Bielby. "Bringing the Firms Back In: Stratification, Segmentation, and the Organization of Work." *American Sociological Review* 45, no. 5 (October 1980): 737–765.

Baron, James N., P. Devereaux Jennings, and Frank R. Dobbin. "Mission Control? The Development of Personnel Systems in U.S. Industry." *American Sociological Review* 53, no. 4 (August 1988): 497–514.

Bartunek, Jean. "Presidential Address: A Dream for the Academy." *Academy of Management Review* 30 (2003): 198–203.

Bazerman, Max. "Conducting Influential Research: The Need for Prescriptive Implications." *Academy of Management Review* 30 (2005): 25–31.

Beard, Charles Austin, and Mary Ritter Beard. *The Rise of American Civilization*. 4 vols. New York: Macmillan, 1927.

Bebchuk, Lucian A., and Jesse M. Fried. *Pay without Performance: The Unfulfilled Promise of Executive Compensation*. Cambridge: Harvard University Press, 2004.

Beck, Hubert Park. *Men Who Control Our Universities: The Economic and Social Composition of Governing Boards of Thirty Leading American Universities*. Morningside Heights, NY: King's Crown Press, 1947.

Bejou, David. "Treating Students Like Customers." *Biz Ed, an AACSB Publication*, March/April 2005, 44–47.

Bell, Daniel. *The Coming of Post-industrial Society: A Venture in Social Forecasting*. New York: Basic Books, 1976.

Ben-David, Joseph. *The Scientist's Role in Society: A Comparative Study*. Foundations of Modern Sociology. Englewood Cliffs, NJ: Prentice-Hall, 1971.

Ben-David, Joseph, and Gad Freudenthal. *Scientific Growth: Essays on the Social Organization and Ethos of Science*. Berkeley and Los Angeles: University of California Press, 1991.

Bendix, Reinhard. *Work and Authority in Industry: Managerial Ideologies in the Course of Industrialization*. New Brunswick, NJ: Transaction, 2001. Orig. publ. 1956.

Bennis, Warren G. *On Becoming a Leader*. Reading, MA: Addison-Wesley Publishing, 1989.

Bennis, Warren G., and Robert J. Thomas. *Geeks and Geezers: How Era, Values, and Defining Moments Shape Leaders*. Boston: Harvard Business School Press, 2002.

Berg, Norm. "Textron, Inc." Harvard Business School Case. Boston: Harvard Business School Publishing, 1973.

Berger, Peter L. *A Rumor of Angels: Modern Society and the Rediscovery of the Super-natural*. Garden City, N.Y.: Doubleday, 1970.

Berle, Adolf A., and G. Means. *The Modern Corporation and Private Property*. New York: Macmillan Press, 1932.

Berman, Edward H. "The Extension of Ideology: Foundation Support for Inter-mediate Organizations and Forums." *Comparative Education Review* 26, no. 1 (February 1982): 48–68.

Bernstein, Michael A. *A Perilous Progress: Economists and Public Purpose in Twentieth-Century America*. Princeton, NJ: Princeton University Press, 2001.

Biddle, C. P. "Eighth Annual Meeting of the AACSB." Eighth Annual Meeting of the AACSB, Hanover, NH 1926.

Bidgood, Lee. Personal Correspondence to Donald K. David, Donald K. David Per-sonal Correspondence, Harvard Business School Archives.

Bjork, Richard E. "Foundations, Universities, and Government: A Pattern of Interac-tion." *Journal of Higher Education* 33, no. 5 (May 1962): 270–276.

Bledstein, Burton J. *The Culture of Professionalism: The Middle Class and the Develop-ment of Higher Education in America*. New York: Norton, 1976.

Bok, Derek. "The President's Report." Cambridge: Harvard University, 1978.

Bok, Derek Curtis. *The Cost of Talent: How Executives and Professionals Are Paid and How It Affects America*. New York: Free Press 1993.

———. *Universities in the Marketplace: The Commercialization of Higher Education*. Princeton, NJ: Princeton University Press, 2003.

Bossard, James H. S. "University Education for Business: A Survey." *Journal of Business of the University of Chicago* 4, no. 3, pt. 2, Proceedings of the Thirteenth Annual Meeting of the American Association of Collegiate Schools of Business (July 1931): 64–77.

Bossard, James H. S., and J. Frederick Dewhurst. *University Education for Business: A Study of Existing Needs and Practices*. Philadelphia: University of Pennsylvania Press, 1931.

Bourguignon, Dylan. "Student Voices Displeasure Regarding Proposed Changes to Non-Disclosure Policy." *The Harbus*, December 12, 2005.

Brandeis, Louis D. *Business: A Profession*. 2d ed. Boston: Hale, Cushman, and Flint, 1933. Orig. publ. 1914.

Brinton, Mary C., and Victor Nee. *The New Institutionalism in Sociology*. Stanford: Stanford University Press, 2001.

Broad School MBA. "Examine Broad's Difference." http://mba.msu.edu/benefit/ (accessed October 9, 2006).

Brodie, Donald C., and Frederick H. Meyers. "Role of the Pharmacist as Drug Con-sultant." *American Journal of Hospital Pharmacy* 18 (January 1961): 11–13.

Broehl, Wayne G. *Tuck and Tucker: The Origin of the Graduate Business School*. Hanover: University Press of New England, 1999.

Brooker, George, and Philip Shinoda. "Peer Ratings of Graduate Programs for Business." *Journal of Business* 49, no. 2 (April 1976): 240–251.

Brown, Courtney. "Presentation of the Graduate School of Business of Columbia University to the Ford Foundation." Ford Foundation Archives, box no. 55-228, June 1955.

Brown, Richard H. "Bureaucracy as Praxis: Toward a Phenomenology of Formal Organizations." *Administrative Science Quarterly* 23 (September 1979): 365–382.

Burrough, Bryan, and John Helyar. *Barbarians at the Gate: The Fall of RJR Nabisco.* New York: Harper & Row, 1990.

"Business Is Rallied to Fight Communism." *New York Times,* September 11, 1949, 21.

Business Week Guide to the Best Business Schools. 6th ed. New York: McGraw-Hill, 1999.

"Butler Lays Stone for New School; Men Prominent in Finance and Commerce Attend Ceremonies at Columbia. Meets Needs of Business. Building Will Cost $1,000,000—355 Students in Institution Last Year, Says Director." *New York Times,* December 19, 1923, 19.

Cabell, David W. E. *Cabell's Directory of Publishing Opportunities in Business, Administration, and Economics.* Beaumont, TX: Cabell Pub. Co., 1978.

Cameron, Kim S., Jane E. Dutton, and Robert E. Quinn. *Positive Organizational Scholarship: Foundations of a New Discipline.* San Francisco: Berrett-Koehler, 2003.

"Can You Teach Management?" *BusinessWeek,* April 19, 1952, 126–ff.

"Capital I-Q." Database: Standard & Poor's, 2006.

Carnegie, Andrew. *The Empire of Business.* New York: Doubleday Page & Co., 1902.

Carnegie Institute of Technology Graduate School of Industrial Administration. "Fact Sheet: Official Dedication, Carnegie." October 2 and 3, 1952. Donald K. David Papers, HBS archives.

Carroll, Thomas. "Memo to the Program Committee—April 1953." Memorandum to Ford Foundation Program Committee, Ford Foundation Archives, no. 47, Gaither Papers, April 29, 1953.

———. "Letter to Stanley Teele." Ford Foundation Archives, 1954.

———. Sixth Annual Conference on the Economic Outlook, Ann Arbor, MI, November 3, 1958.

———. "Sixth Annual Conference on the Economic Outlook." Ford Foundation Archives, Papers of Thomas Carroll, November 3, 1958.

———. "Memo to AACSB Deans." Memorandum to Deans of Member Schools of AACSB, Ford Foundation Archives, no. 002970, December 24, 1958.

Cartter, Allan Murray. *An Assessment of Quality in Graduate Education.* Washington, DC: American Council on Education, 1966.

Center for Private Equity and Entrepreneurship: Tuck School of Business at Dartmouth. "Interviews—Ed Diffendal, Vice President, Broadview Capital." http://mba.tuck. dartmouth.edu/pecenter/resources/interview_diffendal.html (accessed October 9, 2006).

Chandler, Alfred D., Jr. *The Visible Hand: The Managerial Revolution in American Business*. Cambridge: Harvard University Press, Belknap Press, 1977.

Chapman, John Jay. "Harvard and Education." *Harvard Graduates' Magazine* 33 (1924): 37–45.

Clark, Robert C. "Agency Costs versus Fiduciary Duties." In *Principals and Agents: The Structure of Business*, edited by John W. Pratt, Richard Zeckhauser, and Kenneth Joseph Arrow. Boston: Harvard Business School Press, 1991.

Coase, Ronald H. "The Nature of the Firm." *Economica* 4, no. 16 (November 1937): 386–405.

———. "The New Institutional Economics." *Journal of Institutional and Theoretical Economics* 140 (1984): 229–232.

Coleman, James Samuel. *The Asymmetric Society*. The Frank W. Abrams Lectures. Syracuse, NY: Syracuse University Press, 1982.

"College Men in Business." *New York Times*, May 4, 1915, 14.

Collins, Randall. *The Credential Society: An Historical Sociology of Education and Stratification*. New York: Academic Press, 1979.

"Columbia University School of Business, Columbia University." *US Airways*, March 2006, 198–199.

Commission on Human Resources and Advanced Training, and Dael Lee Wolfle. *America's Resources of Specialized Talent: A Current Appraisal and a Look Ahead*. New York: Harper, 1954.

Conant, James B. Paper presented at the National Retail Dry Goods Association, February 12, 1950.

"Conference on Professional Education for Business: Faculty Requirements and Standards." Arden House, New York, October 27–29, 1955.

Cooke, Morris L. "The Spirit and Social Significance of Scientific Management." *Journal of Political Economy* 21, no. 6 (June 1913): 481–493.

Copeland, Melvin Thomas. *And Mark an Era: The Story of the Harvard Business School*. Boston: Little Brown, 1958.

Corley, Kevin G., and Dennis A. Gioia. "The Rankings Game: Managing Business School Reputation." *Corporate Reputation Review* 3, no. 3 (2000): 319–333.

Cotton, John. "A Briefe Exposition . . . Upon . . . Ecclesiastes." In *The Puritans*, edited by Perry Miller and Thomas H. Johnson. New York: Harper Torchbooks, 1963.

Croly, Herbert David. *The Promise of American Life*. New York: Macmillan Company, 1910.

Cruikshank, Jeffrey L. *A Delicate Experiment: The Harvard Business School, 1908–1945*. Boston: Harvard Business School Press, 1987.

Cuff, Robert. "Organizational Capabilities and U.S. War Production: The Controlled Materials Plan of World War II." *Business and Economic History* 19 (1990): 103–112.

Daniel, Carter A. *MBA: The First Century*. Lewisburg, PA: Bucknell University Press, 1998.

David, Donald K. "Business Leadership and the War of Ideas." Paper presented at the Magazine Forum, April 27, 1948.

———. "Personal Correspondence." To James B. Conant, Harvard Business School Archives, box no. 11, June 13, 1953.

Davis, Gerald F. "New Directions in Corporate Governance." *Annual Review of Sociology* 31 (2005): 143–162.

Davis, Gerald F., Kristina Diekmann, and Catherine H. Tinsley. "The Decline and Fall of the Conglomerate Firm in the 1980s: The Deinstitutionalization of an Organizational Form." *American Sociological Review* 59, no. 4 (August 1994): 547–570.

Davis, Gerald F., and Douglas McAdam. "Corporations, Classes, and Social Movements after Managerialism." In *Research in Organizational Behavior*, vol. 22, edited by Barry Staw and John R. Sutton, 193–236. New York: Elsevier, 2000.

DeAngelo, Harry, Linda DeAngelo, and Jerold L. Zimmerman. "What's Really Wrong with U.S. Business Schools." University of Southern California, Working Paper, 2005.

Department of Education. "Bulletin, 1929." Washington, DC: Department of Education, 1929.

Devinney, Timothy, Grahame Dowling, and Nidthida Perm-Ajchariyawong. "The MBA Rankings Game." Australian Graduate School of Management, Working Paper, 2006.

DiMaggio, Paul J. "Interest and Agency in Institutional Theory." In *Institutional Patterns and Organizations: Culture and Environment*, edited by Lynne G. Zucker, 3–21. Cambridge, MA: Ballinger Publishing, 1988.

DiMaggio, Paul, and Walter W. Powell. "Institutional Isomorphism and Collective Rationality." In *The New Institutionalism in Organizational Analysis*, edited by Walter W. Powell and Paul DiMaggio, 63–82. Chicago: University of Chicago Press, 1991.

Dobbin, Frank. "The Sociological View of the Economy." In *The New Economic Sociology: A Reader*, edited by Frank Dobbin. Princeton, NJ: Princeton University Press, 2004.

———. *The New Economic Sociology: A Reader*. Princeton, NJ: Princeton University Press, 2004.

Dobbin, Frank, John R. Sutton, John W. Meyer, and Richard Scott. "Equal Opportunity Law and the Construction of Internal Labor Markets." *American Journal of Sociology* 99, no. 2 (September 1993): 396–427.

Dobbin, Frank, and Dirk Zorn. "Corporate Malfeasance and the Myth of Shareholder Value." In *Political Power and Social Theory*, vol. 17, edited by Diane E. Davis, 179–198. Greenwich, CT: JAI Press, 2005.

Donaldson, Gordon. *Corporate Restructuring: Managing the Change Process from Within.* Boston: Harvard Business School Press, 1994.

Donaldson, Lex. "Damned by Our Own Theories: Contradictions between Theories and Management Education." *Academy of Management Learning and Education* 1, no. 1 (September 2002): 96–106.

Donham, Wallace B. "Annual Report to the President and Fellows of Harvard College." Cambridge: The Graduate School of Business Administration, 1926.

———. "The Social Significance of Business." Reprinted from the *Harvard Business Review* (July 1927) in the printed document *Dedication Addresses.* HBS Archives, AC 1927 17.1.

———. "The Graduate School of Business Administration, Dean's Report." Boston: Harvard University, 1929.

———. "Business and the Public: Harvard School's New Training to Stress an Understanding of Social Forces." *New York Times,* December 16, 1934, XX6.

———. *Administration and Blind Spots: The Biography of an Adventurous Idea.* George H. Weatherbee Lectures. Boston: Harvard University, Graduate School of Business Administration, 1952.

Douglas, Davison M. "The Jeffersonian Vision of Legal Education." *Journal of Legal Education* 51, no. 2 (June 2001): 185–211.

Douglas, Mary. *How Institutions Think.* The Frank W. Abrams Lectures. Syracuse, NY: Syracuse University Press, 1986.

Dowling, John, and Jeffrey Pfeffer. "Organizational Legitimacy: Social Values and Organizational Behavior." *Pacific Sociological Review* 18, no. 1 (January 1975): 122–136.

Drucker, Peter. "The Graduate Business School." *Fortune* 42, August 1950, 92–94.

Duncan, Otis Dudley. "Social Origins of Salaried and Self-Employed Professional Workers." *Social Forces* 44, no. 2 (December 1965): 186–189.

Eccles, Robert G., Nitin Nohria, and James D. Berkley. *Beyond the Hype: Rediscovering the Essence of Management.* Boston: Harvard Business School Press, 1992.

Edmond, J. B. *The Magnificent Charter: The Origin and Role of the Morrill Land-Grant Colleges and Universities.* Hicksville, NY: Exposition Press, 1978.

Educational Testing Service. "Statistical Studies of Selective Service Testing." Princeton, NJ: Educational Testing Service, 1955.

Eisenhardt, Kathleen M. "Control: Organizational and Economic Approaches." *Management Science* 31, no. 2 (1985): 134.

———. "Agency Theory: An Assessment and Review." *Academy of Management Review* 14, no. 1 (1989): 57.

Elsbach, Kimberly D., and Roderick M. Kramer. "Members' Responses to Organizational Identity Threats: Encountering and Countering the *Business Week* Rankings." *Administrative Science Quarterly* 41, no. 3 (September 1996): 442–476.

Elsbach, Kimberly D., Robert I. Sutton, and D. A. Whetten. "Perspectives on Developing Management Theory, circa 1999: Moving from Shrill Monologues to (Relatively) Tame Dialogues." *Academy of Management Review* 24 (1999): 627–631.

Ely, Richard T. "Report of the Organization of the American Economic Association." *Publications of the American Economic Association* 1 (1886).

Fama, Eugene F. "Agency Problems and the Theory of the Firm." *Journal of Political Economy* 88, no. 2 (April 1980): 288–307.

Fama, Eugene F., and Michael C. Jensen. "Separation of Ownership and Control." *Journal of Law and Economics* 26, no. 2 (June 1983): 301–325.

Fee, Edward C., Charles J. Hadlock, and Joshua R. Pierce. "Business School Rankings and Business School Deans: A Study of Nonprofit Governance." *Financial Management* 34, no. 1 (Spring 2005).

Ferraro, Fabrizio, Jeffrey Pfeffer, and Robert I. Sutton. "Economics Language and Assumptions: How Theories Can Become Self-Fulfilling." *Academy of Management Review* 30, no. 1 (January 2005): 8–24.

Flexner, Abraham. *Medical Education in the United States and Canada.* New York: Carnegie Foundation for the Advancement of Teaching, 1910.

———. *Universities: American, English, German.* New Brunswick, NJ: Transaction, 1994. Reprint, with an introduction by Clark Kerr.

———. "Is Social Work a Profession?" *Research on Social Work Practice* 11, no. 2 (March 2001): 152–165.

Fligstein, Neil. *The Transformation of Corporate Control.* Cambridge: Harvard University Press, 1990.

Folwell, William Watts. *University Addresses.* Minneapolis: H. W. Wilson, 1909.

Ford Foundation. "Annual Report." New York: Ford Foundation, 1950.

Fouraker, Lawrence. "Graduate School of Business Administration." Boston: Harvard Business School, 1971.

———. "Graduate School of Business Administration." Boston: Harvard Business School, 1974.

———. "Graduate School of Business Administration." Boston: Harvard Business School, 1976.

Fourcade-Gourinchas, Marion Cecile. "The National Trajectories of Economic Knowledge: Discipline and Profession in the United States, Great Britain and France." Ph.D. diss., Harvard University, 2000.

Francke, Don E. "The Expanding Role of the Hospital Pharmacist in Drug Information Services." *American Journal of Hospital Pharmacy* 22 (January 1965): 33–37.

Freeman, John, and Audia Pino. "The Creation of Local Banks: Social Sponsorship and Embeddedness." University of California-Berkeley, Working Paper, 2005.

Freidson, Eliot. *Professional Dominance: The Social Structure of Medical Care.* Chicago: Aldine Publishing, 1970.

Freidson, Eliot. "The Changing Nature of Professional Control." *Annual Review of Sociology* 10 (1984): 1–20.

———. *Professionalism: The Third Logic.* Chicago: University of Chicago Press, 2001.

Friedland, Roger, and Robert R. Alford. "Bringing Society Back In: Symbols, Practices, and Institutional Contradictions." In *The New Institutionalism in Organizational Analysis,* edited by Walter W. Powell and Paul J. DiMaggio. Chicago: University of Chicago Press, 1983.

Friedman, Milton. "The Social Responsibility of Business Is to Increase Its Profits." *New York Times Magazine,* September 13, 1970.

Frum, David. *How We Got Here: The 70's, the Decade That Brought You Modern Life, for Better or Worse.* New York: Basic Books, 2000.

Gabor, Andrea. *The Capitalist Philosophers: The Geniuses of Modern Business, Their Lives, Times and Ideas.* New York: Times Business, 2000.

Gaither, H. Rowan. "Freedom and the Challenge to Management." Speech at Stanford University, Ford Foundation Archives, Gaither Papers, box no. 47, July 23, 1958.

Galante's Venture Capital and Private Equity Directory. Wellesley, MA: Asset Alternatives, 2006.

Gaulle, Charles de. *Trois études, suivies du memorandum du 26 janvier 1940.* Paris: Éditions Berger-Levrault, 1945.

Geiger, Roger L. *To Advance Knowledge: The Growth of American Research Universities, 1900–1940.* New York: Oxford University Press, 1986.

Ghoshal, Sumantra, and Peter Moran. "Bad for Practice: A Critique of the Transaction Cost Theory." *Academy of Management Review* 21, no. 1 (January 1996): 13–47.

Gioia, Dennis A., and Kevin G. Corley. "Being Good versus Looking Good: Business School Rankings and the Circean Transformation from Substance to Image." *Academy of Management Learning and Education* 1, no. 1 (September 2002): 107–120.

Gleeson, Robert E. "Stalemate at Stanford, 1945–1958: The Long Prelude to the New Look at Stanford." *Selections* 13, no. 3 (Spring/Summer 1997): 6–23.

Gleeson, Robert E., and Steven L. Schlossman. "The Many Faces of the New Look: The University of Virginia, Carnegie Tech, and the Reform of American Management Education in the Postwar Era (Part II)." *Selections* 8, no. 4 (Spring 1992): 1–24.

———. "George Leland Bach and the Rebirth of Graduate Management Education in the United States, 1945–1975." *Selections* 11, no. 3 (Spring 1995): 8–36.

Glidden, Robert. "Specialized Accreditation." In *Understanding Accreditation,* edited by Kenneth E. Young, Charles Chambers, and H. R. Kells. San Francisco: Jossey-Bass, 1983.

Good, Carter V. "Organized Research in Education: Foundations, Commissions, and Committees." *Review of Educational Research* 9, no. 5, Methods of Research in Education (December 1939): 569–575.

Goode, William J. "Community within a Community: The Professions: Psychology, Sociology and Medicine." *American Sociological Review* 25 (1957): 902–14.

Gooding, Judson. "Blue-Collar Blues in the Assembly Line." *Fortune* 82, July 1970, 112–113.

Gordon, Robert Aaron. "Some Current Issues in Business Education." Paper presented at the Annual Meeting of the AACSB, Gatlinburg, TN, May 2, 1958.

———. "Business Education at the Undergraduate Level." Convocation Commemorating the Fiftieth Anniversary of the Founding of the College of Business Administration, The University of Denver, April 25, 1958. Ford Foundation Archives, Robert Aaron Gordon files.

Gordon, Robert Aaron, and James Edwin Howell. *Higher Education for Business.* New York: Columbia University Press, 1959.

Gottesman, Aron A., and Matthew R. Morey. *Does a Better Education Make for Better Managers? An Empirical Examination of CEO Educational Quality and Firm Performance.* SSRN, 2006.

Gouldner, Alvin W. *Patterns of Industrial Bureaucracy.* Glencoe, IL: Free Press, 1954.

Granovetter, Mark. "Economic Action and Social Structure: The Problem of Embeddedness." *American Journal of Sociology* 91, no. 3 (November 1985): 481–510.

Griffin, C. E. "Education Looks at Business." 1938.

Guillén, Mauro F. *Models of Management: Work, Authority, and Organization in a Comparative Perspective.* Chicago: University of Chicago Press, 1994.

Haber, Samuel. *Efficiency and Uplift: Scientific Management in the Progressive Era, 1890–1920.* Chicago: University of Chicago Press, 1964.

Hall, Peter Dobkin. "What the Merchants Did with Their Money: Charitable and Testamentary Trusts in Massachusetts, 1780–1880." In *Entrepreneurs: The Boston Business Community, 1700–1850,* edited by Conrad Edick Wright and Katheryn P. Viens. Boston: Massachusetts Historical Society, distributed by Northeastern University Press, 1997.

Hall, G. Stanley. "Mental Science." *Science* 20, no. 511 (October 1904): 481–490.

———. "The Unity of Mental Science." In *Congress of Arts and Sciences, Universal Exposition,* vol. 5, edited by Howard J. Rogers, 577–589. St. Louis, 1906.

Hambrick, Donald C. "1993 Presidential Address: What If the Academy Actually Mattered?" *Academy of Management Review* 19, no. 1 (January 1994): 11–16.

Hamilton, Alexander. "The Federalist, No. 35—the Same Subject Continued (Concerning the General Power of Taxation)." In *The Federalist,* edited by J. R. Pole, 181–185. Indianapolis: Hackett Publishing, 2005.

Haney, Lewis. "Organized Research." Paper presented at the Sixth Annual Meeting of the AACSB, New York, NY, 1924.

Harvard Business School. "Who We Are." http://www.hbs.edu/about/index.html (accessed October 9, 2006).

Haskell, Thomas L. *The Emergence of Professional Social Science: The American Social Science Association and the Nineteenth-Century Crisis of Authority.* Urbana: University of Illinois Press, 1977.

Haveman, Heather A., and Hayagreeva Rao. "Structuring a Theory of Moral Sentiments: Institutional and Organizational Coevolution in the Early Thrift Industry." *American Journal of Sociology* 102, no. 6 (May 1997): 1606–1651.

———. "Hybrid Forms and the Evolution of Thrifts." *American Behavioral Scientist* 49, no. 7 (2006): 974–986.

Hawkins, Hugh. "University Identity: The Teaching and Research Functions." In *The Organization of Knowledge in Modern America, 1860–1920,* edited by Alexandra Oleson and John Voss, 285–312. Baltimore: Johns Hopkins University Press, 1979.

Haynes, Benjamin Rudolph, and Harry P. Jackson. *A History of Business Education in the United States.* Cincinnati: Southwestern Pub. Co., 1935.

Heaton, Herbert. *A Scholar in Action, Edwin F. Gay.* Cambridge: Harvard University Press, 1952.

Higgins, Monica. "Building Career Foundations." In *Building Career Foundations.* Boston: Harvard Business School Publishing, 2000.

Higgins, Monica, and Christine Teebagy. "Recent Facts about MBA Job Searches." Harvard Business School Case 9-404-013 (March 11, 2004).

"History of Beta Gamma Sigma." http://www.betagammasigma.org/history.htm (accessed January 19, 2005).

Hoffman, A. J. "Reconsidering the Role of the Practical Theorist: On (Re)Connecting Theory to Practice in Organizational Theory." *Strategic Organization* 2, no. 2 (2004): 213–222.

Hofstadter, Richard. *The Age of Reform: From Bryan to F.D.R.* New York: Knopf, 1955.

———. *Anti-Intellectualism in American Life.* New York: Knopf, 1963.

Hofstadter, Richard, and C. De Witt Hardy. *The Development and Scope of Higher Education in the United States.* New York: Columbia University Press for the Commission on Financing Higher Education, 1952.

Hofstadter, Richard, and Walter P. Metzger. *The Development of Academic Freedom in the United States.* New York: Columbia University Press, 1955.

Hollinger, David A. "The Problem of Pragmatism in American History." *Journal of American History* 67 (1980): 88–93.

Hollis, Ernest Victor. *Philanthropic Foundations and Higher Education.* New York: Columbia University Press, 1938.

———. "The Foundations and the Universities." *Journal of Higher Education* 11, no. 4 (April 1940): 177–181, 230.

Holmstrom, Bengt, and Steven N. Kaplan. "Corporate Governance and Merger Activity in the United States: Making Sense of the 1980s and 1990s." *Journal of Economic Perspectives* 15, no. 2 (2001): 121–144.

Horn, R. "An Overview of Trialectics within an Application of Psychology and Public Policy." In *Trialectics: Toward a Practical Logic of Unity*, edited by R. Horn, 1–39. Lexington, MA: Information Resources, 1983.

Hotchkiss, Willard E. "The Northwestern University School of Commerce." *Journal of Political Economy* 21, no. 3 (March 1913): 196–208.

———. "The Basic Elements and Their Proper Balance in the Curriculum of a Collegiate Business School." *Journal of Political Economy* 28, no. 2 (February 1920): 89–107.

Howell, James Edwin. "A Terminal Program in Business Education: GCT." Discussion Paper, Ford Foundation Archives, GCT, box no. 366, March 23, 1962.

———. "The Ford Foundation and the Revolution in Business Education: A Case Study in Philanthropy." Report, Ford Foundation Archives, no. 006353, September 1966.

Hughes, Everett C. "Institutional Office and the Person." *American Journal of Sociology* 43, no. 3 (November 1937): 404–413.

———. "Professions." In *The Professions in America*, edited by Kenneth S. Lynn, 1–14. Boston: Houghton Mifflin, 1963.

Hurst, James Willard. *The Growth of American Law: The Law Makers*. Boston: Little, Brown, 1950.

Hutchins, Robert Maynard. *The University of Utopia*. Charles R. Walgreen Foundation Lectures. Chicago: University of Chicago Press, 1953.

Jain, Anjani. "Proposed Honors Expansion: Content and Rationale." *Wharton Journal*, April 18, 2005.

Janowitz, Morris. *The Professional Soldier, a Social and Political Portrait*. Glencoe, IL: Free Press, 1960.

Jencks, Christopher, and David Riesman. *The Academic Revolution*. Garden City, NY: Doubleday, 1968.

Jensen, Michael. "Takeovers: Folklore and Science." *Harvard Business Review*, November–December, 1984.

———. "Is Leverage an Invitation to Bankruptcy?" *Wall Street Journal*, February 1, 1989, A14.

———. "CEO Incentives: It's Not How Much You Pay, but How." *Harvard Business Review*, May–June 1990, 138–153.

———. "The Modern Industrial Revolution, Exit, and the Failure of Internal Control Systems." *Journal of Finance* 48, no. 3 (July 1993): 831–880.

Jensen, Michael C., and Perry Fagan. "Capitalism Isn't Broken." *Wall Street Journal*, March 29, 1996, A10.

Jensen, Michael C., and William H. Meckling. "Theory of the Firm: Managerial Behavior, Agency Costs, and Ownership Structure." *Journal of Financial Economics* 3 (April 1976): 303–360.

———. "The Nature of Man." *Journal of Applied Finance* 7, no. 2 (1994) (revised July 1997).

Jensen, Michael C., and Clifford W. Smith. "The Theory of Corporate Finance: A Historical Overview." In *The Modern Theory of Corporate Finance*, edited by Michael C. Jensen and Clifford W. Smith, 2–20. New York: McGraw-Hill, 1984.

Jensen, Michael, and Karen Hopper Wruck. "Coordination, Control, and the Management of Organizations: Course Content and Materials (3rd of 4 CCMO Documents)." SSRN (2001).

Jones, Edward D. "Some Propositions concerning University Instruction in Business Administration." *Journal of Political Economy* 21, no. 3 (March 1913): 185–195.

Jordan, John M. *Machine-Age Ideology: Social Engineering and American Liberalism, 1911–1939*. Chaped Hill, University of North Carolina Press, 1994.

Kakar, Sudhir. *Frederick Taylor: A Study in Personality and Innovation*. Cambridge: MIT Press, 1970.

Kaplan, Steven N. "The Effects of Management Buyouts on Operating Performance and Value." *Journal of Financial Economics* 24 (October 1989): 217–254.

———. "The Staying Power of Leveraged Buyouts." *Journal of Financial Economics* 29 (October 1991): 287–314.

Karabel, Jerome. *The Chosen: The Hidden History of Admission and Exclusion at Harvard, Yale, and Princeton*. Boston: Houghton Mifflin Co., 2005.

Kaufman, Allen, and Ernest J. Englander. "Kohlberg Kravis Roberts & Co. and the Restructuring of American Capitalism." *Business History Review* 67, no. 1 (Spring 1993): 52–97.

Kellogg School of Management. "Learning by Doing." http://www.kellogg.northwestern.edu/difference/academics/doing.htm (accessed October 9, 2006).

Kerr, Clark. *The Uses of the University*. 5th ed. Cambridge: Harvard University Press, 2001.

Khurana, Rakesh. *Searching for a Corporate Savior: The Irrational Quest for Charismatic CEOs*. Princeton, NJ: Princeton University Press, 2002.

Knight, Michael. "Harvard M.B.A.: A Golden Passport." *New York Times*, May 23, 1978, D1.

Koehn, Nancy F., Thomas R. Piper, Kasturi V. Rangan, Richard S. Tedlow, and Amy T. Schalet. "Historical Perspective. Making Choices: Aspects of the History of the Harvard Business School MBA Program." Boston: Harvard Business School, 1992.

Kotter, John P. *A Force for Change: How Leadership Differs from Management*. New York: Free Press, 1990.

Kunda, Gideon. *Engineering Culture: Control and Commitment in a High-Tech Corporation, in Labor and Social Change*. Philadelphia: Temple University Press, 1992.

Lacey, Robert. *Ford: The Men and the Machine*. Boston: Little, Brown, 1986.

Lagemann, Ellen Condliffe. *Private Power for the Public Good: A History of the Carnegie Foundation for the Advancement of Teaching*. Middletown, CT: Wesleyan University Press, 1983.

———. *The Politics of Knowledge: The Carnegie Corporation, Philanthropy, and Public Policy*. Chicago: University of Chicago Press, 1989.

Larson, Magali Sarfatti. *The Rise of Professionalism: A Sociological Analysis*. Berkeley and Los Angeles: University of California Press, 1977.

Lasch, Christopher. *The Revolt of the Elites and the Betrayal of Democracy*. New York: W. W. Norton, 1996.

Lazarsfeld, Paul Felix, Hazel Gaudet, and Bernard Berelson. *The People's Choice: How the Voter Makes Up His Mind in a Presidential Campaign*. 2d ed. New York: Columbia University Press, 1948.

Leicht, Kevin T., and Mary L. Fennell. *Professional Work: A Sociological Approach*. Malden, MA: Blackwell Publishers, 2001.

Lemann, Nicholas. *The Big Test: The Secret History of the American Meritocracy*. New York: Farrar, Straus and Giroux, 1999.

Lippmann, Walter. *Drift and Mastery: An Attempt to Diagnose the Current Unrest*. A Spectrum Book: Classics in History Series. Englewood Cliffs, NJ: Prentice-Hall, 1961. Reprint, with introduction and notes by William E. Leuchtenberg.

Locke, Robert. "Postwar Management Education Reconsidered." In *Management Education in Historical Perspective*, edited by Lars Engwall and Vera Zamagni. Manchester, England: Manchester University Press, 1998.

Lodge, George C. *The New American Ideology: How the Ideological Basis of Legitimate Authority in America Is Being Radically Transformed, the Profound Implications for Our Society in General and the Great Corporations in Particular*. New York: Knopf, 1975.

Logan, Sheridan A. *George F. Baker and His Bank, 1840–1955: A Double Biography*. [St. Joseph, MO]: S. A. Logan, 1981.

Macdonald, Dwight. "Foundations: IV—Next Winter or by Plane." *New Yorker* 31, December 17, 1955.

———. *The Ford Foundation: The Men and the Millions*. New York: Reynal, 1956.

Macy, Jesse. "The Scientific Spirit in Politics." *American Political Science Review* 11, no. 1 (February 1917): 1–11.

"Management Education at Risk." Report of the Management Education Task Force to the AACSB—International Board of Directors, 2002.

Marchand, Roland. *Creating the Corporate Soul: The Rise of Public Relations and Corporate Imagery in American Big Business*. Berkeley and Los Angeles: University of California Press, 1998.

Marshall, Leon C. "The College of Commerce and Administration of the University of Chicago." *Journal of Political Economy* 21, no. 2 (February 1913): 97–110.

———. *Business Administration*. Chicago: University of Chicago Press, 1921.

———. "A New Objective: A University School of Business." Paper presented at the Tenth Annual Meeting of the AACSB, Chicago, IL, 1928.

———. *Unemployment Relief and Public Works*. The National Crisis Series. New York: Bureau of Publications, Teachers College, Columbia University, 1933.

Marshall, Leon C., and Mildred J. Wiese. *Modern Business: The Business Man in Society*. New York: Macmillan, 1926.

Marx, Karl, and Friedrich Engels. *The Communist Manifesto.* Harmondsworth, England: Penguin Books, 1985.

Mast, Carlotta. "The People behind the Rankings." *Selections* 1, no. 2 (Fall 2001): 16–25.

Mayo, Anthony J., Nitin Nohria, and Laura G. Singleton. *Paths to Power: How Insiders and Outsiders Shaped American Business Leadership.* Boston: Harvard Business School Press, 2006.

Mayo, Elton. *The Human Problems of an Industrial Civilization.* New York: Macmillan, 1933.

McClay, Wilfred M. "Croly's Progressive America." *Public Interest,* no. 137 (Fall 1999): 56–72.

McCrea, Roswell C. "The Basic Elements and Their Proper Balance in the Curriculum of a Collegiate Business School." *Journal of Political Economy* 28, no. 2 (February 1920): 100–111.

———. "The Place of Economics in the Curriculum of a School of Business." Paper presented at the Seventh Annual Meeting of the AACSB, Columbus, OH, May 7, 8, and 9, 1925.

———. "The Place of Economics in the Curriculum of a School of Business." *Journal of Political Economy* 34, no. 2 (April 1926): 219–227.

McGlade, Jacqueline. "The Big Push: The Export of American Business Education to Western Europe after the Second World War." In *Management Education in Historical Perspective,* edited by Lars Engwall and Vera Zamagni. Manchester, England: Manchester University Press, 1998.

Mears, Eliot G. "The Teaching of Commerce and Economics." *American Economic Review* 13, no. 4 (December 1923): 648–651.

Meindl, James R., Sanford B. Ehrlich, and Janet M. Dukerich. "The Romance of Leadership." *Administrative Science Quarterly* 30, no. 1 (March 1985): 78–102.

"The Members of the Commission on Admission to Graduate Management Education." *Selections,* Spring 1990, 22–43.

Menand, Louis. *American Studies.* New York: Farrar, Straus and Giroux, 2002.

Merton, Robert K. "Bureaucratic Structure and Personality." *Social Forces* 18, no. 4 (May 1940): 560–568.

———. "Puritanism, Pietism, and Science." In *Social Theory and Social Structure,* 628–660. New York: Free Press, 1968.

———. "Science and the Social Order." In *Social Theory and Social Structure,* 591–603. New York: Free Press, 1968.

Metzger, Walter P. *Academic Freedom in the Age of the University.* New York: Columbia University Press, 1961.

Meyer, John W. "The Effects of Education as an Institution." *American Journal of Sociology* 83, no. 1 (July 1977): 55–77.

————. "Ontology and Rationalization in the Western Cultural Account." In *Institutional Environments and Organizations*, edited by W. Richard Scott and John W. Meyer, 9–27. Thousand Oaks, CA: Sage, 1994.

Meyer, John W., and Brian Rowan. "Institutionalized Organizations: Formal Structure as Myth and Ceremony." *American Journal of Sociology* 83, no. 2 (September 1977): 340–363.

Mills, C. Wright. *White Collar: The American Middle Classes*. New York: Oxford University Press, 1951.

————. *The Power Elite*. New York: Oxford University Press, 1967.

Mintzberg, Henry, Robert Simons, and Kunal Basu. "Beyond Selfishness." *MIT Sloan Management Review*, Fall 2002, 68.

MIT Sloan School of Management. "About MIT Sloan—Background: Mission." http://mitsloan.mit.edu/about/b-mission.php (accessed October 9, 2006).

Mizruchi, Mark S. "What Do Interlocks Do? An Analysis, Critique, and Assessment of Research on Interlocking Directorates." *Annual Review of Sociology* 22 (1996): 271–298.

Montgomery, David. *Workers' Control in America: Studies in the History of Work, Technology, and Labor Struggles*. Cambridge: Cambridge University Press, 1979.

Moon, Hyeyoung. "The Worldwide Diffusion of Business Schools, 1881–1999: The Historical Trajectory and Mechanism of Expansion." University of Washington, Working Paper, 2004.

Morison, Samuel Eliot. *The Founding of Harvard College*. Cambridge: Harvard University Press, 1935.

————. *One Boy's Boston, 1887–1901*. Boston: Houghton Mifflin, 1962.

Morrissey, Charles T. "Kermit Gordon Interview with Charles Morrissey." Interview, Ford Foundation Archives, no. 18, December 19, 1972.

Moyer, Albert E. *A Scientist's Voice in American Culture: Simon Newcomb and the Rhetoric of Scientific Method*. Berkeley and Los Angeles: University of California, 1992.

Moynihan, Daniel P. *Maximum Feasible Misunderstanding: Community Action in the War on Poverty*. The Clarke A. Sanford Lectures on Local Government and Community Life, 1967. New York: Free Press, 1969.

Münsterberg, Hugo. *Psychology and Industrial Efficiency*. Boston: Mifflin, 1913.

Newcomb, Simon. "Abstract Science in America, 1776–1876." *North American Review* 122, no. 250 (January 1876): 88–123.

Newman, John Henry. *The Idea of a University*. Notre Dame: University of Notre Dame Press, 1982. Reprint, with introduction and notes by Martin Svaglic.

Nicolai, Alexander T. "The Bridge to the 'Real World': Applied Science or a 'Schizophrenic Tour De Force'?" *Journal of Management Studies* 41, no. 6 (September 2004): 951–976.

Nisbet, Robert A. *The Degradation of the Academic Dogma.* Foundations of Higher Education. New Brunswick, NJ: Transaction, 1997.

Nohria, Nitin, Davis Dyer, and Frederick Dalzell. *Changing Fortunes: Remaking the Industrial Corporation.* New York: Wiley, 2002.

"No Red Grip Found on Foundation Aid." *New York Times,* January 3, 1953, 5.

Office of Education. "Working Paper on Congress' Power to Rely upon Determinations of Private Accrediting Agencies as Basis of Eligibility for Federal Educational Assistance." Unpublished Manuscript, Washington, DC: Office of Education, Division of Eligibility and Agency Evaluation, June 1970.

Oleson, Alexandra, and John Voss, eds. *The Organization of Knowledge in Modern America, 1860–1920.* Baltimore: Johns Hopkins University Press, 1979.

Olson, Mancur, Jr. "Rapid Growth as a Destabilizing Force." *Journal of Economic History* 23, no. 4 (December 1963): 529–552.

Ouchi, William G. *Theory Z: How American Business Can Meet the Japanese Challenge.* Reading, MA: Addison-Wesley, 1981.

Parsons, Talcott. "The Professions and Social Structure." *Social Forces* 17, no. 4 (May 1939): 457–467.

———. *Structure and Process in Modern Societies.* Glencoe, IL: Free Press, 1960.

Pascale, Richard T., and Anthony G. Athos. *The Art of Japanese Management: Applications for American Executives.* New York: Simon and Schuster, 1981.

Perlow, Leslie A. *When You Say Yes but Mean No: How Silencing Conflict Wrecks Relationships and Companies, and What You Can Do about It.* New York: Crown Business, 2003.

Perrow, Charles. *Complex Organizations: A Critical Essay.* 2d ed. Glenview, IL: Scott Foresman, 1979.

———. *Organizing America: Wealth, Power, and the Origins of Corporate Capitalism.* Princeton, NJ: Princeton University Press, 2002.

Person, Harlow S. "The Amos Tuck School of Dartmouth College." *Journal of Political Economy* 21, no. 2 (February 1913): 117–126.

Pfeffer, Jeffrey. "Barriers to the Advance of Organization Science: Paradigm Development as a Dependent Variable." *Academy of Management Review* 18 (1993): 599–620.

———. *New Directions for Organization Theory: Problems and Prospects.* New York: Oxford University Press, 1997.

Pfeffer, Jeffrey, and Christina T. Fong. "The Business School 'Business': Some Lessons from the US Experience." *Journal of Management Studies* 41, no. 8 (December 2004): 1501–1520.

Pickens, T. Boone. "Shareholders: The Forgotten People." *Journal of Business Strategy* 6, no. 1 (Summer 1985): 4–5.

Pierson, Frank Cook. *The Education of American Businessmen: A Study of University-College Programs in Business Administration.* New York: McGraw-Hill, 1959.

Podolny, Joel, Rakesh Khurana, and Marya Hill-Popper. "Revisiting the Meaning of Leadership." *Research in Organizational Behavior* 26 (2005): 1–31.

Policano, Andrew J. "What Price Rankings?" *Biz Ed, an AACSB Publication*, September/October 2005, 26–32.

Porter, Lyman W., Lawrence E. McKibbin, and American Assembly of Collegiate Schools of Business. *Management Education and Development: Drift or Thrust into the 21st Century?* New York: McGraw-Hill Book Co., 1988.

Porter, Russell. "Stress Social Responsibility as Factor in American Life." *New York Times*, September 7, 1947, F1 ff.

Porter, Theodore M. *Trust in Numbers: The Pursuit of Objectivity in Science and Public Life.* Princeton, NJ: Princeton University Press, 1995.

Powell, Walter W., and Paul J. DiMaggio, eds. *The New Institutionalism in Organizational Analysis.* Chicago: University of Chicago Press, 1983.

Pratt, John W., and Richard Zeckhauser. "Principals and Agents: An Overview." In *Principals and Agents: The Structure of Business*, edited by John W. Pratt, Richard Zeckhauser, and Kenneth Joseph Arrow. Boston: Harvard Business School Press, 1991.

President and Fellows of Harvard College. "Research and Advanced Training Activities of the Graduate School of Business Administration." Grant Proposal to Ford Foundation, Ford Foundation Archives, September 10, 1954.

"President's Order on NRA." *New York Times*, September 28, 1934, 4.

Pritchett, Henry Smith. "Is There a Place for a Profession in Commerce?" *Engineering News* 435 (May 9, 1901): 343.

Proffitt, John R. "The Federal Connection for Accreditation." *Journal of Higher Education* 50, no. 2 (March–April 1979): 145–157.

Prokesch, Steven. "Remaking the American CEO." *New York Times*, January 25, 1987, 1.

Rae, John. "The Application of Science to Industry." In *The Organization of Knowledge in Modern America, 1860–1920*, edited by Alexandra Oleson and John Voss. Baltimore: Johns Hopkins University Press, 1979.

Rajan, Raghuram, and Luigi Zingales. *Saving Capitalism from the Capitalists: Unleashing the Power of Financial Markets to Create Wealth and Spread Opportunity.* Princeton, NJ: Princeton University Press, 2004.

Readings, Bill. *The University in Ruins.* Cambridge: Harvard University Press, 1996.

"Research Relevancy Remains a Challenge for Business Schools." *Biz Ed, an AACSB Publication*, Spring 1997.

Reuben, Julie A. *The Making of the Modern University: Intellectual Transformation and the Marginalization of Morality.* Chicago: University of Chicago Press, 1996.

Rickover, Hyman Adm. "Getting the Job Done Right." *New York Times*, November 25, 1981, 23.

Roe, Mark J. *Strong Managers, Weak Owners: The Political Roots of American Corporate Finance.* Princeton, NJ: Princeton University Press, 1994.

Roethlisberger, F. J. *The Elusive Phenomena: An Autobiographical Account of My Work in the Field of Organizational Behavior at the Harvard Business School.* Edited by George F. F. Lombard. Cambridge: Division of Research, Graduate School of Business Administration Harvard University (distributed by Harvard University Press), 1977.

Roose, Kenneth D., and Charles J. Andersen. *A Rating of Graduate Programs.* Washington, DC: American Council on Education, 1970.

Ross, Dorothy. "The Development of the Social Sciences." In *The Organization of Knowledge in Modern America, 1860–1920,* edited by Alexandra Oleson and John Voss. Baltimore: Johns Hopkins University Press, 1979.

Ross, Nancy L. "B-School Ratings: Name of the Game; Rating Game Played at U.S. B-Schools." *Washington Post,* January 4, 1978, D8.

Rost, Joseph C. *Leadership for the Twenty-first Century.* New York: Praeger, 1991.

Roy, William G. *Socializing Capital: The Rise of the Large Industrial Corporation in America.* Princeton, NJ: Princeton University Press, 1997.

Royal Swedish Academy of Sciences. "This Year's Laureates Are Pioneers in the Theory of Financial Economics and Corporate Finance." *The Bank of Sweden Prize in Economic Sciences in Memory of Alfred Nobel,* October 16, 1990.

Ruben, Ellen. "Trends in Minority Enrollment." *Selections,* Special Edition, 1986.

Rueff, Martin. "The Construction of a Professional Monopoly: Medical Education in the U.S., 1765–1930." Princeton University, Department of Sociology, Working Paper, 2006.

Ruggles, C. O. "The Significance of Research in Business Education." Paper presented at the Sixth Annual Meeting of the AACSB, New York 1924.

Sass, Steven A. *The Pragmatic Imagination: A History of the Wharton School, 1881–1981.* Philadelphia: University of Pennsylvania Press, 1982.

Scherer, F. M. "Corporate Ownership and Control." In *The U.S. Business Corporation: An Institution in Transition,* edited by John R. Meyer and James M. Gustafson. New York: Ballinger Publishing Company, 1988.

Schlossman, Steven L., Michael W. Sedlak, and Harold S. Wechsler. *The "New Look": The Ford Foundation and the Revolution in Business Education.* Los Angeles: Graduate Management Admissions Council, 1987.

Schmotter, James W. "An Interview with Professor James E. Howell." *Selections* 1, no. 1 (Spring 1984): 9–14.

———. "Interview with Dean Robert Jaedicke." *Selections* 6, no. 2 (Autumn 1989): 1–10.

———. "Interview with Dean Don Jacobs." *Selections* 8, no. 3 (1992): 1–9.

———. "The Graduate Management Admissions Council: A Brief History, 1953–1992." *Selections* 9, no. 2 (Winter 1993): 1–11.

———. "An Interview with Dean B. Joseph White." *Selections* 14, no. 2 (Winter 1998): 22–27.

———. "An Interview with Robert H. Frank." *Selections* 15, no. 1 (Autumn 1998): 15–22.

———. "An Interview with Professor James G. March." *Selections* 14, no. 3 (Spring 1998): 56–63.

Schumpeter, Joseph Alois. *Capitalism, Socialism, and Democracy.* New York: Harper & Brothers, 1942.

Scott, William A. "Training for Business at the University of Wisconsin." *Journal of Political Economy* 21, no. 2 (1913): 127–135.

Scott, W. Richard. *Organizations: Rational, Natural, and Open Systems.* 3d ed. Englewood Cliffs, NJ: Prentice Hall, 1992.

———. *Institutions and Organizations.* Foundations for Organizational Science. Thousand Oaks, CA: Sage, 1995.

———. *Institutional Change and Healthcare Organizations: From Professional Dominance to Managed Care.* Chicago: University of Chicago Press, 2000.

Scott, W. Richard, Martin Ruef, Peter J. Mendel, and Carol A. Caronna. *Institutional Change and Healthcare Organizations: From Professional Dominance to Managed Care.* Chicago: University of Chicago Press, 2000.

Sedlak, Michael W., and Steven L. Schlossman. "The Case Method and Business Education at Northwestern University, 1906–1971." *Selections* 7, no. 3 (Winter 1991): 14–38.

"Sees Great Need Now of Liberal Education." *New York Times,* December 27, 1931, 26.

Selden, William K., and Harry V. Porter. "Accreditation, Its Purposes and Uses." Occasional paper, Council on Post-secondary Accreditation. Washington, DC: Council on Post-Secondary Accreditation, 1977.

"*Selections* Interview with John Byrne, Senior Writer at *Business Week.*" 2001. http://www.gmac.com/selections/fall2001/byrne/index.html (accessed October 9, 2006).

Selznick, Philip. *TVA and the Grass Roots: A Study in the Sociology of Formal Organization.* Berkeley and Los Angeles: University of California Press, 1949.

———. *Leadership in Administration: A Sociological Interpretation.* Evanston, IL: Row Peterson, 1957.

Senate Committee on Education and Labor. Report of the Committee of the Senate upon the Relations between Labor and Capital, 1885.

Sennett, Richard, and Jonathan Cobb. *The Hidden Injuries of Class.* New York: Vintage Books, 1973.

Shapin, Steven. *A Social History of Truth: Civility and Science in Seventeenth-Century England.* Science and Its Conceptual Foundations. Chicago: University of Chicago Press, 1994.

———. *The Scientific Revolution.* Chicago: University of Chicago Press, 1996.

———. "University-Industry Relations: Getting Perspective." Boston Colloquium for Philosophy of Science, Boston University, November 3, 2005.

Shapiro, Susan P. "The Social Control of Impersonal Trust." *American Journal of Sociology* 93, no. 3 (November 1987): 623–658.

Shenhav, Yehouda. "From Chaos to Systems: The Engineering Foundations of Organization Theory, 1879–1932." *Administrative Science Quarterly* 40, no. 4 (December 1995): 557–585.

———. *Manufacturing Rationality: The Engineering Foundations of the Managerial Revolution.* New York: Oxford University Press, 2001.

Shils, Edward. "The Intellectuals and the Powers: Some Perspectives for Comparative Analysis." *Comparative Studies in Society and History* 1, no. 1 (October 1958): 5–22.

———. "Charisma, Order, and Status." *American Sociological Review* 30, no. 2 (April 1965): 199–213.

———. "The Order of Learning in the United States: The Ascendancy of the University." In *The Organization of Knowledge in Modern America, 1860–1920*, edited by Alexandra Oleson and John Voss. Baltimore: Johns Hopkins University Press, 1979.

———. *The Calling of Sociology and Other Essays on the Pursuit of Learning.* Vol. 3 of *Selected Papers of Edward Shils.* Chicago: University of Chicago Press, 1980.

———. *The Calling of Education: The Academic Ethic and Other Essays on Higher Education.* Chicago: University of Chicago Press, 1997.

Shils, Edward, and Philip G. Altbach. *The Order of Learning: Essays on the Contemporary University.* New Brunswick, NJ: Transaction, 1997.

Silk, Leonard, and Mark Silk. *The American Establishment.* New York: Basic Books, 1980.

Simon, Herbert Alexander. *Administrative Behavior: A Study of Decision-Making Processes in Administrative Organization.* 2d ed. New York: Macmillan, 1957.

———. *Models of My Life.* New York: Basic Books, 1991.

Small, A. W. "The Era of Sociology." *American Journal of Sociology* 1, no. 1 (July 1895): 1–15.

Spence, Michael. "Job Market Signaling." *Quarterly Journal of Economics* 87, no. 3 (August 1973): 355–374.

Stanford Graduate School of Business. "About the Stanford Graduate School of Business." http://www.gsb.stanford.edu/about/ (accessed October 9, 2006).

Starr, Paul. *The Social Transformation of American Medicine.* New York: Basic Books, 1982.

Stinchcombe, Arthur L. "Social Structure and Organizations." In *Handbook of Organizations*, edited by James G. March, 142–193. Chicago: Rand McNally, 1965.

———. *Constructing Social Theories.* Chicago: University of Chicago Press, 1987.

Stolzenberg, Ross M. "The Changing Demand for Graduate Management Education." *Selections* 2, no. 1 (Spring 1985): 10–29.

Stone, Katherine. "The Origins of Job Structures in the Steel Industry." In *Labor Market Segmentation: Papers from Conference on Labor Market Segmentation at*

Harvard University, 1973, edited by Richard Edwards, Michael Reich, and David M. Gordon, 27–84. Lexington, MA: D. C. Heath, 1975.

Stuart, Mary Clark. "Clark Kerr: Biography of an Action Intellectual." Ph.D. diss., University of Michigan, 1980.

Sundaram, Anant K., and Andrew Inkpen. "The Corporate Objective Revisited." *SSRN* (October 2001).

Swedberg, Richard. *Max Weber and the Idea of Economic Sociology*. Princeton, NJ: Princeton University Press, 1998.

Tarbell, Ida M. *Owen D. Young, a New Type of Industrial Leader*. New York: Macmillan, 1932.

Taylor, Frederick W. "Testimony to the House of Representatives Committee." In *Organization Theory*, edited by D. S. Pugh, 157–182. London: Penguin Books, 1912.

———. *The Principles of Scientific Management*. New York: Harper, 1947.

Tedlow, Richard S., Courtney Purrington, and Kim Eric Bettcher. "The American CEO in the Twentieth Century: Demography and Career Path." HBS Working Paper, no. 03-097 (2003), 96.

Thornton, Patricia H., and William Ocasio. "Institutional Logics and the Historical Contingency of Power in Organizations: Executive Succession in the Higher Education Publishing Industry, 1958–1990." *American Journal of Sociology* 105 (1999): 801–843.

Thunderbird—The Garvin School of International Management. "Mission Statement." http://www.thunderbird.edu/about_thunderbird/inside_tbird/mission_statement.htm (accessed October 9, 2006).

"To the Trustees of the Ford Foundation: A Proposal of the Harvard Graduate School of Business Administration." Ford Foundation Archives, no. 55-02, November 16, 1953.

Trump, Guy W., H. S. Hendrickson, William L. Campfield, Donald H. Cramer, Thomas F. Keller, Sam W. Lyverse, Homer J. Mottice, John M. Saada, Wayne P. Tenney, Milton F. Ushy, and Thomas H. Williams. "A Ranking of Accounting Programs." *Journal of Accountancy* 130, no. 1 (July 1970): 86–90.

Tuck School of Business at Dartmouth. "Our Strategy." http://www.tuck.dartmouth.edu/about/strategy.html (accessed October 9, 2006).

United States Military Academy at West Point. "USMA Mission." http://www.usma.edu/mission.asp (accessed October 9, 2006).

United States Office of Scientific Research and Development, and Vannevar Bush. *Science, the Endless Frontier*. Washington, DC: Government Printing Office, 1945.

University of Chicago Graduate School of Business. "Full-Time MBA Program." http://chicagogsb.edu/fulltime/index.aspx (accessed October 9, 2006).

———. "Leadership Effectiveness and Development." http://www.chicagogsb.edu/fulltime/academics/experiential/lead.aspx (accessed October 9, 2006).

Urwick, L. F. *Management Education in American Business*. New York: American Management Association Publications, 1953.

Useem, Michael. *Executive Defense: Shareholder Power and Corporate Reorganization.* Cambridge: Harvard University Press, 1993.

Van Metre, Thurman William. *A History of the Graduate School of Business, Columbia University.* The Bicentennial History of Columbia University. New York: Columbia University Press, 1954.

Veblen, Thorstein. *The Higher Learning in America: A Memorandum on the Conduct of Universities by Business Men.* New York: A. M. Kelley, 1965. Orig. publ. 1918.

VerMeulen, Michael. "Mergers and Acquisitions: Economist Michael Jensen Defends Corporate Raiders and Greenmailers and Has Developed an Economic Rationale for Takeovers." *Institutional Investor,* August 1985, 71–76.

———. "The Iconoclast of M&A." *Institutional Investor* 19, no. 8 (August 1985): 71.

Veysey, Laurence R. *The Emergence of the American University.* Chicago: University of Chicago Press, 1965.

Weber, Max. *The Protestant Ethic and the Spirit of Capitalism.* Translated by Talcott Parsons. London: Allen & Unwin, 1930. Reprint, with foreword by R. H. Tawney.

———. *The Theory of Social and Economic Organization.* Edited by Talcott Parsons. Translated by A. M. Henderson. New York: Free Press, 1964. Reprint, with introduction by Talcott Parsons. Orig. publ. 1947.

———. *Economy and Society.* Edited by Guenther Roth and Claus Wittich. Translated by Ephraim Fischoff et al. 2 vols. Berkeley and Los Angeles: University of California Press, 1978.

Weisman, Steven R. *The Great Tax Wars: Lincoln to Wilson. The Fierce Battles over Money and Power That Transformed the Nation.* New York: Simon & Schuster, 2002.

Wheeler, John. "Changes in Collegiate Business Education in the United States 1954–64 and the Role of the Ford Foundation in These Changes." Draft Report, Ford Foundation Archives, no. 004933, 1965.

Wiebe, Robert H. *The Search for Order, 1877–1920.* New York: Hill and Wang, 1967.

Wilensky, Harold L. "The Professionalization of Everyone?" *American Journal of Sociology* 70, no. 2 (September 1964): 137–158.

Williamson, Oliver E. *The Economics of Discretionary Behavior: Managerial Objectives in a Theory of the Firm.* Ford Foundation Doctoral Dissertation Series. Englewood Cliffs, NJ: Prentice-Hall (published thesis from Carnegie Institute of Technology), 1964.

———. *Markets and Hierarchies.* New York: Free Press, 1975.

Williamson, Oliver E., Sidney G. Winter, and R. H. Coase. *The Nature of the Firm: Origins, Evolution, and Development.* New York: Oxford University Press, 1991.

Wolin, Sheldon S. *Politics and Vision: Continuity and Innovation in Western Political Thought.* Expanded ed. Princeton, NJ: Princeton University Press, 2004.

Wren, Daniel A. "American Business Philanthropy and Higher Education in the Nineteenth Century." *Business History Review* 57, no. 3 (1983): 321–346.

Wuorio, Jeff. "The Impact of the Rankings: Multiple Perspectives." *Selections* 1, no. 2 (Fall 2001): 26–37.

Young, Kenneth E., ed. *Understanding Accreditation*. San Francisco: Jossey-Bass, 1983.

Zalaznick, Sheldon. "The MBA, the Man, the Myth, and the Method." *Fortune*, May 1968.

Zaleznik, Abraham. "Managers and Leaders: Are They Different?" *Harvard Business Review* 55, no. 3 (May–June 1977): 67–78.

———. "Managers and Leaders: Are They Different?" *Harvard Business Review* 70, no. 2 (March–April 1992): 126–135.

Zimmerman, Jerold L. "Can American Business Schools Survive?" SSRN Working Paper no. FR 01-16, 2001.

Zucker, Lynne G. "Production of Trust: Institutional Sources of Economic Structure, 1840–1920 *Research in Organizational Behavior*, vol. 8, edited by Barry Staw and L. L. Cummings, 55–111. Greenwich, CT: JAI Press, 1986.

Zuckerman, Ezra W. "Internet Valuations: Surveying the Landscape." Palo Alto, CA: Stanford University, Graduate School of Business, 1999.

Zunz, Olivier. *Making America Corporate, 1870–1920*. Chicago: University of Chicago Press, 1990.

Index

Mayo, Elton, 185, 190–91, 221–22, 235, 240, 282, 437n105
MBA Magazine, 308, 335–36
McArthur, John H., 331
McCarthy era, 234, 450n26
McChesney, Robert W., 376
McClay, Wilfred M., *The Promise of American Life,* 69
McCrea, Roswell C., 149–50, 154, 162, 163, 165, 223
McKibben, Lawrence E., 312, 340–41
McKinsey (management consultancy), 96
McNamara, Robert, 286
McPeak, William, 245
meaning, 15, 382
Means, G., 206, 315, 316, 319; *The Modern Corporation and Private Property,* 28
Mears, Eliot, 114, 164
Meckling, William, 301, 317–18, 319, 343, 456n77; "The Nature of Man," 323
medical profession, 6, 71, 100, 202, 398n19; as ancient, 64; education in, 65–66; and Eliot, 66–67; and higher education, 73; institutional forms of, 70; jurisdiction of, 17; knowledge in, 99; licensing in, 66; and management as profession, 49; and market, 371–72; and monopoly, 79; as profession, 103; and science, 56, 412n17; and social interests, 173; social use of, 68; and status of business, 46; and university professional schools, 80
medical schools, 66, 67, 80, 102, 112, 141, 184, 270, 368, 398n19
Mellon, William Larimer, 251, 252
Mellon family, 251
Mencken, H. L., 66
Menger, Carl, 161
mercantile elite, 42, 44–45
merchants, 64, 132
Merton, Robert, 8, 11, 373, 413n31
Metzger, Walter, 133
Meyer, John, 13, 63, 134
Meyers-Brigg (Personality) Type Indicator, 360
Michigan State University, Eli Broad Graduate School of Management, 356
middle class, 38, 84, 211
Miles, Raymond, 292

military, 202, 203, 354, 361
military profession, 66
Mill, John Stuart, 309
Miller, Arjay, 262, 296
Miller, Merton, 466n71
Mills, C. Wright, 2, 32, 34
Mintzberg, Henry, 369
MIT, 81, 101, 102, 214, 215, 252, 263, 274, 285, 293, 306, 422n20
MIT, School of Industrial Management, 265, 284
MIT, Sloan School of Management, 204, 308, 339–40, 355–56
Mitchell, Wesley, 161–62, 435n64
Modigliani, Franco, 284, 466n71
monopoly, 9, 11, 31, 66, 79, 90, 103
morality: and business schools, 188, 365, 375; and corporations, 38; and curriculum, 154, 365, 370, 371, 474n36; and Donham, 115; and economics, 162; and management, 100, 364–65; and market, 375, 378; Owen on, 376–77, 378; and professions, 70–71, 85, 114, 373; and science, 55, 59, 60, 61, 62, 64, 71, 79, 123–24; and self-interest, 379; and social science, 59; and sociology, 62; and Tuck School, 153–54; and Wharton, 107; Young on, 118. *See also* public/common good; social interest; trust
Morgan, J. P., 34, 36
Morison, Samuel Eliot, 45, 112
Morrill Act of 1852, 75, 80, 102, 210
Morrill Act of 1890, 80, 210
Morris, Victor P., 188
Moynihan, Daniel Patrick, 298–99
Muller v. Oregon, 54, 71
Münsterberg, Hugo, 92, 96; *Psychology and Industrial Efficiency,* 95
mutual funds, 304

National Academy of Sciences, 53
National Bureau of Economic Research, 220, 435n64
National Commission on Accrediting, 213
national industrial policy, 301
National Industrial Recovery Administration, 184
National Industrial Recovery Board, 145